The Voice in the Drum

The Voice in the Drum

Music, Language, and Emotion in Islamicate South Asia

Richard K. Wolf

University of Illinois Press
Urbana, Chicago, and Springfield

Harvard University Department
of Music Publication Fund

Manufactured in the United States of America
c 5 4 3 2 1
∞ This book is printed on acid-free paper.

Library of Congress Cataloging-in-Publication Data
Wolf, Richard K., 1962– author.
The voice in the drum: music, language, and emotion
in Islamicate South Asia / Richard K. Wolf.
pages cm
Includes bibliographical references and index.
ISBN 978-0-252-03858-7 (cloth : alk. paper)
ISBN 978-0-252-09650-1 (ebook)
1. Islamic music—South Asia—History and criticism.
I. Title.
ML3197.W65 2014
780.88'2970954—dc23 2014012477

For Adam Nayyar

About the Illinois Companion Web Site

www.press.illinois.edu/books/wolf/voiceinthedrum

This book is accompanied by a Web site that features audio and video material pertinent to the text, as well as supplemental photos and other added content. The symbol ⇱ in the text indicates a reference to these online materials. Readers may access the Web companion with the access code: "exploration."

Contents

Acknowledgments ix

An Essential Note from the Author xiii

Note from the Editor xv

Note on Transcription and Musical Symbols xix

Map xxv

Chapter 1. Drumming, Language, and the Voice in South Asia 1

Chapter 2. Emotional Agents 23

Chapter 3. Tone and Stroke 55

Chapter 4. Beyond the *Mātra* 81

Chapter 5. Muharram in Multan 115

Chapter 6. Shah Jamal 145

Chapter 7. Madho Lal 165

Chapter 8. The Manifest and the Hidden 188

Chapter 9. The Voice in the Drum 222

Chapter 10. A Silver Box 250

Appendix A Dhīmā and Mātam 259
Appendix B Summary of Commemorative Themes on Particular Days of Muharram in South Asia 265
Appendix C Cast of Characters by Chapter; Key Figures in the Karbala Story 269

Notes 275
Glossary 307
References 327
Index 337

Acknowledgments

This project entailed my spending a few hours or a few days with many musicians rather than hundreds of hours with a few musicians. I am deeply grateful to all the musicians mentioned by name in this book, as well as to many more whom I encountered on the streets during festivals, recorded, interviewed, thought about, but could not include here. Some may have regarded me as an innocuous pest, easy to brush off after a recording and a few harmless questions. Others didn't get off so easily. I demanded much from those who served as mentors, teachers, cultural intermediaries, and translators and could not have completed this work without them.

At the top of this list are Qamar Jalil and Adam Nayyar. Qamar was my Urdu teacher and indefatigable research assistant in 1997, my first year in Pakistan. Not only did he accompany me to places that may have been, for him, socially and physically disagreeable, but he did so in all seasons, day or night. When not bumping along on some bus or helping me ask awkward questions of strangers on the street, he sat at home doggedly transcribing my recorded interviews and performances, producing fourteen hundred A4-sized pages of single-spaced, neatly handwritten Urdu and English texts.

The late Adam Nayyar was my first research guide, a singularly persistent critic, and as our friendship developed, my heartiest collaborator. Adam and his wife Lucia hosted me numerous times in their Islamabad flat. Lucia tolerated our relentless wrangling late into the night and was patient when I took her husband away for days at a time. I imagined myself arguing with Adam as I read and revised this manuscript.

I am also grateful to Lok Virsa in Islamabad, where Adam was the director of research, as my Pakistani affiliate institution in 1997, and to the Henry Martyn Institute in Hyderabad for affiliating me in 1998. The American Institute of Pakistan Studies funded a portion of my initial research in Pakistan in 1997, and the American Institute of Indian Studies provided a small grant to help cover research expenses in India in 1998. Amy Bard generously shared with me her own doctoral research funding from these two institutions for the balance of my research stay over the twenty-eight-month period from 1996 to 1999. The Radcliffe Institute for Advanced Study supported me for the 2002–3 academic year for the initial phases of writing of this book. A Das Traveling Fellowship from Harvard University, while supporting me during another project in India, helped free up my time for work on this manuscript in 2004, as did a year of Presidential Leave at Harvard. Support for my other years of research in India and Pakistan, and now Central Asia, has fed directly or indirectly into the present project; for that I thank Fulbright-Hays, the American Institute of Indian Studies (again), the South Asia Initiative at Harvard, the Asia Center at Harvard, and the Fulbright Regional Research program in South and Central Asia. I am also thankful to the Harvard University Department of Music Publication Fund for generously providing a publication subvention. Some debts are more personal: a friend, the anthropologist Frank Heidemann, allowed me to use his isolated mountain hideaway in Austria for a few precious weeks during the winter of 2011–12 to write undisturbed. Thank you, Frank.

For reading and commenting on all of the manuscript I thank first and foremost my wife, Amy Bard. I am also grateful to one anonymous reader for the press, to two readers who identified themselves, Margaret Mills and Peter Manuel, and to colleagues who read parts of the manuscript and provided helpful feedback: Stephen Blum, Kay Kaufman Shelemay, Michael Herzfeld, and Michael Jackson. The cartographer Daniel P. Huffman created the map at the front of the book.

I presented analytical examples from Chapters 3 and 4 in an international symposium on rhythm at the Harvard University Department of Music that I organized along with Christopher Hasty and Stephen Blum, and I received helpful thoughts from the participants and from members of the graduate seminar on rhythm I was co-teaching with Christopher Hasty at the time. I'm especially grateful to James Kippen for listening carefully with me to some of my drumming examples from Hyderabad, Sindh, and catching an error in my notation. I presented parts of what became Chapter 8 at the University of Leeds at a conference titled "Performance, Politics, Piety: Music as Debate in Muslim Societies of North Africa, South Asia, West Asia, and Their Diasporas," October 10, 2009. Parts of Chapter 9 grew from a paper titled "The Shi'i Faces of Nizamuddin: Nizami Drumming and Texts in Delhi and Karachi," presented at the conference "Tellings, Not Texts: Singing, Story-Telling and Performance," School of Oriental and African Studies, University of London, June 9, 2009. I thank the organizers of these two conferences, Kamal Salhi (for the first) and Katherine Schofield and Francesca Orsini (for the second), for providing fora for my ideas to germinate.

In Karachi, Qasim Raza and his family hosted my wife and me, sent me off on expeditions with their driver, and guided me clear of harm's way. The late *soz k͟hwān* and professor Sibte-Jafar shared his time, his beautiful voice, and his scholarship both in 1997 and in 2003. Doctor Rajab Ali Memon efficiently arranged research assistance for me in Hyderabad, Sindh. Saleem Gardezi and Muhammad Ajmal of Multan facilitated my research in Multan in 1997. The singing legend Suraiya Multanikar gave her precious time to me on two occasions in 2007 for feedback interviews using videotapes from her neighborhood during Muharram in Multan. Nadeem Akbar of the American Institute of Pakistan Studies has provided logistical assistance for my research in Pakistan from 1996 to the present.

In India, my circle of friends in Lucknow provided a support system and a range of contacts for a project the significance of which, for many of them, was probably dubious. These included the Raja of Jahangirabad (who, as a child, used to play the *tāshā* in his father's Muharram processions), Ram Advani, Amarjit Singh, Saleem Kidvai, and Saqlain Naqvi. Nayyar Masud was an unmatched resource for his knowledge of literature and history.

In Delhi Doctor Athar Raza Bilgrami, an avocational researcher and writer on Muharram, shared his insightful thoughts about Muharram music. Irfan Zuberi introduced me to a network of acquaintances in the Nizamuddin neighborhood in 2009–10 and helped me puzzle through the confusing remarks of drummers in Karachi and Delhi. Nathan Tabor hosted me in Delhi on several occasions and shared the excellent digital photos he had taken when the two of us followed the Muharram processions at Nizamuddin in December 2009.

In South India, J. Rajasekaran, A. Rajaram, and the latter's student Nataraj provided invaluable assistance with contacting, recording, and interviewing *Dalit* drummers and other musicians—Sekar beginning in 1982 and Rajaram from 1990. Riaz Fatima in Hyderabad, Andhra Pradesh, transcribed extensive interviews and recitations of Urdu poetry that I had collected in India and Pakistan. In Andhra Pradesh, I also thank M. Laxmaiah, Nagaraj, and Husain.

In the United States I owe a debt of gratitude to Abdul Haque Chang for his assistance with Sindhi language materials; Sabir Badalkhan translated valuable Baluchi materials that did not make their way into the current manuscript; Talal Almani, an undergraduate at Harvard, assisted me in translating Saraiki songs; and Irfan Moeen Khan, a graduate student at Harvard from Jacob Lines, Karachi, also provided insight into my materials. Amera Raza provided numerous contacts over the years, helped me with tricky translations, and was a constant source of advice on Shīʿī practice and life in Pakistan from the period when Ali's story began until the present.

An Essential Note from the Author

One spring morning in 2011, I awoke with some confusion, having had one of those dreams so vivid that its verisimilitude competed for a few moments with the reality of my waking life. The nested doll of the dream was my slumbering attempt to tangle the relations of the real and the creatively imagined. In the dream I was engaged in the mundane activity of writing an academic book. The twist was that the protagonist-researcher in the book was not me but an Indian, who was traveling to the places where I had conducted fieldwork on ritual drumming in South Asia and writing of his experiences. What's more, he was operating in a kind of "fictionland" only possible in a dream: he would constantly bump into people on the streets who were characters in other people's novels and short stories. Once, on a bus, he brushed up against a woman with a dragon tattoo.

In the weeks that followed, encouraged by some of my colleagues, I decided to play with the idea. Instead of fictionland, however, I set the protagonist, named Muharram Ali, in "ethnography-land." A great many of his interlocutors are real people, some of whom I'd met myself, others of whom I'd heard about. Ali's life experiences allowed me as an author a fresh way to explore a theme that has interested me since the late 1990s: the ways drumming and voices interconnect over vast regions of South and West Asia. His life story is presented in this book in order to bridge various frames of inquiry and communicate ethnographic and historical realities in South Asia that transcend the local details of any one individual's life. Ali and his interlocutors give voice to some of the forms of subjectivity I inferred from the actions and statements of my field consultants in India and Pakistan, especially during the period 1996 through 1999. I created Ali's character in part to avoid misattributing motivations to consultants,[1] some of whom I met only briefly. His story also creates continuity in what would otherwise be a greatly disjointed and unbalanced set of actual ethnographic accounts.

Ali's notes to himself appear from Chapter 4 onward in Tekton Pro, whether they are scratched out in the field or carefully inscribed at the end of the day. Ali's thoughts to himself, usually if they are not introduced by such words as "Ali thought . . .," are indicated in small caps beginning in Chapter 7. It is critical to bear in mind that neither Ali's thoughts nor his fieldnotes are quotations from my own fieldnotes. Indeed, many of his reflections could not have been generated during my own fieldwork. Aside from the discrepancies in our social and educational backgrounds, I was not yet ready to make many of the connections he does. Creating and developing the character of Ali entailed a discrete process of research. It was not possible for me to envision Ali's intellectual and emotional development until I had grappled with my data for many years—drawing from my other cumulative South Asian field experiences from 1982 until 2013.

Ali's story operates in what Victor Turner described in another context as the "subjunctive mood of culture," the world of "maybe, might be, as if, hypothesis, fantasy, conjecture, desire" (Turner 1986, 42). I take Ali's "fictive actions as imitations of actions which might at some time occur, given what we know about human possibility" (Gorfain 1986, 213)—or rather, given what I think I have learned through ethnographic inquiry. I invite you now to willfully forget what I've let on and join Ali and me in our explorations.

Note from the Editor

This work is hybrid, a chimera with thick spectacles, the legs of a gazelle, and the musical skin of a goat.[1] It skirts and teases the boundaries of the -ologies and the arts, dances along the frontiers of fact and fabrication. If "-ological" works, ever reliant on theory and empiricism, seek to persuade through established disciplinary pathways, artistic ones—no less disciplinary—rely on inference and allusion. As a novel, the present work uses settings in South Asia to tell a personal story of music and its humanistic limits. As an academic work, this book uses narrative tactics to address persistent questions regarding rhythm, melody, and voice in the field of ethnomusicology.

Many drummers in South Asia—the modest *ḍhol* player standing at the corner soliciting patronage from shrine pilgrims in Lahore, Pakistan, the classical mridangist of South India, even the *tāshā* player in Lucknow, India, who persists in beating out only a single drum pattern—draw from an ancient pool of musical thinking in South Asia. Navigating through its waters, crystalline or clouded, the authors find many conventional uses of the terms *rhythm* and *melody* misleading; they attempt to chart a new course. Unexpected riches lie submerged beneath the surface of some drumming: latent voices, broadcasts meant for many or a select few.

Two men collaborated in this venture. The American ethnomusicologist Richard Wolf contributed a wide-ranging analysis of South Asian drumming and related musical practices, which he based primarily on his own fieldwork in Pakistan and North India. The second contributor is the Indian journalist Dr. Muharram Ali, the protagonist of this novel, who undertook a journey in order to pursue questions about the *tāshā* drum that had haunted him since childhood. The three of us eventually transformed his notes on this journey into the narrative portion of the present book.

As the editor of this curious collaboration, it is my duty to prepare the reader for an unconventional reading experience. At times, when we examine the creature that is this book, we may see what looks like a botanical graft; at other times we may experience the seamless twining of foreign DNA strands. This results, practically speaking, in voices that are sometimes merged, sometimes separated, in the text. Some readers may find the transitions from voice to voice, from owl to gazelle, somewhat disorienting, and it is for these readers that I provide the present note. However, if you, dear reader, are intrigued by ambiguity, you may wish to experience these shifts without my mediation.

As a general guide, I urge you to ask yourself "why is this happening now?" when you encounter structural changes in the text. The abrupt transitions that remain in the text, as the authors have strenuously argued during their long sessions with me, are deliberately so. The authors will not reveal the reasons for their decisions, for they wish to invite readings that they have not yet envisioned. And then there is a larger question of voice that lurks throughout the book, which concerns the relationship between Wolf's and Ali's ultimate message (or messages). As the editor who eventually signed off on this amalgam, I hope the reader will be left thinking about how the social and political implications of the novel's plot could possibly relate to the ethnomusicological revelations in its analytic portions.

Because the majority of this book is meant to be read as literature, the authors have refrained from self-reflection and theorizing. They have remained silent with respect to the merits and pitfalls of creative nonfictional writing. For the academic specialist, however, notes have been provided at the end of the book. Chapter by chapter, this backmatter specifies the source material and discusses its transformation into the present form. It includes figures referred to in the narrative part of the text, which are essential for those interested in the musical and textual details, notes on local terms that are too specialized for the glossary, and local terms for which glosses in English, in single quotation marks, are used in the narrative. The emphasis on English glosses in the main text is not only to make for smoother reading but also because a single term in Urdu or another language may have several different English translations depending on its context. The chapter notes also contain selected lists of interviews and recordings upon which the chapter is based—some more literally than others. Endnotes are confined to situations in which a particular passage in the text must be specified exactly—usually for transcriptions of extended speech from field interviews. These interviews and recordings are available for consultation at the Archive and Research Centre for Ethnomusicology in Gurgaon, India, and at the Archive of World Music at Harvard University; many of the videos are deposited at the Archives of Traditional Music at Indiana University.

As a novel, the mode of presentation is for the most part linear. The character Ali develops over the course of the book's pages. The plot "goes" somewhere. Reading the chapter notes at the end of the book before reading the entire plot from beginning to end could spoil, for some, what is meant to be a surprise at the conclusion. In this spirit, I recommend that, even for the specialist, these notes be consulted only after completing the whole book.

The novel consists of ten chapters. Chapters 1 through 4 are divided into two unequal parts. The first part is an episode in the life of Muharram Ali. The second addresses issues of significance to the work as a whole: the status of drumming in relation to the voice in South Asia, the social position of drummers, and conceptualizing and naming drum patterns. Divided in two, each of the first four chapters resembles more a graft than a crossbreed. The shift between the story and the analysis is deliberate and marked. The authors have, however, attempted to create links between the episodes chosen from Ali's life and the analytical themes of each of these chapters. These analyses often refer back explicitly to Ali's story and contextualize the events thereof within the larger ethnographic purview of Wolf's fieldwork and bibliographic research. The technical discussions in the second parts of Chapters 3 and 4 may prove challenging for nonmusicologists. General readers may find it more rewarding to skim, skip, or return to those sections after reaching the end of the story.

As Ali's character matures, so, too, does the length of the treatment of his journey expand from chapter to chapter. By Chapter 5, the background and main analytic points having been presented in condensed form, the book proceeds more straightforwardly as the story of Ali, transitioning to analytic mode only briefly at the end of Chapter 7. As Ali develops as a character in the text, he gradually takes on responsibility for the analysis. His notes to himself, his reflections in his notebooks, his discussions with his friends all serve to supplant the analytic grafts that appeared in the first four chapters.

Although the text is the product of a collaboration, the puppetmaster of all the voices in the text is, in the end, Richard Wolf. For those concerned about the veracity of the ethnographic details in the text, including a great number of the quotations and descriptions of people and places, keep in mind Wolf's remark to me that although the writing is creative, he "plagiarized extensively from reality." All the characters in the book are, in their own ways, reliable witnesses, informants, and thoughtful actors.

Sufiya Rizvi
Lahore, Pakistan, May 2013

Note on Transcription and Musical Symbols

Transliterations of Urdu/Hindi, Persian, Panjabi, Sindhi, Saraiki, Tamil, Telugu, and Kota words adhere as closely as possible to ALA-Library of Congress romanization tables. Below follows not a complete inventory of each language's sounds but only those found in this text. Persian is transliterated according to Indic pronunciation unless referring to a specific practice or usage in Iran. The few words transcribed in Ḍumāki use the International Phonetic Alphabet (IPA). Dialectical pronunciations of some words are transcribed following the phonetics of speech rather than using standard orthography (especially for Tamil). For nonspecialists, the sounds of South Asian languages are approximated very roughly in the table below, using examples from English words or combinations thereof.

Many words are transcribed according to their orthography in modified Perso-Arabic script, though the same words appear in both Perso-Arabic and Devanagari versions of Urdu/Hindi, Sindhi, and Panjabi orthographies. One exception is *tāshā*, which is transcribed as it is spelled in Hindi. When derivations from Persian, Urdu, Hindi, Sanskrit, Tamil, and other languages are provided in the glossary, the spelling conventions from—and sometimes orthographies of—those source languages are used. Problems do crop up: for instance, the initial consonant for the word for the number four in Urdu/Hindi, *cār*, is pronounced the same as that in the Persian/Tojiki, *chār*, but they are transcribed differently because aspiration is not phonemic in Persian. The reverse problem obtains for the sounds transcribed /*ṭ*/. The letter /*ṭ*/ is retroflex in Indic languages. In Persian, /*ṭ*/ conventionally represents ط and is pronounced identically with other alveolar *t*s in Persian. This problem of overlapping transliterations is solved in the ALA-Library of Congress system of transliteration for Urdu by representing the same Perso-Arabic letter, ṭ̤.

With regard to stylistic matters, to ease the reading experience in a work with many foreign terms, I've adopted the following practices: except when English and foreign words are both used in the same quoted sentence or passage, I use only quotation marks and not italics. Proper names for ethnic groups and the like are transcribed with diacritics and capitalized but not italicized. When available, I retain English spellings for personal names as they were given to me in the field (for example, Bux for Bak̲h̲sh). Quotations transcribed from languages written in Perso-Arabic script that appear within a quotation are placed in italics in order to prevent misinterpreting the *'ayn* sign (') as the beginning of another internal quotation.

When Ali writes fieldnotes in situ or journal entries at the end of the day, these are indicated in Tekton Pro. When Ali's internal thoughts in an ongoing interaction appear in the manner of direct speech, they appear in small caps (however, if they are marked as indirect speech, as in "Ali thought back on some of the recurring issues in Pappu's statements—the intentions of the performer versus the needs and interpretations of the listener," they appear in ordinary typeface).

Boldface in syllable notations of drum patterns, indicates accent.

. used to indicate a pulse in a drum pattern represented by syllables. For example, in "**gin** . na," the dot indicates a pulse the same length as the syllables ***gin*** (here accented and hence boldfaced) and *na.*

_ when used in syllable notation, indicates that the syllables and pulses underlined are performed at double the base speed. For example, if "**gin** . na" is 3 pulses, "**gin** . na" would be 1½ pulses. This occurs rarely in the text. Occasionally, and only when specifically noted, an underline under a single syllable indicates secondary stress. An underscore also has a specific meaning in transliteration. The differences among these usages of the underscore should be obvious in context.

- used to indicate *ez̤āfeh/iz̤āfat* in Persian/Urdu constructions (always before /e/ or /i/, as in *bāzār-e huṣn*, "market of beauty")

a = /u/ in *butter*; the *fatḥeh* vowel in Indo-Persian. The Iranian Persian pronunciation of this vowel is more like /a/ in *bat.*

ā = /a/ in *father*

á = /a/ in *father* (transliteration of Arabic *alif maqṣūrah*)

i = /i/ in *pin*

ī = /ee/ in *seen*

u = /u/ in *put*; short vowel called *dammeh* in Persian, as pronounced in Indo-Persian and Indic languages written in Persian script (this vowel is pronounced /o/ in Iranian Persian)

ū = /oo/ in *too*

e = /e/ in *get* in Dravidian languages, here, Tamil, Telugu, and Kota. In Hindi and Urdu, the vowel /e/ is usually long, pronounced /ē/, except when it precedes /h/, in which case it is short. In this case it is a transliteration of the Urdu *alef* or Hindi अ, an /a/ sound except in this position. The Iranian Persian pronunciation of the *kasreh* vowel is /e/; the Indo-Persian pronunciation is /i/. The Iranian Persian pronunciation of the silent *he do-cheshme* ("two-eyed *he*") in final position after a consonant is also a short /e/; the equivalent in Indo-Persian and Indic languages written in Persian script is /a/ (final *he* silent)

ē = lengthened version of /e/; the /a/ in *gate* without the diphthong

ai = diphthong /i/ in *kite* (Tamil ஐ); diphthong /ai/ in *bait* (Hindi ऐ; Urdu اے)

o = /o/ in *coat*, but short and without the diphthong for Tamil, Telugu, and Kota and for the *dammeh* vowel in Iranian Persian. For Hindi, Urdu, Panjabi, Sindhi, and Saraiki, /o/ represents the long vowel /ō/.

ō = /o o/ in *go over there*. Elide the boundaries between *go* and *over* to approximate the long /o/. Tamil, Telugu, Kota.

au = /au/ in *caught*

k = /k/ in *kitten* (no aspiration where aspiration is phonemic); in Tamil, /k/ in an intervocalic or post-nasal position is voiced. It is usually voiceless in the initial position.

q = voiceless uvular stop (sometimes fricative); /k/ pronounced further back in the mouth than in English

kh = /kh/ in *jackhammer* (aspirated /k/)

k̲h̲ = /ch/ in *Chanukah* or Scottish *loch* (voiceless velar fricative)

g = /g/ in *game* (no aspiration where aspiration is phonemic)

gh = /gh/ in *foghorn* (aspirated /g/)

ġ = γ in modern Greek. Voiced velar fricative not found in modern English; similar to /r/ in French but very slightly further forward in the mouth.

g̈ = /g/ in *good*, spoken while inhaling (velar implosive in Sindhi and Saraiki)

ṅ = /n/ in *thing*

c = /ch/ in *chocolate* (no aspiration where aspiration is phonemic); in Tamil, /c/ is pronounced /s/ in the intervocalic position and /j/ in the post-nasal position ch = /ch-h/ in *catch-him* (aspirated /c/); in Persian, */ch/* is /ch/ as in *chocolate* and indicates the consonant چ.

j = /j/ in *jacket*

z = /z/ in *zebra*; corresponds to ز in Perso-Arabic script

ẓ = /z/ in *zebra*; corresponds to ظ in Perso-Arabic script

z̲ = in South Asian languages written in Perso-Arabic script, /z/ in *zebra*; corresponds to ذ (pronounced /th/ in *them* in Arabic and transliterated /d̲h̲/ here; compare *z̲ikr* [South Asia] and *d̲h̲ikr* [Arab heartland])

z̤ = /z/ in *zebra*; corresponds to ض in Perso-Arabic script

jh = /ge-h/ in *judge-him* (aspirated /j/ sound)

ñ = /n/ in *change*; in drum syllable notation only, /ñ/ indicates nasalization of the previous vowel

ṭ = /t/ in *curt* (retroflex t), except in Persian, where it is an alveolar /t/ as in English *till* and corresponds to ط in Perso-Arabic script. In written Tamil, /ṭ/ in intervocalic or post-nasal position is voiced to sound like /ḍ/.

ṭh = /t-h/ in *hurt-him* (aspirated retroflex /t/)

ḍ = /d/ in *curd* (retroflex /d/)

ṛ = /r/ in *fury*: pretend you are going to roll your /r/, but only initiate the roll with a flap from behind the alveolar ridge (retroflex flap; like /ḍ/ only shorter)

ḍ̤ = /d/ in *curd*, pronounced while inhaling (retroflex implosive); Sindhi and Saraiki

ḍh = /d-h/ in *hard-head* (retroflex aspirated /d/)

ṛh = same as /ṛ/ only aspirated (retroflex aspirated flap)

ṇ = /n/ in *corndog*. Curl the tongue back and pronounce /n/ in the same place as the retroflex consonant that follows it, for example, *kūṇḍi* (drum stick).

n̲ = /n/ as in the French name *Jean* (nasalizes the preceding vowel; do not touch the tongue to the alveolar ridge)

t = /t/ in Indic languages, like /t/ after the hyphen in *path-taker* (dental /t/); in transcription of written Tamil, /t/ in the intervocalic or post-nasal position is pronounced like /th/ in *this*. In Persian /t/ is closer to the English letter (alveolar /t/).

t̤ = /t/ in Indic languages written in Perso-Arabic script; corresponds to the letter ط

th = /t-h/ in *fat-head* (aspirated dental /t/)

d = /d/ after hyphen in *death-defying* (dental /d/)

d̲h̲ = /th/ in *this*; the letter ذ when transcribed from Arabic only (otherwise /z̲/)

dh = /dh/ in *headhunter* (aspirated dental /d/)

n = /n/ in *Nancy* (unless other wise noted, /n/ without diacritics will take on the position of articulation of the consonant that follows it)

p = /p/ in *Peter* (without aspiration where aspiration is phonemic); in written Tamil, /p/ in the intervocalic or post-nasal position is voiced (that is, pronounced /b/)

ph = /p-h/ in *step-hard* (aspirated /p/)

f = /f/ in *forget*

b = /b/ in *boy* (without aspiration where aspiration is phonemic)

bh = /b-h/ in *tub-heater* (aspirated /b/)

m = /m/ in *Mary*

ṃ = nasalized pronunciation that varies slightly according to language and syntactic context

y = /y/ in *youth*

r = /r/ in *rain* (tip of tongue on alveolar ridge in position of trilling)

l = /l/ in "*love that transliteration system*"

ḷ = /l/ in *curling* (retroflex /l/)

l̲ = /l/ in *Tamil* (not found in English, it varies from a fricative, sometimes written /zh/, to the sounds /y/ and /ḷ/ in different dialects)

v = /v/ in *very* (note that some of the languages in question do not distinguish between /v/ and /w/, rendering transcription somewhat arbitrary)

w = /w/ in *wary*

ś = /sh/ in *push* (transliterates Devanagari श)

sh = /sh/ in *push* (transliterates Perso-Arabic ش)

ṣ = For words of Indic origin: /ti/ in *portion* (retroflex /sh/; transliterates Devanagari ष); for words of Arabic origin: /s/ in *Sam* (transliterates ص)

s̱ = /s/ in *Sam* (transliterates ث, which is pronounced /th/ as in *three*, in Arabic; compare *hadis* in South Asian languages and *hadith* in Arabic)

h = /h/ in *help*. Exceptions when preceded by a short /a/ vowel: in Persian word-final position this will be transcribed /eh/ and pronounced /e/; in Urdu word-final position this will be transcribed /ah/ and pronounced /a/. In Urdu medial position the pronunciation of /ah/ becomes /eh/ and will be spelled as such, for example, *shehr* and not *shahr* (city), and *lehrā* not *lahrā* (repeating melodic pattern). However, I have chosen *shahnā'ī* rather than *shehnā'ī.*

ḥ = /h/ as in *help* or *aha!* (used mainly for *he jīmī,* ح, and once for Sanskrit /:/)

' = glottal stop or glide, depending on language and word. In the name *'Alī*, it is the onset of the vowel /a/. In the word *Shī'ah*, in the usual South Asian pronunciation, this letter is pronounced /y/—that is, "sheeya" (transliteration of the Perso-Arabic *'ayn,* ع).

' = glottal stop or glide, depending on language and word. In Urdu it is used as a transition between vowels. The proper pronunciation of *Qur'ān* in Arabic requires a glottal stop between the /r/ and the /ā/ (transliteration of the Perso-Arabic *hamza* ʾ).

ʔ = glottal stop (used here in representing drum syllable patterns with strong glottal articulation)

Tajikistan
Badakhshan
Panj
Hunza Valley
Afghanistan
Kabul
China
Islamabad
Pakistan
Indus
Lahore
Panjab
Multan
Panjab
Almora
Brahmaputra
Nepal
Delhi
Uttar
Agra
Mehmudabad
Lucknow
Pradesh
Ganges
Rajasthan
Ajmer
Sindh
Hyderabad
Karachi
Udaipur
India
Godavari
Mumbai
Telangana
Hyderabad
Andhra
Pradesh
Arabian
Sea
Bay
of
Bengal
Chennai
Bangalore
Dharmapuri
Dharmapuri
District
Tamil
Nadu
Kolmel Village
Nilgiri
Hills
Sri
Lanka

The Voice in the Drum

CHAPTER I

Drumming, Language, and the Voice in South Asia

Introduction

At age twenty-nine, anxiety-ridden because she had been unable to conceive, Sakina directed her prayers to the Panjatan Pāk. These "five pure" figures in the Shī'ī faith, the Prophet and his closest family members, are believed to have the power to intercede on behalf of the faithful. Sakina vowed to tie her future son's head with a turban and send him out on procession as a drummer in their honor. Drumming would commemorate, in a manner befitting the boy's station, the sacrifice of Husain in 680 CE. On the dusty fields of Karbala, Husain and his companions were crushed mercilessly by the henchmen of the Umayyad caliph Yazid, to whom Husain refused to pay fealty in the wake of the deaths of his father and his grandfather, the Prophet Muhammad. Sakina felt the precocious Sajjad was ready at the age of five to play a part in Muharram ceremonies; he cut quite a figure with that small *tāshā* tied around his neck. No sooner did the extended Muharram season pass than Sakina found herself pregnant again.

So it was that Muharram Ali entered the world on July 19, the first day of Muharram in 1958. This felicitous event coincided not only with the beginning of the year 1377 in the Hijri calendar and the beginning of Shī'ī Muslims' annual cycle of lamentation, but also with the anniversary of his elder brother Sajjad's dedication as a drummer. This conjunction of rites took root in Muharram Ali's imagination and eventually compelled him to travel the length and breadth of the Indian subcontinent searching for an interior, a mystical side to drumming that lay forever just beyond his grasp. His journey led him to chronicle dimensions of South Asian vernacular music hitherto unexplored in anything that he had read.

His mother Sakina was the third wife of Ahmed Ali Khan, the raja of Aminabad, a minor principality outside Lucknow. Ahmed Khan was Sunni, but like other aristocratic men of the Avadh region, he married a member of a prominent Shī'ī family. This marriage was both a political tool for allying with other princely families and a statement of his personal catholicity. Ahmed Khan was fond of paraphrasing Wajid Ali Shah, the last nawab of Lucknow, with such lines as "of my two eyes, one is Shī'ī and one is Sunni." He put on the airs of a nawab, immersing himself in paraphernalia recalling the exiled nineteenth-century aesthete and exercising what talents he had without expending much thought or effort.

Sajjad followed in his footsteps, imbibing his coursework in English literature as a baby drinks milk. It was somehow easy for him to memorize an extensive body of poetry in English, Urdu, and Persian and to learn the Lakhnavi style of reciting lament poetry. Listeners responded with cries of "Wāh, wāh" as Sajjad drew out the tones in Hindustani *rāg*s like *ghāra* with his deep, powerful, languorous voice and responded sinuously to the drone of his two supporting vocalists, called *bāzu*s. His talents were a liability, though. He never worked hard enough, never did enough *riyāẓ* (practice), really to make it as a musician. Nor, when his family fell on hard times, could he hold down a proper job; he was satisfied to say he "helped" with his friend's business. "The zeros," he said. "On those old dial phones the zeros were hard to reach. I would help the patrons dial the zeros." He had long fingers.

Muharram Ali—Ali for short—had a different disposition. Though less gifted artistically, Ali pursued music, like his other interests and responsibilities, with a curiosity and work ethic that were anathema to his brother. His gravitas led schoolmates to call him "Maulvi Sahab," an epithet invoking the image of a moralizing elderly man with a long beard. Reflecting privately on this later in life, he was fond of attributing his quasi-scholarly bent to an indirect encounter with the ethnomusicologist Regula Qureshi. He had overheard this Swiss-born, Urdu-speaking scholar discussing, with great seriousness, the genres of *soz* and *salām* with the raja of Mehmudabad. Knowing only how to write Devangari script and a little English himself at that time, Ali was intrigued to see her take notes from right to left in the Urdu *nastaliq* script and from left to right using musical notation.

"Mehmudabad Uncle" was his father's friend and a prominent Shī'ī sponsor of the major Muharram procession in his principality. Ali used to play with the children in the compound around the Mehmudabad palace when he was a child, chasing spiders with thumbed marbles, screaming, and throwing stones at fulvous fruit bats in the *naubat k̲h̲āna*—the "house of drums" where the *shahnā'ī* and kettledrum players acoustically broadcast *mars̲iyah* and *soz* melodies during the principal days of Muharram.

A reflective child, Ali was struck by the piety of his South Indian ayah, Kannamma, the orphaned illegitimate child of an Anglo-Indian military serviceman and his Madrasi cook. Kannamma kept a small wooden crate with her possessions, in which she arranged a few deity portraits and statues. The likenesses in stone and brass depicted the elephant-headed god Ganesh, the *vīṇā*-playing goddess of knowledge Sarasvati, and several other pan-Indian deities. Motivated by her sense of being different as a South Indian and a Hindu in this household, she had pieced together this amalgam from observing rites in local temples and images of Hinduism

Side view of Mehmudabad Palace, Mehmudabad, Uttar Pradesh, India, 1998. Photo by the author.

in Indian films, rather than through her mother, who had died when Kannamma was an infant. Ali's grandmother would certainly have objected to keeping these icons in the house, but who was to know? Ali would tiptoe by the potted ferns on the verandah and peek through the dusty, tattered blue curtain into the servants' quarters in the morning when Kannamma stole a moment to perform puja. When he was a bit older he wondered how the small *imambarah* his mother asked Ahmad Khan to have built in their haveli was so different from the little crate Kannamma kept hidden away.

The *imambarah*, modeled after a Shīʻī shrine commemorating the Prophet's family and martyrs of Karbala, was a room filled with artifacts related to Muharram: a golden replica of Imam Husain's mausoleum and green flags and staves draped in glittering shades of gold and red. These *ʻalams* were surmounted by shapes representing the Panjatan: thin layers of gold and silver over wood fashioned into a golden minaret rising out of a teardrop, with two "fingers," one to each side, and a solid steel figure of a hand with the names of the Panjatan Pak, the Prophet, Ali, Fatimah, Hasan, and Husain, inscribed by the delicate hand of a Persian calligrapher.

Sometimes Sakina would sit in that room and recite from the *bastah* of handwritten Urdu *marṡiyah* poems she had inherited from her mother. Sajjad's and Muharram Ali's earliest musical sensibilities were formed from listening to their mother's tuneful recitations. A great ustad in Delhi once said, "*Soz* is the basis of all Hindustani music." In this household, where religious piety was not at odds with aesthetic enjoyment, this statement rang true.

At the age of nine, Ali attended his first Shāhī Zarī procession—the famous Shīʻī procession held in Lucknow on the first of Muharram. The processions with which he was familiar in Aminabad and Mehmudabad hardly prepared him for what he saw. The ones at home included only a few small memorial floats (*taʻziyah*s), a couple of camels, twenty *ʻalam*s, a group of *soz* and *marṡiyah* reciters, *ḍhol-tāshā* players, and performers on *naqqārah* and *shahnāʼī*. In Lucknow, by contrast, there were many bands from all over the city, including impressively uniformed brass bands, the police bagpipe band, many camels, and several elephants. The *zarī*s, or *taʻziyah*s, representing the mausoleum of Imam Husain were constructed of bamboo, wax, colored paper, and foil and towered ten meters overhead. An elephant led the procession from the "Large" (*baṛa*) Imambarah to the "Small" (*choṭa*) Imambarah that day, carrying two enormous kettledrums called *dhus*, which were to disappear from the scene twenty years later. Walking somberly near the front of the procession were Shīʻī drummers from the Choṭa Imambara. The *ḍhol* and *tāshā* players beat the only pattern

Ḍhol, tāshā, and *karnā* (long trumpet) leading a procession on the first of Muharram, April 27, 1998. Photo by the author.

they knew: the three-stroke pattern they used for announcing the times of prayer on normal days, when they sat in the *naubat ḵẖāna* across the street from the imambarah.

Since his early childhood, Ali had taken an interest in *ḍhol-tāshā* playing in Aminabad and always kept his ears attuned to the possibility of finding excellent players. His father regaled him and his brother with stories of Lucknow's heyday, when Wajid Ali Shah would lead his own royal Muharram processions as a *tāshā* player. Ali read contemporary accounts of Muharram processions in nineteenth-century Lucknow by the Persian writer

Ali Muhammad Kazim (published in 1887). He also devoured the Urdu novels and collected essays of the Lucknow native Abdul Halim Sharar (1869–1926), who spent ten years of his youth in Matiya Burj, Calcutta, where Wajid Ali Shah was exiled by the British in 1856. Sharar wrote extensively on the manners and customs of Lucknow in his lifetime and collected historical information from oral and rare printed sources. Sharar had a social reformist bent; he tried, among other things, to use his Urdu literary journal *Dil Gudaz* to foster an understanding between Hindus and Muslims. He felt their relations had deteriorated under the influence of the Indian National Congress. The idea of a golden age in which Hindus, Shīʻahs, and Sunnis lived cooperatively appealed to Ali.

Ali imagined the nineteenth-century processions in which *tāshā* players engaged in competitions of speed and complexity in front of their nawab; he imagined a drummer perched atop an elephant as Kazim described it, with a red woolen blanket draped on the elephant. The drummer would take his stick and hit the *dhus* again and again, striking, pounding the drum, sending reverberations far in all directions. In Ali's own childhood, he saw tears flow from the eyes of Mehmudabad Uncle at the sound of these drums of war; the raja would reward the sensitive *dhus* drummer with money and gifts.

Musician perched atop a camel flanked by kettledrums (*naqqārahs*). Mehmudabad, Uttar Pradesh, India. Fortieth day (*chehlum*) Muharram ceremony, June 18, 1998. Photo by the author.

The contrast between the somber *tāshā* players from the Choṭa Imambarah and the royal splendor of the procession as a whole struck Ali as somewhat odd. It was only when he was much older and had begun to fixate on, even obsess about, the *tāshā* drums that he learned what lay behind their sober performance. When he went to see them at the Choṭa Imambarah they told him they were not like other *ḍhol-tāshā* groups: they were not musicians. Observant Shī'ahs, they were using the drums to recite the words "Sain Imam Husain Haidar." They were infusing the names of the Shī'ī imams Ali and Husain into the sound of the drums. To Muharram Ali, this was a revelation.

: : :

This book tells a story of drumming and other instrumental traditions that are interconnected over vast regions of South and West Asia in sometimes surprising ways.

The traditions considered here qualify broadly as functional music rather than concert music and include the public instrumental music of weddings, funerals, and religious holidays. Despite being geographically widespread and heard almost every day, many of these traditions are also marginal artistically and socially speaking: the sounds produced are seldom taken seriously as music, and their practitioners are not accorded much respect (see Booth 2005). The limited repertoires of some ensembles such as the Choṭa Imambara *ḍhol-tāshā* group, moreover, may challenge the boundaries of what, for many, counts as music. These possible limitations in artistry and complexity need not interfere with our recognizing, in the principles by which these repertoires are organized and manner in which they are ritually used, a larger set of patterns that pervade functional music of South Asia and to some extent North and South Indian classical music as well. The many, sometimes shallow, local traditions of largely functional music are illuminated by a multifocal view—attending to the local details of practice and exegesis while keeping in mind a multisited frame extending to various scales of vision.

One of the analytic goals of the book is to show how performed texts are related to their verbal or vocal models—that is to say, how an instrumental pattern reiterates features of an abstract textual model, a concrete vocal performance, or an imagined vocal model. More broadly, I also wish to consider what it means in particular contexts for instruments to be voicelike and carry textual messages, whether or not the wider circles of listeners in a public gathering have access to these semantic details.

Common conceptions of rhythmic-melodic patterning link many traditions presented in this book. Some involve nomenclature, such as naming a pattern by its constituent number of stressed strokes, and some concern habits of performance, such as the tendency to thicken the texture of a pattern and conclude with a tripartite cadence. The use of the conjoined term *rhythmic-melodic* rather than *rhythmic and melodic* is meant to problematize the idea that rhythm and melody are separable, practically speaking, either in South Asian experience or in cross-cultural musicological analysis (see Jones 1959, 61*ff.*). As Lewis Rowell noted in *Music and Musical Thought in Early India*, "it is more accurate to think of the melodic and drum sounds of Indian music as coordinate dimensions of pitch, held in check within the regulating framework of rhythm" (Rowell 1992, 116). By *rhythm*, in this case, Rowell is referring to the "structural rhythm" of *tāla*, a conceptual entity not heard directly in the music.

The perception of rhythmic activity in a concrete performance obviously depends on the embodiment of that rhythm by an instrument or the voice. The instrumental sound unfolding in time creates fine distinctions of timbre and tone that can always be described in qualitative terms. In this sense, rhythm-melody is phenomenologically prior to rhythm. Actual rhythms are all rhythm-melodies, rhythm-harmonies, rhythm-textures, rhythm-timbres, rhythm-body-movements, and so forth.

Melodies are articulated by various means. For convenience, I will call the melody of an instrument capable of playing discrete tones a *tone-melody* and that of successive articulations and timbres on a percussion instrument a *stroke-melody* or a *drum pattern* (but not a rhythm). Clearly, tone-melodies also involve timbral distinctions and kinetic attacks (less so for the voice), and both tone- and stroke-melodies subsume ideas of rhythmic process. That both should be viewed as kinds of melodies in local terms is suggested by the ways South Asians use some musical vocabulary nontechnically. For instance, the Hindi term *dhun*, nominally "tune," is sometimes used to describe the distinguishing features of a drum pattern. (This usage is further explored in Chapter 3.)

Other ethnomusicologists have also used the term *melody* to describe patterns iterated on percussion instruments. Jones noted, for instance, that the drums accompanying the Ewe master drum Atsimevu produce rhythmic "tunes" (1959, 1:61*ff.*). More broadly, in discussing Philippine and other Asian musical instruments, José Maceda drew a distinction between "drone" as a "periodic reiteration or as a continuous sounding of one or more tones which act as organ points, ostinati, centres or pivots around which a melody circulates" and "melody," which, "in contrast to drone in the same piece of music, consists of a permutation, combination or an arrangement of two or more tones with or without pitch" (Maceda 1974,

247). Maceda's specific formulation does not work very well for some of the patterns I describe as either tone- or stroke-melodies because many of them repeat without much variation and may or may not serve as a ground for further variation.

The capacity of drum patterns to sound like texts and be melodic, even if they do not vary, points to a salience that deserves careful attention. For example, a drum pattern may function like a melody in the sense of being a foreground—the thing for which a repertorial item consisting of conventionally melodic instruments and drums is named—rather than a form of support or accompaniment. It may be hard for an American listener to imagine the tune "Yankee Doodle" as a secondary phenomenon to a drum pattern playing alongside it, for instance, but that is sometimes how the hierarchy works in South Asian vernacular traditions. Somewhat more comparable in Europe and the Americas are dance grooves. Dancers of the mambo, for instance, extract a short-short-long sequence (three steps and a rest) from one of a variety of compound rhythmic and melodic patterns. The mambo cannot be reduced to short-short-long and neither can it be reduced to a particular tone-melody.

Another alternative to the tone-melody-accompanied-by-drums model in North India and Pakistan is that of the *lehrā*. In some instrumental and dance forms an instrumentalist may repeat a melody (*lehrā*) against which a drummer or dancer may perform rhythmically complex moves.

The potential for a drum pattern to be foregrounded is musically significant in the sense that stroke-melody instruments like drums can in some contexts trump tone-melody instruments like bagpipes or double-reed aerophones. This is also significant from the perspective of contextual meaning. In some contexts the tone-melody may be more important and in others the stroke-melody may receive emphasis. Among the Kotas of South India, for instance, many of the tone-melodies on the double-reed *koḷ* index specific rituals, deities, stories, dances, or events. There are, in contrast, only a small number of percussion patterns, or stroke-melodies (three or four depending on how one counts), only one of which specifically indexes non-Kota deities.

A further implication of tone- and stroke-melody indexicality is the possibility of both elements playing a significant role in the semiotics of the encompassing event or events. By virtue of such features as timbre, tempo, tone-melody, and the contextual associations of the instruments on which they are played, instrumental patterns can serve as conceptual bridges between one event and another and carry both positive and negative associations. Many Shī'ī participants in Muharram object to *tāshā* drumming because of the instrument's association with wedding celebrations, and important distinctions between occasions such as these, seen as conflicting in emotional and moral terms, are sometimes articulated through the use of distinct drum repertoires. While recognizing these preferences for articulating contextual differences using musical patterns, we also consider cases that are more complicated, including the use of wedding music during Muharram or a Sufi *'urs*, Shī'ahs playing the *tāshā* for themselves for Muharram, and drumming that quotes other drumming.

In order to investigate further what it means for an instrument to be vocal, and why this might or might not be surprising, it is necessary to consider the broad historical context in which voices and instruments have been co-constructed in the history of the Indian subcontinent and regions west. Although Ali's story takes place in Uttar Pradesh, Delhi, the Panjab, and Sindh, I include in the following discussion—and in early parts of the book—many examples from South India. These help create a picture that transcends the bounds of Ali's travels.

Vocal Hierarchies

Hierarchies favoring the human voice and verbal artists over musical instruments and instrumentalists are diverse and widespread in South and West Asia. Some are rooted in a rich and ancient set of Indic philosophical and aesthetic traditions dating from the fourth century BCE through the first millennium of the common era. Bharata, in the *Nāṭyaśāstra* (c. second century BCE to the second century CE), for instance, described the seven *svaras* (tones) as emanating first from the "vīṇā of the body" and then becoming manifest in the (wooden) *vīṇā*, drums, and idiophones (Bharata Muni 1986, 199; Kumar and Ghosh 2010, 1693; Ellingson 1980, 432–33). The *Bṛhaddeśī* (c. ninth century) of Matanga introduced the concept of *nādabrahman*, the divinely inhabited sound that, animated by breath, becomes an essential agent in the composition of the universe (Rowell 1992, 43). Buddhist traditions during this period privileged the voice by giving weight to intoned recitations, restricting the kinds of instrumental music appropriate to festivals and ceremonies, and grounding instrumental music in vocal sounds/syllables (Ellingson 1980).[1]

Other vococentric hierarchies can be traced to Muslim and Arabic sources.[2] The Arab general Muhammad bin Qasim's conquest of Sindh in 711 initiated a significant period of interaction between Muslims and local populations during which Islamic views concerning the voice and musical instruments may first have been introduced to the subcontinent.[3] The eleventh-century Ghaznavid expansion into South Asia and the subsequent development of Lahore as a cultural center paved the way for a more substantial Islamic impact in South Asia. A major contributor was the mystic Ali ibn Uthman al-Hujwiri (c. 990–1077). His *Kashf-al maḥjūb,* the oldest extant work on Sufism in the Persian language, provides as good an introduction as any to Muslim thought regarding vocality and the moral role of the listener.

Al-Hujwiri described David's voice as so beautiful and enchanting that it attracted all manner of birds and wild beasts; it caused birds to fall from the sky, water to cease flowing, and enraptured listeners to perish, unaware of their need for food or water. God permitted Iblīs (Satan) to "work his will and display his wiles" by playing instrumental music in order to distinguish the "followers of truth" from those who were merely slaves of their temperament. The followers of truth, wrote al-Hujwiri, could perceive the divine source of David's voice and recognize the devil's music as a temptation (Nicholson 1996, 402–3).

These Indic and Muslim sources, along with many others, position the voice favorably in relation to instrumental music, but in different ways. The early Indic sources associated with what came to be called Hinduism represented sound as an animating force in the universe that originated from the vital breath of the human body. Instrumental music was represented as a secondary manifestation of this breath but was not negatively valued. Philosophers in Buddhist and Muslim traditions focused on the capacity of vocal sounds to help humans realize favorable ends in the two systems of faith, while expressing caution over music's potential to be an immoral distraction. While the early "Hindu" concepts of sound and voice are more inclusive and abstract than are those of the Buddhist and Muslim traditions, voice in all of these traditions implied vocal iterations of texts or syllables; as we shall see, some modern notions of vocality do not rely as much on text.

While philosophical treatments of music tended to favor the voice, practical discussions of pitch relationships relied on the physical configuration of the *vīṇā*. The stringed instrument to which the name *vīṇā* applied did not remain constant from treatise to treatise or century to century. Types of *vīṇā* mentioned in the *Nāṭyaśāstra*, for instance, were the bow harp and the ovoid lute; types referenced in later periods were varieties of stick zithers. Harold Powers (1980, 78) noted that "whenever *a priori* pitch relationships have been important in South Asian music theory, the instrument of reference has always been the current form of vīṇā." Powers alludes to the prevalence of oscillation and other forms of pitch movement in the music of South Asia. When music theorists needed to treat *svara*s as stable entities, they used the strings or frets of the *vīṇā* to represent them. One of the broad differences by which the thirteenth-century treatise *Sangītaratnākara* by Sarngadeva is distinguished from treatises of the sixteenth and seventeenth centuries and from modern discussions in Karnatak music concerned the role of the *vīṇā* in describing *gamaka*s (integral ornaments). According to Powers, Sarngadeva discussed gamaka as "predominantly" vocal but also as instrumental. The later treatises and modern discussions have, in contrast, relied primarily on "the plucked and fretted *vīṇā* as an instrument of reference" (ibid., 106). As a practical matter, then, the musical voice has always been defined in relation to musical instruments, with the *vīṇā* often serving as a conceptual model for the voice even while "the voice," writ large, is emphasized in philosophical terms.

Any specific attempt to connect conceptions of the voice in premodern texts to contemporary views of the voice would ideally consider the motivation of particular actors who do so. This is the intention of Amanda Weidman, who argues that the "valorization of the voice" in South Indian classical (Karnatak) music is a specifically twentieth- and twenty-first-century phenomenon. Musicians and musicologists of this period sought to differentiate the authenticity and Indianness of their "vocal" music from the "instrumental" music they saw as characterizing the classical music of the West. Weidman discounts the long history of vococentrism in South Asia by writing that any attempt to relate contemporary practice to this history in fact *removes* "Indian music" from history and ignores "the entailments of this music in the project of modernity"; claims to the "essentially vocal character" of Indian music, in her view, "have a distinctly Orientalist ring" (Weidman 2006, 5–6). While one must agree that conceptions of the voice in the twentieth century have, indeed, been tied up in the growth of an urban middle class, the Tamil language movement, and self-conscious attempts to balance "tradition" with "modernity," Weidman offers no evidence of a historical process whereby one dominant conception (not valorizing the voice?) came to be replaced by another. She does not mention the shift in theoretical treatment of vocal ornament in the direction of the *vīṇā* discussed above.

Without evidence of a paradigm shift with regard to dominant views concerning the voice—even locally in Madras—it is hard to understand modern-day "valorizations" of the voice, however they may be inflected, as anything more than a new set of variations on a widespread and complicated set of philosophical positions, social hierarchies, and aesthetic preferences that have persisted for centuries. Put another way, vococentrism is overdetermined in South Asia. Many different hierarchies favoring the voice and vocalists continue to figure prominently in South Asian culture and society, and they cannot all be accounted for. This point is important to bear in mind as we encounter instances of instruments conveying text or instrumental sound in different settings; explaining the process in a Muslim context solely in terms of an "Islamic emphasis on the word," for instance, would be vastly reductive, given the complex interplay of populations in South Asia for millennia.

In preparation for exploring the voices in drumming, it will be useful to survey a range of contexts, across our broad region, in which aspects of the voice are valorized and those who specialize in vocal arts occupy positions of status.

Vocalists and Instrumentalists

We begin in South India, where ideologies of the voice in relation to musical instruments have received attention in recent scholarship. Many Karnatak music lovers express a preference for vocalists as main artists and for instruments that sound particularly vocal, especially the violin. The meaning of *vocal* in this context, Weidman argues convincingly, is informed by the seamless melodic continuities made possible on the violin: the "reproducible qualities [of this style] are no longer words and phrases but a generalized, homogenized, virtuosic voice" (Weidman 2006, 51). This characterization of voice is also negatively supported in relation to the South Indian *vīṇā*, which is now sometimes criticized for its inadequacy in mimicking the "continuity" of the voice.

Some performers, such as the vocalist and self-taught *vīṇā* player T. N. Seshagopalan, eschew the idiomatic capabilities of the Sarasvati *vīṇā*—the sounds intimately connected with the physical layout of the instrument—in favor of this abstract notion of continuity. The characteristics of this continuity correspond roughly with Weidman's "homogenized, virtuosic voice." It is, however, possible for *vīṇā* players to articulate aspects of text using techniques idiomatic to the instrument including left-hand plucks and stops. These latter are heard by some South Indian listeners as contrary to a vocal ideal because they create temporary discontinuities of sound. Many readers may find this idea of vocality counterintuitive: many kinds of vocal music involve a variety of stops and articulations and are no less vocal as a result. Regardless of technique, any musician, vocalist or instrumentalist, who lays emphasis on clarity of text can be praised in South India for his or her "sāhitya suddham" (purity of lyrics); vocalness and verbalness are linked but also distinguishable.

Despite their attention to vocality, tone-melody instrumentalists seldom attain the same levels of acclaim or economic benefit as do Karnatak vocalists. This is true whether they are *vīṇā* players on the concert stage or *nāgasvaram* players who perform in connection with South Indian Hindu temple rituals. Ritual drummers, in their turn, occupy a spectrum of social, ritual, and economic positions below those of the tone-melody makers and concert-accompanist drummers. They may range from the *tavil* players who accompany *nāgasvaram* players in and around Hindu temples in South India to folk drummers such as players of the *uṟumi* and *pampai* to performers on the *tappaṭṭai*, *paṟai, tājā* (that is, the *tāshā*), and *mattaḷam*. Depending on the region, the latter performers are generally members of scheduled castes (also called untouchables or Dalits). By virtue of their historical association with polluting substances (such as leather) and contexts (such as funeral rituals), these musicians are sometimes still kept at a distance from multi-caste temples where they might perform during a festival. However, the frame drum (*paṟai* or *tappaṭṭai*) has also become a symbol around which communities who have historically been discriminated against now rally (for example, Sherinian 2009).[4]

These observations regarding ritual drummers versus classical accompanists and regarding percussion players versus tone-melody instrumentalists and vocalists also describe aspects of musical-social structure in North India and Pakistan. As Daniel Neuman observed: "By relegating the subordinate musical function to separate and socially inferior musical specialists, the problem of leading and following was resolved through Indian civilization's classic strategy, occupational caste specialization" (Neuman 1990, 136).

In the very different set of social and musical circumstances in the hill range bordering Tamil Nadu, Kerala, and Karnataka, the Toda and Mullu Kurumba communities, who successfully claimed superior rank (at least in colonial eyes) in the two tribal systems of the Nilgiri plateau and the Wynad, respectively, have historically specialized in vocal arts, while many of their well-known tribal neighbors, such as the Kotas, have been client instrumentalists. These instances merely reinforce the correlation between certain kinds of status claims and vocal rather than instrumental performance; they do not indicate that singing and not playing musical instruments is itself a reason for attaining status. This is in contrast with vegetarianism, which strongly connotes superior ritual rank in Hindu social hierarchies, and clienthood, especially performing services for funerals, which tends to confer inferior rank. An example of the former are the Todas, who present themselves as vegetarians, and of the latter, the Kotas, who at one time performed music for Toda funerals but ceased to do so in protest against their increasingly poor treatment. That is, the Kotas did not accept the inferior hierarchical position that was thrust upon them, particularly after European contact.

The voice also occupies pride of place when we circle back to classical musical milieux of North India and Pakistan, where instrumentalists, who are subordinate to vocalists (Neuman 1990, 134), often claim legitimacy and status through alliance to the so-called *gāyaki ang,* or "vocal style."[5] This term may be invoked in a rather general way to refer to an ideology favoring a voicelike continuity of tone, again recalling the kind of violin-voice Weidman describes but without strong evidence of the violin's influence.[6]

Among the several North Indian classical styles, *dhrupad* carries an air of antiquity and authenticity, not only because it is historically old but also because of its rootedness in a vocal medium and because of its use of longstanding poetic forms. *Dhrupad*'s symbolic weight carries over to instrumental music when, for example, the rhythms of *dhrupad* texts are used to create instrumental strumming patterns, as in the teaching of Ali Akbar Khan (George Ruckert, pers. comm., May 18, 2011).

We have already encountered a strain of Islamic thought regarding the place of the voice in moral listening. In some Muslim contexts, terms that denote singing, such as *gānā* in Hindi/Urdu, connote lightness and frivolity, if not decadence; "singing" and "music" (*mūsiqī*) are considered unfit for certain forms of Muslim religious activity, such as praying in a *masjid* (mosque), so practitioners take measures to distance what they perform from music by recourse to verbocentric conceptions of voice. Verbs such as *paṛhnā* in Urdu and *k̲h̲āndan* in Persian, which mean primarily "to read or recite," are used to describe melodic recitations that are musically equivalent to singing but conceptually distinct from music. This form of terminological distinction extends also to the persons who perform, so vocalists are *gawaiyā,* or singers of a particular genre, *k̲h̲ayāliyā* for *k̲h̲ayāl* and *dhrupadiyā* for *dhrupad* (Neuman 1990, 89). Iqbal Ahmed Khan, senior vocalist in the Delhi *gharāna*, is recognized as a *k̲h̲ayāliyā* when he performs Hindustani classical music. When he performs *soz* for a *majlis*—a religious assembly for recalling the events of Karbala and praising members of the Prophet's family—he is called a *soz k͟hwān*, a "reciter" of *soz*. If he were singing a classical piece in the genre called *k͟hayāl* he would be considered a "singer." This distinction in terminology would apply even if the *soz* and the *k͟hayāl* were, musically speaking, in the same melodic framework (*rāga*).

Whereas Hindustani tone-melody makers make claims of vocality through reference to the *gāyaki ang*, this does not necessarily imply that they attempt to articulate specific words, just as the homogenized vocal style Weidman describes for the violin does not imply emphasis on verbal phrases. However, in other instances of instrumental performance, the articulation of words is important; these traditions may be verbocentric without being vococentric.

Unlike Shīʿī recitations, which avoid symbolic associations with music, religious rituals associated with Chishti and other Sufi shrines in South Asia make explicit use of music, drawing from philosophies about the *sama'*, or spiritual concert, which "free[s] the physical effort from conscious thought, since both mind and will must be suspended if ecstasy is to be attained." This ecstasy does not (necessarily) constitute a direct encounter with God but, rather, an experience of union, an "emotional identification" with God, or an "illusion of a glimpse into Reality," meant for the common person (Trimingham 1998, 200). The most prevalent musical genre associated with Sufism in South Asia is *qawwālī*, whose very name draws from the Arabic term *qawl*, meaning "word or utterance," and whose emotional impact relies on combining musical expression with the correctly timed delivery and repetition of poetic lines and phrases. Instrumental iteration of words is focused mainly in the *naġmah* ("melody"), the harmonium introductions to *qawwālī* songs.

In terms of the vocalist-instrumentalist hierarchy, the singer (*qawwāl*) is the highest-ranking member of a group and is called the *mohri* ("leading chess figure"). There are typically two accompanying vocalist *āvāzia* who play harmonium and sit in the front row, a tabla or *ḍholak* player, and six or more men who clap and provide vocal support (*vāri kehan wāle*). In addition there may be a *bōl dasan wālā* who reads from a book and prompts the lead singer (Nayyar 1988, 10). The *qawwālī* drummer would typically rank lower than a classical drummer and would not, ordinarily, perform a drum solo. Other ritual drummers who perform repertoire based on specific drum patterns (stroke-melodies) might in fact play more intricately than do these accompanists, but they normally occupy a lower status category, particularly if they must earn a living by performing services at shrines, weddings, and so forth.

Text, Prosody, Musical Instruments, and the Body

Ritual stroke-melody drumming and other forms of instrumental music have a voice in the sense that they may carry specific verbal messages, which, in Muslim contexts, consist of words or short phrases that function as *ẕikr*s. A *ẕikr* (*ḏẖikr* in Arabic), which means literally a "remembrance," is a formulaic phrase that focuses the mind on God and may also bring about an aroused state of consciousness called *ḥāl* (literally, "condition"). *Ẕikr*s, associated with Sufi Islam, are justified by numerous injunctions in the Qur'ān to remember God, for example, Qur'ān 13:28: [Those] "who have believed and whose hearts have rest in the remembrance of Allah. Verily in the remembrance of Allah do [their] hearts find rest!" (Pickthall 1977, 244).

Historically, *ẕikr* was one of several forms of internal remembrance. With the growth and spread of Sufism in the eleventh century, *ẕikr* recitation styles in different schools (*ṯarīqat*) developed as forms of discipline. Techniques involved coordinating the utterances, or parts of them, with controlled breathing and a focus on different parts of the body; the move from vocalization and embodiment of the *ẕikr* to the use of *ẕikr*s in music and dance in orders such as the Mevlevis was a natural, if controversial, one (Hodgson 1974, 2:210–14).

In parts of India ranging from Hyderabad in the South to Lucknow, Panjab, and Rajasthan in the North, and in the Panjab and Sindh in Pakistan, *ẕikr*s have figured prominently in musical forms associated with Sufi rituals, the most well-known genre of which is *qawwālī*. One *qawwālī* song, "Lāl Merī Pat," employs *ẕikr*-like material that also forms the basis for patterns on some musical instruments. Versions of what became this *qawwālī* song, originally a folk tune, gained popularity in the 1960s when the singer Reshma sang it at the shrine of the Sufi saint Lāl Shahbāz Qalandar in Sindh (Abbas 2002, 25). The song circulated in South Asia through the concerts and recordings of Pakistan's top *qawwāl*s and other singers, including Nusrat Fateh Ali Khan and Abida Parveen. We need consider only the refrain:

Sindhṛi dā, sewan dā sakhi
Shahbāz qalandar
Dam-ā-dam mast qalandar
Sakhi shahbāz qalandar
'Ali dam dam de andar
O lāl merī, o lāl merī

[Oh you, Saint Lāl Shahbāz Qalandar] of Sindh
[Oh you, female] Devotee/companion of Sewan [the town in Sindh where the shrine lies], Shahbāz Qalandar.
With each and every breath [you say the name of God], intoxicated mystic
Devotee/companion Shahbāz,
ʻAli within each breath,
Oh my precious beloved (see Abbas 2002, 26; Wolf 2006).

References to "mast qalandar," or intoxicated mystic, especially in combination with text alluding to the process of taking breaths—breath after breath, each and every breath, and so forth—are widespread in Pakistan and Iran. The content of the phrase is significant in that it describes the physical act of performing a *ẕikr*—that is, through controlling of the breath—and thus constitutes a motivation for its own performance. The breaths may also have the connotation of inhalations of hashish or opium, as Sufi mendicants in South Asia often supplement their ecstatic disciplines with such drugs.

"Mast qalandar" has also become a mnemonic and an alternative name for the stroke-melody on the *ḍhol* in Pakistan called *dhamāl*. Whereas some texts that are associated with drum patterns are known to limited audiences, the mast qalandar pattern is recognizable to a great many shrine-goers in Pakistan—particularly in the Panjab, Sindh, and Baluchistan. This becomes clear, for instance, when the blend of pious shrine-goers and hip arts college students in Lahore cry out "Mast qalandar" upon hearing the signature riff of *dhamāl* during Thursday night performances by the local celebrity, *malaṅg* Pappu Sain, and his partner at the Shah Jamal shrine.[7] The words *mast qalandar* are synecdochical for the whole phrase *dam-ā-dam mast qalandar*.

The most obvious way the drum can mimic the sound of language is by reinforcing the text's implied rhythm. The building blocks for such rhythms in all the languages of the subcontinent as well as in Persian are sequences of long and short syllables. In the case of *dam-ā-dam mast qalandar*, the syllables divide and are rhythmically rendered as follows:

⏑	—	—	—	(⏑)	⏑	—	—
da	mā	dam	mas	t	qa	lan	dar
♪	♩	♩	♩.		♪	♩	♩‿♩.

The *t* in *mast* is scanned as a short (⏑) syllable in Urdu, which is to say it theoretically adds length to the syllable *mas*, which is already long (—)

according to the Perso-Arabic system of prosody. The sequence of musical durations notated below the text shows the typical rhythm to which this phrase is sung or chanted and the corresponding drum pattern played. In this case, the rhythm can be derived directly from the prosody of the phrase by assigning an eighth note to a short syllable and a quarter note to a long syllable. Not all associations between text, vocal delivery, and instrumental rendition are so simple, but understanding this potential kind of prosodic relationship is a key starting point.

Ẕikr-like phrases with a similar theme extend westward beyond the borders of Pakistan. The eastern Khorasani city of Torbat-e Jam (in Iran) has been the center of the Mojaddedi branch of the Naqshbandi order of Sufism since the early nineteenth century. Unlike other Naqshbandis, known for their silent *ẕikr* (and in South Asia, their disapproval of music), members of this order in this part of Iran are famous for incorporating *dotār* (lute) performances into their *ẕekr* ceremonies (the *e* in *ẕekr* reflects a difference in pronunciation in Iran; Khalilian and Blum 2007). Although in this case the performers I recorded, Habibi and Ahmadi, may not themselves perform in Naqshbandi ceremonial contexts, it is clear that the well-known *ẕekr*-like text that they sing is reinforced by the sound of the *dotār*. The *dotār* player's continual performance of the same rhythmic cells between lines of text serves, like a *ẕekr*, to invite the listener's contemplation and total absorption (Media Example 1.1 ⮹).

> cho qomrī har zamān kū kū be har dam mīzanam hū hū
> qalandarwār o yā man hū na pūyam ġayr-e 'ellā hū
>
> Like the turtledove's incessant "ku ku," with every breath I say
> "hu hu" [the name of God].
> Oh! in the manner of a qalandar, I don't seek anyone other than Allah.
> (text adapted from Massoudieh [1980, 70]; translated by Richard Wolf)

When the singer refers to saying (*zadan*) the name of God, he may also be referring to striking the strings: the rhythmic pattern of both this *ẕekr* and the *dotār* are the same, and the verb *zadan* is used to mean "to pluck or strum strings" as well as "to speak words."

The rhythmic implications of this text, based on the rules of prosody, may also be used as a basis for analyzing the text as sung and as implied on the *dotār*. The main point here is that the sets of relations between long and short syllables are more or less kept constant, even though the precise lengths of those syllables as performed vocally or instrumentally do not consistently maintain a proportion of 2:1.

Timbre and Syllables

In addition to reproducing the rhythms of speech, chant, or song, drum patterns can also be models for syllable sequences with various uses including mnemonics. Some of these have semantic meanings and some do not. The work of David Hughes suggests that many kinds of mnemonic systems for melodies—including what I call stroke-melodies—are not arbitrary; they involve, for example, iconic relationships between "intrinsic pitch" of vowels based on second formant values and the relative pitches with which they are associated (Hughes 2000, 101 and passim).[8] Drumming in much of the Middle East makes use of iconic relationships between syllable and stroke to delineate brighter from deeper and resonant from damped strokes (Blum 2002, 7). In articulating texts on the drums, performers may use damped strokes for short syllables and resonant strokes for long ones, but the match is seldom perfect. In South Asia the systems of mnemonics range widely from generalized patterns representing the sounds of whole ensembles, to sets of syllables that can refer to more than one sequence of strokes on a particular drum, to fairly specific correspondences between syllables and strokes based on similarities of timbre.

In South and North India, terms for drum syllable mean "word." Vocalized patterns in Tamil are called *colkaṭṭu*, literally, "word(s) built or composed" (< *col*, "speak," and < *kaṭ*, "build"). The strokes and their names in North India are called *bol*s (< *bolnā*, "to speak"). In classical mridangam drumming of South India, the names of strokes vary considerably. No correspondence is necessary between the timbral quality of the stroke and the text used to represent it, although some of the more common stroke names do reinforce iconicity between vowel length, quality, and resonance; in general, though, the syllables are chosen for the way they combine when recited rather than for their similarity to the sounds of the drum (Nelson 2000, 151).

In North Indian classical music, strokes for the *pakhāvaj* (for accompanying *dhrupad*) and the tabla (for accompanying *k̲h̲ayāl* and other forms) are "quasi-onomatopoeic" (Kippen 2006, 77). Drum syllables are not limited to one-to-one correspondences with strokes, but certain kinds of syllables tend to be correlated with certain kinds of sounds to a much greater extent than in South India. Aspirated syllables with voiced consonants (/d/ or /g/) connote a heavy or "full" (*bharī*) sound and involve the continuous resonance of the bass drum (or bass side of the drum). Voiced and unvoiced velar consonants (/g/ and /k/) distinguish resonating and nonresonating bass sounds. Nonresonating sounds on the treble or bass drum (or side) may also be indicated by a closed syllable with unvoiced consonants (tak, tit, kat). Treble resonance may be indicated by a long vowel, possibly combined with a voiced dental or flap (tā, dī, ṛā) (see Kippen 1988, xviii–xxi; 2000, 115–16, 124; 2006, 78–79). *Ḍhol*, *naqqārah*, and other traditions from North India and Pakistan that employ *tāl*s from the Hindustani tradition may also draw from aspects of this mnemonic system.

The major distinction between North and South Indian use of syllables is the metric structure, *tāla*, within which sequences of these strokes function. North Indian *tāla*s are structured largely by the placement of so-called empty (*k̲h̲ālī*) beats, which are often indicated by the absence of bass resonance; for complex historical reasons, however, *k̲h̲ālī* beats today are indicated in inconsistent ways (Kippen 2006, 75–97). South Indian *tāla krīya*s, or hand gestures, include "waves," or claps with the back of the hand, but there is no set of strokes that correlates with this gesture and no concept of *k̲h̲ālī* beats. Currently the system of hand gestures in South India holds no extramusical significance, although it is widely believed that the gestures derive from a more complex set of hand movements connected with rituals of ancient times. Neither the systematicity of drum mnemonics nor that of the *tāla* systems of North and South India necessarily applies to the many drums played in ritual contexts in South Asia. Gibb Schreffler points out in his discussion of *ḍhol* playing in the Indian Panjab that performers pick up *bol*s "haphazardly," that such *bol*s may be "unnecessary" or "awkward" (Schreffler 2002, 70). Andrew Alter reports that *gijan bol*s, used as drum mnemonics in Garhwal, represent the overall sound of the two drums, *ḍhol* and *damauñ*, rather than the sound of individual strokes and that there is only "moderate conformity" in the ways musicians link syllables to patterns (Alter 2008, 104). Such use of syllable combinations to represent the overall sound of an ensemble is common in a range of South Asian vernacular musics.[9]

In Garhwal a treatise titled *Ḍhol Sāgar* (The Ocean of Drumming), published in 1913 or 1932, makes "connections between the *ḍhol*'s sounds and the phonetic structures/symbols of the Devangari script"—a form of knowledge no longer maintained in the area (Alter 2008, 86). It is noteworthy that the religious background for this text is not Islamic but rather the local Garhwali pantheon, situated within the pan-Indian system of Brahma, Visnu, and Siva. In Nepal, lexical meaning associated with Newari drumming is situated within a Buddhist religious milieu (Wegner 1986). The various kinds of correspondence between drum strokes and verbal syllables in South Asia range in their degrees of iconicity and in the degree to which those syllables are "heard" as containing verbal messages. The fact that this range of correspondences is not limited to Islamic contexts reinforces our general understanding of South Asia as a place where populations of different kinds invest their drums with the ability to "talk"—if only in very limited ways.

CHAPTER 2

Emotional Agents

Muharram Ali was not the only pupil fidgeting on Founder's Day at La Martinière College. Well over one hundred years after their predecessors had helped defend the Lucknow Residency against the rebels in the 1857 Indian uprising, the boys assembled at this select school found its storied past, whether recounted in speeches, novels, or memoirs, less than enthralling. It was a rare morning of cool sunlight after the monsoon on this September 13, 1969, and the boys had to sit quietly—which only, of course, increased their urge to sneak off and play cricket. Claude Martin (1735–1800), a Frenchman who served in the British East India company as a major general and amassed his fortune under the nawab of Lucknow, Asaf-ud Daula, had left an endowment for founding the school. This holiday honoring him was to conclude with a march to Martin's tomb, where school officials would lay a memorial wreath. There was something impressive about the procession of gown-clad school faculty marching to the sound of bagpipes, and Ali always enjoyed the choir, "suited and booted" for the occasion.

This year's guest speaker, alumnus Saeed Naqvi, was just making a name for himself as a journalist. Naqvi's prominent Avadh family, distantly related to Ali's mother Sakina, had helped Ali gain admission at the age of five. Ali was all ears. A year earlier, Naqvi and a companion had notoriously slipped inside the ashram of Maharishi Mahesh Yogi in Rishikesh and snapped rare photographs of the Beatles—an adventure whose telling did much for Naqvi's popularity among the boys and broke up the self-congratulatory monotony of the day. It was during Naqvi's verbose and theatrical address as Founder's Day speaker that Ali first latched onto the idea of becoming a journalist.

On graduating from La Martinière, Ali enrolled in Jawaharlal Nehru University's School of Language, Literature, and Culture Studies, in Delhi, where he focused on both English and Urdu literature. He then traveled to Wales to complete advanced work at the Cardiff School of Journalism. At the age of twenty-four he returned to his parents' second haveli in Lucknow—at this point they would only stay in Aminabad on special occasions—and began freelancing for local newsletters, eventually securing a post as a correspondent for the *Times of India*.

At first Ali was tasked with covering news items of little interest to him: striking university employees in Allahabad, adulteration of mustard oil in Barabanki, and the latest exploits of that insufferable chess prodigy Shiv Sharma, who lived behind the Bhatkande College of Music in Lucknow. One morning, over a plate of the alu parathas for which their family cook, Sam Khan, was famous, Ali was chatting about this with his brother. Sajjad had returned home some years earlier after his studies in English literature in Delhi, and he now whiled away his time singing and sleeping during the day and hanging out with other erstwhile spoiled brats late into the night. Why did he think Sajjad would understand his frustration? After all, it was Ali's own choice to pursue journalism. But Sajjad made a useful suggestion to him: "Look, brother, you've taken pains to train yourself up in our heritage, and you have some real passions. Why not propose some project to your editor?"

Ali thought back to the golden days of Lucknow described by his father and in the literature he had read. He thought about *tāshā* drumming. And he thought about Muharram. Suppressing timidity for the sake of his passions, Ali proposed a three-part series on the music of Muharram in India and Pakistan to his editor, Mr. Chandlal. His response was less than enthusiastic. He would be happy to consider the series for publication, but Ali would have to finance and arrange his travel to Pakistan privately. In the meantime, the *Times* still held him responsible for the usual coverage in Lucknow, which he was welcome to subcontract at his own expense.

Ahmed Ali Khan still possessed sufficient wealth at this time to support his children and grandchildren, and he took personal interest in Ali's project. Like many Muslims in Uttar Pradesh, some members of Ahmed Khan's extended family had migrated to Pakistan at the time of Indian partition in 1947. These relations helped Ali's father secure his son's visa, as did Ali's invitation to a wedding on his mother's side in Lahore. It was Ḏẖu'l-

Ḥijja (mid-September 1984), historically important as the month in which Fatimah and Ali, the daughter and the cousin of the Prophet Muhammad, were married, and only a few weeks before the beginning of Muharram.

Sakina's elder brother Qasim, who had migrated to Lahore in 1947, was arranging the marriage of his daughter Amina. He met Ali at the airport in his polished white Daihatsu Charade and drove him back to his walled two-story home. Shadowed by a ditabark tree and surrounded by fragrant kawar gandal (aloe vera) and dombeya blossoms, his was one of the newer constructions in Model Town.

The wedding ceremony and reception were coming up the following week at a *shādī* hall in Gulberg, near Liberty Circle. *Ḍhol* players wait around the circumference of this large, grassy traffic circle to be hired for weddings, Sufi shrine visits, and other functions. Dressed foppishly with colored turbans, they look almost like doormen at a classy hotel—but a little too run-down. Qasim's family, being a bit more musically discerning, had secured the cousins Niamat Ali and Shahid Ali to perform at the wedding.

Qasim and Ali arrived just as the guards were opening the gates for the two musicians, who had been negotiating their fees with Qasim's eldest son. Seeing these musicians quickened Ali's interest; he made an awkward gesture toward them with his hand, meaning to be friendly, and proferred the formal, somewhat secular Urdu greeting "Adāb 'arz." Fairly common in Lucknow, the salutation sounded a touch antiquated in the Islamic Republic of Pakistan. The young men stopped and smiled politely.

With a journalist's skill for extracting information, Ali quickly learned that the cousins were *Dīndār*s (literally, "persons of [Muslim] faith"). *Dīndār* is generally applied to those who converted to Islam at the time of Partition. Niamat's father and grandfather had been acrobats; it was his father who, later in life, took an interest in *ḍhol* and eventually trained Niamat. Shahid's father, who also developed *shauq* for (that is, yearned to learn) the *ḍhol*, asked Niamat's father to teach him. The two fathers grew together as musicians "the way plants intertwine and grow into one another," Niamat said. Shahid took up the *ḍhol* professionally only after a hand injury cut short his career as an automobile filter maker. Shahid's father placed him under the guidance of an ustad, Muhammad Shafi, with whom he lived for two and a half years. When Shahid returned from his apprenticeship, Niamat took him on as a partner. Now the two were inseparable, a permanent pair, a *pakkī joṛī*.

A year later Ali was to re-encounter the two at one of the most exciting *'urs*es (death anniversaries) in the city of Lahore, the Mela Cīrāġān, or festival of lights in honor of Shah Husain. For now, though, this was Ali's first encounter with *ḍhol* players whose talents far surpassed those of the *ḍhol-tāshā* ensembles of Lucknow.

Qasim watched Ali's interaction with the drummers with a scarcely suppressed smile and then silently led Ali upstairs to his air-conditioned bedroom. Ali was struck by the comforts in this home that were lacking in his own: air conditioners in all the bedrooms and built-in gas-fired heaters for the winter. During the next few days he was treated to an air-conditioned tour of the city's many tourist attractions and a number of sites of religious importance. Among these was the shrine of al-Hujwiri, affectionately known as Data-Sahab (Bountiful Giver), where a rollicking series of Panjabi *qawwālī* performances was taking place in the annex area. He saw *malaṅg*s the likes of whom were unknown in Uttar Pradesh. These dreadlocked, bearded Sufi mendicants clothed in black, orange, and green danced with their hands high in the air, sometimes spinning gently or just swiveling their necks.

The wedding activities began the following Tuesday with a *majlis*. This is a Shī'ī "mourning assembly" of the type held every day of Muharram as well as on important days throughout the year. Shī'ahs praise the Panjatan and lament the martyrs even at the time of a wedding because they feel that all human experience, happy or sad, should be tempered with a remembrance of what Husain and his party endured. This *majlis* was confined to the extended family and held in Qasim's home. Men and women sat together freely. After one of Qasim's nephews recited a *soz* and *salām* tunelessly but sincerely, the male *soz k̲h̲wān*, Sibte-Jafar, took over, accompanied by two *bāzu*s, who provided a drone. Sibte-Jafar, a close family friend with ancestral connections back in Uttar Pradesh, had been invited from Karachi for a series of high-profile *majlis*es in the upcoming Muharram season and was staying at Qasim's home.

He rendered the *soz* "kisī ne kūfe ke raste men̲," in the *rāga bhairavi*, which describes the warning Husain received on his way to the Karbala battlefield (Media Example 2.1 ☞). The poem's language switches from Urdu to Persian, the rhyme changes, and the melody climaxes in the upper register for the *antara* on the last two lines. Husain expresses his desire to meet his death like his cousin Muslim, who had been sent ahead as an emissary and duly slaughtered. A common play on words overlays the meaning "anguish and calamity" (*karb-o balā'*) onto the place name Karbala.

kisī ne kūfe ke raste men̲ dī yeh sheh ko k̲h̲abar (Urdu)
keh qatl ho ga'e muslim aur ūn ke dōnon̲ pisar
nah jā'e āp bhī us samt ko to hai bihatar

tab us se kehne lage ro ke shāh jin-o bashar
ajal rasīdeh man ham mīravam ba karb-o balā' (Persian)
guzashteh naubat-e muslim rasīd naubat-e mā

On the way to Kufah, someone gave the King [Husain] the news
That Muslim [Husain's cousin] and his two sons were murdered.
"It is better if you don't go in that direction."
Then [Husain,] the king of jinns and men, weeping, said to him,
[in Persian]: "Destined to die, I too shall go to Karbala.
Gone by has Muslim's turn, arrived has mine."

As Sibte-Jafar explored the upper register, several men exclaimed, "Wāh, wāh," with an outward gesture of their right hand, fingers spreading. While touched by their melodic beauty, many listeners also experienced a surge of pain on hearing these lines. Qasim sat cross-legged on the floor looking downward, shaking his head, and emitted a few muffled sobs. Ali was caught up in the music—he thought of it as music, though many others didn't—and found himself responding only to the artistry; he wasn't really in the *majlis* mood yet. His emotions didn't flip like a switch; he was still thinking about the *ḍhol* players and wondering whether he might find *tāshā* players here, too.

The *majlis* continued, progressing from the melodically fluid and ornate *soz* selections to more declamatory and syllabic recitations of *salām* and *marṣiyah*, each on themes related to Muharram rather than to the upcoming wedding. At the end, all rose and gently struck their right hands on their hearts, keeping time as they sang the *nauḥah* "Shāh kehte the, 'bas, zyādah ġam nah khā'o sakīnah'" (The king said, "Don't be too sorrowful, Sakina").

The family shared an aromatic biryani after the *majlis*, which, Ali was delighted to taste, was unencumbered by the ponderous *kevṛa* (pandanus flower essence) flavor of Lucknow's nawabi cuisine—fortunately his relatives had left that behind when they settled in Lahore.

The next day, Wednesday, was the mehndi. Qasim's nonagenarian mother still presided over this event, overseeing a few women as they applied henna in ornate patterns on the hands, arms, feet, and ankles of all the girls and women. She was the only one who knew traditional mehndi songs from the old days in rural Aminabad, but she no longer had the breath to sing them. The girls were conversant with the latest *nauḥah*s, but nothing smacking of folk culture was of any interest to them, and Amina refused to let her mother call local *mīrāṣan*s to sing traditional Panjabi songs.

Mīrāsans play the *dholak* drum and lead the kinds of Panjabi wedding songs with which Amina would have no patience. Wedding reception held in a Panjabi home, Lahore, 1997. Photo by the author.

Amina's future mother-in-law, Batul, put on a cassette of Suraiya Multanikar, the Saraiki* vocalist, singing her most famous Urdu song, "Baṛe be murawwat haiṉ yeh ḥusn wāle" ("Highly disdainful are these beautiful ones"), from the 1966 film hit *Badnām* (Disgraced). Ali immediately recognized the resemblance to one of his favorite ġazals, "Voh jo ham meṉ tum meṉ qarār thā" ("That understanding we had between us"), sung by Begum Akhtar, "Queen of the Ghazal," who rose from the ranks of the *tawā'if* community to become one of India's national treasures. The younger generation, however, was not interested in these dusty old numbers. Someone put on the filmy *qawwālī* "Cahrah chupā liyā hai kisī ne hijāb meṉ" ("Someone has hidden her face behind the veil") from the 1982 film *Nikāḥ*—an Indian film with a Pakistani playing the heroine. Ali wondered if anyone was thinking about the film's social commentary on Islamic codes of divorce; probably not.

---

*Saraiki, a language closely related to Panjabi and Sindhi, is spoken mainly in the southwestern half of the province of Panjab in Pakistan.

On Thursday all were to head over to the *shādī* hall in Gulberg for the nikah, or marriage ceremony proper, as well as the reception. Before leaving, the immediate family held another very brief gathering—this one not mournful, but rejoicing in the Prophet and his family. Qasim recited the *hadis̱-e kisa*, the traditional story of the Prophet calling for Fatimah, Ali, Hasan, and Husain to join him under his cloak. This affirms the Shī'ī conviction that descendents of the Prophet through Ali and Fatimah are the only ones fit to lead the Muslim community and that they are infallible.

On the way over to the marriage hall Ali sat in the car with his cousin Fatimah, who was visiting from England. She was among a growing number of Shī'ahs sensitive to the image of Shiism in the contemporary world and thought of herself as applying a scientific rationality, which she had acquired as a chemistry student abroad, to the scrutiny of her own society in Pakistan. Although she was deeply committed to the Shī'ī community and a believer in meritorious mourning, she disagreed with the practice of holding a *majlis-e-'azā* (*majlis* with lamentation) before the wedding, saying, "Where does it say we should shed tears and recall the blood of Karbala at the happiest time in our lives? It makes us appear backward, mired in the past." She added that she thought the local accretions to *'azādārī* practice, such as the celebration of the mehndi of Husain's daughter on the seventh of Muharram, ought to be avoided. "Why give the impression we are celebrating in the midst of mourning," she asked, "or mourning in the midst of celebrating?" Ali kept his mouth shut. He was pretty sure what her views would be on *tāshā* drumming during Muharram and did not want to hear her pronouncements.

Qasim's family arrived at the marriage hall, where Qasim's son was on the phone with the *shahnā'ī* players, who were caught in traffic traveling from the old city. They had decided to hire a separate *shahnā'ī* and *naqqārah* band to welcome the groom's *barāt*, and now the groom's procession needed to be delayed. Niamat and Shahid Ali had arrived earlier, but they were not needed until the wedding reception after the ceremony. An hour later the *shahnā'ī* band arrived and the *barāt* got under way. The groom's procession was accompanied by rifle shots and the *ḍhol* playing of Bharāin musicians who had obviously been picked up from Liberty Circle. But no matter, the arrival of the groom's party was brief enough that the inferior drumming went almost unnoticed. The *shahnā'ī* and *naqqārah* band quickly took over as the main focus of musical interest after the *ḍhol* players exhausted their minimal elaborations on the *bhāṅgṛā* rhythmic groove. The *shahnā'ī* players began playing the melody of a song used for the *jhūmar* dance, and both the *naqqārah* players and the Liberty Circle *ḍhol* players joined in with the appropriate pattern as the men began the slow circle dance, hands raised in the air. Shahid and Niamat waited their turn, as the Bharāins are a lower echelon of musicians, who, the cousins felt, could not keep up with their playing. They exchanged knowing glances as the Bharāins accompanied the procession playing a simple *bhāṅgṛā* instead of the related, but more subtle, *lehrā* pattern—too advanced for these pretenders.

After the families greeted each other outside, all proceeded indoors for the rather simple nikah ceremony. Amina was giddy, not so much because the formal act of signing the marriage certificate was so exciting (it wasn't), but because in her mind, she was already married and ready to party. Dressed in a red *ġarāra* designed in imitation of the one her grandmother had worn in Lucknow seventy-five years earlier, with silk brocade and gold embroidery around the legs, Amina lifted the green veil so that her new husband Amir could see her face, as if for the first time, via a mirror.

Although the *ḍhol* players Qasim employed owned their own drums, instrument rental is common. This photograph depicts three musical instrument shops side by side in Udaipur, Rajasthan. Those in need of musicians often book them through such shops, which may bear the name of a particular band. The clay-shelled kettledrums are *naqqārah*s (here called *naṅgārā*), and the cylinder drums are wooden *ḍhol*s. On one of the front walls, in a combination of Hindi/Mewari and English, is written "ḍhol, naṅgārā and music item are available." November 11, 1998. Photo by the author.

After this brief nod to tradition, the two shared what was probably the last mango of this year's late season, and family members gathered around to congratulate them.

During the lavish feast that followed, Shahid and Niamat Ali played patterns for traditional Panjabi men's and women's dances, *jhūmar* and *sammī*, as well as *bhāṅgṛā*, in which family members of both sexes participated. They interspersed dance patterns with sophisticated improvisation around classical *tāl* frameworks. Ali's Sunni cousin Ajmal Ahmed Khan, the brother of Ali's father's second wife Khadijah, was visiting from Multan, where he eked out a meager living as a *pakhāwaj* and tabla player. Knowing what it means to be a good listener, he asked them to play *tāl*s like the ten-count *jhaptāl* and the seven-count *muġala'i*. They responded enthusiastically to Ajmal's connoisseurship, and Ali got an excellent taste of what Panjabi *ḍhol* players were capable of producing. Their final function was to play the six-count *dādra* pattern, setting a slow pace for the emotionally difficult *rukẖṣatī* ritual, in which the bride formally departs for the groom's house. Amina was surprised to find herself crying at this point, since she was only moving a few kilometers away and as a Westernized Lahori felt that some of these ritual formalities were rather silly. Caught up in the moment and seeing her mother and grandmother weeping—her grandmother was remembering her own wedding—she gave way to the emotions that were, as she vividly described it later, "rising from her gut."

As the guests cleared away, Ali was drawn to Shahid and Niamat like a boy to a star cricket player. As he gathered courage to ask them to teach him something, he decided to show he was a discerning listener.

"Shahid Sahab," he said, "your playing is so different from that of those *pagaṛī wālā*s*—so much more complicated and subtle."

"Janab [sir], those Bharāins are incapable of understanding classical [*klāsīkal*] music. It is too 'refined' for them."

"They lack *sur*,"† opined Niamat. "They don't learn from anyone, they just imitate, the way copies [*naql*] are made from a cassette."

Ali took advantage of the opening. "I wondered if I might learn something from you."

"Do you drum?" Shahid asked.

"I learned a little *tāshā*, growing up in Lucknow."

"What's that, a *tāl*?" asked the puzzled Niamat.

---

*The ones (dressed in) turbans (*pagaṛī*).

†*Sur* means "understanding of music" in this context, although its basic meaning is "pitch."

"No, it's a kind of drum, like this." (Ali showed the shape of the drum with his hands and indicated how it hangs from the neck.) "Don't you have that here?"

Furrowing his brow, Niamat said, "I might have seen it in some film . . . at Shahnoor [studio] . . . a smaller one."

"There's no such drum in Panjab," pronounced Shahid.

: : :

Niamat and Shahid Ali's negative views of the Bharāins raise the more general question of how ritual drummers fit into the larger sociocultural world of music making in South and West Asia. The Shī'ī wedding Ali attended is an example of a ritual sequence with contrasting emotional overtones. How might music structure other such events and sequences? The idea that individuals relate to elements in that structure—a nominally sad *soz,* for example—in different ways (Ali was not ready to be sad) raises the problem of reception. How do we understand musical meaning in complex events?

These themes are addressed in order in the following sections. "Sociocultural Background" situates the musical actors in their social milieux. "Complex Agency" shifts emphasis to the role of the individual in religious or other events that diverse populations attend and participate in. "The Navigation of Feeling" suggests the ways actors in such complex events bring forth emotionally coded musical components that themselves have a differential impact on participants' emotional conditions.

Sociocultural Background

This section offers a broad sense of how the musicians discussed in this study relate to one another and to the sociocultural structures and institutions of South and West Asia. It is not meant as a comprehensive review. Although the diverse populations of South Asia do not fall into easy categories with respect to their musical involvement, they can sometimes be characterized in terms of their most commonly employed musical instruments and genres (Henry 1988). The social backgrounds of ritual drummers in South Asia overlap significantly with those of other musical and nonmusical service specialists.

Many service professionals in South and West Asia perform multiple roles such as those of barber, midwife, and surgeon, as well as musician. Examples include the Ampaṭṭans of Tamil Nadu, who form the ranks of *periya mēḷam* ensembles of *nāgasvaram* and *tavil*, and the Mangalis of Andhra Pradesh, also called *Ḥajjām* in Urdu, who play the double-headed *mangal bāja* drums (see Thurston and Rangachari 1909, 1:32; Moffatt 1979; Terada 2000, 481). *Mangali,* "barber" in Telugu, is derived from a Sanskrit root meaning "auspicious." *Mangal bāja*, then, are both auspicious drums and drums played by barber-caste musicians. They perform for, among other events, weddings and the Hindu-sponsored Muharram rituals of Mushirabad (Hyderabad, Andhra Pradesh). According to the anthropologist Ghaus Ansari, Nā'ī barbers also act as "reliable and confidential messenger[s]" who will convey only good and auspicious news (Ansari 1960, 48). So-called barber-musicians are also common both in Afghanistan and in the Khorasan region of Iran (Sakata 2002; Baily 1988; Blum 1978; Youssefzadeh 2002).

Communities cannot be defined simply by a set of skills or roles, especially roles that are thrust upon them in an often exploitative system. Nevertheless, the idea that musicianship in a community might arise out of occupational specialization in a set of related skills or that the social status of those performing musical services is equivalent to that of other occupational specialists with whom they are grouped crops up repeatedly in the ethnographic record. It may be that the barber's manual dexterity, for example, allows him both to play musical instruments and to perform "skilful operat[ions] with the knife"—shave, cut hair, lance boils, cut nails, perform circumcisions, and in much earlier times, let blood (Thurston and Rangachari 1909, 1:37; Ibbetson 1916, 230; see Baily 1988, 102 for Afghanistan); the tailor's facilities with stitching cloth and manipulating membranes may help him craft and play drums; and the entertainer's flair and flexibility may ease his or her movement seamlessly from acrobatics to dancing, and from acting to singing.

Baily observed in Herat that barber-musicians, like the kinds of musicians Alan Merriam famously described (Merriam 1964, 123–44), combine low rank with high social importance (Baily 1988, 103; see also Tingey 1994, 86–102). The barber is rendered lowly by his contact with hair, nails, and blood, while also being invested with symbolic potency as the cutter of hair, "the special seat of bodily strength" in South Asia as in many other regions (Russell and Hira Lal 1916, 4:270). In their musical roles, Ampaṭṭan performers of the double-reed *nāgasvaram* in South India are, from a Brahmin perspective, subject to pollution (*tīṭṭu*) by their own saliva (*eccil*), since they reinsert saliva-covered reeds into their mouths. Yet such musicians are also charged with producing "dense, loud instrument[al sounds]" to drown out inauspicious sounds during Hindu weddings and at the moment of *darśan* in Hindu temples. These double-edged ritual roles support Mary Douglas's argument for viewing corporeal margins in terms of margins generally, all of which are, in her view, dangerous (Douglas 2002, 150).

Bharāins of the Panjab, who are not barbers, bear family resemblances to barber groups via their overlapping roles as circumcisers and midwives. This "occupational group or spiritual brotherhood which comprises men of many castes" (Rose 1911–19, 2:86) consider themselves to be "descendants of a Meccan community of midwives and child caretakers" (Faruqi et al. 1989, 40) and "go about beating a drum and begging in the name of [Saint] Sakhi Sarwar [Sultan]" (Ibbetson 1916, 229). They intervene with the saint on behalf of childless women, who, in return, reward them with fringes of tassels and rag dolls (Rose 1911–19, 2:86; Faruqi et al. 1989, 35; Nayyar 2000). I have seen Bharāins play *ḍholak* and *ciṃta* (metal percussion tongs) at Sufi *'urs*es in the Panjab, sometimes snatching a baby from its mother, soothing it with lullabies (*loriyā̱n*), and playfully holding it ransom for money.

While Bharāins' own stories suggest a longstanding competition between themselves and Nā'ī barbers and Mīrāṣī hereditary musicians (Nayyar 2000, 766–69),[1] Bharāins may nevertheless look up to Mīrāṣīs. The Bharāins of the professional Kurbān party of *ḍhol* players in Rawalpindi district, for example, studied under a Mīrāṣī ustad named Muhammad Afzal. Although they could name twenty *tāl*s and identify the number of constituent *mātra*s, they considered themselves sufficiently dependent on their teacher to refrain from recording without him (pers. comm., Islamabad, April 9, 1997).

The musics of the various barber communities and the Bharāins are generally considered auspicious, even though, in some regions, barbers also serve as functionaries at funerals. Dalit musicians of Pa̱raiyar and Cakkiliyar castes in Tamil Nadu, Mādigas of Andhra Pradesh, and Camārs in much of North India occupy a more tenuous hierarchical position owing, in part, to their more central role in announcing funerals and in some cases handling corpses and leather (see, for example, Henry 1988). Dalits are not only drummers but also singers and performers on double-reed instruments. Non-Dalits have effectively reinforced the inferior status of Dalit communities by predicating their primary role as (lowly) drummers upon them. The ethnonym Pa̱raiyar, built by adding a suffix indicating in this case "person of the," to the name of the drum, *pa̱rai*, is an obvious example. (The English word *pariah* derives from this Tamil caste name).

As for hereditary entertainers, the Bāzīgars, who were once nomadic entertainers and acrobats, perhaps developed their now-primary role as *ḍhol* players out of an earlier practice of using the instrument to announce their arrival in a village (Schreffler 2002, 74–75). Niamat Ali belongs to a Bāzigar family. Bāzigars are somewhat comparable to the Bedas of Garhwal, erstwhile itinerant entertainers who sang, danced, and performed acrobatics and who are now limited in number and specialize in the *ḍholak* and harmonium (Alter 2008, 41).

Another prominent category of entertainer stretching from North India to Iran is that of the Naqqāl; this figure used to recite, tunefully, texts such as the epic *Shāh Nāmeh* and Sa'di's *Bustān* in urban teahouses of Khorasan and other regions of Iran before the revolution of 1979 (Blum 1978). The term *naqqāl* in Persian derives from the Arabic *naql*, "carrying, transporting" and "transmission, report, account, copy" in the sense of carrying the meaning or image of something (Wehr 1976, s.v. *naql*). Niamat Ali used the word *naql* in likening the Bharāins' performances to copies of cassette recordings. Naqqāls working across this vast area do not necessarily belong to a single ethnic group or kin group. Rather, this is a descriptive term for communities who may bear several local names and engage in the variety of activities the term implies. In South Asia the names Bhāṇḍ, Naqqāl, and Ṭa'ifah all potentially refer to the same groups of mimics, buffoons, singers, dancers, storytellers, and actors (Russell and Hira Lal 1916, 1:349; Rose 1911–19, 2:83; Nayyar 2000, 765; Nayyar Masud, pers. comm.).

In Lucknow, the Muslims referred to by these three terms (Hindus of this category are called Bharatiyas) were primarily Shī'ī (Ansari 1960, 432) and used to march in their own procession during Muharram. During these processions they sang a special mehndi *nauḥah*—written by the poet Ahsan—on the apocryphal wedding of Husain's nephew Qasim, said to have been performed beside the battlefield. Their grave conduct in these religious processions contrasted with their clownish professional performances for patrons. Their license to lampoon was virtually unlimited; no one, not even the king, had the right to rebuke them. They could publicly humiliate their patrons, mainly kings and wealthy landowners, by farcically revealing family secrets, which they made it their business to know. Although members of this community in Lucknow were not themselves drummers, they were musicians, and they contributed to the great color and diversity of Muharram processions of the past (in living memory) of which drumming, too, was once a prominent part.

Grades of Generality

Musicians are embedded in multiple classification systems whose components represent different levels of generality. It is useful to keep these levels in mind as we compare the social positions of musicians across the region.

The lowest level, or category, Cat-1, refers to groups that are relatively straightforward to define in a place: a local endogamous caste such as the Paṟaiyar or the (agreed-upon) members of one school or lineage of musicians (*k͟hāndān, gharāna*). Cat-2 indicates a supercategory, usually occupational, that encompasses more than one endogamous group. Cat-2 terms such as Naqqāl, Bharāin, and Ḥajjām can be used cross-regionally to describe multiple lineages, ethnic groups, or castes. Cat-3 consists of names or sets of common practices that draw different groups together while implying internal differentiations—subcastes or occupational groups—that are operationally important. Examples include the Hindu system of *varṇa*s, under which individual castes are classified, castes that contain subcastes, and modern generalizing terms such as *Dalit, scheduled caste*, and *untouchable*. What is operationally important will, of course, depend on context.

Berreman describes the Himalayan classification of Ḍom (a derogatory term) as comprising blacksmiths (*lohar*), barbers, and drummer-tailors (*bajgi*) (Berreman 1978, 334; see also Alter 2008, 39). Because each of the subgroups is identified as a separate operational caste division, the Ḍom category here belongs to Cat-3. In Hunza (now Pakistan), where the Ḍom immigrated from other parts of North India via Baltistan, the term is now generic for "several endogamous professional groups at the low end of the social hierarchy" (Schmid 2000, 795); these groups include both blacksmiths (ɛ·ɣərʌšo ʊsta·dtiŋ) and musicians (ḍʌkɛ ʊsta·dtiŋ) (Lorimer 1939, 8).

As a generic term used by more than one population for loosely related groups spread over a large area, Ḍom functions more like a Cat-2 designation, but to the extent that Ḍom consider themselves as a people, rather than merely occupational specialists, it is a Cat-1 designation.[2] Some Ḍom in the Gilgit-Baltistan province of northern Pakistan were once thought to be musician sub-groups of the Kamin caste (Leitner 1996, 8; see also 63). If this was indeed the case, the name Ḍom functioned as a Cat-1 designation within the Cat-3 Kamins. It is important to keep in mind, then, that the same term can belong to Cat-1, Cat-2, or Cat-3, depending on the region, point in history, or the intention of the speaker.

Ḍom musicians in Hunza are of interest here for their *haríip* music. Representations of this repertoire such as the following emphasize tone-melody over stroke-melody: "the melody on the wind instrument expresses the musical content, with the bass drum reinforcing and dramatizing the texture" (Schmid 2000, 795). However, close listening reveals that, in some pieces, musicians play a distinct stroke-melody in counterpoint with a tone-melody, rather than merely providing a responsive form of accompaniment to the "musical content." Because Ḍom populations exist throughout South and West Asia and at least some of them are considered to be historically related to one another (as well as to the European Rom), an obvious question is whether these populations may have been involved in spreading some of the widely found conceptions of drumming discussed in the present book—for example, conceptions of drum patterns as contextually salient stroke-melodies. This is not a question that is, in my view, answerable with the data at our disposal, and I am not prepared to speculate.

Cat-3 conceptions can be articulated by activities as well as by names. Among the Newars in Bhaktapur, Nepal, for instance, participation in processional music called *gũnlābājā* involves Buddhist oil pressers, goldsmiths, and silversmiths, who are drummers, and low-caste Hindu tailors, who play the shawm (Wegner 2009, 116). The common participation in *gũnlābājā,* rather than a common appellation, constitutes a Cat-3 relationship.

The Runzavānlu, or Panasa, belong to a group of artisan castes identified by the Cat-3 term Viśvakarma (Thurston and Rangachari 1909, s.v. Kamsala). Runzavānlu play the *runza*, an upright barrel drum with a snare, and relate traditional stories of the other Telugu-speaking Viśvakarma castes of the Telangana region: Kammari (blacksmiths), Vaḍlangi (carpenters), Kancari (copper- and brass-smiths), Kāsi (stone workers), and Kaṃsāli (gold and silver workers). These geomancers "stand in close contact with terrestrial and heavenly powers, possess at times priestly functions, and are feared by society as magicians. Their task is to create boundaries for space and time which, in themselves, are infinite" (Link 2003, 247; see also Kramrisch 1958). More mundanely, they are of interest here because their musical repertoire consists, in part, of imitations of other musical sounds, such as those of the *ḍhol* and the *tāshā*. The Viśvakarma castes are related by their name, their artisanship, and the practices of the Runzavānlu. They also share the capability of transforming both substances and sound.[3]

A frequently encountered term in North India and Pakistan, Mīrāsī (f. mīrāsan), "hereditary one," can be a Cat-2 label for any hereditary musician. As with several other terms, it may function as a Cat-1 or Cat-3 designation depending on context and region.

At the time of his fieldwork in Delhi in 1969 and the 1970s, Daniel Neuman described Mīrāsī, in Cat-1 terms, as referring to the occupation of playing the tabla or *sāraṅgī* as accompanist or as a caste category for marriage purposes (Neuman 1990, 126). They were relatively low in rank because of their status as accompanists and because they were associated with the Tawā'if courtesan communities. Even those who became vocalists could not shed their status as Mīrāsīs to become higher-ranking Kalāwants (102–4). During Neuman's research, Chand Khan was one of the few musicians of this Delhi Mīrāsī community to make a name for himself as a vocalist and bear this designation proudly (103). Chand Khan's grandson,

Iqbal Ahmed Khan, the *khalīfah* (head) of the Delhi *gharāna,* is the one who actually asserted (as in Ali's story in Chapter 1) that *soz* is the foundation of all Hindustani music. He is also (as of the time of this writing) a *soz k̲h̲wān* who performs in connection with *majlis*es near the Nizamuddin shrine in Delhi.

In the Pakistani Panjab, some Mīrās̱īs refer to themselves as Kasbīs ("professionals"), Mīr Ālams, or Mīrzādas and to non-hereditary musicians as Atais ("those to whom it is given") (Nayyar 2000, 763). Although some view the term *Mīrās̱ī* as pejorative (Faruqi et al. 1989, 35–36), the rank of the person actually depends on one's perspective. Among *ḍhol* players, Mīrās̱īs are carriers of valuable knowledge and rank above Bharāins. Niamat Ali said that Mīrās̱īs are "sharp" (*tez*); they make "puns" (*jagti*) and are playful about everything. Mīrās̱īs of the Panjab often play the role of genealogists (*dādehāl*). They have the power to boost their patrons' honor or devastate them through witty references to their secrets. The Bhāṇḍs alluded to above are a Mīrās̱ī subgroup in the Panjab, as are Qawwāls (ibid., 764–65; see also Ansari 1960, 45).

The folk and classical singer Javed Ali, who was twenty-two in 1997 when I interviewed him, was cagey about and embarrassed by the term *Mīrās̱ī*. His own family consisted of *qawwāl*s (those who perform *qawwālī*) and players of the tabla and harmonium who clearly would have been known as Mīrās̱īs. Musicianship went back at least three generations in his family to ancestors in the village of Nala in East Panjab. Javed Ali objected to the term because uninformed people were in the habit of 'ridiculing' them. The proper term of reference, he said, is one's actual profession. "If you sing, you should be called a singer." He wanted to be known as a professional singer of the Nala *gharāna*. Javed's modern emphasis on professional specialization and very narrow Cat-1 terminology was in keeping with his musical values. He objected to functional songs and instrumental music at ritual moments in the wedding, for instance. All music should be performed in proper concert settings, where people attend in order to listen to the music.

As different Mīrās̱īs in the traditional system serve different communities, a Cat-1 designation for a Mīrās̱ī in the Panjab can be made more specific by identifying the patron caste. Muhammad Baksh Multani, an elderly Mīrās̱ī performer on the *naqqārah*, *ḍhol*, and *tāshā*, described in 1997 his family's serving members of the Kārlū caste (*z̤āt*) in Multan as *dādehāl* genealogists. Part of their job was to perform many rites and services in connection with weddings. These included males singing the *sehrā* songs that accompany the bridegroom as he ties his turban and females putting mehndi on the bride and helping her dress. These Mīrāṣīs, knowing the kin relations, would also assist in matchmaking. In return for all their services, they would receive five kilos of grain from each of the houses they served each year.

Like the Mīrāṣīs whom Neuman describes, Muhammad Baksh's relatives were not vocal specialists in classical music. They were professional singers of ritually appropriate vernacular songs, particularly at weddings, whose special field was and is drumming. When Muhammad Baksh was a child, he attended the wedding of an important figure in Sujā'ābād, near Multan. The patron staged a great musical competition, appointed a judge, and invited the legendary *naqqārah* player Mīān Allah Divāyā, among others, to play. Each musician had a half-hour slot to play for each of ten days. The rule was that no *bol* (here: drum pattern) could be repeated from one day to the next. For each *bol* the musician would receive five rupees. Several knowledgeable people were tasked with keeping track of the number of *bol*s. One by one the musicians from Wazirabad, Sialkot, and other places fell by the wayside, leaving only Mīān Allah Divāyā. He played so many variations, Baksh said, that he made the *bol*s "dead," and won the contest.

Manganhār

The names for this category of hereditary Muslim musician vary slightly as one moves west from western Rajasthan in India, where they are called Māngaṇiār, to Sindh province in Pakistan, where they are called Manganhār. If the term does in fact refer to a single people, as it seems to, it is a Cat-1 designation. Members of this community sing and play a wide variety of instruments including drums, clappers, double reeds, and bowed lutes. As hereditary musicians, they are Mīrāṣīs—a term some of them prefer to their own ethnonym, which derives from the verb *māngnā,* "to beg" (Natavar 2000, 641).

In western Rajasthan, Māngaṇiārs are patronized by Hindu Rājputs, a martial ruling caste. One story explaining the occupation of those Māngaṇiārs centers around the self-immolation of a Rajput princess. Her spirit appeared before her client Māngaṇiār and bestowed upon his family the right to sing her tale (Chaudhuri 2009, 98). In Sindh, Manganhār patrons were once said to be clansmen of Sumrah and Samma (Rājput) backgrounds (Burton 1851, 125–26; Balocu 1975, 30, 32). Today, each Manganhār household has a *rāj*, or domain, that consists of land and up to about three patron villages (*g̈oṭhu*). These rājs are distributed by the Manganhār lineage (*barādarī*) and periodically renegotiated as households of musicians and patrons increase in number. In return for food, Manganhārs are responsible for playing music, maintaining genealogies (for example, Burton 1851, 126), and serving as authorities with regard to customs and rituals of each village in their *rāj*.

The celebrated Sindhi historian and folklorist N. A. Baloch cited a Persian version of the thirteenth-century chronicle *Chachnāmah* (Kūfī 1939, 220–21) which depicts the Samma chiefs receiving Muhammad bin Qasim's invading forces with a retinue of their musicians playing the *duhl* and the *sharnā'ī*. Baloch's popularization of this history, along with his observations that certain drum pattern names include the word *sammatka* ("of the Sammas"), may help explain why some Manganhārs, including those I interviewed in Hyderabad, Sindh, trace their origins to the Samma people. Manganhārs consisted of both Shī'ahs and Sunnīs in the Hyderabad region in 1997. Their affiliations with these two branches of Islam are unrelated to patterns of descent; Manganhārs do not base their identity as Shī'ahs, for example, on claims of descent from particular members of the Prophet's family.

Despite the importance of localism in Manganhār identity politics, the *ḍhol* player Nathan of Ṭhaṭṭah district in Sindh offered an Islamic lineage for his community: the Manganhār ancestor Mullah Nuru was last in line to be given gifts and assigned a means of livelihood by the Prophet. Having nothing left to give him but a frame drum, the Prophet said that his job would be to play the *daf* and collect money from passersby in the name of God. Bibi Fatimah, the daughter of the Prophet and mother of Hasan and Husain, wanted to honor Nuru after he came to her door singing of the birth of her sons; she changed the name of his community to Manganhār, which, in Nathan's view at least, concealed the term's etymological roots in the word for begging. Over time, the story goes, Manganhārs increased the drum's sound output with a second membrane, thereby giving rise to today's two-headed *ḍhol*.

The research on and interest in Manganhārs in Pakistan stimulated by N. A. Baloch is exceeded in India by an extensive literature on the Māngaṇiārs fostered by the patronage and scholarly work of the late Komal Kothari. Kothari and Vijaydan Detha founded the Rupayan Sansthan for documenting Rajasthani folklore, which continues to be a major hub for research and patronage. Whereas Māngaṇiār musicians from India have made a popular name for themselves on the world stage, their counterparts in Pakistan have not. Manganhārs do, however, remain active as musicians in ritual contexts and in folk festivals patronized by the Pakistan National Council of Arts and Lok Virsa, the National Institute of Folk and Traditional Heritage.

The Manganhārs, along with other castes of ritual drummers such as *ḍholi*s across Rajasthan and Sindh, are important for this study because they traverse religious and other community boundaries, and their extensive drum repertoires are linked to specific rituals (Joshi 1995; Balocu 1975) and sometimes to texts.

Other Communities, Lineages, and Idiosyncratic Musicians

Many South Asians now find the idea that family background should determine whether one becomes a musician repellent. Inasmuch as individuals may exert somewhat free agency, the categories described above are insufficient. Cat-2 classifications such as Bharāin are limited in that they only indicate what an individual has become—not what experiences gave rise to such an outcome. Similar are the terms for Sufi mendicants, faqir and *malaṅg*, roles which anyone may choose merely by adopting a change in lifestyle (there is no necessary connection between being a mendicant and being a musician, however). Only in the case of hereditary musicians does the social classification alone imply something about, without determining, how and why a person became a musician.

Some Muslims whose families ranked mid-to-low in social status adopted such higher-status last names as Sheikẖ, Rājput, and Khān. The name Sheikẖ was once more exclusively associated with elite Muslim *ashrāf* classes, whose families could be traced to Arabia. Now, however, in the case of low-status castes, the name Sheikẖ implies recent conversion to Islam, and the term *Dīndār* even more directly indexes a family's conversion. Both terms serve to erase the *specificity* of low-caste associations with a former identity but cannot hide the fact that the bearers (or their families) are performing this act of erasure (see Ansari 1960, 37–38). *Sheikẖ* in the Panjab can be synonymous with *Bharāin*, and the two terms may combined to form *Bharāin Sheikẖ*. The term *Khān* is often used by Mīrāsī musicians, especially those specializing in classical vocal music or *qawwālī*. Most of the Sheikẖs I encountered, when not Bharāins, were called Sheikẖ Siddiqis. They made up the majority of the ranks of Muhājir *ḍhol-tāshā* players who performed each year during Muharram in Hyderabad, Sindh, and Karachi (Muhājirs in this context are Muslims who migrated from India to Pakistan at the time of Partition). These participants did not normally consider themselves musicians as ritual drumming during Muharram was not generally considered music, and these drummers did not play on any other occasion.

Although it is possible for anyone to decide to become a ritual drummer, a drummer's status is so low that there are only a few obvious reasons why—in the absence of any family association—one might choose to do so. One is as a form of devotion to a Sufi saint or to the Karbala martyrs; the other is to eke out a living beyond that of a common beggar. A great many men and boys in Uttar Pradesh and other parts of North India bring out *ḍhol*s and *tāshā*s to play during Muharram, and it would be hard to say that all the playful and often highly unskilled community involvement in this kind of drumming is actually intended as reverent. But the occasion does serve as a ritual cover for drumming activity; and because it is temporary, and involvement of Sunnis is widespread, the stigma of being a drummer does not apply.

Far more common instances of individuals' taking on musical professions involve those who become singers or players of tone-melody instruments; depending on their family backgrounds, these musicians also risk social stigma and a decline in status. My first musical host in Multan, for example, was a locally popular singer named Saleem Gardezi. His *ashrāf* family had ostracized him for becoming a singer and he died in middle age, without their love and support.

A musician who suffered a similarly negative family reaction was Muhammad Urs Bhatti of Pakkachang village in Khaipur district of Sindh, an *alġozah* player of *zamīndār* (wealthy landowner) background. At the age of eight he began studying with the esteemed ustad Misri Khan Jamali. It may have been the ustad who took the boy under his protection when Bhatti's family threw him out of the house. Bhatti's father chided him for "becoming a Mīrāṣī." Bhatti confided to me, with a laugh, "I am bad; my sister's son Manzur is also bad" for learning music. At age forty-five, when I met him, Bhatti was networked with the Pakistan National Council of Arts and would perform regularly under their auspices as well as at a variety of celebrations.

Not all would-be musicians receive such harsh treatment from their families. The Baloch singer and tambur player Qadar Baksh Mazari described "falling in love with and going crazy over the voice" (*āvāz*) of the singer Mahmand Murid Bulaydi, who had come to perform at a function. Totally smitten, feeling "helpless," he asked his parents for permission to study this music, which they granted. He proceeded to study with Bulaydi's ustad, the *sāraṅgī navāz* Muhammad Bachak. After one and a half years of teaching Mazari, Bachak fed him sugar with his own a hand—a ritual cementing the master-disciple relationship. Eventually Mazari received permission from his teacher to perform professionally. Although Mazari's background was Baloch and he performed in all the major languages of Pakistan, he was born in the Panjab and could not find significant performance opportunities in other provinces.

Mazari came across as very much a man on the make, smooth-talking, introducing each piece in a performance in Urdu; and yet he was sensitive to his lack of standing, his lack of a musical heritage (either that or he was ashamed of his heritage and wanted to emphasize his own agency). He shot his accompanist, Bashir Ahmed, a piercing look of disapproval when my friend Adam Nayyar and I asked Ahmed about his background. I could learn only a few details from Ahmed.

A player of the bowed *rabāb* called the *sārinda*, Ahmed was from a Lorī musical family that had been playing music, generation after generation, "since the beginning." Lorī is a Cat-3 designation for artisans who also have more specific occupational names (Hughes-Buller 1906, 107). Ahmed picked up *sārinda* after reaching the tenth standard, at which point he gave up studies in school completely. Like Mazari's, Ahmed's mother tongue was Baluchi, but he made it a point to say his instrument could "speak" in Pashto, Urdu, Saraiki, and Sindhi—by which he seemed to mean he could mimic the cadence of these languages when sung.

The upshot of Mazari's and Ahmed's statements about their repertoire is that they felt that they could play for any audience. Only *they* had control of all these Pakistani musical styles, whereas Pashto-, Saraiki- and Sindhi-speaking players and other musicians did not. The position of stylistic omnivore is associated with Baloch musicians generally, apparently without regard to musical background, and was particularly suited to Baloch musicians living outside Baluchistan.

Summary

Occupational association with musicianship is often linked to other service specializations such as barbering, surgery, tailoring, and serving as a repository for familial and ritual knowledge. Many ritual drummers and other musicians draw from communities who have transmitted these skills and forms of knowledge from generation to generation. Some categories also describe an identity that a person has acquired, such as Bharāin or Sheiḵẖ. It is often difficult to determine in any given setting whether a classificatory term for a musician refers to a local, specific, endogamous group (Cat-1), a widespread name for an occupation whose local members may belong to different castes or *qaum*s (Cat-2), or a category under which there are well-defined subdivisions (Cat-3). Individuals may become musicians whether or not they belong to one of these communities, but they cannot completely escape the sociocultural associations of these communities. We now proceed from this discussion of the musician, within societies of musicians, to musicians and other participants as social actors in religious observances, festivals, and other events.

Complex Agency

One of this study's major concerns is the way in which individuals take account of complex social, religious, and historical factors when they react to or contemplate music, particularly in such heterogeneous contexts as Sufi *'urs*es and Muharram. What ethnographic strategies might yield at least partial access to these local understandings? How can these local views be used to gain broader understandings? For convenience of explanation, I'll outline three fields through which we might study the negotiation of meanings: field 1, changing, face-to-face verbal and musical interactions; field 2, competing discourses and knowledge sets that partly inform moment-to-moment decisions; and field 3, broad regional patterns of activity of which individuals are only partly aware. None of these fields is simply determinative of "meaning," but, viewed together, they illuminate the changing conditions under which participants process musical (or any other) activity.

The first field consists of concrete encounters. These could engage an ethnographer with a consultant, two or more other individuals involved in a conversation, or a musician interacting with another musician, a dancer, or another listener. For instance, Ali, in anticipation of his upcoming visit to Multan for Muharram—outside the narrative frame of this chapter—asks Ajmal a predictable question about Muharram drumming in Multan: what's it like? Ajmal, knowing Ali's background understanding from Lucknow, provides new information pertinent to his own Sunni subjectivity in Multan: "It struck fear in my heart when I was a child." During the same wedding, Ajmal meets his former schoolmate Asif, who had grown up in Lahore, where musical instruments are, for all intents and purposes, and particularly among Shī'ahs, banned during Muharram. Asif had heard that Ali was writing about Muharram in Multan and expressed his curiosity to Ajmal. Ajmal now says to him, "In Multan, we really have something special—a drum beat especially for Muharram, and a whole set of tunes for the *shahnā'ī*." These two representations of music are not incompatible, but they express entirely different ideas. They depend on Ajmal's assumptions about his interlocutors' background knowledge and motivations (field 2). A larger frame (field 3) would take account of the distribution of cities and towns in South Asia with a preponderance of music, or lack thereof, as part of Muharram observances and would recognize that a similar set of arguments for and against use of musical instruments during Muharram are recycled in different ways at different historical moments—no one of them holding authority beyond a particular locale. The fictional character of Ali takes up projects similar to those of a number of South Asians I encountered, as they became interested in field 3. Among these were several journalists and folklorists, a minor raja, and a couple of Indo-Caribbean musicians interested in tracing their Indian roots. The ethnographic material I analyze in each chapter is meant to bring out aspects of all three fields.

In considering these three fields as sites for the production of meaning, I do not mean to deny the importance of such intangible aspects of personhood as consciousness or subjectivity; rather, these aspects lie at the interstices of what we can grasp through language and the senses. Probing further, I would include *subject positions*, inasmuch as discourses can be said to constitute them (Ewing 1997, 5), as constituents of field 2. Following Katherine Ewing, I regard the individual (whom she terms the "experiencing subject") as a "non-unitary agent" or a "bundle of agencies" who is capable of retaining "critical distance" from so-called hegemonic discourses.

Ewing's critique is aimed largely at studies that view modernity as a single totalizing force, against which the individual subject is determined—either through acceptance of modernity's dominant tropes or through resisting them. Ewing's critique could well be applied to Weidman's argument about the voice in South India (Chapter 1). Any move by a South Indian to reinscribe the voice as part of an ancient heritage, we might infer from Weidman, is "orientalist" because that person fails to recognize his or her move as complicit in the (singular) project of modernity. I propose the Ewingian alternative of examining a single subject over time. A (hypothetical) Madrasi lawyer in the 1930s adopts a rationalist attitude at one moment, saying, "Our classical music is scientific," an idiosyncratic traditionalism at the next, giving a few rupees to a Madrasi Muslim healer (of whom everyone is a little afraid), and a Hindu chauvinist attitude at another moment, locating the origin of authentic Karnatak music in the singing of South Indian saint musicians (compare Ewing 1997, 5–6 and passim). The manifold discourses on the voice in South and West Asia, a portion of which would probably operate outside the experience of some individuals, populate field 3. These discourses involve overlapping variables—the transformative power of sound, the attribution of divine or human qualities to the voice, and both the symbolic and technical roles of verbal language. The analytic advantage in recognizing this wide-ranging backdrop for emphasis on vocality in South Asia, to rephrase a point already made, is that it militates against assigning a determinative role to any particular discourse or set of discourses—particularly the pernicious ones that fall under the rubric "modernity."

This interpretive frame can be further explained and elaborated using a case study from Hyderabad, Sindh, which is treated below in more detail, reframed as Ali's story. The drum leader Allaudin, who was eighty years old in 1997, told me when I first met him at his house that he had learned his repertoire from a Hindu in Bharatpur, India, before his emigration to Pakistan at the time of Partition. When we next met a few days later and other members of his group were present, he denied having learned anything from a Hindu—how could he, he said, when such drumming was a matter concerning their faith (*'aqīdah*)?

The group was composed of Sunni Muslim Muhājirs who played *ḍhol* and *tāshā* exclusively during Muharram and who, unlike Shī'ahs, did not place emphasis on meritorious mourning. Their repertoire was relatively elaborate for a group that only played ten days of the year without rehearsing otherwise. The fact that the group leader learned from someone with more general training—not from someone who played only ten days per year—stands to reason. That person served as a link between the learned and extensive classical traditions of North Indian music and the limited context of Muharram in which often a pattern or two would suffice.

Allaudin represented his knowledge to me in artistic, musical terms when initially describing his training. Later, without reference to the musical variety of the repertoire, he emphasized the role of drumming in proclaiming the group's faith. The field 2 background knowledge that fed into Allaudin's verbal self-representations grew out of his earlier experiences in India and his later role in leading the Hyderabad group.

The group he led constituted what I will call a complex agent—a group of individuals who, as non-unitary agents themselves, bring together their own sets of life circumstances and explanatory frameworks in unpredictable ways. Allaudin's re-presentation of himself as a drumming authority was evidently a reaction to what he imagined his group expected of him. This self-presention did not incorporate a critical piece of field 3 information, perhaps because it was beyond the reach of the participants who grew up in Pakistan: namely, that Hindus in India regularly participated in Muharram rituals in terms of their own faith, and frequently cooperated, and drummed, with Muslims.

Social Poetics

Agency in Ewing's analysis involves positionality. Inasmuch as adopting a position is a rhetorical move, it feeds into what Michael Herzfeld terms social poetics. Allaudin, in making his rhetorical shift, manipulated a set of stereotypes of the Hindu and the Muslim, as well as of his art's function—he might have chosen, alternatively, to emphasize the artistic merit of the drumming rather than its role in expressing faith. Allaudin's simple statement that it was a matter of faith served to align the relations among the various categories of identity—religious and musical—in a manner that he presumed would allow him to save face among his juniors.

The focus in Herzfeld's analysis on poetics in terms of making or doing (from the Greek, *poieo*) immediately draws attention to what actors accomplish via the rhetoric of their actions. *Rhetoric* here is any form of social action put forward with the attempt to persuade; this does not mean it is necessarily exaggerated, false, or deceptive (Herzfeld 2005, 183–89). (Nor does it mean it must occur in extraordinary circumstances—although through my focus on ritual, most of this book concerns situations that are not entirely mundane.) To the extent that social poetics "treat[s] essentialism as a social strategy" (ibid., 183), Allaudin's positional shift highlighted the essential Hindu-ness of his teacher—and not the capacity of this teacher to transmit drumming as an art or to be a religious participant whose involvement could be appreciated by a Muslim. Through this, Allaudin made the argument that a Hindu could not possibly have taught him the *important* thing he and his group were doing, which involved the Muslim faith. The fact that Muslims integrate Hindus into their Muharram observances elsewhere without a sense of cognitive dissonance was not part of the story Allaudin wished to tell in front of the others. This was a distortion by omission.

Social poetics involves both "the analysis of essentialism" and "the deformation of social conventions" (Herzfeld 2005, 32, 37). These processes are connected in that social actors must reduce an aspect of human complexity to a stereotype or essence before it is possible to deform it—or perceive it as deformed. The fact that Allaudin's teacher was Hindu did not necessarily prevent him from teaching something significant for Islamic faith; Allaudin, rather, *used* the category "Hindu" in that way. Such deformations call attention to the frame and thereby to the social categories of which each actor may be a token.

To extend the Allaudin case study briefly, the chief repertorial item Allaudin used to demonstrate the status of drumming as faith is called *kalmah*, meaning "the word," and more specifically, the formal affirmation of God's unity. The fact that Allaudin and his group were Sheiḵẖ Siddiqis, Muhājirs, recent descendents of Hindus, and drummers, would potentially motivate them to emphasize the Islamic message of their drumming. Indeed, the *kalmah* encodes the statement "no god but God," which appears ubiquitously in many genres of Muslim verbal and musical performance. In this case, the musical utterance's meaning is inflected by the contemporary politics of being Muslim in Pakistan—a topic on which I elaborate in subsequent chapters.

By drawing attention to common elements such as the *kalmah*, social poetics lends focus to "parallelisms that exist among multiple levels of identity" and reveals how a community is entwined with "several other social entities, overlapping or concentric, clearly or weakly defined, officially recognized or contrary to the social values of the bureaucratic state" (Herzfeld 2005, 118). I would also include under this rubric religious norms espoused by those invested with official authority by the state or agents in the religious establishment.

The direct antecedent of Herzfeld's social poetics is Roman Jakobson's discussion of the *poetic function* of language—an analysis that is relevant for the musical texts we will encounter, and in particular, the *kalmah*. Before turning to this, it is worth pointing out the roots of poetics theory in the philosophical writings of Greek antiquity. Muslim philosophers such as al-Fārābī, Ibn Sinā, and Ibn Rushd produced an extensive and well-known body of commentaries on the works of Aristotle, Plato, and others that figures prominently in the history of Islamic philosophy. This early intellectual cross-fertilization informed the development of modern Islamic thought and made aspects of Greek philosophy accessible in medieval Europe.[4] The Greek philosophers and their Muslim commentators were interested in the relation between language and music, especially with respect to metric organization (Madian 1992, 18 and passim). The theological traditions to which many of my research consultants were exposed developed from such commentaries and their many responses.

Plato and Aristotle were prominent among those who participated in the broader conversation that ultimately served as a resource for modern poetics theory in European and American academia. I draw briefly on Aristotle to make the link explicit. In the *Poetics*, Aristotle was concerned not only with acting (on stage) but more generally with the nature of human action as mimetic—as involving *exaggeration*, a "framing of reality that announces that what is contained within the frame is not simply real" (Davis 1999, 3). Aristotle's ideal poet creates a character who imperfectly embodies a characteristic such as virtue (if it were perfect, it would not announce its frame). The plot in a tragedy must contain a *reversal* that causes the viewer to reflect on the play; the viewer comes to a realization of true virtue only through the failure of the character to become fully virtuous himself (Davis 2002, xxv). In the *Politics*, by contrast, Aristotle asserts that only rhythms and songs are capable of being direct likenesses of characters such as anger and gentleness. Because "there is a kinship of resemblance in scales and rhythms to the soul," music should be used to morally educate the young (ibid., 87). Songs and rhythms, unlike poetry, do not require reflection and contemplation to work their moral magic on human consumers.

Aristotle's mimetic theory extends beyond the domain of poetry and music. All human action is already an imitation of human action because actors behave in response to their own self-images; these images are idealized reformulations of actions others have already performed. Consider social poetics as deformations of social convention in light of Davis's reading of Aristotle:

> The hardest problem for Aristotle's account of courage is that, while the moral virtues are supposed to make us happy, courage is frequently rather unpleasant and can easily make us dead. Why, then, does the brave man risk his life? Aristotle says it is for the sake of the *kalon*—the noble or beautiful. But this *kalon* end is clearly not present in the activity itself.
>
> Neither killing nor being killed is by itself beautiful. We must look elsewhere than the dead bodies fouling the Scamander to see Achilles' devotion to the *kalon*. The brave man, presenting an image to himself of his action as completed, contemplates his deed as others will contemplate it, and so reaps the benefits of honor even before it has been granted. The current action becomes *kalon* insofar as it is made complete through reflection or imagination. The brave, therefore, do what they do not because it is good but because they can say "it is good." This is what the *kalon* means; it is impossible without logos. (Davis 1999, xvii).

The discourses surrounding ritual drumming in the largely Islamic contexts explored in this book cannot be understood without attention to the ways actors deploy and distort self-images, particularly with regard to how they imagine that others construct ideal types—social categories defined by religion or occupation, or moral categories defined by some subset of religious doctrine and objectified in writings, poems, and sermons. Allaudin, in emphasizing the faith of drumming over its technical source, was living up to the image he imagined his co-drummers would expect of him. The photographs presented throughout the present work also thematize mimesis—deformations of images on a poster, in wood, and so forth that the reader is meant to contemplate in light of the book as a whole.

In Herzfeld's poetics, mimesis is embodied in social action. In Jakobson's poetic function, mimesis operates primarily at the level of linguistic syntax.

Jakobson's Poetic Function

Jakobson's poetic function is one of six functions of verbal communication. Its principal feature is a "focus on the message itself" (Jakobson 1960, 356). That is to say, something about the utterance, whether it is in everyday speech or in a literary genre, makes it salient in an artistic or aesthetically satisfying way (just as in Herzfeld's scheme, rhetorical moves create social saliences that call into play a series of cultural iconicities). The effect of this artistry in language is also to enhance the message. I forgo Jakobson's classic example of the poetic function in the slogan "I like Ike" (ibid., 357) in favor of a more regionally appropriate one, reported to have been common around the time of Partition and incorporating the first part of the *kalmah* (in the slogan's second half):

Pākistān kā na'rah kyā	What is the slogan of Pakistan?
lā il-lāha illa'l-lāh	No god, except God [Allah]

The two parts of the chant consist of seven syllables each, organized with alternating strong and weak beats; all but the penultimate strong stresses fall on syllables with long /ā/ vowels. This creates several layers of parallelism. Rhythmic and end-rhyme parallels between the two half lines draw attention to the formal poetry of the chant. The sequence of consonances, moving from the hard /k/ sounds in the first half to the soft /l/ sounds in the second, parallels the shift from tension to resolution, question to answer, the aggressive, proclamatory statement about Pakistan's new identity to the inclusive, gentle *ẕikr* and moral refrain of the Sufis and every Muslim affirming the unity of God. The assonance of the vowel /ā/ beginning in the first syllable of Pakistan creates a set of associations that are compounded as one moves through the text. In a general sense, it tightly ties the first half to the second, and thereby reinforces the idea that Pakistan is a Muslim place. On the micro level, each syllable impacts the next: The /ā/ in *Pāk*, meaning "pure," is retained as one moves forward to *stān* (place), *na'rah* (slogan), and *kyā* (what). The predominant vowel in the word for God, *Allāh*, is also /ā/. As Michael Sells writes, "The ā sound is the major or tonic of Qur'anic sound figures. It is combined with key terms in a way that brings out aspects of gender, emotion, and spirit" (Sells 2007, 163). The impact of this chant draws not only on the set of parallels within the chant itself, then, but also from a palette of deeply ingrained recitational contexts.

Given that early Greek thought was transmitted to medieval Europe through Arabic sources, it is worth noting, in Jakobson's poetic function, resonances of Ibn Sinā's theory of *imaginative assent.* This notion derives from the Arabic word *takhyīl*, which implies both image-making and psychological effect (Dahiyat 1974, 33). In imaginative assent, listeners respond to an utterance "psychologically rather than ratiocinatively." They respond to its sound qualities, metric properties, its sense, and the elements that "hesitat[e] between sound and sense." Imaginative assent, then, "results from the utterance itself" (33–35), giving pleasure through such forms of artifice as "internal rhyme, metrical proportion, decoration, [and] inversion" (64).

Further to the subject of *deformation,* Aristotle and his commentators were interested in *deviations* of many kinds. Ibn Sinā describes a sense of wonder (*ta'jīb*) that arises from the listener's estimating the way a poetic representation "deflects" reality in the direction of praise or blame (Blum 2012; Dahiyat 1974, 75). Al Fārābī wrote of the "psychological effect of the formal elements of poetry on the listener" (Madian 1992, 70), whereby the listener expects formal parallelisms in measure (the length of feet, lines, stanzas, and so forth) at various hierarchical levels to be repeated; listeners also expect formal deviations in measure, which Al Fārābī likens to "alterations made in the rhythmic cycles in melodies" (Madian 1992, 71; see also Blum 2013, 108–9, 112–14).

As the brief examples above are meant to suggest, the creation and manipulation of iconicities in both language and sociocultural formations play a role in the ways drummers and other musicians position themselves in complex events and in the ways the texts (musical or otherwise) they perform might be understood. We now turn more specifically to that aspect of understanding which involves emotion.

The Navigation of Feeling

The narration of the wedding sequence in Ali's visit to Lahore was meant to highlight a characteristic of many ceremonial structures as well as the possible roles of music in those structures. Different sections of a ceremony, its constituent rituals, may have conventional affective meanings. The sequence of rituals that composes a ceremony in such circumstances may outline a series of conventional affects that change as the rituals unfold in time. I term this the *emotional contour* of a ceremony (see Wolf 2000, 2001, 2003, 2005). Suggesting that a ceremony might have a conventional emotional contour is not to say that such conventions are immutable, nor does it mean that the affective codings determine how individuals involved in a ceremony actually experience them. It merely suggests that by some process of history and consensus, communities involve themselves in ceremonies with parts whose shared meanings might include happiness, sadness, pride, pain, and anger. My focus here is on the musical constituents of a ceremony, but the argument applies (perhaps) equally well to any aspect of ritual performance.

Often, especially with reference to rituals constituted by music, participants will describe affect not in words—which are, after all, quite limited—but in terms of what the music makes them feel. That is, the musical sound comes to be a label for affect as if it were an unmediated translation (compare the above-mentioned discussion of rhythms and song in Aristotle's *Politics*).[5] In a way, this is what the real Ajmal was implying when he said that the sound of the Multan drum pattern struck fear in his heart as a young child. The words were really inadequate to describe what this drum pattern meant to him. Literally, the name of the drum pattern *mārū* means "striking" or "death," and figuratively it means the same thing as *mātam*—mourning.

The ways individuals react in a specific set of circumstances to musical or other affectively coded rituals relate directly to the problem addressed in the previous section. Individuals, as non-unitary agents, may find themselves drawn into the emotional mood the music is supposed to create, but they may also retain critical distance. This distance may arise from philosophical disagreement; it may also be a result of reacting to many other stimuli taking place at a complex event or to situations in the subject's life. All of these conditioning situations, which may constitute subject positions, belong in field 2 (competing discourses and knowledge sets that partly inform moment-to-moment decisions). The individual experiences may also be more or less intense from one occasion to the next. That is to say, any particular musical ritual coded with affect *x* could be experienced as more or less *x* or as varying intensities of *y* or *z*. My shorthand term for the multiple possible experiences of complex agents (that is, groups of individuals) in relation to a ceremony's emotional contour is *emotional texture*. This is meant to evoke a sense of multidimensionality, in which affect and intensity vary for each participant (see Wolf 2000, 2001, 2003, 2005).

Such affective understandings, in either their ideal or actually experienced forms, can be subject to criticisms based on reevaluations of religious practice generally; in such cases, the emotional contour of a ceremony may also be subject to periodic revision (Wolf 2001). In the case of the wedding, I placed into relief the Shī'ī value of remembering the Karbala martyrs, their moral rectitude, and what they suffered at every critical moment in Shī'ī lives, including weddings. The very same poetry, musical settings, and ritual actions may be used in a *majlis* preceding a wedding as in a *majlis* taking place in the heart of Muharram observances. However, to some extent, this wedding *majlis* is a token. It is not likely to have as strong an impact in this context as it does during Muharram. It is a reminder, a blessing, and a communal affirmation of the value of what Mahmoud Ayoub called "redemptive suffering" (1978). Muharram Ali's cousin Fatimah, who was critical of juxtaposing differently emotionally coded rituals within the wedding sequence and within the Muharram sequence, articulated an actively reformist position in today's South Asian Shiism. Reformers have instigated such changes as downplaying or eliminating wedding-related rituals during Muharram and holding *milād*s—celebrations of the Prophet—instead of *majlis*es before their weddings.

Fatimah gave voice to but one aspect of the variations in Muharram ritual structure in South and West Asia—variations that fall within the realm of field 3. This field is critical when considering the possible emotional implications of ritual drumming, because the inclusion or exclusion of drumming during Muharram at a given place and time by a given community depends almost entirely on conventional emotional attributes. These are locally determined to such an extent that it is hard for participants in some regions to relate to those in some others. Asif's interaction with Ajmal draws on my experiences of reporting to my wife's Shī'ī consultants in the old city of Lahore that in Multan, Muharram was observed with performances on musical instruments. They expressed surprise, disbelief, and, in the case of male relatives, a degree of scornful curiosity that made me anxious for the safety of the Muharram drummers in Multan.

The ideas of emotional contour and texture that I have been developing in the context of this project as well as my work on South Indian Kota society are inspired, in part, by the work of William Reddy. The title of this section is based on his book *The Navigation of Feeling*, the idea here being that the sequence of rituals, coded by conventional affects, provides a series of signposts for emotional experiences without entirely determining them. Reddy's critical contribution is theorizing the impact of what he calls *emotives*. Emotives are first-person emotional utterances, like "I am angry," which appear to have an exterior referent—in this case anger. But, in fact, anger is not as exterior as it may seem; it is not "passive in the formulation of the emotive, and it emerges from the act of uttering in a changed state" (Reddy 2001, 105). Put another way, the emotion I experience before stating (or writing) "I am angry" could be intensified or attenuated by the very act of using this emotive—depending on the identity of the person to whom I address the statement, the sentences I use to frame it, my tone (or typeface), and so forth. What it means to be angry could change through the act of speech—saying "I am angry" does not merely express my anger.

Conventionally coded musical utterances are analogous but not perfectly homologous to verbal emotives. The parallel I wish to draw is that emotive musical or other ritual gestures deployed in a ceremony can be regarded as kinds of collectively determined (yet revisable) statements about what people ought to be feeling, or at least represent themselves as feeling.

This is something like the relation of Achilles to the concept of kalon, the noble or the beautiful, as Davis interprets Aristotle. To rephrase it slightly, not only being brave but also the experience of feeling courageous comes about through contemplation of how others will view one's activities once they are accomplished: "current action becomes *kalon* insofar as it is made complete through reflection or imagination" (Davis 1999, xvii). A similar moral framework underlies the structure of a *majlis*, in which emotional conformity with the affective structure (which is also largely guided by poetic texts and sermons) constitutes part of the devotional act. Crying in the *majlis* is a sign of the ritual's efficacy, and participants judge sermons and recitations accordingly (Bard 2010).

The very performance of such emotive acts as music, recitation, sermons, and certain kinds of bodily practice such as *mātam* (gently striking the hand on the chest or vigorous forms of self-mortification) have an effect on those who are collectively, as it were, making that statement. One of my aims in this book's case studies is to explore the productive feedback between the emotional system, as projected in any one community's ceremonial sequence, and the collective effects of individual emotional readings of these sequences.

CHAPTER 3

Tone and Stroke

Muharram Ali lingered after his cousin's wedding reception in Lahore to speak further with the *ḍhol* players Niamat Ali and Shahid Ali.

"So you have learned only a few patterns on this . . . *tāshā*. Can you recite *bol*s for those patterns?" Shahid asked Muharram Ali.

"Unfortunately not. We picked up *tāshā* playing during Muharram, on the street in my town outside Lucknow. There were no ustads, so I never had the chance to learn drumming properly. The best players lived in the *qaṣbāt* and the *dehāt*,* some in nearby villages. They'd show up in the larger cities and towns for the first two weeks of Muharram. We'd watch the flashier players and try to imitate their hand movements."

"We don't think it is really possible to learn this way," responded Niamat. "In fact, we don't even think it is sufficient to learn from a family member. Our fathers can't instill the necessary discipline. They send us for apprenticeship under an ustad. We stay in the ustad's home; we bring him goods from the market; we massage his legs with oil at night when he feels fatigued. We catch as catch can. Little by little. The drum technique takes years to master. Still, since you're interested, I can teach you some simple *bol*s for some of the *tāl*s we play on *ḍhol* to recite by mouth."

"Ṭhīk [OK], Sahab, if you would."

---

*Rural towns, villages, and countryside.

Niamat began to utter syllables (see figure 3.1 in the chapter notes; Media Example 3.1). He infused them with the Panjabi lilt or swing, called *jhol*, that gives drum patterns their individual character.

Ali repeated the *bol* sequence several times and asked, "What is this *tāl* called?"

"Cheh mātre (6-count) fāḵẖtah aṣūl."

"Cheh mātre fāḵẖtah aṣūl," repeated Ali, getting his mouth around the words. The name of the *tāl* meant, unhelpfully, "six-count pattern of the Ringdove."

"May I record you playing this?" Ali's distant cousin Samina, who lived in New York, had brought him a Sony Walkman Professional when they met at the wedding.

"Āp kī marẕī [as you like]. Look: this curved stick, for bass strokes on the left-hand side, is called *kūṇḍi;* this thinner one, for making crisp strokes on the right head, is called *tīlā.* My left and right hands play resonant strokes together to produce the heavy accent on the first syllable, *dhin.* I use the *tīlā* to play a resonant treble stroke for *na* and the *kūṇḍi* to play a damped bass stroke for *kat.*" Niamat began to play the *ṭhekā*—the stroke-melody that contains the essence of the *tāl.*

"Do this for as long as you want. Depending on how much you practice, and what you remember, you can vary it a lot." Niamat stopped playing to recite a string of *bol*s so fast that Ali was unable to keep track of the six-count cycle. Ali could sense a return to beat one (the *sam*) each time Niamat would repeat a pattern three times. (Media Examples 3.1 and 3.2 ; figure 3.2 in the chapter notes).

Ali had acquired rudimentary knowledge of Hindustani classical music from attending concerts and hearing his brother's singing lessons. He could follow simple *tāl*s on the tabla, had a sense of pitch, and could recognize some *rāg*s. But he wasn't sure whether this knowledge was relevant to Niamat's and Shahid's *ḍhol* playing. He expected the *tihā'ī* to begin on the third count of the cycle and then lead back to the *sam*—where Niamat returned to the *ṭhekā*. But Ali could not orient himself within the *tāl*. Niamat did not count the *tāl* on his fingers while reciting, as one might when illustrating a complicated pattern in Hindustani music.

"After this you can go to *panj tāl* [five tāl], which has five rhythmic units (*layvāṉ*). [See figure 3.3 in chapter notes.] This is the *aṣūl* (foundation/cyclical pattern) of five *matrā*s—the five-count fāḵẖtah *aṣūl.* But you have to take your time before modulating. One, two, three, four, five. This is how our breathing flows. Continuously. One, two, three, four, five. These are all the beats of our heart. *Sāz, sur, sangīt*—instrument, tone, and music—are all, in fact, heartbeats. That's what our teacher taught us. You need to breathe, feel the music in your body, and then gradually change to a new pattern."

Ali found it confusing that a single *tāl* name, *fāk̲h̲tah aṣūl*, could be used for patterns with two different numbers of counts. The six-count pattern was the same as the five-count pattern, save for the added phrase *tiṭakiṭa* (uttered quickly within the duration of a single count). The *tāl* name included the word *aṣūl*, the generic term for repetitive percussion pattern, *uṣūl*, in Turkish and Central Asian music.

"What comes after *fāk̲h̲tah aṣūl*?" Ali asked, thinking about the learning sequence.

"The one with six *mātra*s? The next one is *muġala'i*, with seven," replied Niamat.

He recited the *bol*s, placing primary emphasis on the first syllable, *tā*, and secondary stresses on the *dhin* syllables over the duration of count four, with a slight undulation in the *jhol* on the *da* syllables of counts five and seven (see figure 3.4 in the chapter notes; Media Example 3.3 ⮊).

Ali noticed *muġala'i*'s similarity to *rūpak tāl;* both articulate a 3 + 4 pattern and employ aspirated syllables for stress on counts four and six.

Niamat then played a short suite joining some of the patterns he had mentioned. Ali had heard *ḍhol-tāshā* players in Lucknow string together different *tāl*s in this way. Some folk songs he had heard in Uttar Pradesh involved more abrupt rhythmic changes. In Hindustani classical music concerts, by contrast, the *tāl* would change once, at most, over the course of a particular *rāg* performance. Ali was unfamiliar with solo tabla genres.

Niamat's introduction was rhythmically disorienting. After twenty seconds, though, he segued into the *fāk̲h̲tah aṣūl ṭhekā*. For Ali, it was as if Niamat had removed a veil that had hitherto rendered the *tāl* hidden, even though he had, in fact, maintained the metric cycle precisely from the very beginning. Niamat then elaborated the groove with a denser stream of strokes and cadenced with a *tihā'ī*. He returned to the basic *ṭhekā* briefly and shifted into high gear once more. Pouring energy into his quick-fire stickwork, Niamat changed the metric frame from five counts to four while retaining the same underlying pace.

Ali associated what he heard with a *drut tīntāl*—the sixteen-count *tāl* of classical music played so rapidly that it is perceived as a four-count cycle. Ali clapped: 1, 2, 3, 4—clap, clap, wave, clap. He did not have to change the speed of his counting: he merely changed from counting five *mātra*s to counting four *mātra*s. In classical music, *tīntāl* was so named because it had three "claps" (*tālī*)—corresponding to three points of emphasis (bass resonance) on the bass drum or bass side of the drum—even though the *tāl* itself had four equal subdivisions. Ali had heard Shahid call this *tīntār* in Panjabi.

After another *tihā'ī*, Niamat transitioned to *muġala'i*. Here the basic unit was twice the speed of the original *mātra*. He shifted from eight to seven fast *mātras*. Unlike Niamat's vocalized version, in which he emphasized counts one, four, and six, his drummed version emphasized only count four. As in *rūpak tāl*, Niamat placed a damped bass stroke on count one, which is considered "empty" (*k̲h̲ālī*) in contrast to the "full" (*bharī*) stroke on count four. He concluded the demonstration with a brief *tihā'ī*.

"Subḥāna'llāh, Niamat Sahab," Ali responded. "Your transitions between *tāls* were wonderful. I have a question about that. You alluded to learning little by little, and you demonstrated how one pattern follows another in a sequence. Can you say a little more about the learning sequence?"

"At first the ustad teaches 'surface things,' like *dhamāl* and *bhāṅgṛā*. When the student becomes 'sharp,' he 'will show him' *nā-dhin-dhin-nā*—eight *mātras*, and then sixteen-*mātra tīntār*, which is more 'weighty' and serves as the 'chief' of all *ṭhekās*. After the student learns one the teacher proceeds to the next. Like climbing stairs, step by step. First you place your foot here, then here, then here. *Ṭhekās* are like stairs. First there is one of four *mātras*. Then it goes to five *mātras*. That is *aṣūl*. Add one *mātra* and it becomes *yakka*, six *mātras*. Add another and it becomes *muġala'i*. Then eight-*mātra tīntār*. And if you add one more it becomes *kaṭh tār*, nine *mātras*. Add three to that and you get *iktāla*; two more and it becomes *dhamār* of fourteen *mātras*. If you pour two more *mātras* into that you get to the 'chief' tāl, *tīntār*. If you subtract one *mātra* from that, you get *panj tāl dī savārī* of fifteen *mātras*. We have only learned up to this point ourselves."

"When do you get a chance to use all these *tāls*? In Lucknow, drummers only play a few patterns during festivals."

Shahid responded, "Here too. *Dhamāl* and *bhāṅgṛā* are used for playing at *mazārs* (Sufi shrines). *Bhāṅgṛā* is important for weddings. But as you heard, sometimes connoisseurs and other 'judges' will listen. *Ḍhol* players from Lahore, from Gujrat, from outlying villages, sit together at *'urses*. Someone will ask Niamat and me to play what we have practiced. We will ask others to play. Ustads will bring their students. Bharāins will also attend. Each will try to outdo the other. Knowledgeable people will pass judgment—this person is 'keeping' the *tāl*, 'raising' the *relā* or the *parṇ* [genres of improvisation and composition] correctly. Each *pahlavān* applies his own tricks of the trade; those who cannot keep up must stop. The 'general gathering' decides on the winner."

"What about the other players in Lahore? Do you compete amongst yourselves?"

"There are five 'senior' players in Lahore: Shabbir Husain of 'noble birth,' who plays with us; long-haired Pappu, who plays at Shah Jamal; Gunga, who lives near Shahnoor studio," began Niamat.

"Niamat ustad is among the top . . . and I struggle to play," added Shahid. "My brother Akram also plays well."

"The seniors meet at the major *'urs*es, like Data Sahab and Madho Lal Husain. Because we are all from Lahore we don't argue, we have musical 'gatherings of affection.' We approach one another, 'assalām alaykum, kih ḥāl'e. May we sit near you? We want to play in your presence. We regard you as an ustad.' We talk, offer one another cigarettes, ask one another to play," said Niamat.

"With love, you may ask anyone to play *ḍhol*," added Shahid.

"Is there any special arrangement for you at *'urs*es? Do you get invited?" asked Ali.

"Yes. For every *mela* we are invited by Arif Sain. He is a *malaṅg*, a dervish who dances a wonderful *dhamāl*. I should know," said Niamat. "I've been playing for him for six or eight years. We accompany him when he goes to Data Sahab and lays a *cādar* (cloth offering) for the saint. You should come to the Madho Lal Husain *'urs* next March. It is a grand gathering of drummers and dancers."

"I'd love to do that. . . . I was wondering, do you earn your livelihood from people like Arif Sain?" inquired Ali.

"No," continued Niamat. "We do not expect anything from Arif Sain. Although he once earned a good living as a cultivator (member of the Arain caste), he has given up his worldly possessions. We feel we are doing something good by serving as drummers for him. Arif Sain will invite only us, no one else, and insist that we remain with him permanently. If he calls us for 9 P.M., we arrive at 6 P.M. and play for whomever requests us. When we play well, people will perform 'spirit bolstering.' One person might place a fifty- or hundred-rupee note neatly on the *ḍhol*, say, 'Well done, Khan Sahab,' and wipe the sweat from our brow. Others might shower money over the dancing *dhamālī*. A father might reward us for playing as his son dances *dhamāl*."

Ajmal entered the small courtyard where Ali was conversing with Shahid and Niamat and indicated that it was time to pose for some family photographs. Ali thanked the drummers, exchanged addresses, and reiterated his desire to return for the *'urs* in March. Niamat joked that they would include him in their *sangat* (gathering) and make him pass a test on what he had just learned.

: : :

Like Muharram Ali, Shahid, and Niamat, many musicians and listeners in South Asia are interested in the relation of what they consider classical music to what they consider folk music. Some emphasize the distinction when wishing to make a point about what constitutes true musical knowledge (usually knowledge associated with the "classical"). The body is often a symbolic and practical ground for such knowledge: performers such as Shahid and Niamat compare drum pattern and flow to bodily rhythms of breath and heartbeat and stress the importance of being able not only to play but also recite the syllables of drum patterns. Some performers and listeners keep track of metric structures with their hands and fingers.

Shahid and Niamat's stories emphasize the role of apprenticeship and specifically mention the role of physical contact in showing the disciple's closeness to his master. Transmission of divine energy (*fayḍ*) through touch, albeit in a different form, is common in Sufi spiritual training as well (for example, Buehler 1998, 133). Indeed, the *pir-murīdī* (master-disciple) relationships for both musical and spiritual disciplines have much in common (Qureshi 2009). Touch in both cases is a manifestation of and a conduit for mutual love. *Ḍhol* players in Lahore are not alone in considering love a desideratum both for participants in musical gatherings and for those sharing bodies of precious and painstakingly acquired knowledge.

Another source of energy and creativity, the competition, also extends well beyond the *ḍhol*-playing sphere. Wrestlers and probably others as well compete at such religious and life-cycle celebrations as *'urs*es and weddings. Through their respective disciplines, these experts enter into temporary forums that combine agonistic and affectionate forms of male sociality.

Other aspects of affect connected with music may be dictated by the needs of an occasion: musicians may be required to perform patterns suitable for the somber mood of families bidding farewell to their daughter, but unless they themselves feel connected to the family, they are unlikely to partake of the emotional atmosphere themselves. In Chapter 6 we shall hear from Pappu Sain (alluded to in the present chapter as "long-haired Pappu"), who describes having had difficulty in carrying out his father's wishes that Pappu play *ḍhol* at his funeral. In my studies of South Indian folk and tribal music and of drumming in South Asian Islamic contexts alike, I have found that a performer's own emotional condition may vary considerably in the creation of emotional texture in highly charged ceremonial contexts. The role of musician as "technician of emotion" is worthy of more general consideration than is possible here.[1]

Ḍhol and *sharnā'ī* players performing context-specific music at wrestling match during the *'urs* of Misri Shah (1840–1905), a Sindhi saint and composer of *kāfī* poetry. Nasarpur, Sindh, Pakistan, June 12, 1997. Photo by the author.

Some of the specifically musical issues that Ali's interactions introduce include matters of naming. The names of items sometimes provide indications of musical organization (for example, numbers that might refer to the length of a musical cycle), they may connect with musical identifiers in West Asia and other regions (for example, the term *aṣūl* or *uṣūl*), they may refer to contexts and accompanying physical actions, and some may seem merely fanciful. The existence of names makes it possible, among other things, to talk about sequences—sequences in which items should be taught and linked in performance. Subtle concepts such as *jhol* allow performers to discriminate among *tāl*s sharing the same number of counts by reference to timbral and accentual details.

The remainder of this chapter and the next focus on three topics of significance in South Asia: the basis for naming items of drum repertoire, ambiguities in defining such items with respect to melody and rhythm, and, in Chapter 4, the grounding of item names in particular musical processes. By necessity, the depth of my fieldwork varies in each of the regions discussed. My hope is that further fieldwork by others will enrich, refine, and provide correctives for this discussion.

The following discussions of naming and defining rhythmic patterns draw from my fieldwork in the following cities, towns, and rural regions in India and Pakistan: Delhi, Hyderabad (Andhra Pradesh, South India), Hyderabad (Sindh, Pakistan), Almora (Kumaon, Uttarakhand, India), Dharmapuri (Tamil Nadu, South India), the Nilgiri Hills (Tamil Nadu, South India), the Hunza Valley (Gilgit-Baltistan, the northernmost part of Pakistan), Udaipur (Rajasthan, India), and Multan (Pakistan).

Naming Drum Patterns

The words for drum patterns across the many languages of South Asia are grounded in an overlapping set of common ideas. Like the English word *beat*, many South Asian terms for drum patterns derive from nouns and verbs meaning "beat" or "strike." Several derive from the instruments on which pieces are performed. Some imply enumeration, although what is enumerated may vary depending on the conventions of a genre, the item of repertoire, and the intentions of the speaker. Several terms for drum patterns invoke images of moving through space. Drumming terminology sometimes implicates the human body, either with terms for motion or by reference to the hand. In general, the terminology involves several kinds of genus, which may be organized according to hierarchical levels or may overlap. Table 3.1 provides examples of the various kinds of pattern names and their relationships.

Tāla derives from the Sanskrit root *taḍ-,* meaning "to beat or strike." In South Indian classical music *tāla* is not demarcated by any instrument; it is, rather, a metric ground, usually demonstrated with claps and finger counts, against which the music's surface rhythm is understood as meaningful. By contrast, *ṭhekā* and *lehrā* in Hindustani music, which timbrally and melodically differentiate the structure of the cycle, usually make it unnecessary to use one's hands to show the *tāl*. *Tāla* stands as a theoretical structure separable from any particular rhythmic pattern in both classical traditions. In many of the vernacular drumming traditions in South Asia, by contrast, the word *tāl* is used for the drum pattern itself—as if it meant *ṭhekā*.

In the classical *tāla* systems, the names of *tāla*s often contain numbers. The word *tāl* in these contexts may imply a point in the rhythmic cycle emphasized by a clap—*tālī*. Hence *tīntāl* refers to a tāl with three (*tīn*)

Table 3.1. Generic and semi-generic terms for drum patterns in South Asia

I. Proper, semi-generic terms
Percussion patterns with at least 2 varieties in a given repertoire, examples of where they occur, and how many varieties exist in each instance (these may or may not have separate adjectives to denote them)
  A. Panjābī (Udaipur, 2)
  B. Rajasthānī (Udaipur, 2)
  C. *mātam* (widespread)
  D. *mārū* (Multan, Pakistan, 3)
  E. *kehervā* (widespread)
  F. *tappi* (Udaipur, at least 2)
  G. *garba* (Udaipur, 3)
  H. *dhamāl* (Yusufain dargah, Hyderabad, AP, 2 types for *ḍhol-tāshā*)
  I. *bhāṅgṛā* (in Indian Panjab, many subvarieties)
  J. *savārī* (Delhi, Mamraj's *tāshā* group, 2; several classical *tāl*s include this term)

II. Terms distinguished by context
  A. *jīt kā ḍhol* (possibly "*ḍhol* of conquest")—played after marriage procession to bridegroom's house. The same pattern is called *badhāvā kā ḍhol* ("auspicious ceremony *ḍhol*") on other occasions (Udaipur).
  B. *bārah terah*—2 versions based on the idea of 12 followed by 13 strokes, 1 for Muharram (*Husainī kī bārah-terah*) and a "straight" one for other occasions (*sīdhī bārah-terah*)

III. Terms used for repertoire items named by the word for *strike*
Asterisked terms are usually preceded by numbers indicating the number of stressed strokes.
  A. *mār** (Urdu—Hyderabad, AP)
  B. *mārū* (Saraiki)
  C. *aṭi** (Tamil, Kota)
  D. *tāl/tāla* (widespread, numbers and adjectives)
  E. *jarbeṉ** (Mamraj's *ḍhol-tāshā* group, Delhi)
  F. *daruvu* (Telugu)
  G. *debba* (Telugu, Runza tradition)
  H. *dāk* (Kota)
  I. *vajat* (Sindhi)

IV. Term based on a word for counting
gintī (Hindi-Urdu: Hyderabad, Sindh/Bharatpur, India) (see also Kippen 1988)

V. Terms based on musical instrument or ensemble
Nongeneric terms are marked by (†).
  A. *tabl* (Arabic *ṭabl*)†—Hyderabad, Sindh; *nagāra* and *ḍhol* item characterized by drum rolls, used at the beginning of Muharram performance
  B. *bājā/bāja* (Sanskrit, vādya) (widespread). Adjectives can refer to instruments (e.g., "Band *bājā*," Western-style brass bands), or some attribute or context. Example: *hudda bāja* (Persian *'ohda*, "duty"), Muharram ensemble of *jhānjh, tāshā, ḍhol* in Uttaraula, UP
  C. *vājā* (Sanskrit, *vādya*)—Saraiki language, Multan
  D. *ḍanka/ḍamka*—kettledrum or stick, Udaipur and Ajmer
  E. *dappu* (Arabic *daff*). Telugu: frame drum; example: *cāvu dappu* (funeral pattern), Kulukulu village, Mahabubnagar district, Andhra Pradesh.
  F. *ḍhol*—example: *aheda kā ḍhol*, a piece used to hail onset of rabbit season in Udaipur
  G. *mēḷam/moḷam* (Sanskrit *mela*)—Tamil: ensemble of double reeds and drums or drums alone. *Mēḷam aṭi,* to "beat" the *mēḷam*, can mean to play a percussion piece in a group or to accompany the double reed; also used metaphorically to mean "play second fiddle"; drums referred to as kinds of *mēḷam* include *tavil*, *palakai* (frame drum), and *tājā* (= *tāshā*).

Table 3.1. (cont.)

H. *vajat* (Sanskrit *vādya*)—Sindhi term for item of repertoire on *nagāra*, *ḍhol*, and *shahnā'ī*. The verb *vajjāirnu* means "to cause a sound, to strike, or to wield a sword" (Mewarm s.v. vajjāirnu).

I. *tappeṭa* (Tamil *tampaṭṭam*, Burrow and Emeneau 1984, 3082)†—Telugu; example: item for the *runza* drum in Andhra Pradesh, *kaneka tappeṭa*

VI. Terms referring to pattern
- A. Melody terms used for drum patterns
  1. *ṭarz* (Urdu)
  2. *naġma* (Urdu)
  3. *haríip* (Ḍūmaki, Burushaski)
  4. *dhun* (Urdu/Hindi)
  5. *rāga* (rare)
- B. Combinations of patterns: *brij* (Tamil)
- C. Piece, possibly defined by drum patterns and/or melody
  1. *mēḷam* (Tamil)
  2. *vājā* (Saraiki)
  3. *vajat* (Sindhi)
  4. *bāj/bājā* (Urdu/Hindi, widespread)
  5. *haríip* (Gilgit-Baltistan, Pakistan)
- D. Drum pattern and not tone-melody
  1. *ṭhekā* (widespread)—example: Muharram *kā ṭhekā*, Hyderabad, AP
  2. *cāl* (Urdu/Hindi, "gait," widespread)—example: *ek kī cāl*, "the cāl of one" (Hyderabad Sindh/Agra)

VII. Terms related to moving through space
- A. *dauṛ* (Urdu/Hindi: *dauṛ savār mārg*, "galloping path," *runza* drum repertoire item, Hyderabad area, Andhra Pradesh; *dauṛ*, Hyderabad, Sindh, *ḍhol-tāshā* group with roots in Bharatpur, India)
- B. *mārg* (*dauṛ savār mārg*; on *mārga* see Kippen 2006, 115)
- C. *cāl* (as gait or dance movement)

VIII. Terms related to the hand
- A. *Alī kā panja* ("Ali's Panja") [ambiguous, could refer to Panjatan or to his hand or fist]—item played by drummers associated with Muharram at Nizamuddin Auliya shrine, Delhi
- B. Shāh Panjatan ("the King's [prob. Husain's] Panjatan")—Sindhi drum pattern used for Muharram
- C. "Hand"—Trinidad tassa-bass pattern (generic name)

claps. Such a naming practice, and its subtending idea, make it useful here to distinguish a *beat*—the locus of a clap or emphatic stroke—from a *count*—a countable homogeneous time unit. However, it bears mentioning that numbers used in the names of classical *tāl*s nowadays do not have consistent referents.[2] More important for the present work, many drumming patterns operating beyond the usual confines of the classical traditions are also named using numbers. While these numbers may or may not refer to hand claps, they do often refer to stressed strokes, or *beats*, and in this way suggest deeply shared ways of conceptualizing the articulation of rhythm across an array of otherwise diverse performance traditions in South Asia and beyond.

In many traditions, nomenclature for drumming patterns involves terms meaning "beat." The Tamil word *aṭi,* for instance, may refer generically to a percussion pattern or, when accompanied by a number (for example, *reṇṭaṭi,* "two-beat"), to a pattern with a certain number of stressed strokes. The Kota word *dāk* (prob. < Tamil *tākku,* "strike") is used in the same two ways. In Hyderabad, Andhra Pradesh, Dalit drummers who perform for Hindu and Muslim religious functions as well as for folk dances use the Hindi word *mār* as a semi-generic term for at least two patterns: *do mār* (two-beat) and *tīn mār* (three-beat). Some terms involve enumeration that at one time might have referred to stressed strokes, or *mātra*s. A *ḍhol-tāshā* group of Muhājirs in Hyderabad, Sindh, for instance, terms two of their patterns *das kī gintī* and *bīs kī gintī*, meaning (in Urdu) ten- and twenty-count, respectively—it is not clear what is being counted.

Other terms relating to beat include a Telugu word for rhythmic pattern, *daruvu*, which is probably related to the Tamil *tarukku*, "to beat." Players of the *runza* drum in the area of Hyderabad, Andhra Pradesh, who sing, tell stories, and play repertoires of rhythmic patterns that imitate the repertoires of other kinds of drums, term a number of their patterns *debba*, meaning "beat or blow." The Arabic word *ẓarb*, which means "beat" and is the name of a goblet drum in Iran, is the basis for counting practices extending beyond the confines of South Asia proper. In the *ḍhol-tāshā* repertoire of Mamraj's group in Delhi (see Chapter 4), the plural term *jarbeṉ* (in Hindi *z* becomes *j*) is prefixed by a number referring to stressed strokes. Among some (non-nomadic) populations of Central Asia, rhythmic patterns are similarly named. Alexander Djumaev reports *ẕikr* cycles with patterns of 1, 2, 3 and 4 *ẓarb*s, where *ẓarb*s designate metrically important syllables (Djumaev 2002, 943–44; see also Mijit 2012). In the Wakhan valley of Tajikistan in January 2013, I myself learned strumming patterns for various forms of *rabāb* named according to numbers of *ẓarb*s (for instance, *duzarb,* "two strikes," in Tojiki); as in South Asia, these referred to beats (emphasized strums) and not counts (homogeneous time units) or total numbers of strokes.

The semantic overlap of *beat* and *kind of drum* (evident in *ẓarb*) is also found in the word *ḍankā*, which means both "drumstick" and "kettledrum." The term means "emphasized stroke" when drummers in Hyderabad, Sindh (of Ajmeri background) say, "*Tīn cāl* has three *ḍankā.*" *Cāl*, a verbal noun of *calnā* ("to move, to walk"), connotes gait and is used as a generic term for pattern.[3] Muhammad Shafi, one of these drummers, also used the phrase "dīn kā ḍankā"—the drum of faith or religion—in reference to the drum itself and the unwavering faith of the performers who are playing it. A great number of other terms for rhythmic pattern are grounded in the names of instruments or ensembles as well (table 3.1, part V). These include *ḍhol, mēḷam, bājā, vājā, tappeṭa, tabl, and dappu.*

When a local term meaning *ensemble* is applied to what seems to be a drum pattern, it is often worth taking a close look at just how widely the semantic range of the term might extend. The term *vājā* is a case in point. Although classically trained musicians will use the term *ṭhekā* to refer to drumming patterns, the operational term in Saraiki, *vājā*, may implicate drumming patterns, melodies, and the contexts for which an item is performed. *Vājā* is cognate with other words for "musical instrument" in South Asia: *bājā* in the North Indian languages, *vātiyam* in Tamil, and *vādya* in Sanskrit. The verb "to play a musical instrument" (Urdu/Hindi *bajānā*; Panjabi *vajāuṉ*; Sindhi *vajjāirnu*) also derives from the same Sanskrit root, *vad-*, meaning "to speak or say." The musical meaning of *ṭhekā* as an accompaniment pattern on a drum is etymologically related to the word *ṭhīk* (firm, strong).[4] *Ṭhekā* is a drumming part that provides a firm, steady ground against which other kinds of musical elaboration can take place. *Vājā*, by contrast, is not merely "musical instrument" but "that which is played by musical instruments"—a gestalt that is not limited to the drum part.

In addition to words meaning "beat" and "musical instrument," several generic terms for drumming patterns imply motion or movement in space. Important among these, *cāl* (gait), a noun derived from the verb *calnā,* meaning "to move, flow, walk or run," evokes the subtle timing and movement of the human body. A *cāl* could be thought of as a kind of *ṭhekā* that moves along at a good clip. *Cāl*s need not be associated with *tāl*s, however. The term may also be used, like *jhol* in Panjabi, to refer to the set of timbral and accentual qualities that separates one *ṭhekā* from another. Gibb Schreffler reports that Indian Panjabi drummers use the word *cāl* to refer to the actions of dancers when they progress from one movement to another, as well as to the drum variations played during such transitions (Schreffler 2002, 87). In Almora, Kumaon, one musician explained that in the local system of *bājā*s, the term *tāl* applied to metric structures articulated by *tālī* and *k͟hālī* sections (*vibhāg*s), whereas the term *cāl* applied to metric structures that lacked such forms of articulation. *Cāl*s are often equivalent to what James Kippen terms *grooves*: "regularly repeating [rhythmic-] accentual patterns rooted in bodily movement (i.e. dance)" (2006, 86; see also Kippen 2001). Since drumming itself implies bodily movement, grooves should also include patterns that are not explicitly keyed to dances. As a term for a specific pattern, *cāl* may be preceded by a number (*tīn kī cāl*) or an adjective (*mātam kī cāl*).

Another term invoking movement is *savārī*, which implies an association with a passenger or a ride. By a series of metonyms, *savārī* may mean an entourage of a royal figure, a religious procession, a piece composed of multiple sections, and a spiritual agent who possesses a human actor. In the Telangana region of Andhra Pradesh, aided by the drum, the spirits of Qasim and other Karbala figures are seen to enter the bodies of some Hindus and Dalits who celebrate their own version of Muharram called Pirla Paṇḍaga (see also Mohammad 2010, 116)—possession of this sort is called *savārī* in local Hindi/Urdu and *pūnakam* in Telugu. *Savārī* is also a local term in Hyderabad for the *'alam* (standard), perhaps because, from some Hindu vantage points, the standards carried in procession are embodiments of deity-like figures. One of the patterns called *savārī* that is performed in association with Muharram in Mushirabad (Hyderabad, Andhra Pradesh) is, according to one of the drummers, named after the *'alam.*

In the ever-colorful repertoire of the above-mentioned *runza* drum in the Telangana region, one item bears a compound name, each part of which implies movement: *dauṛ savār mārg* (here "galloping path" or "running procession path"). The drummer Runza Yadagiri claimed that this drum pattern was in use for accompanying royal processions in the Hyderabad region from before the time of the first nizam (that is, before 1724).

In addition to sharing similar names, drum patterns in many parts of South Asia share a conception that links them not only to local concepts of rhythm but also to melody.

Melody and Rhythm in the Definition of Patterns

Sayings such as "śruti māta, laya pitā" (Sanskrit, "tone mother, rhythm father") attest to the conceptual distinction between the related ideas of pitch, melody, and singing (here, as mother) and rhythm, tempo, and drumming (here, father) in a variety of South Asian traditions. Most classical repertorial items are in a *rāga* and/or in a *tāla*; they are not definitive of that *rāga* or *tāla*. When both melody and drums are present, a performance is defined primarily in terms of the melody part. (*Lehrā*, the repeating melody used as a time marker for drum solos and *kathak* dance, is an exception). In Karnatak music, the identity of a song such as "Brōvabarāma," for instance, depends on crooked melodic motives in the *rāga bahudāri*, but the arrangement of accompanying drum strokes has no bearing on the definition of the piece.[5] It would be equally ludicrous to identify a tabla performance of *ek tāl* as an instance of the genre *baṛa k̲h̲ayāl* without the singing. The distinction is obvious in much folk and mass-mediated music as well—film songs are not defined by their drum patterns. The superior hierarchical status of the voice in most South Asian traditions is probably one reason for this melody-centrism.

Instrumental music accompanying dance is not necessarily melody-centric. The drum pattern may play a primary role in defining a piece with respect to dance, with the tone-melody articulating a lower-level generic distinction or indexing a specific song.[6] Kotas, for instance, name the two main drum patterns (*dāk*) used for their dances the "plain" (*cādā*) and the "turning dance" (*tiruganāṭ*) types. The corresponding plain dance and turning dance for each pattern are similar: both involve turning in one direction and then another.[7] However, a few special dances within each category are singled out according to their association with one or more melodies. For example, Kotas dance the "leg joining dance" (*kāl gūc āṭ*) at the beginning of any men's or women's dance sequence; several *koḷ*s (melodies) may accompany the *kāl gūc āṭ*, but the drum pattern is always *cādā dāk*. Similarly, women in many parts of South Asia might perform a single clapping pattern and set of dance movements to more than one song or melody—the dance would serve as a higher-level generic category than would any particular melody.

The relative priority of a drum pattern over a tone-melody in defining dance genres stands to reason. The same reasoning does not hold with regard to many nondance genres defined primarily in terms of their composite drum patterns. In repertoires that include distinctive tone- and stroke-melodies, how is it possible to determine if one musical component is more or less significant than the others? It is important to bear in mind that within any given piece, the melody might be significant with respect to one criterion and the stroke-melody significant with respect to another. One challenge is to discover ways in which these components might be seen by practitioners to shift in importance in different contexts. Methodologically speaking, it is often difficult to find out what defines an item simply by asking.

Recalling that the generic term for a piece or an item of instrumental music in many parts of the subcontinent is often that for the instrument or ensemble on which it is played, let us now examine one such term, *mēḷam*, in the context of three village repertoires in the Dharmapuri district of north-central Tamil Nadu. The musicians are Dalits (members of scheduled castes) belonging to Paṟaiyar and Aruntiyar (Cakkiliyar) castes.

Mēḷam *and Constituent Drum Patterns*

The term *mēḷam* (< Sanskrit *mil*, "join, assemble"), pronounced *mōḷam* in some places, can refer to one or more drums and to an entire ensemble of instruments, including the double-reed *nātacuram*. As with *vājā*, *mēḷam* is best defined here as "that which is played on the ensemble of instruments."

Although *mēḷam* music sometimes includes tone-melodies, the drum patterns serve as primary differentiae.

The focus of the following analysis is the "funeral pattern" (*cāvu mēḷam*) of all three villages—a significant component of the local semiotic drum code. Those within earshot might inquire as to who has died or simply take the sound as a warning to keep clear of the defilement (*tīṭṭu*).

Table 3.2. Repertoire of the three mēḷams

Nārtampaṭṭi village	
Name of mēḷam *item*	*Context*
1. *jampa*	can be played at any time/when deities are carried in procession through the village
2. *aratāḷam*	can be played at any time
3. *rūpakam*	can be played at any time
4. *āti*	can be played at any time
5. *tiruppaṭi tāḷam*	*karakam* dance (dance with pot on head) and for tying marriage necklace (*tāli*)
6. *narivēcam*	fox costume dance
7. *cāṭṭu mēḷam*	for important village announcements
8. *kūli erutu mēḷam*	when capturing bull during bullfight; after the *pongal* holiday
9. *cāvu mēḷam*	funeral
10. *naṭamēḷam*	for ritual of collecting water
11. *mukurttam*	at moment of tying marriage necklace (*tāli*)
12. *kalyāṇa mēḷam*	wedding *mēḷam*; can be played at any time
13. *kōyil mēḷam*	"temple" *mēḷam* played for the love of god
14. *cāmi pūcai mēḷam*	"god worship *mēḷam*"; used when putting the image down after carrying it around the village
15. *cavāri mēḷam*	when returning after circumambulating the village with the image of the deity (see discussion of *savārī*, p. 67)
16. *karakkacanta mēḷam*	associated with the goddess Kāḷiyammaṉ
17. *cēva mēḷam*	for dancing
Menaci village	
Name of mēḷam *item*	*Context*
1. *cāri*	when the image of the deity is brought out of the temple
2. *kalyāṇa mēḷam*	wedding
3. *kāvaṭi mēḷam*	for the *kāvaṭi* dance (with arched structure on shoulders)
4. *cāvu mēlam*	funeral
5. *allā cāmi mēḷam*	"Allah god" *mēḷam*, for Muharram
6. *tēr/cāmi/koyil*	temple cart/god/temple; for announcements
7. *erutu kaṭṭu mēḷam*	for chasing and provoking the bull; after the *pongal* holiday
8. *nari vēca mēḷam*	fox costume dance
Ilakkiyampaṭṭi village	
Name of mēḷam *item*	*Context*
1. *cāmi mēḷam*	temple festival
2. *kalyāṇa mēḷam*	wedding
3. *allā cāmi mēḷam*	Muharram (only *palakkai* and *tājā* are played)
4. *cāvu mēḷam*	funeral
5. [*keṭṭi mēḷam*]	instruments played together as a conclusion for anything

The *mēḷam* plays a composite pattern organized around a short rhythmic idea (figure 3.5a) that the leader plays on the frame drum (*palakai* or *tappaṭṭai*).[8] Drummers assign the frame drum the role of the raja (figure 3.5a). This idea can be vocalized in more than one way; it may include variations, and it may include representations of other instruments from the composite sound. The core motive in figure 3.5a can be heard at the beginning of a vocalization performed by Perumal of Nārttampaṭṭi (figure 3.5b, Media Example 3.5). Perumal then intersperses vocal representations of some of the interpolations and responses of the other instruments, making no reference to the melody on the *nātacuram*. Media Example 3.7, vocalized by Perumal of Ilakkiyampaṭṭi, is a version of the same basic pattern with similar syllables and contains no variations (figure 3.5c). Media Example 3.8, vocalized by Kaveri of the same village, includes a few variations. Media Example 3.10 is a much more elaborate vocalization from Menaci village that incorporates the differences in timbre and pitch of several instruments. The rhythmic similarity to the vocalizations in figures 3.5a and 3.5b and the motive in figure 3.5a is contained in the recurring cluster of syllables "ja di di" (figure 3.5d).

The relation of the drummed version of the *cāvu mēḷam* in Menaci (Media Example 3.9) to those of the other two villages (Media Examples 3.4 and 3.6) is fairly easy to hear. The vocalized version from Menaci (Media Example 3.10), while having structural similarities with the

Figure 3.5. Cāvu Mēḷam

The motivic basis for *cāvu mēḷam* as played by the lead frame drum, Ilakkiyampaṭṭi village (Media Example 3.6)

a.

Vocalization of *cāvu mēḷam,* Nārttampaṭṭi village. Boldface shows primary emphasis (approximating the rhythm shown in fig 3.5a); underlining indicates secondary emphasis (Media Example 3.5).

b.

| **jag** . **ja** ni ka na | **chaīñ** . . . . . |

Vocalization of *cāvu mēḷam,* Ilakkiyampaṭṭi village (Media Example 3.7)

c.

| **jan** . **ja** ni ka . | **jan** ga . . . . |

Vocalization of *cāvu mēḷam,* Menaci village (Media Example 3.10)

d.

| **ja** di **di** . . . | **ja** di **di** . . . |

other versions of the *cāvu mēḷam* as outlined in figure 3.5, is more difficult to hear as being related to the drummed versions from the other villages. Whether or not we hear close correspondences between the vocalized and drummed versions of these patterns, all the vocalizations, and Media Example 3.10 from Menaci especially, testify to the extent to which these musicians conceptualize their drum patterns as sequences of tones operating in counterpoint. My analytical abstractions of these melodies as time-patterns may help us see at a glance what these patterns share, but they do not do justice to the musicality of these patterns in performance.

A detailed analysis of the musical parts in each of these examples falls beyond the scope of this chapter. It will be helpful, however, to know a bit more about the groups themselves, their instrumentation, and how their performances are organized. The first two groups (Media Examples 3.4, 3.5, 3.6, 3.7, and 3.8) are Telugu-speakers who belong to the Aruntiyar (Cakkiliyar) caste, traditionally associated with leather work. Their respective villages, Nārttampaṭṭi (group one) and Ilakkiyampaṭṭi (group two), lay just beyond the town boundaries of Dharmapuri in the 1990s but may now have been effectively incorporated into the town.[9] The third group (Media Examples 3.9 and 3.10) consists of Tamil-speaking Toṭṭi Paraiyar caste musicians from the village of Menaci, about fifteen miles southeast of Dharmapuri.[10]

In addition to the frame drummer who leads each group, the ensembles include one to five players of the *maṉmattaḷam* (spherical clay drums with two leather heads) and two to six players of a small *tāshā* (locally pronounced *tājā*). Other instruments include the *ḍhol* (pronounced *tol* or *dol* and played on one side only; groups two and three); *tuṭumpu*, a deep kettledrum (group three); one *ottu* (double-reed drone); and two *nātacurams* (group one). No historical records of which I am aware explain how and when the *ḍhol* and *tāshā* drums reached this part of South India, but it would seem likely that these drums were appended to existing ensembles.

Each of these groups maintained a repertoire of about five to twelve items, which were named mainly according their contexts. In Ilakkiyampatti the drummers Kaveri and Perumal explained the processes by which they conceptualized variation. These local concepts of drumming in Tamil Nadu are, to my knowledge, unknown to the scholarly community. They provide crucial data regarding ways in which the Tamil vernacular traditions relate to and differ from some of their counterparts in North India and Pakistan.

Kaveri and Perumal emphasized the lead role of the frame drum player in playing "twelve variations" to which the rest of the ensemble responds.[11] The men used two terms in connection with such variations. One was *tiruppu*, meaning literally a "turn" but in this case meaning either a single drum stroke or a short phrase.[12] Conjugations of the verb *tiruppu-* ("turn, distort, revise, translate, invert") were used in combination with the verbal noun *tiruppu* to mean something like "perform variations" or "change to another pattern." A particular combination of *tiruppu*s evidently compose a unit called a *brijj*. Although not in the dictionary as pronounced, Kaveri and Perumal insisted that the term *brijj* was a Tamil word used by their Telugu-speaking family for at least three generations. It could be a corruption of *piriccal*, meaning "division, partition." Twelve *brijj* would in that case mean that there are twelve types or divisions of drum pattern. It is tempting to speculate that the term originated in the English word *bridge*, however, because it seems to refer to connecting or "bridging" small patterns.

My collaborator Rajaram and I faced difficulty interpreting some of their responses to our questions about *brijj*s. Some of the ambiguous statements are worth considering here because the details are potentially important for future research. Part of the challenge is that, although *brijj*s are central to their performance, drummers have trouble articulating how the system operates. Instead they seem to be responding to questions like "What does it mean to play a *brijj*?" or "Why is *brijj* important?" Perumal and Kaveri explained that there are only two significant contexts (*to̱il*, literally "work," here, contexts in which they serve as musicians): festivals and all other nonfunerary occasions, and funerals. All patterns except that for the funeral constitute a single overarching *mēḷam*. Perumal said, "In this [nonfunerary context] there are twelve *brijjs*" (idil paneṇṇdu biric irukkudunga). The variations performed in the funeral *mēḷam* are not considered *brijj*s.

"Have you used this word [*brijj*] for a long time?" I asked.

"Yes, for a long time indeed," said Kaveri. "[The elders] said 'use this [*mōḷam*] for God and use this *mōḷam* for Death.'"

"Twelve words [vocalizations] are also in that (paṇneṇdu vārttaiyum adulaiyē irukku)," said Perumal.

"Twelve within that. [The syllable pattern] jagig jagig jagig, is for one," said Kaveri, reiterating Perumal's point.[13]

A few seconds later Kaveri attempted to clarify by saying that there were twelve "instruments" (*vādyam*), perhaps translating *mēḷam* literally from one Tamil word for instrument into another—but still meaning "that which is played on instruments."

"What is a *brijj*?" I later asked, yet again.

"For this reason [being able to play *brijj*s] only, before [playing in the] *mēḷam* it is necessary to be thoroughly trained in the *raja tappaṭṭa* [the lead part]. If we start playing the drum, all the players can identify the beat correctly (idukkāhavē mōḷam muṉṉa rājā tappaṭṭa paḻahuṉadukku kāraṇamē. adu eḍuttu taṭṭuṉōmuṉṉū idu enda aḍikkiṟa ellārum karaikṭā kaṇḍapiḍuccuvāngu)."

Later, Rajaram again asked, "What is a bridge?"

"Learning the *toḻil* [work, occupation, art, context], sir," said Kaveri.

Rajaram: "Is a *brijj* an individual pattern of beats (*aḍi* or *koṭṭu*) like you said, jagu, jagu, jagu, or is it a combination of beats?"

Kaveri: "No, all of them together make a *brijj*."

Perumal: "You can play this very one and you can join this [with other patterns] and play."

Kaveri: "Only all [patterns] joined together [constitute] a *brijj*; only one [played alone] is not a *brijj* (ellām cērndu dāṉ oru biric. Oṉṉu oru birij varādu)."

A number of matters remain unclear. One is why Kaveri's group demonstrated different *mēḷam*s for the wedding (*kalyāṇa mēḷam*) and for "God" (*cāmi mēḷam*) (see table 3.2) when he said in our interview that all drumming for nonfunerary contexts can draw from a single pool of patterns. The differences heard on the recording might only reflect different performance choices at that moment and not generic differences.[14]

Another matter is whether a *brijj* is the building block for permutations or whether one *brijj* is a permutation in and of itself. Although Kaveri's final statement suggests that a *brijj* is a permutation, it seems improbable that there are twelve phrase ideas (*tiruppu*s, *aḍi*s, or *koṭṭu*s) as well as twelve permutations *(brijj)* of those ideas. Regardless of the details, the following point is unambiguous: the "king" drummer strings short patterns together, and it is his responsibility to make the changes clear to the other musicians so they can follow him.

The two other groups, while also organizing their variations in response to the *tappaṭṭai* player's phrases, did not share this concept of the *brijj*. They also differentiated a greater number of repertorial items according to content and context (table 3.2).

Some general points can be derived from the foregoing: particular ritual moments call for individual stroke-melodies, which are, in this case, composites performed by a number of instruments. Part of a drummer's competence lies in being able to vocalize the essential, defining feature of the pattern. Tamil patterns are rooted in motives. The periodicity of a cycle is limited to the length of the motive (or perhaps to the length of a *brijj*, if that can eventually be determined) rather than to a longer set of phrases (as in *ṭhekā*s). The Panjabi examples performed by Shahid and Niamat Ali feature cycles of multiple lengths, the shortest of which appear to be lengthier than the Tamil patterns. Performers use accents and timbre to create distinctive patterning in both Panjabi and Tamil examples (compare vocalization of Panjabi *fāk͟htah aṣūl* pattern in Media example 3.1 with vocalization of the Tamil funeral pattern in Media example 3.10). What Panjabis call *jhol* and Hindi speakers term *cāl* have analogues in South India.

The Panjabi and Tamil examples both involve creating variations, but those variations are accomplished in different ways. The Panjabi examples are all based on a *ṭhekā*-like conception, whereby a single pattern is the basis for improvisation. Drummers resolve rhythmic tension created during episodes of improvisation by returning to the *sam*. Although *tāl*s are strung together in suites, each transition is distinct, and the performer creates a firm sense of one *tāl* or *ṭhekā* before proceeding to the next. In the Tamil examples, variation is not set against a steady *ṭhekā*-like ground; rather, the leader himself varies the motives, perhaps after only iterating them once or twice; he then leaves open spaces in between his strikes for the ensemble to respond.

To reiterate the overarching point of this section, this kind of *mēḷam* music in Tamil Nadu is defined in significant measure by its drum pattern, even when tone-melody instruments are present. With this point in mind, we travel north to examine two further examples in which the relative dominance of tone- or stroke-melodies is neither consistent nor obvious. One is from the Himalayan region of Kumaon, formerly part of Uttar Pradesh state and now in Uttarakhand. The second is from the Ḍoms of Hunza in the Gilgit-Baltistan province of Pakistan.

Music of Kumaon During the Nanda Devi Festival

During the annual festival for the goddess Nanda Devi in Kumaon (see Sax 1991), musical performances punctuate a variety of ritual activities for several days. Ensembles of different kinds from throughout the region converge in cities and towns like Nainital and Almora to perform a range of musical genres for rituals and for lively evening cultural shows. Kumaoni and other languages native to this Himalayan region belong to the Central Pahāṛi (hill) group. Speakers of these languages can easily converse in Hindustani, although native Hindi speakers cannot easily understand Pahāṛi languages.

Some ensembles perform the graceful *choliyā* dance, which involves stylized swordplay. Professional reciters called *jāgariya* sit in the temple precinct and sing the epic of the goddess's life story over the course of several days (called *jāgar*, "singing vigil," from the verb *jāgnā*, "to wake up"). Some groups play functionally specific items for processing to and from the forest to collect materials with which to fashion the likenesses of temple deities and for the ritual of puja (worship) at the *mandir* (temple). The *mandir tāl* (Media Example 3.12) that I heard in Almora in 1998 was played by an ensemble of kettle and cylinder drums. The *turi* trumpeter played long, drawn-out tones while *masakbīn* (< Persian *mashk*, "water-skin") bagpipe players spun out short tunes. The fact that the bagpipes were an accretion to this kind of ensemble during the long period of British presence in the subcontinent may help explain why the drum pattern and not the melody is locally understood to tie the piece to its context.

As we have encountered in several cases already, the name of this *tāl* actually refers to two distinct drum patterns that players perform in alternation. The edited video on the accompanying Web site shows the ritual context as well as the two parts of the melody (Media Example 3.12). At the end of the clip, one participant vocalizes the two patterns as they are played on the *ḍhol* and then indicates how the patterns are played on the *damāũ*. The patterns of the different drums interlock, and it is not clear whether the version he vocalized has hierarchical priority over other possible representations (figure 3.6).

Keeping in mind the comparisons made earlier, this *tāl* is more akin to a *ṭhekā* than to the ever-transforming, motivic patterns of the Tamil groups. However, there is no significant elaboration or interpretation of the basic drum pattern. Since the musical interest seems to be created by the *turi* and the *masakbīn* melodies, it is all the more remarkable that the contextual marking function is performed primarily by the drums.

Figure 3.6. Mandir tāl (see Media Example 3.12)

Slow version
gin . . naṛeki **gin** . . nā . .
Fast version
gin . na **gi** ṛa ni **gin** . na **gi** ṛa ni (gin)

The Haríip *Repertoire of Hunza*

In Hunza, near the Khunjarab Pass in the far northern reaches of Pakistan, live Dumāki-speaking hereditary musicians known as Ḍom (see Chapter 2). Within this mainly Ismaili Muslim environment, Ḍom musicians perform for a variety of functions, including polo matches, weddings, visits by officials, and dances. In addition to the national language of Urdu, the local lingua franca is Burushaski, a language that historical linguists have not yet been able to connect with any other language group (Berger 1985, 37).

I passed through the region in 1997 on my way to Xinjiang, China, from Lahore. While staying in Sust, about fifty miles from the Chinese border, I invited a set of musicians from Nazimabad village in Gilgit district to perform outside my guest house. A "set" consists of a *surnā'ī* player and two drummers (Huehns 1991, 97*ff.*).

Haidar Bek (age forty) played the lead role on the cylindrical *ḍaḍáṅ* drum (see Schmid 1997, 167). A mustached man of medium build outfitted in a light-olive *shalwār qamīz*, Haidar listed for me about eighteen items in the local *haríip* repertoire. The names comprised terms for ethnic groups, places, speakers of particular languages, contexts, and dances. These included *alġanī* (after the Ġanī tribe), *chilāsī* (after the town of Chilas), *shīna haríip* (after the speakers of the Shīna language), *malaṅga haríip* (after the mendicants known as *malaṅg*), *k͟hybar* pass, *bazmē* (for the private parties of the local ruler), *farangī* (literally "foreigner," here "film song"), and a repertorial name found far and wide in modern South Asia, *disco*.[15]

I was struck by the preponderance of complexly accented, asymmetrical rhythmic patterns in this repertoire as well as by the dances that accompanied most of them. The melody played on the *surnā'ī* was rhythmically elastic, composed of rapid flourishes interspersed with long-held tones. Hājī Bek (age forty-five), the *surnā'ī* player, separated his phrases with emphatic stops, in the articulation of which the pitch would rise for a fraction of a second. As the musicians gradually proceeded through their roster of *haríip*s, local men from Sust started to gather.

Four or five of them, more or less in a line at first, faced the row of musicians and commenced dancing. The dances involved graceful, swinging movements of one arm and then the other—sometimes including more elaborate gestures with the hands. The men moved their feet in lockstep with the asymmetrical rhythmic grooves. They looked downward and maintained close eye contact with Haidar Bek. *Ḍaḍáṅ* drummers like Bek have the power either to humiliate the dancers by throwing them off the beat or to accentuate their skill (Schmid 2000, 798). Each man stepped in time with the stressed drum strokes, putting his toes slightly forward and then emphasizing the move by retracting his foot quickly and kicking his heel sharply behind. The jerky effect of the men's stepping made an interesting contrast with the grace of their arm and upper body movements. The atmosphere was quite alive with whistling, clapping, and shouts by the audience and the musicians.

What constitutes a *haríip* varies by context, making our exploration of stroke- and tone-melodic criteria or the definition of pieces potentially ambiguous (see Huehns 1991, 163*ff.*). Anna Schmid, who conducted anthropological research on the interaction of Ḍoms with the Burusho, the Wakhi, and the speakers of Shina, reported that the term may mean music in general; in the absence of further qualification, melody; and "primäres Stilprinzip der Musik, in dem Melodie und Rhythmus gleichwertig eingesetzt werden" (the primary stylistic principle of the music in which melody and rhythm are endowed with equal value).[16] According to Schmid's *Ḍom* consultants, the *surnā'ī* player occupies the primary hierarchical position; the *ḍaḍáṅ* player "orients" himself to the basic melody, and the player of the *ḍaámal* (set of kettledrums) performs variations on the basic melody as well. From the perspective of the dancers, the hierarchy is reversed: dancers need to focus on the sound of the *ḍaḍáṅ* (Schmid 1997, 174).

The term *haríip* is used both in the Ḍom's language, Ḍumāki, and in Burushaski.[17] Hermann Berger's three-volume work on Burushaski defines *haríip* as a melody, a rhythm, the principal form of Hunza music, and as something comparable to Indian *rāga* (Berger 1998, 3:193).[18] Colin Huehns, who wrote a magisterial dissertation on the music of what were then called the Northern Areas of Pakistan (now Gilgit-Baltistan), found the drum patterns to be of such constitutive significance in *haríip*s that he notated the melodies and drum patterns separately (Huehns 1991). He then analyzed how the components were brought together to form each piece.

The linguist G. W. Leitner (1840–99) described two classifications of *haríip* in terms of the tempo of their associated dances: *būti haríip*, which he glossed as "slow instrument," and *danni haríip*, glossed as "fast instrument." He may have misconstrued the role of tempo and the uses of the terms may have changed (the *haríip*s titled *bóote* and *dáni* that I recorded were both relatively slow in tempo). I mention them here because they suggest a subclassification of *haríip* based on tempo and because they present another instance in which a word for "musical instrument" also refers to what is played on that instrument.

The *bóote haríip*, according to Schmid, is played at the beginning of many kinds of events, as well as after a competition as a way to honor the winners. At the beginning of an event it is also possible to play the *ḍaḍáṅ haríip,* which calls people to assemble, on the cylinder drum (Schmid 1997, 166n26). The fact that one *haríip* can be played on a drum alone confirms that the *haríip* concept can embrace definitions based on both tone- and stroke-melodies.

Dáni, among other meanings, appears to designate pieces dedicated to the ruling classes and based on melodies praising their exploits and virtues. The so-called first melody, the *bapóe dáni*, was said to have been composed when the Ḍoms first arrived in Hunza. They heard a beautiful song about the great deeds of the Thams (the local aristocratic class, later called Mīrs) and adapted the melody to their instrument. From that day forward, other melodies were composed in similar fashion (Schmid 1997, 183). According to Schmid, *dáni* is also a style classification in which the "rhythm" (that is, drums) recedes behind the "melody" (ibid., 251).

Although one of my points in this section is that when drums and wind instruments are co-present it is not necessarily the case that the drums provide accompaniment, it appears that in some *haríip*s particular drum patterns *do* function as *ṭhekā*s. Two *haríip*s that have *ṭhekā*-like drum patterns in common are *tāmbal* (Media Example 3.13)[19] and *alġāni* (Media Example 3.14).[20] The tone-melodies are tune types: in the recordings of each piece I consulted, the basic melodic contour and phrasing were maintained but the pitch content and intonation varied. The percussion outlined a rapid asymmetrical duple pattern. In my recording, the composite pattern shown in figure 3.7a was dominant.

Whereas these two *haríip*s do seem to be defined mainly by their melody types, others incorporate percussion patterns whose distinctiveness lends individuality to the *haríip*. The drum pattern in the *haríip* called *ġalawáar* is a case in point (Media Example 3.15). According to Schmid, *ġalawáar* is one of twelve pieces called *bulá haríip* that provide background music for the different phases of polo matches.[21] Figure 3.7b shows the *ḍaámal*

Figure 3.7. Percussion patterns for select *haríips*

The percussion pattern associated with *tāmbal* (see Media Example 3.13) and *alġāni* (see Media Example 3.14)

ḍaḍáṅ
ḍaámal

The ḍaámal part for the first section of *ġalawáar* (see Media Example 3.15)

ḍaámal

The duple-triple cross-rhythmic pattern in the second section of *ġalawáar*, with *ḍaḍáṅ* variations (see Media Example 3.15)

ḍaámal

ḍaḍáṅ variations

part in the first section of the piece. The *ḍaḍáṅ* part appears to include set patterns that interlock with this, but the player also performs a set of variations.[22] At 55:00 the drummers step up the intensity, with the *ḍaḍáṅ* player alternately bringing out particular drumming phrases and leaving space for the sound of the *ḍaámal* to ring out on its own. At 1:25 a single-note cue from the *surnā'ī* seems to be sufficient to bring on the transition to a duple-triple cross-rhythmic pattern (figure 3.7c).

The *surnā'ī* player keeps his elastic melody of several sections in phase with the percussion cycle. While the drum pattern may originally have been derived from an interpretation of the *surnā'ī* melody, it also appears (although this cannot be ascertained from a recording alone) that the *surnā'ī* player uses the principal strokes on the drums to orient himself temporally within the tone-melody.

Summary

A number of functionally specific genres that combine wind-instrument melodies with drum patterns in the subcontinent may appear to be examples of (tone-) melodies accompanied by drums. While this may accurately reflect local conceptions of the musical process in some cases, such a characterization risks glossing over the complex ways in which tone- and stroke-melodies may vie for primacy within a genre or across different items in the repertoire. Sometimes this is a matter of definition, as in the *mandir tāl*, where the percussion pattern is, for some reason, named for the ritual. The melodies played on the *turi* and the bagpipes could easily belong to their own classification systems and hold independent sets of associations. In the Tamil case, the primacy of the drums is suggested by the importance of playing versions of the same stroke-melody for the funeral *mēḷam* in three different ensembles; once again, the wind-instrumental melody in one of the groups is likely to have additional associations, but drums alone are sufficient for the primary semiotic function of announcing a death. In the *haríip* repertoire the prominence of the drums varies across the repertoire, ranging from total reliance on the drum (in the *ḍaḍáṅ haríip*) to a focus on wind instruments alone (in one kind of *dáni*).

I have emphasized that both melodies and percussion patterns are equally "melodic" and "rhythmic." Most of the examples we have thus far encountered have involved different kinds of melody operating in counterpoint. Local conceptions of drumming patterns often imply a conceptual overlap with melody. Drum patterns, like tone-melodies, may be referred to as *ṭarz*, as they have "form" or "shape" (Platts s.v. *ṭarz*); they may both be called *naġmah* (Arabic, "to read or sing"); and they may both be called *dhun* (assiduousness, resoluteness)—in one case I even heard someone call a drum pattern a *rāga*, but this stretches beyond ordinary usage. The idea that links most of this vocabulary for tone- and stroke-melodies is that of pattern—of tones, timbres, and articulations in time. Beyond the periphery of the Hindustani and Karnatak traditions, then, and in those most distant reaches of South Asia, the identity of many musical pieces by their percussion patterns would seem to subvert the otherwise conventional hierarchy of "melody" (in a conventional sense) over the "rhythm" of the percussion parts.[23]

CHAPTER 4

Beyond the *Mātra*

The day after the wedding, Ajmal and Ali departed together by train to Multan. Travel in the poorly maintained—but inexpensive by Indian standards—first-class cabin had left them both weary. Ajmal assured Ali it would have been even more tiresome by car owing to the dilapidated condition of the Lahore-Multan road. Although both men were traveling light, the 37°C temperature that late afternoon made it unbearable to walk. They flagged down an auto rickshaw. A short distance northeast on Akbar Road separated them from Haram Gate, the entrance to the walled city of Multan closest to Ajmal's home. Ajmal had married into a Saraiki-speaking family and now occupied part of the family's ancestral haveli in the old part of the city so that his wife Huma could look after her asthmatic widower father. Ajmal would have preferred something more modern on the edge of town. Ali had a romantic fondness for the *pūrāne shehr*s of South Asia and was grateful for this central home base.

A few blocks before reaching the walled quarter, Ajmal asked the rickshaw driver to detour to the right into the lanes around the Bheḍi Potra *muḥalla*. In this neighborhood the Haji Wala *ta'ziyah* was being assembled in preparation for Muharram. The footprint of the wooden structure was about eight feet by eight feet. Decorating the base was elaborate *kāshigarī* tile work in blue and red in the style for which Multan is famous. The structure rose in gold-painted cubes of progressively diminishing sizes to form a pyramid twenty feet in the air. The body of this imitation cenotaph was cornered with green-domed minarets. This *ta'ziyah,* between two hundred and three hundred years old and reputedly the oldest in the city, was established by an ancestor of the Shī'ī musicians' lineage residing in Bheḍi Potra.

Ajmal explained, "Musicians here boast of Bheḍi Potra's reputation. Musicians in Bombay and Delhi know Bheḍi Potra as one of the well-springs of the Panjab *gharāna*. During Muharram this place used to overflow with music. Until about ten years ago, *sāraṅgī, shahnā'ī,* and tabla players would perform along with *marṣiyah-go*. They would select a single stanza of elegiac poetry in Saraiki and elaborate upon it endlessly with so many melodies. Gradually, though, local people's tastes and values began to shift. Some demanded different texts—ones more contemporary and easy to understand. Some did not like the emphasis on music. As performance on instruments declined, *nauḥah* singing became more popular. I've even heard people exaggerate, saying *nauḥah* was invented here."

"Is there any music left here during Muharram?" asked Ali, a bit disappointed.

"Yes, the typical *ḍhol-shahnā'ī* duo you find in several other parts of the city you find here as well. They do a workmanlike job. You can hear their

Hereditary musicians of the Bheḍi Potra neighborhood in Multan playing harmonium and tabla. Photo by the author.

mārū and decide for yourself. *Acchā*. Remember where you are, because it is only a short walk from my place."

Ali and Ajmal got back into the auto, and the driver brought them back to the main road and up to Haram Gate, from which they would walk through the narrow lanes to Ajmal's haveli. As they approached the gate, Ali sensed the history of the place viscerally. He felt positioned between the descendants of two ancient worlds. Multan was the eastern frontier of Arab control in the eighth century—a pivotal meeting point for Islam, Hinduism,* and Buddhism at a time when the practitioners of these faiths peacefully coexisted. He looked up at the grand city gate, surrounded by drink vendors, cyclists, peddlers, and beggars. A big sign painted in Urdu with a picture of a soft drink bottle advertised the "Famous shop of the Ayyaz Brothers." The gate's earth-toned, pointed arch was flanked by two hexagonal towers and surmounted by a limestone-hued parapet, patterned with sets of three horizontal vents.

"On the night of the ninth of Muharram, after the Haji Wala *ta'ziyah* leaves Bheḍi Potra, it takes two or three hours to cover the short distance to reach here," Ajmal said. "Many other *ta'ziyah*s gather, and there is a grand display of *mātam*. During the next day, Ashura, you will also see the elephantine movement of the ustad and *shāgird ta'ziyah*s† as they are carried to this gate on the shoulders of many men. The ustad *ta'ziyah* is about 135 years old. In 1947, Ghulam Shabbir Baloch had the *shāgird* of the original master craftsman make a duplicate."

Ajmal led Ali through the gate and into a shadowy network of *gali*s (narrow lanes), illuminated by sunlight for only minutes each day. As in the old city of Lucknow, they had to maneuver deftly to avoid the open sewage drain on one side, a shabbily braced water conduit on the other, smoldering piles of paper and plastic trash, and electrical cables fallen from the twisted mass overhead. Many of the old buildings were constructed of beautifully hewn wooden boards and outfitted with lathed balustrades and neat rows of artfully paneled shutters. The two men climbed uneven stairs to Ajmal's family dwelling. News traveled fast. Ajmal's wife and son Afzal had already been informed of the two men's arrival at the gate. They deposited their luggage and gratefully received the glass of cold orange *sharbat* Huma proffered to them on an ornamented tray.

---

*Ali, like many South Asians, thinks of the native religion of South Asia as Hinduism. In the eighth century, there was no such notion of a common religion.

†These names mean "master" and "disciple" *ta'ziyah,* respectively.

After a short nap and some tea, the two repaired to the roof, where a hint of a breeze teased them with the pathetic measure of coolth a dry 37°C can bestow. They made plans for the coming days. Feeling free from the eyes and ears of family and neighbors for the first time since arriving in Pakistan, Ali relished the chance to hear Ajmal regale him with ribald backstories of Muharram in the Panjab.

"About five years ago Iqbal Husain was looking for a sturdy horse to use as a model for his painting class at the National College of Arts in Lahore. It being Muharram season, he was able to borrow a fat *zuljinah** decked out in red and *zarī*. No sooner did he bring the horse into the classroom than the beast became aroused. Whereby . . ." Ajmal paused to suppress a laugh, barely, "the girls in the class, ever so coy and aloof, and fashionable, began to shriek." The laugh escaped. "No one could prove it, but I think he medicated the horse for the express purpose of creating an uproar."

"Baṛhiyaṉ bhai! Voh maze kī bāt hai,"† said Ali. "But at least that doesn't create a total mockery of commemorating the *vāqe'ah-e* Karbala.‡ I once overheard some Shī'ī girls from Nakkhas in Lucknow adopting the style of a *zākirah* in a *majlis*.§ Oh, Sakina is going to take her O levels [examinations] tomorrow. Her parents are so proud. She is the first in her family to study in an English medium school. Oh, Sakina is going to take her O levels tomorrow. Tomorrow is the fateful day. Oh, Sakina is going to take her O levels tomorrow, BUT SHE HAS NOT STUDIED. They wailed and wailed, and giggled and wailed, until they choked and coughed on their irreverent effluence."

"*Khair*, if you want to move into that territory, the Sunni kids around here mock the Shī'ahs with a scandalously obscene chant in Saraiki, set to one of the *mārū* patterns: 'dab te piṭṭo, bheṇ ḍe cuḍo.'"**

"That's dreadful, Ajmal," said Ali, trying to be serious for a moment. "Actually, it's also interesting. I got hooked on the idea for this project long ago, after learning that the Shī'ī players at the Chota Imambarah in Lucknow think of their drums as voices which cry out 'Sain, Imām Husain, Haidar.' It hadn't occurred to me that words might be superimposed upon the drumming patterns. It seems an obvious possibility now."

**Zuljinah* is the name for the horse used in South Asian Muharram processions to represent Husain's riderless steed, whose appearance signaled Husain's slaughter.

†"Excellent, brother. That's a funny matter."

‡This is an idiomatic reference to the calamitous events at Karbala.

§A zākirah is a female preacher for a women's mourning session. Through her sermon, she brings the audience to tears.

**The Saraiki language is very close to Urdu. Ali would understand this correctly as "beat [your breast] hard, sister-fucker."

"It *is* interesting, even in the details . . . for me as a drummer. The first word is onomatopoeic for the sound of beating a drum: *dab dab dab*. The rhyme of *ṭo* and *ḍo* replicates a kind of drum rhyme—a ringing treble stroke at the end of each half of the pattern. The contrast between *piṭ* and *cu* corresponds to the alternation between damped and resonating bass strokes that differentiate the two halves of the pattern. I can imitate it on this *ḍholak*, but you'll have to imagine the timbre of the *ḍhol* played with a stick on one side and the hand on the other [figure 4.1; see the chapter notes]. Tomorrow we'll be meeting the *naqqārah* player Muhammad Baksh Multani, who can, I'm sure, tell you more about the more serious texts associated with Muharram performance. I can't make out the words when processioners sing with the *shahnā'ī*." The two chatted on into the night, and the next day they traveled to the compound of a friend in the countryside next to Muhammad Baksh's village of Nandala.

"Here comes Baksh Sahab. Welcome, Janab! Who are your companions?"

"Nazir Ahmed and Muhammad Shabir, who play the *ḍhol,* and Ala Baksh and Ata'ullah, *shahnā'ī navāz*s."

"Excellent," said Ajmal.

After some tea and small talk they got started. Ali found the Saraiki-sprinkled Urdu of seventy-five-year-old Baksh difficult to understand. Baksh was a sixth-generation *naqqārah* player whose *mīrāsī* forefathers had performed on the *naqqārah, ḍhol,* and *tāshā.* Baksh said that in those days, one family would specialize in drumming and another in *shahnā'ī.* His own teachers were the illustrious *naqqārah* players Mīān Allah Divāyā and Mīān Rahīm Baksh.

"Why did your father send you to these performers instead of to someone from your own family?" Ajmal began.

"My own great-grandfather, Allah Ditta, was a contemporary of these masters and the most celebrated performer in my lineage; but even he was not up to their standard. He played for weddings and sang *deśī* [folk] songs, whereas *that* janab [Allah Ḍivaya] played a lot of *klāsikal* and performed in competitions," explained Baksh.

"What is classical?" asked Ali, with an affected naiveté that he assumed Baksh could not perceive.

"In the time of my grandfathers, performers did not speak of the *mātra*, only of the *tāṛī*." Baksh clapped to show that *tāṛī* meant clapping. "The word *mātra* came later. That is a classical term." He demonstrated by clapping and saying the *bol*s for *panjtār dī savārī*. "At the slow speed, it is *pandrān̲ mātre dī panj tār dī savārī* [fifteen-*mātra*, five-clap savārī]. At half speed it is a *tīh-mātre dī panj tār dī savārī* [thirty-*mātra*, five-clap savārī]" (figure 4.2; see the chapter notes).

Ajmal broke it down for the somewhat confused Ali. "He means that they taught drumming in the old days by clapping and saying *bol*s. They didn't use the word *mātra*. This *tāl* consists of fifteen rhythmic units divided into groups: 3 + 4 + 4 + 2 + 2 = 15. The onset of each of these *bol* groups begins with a clap. In the process of playing, performers may cut the speed in half, or as they say, 'make the tempo sit,' several times over. When they do this, the *bol*s change slightly, but the structure stays intact. In his second demonstration, he slowed the rate of *bol*s down to half the speed and replaced a number of the *bol*s, especially in the second and third groups, with rests.

"The 'classical' system involves counting *mātra*s. In this case, the number of *mātra*s for the base speed is fifteen; the slower version is thirty *mātra*s. When Baksh Sahab says '*pandrān̠ mātre dī panj tār dī savārī,*' he is using what he views as the classical term *mātra* to specify further the characteristics of the *tāl* called 'the *savārī* of five claps.'"

"I think I understand. Did they not count at all in the old days?" asked Ali, who couldn't imagine reckoning a *tāl* without counting.

Ajmal discussed this with Baksh and could not get a clear answer. "My impression is that they would count, but not consistently, and not using a uniform time unit. The point is that they counted larger units with claps and thought of the smaller units in terms of *bol* patterns. They were certainly capable of counting pulses or groups of pulses, but counting out a whole *tāl* in such a way was not part of the procedure at that time."

Moving on, Ali asked about the *tāl* name: "Baksh Sahab, I have heard of a 'horse ride,' an 'elephant ride,' and a 'camel ride.' What kind of 'ride' [*savārī*] is this?"

"This is a classical ride [*klāsikal dī savārī],*" came the reply, at which Ali and Ajmal laughed heartily.

"What do you call the *panj tār dī savārī* pattern you just demonstrated?" asked Ali.

"The classical term in Urdu is *naqqārah ṭhekā*. The Saraiki-language term our *buzurg*s [elders] used, and I use, for both classical and folk music drum patterns is *vājā*—the *vājā* of *tīntār*, the *vājā* of *dhamāl*, and so forth."

"How is that *vājā* used?" Ali continued.

"First, at the beginning of any performance, at a wedding, for instance, one *naqqārah* player 'holds the *vājā* steady' on the drum, or, if there is only one *naqqārah* player, the *shahnā'ī* plays a repeating tune. One drummer will recite the *bol*s. Those who first recite and then play are 'genuine'; they are the ones who really know. It is not possible to pick up this drumming merely by listening to others play. You have to learn the *vājā* orally and recite it with the mouth, whether for a lesson or in a public performance," explained Baksh.

"Once you have established the *vājā* as a foundation [*bunyād*], in what ways can you transform it?" inquired Ajmal.

"The *naqqārah* or the *ḍhol* can 'make it beautiful,' keeping the tempo [*lay*] steady and changing the *bol*s, like this [he demonstrated]. One drummer will take a 'round' and then return to his 'place'—the *sam*. Then another person will take a turn. Or, for 'fun,' the drummer or *shahnā'ī* player can do *chēṛ chāṛ* ['mischief'] by playing a pattern that doesn't belong—something meant to throw the other players off," explained Baksh. "Ajmal, I once told you a story about Mīān Allah Divāyā, who participated in a competition at a wedding in which *naqqārah* players were awarded five rupees for each new *bol* they performed. Although Mīān Allah Divāyā ultimately won, his own final turn came when he tried to test his audience's knowledge. He tried to play a *bol* he had played on an earlier day. He disguised it so heavily that he thought it would go unrecognized. Unfortunately for him, one man could recognize the identity of the *bol* amidst the *chēṛ chāṛ*."

"So these kinds of contests take place at weddings?" asked Ali.

"Depending on the patrons, yes. We have a special *vājā* for Sayyads and non-Sayyads. And in the days of the Kirāṛs [Hindus] we used to play the *tāshā* for them with a special *vājā*. For Muslim weddings we generally begin with the *shādīyānah*. The minute we walk through the door we ask the person getting married to bring wheat flour and jaggery, we say a blessing, and then play the pattern called *shādmānah* on the *ḍhol* [figure 4.3; see the chapter notes]. We follow this with something like the *jhūmar* pattern for the men's circle dance [figure 4.4; see the chapter notes]. Some might say 'play *ḍāḍkeyāṉ ālī jhūmar*' to accompany the men's stick dance. Pathans attending the wedding may request us to play the Pathan version of *jhūmar*. If listeners wish to hear more, they may ask for other *vājā*s like Baluchi, or the wrestler's *vājā*.

"When the wedding procession arrives we play the pattern called *karaṛ* on the *ḍhol* and *naqqārah* with bagpipe or *shahnā'ī*"—Baksh and Nazir demonstrated by vocalizing their respective parts in counterpoint—"and sing a *sehrā* song in honor of the bridegroom. When the procession departs, the *ḍhol* player performs his part of *karaṛ* alone with the *shahnā'ī* [figure 4.5; see the chapter notes; Media Example 4.1 ⮊]. After the main ceremony the bride is carried on a palanquin or in a car from her parent's home to her husband's home and we play the *ḍoliwālā vājā*.

"For the wedding of a Sayyad, we play a different *vājā* at the beginning, during the *shādīyānah*. It starts out slow, with the grand one [*baṛā wālā*], and continues with the small one [*choṭā wālā*]" (figure 4.6; see the chapter notes; Media Example 4.2 ⮊).

"Cācāji [uncle], this sounds like *mārū*. It used to frighten me as a kid, keep me up at night," said Ajmal, who started to imitate the sound of the drums himself.

"This *is mārū*," responded Baksh.

Nazir picked up the *ḍhol*, recited the *ḍhol* version of the syllables, and then played (figure 4.7; see the chapter notes; Media Example 4.3).

"The second part of *choṭā mārū* is like *cañcar*, seven fast *mātra*s," observed Ajmal.

"Yes," agreed Baksh, evidently without hearing him, because he later contradicted himself. "This is accompanied by a *mansuriya* [*mars̱iyah*] whose melody is played on the *shahnā'ī*. It goes,

> Velā valī vay shāh Sayyadā, āj hay ẓulam dī rāt
> Dekh rabbā tayriyāṉ be parvaiyāṉ kambiyā 'arsh 'ilā hī dā
>
> Oh what a time, Shah Sayyad, the night of tyranny is today!
> Oh God, seeing your [the Sayyad's] indifference, the sky of God trembles.

Ali quickly noted down the Saraiki texts with the help of Ajmal and Baksh and scanned the lines (figure 4.8; see the chapter notes; Media Examples 4.4 and 4.5). Their scansion did not conform to meters with which he was familiar, and the two lines were not identical in structure. When Baksh and his group later performed *mārū* as an ensemble, Ali noticed that the *shahnā'ī* players realized the melody a little bit differently than did Baksh in his sung version (Media Example 4.2, at 1:08). The *shahnā'ī* player was evidently using the sparse strokes in the grand *mārū* as guideposts for his attacks, which corresponded perfectly with where the syllables should have fallen. The two parts of the melody corresponded to the two lines. The performers generally repeated the first part of the melody a few times before proceeding to the second; then they repeated the whole sequence. As the *vājā* varied on the drums, the same melody was adjusted to the three different metric contexts. Ali did not feel a pitch functioning strongly as the tonic (*sa* in classical music), but if he took the final note of the first line as the fifth (*pa*), the second line descended to what would structurally be the tonic (*sa*). He also noticed melodic parallels between the two lines, separated by the interval of a fifth.

Ali, who thought the text was making an odd allusion for a wedding, asked, "What is the night of tyranny?"

"It is Ashura, the day of Husain's martyrdom at Karbala," answered Nazir.

Anticipating Ali's next question, Baksh explained, "This is a sad *vājā* during Muharram but it becomes a marriage *vājā* at a Sayyad's wedding. It creates enthusiasm."

Ali assumed that the Sayyads in question were Shī'ahs and that they, like Ali's family, were accustomed to incorporating references to the *vāqe 'ah-e* Karbala into their marriage ceremonies without necessarily immersing themselves in the sense of tragedy.

"Does this belong to the repertoire passed down in your family?" asked Ajmal.

"No. Our family didn't used to play for Muharram. This became a 'new fashion' when I was younger. We had to make a living, and since the Sayyads started requesting this sung poetry we began playing it," explained Baksh. "Now no one asks for it anymore. We also stopped playing for Muharram."

When Baksh demonstrated the patterns again, he volunteered that grand *mārū* was sixteen *mātra*s and small *mārū* was eight *mātra*s.

With Ajmal's assistance Ali was later to review his recording of this demonstration. In his field notebook he inserted these remarks:

Baksh contradicted his earlier statement agreeing with Ajmal that part of mārū is like cañcar. Actually, in his demonstration, great mārū was 15 mātras and small mārū alternated between 8 and 7 mātras. Two factors may have contributed to the discrepancy between Baksh's reportage and his playing. Baksh's group had adopted this piece from contemporary practice. They had not learned it from an ustad who might have verbally categorized it in classical, theoretical terms. Moreover, Baksh's family did not emphasize a mātra-based approach to their functional repertoire. Even though he volunteered the information, this may have been the first time Baksh had thought about or expressed mārū in terms of mātras.

There was also room for mātra ambiguity. Big mārū in particular involved long somewhat flexible gaps between the two strokes corresponding to the syllables "ta." In isolation from the rest of the pattern, the duration of these gaps might be counted more than one way. But as a gestalt, the mātra-breakdown was clearly 8 + 7 for the two phrases. As for the change to choṭa mārū, Baksh was right to indicate the latter pattern was about half as long as the grand pattern, and that it began with eight mātras. But he seemed to view the 7-mātra version as a mere variation. In any case, the transformation from the grand to the small mārū effectively moved from a single grand pattern combining patterns *of 8 and 7 mātras, to two separate "small" patterns, one of 8 mātras and one of 7 mātras. These two latter are variants of one another but distinct from the grand pattern.*

Ajmal asked Baksh to continue. "Cācājī, do you remember what you used to play for Hindu weddings?"

"For a Kirāṛ wedding, they would ask us to bring seven instruments (*vāje*)—two *ḍhol*s, two *tāshā*s, one *naqqārah*, and two *shahnā'ī*s, or some other combination adding up to seven. The Hindus held out cloths as part of the ritual while we recited the *du'ā-e-k͟hair* prayer for their welfare. We played a special *vājā* on all the instruments for this ritual, and then *jhūmar* for their stick dance. We used a special *vājā* for the groom's 'procession departure' with two *ḍhol*s and one *tāshā*. The *ḍhol* part is the same *karaṛ* I mentioned earlier. The *tāshā* plays a steady filler pattern and then inserts *tihā'ī*s and rapid rolls [figure 4.9; see the chapter notes; Media Example 4.6]. A different *vājā* celebrated the arrival of the palanquin at the groom's house from the bride's house."

Finally, Ali had encountered someone in Pakistan who knew about the *tāshā*. "Baksh Sahab, your repertoire for marriages is the most elaborate I have encountered. I noticed that you only play a few things on the *tāshā*. In my place, *tāshā* is used during Muharram. Do you play *mārū* on the *tāshā* as well?"

"No, we used to play it only on *naqqārah* and *ḍhol*. *Tāshā* was popular in Hindu times for weddings and my elders used to play as well; but not for Muharram. Some *muhājir*s were playing *tāshā* during Muharram here until only five or six years ago. They are Rohtkis, from district Rohtak. They used to play a pattern called *palath*. When they played tikitikitikitiki, I used to play: | jhā . ṇe ke nā . ke ne / dā . ṇe ke nā . ke ne |. They would do palath [swordplay] as a kind of *mātam*, although they didn't actually strike themselves with the swords." Baksh waved his arm through the air, showing the method of swordplay, and vocalized an imitation of the *ḍhol* and *tāshā* parts in alternation [Media Example 4.7]. "Both Shī'ahs and Sunnis from Rohtak used to participate in this, along with our [Sunni] people on *ḍhol*. And some people used to do *kathkī ḍānas* [dance]—some people call it *kathak*."*

"You mentioned you stopped playing for Muharram and that the Rohtkis did as well. Why?" inquired Ali.

*This presumably has no connection with the classical dance *kathak*.

"Our Murshad Pāk told us to stop. Our religious leader Pir Anwar Shah Sahab said, 'Muhammad, don't play this or mourn the imams at your home.'"

"What was his objection?"

"We are Sunnis and those who mourn the imams are Shīʻahs. He said that Sunnis shouldn't play at all."

"Do Shīʻahs play?"

"They have *majlis*es, *ziyārat*s, and sermons, but they believe it is against Islamic law to play the *ḍhol*, *naqqārah* or *shahnā'ī*."

"What about the Rohtkis? Why did they stop?" asked Ali.

"I don't know why. Some reason must have struck their hearts. Or maybe their pir asked them to discontinue also. You see, many people have given up many things. I myself used to play *ḍhol* during Muharram in Multan until a few years ago. I used to make my rounds. I would walk, I'd sleep, then I'd go to another neighborhood."

"Before your pir forbade you entirely, why didn't you also play *tāshā* during Muharram?" asked Ali.

"It is not good to play any instrument during Muharram, but *tāshā* is particularly bad because of its sound."

Nazir opined, "The sound of the *ḍhol* extends a long way; the sound of the *tāshā* resonates only in the immediate area."

Ali took this to mean that the *ḍhol* served a wider community function, whereas the *tāshā* was mere aesthetic decoration for a smaller group of listeners.

"At least the *ḍhol* has elements of sadness [*ġamnāk*] in it, and it is played in a quiet and calm way. The *tāshā* is just noise," reasoned Baksh.

"Cācājī, Ali and I would like to listen to the *ḍhol* and *shahnā'ī* players next week during Muharram. Where should we go?" Ajmal inquired.

"Bheḍi Potra, outside Haram Gate."

: : :

As Baksh was a hereditary musician, the role of patrons was significant in the evolution of his repertoire and his performance strategies over the course of his life. When his patrons were Sayyads, for instance, his fellow Mirāṣīs had evolved special repertoire to honor and attract them. This repertoire provided a surprise twist with regard to the semiotics of musical affect. In Baksh's view, the same tragic *mansuriya* text with a single musical setting carried different affective shades for his patrons depending on context—and, I might add, the mood and predisposition of the listener. His identity as a Sunni did not prevent him from viewing the affective "system" as a whole—an ideal set of relations. Even if he himself wasn't inclined, for example, to feel moved to weep during Muharram, he detected subtle differences in the emotional implications of the *ḍhol* and the *tāshā*.

A few further words explaining my interpretation of the *mansuriya* text may be helpful here, since Baksh's responses in my original interviews with him were rather telegraphic. "Shāh Sayyad" was Husain and the night of tyranny, Ashura, the day Husain was killed. Husain's ability to remain focused and indifferent to his fate (of which he is said to have been fully aware) was apparently so tremendous that, according to this poem, God made the sky tremble. Baksh's terse comment about the effect of this line at a wedding was that "it creates enthusiasm." That is, Sayyads, as descendants of Husain's family, are viscerally moved by the resolve and self-sacrifice of their ancestor. In speaking of enthusiasm at the wedding, Baksh points toward emotional amplification, an increase in intensity not marked specifically by happiness or sadness. A listener might have her spirit bolstered (to borrow another local expression) or, if so inclined, his heart touched with poignancy.

As one caught up in Multan's famous Muharram observances, Baksh was also subject to the kinds of reformist discourses that have circulated the subcontinent on a regular basis since at least the nineteenth century. Many such discourses, which were sparked by interactions with Europeans, concerned decorum in the public sphere and were aimed at such practices as celebrating funerals and expending valuable resources, whether cash or cattle, on religious and life cycle rituals. In Baksh's case, one of the reformist themes was directed against social and religious intermingling: he, as a Sunni, ought not perform as a musician during Muharram. Ironically, as we've seen, it is the Shī'ahs of substantial South Asian cities who ordinarily refrain from performing on musical instruments during Muharram because they hold the relatively recently acquired view that instruments, drums included, convey the wrong emotional message—one of joyous celebration. Muharram drummers in South Asia are now, with a few notable exceptions, Sunni (and in India, Hindu). The underlying message from Baksh's pir is not only against musicians like Baksh acting too Shī'ī, but also against their participating loudly and indecorously in the public sphere during an occasion that Sunnis, too, respect. That is, the pirs have called for a toning down of the emotional intensity of the affair, as projected by performance on the drums and *shahnā'ī*. Ali's unfolding story will add detail and nuance to the issues of sectarianism and emotionality raised so far.

The conversations that Ali and Ajmal had with one another and with Muhammad Baksh Multani in the present chapter also explored further significant ways in which drum patterns might be linked to texts: through a posteriori assignment of verbal phrases to preexisting drum patterns and as a secondary phenomenon to flexibly sung song melodies. Baksh emphasized the importance of reciting drum syllables not only in the learning process but also in performances. Baksh's comments on classical music reinforced the idea of classicism being connected with the counting of homogeneous time units—*mātra*s—and of local, in this case *vājā*-based, music being oriented to an irregular sequence of accents marked by syllables and claps. The remainder of this chapter provides further analysis of the organization of drum patterns according to texts and in relation to accented syllables.

Grounding of Drum Patterns Outside of the *Mātra*

There are at least four principles for organizing drum patterns that do not depend on cycles with a fixed number of pulses: the number of stressed beats, repeating motives, tone-melodies, and verbal formulas.[1] Repertoires tend to include different kinds of pieces, each of which may be organized according to a different principle. Pieces commonly combine this principles. For example, patterns conceptualized according to melodies may also follow aspects of a song text. The case studies that follow trace patterns named for numbers of stressed beats, starting from the short motivic kernels of Dalit groups in South India and culminating in the long, through-composed pieces of a *ḍhol-tāshā* ensemble in Delhi. Each case will consider, in addition, other elements of repertoire that are relevant to understanding the principles by which local patterns transcend the limits of *mātra* counting. The case studies are (1) Kota and Aruntiyar (Cakkiliyar) drumming in Tamil Nadu; (2) Dalit drumming in Hyderabad, Andhra Pradesh; (3) Muhājir drumming in Hyderabad, Sindh, by men of Agra heritage; and (4) Mamraj's *ḍhol-tāshā* group, associated with the Nizamuddin shrine in Delhi.

Kota and Tamil Drummers in South India: Numbered Subpatterns

The Kotas of the Nilgiri Hills and some Dalit groups of Tamil Nadu share a concept of variation whereby the lead frame drummer systematically alters the density of his strokes and identifies the variations by number. My knowledge of the process of variations in all the Kota drum patterns comes from several years living in the Kota village of Kolmel and participating in ritual events as a drummer. The day after one of the first times I recall performing, a youth playfully approached me saying something like, "I heard you played last night. You played the one-beat variety. Did you play the two-beat? [Yes.]

Did you play the three-beat? [Yes].” Within drum patterns called *dāk*s, Kotas label variations according to the number of stressed beats played at the beginning of a pattern. In Kota, a beat or strike is also called a *dāk*—or an *aṛy* (Tamil *aṭi*). In Media Example 4.8, S. Raman demonstrates the one-beat, two-beat, and three-beat versions of the *dāk* called *tiruganāṭ* and then presents them in different combinations (see figure 4.10).

Figure 4.10. *Dāk/Aṭi* varieties in *Tiruganāṭ dāk*

One-beat pattern (*oḏ dāk* or *aṛy*)

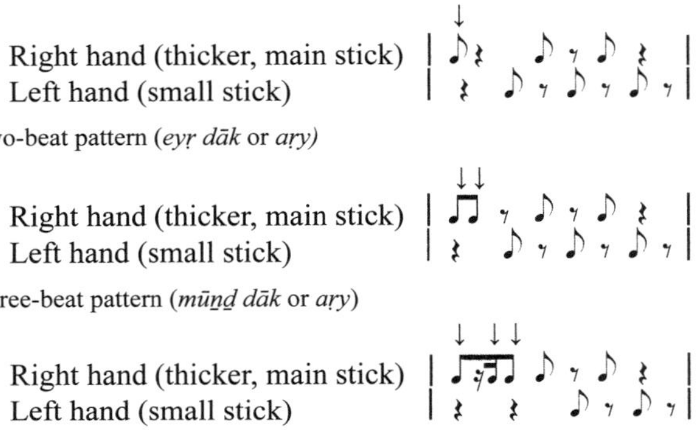

S. Raman, *tabaṭk*, K. Puccan, *koḷ*, demonstrating varieties of *tiruganāṭ dāk*, 8 Feb 92, Kolmel village, The Nilgiris, Tamil Nadu. Arrows show the strokes for which the beats (*dāk* or *aṛy*) are counted.

Kota instrumental music is closely related to that of the other tribal communities in the area: the Ālu Kurumbas, Pālu Kurumbas, Kāṭṭu Nāyakas, Beṭṭu Kurumbas, and Irulas. Kotas have historically interacted with Dalits in the region as well.[2] One Kota drum pattern, *koḷāḷ dāk*, draws its name from Koḷāḷ, the Kota ethnonym for the Cakkiliyar caste. The pattern marks ritual otherness: Kotas use it exclusively for rituals associated with deities seen to be originally Tamil or Hindu. Some Dalit communities in other parts of Tamil Nadu designate their variations by the number of stressed strokes they contain. A longer history of interaction may account for this shared naming practice.

My experience with Tamil Dalit communities was, unfortunately, limited. Although the Aruntiyars (Cakkiliyars) from Dharmapuri discussed above did not mention the numbering of *aṭi*s in my interviews of 1998–99, I distinctly recall some of them explaining and demonstrating this numbering system when I attended a Kāḷiyammaṉ (goddess) festival in Nārttampaṭṭi village in April 1991. An excerpt from my video of that festival shows the progression of frame-drum beats from one to three, followed by a series of more complex variations (Media Example 4.9).

The point to be taken from these examples is that the idea of naming variations by the number of stressed strokes cuts across different sociocultural strata in Tamil Nadu. This phenomenon iterates on a small scale a conceptualization of drumming patterns found elsewhere in South Asia.

Hyderabad Dalit Ensembles of dugga *and* tāshā*:* do mār *and* tīn mār

In Hyderabad, Andhra Pradesh, scheduled-caste ensembles play the *tāshā* with a narrow cylinder drum called the *dugga* for a variety of occasions including weddings, funerals, Hindu festivals, and Muharram. The patterns upon which the following discussion focuses are *do mār* and *tīn mār* (two-beat and three-beat). I recorded several versions of these patterns by different groups, two of which are represented in the recorded examples. One band, which I'll call Band A, used these patterns to support the dance of the demon Pōta Rāju (Media Examples 4.10 to 4.15 ⇐).[3] The second band, called the Jyothi band, used these two patterns, along with another pattern called Vijayawada (the name of a major city in Andhra Pradesh), to perform during Muharram (Media Examples 4.16 and 4.17 ⇐).

The performers from Band A call their repertoire items *tāl*s or *ṭhekā*s. The patterns progress through parts which may be of different lengths. This progression makes the items more similar to the Tamil Dalit examples introduced above than to the *ṭhekā*s of Hindustani classical music. In playing *do mār* and *tīn mār*, the Band A performers begin with a core pattern of either one- or two-measure cycles. For analytic convenience, I call these the main pattern and the first variation; the performers did not make a terminological distinction themselves. As he progresses, the *dugga* performer seems to select a motive or idea from that pattern, vary its articulation on the *dugga*, and either thin the texture by leaving space for the *tāshā* players to sound alone or make the texture more dense by increasing the frequency of the stressed bass strokes. The texture thickens into a series of closely spaced, stressed strokes. The *dugga* player leads the group to a cadence before returning to the base pattern. In the course of these variations, the tempo varies—in contrast to Karnatak music, in which performers ideally accomplish changes in rhythmic texture without changing the tempo. There does not seem to be a *tāla*-like control over the basic measure length in the present examples. Rather than thinking *tāla* "metrically," the ensemble members respond to the motivic variations on the *dugga*. The *tāshā* players in Band A play a single accompaniment pattern for each item with very little variation. The *tāshā* player in the Jyothi band, by contrast, performs his own set of variations, especially for *do mār* (see Media Example 4.16 ⇐).

A drummer from Band A vocalizes each drum pattern with a combination of voiced and unvoiced consonants, glottal stops, and vowels. In figure 4.11, *do mār*, the syllable *dim* corresponds to a resonant bass stroke on the drum and glottal stops correspond to damped strokes (in the vocalization of *tīn mār*, glottal stops are also used to mark rests).

From this first variation of the pattern, which stretches over two measures, it is not obvious why the term *two-beat* applies. One measure in which the bass stroke *dim* is heard twice alternates with another measure in which the bass stroke *di* is heard once. *Do mār*'s two-beat character is clear, however, in what I call the main pattern, which unfolds over a single measure. The two strikes appear in the anacrusis and downbeat of each cycle. The three-beat character of *tīn mār* is also more evident in its one-measure main pattern than in its two-measure first variation. Skeletal notations of the respective main and first variation patterns are presented in table 4.1.

Whereas the vocalization of *do mār* by the drummer of Band A maps well onto the first variation, his vocalization of *tīn mār* does not reconcile with either of the drummed variations or any of the variations I was able to discern on the recording (figure 4.12; Media Example 4.11).

Although the pulses in the rapidly articulated vocalization notated in figure 4.12 match up with the sixteenth-note-level pulses in a measure of the main pattern (table 4.1B1), the syllables do not fall where one would expect. The single *dim* syllable indexes only one resonant bass stroke instead of three; the pulse stream *diku ṭa cha pa* could possibly refer to the *tāshā* pattern of five sixteenth notes followed by a sixteenth rest, but if that were the case, the whole pattern would have to be offset by an eighth note. The reconstruction shown in figure 4.13, based on the vocalization, suggests what the drummed pattern might consist of. It involves omitting the first bass stroke and switching the hands with which strokes on eighth-note counts two and three are played.

Whereas *do mār* and *tīn mār* draw their names from the number of *dugga* strokes in their respective main patterns, some of the other items are

Figure 4.11. Vocalization of *do mār* (see Media Example 4.10)

| **dim** . . paʔ . . dim . | **di** miʔ . pa pa . . . |

Figure 4.12. *Tīn mār* vocalization, first phrase (see Media Example 4.11)

Syllables:	| dim	.	ba	ʔa	di	ku	ṭa	cha	pa	ʔ	ʔ	.	|
Pulses	1	2	3	4	5	6	7	8	9	10	11	12	

Table 4.1. *Do mār* and *Tīn mār* drummed patterns

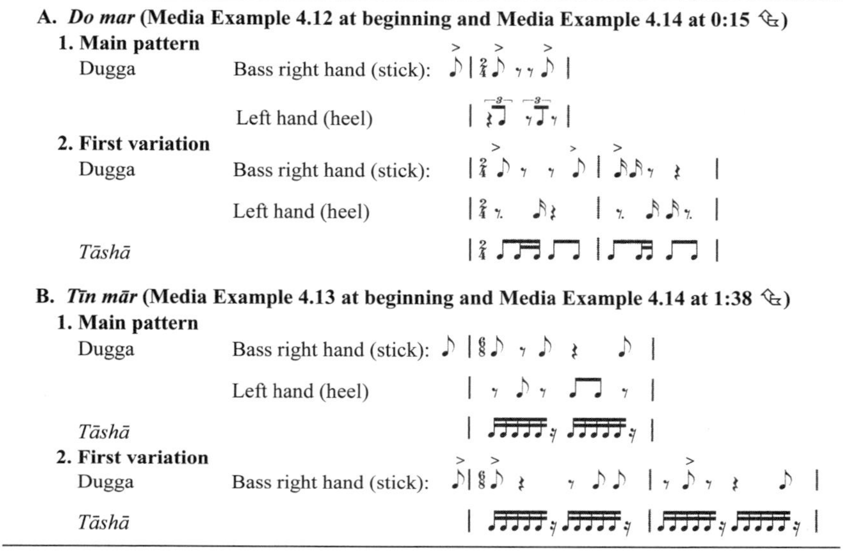

Program of *dugga-tāshā*, tiger dance, Pōta Rāju dance, and so on in Secunderabad, Andhra Pradesh, November 22, 1998. Performers: Shankar (age 34), *tāshā/dugga*; Ramesh (age 28), *tāshā/dugga*; Elaichi (age 38), *tāshā/dugga*; Laxman (age 24), *tāshā/dugga*. Performers adopted roles in shifts; at any one time the ensemble consisted of two *tāshā*s and one *dugga*.

Figure 4.13. *Tīn mār* vocalization mapped onto a reconstructed drum pattern. Compare this version to the *tīn mār* pattern notated in Table 4.1B1—the main pattern head in Media Examples 4.13 (beginning) and 4.14 (at 1:38).

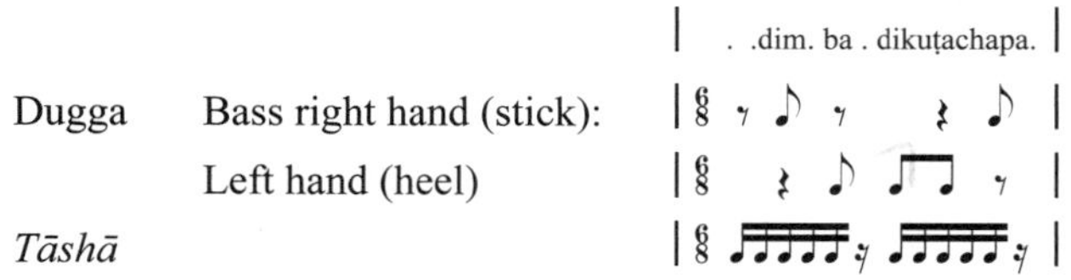

named for, and anchored to, specific melodies. In demonstrating the *bol*s for the funeral pattern used to accompany the bhajan "Raghupati Rāghava Rāja Rām," for instance, a drummer in Band A accidentally started singing the song (Media Example 4.18).[4] When one of his fellow musicians reminded him to recite the *ṭhekā*, he continued by humming and reciting *bol*s at the same time; eventually discontinuing the bhajan melody with his voice, he appeared to follow the melody in his head while vocalizing an accompaniment. Although some of the patterns named for songs clearly originated as accompaniment patterns, they are not all generic grooves: some follow the specific melodies of the songs for which they are named. As a general point, then, the models for what drummers call *ṭhekā*s or *tāl*s may in some cases be tone-melodies, to which the drummers dynamically respond, whether or not that tone-melody is actually present.

Table 4.2. Repertoire of Band A, November 1998

Dances
Pōta Rāju dance (combinations of *do mār*, *tīn mār*, and possibly other patterns)
Sher (lion) dance (*sher kā tāl*)
[*Bhaṅgṛā*] (not conceived locally as a dance)

Film songs
"50 50" (song from the 1956 film *50 50*)
"Jai Santoṣī Māṁ" (song from the 1975 Hindi film of the same name); played for the Hindu holidays Navarātri and Ganesh puja
"Ramba Ho" (said to be from the Hindi film *Armān*, 1981)
"Rām Lakhan" (said to be from the Hindi film *Armān*, 1981)

Contexts
Muharram *kā tāl*
maute kā ṭhekā (patterns for funeral) 3 types:
a. "march" ($\frac{4}{4}$)
b. "waltz" ($\frac{3}{4}$)
c. Accompaniment pattern for the *bhajan* "Ragupati Rāghava Rāja Rām"

Miscellaneous
Vijayawada (city name, possibly film related)
Gāon dafalī tāl (imitation of the sound of *daf* ensembles in Telugu villages)
Rock and roll (source uncertain)

The hybridity of the repertoire listed in table 4.2 is typical for modern urban drumming ensembles throughout South Asia—especially those involving *ḍhol* and *tāshā* drums. The idea of naming an item by the number of stressed strokes is limited in this repertoire only to *do mār* and *tīn mār*. The next case study is atypical in that this kind of beat-number classification describes almost the entire repertoire.

Muharram Ensemble, Hyderabad, Sindh; Muhājir Families from Agra

The *ḍhol* players described in this case study were living in Hyderabad, Sindh, when I met them in 1997. However, the leader and several others traced their origins to Agra, India, whence they or their families migrated at the time of Partition. The leader said that he brought the *ḍhol* tradition they performed from Agra. These drummers' views on drumming vis-à-vis Muharram and Islam are discussed in detail in Chapter 8. The important point here is that the group members do not acknowledge any meaningful religious connection between what they play and its sole context, Muharram. In keeping with this rather clinical approach to ritual drumming, this group names pieces by number rather than according to context. Unlike Band A, whose members called their pieces *tāl*s and *ṭhekā*s, the generic term for pattern this group employs is *cāl*.

Of their eight *cāl*s, seven were labeled sequentially from one to seven, and one *cāl* bore the adjective "one-and-a-half" (*ḍeṛh*).[5] The whole-number sequence is built by systematically adding identical motivic units to a core pattern and then appending a motivically related tag at the end. The motivic unit at the core of the first several *cāl*s (Media Examples 4.19, 4.20, 4.21, and 4.23), which I shall call *t*, could be heard as either an asymmetric duple (3 + 4 sixteenth notes) or as a triplet with the first count slightly prolonged (| ♪. ♪♪ |). The dot after the eighth note in this instance represents a slight prolongation of the first count and not the precise fraction denoted in standard staff notation (compare Wolf 2005, 50; Brăiloiu 1984, 133*ff.*). For the *cāl*s numbered one (*ek*), two (*do*), and four (*cār*), unit *t* is played with an initial (bass) accent with the right-hand stick (notated $\underline{t}$) for the number of times determined by the *cāl* number. An additional iteration of *t* without this accent is appended as a tag. These examples conform to the formula: x $cāl = x \cdot \underline{t} + t$, where x is the number (1, 2, or 4) indicated in the *cāl* name (see figure 4.14A). The performers applied the same formula using the value $x = 3$, but this was deemed an error by the group leader (Media Example 4.21). The correct version of *tīn cāl* follows a different formula.

The *cāl*s numbered *tīn* (three, corrected), *pānc* (five), *cheh* (six), and *sāt* (seven) follow a related formula (Media Examples 4.22, 4.24, 4.25, and 4.26). The main difference is that there are two tags, T_1 and T_2. Unlike the relation of *t* to $\underline{t}$, these tags use portions of the (new) core pattern but are not identical to it (see the comparison in table 4.3). The new core pattern for these *cāl*s, *y*, includes two accented beats: y = ♩̂ ♪ ♩̂ ♩; as such, any multiple of *y* will also have an even number of accented beats. This means an odd-numbered *cāl* pattern—that is, one named for an odd number of accented beats—requires the tag to begin with an accent, which single accent will make the even number odd. An even-numbered *cāl* pattern (in this case only *cheh cāl*) does not require the tag to include an accent. The two formulae are compared with one another and with the earlier formula in figure 4.14.

Notice the close structural similarity of all these patterns. The use of motivic material is extremely conservative. Each *cāl* consists of a repeating motivic unit ($\underline{t}$ or *y*) followed by a tag (*t*, T_1, or T_2) that is derived from

Figure 4.14. *Cāl* formulae for Hyderabad, Sindh group of Agra heritage.

a. *x* = 1, 2, or 4 as indicated in the *cāl* name (x = 3 is an error that follows this formula)

x cāl = x · $\underline{t}$ + *t*

b. *x* is an odd number greater than 1 (here, less than 9)

x cāl = (*x* – 1)/2 · *y* + T_1

c. x is an even number greater than 4 (here, less than 8)

x cāl = *x*/2 · *y* + T_2

Table 4.3. Repertoire of *ḍhol* players in Hyderabad, Sindh, of Agra heritage

Media Example No.	Tempo	Pattern
4.19: Ek kī cāl	♪. ♪♪ = 93	| >♪. ♪♪ | ♪. ♪♪ |
4.20: Do kī cāl	♪. ♪♪ = 84	| >♪. ♪♪ | >♪. ♪♪ | ♪. ♪♪ |
4.21: Tīn kī cāl (error)	♪. ♪♪ =	| >♪. ♪♪ | >♪. ♪♪ | >♪. ♪♪ | ♪. ♪♪ |
4.23: Cār kī cāl	♪. ♪♪ = 91	| >♪. ♪♪ | >♪. ♪♪ | >♪. ♪♪ | >♪. ♪♪ | ♪. ♪♪ |
4.22: Tīn kī cāl (corrected)	♩ = 50	| >♩ ♪ >♩ ♩ | >♪♩ ♩ ♩ ♪ |
4.24: Pānc kī cāl	♩ = 66	| >♩ ♪ >♩ ♩ | >♩ ♪ >♩ ♩ | >♪♩ ♩ ♩ ♪ |
4.25: Cheh kī cāl	♩ = 66	| >♩ ♪ >♩ ♩ | >♩ ♪ >♩ ♩ | >♩ ♪ >♩ ♩ | ♩ ♩ (♪) |
4.26: Sāt kī cāl	♩ = 66	| >♩ ♪ >♩ ♩ | >♩ ♪ >♩ ♩ | >♩ ♪ >♩ ♩ | >♪♩ ♩ ♩ ♪ |
4.27: Ḍeṛh kī cāl	♩ = 95	| ♪ ˘>♪ ♪ ♪ >♩ |

Key:

All accent marks refer to right-hand strokes.

Dynamic accents with left-hand strokes are not notated.

˘ = unaccented right-hand stroke

> and > = degrees of stress

Pattern components are aligned to illustrate interrelationships.

t = ♪. ♪ ♪

y = ♩ ♪ ♩ ♩

T_1 = ♪ ♩ ♩ ♩ ♪

T_2 = ♩ ♩ (♪)

all or some part of the repeating motive. Not only are the units *y* and *t* both asymmetrical, but *y* may also be viewed as an inflated version of *t* (that is, the same pattern at half the speed)—the prolongation represented with a dot after the first eighth note in *t* is analogous to the eighth-note stroke in *y*.

These patterns bear abstract similarities to some of the *deśī,* or regional *tāla*s, described in Indian musical treatises during the second half of the first millennium. Lewis Rowell describes the *deśī tāla*s as constituting both a "movement" and a "set of principles" from which the "modern systems of *tāla* have evolved." Although no single principle describes the roughly two hundred *deśī tāla*s, they generally consisted of "short and irregular patterns" and were defined by "short, repeatable sequences of durations" (Rowell 1992, 208–9). The durational values were ♩. ♩ ♪ and 𝅘𝅥𝅯 plus an additional unit, called a *virāma*, that was defined as a fraction of the latter two durations. Rowell compares the *virāma* to the augmentation dot in Western notation and uses a dot to represent it. The *virāma* unit in *deśī tāla*s, like the prolongation in *t* and the eighth note in *y*, lends each pattern its characteristic asymmetry.

The lengthier *deśī* patterns mentioned in the thirteenth-century *Saṅgītaratnākara* tended to be composed of internally repeated units and sometimes ended with longer, irregular patterns or a relatively long durational value whose function Rowell interprets as cadential (Rowell 1992, 213–13). Because the *deśī tāla*s were themselves so diverse and only a few of them survive in any form today, it is unlikely that any currently performed pattern can be linked with any particular *tāla* listed in treatises from about the thirteenth century.[6] The organizational ideas underlying some *deśī tāla*s, however, accommodate the Hyderabad *ḍhol* group's repertoire quite well. The *deśi tāla* called *miśravarṇa* is a particularly strong example of structural similarity (figure 4.15).

Furthermore, as Sharma suggests, "larger units in a given tāla were rendered with a sounded beat followed by [a] semicircular movement of the hand" (Sharma 2000, 217). It is tempting to think of the left-hand *ḍhol* strokes, which serve as the basis for the number-based nomenclature, as analogous to these "sounded beats": imagine a strong bass articulation at the beginning of each measure.[7]

Figure 4.15. The *deśī tāla* called *miśravarṇa*

The consistency of this miniature system is somewhat compromised by the eighth repertoire item, *ḍeṛh* (table 4.3; Media Example 4.27). The right-hand strokes articulate a triple pattern while the left-hand strokes maintain a duple pattern. If the right-hand strokes mark out *mātra*s, the left-hand strokes would mark out durations of 1.5 *mātra*s. By this logic, the pattern name is conceptualized in terms of *mātra*s rather than stressed strokes, and the left-hand stroke, slightly brighter in timbre, receives pride of place instead of the right. The performers did not verbalize the logic behind their naming system, however.

I did not have the chance to observe the performance of these patterns in context because I recorded the repertoire after Ashura (but still during the Muharram season). However, the players told me that they continuously change from one *cāl* to another, presumably guided by their lead drummer. This ensemble is unlike the others we have encountered in that all the drummers play the same part—no instrument like the *tāshā* fills in or elaborates in the treble range, and no instrument holds down a steady pattern so that another instrument can improvise.

Mamraj's Tāshā *Group*

Ustad Mamraj (b. 1933), at the time of this writing, leads one of the most versatile and skilled *ḍhol-tāshā* groups I have encountered in India or Pakistan. This Hindu group, based in Delhi, performs for a wide variety of occasions, including weddings, Hindu holidays, and Muharram. Mamraj, who holds the position of *first pagaṛi* (literally, first turban), has the honor of musically leading the Muharram processions associated with the Sufi shrine of Nizamuddin Auliya. Four features of their performances are of note here: textural layering, verbal underlay, beat-number terminology or organization, and riff-based organization.

In the *ḍhol-tāshā* examples we have encountered thus far, the *tāshā* part has consisted of either a relatively rapid repeating pattern or a set of limited variations. High-caliber groups such as Mamraj's employ three functional layers. The *ḍhol* player provides the foundational stroke-melody, which Mamraj calls the *naġmah* (tune). One group member likened this to the melody a harmonium player repeats as a metric foundation for a tabla solo, although as we shall see, the *naġmah* does not necessarily return according to a periodic cycle.[8] The second layer is a steady pattern played by one or more *tāshā*s in unison; this part is likened to the role of a *tānpūra* in a classical concert: it provides a blended sonic background for both the *ḍhol* and the lead *tāshā*. Although my data are unclear as to whether there is a technical term for this second layer, I shall adopt the term *ḍhaburī*,

"Bass" (i.e. *ḍhol*) and tassa performers of the band US #1 and others performing for Hosay (Muharram), 52nd Street and 11th Avenue, Manhattan, September 1, 1996. Photo by the author.

which seems to refer to this part—albeit ambiguously—in my field data.[9] The function of the third layer is to build the rhythmic tension and excitement (*lay bāndhnā*). Experienced *tāshā* players take turns performing what Mamraj called *upji* (*upaj,* "produce, product"; here, "improvisation") and usually complete their turn with cadences such as the tripartite *tīyā* (*tihā'ī*).[10] This three-layer organization of *ḍhol-tāshā* performance is also maintained among descendents of Indian migrants in Trinidad, where the parts are called the bass (*ḍhol*), the fuller (*tāshā,* possibly *ḍhaburī*), and the cutter (*tāshā*, lead part).

Four of the patterns in Mamraj's Muharram repertoire are associated with underlying texts: *kalmah, Muharram kī savārī, mātam,* and *dhīmā*. Most members of his group are only aware of the *kalmah* text. This statement of

Muslim faith in one god is widely used as a *zikr* in the Muslim world (see Chapter 2): "[There is] no god but God [and] Muhammad is the prophet of God." As Hindus, Mamraj's group members express openness to the forms of religiosity espoused at the Nizamuddin shrine. The *kalmah* example will illustrate several ways in which a text-based pattern can be taken up musically on the drums. The subtleties of the other three patterns and texts are considered in Chapter 9. Mamraj recites the *kalmah* in Media Example 4.28.[11]

Although performers sense the relation between the *ḍhol* pattern and the verbal phrase intuitively, that intuition is grounded in patterns of prosody. The points of emphasis indicated in boldface are reinforced by *ḍhol* strokes in figure 4.16.

In order to analyze the prosodic basis for this drum pattern, I use *'arūz* principles (although not the classic meters themselves) to assign a value of 1 for short syllables (a consonant plus a short vowel) and 2 for long syllables (a consonant plus a long vowel, a short vowel plus a consonant, or a consonant followed by a short vowel and a consonant); an added unit in parentheses indicates the final *h* of *Allah*. The sequence of durational values is shown in figure 4.17. Slashes in the figure delineate segments between emphasized syllables (which are in boldface).

Since the drum pattern only consists of two units, ♩ and ♪, let us now project this sequence of 4s, 3s, and 2s into a sequence of longs and shorts, where 4s and 3s are both long and 2s are short. This results in the hypermeter _ _ ⏑ ⏑ _, _ _ ⏑ ⏑ _, which matches exactly the musical durations played on the drums.[12]

This sequence is used in different ways. When Mamraj's group performed during Muharram processions in December 2009, I only heard them play the *kalmah* pattern immediately after a *ḍhol* player handed off

Figure 4.16. The *kalmah* recited and played on the *ḍhol*

lā il-**lāha** **illa**'l-**lāh** mu**ḥam**ma**dur** ras**ūl** **'all**āh
♩ ♩ ♪♪ ♩ ♩ ♩ ♪♪ ♩

Figure 4.17. Prosodic durations for *kalmah* text

lā il**lā**ha **illallāh** mu**ḥam**ma**dur** ras**ūl** **'all**āh
2 2/**2** 1/**2**/**2**/**2**(**1**) 1 /**2** 1/**2** 1/ **2** /**2** /**2**(1)

Durational values in each segment added together:
4 / 3 / 2 / 2 / 4 / 3 / 3 / 2 / 2 / 3

the drum to his fellow musician (the instrument is very heavy). Observe the sequence in Media Example 4.29: Mamraj's group plays *Muharram kī savārī,* the drummers switch, they play one round of *kalmah*, and then they resume *Muharram kī savārī.*

In 1999, when I recorded the *kalmah* as part of a demonstration of the group's whole repertoire, the musicians used the pattern as a backdrop for twelve minutes and twenty seconds of improvisation (Media Example 4.30). For the first fifteen seconds they performed a set of *tāshā* phrases that are standard for the *kalmah*; then they cadenced on the first beat of the *naġmah* pattern. Following that, however, the lead *tāshā* players continuously improvised around the principal strokes of the *ḍhol* without ever cadencing again. The *ḍhol* players, for their part, did not return to the signature phrase with precise regularity either.

In 1997, in Hyderabad, Sindh, I recorded an excellent *ḍhol-tāshā* group whose members traced their origins to Bharatpur in India (see Chapter 8). The *kalmah* figured prominently in their repertoire as well. Although they also did not repeat the *naġmah* pattern after regular intervals, each iteration of the pattern made musical sense because it was cued by the end of a lead *tāshā* solo (Media Example 4.31). Since every group I have heard perform the *kalmah* has reiterated this *naġmah* pattern irregularly, I am led to conclude that the use of flexible intervals between iterations of the *naġmah* is part of the performance practice and not a sign of defective musicianship.

The *kalmah* case raises some general points. First, the relative durational values implicit in the underlying text inform the associated drum pattern. Second, the textual *theme*—that is, the pattern derived directly from the text—is usually iterated in the bass register by the *ḍhol* (exceptions are discussed in Chapter 8). Third, the theme can be used in more than one musical way, and fourth, the theme can recur irregularly. I call a pattern identified by a recurring riff, motive, or theme a *riff-based pattern*. Unlike a *mātra-based pattern*, which would rely on a constant number of constituent counts in a cycle, a riff-based pattern need not be situated in a metric context that consists of regularly repeating measures. A riff-based pattern is related to a *beat-based pattern*, the kind of pattern named for the number of stressed strokes, in that any riff is composed of a configuration of a fixed number of beats.

Hindustani *ṭhekā*s could be seen as combining all three of these pattern characteristics: they have a fixed number of counts (*mātra*s), are internally articulated by claps (beats) and waves that together mark out *vibhāg*s, and at the micro level are made up of sequences of specific contrasting strokes (which could be thought of as extended riffs). The set of thirty-five Karnatak *tāla*s are organized according to seven configurations of claps and waves (*beats* within the hand gesture system), each of which can yield five varieties by varying the finger counts of 3, 4, 5, 7, or 9. The system of *vājā*s, as described by Muhammad Baksh, was beat-based until it was overlaid with the contemporary classical practice of describing metric structures in terms of *mātra*s. The Tamil and Telugu Dalit examples appear to be based on both riff-based and beat-based principles. Patterns are identified by small motives that are not necessarily organized into regularly recurring cycles. The basic forms of some of the motives are identified by the number of stressed strokes. The classical systems do not accommodate metric structures defined by an irregularly recurring riff. Indeed, such a conception is much closer to that of *rāga*s, which may be identified by key melodic phrases.

Mamraj's group performs four beat-based patterns, *batīs jarbeṉ* (32 beats), *bāsaṭh jarbeṉ* (62 beats), *sīdī bārah-terah* ("straight 12–13," that is, 12 and 13 beats), and *Husainī kī bāra terah* ("12–13 of Husainī"), plus a related pattern, *Ali kā panjā* ("Ali's five/hand/fist"). These patterns illustrate the extent to which beat-based thinking structures performances on a large scale—not merely for a short repeating cycle. The ways musicians both combine the patterns and break them down into constituent units enrich our understanding of beat-based and riff-based conceptualizations.

Batīs jarbeṉ (32 beats) and *bāsaṭh jarbeṉ* (62 beats), played one after the other, are related by a common *tāshā* theme. This through-composed composite piece takes about two and a half minutes to complete. The *ḍhaburī tāshā* player maintains a triplet pattern that may also be heard as swung sixteenth notes, while the lead *tāshā* player plays the theme notated in figure 4.18.

The *tāshā* parts are notated in equal measures of six dotted eighths in order to show the major recurring unit (but not the meter) of this piece. The vertical lines are not meant to be bar lines. Although the *ḍhaburī* part is notated as sixteenth and eighth notes with the latter accented, it could be heard as swung eighth notes with ambiguous dynamic accent. The lead pattern does not actually enter at the beginning of the performance but, rather, after the *ḍhaburī tāshā* part establishes the groove. The lead then generally waits a

Figure 4.18. The tāshā theme and background pattern for *Batīs jarbeṉ* and *Bāsaṭh jarbeṉ*

"measure"—an interval equal to the length of his theme—before repeating the theme. He does not, however, do this consistently, and this interval is not relevant when he proceeds to a new section. The lead theme is brought in at successively faster speeds throughout the performance whenever there is an extended interval without a *ḍhol* stroke. When he is not playing this theme, the lead *tāshā* performs patterns that either are punctuated by *ḍhol* strokes or culminate in *ḍhol* strokes. When listening to Media Example 4.32, count the *ḍhol* strokes and notice their clustering. The sequence of numbers given in the following paragraph indicates only how many *ḍhol* strokes are found in a cluster, not how many *mātra*s separate the strokes in or between clusters. Again, the "measure" indicated just above is only relevant in the sections where the lead *tāshā* player repeats his theme.

In the first section (Media Example 4.32, 0:00 to 0:54), *batīs jarbeṉ*, the 32 beats are clustered: 1-9-5-3-2-9-1-1-1. In the second section (0:55 to the end), *bāsaṭh jarbeṉ*, the 62 beats are clustered: 8-8-8, 6-6, 3-3-3, 2-2-2, 11. Mamraj recited the *bol*s for these patterns and explained, for *bāsaṭh jarbeṉ*, the numerical breakdown using Hindi words for clusters of numbers (these terms are not the same as for the numbers themselves):

mora aṭṭhā (eight *jarbeṉ* three times, adding up to twenty-four)
chakka (six *jarbeṉ* two times, adding up to twelve)
tirī (three *jarbeṉ* three times, adding up to nine)
durī (two *jarbeṉ* three times, adding up to six)

The last unit of eleven *ḍhol* strokes is indicated by a term that means "limping time/interval," *langṛa nauba. Langṛa* in Urdu/Hindi, the etymologically related *lang* in Persian, and *aksak* in Turkish are all terms meaning *limping* that are used for asymmetrical time patterns in their respective regions.

The items called *sīdī bārah-terah* and *Husainī kī bārah-terah* (Media Examples 4.33 and 4.34) are organized in similar fashion at the macro level but differ in many details. *Sīdī bārah-terah*, or "straight-twelve-thirteen," uses the patterns notated in figure 4.18 for the two *tāshā* parts. The *ḍhol* strokes in *sīdī bārah*, the first part of Media Example 4.33 (0–1:06), fall into the following clusters as determined by their relative density: 3-3-6. The *ḍhol* strokes in the two clusters of three are separated by brief intervals. The cluster of six, which follows immediately after the second cluster of three, is composed of a much denser stream of *ḍhol* strokes. The second part of Media Example 4.33 (1:06 to the end), *terah*, is clustered thus: 3-2-2-2-3-1.

Husainī kī bārah-terah (Media Example 4.34), the "12–13 of Husainī," shares only the macro division of twelve and thirteen with "straight 12–13." The *tāshā* parts are treated in a structurally different way. At first, the part

I am calling *ḍhaburī* plays a triplet or swung sixteenth-note pattern similar to those heard in the preceding two items. The lead *tāshā* joins by playing groups of four thirty-second notes that are not always aligned the same way with the triplet patterns (figure 4.19).

The measure does not indicate the placement of metrical emphasis or a unit that repeats consistently throughout the piece, but the time unit does have local relevance in certain sections of the piece. After the two parts play together for a duration that is often some multiple of the measure, both *tāshā* parts play the theme notated in figure 4.20 in unison, culminating in a *ḍhol* stroke (D):

As the piece proceeds, the *ḍhol* stroke may (1) initiate another round of background pattern one (figure 4.19), (2) proceed to another background pattern that draws from the theme (figure 4.20) in an idiosyncratic way, or (3) reiterate the theme. Regardless of what pattern follows a new *ḍhol* stroke, a second *ḍhol* stroke may follow after an interval of three sixteenth notes, though the interval may be longer. If two *ḍhol* strokes follow in succession and overlap with two iterations of the theme, the *ḍhol* strokes will correspond with the first two accented *tāshā* strokes (for example, at 1:13). The *ḍhol* strokes fall in patterns of one or two in the first part and in patterns of one, two, and five in the second part. The clusters are represented approximately in figure 4.21.

Immediately after the last cluster of 2 (at 1:53) making up the "12," Mamraj can be heard on the recording saying, "Alī kā panjā." I have not

Figure 4.19. Background pattern number one for *Husainī kī bārah-terah*

Figure 4.20. *Husainī-kī-bārah-terah tāshā* theme

Figure 4.21. Clustering pattern for *Husainī kī bārah-terah*

1-2-2-1-1‸1-1‸2-1 ‖ 1‸2_2_1‸2_2_1‸2

Key:

‸ = relatively long duration between sections

‖ = break between the "twelve" section and the "thirteen" section at 1:11

_ = combinations of twos and ones to make "fives" in the thirteen section

yet been able to determine the precise governing principle of this pattern. In addition to the sequential recording in Media Example 4.34 (1:53 to 3:28:), the group demonstrated *Alī kā panjā* alone (Media Example 4.35). Figure 4.22 compares the clustering of *ḍhol* strokes in both examples. Note that at 2:58 a digital error in the recording (marked *) might mask another stroke. To facilitate lining up the two versions of *Alī kā panjā*, I am taking the final stroke in the last cluster of 2 of the previous "13" as the first stroke, in brackets, of *Alī kā panjā*, and inserting spaces where there are discrepancies in numbers of strokes.

On the analogy of the Hindi terms Mamraj used to analyze *bāsaṭh jarbeṉ*, it would be reasonable to expect *panjā* in *Alī kā panjā* to refer clusters of five. While it is possible that one or both of these two versions contain errors, neither version would easily support the idea of *five* as a description of beat clusters. In Media Example 4.35, however, there are five clusters of clusters. Since the *clusters of clusters* idea does not recur in other items of repertoire, its importance remains speculative. Whether or not the numbers are relevant, both versions exhibit very similar patterning. Assuming that the version in Media Example 4.34 is conjoined with the final stroke of the preceding "13," and that the digital error does not cover up a *ḍhol*

Figure 4.22. Two versions of *Ali kā panjā* compared

Media Example 4.34 (1:53 to 3:28)	{1}-1-1‸2-1‸1-1-1‸ 1-1-1‸2-1*1‸2-1‸1†
Media Example 4.35	1-1-1‸2-1-1-1-1-1‸1-1-1‸2-1-1‸2-1-1-1
Discrepancies	↑ ↑ ↑ ↑
Clusters of clusters	1 2 3 4 5

† Muharram kī savārī begins here

stroke, there are only four small discrepancies in Media Example 4.35. Indicated by upward-pointing arrows, these are, in order, (1) absence of a pause, (2) an extra *ḍhol* stroke, (3) the absence of a pause, and (4) an extra *ḍhol* stroke at the end.

Taken very schematically, the two versions share the formula *x y x* (1) *x y* (1) *y* (1) (1), where *x* equals a cluster of three and *y* equals a cluster of two plus one; the parenthetical numerals indicate places in which one, the other, or both patterns include single extra beats not subsumed in the *x*s and *y*s. The point of abstracting in this way is to suggest one possible way in which listeners can identify *Alī kā panjā* despite its variations. Another way of representing it is as a hypermeter:

Short {2} Long {2} Short {2} Short

where {2} indicates a cluster of two; "Short" indicates a sequence of three or fewer *ḍhol* strokes that are not as closely spaced as the two indicated by {2}; and "Long" indicates a much longer sequence of *ḍhol* strokes. Table 4.4 breaks the hypermeter down in terms of the clusters listed in figure 4.22.

The name of this pattern may be more relevant to its context than to its content. *Alī kā panjā* could refer to the five fingers of an open hand, a common symbol for the Panjatan Pāk (Muhammad, Fatimah, Ali, Hasan, and Husain). It could also refer to Ali's fist or punch. In Karachi, where a group of Nizami musicians (discussed in Chapter 9) perform much of the same Muharram repertoire as Mamraj's group, a different pattern bears the similar name *Alī kī zarbeṉ*, "the beats of Ali." Both pattern names would seem to refer to Ali's virility.

Table 4.5 lists the items discussed thus far in the context of Mamraj's entire repertoire. Like the other repertoires I have examined, Mamraj's is eclectic. It includes classical *tāl*s (*jhaptāl* and *kehervā*) whose *ṭhekā*s are

Table 4.4. *Alī kā panjā*, reconfiguration of figure 4.22

Hypermetric value	Media Example 4.34	Media Example 4.35
Short	{1}-1-1	1-1-1
{2}	2	2
Long	1‸1-1-1‸1-1-1	1-1-1-1-1‸1-1-1
{2}	2	2
Short	1*1	1-1
{2}	2	2
Short	1‸1	1-1-1

Table 4.5. Mamraj's repertoire

Hindu occasions, weddings, and miscellaneous functions
kehervā
bāsaṭh jarbeṉ
batīs jarbeṉ
savārī (also called *Rāmlīla kā ṭhekā*)
nā-din-din-na
bhangṛā
Panjabi *ṭhekā*
caukaṛī
jhaptāl
sīdī bārah-terah
For Muharram
Muharram *kī savārī*
kalmah
dhīmā
Husaini kī bārah-terah
Alī kā panjā
mātam

Mamraj's group in January 1999 consisted of Mamraj (*tāshā*); Rambabu (*tāshā*); Rajkumar (*tāshā*); Kailash Kumar (*ḍhol*); Gyan Chand (*ḍhol*); Suresh Kumar (*ḍhaburī*); Jiya Lal (*tāshā*).

translated onto the *ḍhol* and *tāshā*; a *bol* pattern, *nā-din-din-na*, that Shahid and Niamat Ali mentioned as part of their repertoire in Lahore; grooves associated with Panjabi dances (*bhangṛā, caukaṛī,* and *Panjabi ṭhekā*), patterns whose names index Islamic themes (*kalmah*, *Husain, Ali, panjā*); and beat number patterns. The major contextual division is between those played for Muharram and those played for any other occasion.

The similarity in names across the repertoire—two kinds of *savārī* and two kinds of *bārah-terah*—illustrates a phenomenon of overlapping subgenres that is common to many drumming repertoires in South Asia. Here, *savārī* is a *kind* of pattern (there are several in the classical repertoire as well), and all patterns for Muharram are kinds of patterns.

We have considered how Mamraj and other musicians conceptualize pieces without counting *mātra*s but not how Mamraj views the differences among patterns that do share the same number of *mātra*s. Mamraj and his companions demonstrated the patterns, *mātam, savārī, kehervā, bhangṛā,* and *caukaṛī,* by tapping drumsticks on books and furniture. Mamraj pointed out that all these patterns are 16 *mātra*s long but differ in terms of their *cāl*s. This use of the term *cāl,* or gait, for an accentual pattern is but one term for a phenomenon we have now observed repeatedly. A related musical concept is that of weighting, *vazan*, which refers to the performance practice of deforming the ideal-typical version of a rhythmic pattern for expressive stylistic purposes (Clayton 2000, 53). This musical concept of *vazan* would militate against notating the *ḍhaburī tāshā* strokes as triplets rather than as swung sixteenth notes. It is possible that these are conceptualized as evenly spaced strokes that are "weighted" or swung. This concept of *vazan* should not be confused with the concept of poetic meter associated with *vazan* (Arabic *vazn*, "weight").

Cāl is related to what Niamat and Shahid Ali termed *jhol* and to what some classical tabla players term *chand* (Clayton 2000, 53). Kippen encountered uses of the term *chand* flexible enough to accommodate ways of dividing the beat as well as configurations of strokes that make up a composition (Kippen 1988, 170–71). Although Kippen warns not to confuse the musical with the prosodic meanings of *chand* (Kippen 2006, 96n69), it is important to bear in mind that cognates of the Sanskrit term *chandas* refer both to prosodic meter and to musical metric structures, often derived from language, across the Indo-Aryan and Dravidian languages (see Wolf 2009b).

In Sanskrit, Hindi, and related languages the two principal kinds of *chand* are based on counting syllable *mātra*s—long and short. The *varṇika* and the *mātrika* types of *chand* differ in that the former requires adherence to a particular sequence of longs and shorts and the latter merely requires that the sum total of long and short values (long = 2 and short = 1) add up to the given value. Rupert Snell's edition of the *Caurāsī pada*, a devotional text in Braj Bhāṣā (a language related to Hindi) compiled in the sixteenth or seventeenth century, describes contemporary performance practices of both kinds of meters (Snell 1991, 284–89). With reference to *tāla* practice, Premalata Sharma speculates that the ancient *tāla* system, including the *deśī tāla*s, was "nearer" to the *varṇika chandas*. Modern Hindustani practice, by contrast, evolved along with languages under "the direct impact" of *mātrika chandas*. This may be one reason why, she suggests, the *ṭhekā*s for Hindustani *tāl*s may contain varying syllable lengths, even though the definition of the *tāl*s and their subsections adhere to overall *mātra* counts (Sharma 2000, 217–18).[13]

The relevance of these varying conceptions and performance practices to modern vernacular drumming in South Asia is that, in both, we see an ongoing process of negotiation between naming practices based on different kinds of units: *mātra*s, sequences of *mātra* groupings, and articulations differentiated by stress or timbre; both also involve names referring to context.

South Asia as a Musical Area

The three main topics of Chapters 3 and 4, the naming of drum patterns, ambiguities concerning "rhythm" and "melody," and the grounding of drum patterns in verbal, motivic, and beat patterns, are conceptual realms around which many musical traditions of South Asia cohere. These are related to but not limited by the topics treated in the recent theories of classical Hindustani and Karnatak music.[14]

In a masterful study, Harold Powers (1970) suggested how equivalently named North and South Indian *rāga*s could be historically related, despite their present-day differences in pitch content: they share such deep features as melodic contour and emphasis on particular scale degrees. Powers found that the processes by which conceptions of particular *rāga*s circulated through the subcontinent were complex and idiosyncratic. No single evolutionary story could explain the process whereby a *rāga* described in an early treatise evolved in one direction to become part of the Hindustani tradition and in another to become part of the Karnatak tradition (for a different view, see Jairazbhoy 1999 and 2008).

A possible broader implication of Powers's research is that similar musical nomenclature occurring across languages constitutes evidence of deeply shared ideas about musical process. In the absence of theoretical writings, conduits for sharing musical ideas in South Asian drumming traditions may have been the repertoires connected with instruments or ensembles that were carried from place to place. *Ḍhol-tāshā* groups, to take a recent example, seem to have retained a distinctive style as practitioners carried the instruments to different parts of South Asia and from South Asia to the Caribbean and Southeast Asia.

The idiosyncratic changes undergone by the *rāga*s that Powers investigated contrast with the rather systematic ways in which particular words and sounds change in the history of languages. Nevertheless, evidence from the linguistic history of South Asia is suggestive, in a more general sense, of how musical processes came to be shared across vast areas. Murray Emeneau's classic article "India as a Linguistic Area," published in 1956, suggests that long-term interactions among populations on the Indian subcontinent led to "profound" and not merely "superficial" exchanges among the Dravidian, Indo-Aryan, and Munda languages that were in contact.[15] Although it is hard to know the historical depth of today's musical commonalities, the linguistic evidence suggests that substantial exchanges in the sound and structure of language were already taking place thousands of years ago. It stands to reason that members of otherwise disparate local cultures in South Asia developed their musical styles in profound dialogue with one another as well—sharing systematic aspects of music such as nomenclature, theory, and procedures for expressing creativity, and not just discrete songs and melodies. We should expect this sharing to be deeply embedded in the fabric of many kinds of music making.

Although we will never be able to disentangle the many kinds of exchanges that resulted in the translocal musical commonalities we find today, some of the commonalities must have been the result of long-term face-to-face contacts. These deep historical processes need to be acknowledged even though far more recent processes associated with modernity have had a more tangible effect and are easier to account for. Many features of musical practice held in common have been fostered by the mediation of elite musicians and musicologists. The prestige of such figures has encouraged others to follow their musical norms. Standardization also suited modern musical institutions in the twentieth century, which had to cater to the needs of the rising middle class. Such modern developments, however, can hardly account for the extent to which the kinds of musical thinking explored in Chapters 3 and 4 have penetrated the far reaches of the Indian subcontinent.

CHAPTER 5

Muharram in Multan

Cānd Rāt was swiftly approaching.* Ali's ears waited, attuned. Since childhood, Ali had associated this evening with the rapidfire strokes of the *tāshā* and the slothful booming of the *ḍhol*. This drummed announcement of the new moon effectively signaled the onset of the new year as well as the Shīʿī season of ritual mourning. At home, Ali's father would pay a nominal sum to the head of an impoverished household near the family estate in Aminabad to arrange for this service. Ahmed Khan's great-grandfather had provided this modest annual revenue to atone for one of his wayward son's alleged indiscretions with a daughter of this needy family. Now it was an established *rivāyat* in Aminabad.

Whether the custom was different here in Multan or whether he was simply in the wrong place, Ali did not know. He perceived only the usual street sounds: the *thwang* of nut and mango vendors striking their carts, cycles clattering along the bricked lanes, a muffled burst from a dented bell, the deep voice of a Royal Enfield with its diesel sputter, and the whizzing and buzzing of Vespa scooters. Overdriven speakers somewhere nearby carried the voices of Abida Parveen, Pathane Khan, and Nazia and Zoheb Hasan onto the streets. The textured hum of the city shifted subtly when the television and radio officially broadcast the moon's sighting. Ali heard Ajmal's neighbor Abbas shout across the verandah to his daughter,

**Cānd Rāt* (moon night) fell on September 25 that year (1984).

"Fatimah, *keseṭ* band karo" (Fatimah, turn off the cassette player). Some local Shī'ahs tuned their radios and televisions to stations carrying religious sermons, stories, and recitations. These, too, were arts, and during Muharram, they could not be repressed.

Ali and Ajmal went into the streets, wandering *muḥalla* to *muḥalla*, stopping to watch families repair and touch up the paint on their wooden *ziyārat*s (floats)—*ta'ziyah*s, *pangūṛa*s, *mehndī*s, and *sej*s. The stylized cradle (*pangūṛa*) of Hussain's infant son made Ali think of the impoverished *mirāṣan*s he had heard, sitting on the streets of Lucknow and Aminabad, singing their tragically tinged lullabies. The subject was Ali Asghar, slain by an enemy's arrow piercing his tiny neck. The float representing the mehndi ritual of Husain's nephew Qasim also triggered musical memories. Ali had always enjoyed listening to Bhāṇḍs chanting their special mehndi *nauḥah*s for the wedding's henna ceremony.

The mehndi *ziyārat* and the *sej* (nuptial bed), given their association with weddings, formed a pair. In Ali's experience, the *sej*, like the *mehndī* (mehndi float), stood in honor of Qasim. But a young Multani man named Ziyad volunteered a different interpretation. Chatting as he restored a rotting strip of wood on a *sej* the size of a small writing table, Ziyad described the visage of Husain's eighteen-year-old son Ali Akbar: a perfect likeness of the Prophet's. In 680 CE a false rumor had been circulating in Medina that Husain was about to arrange for Ali Akbar's marriage. But he was in fact departing for Karbala. The *sej* evoked the unfulfilled marriage of a beautiful youth cut down in his prime and the fulfillment of Ali Akbar's destiny as a martyr. This double wedding imagery nuanced Ali's view. His cousin Fatimah, he felt, could not appreciate the aesthetics of this ambiguity, despite her otherwise worldly sophistication.

Ziyad continued as he worked. "We also have a *beṛā* in the shed over there," he said, pointing to a nondescript cement enclosure with a corrugated roof. "We take out that 'ship-of-the-people-of-the-Prophet' on the 28th of next month, the anniversary of Hasan's martyrdom.* *This* ship is a *shabīh* (likeness) of *that* ship; this *sej* is a *shabīh* of Ali Akbar's nuptial bed; all these things are *shabīh*s. The *ta'ziyah* is a likeness of the *rauẓah* of Imam Husain, may peace be upon him. Even our mosque is a *shabīh* of the *ka'bah* in Mecca."

Ali was struck by his encounter with these foreign and yet familiar artifacts. The style in which the various solid wood portable *shabīh*s were

*Al-Hasan ibn Ali ibn Abi Talib was poisoned on the 28th of Safar in the year 50 AH (March 26, 670 CE), allegedly at the behest of the Umayyad Caliph Mu'āwiya. The second imam and elder brother of Husain, Hasan was the successor of his father Ali.

constructed, their solid wood heft, and their sheer number, shone favorably in comparison with those of their flimsy counterparts in the Lucknow area.

Another, more distant, set of images began to surface—those of multistory Hindu temple chariots of South India (Media Example 5.1 ⭍). His ayah Kannamma had pointed out these structures to him in photographs and films when he was a child; in explaining their significance as vehicles of divinity, she had likened them to *ta'ziyah*s. Ali had not thought of those conversations in years. The mental juxtapositions, however, now helped him envision these practices as if through the eyes of others. Supporters of an Islam untainted by the Indian environment were disturbed by the similarities between *ziyārat*s and the material culture of the Hindus. Islamic reformers of the eighteenth century had mounted an increasingly staunch campaign in response to a rise in *ziyārat*-related rituals among both Shī'ahs and Sunnis. Those swayed by the reformist messages began destroying their *ta'ziyah*s and, like Muhammad Baksh nearly two hundred years later, distancing their religious personae from musical activity.

Ali cherished his good fortune as one born into a family that valued religious commingling and the positive social potential of the arts. "Our home is like a miniature United Nations," his father would say. One of Ali's heroes was the Chishti saint Nizamuddin Auliya. In the thirteenth century, Nizamuddin had successfully deflected criticisms against singing and other forms of worship at the graves of venerated personages. These were the very acts that Shah Abdul Aziz and other notable Islamic reformers in eighteenth- and nineteenth-century Delhi were later to attack vigorously. The heritage of the Chishtis' unified vision today endured in the *qawwālī* music of their *'urs*es and in the *ta'ziyah*s of their Sunni Muharram observances—to Chishtis, Husain was akin to other personages commemorated in their annual *'urs* celebrations. These institutions were proof enough to Ali that the arts could serve as vehicles for emphasizing the common humanity of all cultures and philosophies. Ali supported this credo with his very fiber. Still, he wondered to what extent modern Indians or Pakistanis would really allow aesthetic experiences to motivate their social and political decisions.

Ali's attention returned to his surroundings as he stumbled on a broken piece of cement and almost toppled headlong onto a sewing machine. Its owner, a roadside tailor who stood across the street sipping tea, was gazing at something or someone above him in the other direction. Ali glanced around nervously, brushed the dust from his *shalwār*, and tried unsuccessfully to look dignified; a young woman (the object of the tailor's attention), peering from behind a cracked-open wooden shutter on the verandah above the tea stall, barely covered her smile with the edge of a newly purchased black *dupaṭṭa*. Observing Ali's loss of focus and growing lassitude, Ajmal lured his friend home for a meal of *shīrmāl* and Lucknow-style kabobs. Just as they were leaving Ajmal noticed a poster announcing a *majlis* at Imambarah Māsumīn, Haweli Murīd Shah, for the next evening.

About an hour after the advertised *majlis* was scheduled to begin, the two men picked their way through the thick network of lanes connecting Haram Gate, near Ajmal's home, to Bohar Gate. They shuffled by the boxy, glazed-tile tomb of the eleventh-century saint Shah Yousef Gardez. Nearby they located the colorful Imambarah Māsumīn, with its three green domes, each hovering over its own arched entryway; red and green painted cornices and imitation archways separated the real archways from their respective domes. Two decorative minarets framing the center dome replicated in miniature the two functional minarets and their filigreed parapets. This play of objects and representations replicated the recursion of images in mirrors within many *imambarah*s and among the *ziyārat*s that now blanketed the town.

The hall inside was already packed with avid *majlis*-goers from all over Multan—men on the left side of a curtain that had been erected, women on the right. The curtain ran the length of the *imambarah*, from the dedicated archway through which women entered to the clearing before the platform where the *soz k̲h̲wān*s sat. Most of the women could peer around or through the curtain at the performers while largely evading the glances of men. Young

Advertisements for *majlis*, Multan, Pakistan, July 3, 2007. Photo by the author.

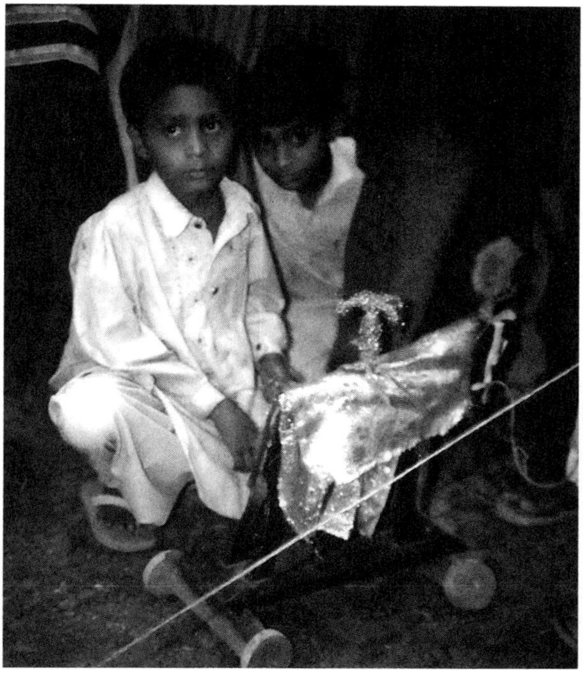

Child with toy horse on wheels, Hyderabad, Sindh, Pakistan, May 1997. Children in Hyderabad hold their own procession with miniature versions of the items the adults carry on procession during Muharram. In this case, the toy horse represents Zuljinah, Husain's steed. Adult processions include one or more live horses, decorated elaborately and called Zuljinah. Photo by the author.

children ran back and forth across the two sides, sometimes chasing one another and occasionally carrying messages from one parent to the other.

The descendents of Shah Gardez, Ajmal said, formed the ranks of most of the households in this neighborhood and were a force to be reckoned with in the district. Sayyad Altaf Gardezi had hosted Ajmal and Ali the previous week. Pulling a musty copy of Arnold Toynbee's 1961 travelogue off his shelf and pointing to a page in it, Altaf Gardezi had recounted his family history. His ancestor Shah Yousuf Gardezi had brought Shiism to Multan, he explained, from Gardez, Afghanistan. "He traveled here on the back of a lion, trained with a snake as a whip. Shah Yousef must have been something more than a mere mortal." Ali took from Altaf Gardezi's emphasis on this story that the Gardezis of Multan were not only custodians of the faith but also embodiments of its potency.

Present in abundance, the Gardezis were also the sponsors of this *majlis*. Ajmal spotted his friend Saleem Gardezi, a tall, soft-spoken man of about forty. Ajmal and Saleem would occasionally perform together on the radio—Saleem singing classical *k̲h̲ayāl* and Ajmal performing on the tabla. Saleem had embarked on a career as a professional musician against the express desires of his family. His choice shamed them. Saleem lived in his joint-family compound like a ghost—virtually formless and voiceless. His music suffered, too. Legendary singers had used their experiences of personal sacrifice as resources for creating emotionally wrenching vocal artistry. Saleem bore his troubles in the grave contours of his face rather through his art. He could never quite pull off anything that strayed beyond convention.

Saleem crossed his legs on the carpet beside Ali and Ajmal and greeted them, left hand pressed to his heart. Learning of Ali's interest in music, Saleem drew attention to the striking delivery style of the evening's reciters: "I'm curious what you think of it." The styles associated with central and northwestern Uttar Pradesh with which Ali was most familiar continued to be performed in Pakistan by *soz k̲h̲wān*s of Muhājir background. Although this *majlis* was in the Urdu language, Saleem portrayed this performance style as a specialty of the region. The performers had already completed the melismatic *soz* and declamatory *salām* selections. Now they were proceeding to *mars̤iyah*s—textually rich, many-stanzaed descriptions and narratives related to Karbala.

Four men loosely clustered themselves around Syed Karrar Haidar Zaidi, who commenced by intoning the syllable ā-a-a-a-h. After a tentative beginning, Zaidi glided upward slightly to a find a comfortable drone pitch. Then each accompanying singer in turn matched his pitch to Zaidi's. An attentive listener, seated on a white sheet covering the floor, head bowed and knees up, pivoted his wrist. He was raising and lowering his first and middle fingers with a steady pulse, as if conducting the vocal entries or anticipating their syllabic delivery. Ali had never experienced an ensemble of this force and texture. Two or more vocal drone singers, called *bāzu*s (arms or supporters), would normally smooth over the sounds of one another's inhaling in order to maintain a steady tone throughout the performance; the *bāzu*s tonight did not merely accompany, they interacted responsively.

With the other singers vocally sustaining the tonal center, Zaidi and one of the other men began to sing: "ins o . . ." (mankind and . . .). The others joined together, "the one who provides aid to [humans], angels, and jinns is Shabbīr" (Husain). They elongated the final syllable of *Shabbīr* to connect seamlessly with the next line. Once again, Zaidi and one or two others sang the next segment while overlapping with the drawn-out tone of the remaining singers. In alternation, they separated roles to sing melody and drone, and then melded to sing portions in unison. On the second line, Zaidi emphasized the verbal rhythm with his left hand proffered entreatingly. The insistent bobbing of his hand underscored the second and subsequent syllables leading up to the rhyming *ār* syllable, called the *qāfiyah*, in several of the lines. Ali wondered if this was merely a mannerism or whether it also helped the supporting singers follow the elastic, melodic rhythm; in any case, Zaidi maintained eye contact with and motioned his head toward his supporting singers at key transitional points.

As Ali expected for this six-line *musaddas* poetic form, Zaidi used common melodic material in the lower range for the first two lines and ascended to the upper range for the third. Despite, or perhaps because of, the predictability, Ali felt a twinge of satisfying pain on the word *slaying-ground* in the upper register. The melodic shift highlighted the duality of Husain's agency. On one hand, Husain helped and controlled the fate of others (lines 1–2); on the other, he was left powerless without assistance on the battlefield (line 3). Ali also responded to the musical setting of the last two lines: the melody of line six interrupted the expected melodic closure of line five, just as, in the text, the idea of Husain as one with great power over the universe was tempered in the next line by the idea of his humility. Stanza by stanza, these musical features in lines three, five, and six reinforced semantic and structural aspects of the text. Ali was seduced by the interesting melodic contrasts and reflected on the ways these saliences shaded the poetic meaning

Mars̱iyah: "ins o malak," Media Example 5.2.

ins o malak o jin ke madadgār hain̠ shabbīr
lauḥ o qalam o 'arsh ke muk̲h̲ tār hain̠ shabīr
maqtal men̠ magar bekas o be yār hain̠ shabīr
nau lākh ke narġe men̠ giraftār hain̠ shabīr
qudrat hai voh qudrat kih hain̠ ġālib do sarā par
par ṣabr hai voh ṣabr kih rāzī hain̠ raẓā par

jab kaṭ gayā gulzār rasūl-e do sarā kā
sheh ne kahā ab k̲h̲āt[i]mah hai āl-e 'abā kā
be kas hu'e be bas hu'e ham shukr k̲h̲udā kā
mushtāq hai ab k̲h̲ushk galā teġ-e jafā kā
k̲h̲ush hun̠ keh sitam k̲h̲anjar-e burrān kā sahegā
ab fāt̤imah kā dūdh lahū ho ke bahegā

The one who provides aid to humans, angels, and jinns is Shabbīr.
The one with authority over heavenly decrees is Shabbīr.
But at the slaying-ground, the one without friend or aid is Shabbīr.
The captive surrounded by nine hundred thousand troops is Shabbīr.
His force is such that it exerts power over both worlds [heaven and earth].
But his patience is that patience which is based on [the] acceptance [of God's will].

When the whole garden of the prophet of the two worlds was slain,
the king said, now is the end of the "people of the cloak."
[We are] being without help or aid, [but] Thanks be to God,
now [my] dry throat is yearning for the sword of cruelty.
I am happy that [my throat] will bear the violence of the sharp sword:
now, Fatimah's milk, being [my] blood, will flow.

When the *marṣiyah*s were finished, all those in attendance arose as one to chant *nauḥah*s. The men used their open hands to strike their pectorals metrically with the tune. Their animated forearms created an illusion of dancing stick-figures as they pounded obliquely, right and left, across the men's torsos. The evening concluded with the men sharing *tabarruk* (blessed food). If the splendid renditions of the *soz k̲h̲wān*s and *marṣiyah k̲h̲wān*s, and the energetic participatory singing of *nauḥah*s, had not been sufficient incentives for attending, this excellent, if simple, roti bread and goat stew would have been enough to attract even the least committed among the crowd. Delicious though the food was, Ali's stomach began to ache a few hours later. This discomfort grew intolerable over the course of the night. It was only slightly mitigated, early in the morning, by his odoriferous purging of the semi-digested remains. In all, Ali lost three days lying listlessly in Ajmal's home. He could barely choke down crumbly slices of processed white bread and tea without milk.

The seventh of Muharram is traditionally associated with rituals commemorating the wedding of Qasim. Since special music was often central to these rituals, Ajmal urged his friend out of the house to witness the proceedings. Their destination, the Sangaṛ Veṛah neighborhood in the Delhi Gate police district, lay directly on the opposite side of the old city from Shah Gardez. A man named Ghulam Shabbir had, for many years, been leading a famous *sej* and *mehndī* procession which departed from the Muftiyān Masjid. Ali and Ajmal waited at that mosque for the procession to begin. *Anjuman*s (clubs) of *nauḥah* reciters began to gather, some of them singing familiar *nauḥah*s in Saraiki and Urdu, others preparing their own new ones. A group leader held up a handwritten text for one less-well-known *nauḥah* and, during brief pauses, prompted members of his group with each new couplet. As a Sunni with Shī'ī relatives himself, Ajmal pointed out with some pride that the sponsor of this *sej* and *mehndī* procession was a Sunni. Shī'ahs and Sunnis were co-participating. Ali had the strength to attend for about an hour. Having not yet heard drumming, and realizing he was not sufficiently recuperated, he returned for the night.

Two nights later Ali felt just well enough to go out. It was the eve of Ashura; the next day would be the Tenth of Muharram, the climax in remembrance of Husain's martyrdom. Irritated with himself for giving in to weariness on the seventh, Ali was now itching to get out of the stuffy confines of his sickroom. He made his first destination Bheḍi Potra. Ajmal was to join him later in the night. Retracing his steps to Bheḍi Potra on his own made Ali feel stronger and more independent. The scene this night was quite different from the one that met him when he first arrived in town through Haram Gate. Many shop owners had now lowered their corrugated metal sliding doors partway over their storefronts, if not locking them down and vacating the area entirely. As a major intersection for Shī'ī foot traffic and a gathering point for *ta'ziyah*s and *mātamdār*s, Haram Gate *chauk* was a potential target for communal antagonists. Local Shī'ī and Sunni communities had otherwise lived in relative harmony in recent history.

The Iranian revolution five years earlier, and the rise to power of Zia-ul-Haq, Pakistan's president, were contributing to the violence that was just beginning to be fomented in Pakistan. Zia was using his affiliation with the Deobandi movement in Pakistan to further a sectarian agenda of Islamization. This marginalized Shī'ahs, Ahmedis, and other Muslims who did not conform to their unyielding, scriptural form of Sunni Islam, which was largely informed by developments in Saudi Arabia. Shī'ahs, stoked by recent successes in Iran and provoked by state-supported oppression in Pakistan, formed the Tehrik-e-Nafaz-e-Fiqah-e-Jafaria to agitate for their rights. Ali had been warned to be cautious as he moved through the city. The commercial shutdown around Haram Gate was a stark reminder that sectarian outbreaks were on the rise in central Panjab.

Quickly walking clear of the gate area, Ali found his way to the *imambarah* of Bheḍi Potra. What he presumed was the famed Haji Wala *ta'ziyah* stood nearby, painted with license number one. Men and women, clothed largely in solid black or white, bumped against one another within the compound wall. Its whitewash, while matching the clothing, still bore greenish traces of last year's paint job. The details of the *ta'ziyah* were obscured, at first, by the glare of two sets of two fluorescent tube lights, aligned like a gable on the upper part of the *ta'ziyah*'s face, and by glowing green and red lights along the top and in the center. Strings of white flowers dangled in a thick curtain in front of the *ta'ziyah*, as if the structure were a bride whose face had not yet been revealed to her soon-to-be husband.

Outside the compound wall, two musicians reiterated a simple version of *mārū* as men, women, and children filed into the courtyard. The mustached *shahnā'ī* player, about Ali's height of 1.6 meters, was bejeweled modestly with an earring dangling from each lobe and a gold band encircling his right-hand ring finger. A small red-and-white garland strung around his neck indicated that he was a *baddhā*—one "bound" to some saintly religious figure. A ragged, bleached canvas bag with accessories for his instrument hung loosely from his right shoulder and sometimes slipped down toward his elbow. The *ḍhol* player, wearing a dull expression on his face, stood to his left. A head taller, he sported closely cropped white hair and a beard. Ali gazed at them from a distance of about three meters.

Amid the din of scuttling passersby and the steady throb of *mārū,* Ali struck up a conversation with a man of dignified bearing whose fringe of nearly white hair neatly framed his balding head. After overhearing Ali inquire about the processional route of this *ta'ziyah*, the man introduced himself as Bashir Husain Mazhar, retired school principal. Mazhar had noticed from Ali's manner of speaking Urdu and gathered from his clothing style that he was a *ġair-mulkī.** Ali, who had learned much by feigning ignorance, introduced himself with some reserve. Self-appointed authorities were valuable in that they never needed an excuse to talk.

Mazhar began speaking crisply in English. "This procession is in honor of Sayyadna Imam Husain, the son of Sayyadna Ali ibn-e Abu Talib, Peace Be Upon Him, the Caliph of Islam from the Arab days. He was the grandson of Sayyadna Muhammad, Peace Be Upon Him. He was martyred in Karbala by Yazid, son of Amir Mu'āwiya. Yazid led the opposition. He was deadly against the Islamic procession and Islamic thinking and Islam in general. He went to Karbala to jeopardize this situation but Sayyadna Husain was there to confront him, to face him, to cut his thinking and thoughts. . . . And seventy-two people were killed there, including the son of Husain, six years, six months of age, plus two years of age, plus three years of age, plus four and onward to seventy-two years." Assigning each of the seventy-two participants successive ages was a novel embellishment.

"In the years following, the people harbored great anger against Yazid. Riding on this wave of emotion, a man named Mukhtar Saqfi rose to power in Kufa and took revenge on all the people who killed Husain and his party at Karbala. The *'azādārī* we perform here expresses the anger we felt back then. It began here in the Mughal period. Queen Nur Jahan was the favorite wife of Emperor Jahangir [1569–1627]. He was a Sunni. He did not believe in these processions and all. But Queen Nur Jahan was a Shī'ah. She came from Iran. Because of her only there were *julūs*es (processions) brought out onto the roads, or through the fields, or in the *imambarah*s."

In spite of himself, Ali interrupted the history lesson. "*Acchā jī*, about the procession, when is this one expected to start? It looks like the *ḍhol*

*Outsider, someone from another country.

and *shahnā'ī* players are waiting for the men to carry the *ta'ziyah* out of the compound."

Mazhar took little notice. "The drums are playing to show the sorrowness; one drum's beatings are for happiness and also the drum's beatings are to show the sorrowness. It is our Arab culture to show the drums in our sorrowness. They used to play the drums in death processions in Arab culture, so, in memory of those processions, we play now. The drums will accompany the whole procession, whether the people are running with the *ta'ziyah*, walking, or just standing."

In mentioning both "sorrowness" and "happiness" Ali wondered if Mazhar was commenting on the musical alternation between the limping, seven-pulse section and the vigorous marchlike section of small *mārū*. Right now they were not playing the slow-tempoed grand *mārū*. Ali himself envisioned the limping section as evoking woundedness and death. As he tried to clarify this point without suggesting it directly, another man, a bit younger and less well-spoken, interrupted. (He spoke in Saraiki but had understood Mazar's English.)

"They say 'beats' for the *ḍhol*; what this really means is the *āvāz* of the *naqqārah*, the voice of the kettle-drum on the battlefield," said the younger man.

Mazhar, speaking in Urdu for Ali's benefit, countered: "What I am saying is correct. The *ḍhol* and other instruments were played on the occasion of someone's death in Arab society. Our practice is mainly that, the Arab system. The *naqqārah* is played on the battlefield, that is different."

"It is the same 'custom,'" said the other. "The *naqqārah* is played at the start of war to call people to gather, to fight."

"The *naqqārah* is different from the *ḍhol*. *Ḍhol* and other instruments were part of the Arab 'traditional practice,' for both a death and for happy occasions. It is for this that there is 'remembrance' for that Arab custom," explained Mazhar. "And the *naqqārah* was beaten on the battlefield, so the drums are also beaten in memory of that fight."

Mazhar was reluctantly incorporating the other man's interpretation into his explanation, and Ali wondered why he was so resistant. "Why were you stressing the difference between the *ḍhol* and the *naqqārah* practices?"

"The drumming on the battlefield was merely functional, to alert the forces; anybody could beat those drums," opined Mazhar. "Our ceremonial drumming falls under the category of 'music.' Only those who know music, those who understand the melodies, can beat the drums. The drums need to be beaten according to the rhythm of the melody."

"Who are these people?" inquired Ali.

"There is a Bheḍi Potra family. Someone named Bheḍi was a very fluent instrument player of music. All of these people were musicians; that is, they were well-known musicians in the history of music. But these families were destroyed and other families joined. The old professions were being let down and new professions were adopted. Now new professionals are playing here. These musicians playing now do not belong to the Bheḍi Potra family. . . . Now there is only one family, the family of love."

Just then the *shahnā'ī player* and the *ḍhol* player, directed by the local "in-charge," began walking through the streets of the neighborhood, a train of the faithful following their lead. A man with closely shorn, hennaed hair, clad in white cotton, performed *mātam* gently with his left hand while leading a snorting *zuljinah* with his right. *Zuljinah* was the white stallion the beloved Prophet himself purchased for his young grandson. Later Husain's sturdy mount famously returned to the women's camp at Karbala without its rider, having vanquished more than a score of enemy soldiers. The *zuljinah* in this procession was the *ta'ziyah*'s tragic mate, festooned with netted strings of white flower buds. Green tassels swung on each side of its head, and a white plume, like that of a drum major, jerked aloft, right and left, as the horse stepped. Gold-bordered cloths of green, red, and yellow striped its muscled equine neck. A profusion of tinsel enhanced the whole glittering effect. The *zuljinah*'s saddle, which resembled nothing less than a royal litter, could not but evoke the absence of its rider. The open umbrella propped over the saddle blocked no rain or sun right now; rather, this regal accoutrement was a moral shield for Husain's *rūḥ*, or soul.

As the musicians walked, the *shahnā'ī* player began to vary the tune. Ali had been trying to orient his ears to the *rāg*. Its five main tones reminded him of *malkauns* or *dhani,* but he couldn't be sure if it was one or the other, or something else still; it all depended on where he heard the tonal center. In the absence of a drone, which he still needed as a crutch, he found the melody ambiguous. The *shahnā'ī* player would sometimes stick closely to the range of the original melody—the *asthāyī* in the lower range and the *antara* in the upper range—and return to the cadential phrase of the *asthāyī*. The drummer used these moments of return to shift from metric patterns of seven to eight and back again. At other times, the mustached piper would climb, with a series of rapid declamatory articulations on his instrument, high into the upper range and hold a tone over several drum cycles. Then down he would come, cascading, like an acrobat who had scurried up a rope ladder and somersaulted through the darkness onto a soft, stretchy net.

The procession reached another compound and the musicians ceased to play as a group of men, women, and children gathered close to the *zuljinah*.

A wiry, clean-shaven man with thick black hair and heavy ebony spectacles held his arms outstretched and hands turned up as he addressed his *du'ā* in the direction of the *zuljinah:* "Mere maula, hazrat Sajjād [Zain-ul Abidin]* di wasta . . ." (For the sake of Imam Husain, for the sake of Muhammad and his descendents, my God, give health to the ill ones; my Lord, give children to the childless. My Lord, this is our prayer; we beseech you, we pray. Bless our business, may our children live long, my Lord. May every person be successful. Save every person from hardship.)

Mazhar, who had accompanied Ali through the crowd, identified the prayer leader as a prominent neighborhood *ẕākir*. In his Saraiki-language sermons, Mazhar said, the *ẕākir* would intersperse his spoken orations with a form of poetic, melodic chanting called *doṛhā*. Judging from the hectoring style of Urdu-speaking *ẕākir*s from Lucknow whom Mazhar had heard, he thought Ali would find this sinuous interweaving of speech and song captivating. Now the *ẕākir* was delivering words without a melody as such, but in regularly timed bursts of verbiage. He would initiate each phrase in a high register with the words "My Lord" and gradually descend to the end of each verbal phrase. The bursts of prayer were answered by sobs and sighs from the crowd. A man to the *ẕākir*'s left tapped him on the shoulder and exclaimed a reminder: "Mohsin, pray for Mohsin." The *ẕākir* incorporated a reference to Husain's daughter, who was too sick to leave Medina when her father departed for Karbala. "Our brother is sick. For the sake of the illness of Hazrat Sughra, please heal him."

The prayers went on. A particularly distraught woman was among several outfitted completely in black. Her *cādar,* wrapped over her head snuggly in two strips, restrained her wavy pepper-and-salt locks as she leaned her head back to lament. Ali could not hear what she was saying but could only see her stark visage. She wore no jewelry save for a finely wrought silver nose stud, and no make-up—her eyelids were darkened by the shadows of her weeping brow. The woman's expressions reminded him of his maternal grandmother. Gross movements of her lower jaw and tongue emitted words that must have expressed grief. Subtle movements, however, carried the colors of her affect: the round of her chin rose up, causing the corners of her lips to stretch down, creating neither a grimace nor a smile, but something of both. Three folds of skin yielded to the force of this expression, directed downward and back toward the base of her jaw. High cheekbones kept her clear, aging skin taut around her cheeks. Tears dripped smoothly to the silk of her neck.

---

*Sajjād, Husain's son, survived the Karbala battle because he was too ill to participate.

The prayers ended with "My Lord, for Muhammad's sake, fulfill the wishes of those who are in need." Several people uttered *amen* as the drums resumed *mārū* and the *shahnā'ī* joined in. Ali caught the glimpse of an eye guiltily looking his way from beneath a purple and white headscarf; only later did he realize it was the young woman from the verandah opposite the tea stall. Someone behind Ali said, "Bas . . . āp k̲h̲ud hī k̲h̲aṛe hain̲ . . ."—"That's enough, you're the only one standing there, [get moving]."

By the time Ali and Mazhar returned to the Bheḍi Potra Imambarah, the musicians, the horse, and most of the crowd had already entered the compound. Ajmal, who was standing by the entrance, joined Ali. He and Mazhar established their mutual relationship genealogically, Ajmal through his wife, Mazhar through his sister's son. Ali returned his attention to the musicians, who had resumed the melody whose *rāg* he had been trying to figure out earlier. The *shahnā'ī* then dropped out, leaving only the sound of the drum. Arms were moving in time with the drums somewhere near the *zuljinah,* and as Ali stepped closer, he saw that women were performing *mātam*—something he rarely saw in public among women in Uttar Pradesh. Most were using their right palms to strike gently over their left breasts, but one woman leaned her head back and struck her forehead energetically with both hands. Noticing first the gold-colored stack of glass bangles reaching halfway up her forearms, rising and falling to the beat, he then recognized her face: it was the woman whose crying reminded him of his grandmother. He could hardly reconcile the earlier moment of intimacy with this public display, which would have been unseemly in his own family.

In this fresh auditory space, no longer overpowered by the *shahnā'ī*, Ali could hear women singing *nauḥah*s. Alongside the woman of note were several other female *nauḥah* reciters, each performing *mātam* in her own way and directly facing the dull-countenanced *ḍholī*. The words, even if they had been in Urdu, would have been hard to make out from Ali's vantage point. The *nauḥah* tune, however, could be heard clearly amid the general clamor and was unlike what the *shahnā'ī* had been extemporizing upon. As if suddenly acknowledging the women's existence, the *shahnā'ī* player picked up the *antara* section of the *nauḥah* tune and improvised a melodic flourish around it. The gold-bangled woman's chanting and arm movements grew more insistent as the instrumental and vocal parties performed in still tighter synchrony.

Now there was a lull. The instrumentalists executed a few technical adjustments. A channel of communication opened up between these women and another small cluster standing on the far side of the *zuljinah*. Those near

Women singing *nauḥah* and processing with *shahnā'ī* and *ḍhol* players in Multan, 8 Muharram (approximately), May 16, 1997. Photo by the author.

the *zuljinah* were now singing a different *nauḥah*. The women motioned to one another, and then to the musicians. Once again, the tune changed. Ali was later to describe this scene to musicians of the hereditary Bheḍi Potra family. They were to deny that women had any such role in determining the melodic choices. At most, they would say, they would ask the *shahnā'ī* player to adjust his pitch to their vocal range. But this *shahnā'ī* player wasn't necessarily one of them, and he most certainly responded to the women's requests. Families of love do not always agree, Ali later noted to himself wryly.

Once again the courtyard began to empty: first the largely male-occupied space between the musicians and the entrance to the courtyard, then the area where most of the women had congregated—between the musicians and the *imambarah* and around the foppish stallion. As they were pushed back and out of the precinct Ajmal said, "Look, now they are lifting the *ta'ziyah*."

Someone had unplugged and removed the tube lights; about twenty men, grimacing and rubicund, struggled to hoist the *ta'ziyah* off its stand. Others had the less strenuous job of clearing the path. One man used a long, forked pole to lift the overhead power and telephone cables. Without the glare, the strings of flowers receded in visual prominence; the glow of the moon competed with small bulbs in the neighborhood to reflect the gold-painted details. The music stopped as some men processed, carrying the *ta'ziyah*. Mazhar said it would take about three hours to cover the short distance to Haram Gate. Other *ta'ziyah*s would meet there, including those of Pir Inayat Valayat and Darbar Pir Sahab, and all the *ta'ziyah*s would be lined up according to rank. The municipality followed the colonial licensing system, whereby the structures, and their associated procession routes, were ranked chronologically; those believed to be older held lower numbers.

In the vicinity of the Haji Wala *ta'ziyah* was an *anjuman* of young, bare-chested men chanting *nauḥah*s and performing *mātam*. The *asthāyī* of this Panjabi *nauḥah* referred to Husain's son Ali Akbar:

baun maut jahān ic thīndeh naiṉ	Many deaths occur in the world
par maut akbar dā bhulidā naiṉ	But Akbar's death is unforgettable.

Many of the youths at the center of attention were the age of Ali Akbar when he was slain. Lifting their hands high into the air, they drove them down, right then left, with considerable force. Thud, smack, thud, smack: baun **mau**t ja**hā**n ic **thīn**deh **naiṉ**. The chests of the men surrounding the *anjuman*, clothed in black, white, and cream *qamīz*es, were far less resonant, but their hearts were morally, if not rhythmically, in synch with the athletic boys as they chanted the words together. Some strained to reach the *antara* melody with the words

jīvaiṉ shādī tha'ī 'alī akbar dī	The way Ali Akbar's wedding occurred
jivaiṉ mehndī rasm nahīṉ kītī	The way the henna ritual didn't take place.

These lines reminded Ali of Ziyad's comments on the *sej* in Multan—with its focus on Ali Akbar rather than Qasim. Ali tried to understand the lines. Mazhar translated them literally, and lapsed into uncharacteristic silence. Ali was left to draw his own conclusions. The second line was self-explanatory: there was no henna ceremony for Ali Akbar's wedding; the mehndi ritual at Karbala was for Qasim and Fatimah Kubra. But what did they mean with regard to Ali Akbar's wedding? Ali took the wedding as metaphorical or mystical. Maybe, as in the *'urs*es of the Sufis, Ali Akbar's death also betokened a wedding of his spirit to God. Ali continued to listen as the *asthāyī* lines recurred; Mazhar could only make out the first line of the next *antara,* "saḍā 'ain javānī vic bacṛā" (our child, in the prime of youth), but Ali had a good idea of what would come next.

What Ali did not expect at the next moment was for Mazhar to collapse. A few minutes earlier Mazhar had been expostulating in his habitual manner. Now he was on the ground clutching his midsection. Several men made hapless attempts to assist him. Two figures emerged from the crowd identifying themselves as *rishtadār*—relatives. One was Salim, Mazhar's nephew, and the other Sufiya, his sister's granddaughter. The young woman looked uncomfortable and out of place in this sea of male bodies. Salim explained to no one in particular, "My uncle has not been keeping at all well. He should not have come out." It sounded as if Mazhar, like Ali, was suffering from the after-effects of food poisoning. Then, to Ali, Salim said, "Uncle distances himself from religious expressions on the street." Ali thought it was probably a matter of class. "But he is pious and emotional in his own way. He feels that even the act of observing *'azādārī* will earn him merit. We tell him it is not worth it. Sick people need not fast during Ramzan; neither should they risk their health during Muharram."

Ajmal and Ali helped Salim and Sufiya walk Mazhar to his home in Bheḍi Potra, and Mazhar's wife whisked him off to rest. Salim, the nephew Mazhar had mentioned, was the one distantly related to Huma, Ajmal's wife. Because these relations did not know Ajmal well, the two guests were invited to the front (public) room of Mazhar's flat, and Sufiya retired to the interior. Salim procured tea and salt biscuits. The purdah lines were ambiguous here, since the families were bound by a complex web of affinal and blood relations. Moreover, such restrictions were perfunctory in this household, kept up mainly for the sake of appearances locally. The family traveled internationally and, when subjected to the Western eye, did their best to hide public symbols of Islam that might be construed as anti-modern.

Sufiya, for her part, had felt comfortable neither in the male arena from which they had emerged nor among the female coterie of *nauḥah* reciters. A student of English literature at Cambridge, she had completed her A-levels at Sadiq Public School—an elite prep school in Bahawalpur, about one hundred kilometers east of Multan. Family pressure alone had not brought Sufiya to her parents' home in Lahore for the Muharram season. She had also returned to Pakistan out of a deep sense of personal attachment to the Panjatan Pāk. In England, she occupied an international but nevertheless Anglocentric literary world, a milieu of well-traveled rationalists who had little truck with the practices of organized religion; to them these customs were mere curiosities, museum pieces. Sufiya hid her own sentiments. She felt lonely among these people. Their intellects, she believed, had overwhelmed their capacity to feel the spark of a world more subtle than they knew.

Now, visiting her aging grandparents, she wished to quench her spiritual privation, satisfy the yearning of her senses. The richly colored *shabīh*s, the fragrance of freshly strewn rose petals, the soft consonants and vowel contours of Saraiki all drew her to Multan. She also hoped to find her friends from school, whom she hadn't seen in two years. When she had looked up from her suffering grand-uncle to see the face of Ali up close she had been disarmed. Ali had caught sight of this purple-scarved woman before, and she him. For a few minutes, she had spoken more freely with him than she should have. Ali had tried not to show he noticed or to reveal any sign that his own pulse was quickening, too. Now that Sufiya was in the private section of the house tending her grand-uncle—asking him if he had taken his heart medications, helping him sip some juice—she tried to banish thoughts of this striking man from her mind.

Sufiya's older cousin Salim was an engineer. Dividing his time between Islamabad, Lahore, and Multan, he earned much of his annual income performing short-term contract work for multinational companies. As his guests sipped and crunched their welcome refreshments, Salim listened attentively to Ali's personal history. More than many, Salim seemed to empathize with Ali's preoccupation with the *tāshā,* in part because of his own musical obsessions. "I enjoy almost all styles of music, and particularly *qawwālī*. Anyone will tell you I am completely *pāgal, yār* [nuts, friend]! I endure miserable, crowded late-night bus rides to hear topmost *qawwāl*s perform at *'urs*es." He shared a spiritually aware disposition with his cousin Sufiya. Something about the atmosphere of the *'urs* gave the music a charge that could not be felt anywhere else.

"As a matter of fact, I returned now only from the *'urs* of Baba Farid in Pakpattan." About two hundred kilometers away, this *'urs* always coincides with Muharram. So while the drums are silent in Lahore, street musicians and *qawwāl*s from all over Pakistan are singing and playing their instruments for this Chishti saint. The mention of Baba Farid, the spiritual guide of Nizamuddin Auliya, struck a sympathetic chord in Ali. "I heard a tremendous performance by Mīāndād Badar, Nusrat Fateh Ali Khan's cousin," related Salim. "He's becoming quite a sensation."

"I am a great admirer of Nusrat," said Ali. "The *qawwāl*s of Delhi and Lucknow perform with real fervor, but nothing matches the kick of these Panjabi singers. Even the tabla, with that wheat paste they add to the head, seems to belt out the message."

"You should come to Lahore, where my mother lives, next month. The *'urs* for Data Sahab is not to be missed," suggested Salim. "You'll also find some great *ḍholī*s there."

"I have to return to my duties in a few days, unfortunately, but I plan to return for the Madho Lal Husain *'urs* in March," explained Ali.

"You won't find *qawwālī* there, but you'll surely see some of the best *ḍhol* players and *dhamālī*s. My cousin and I will be in Lahore then. Maybe we'll join you. Please give me a ring when you come to town." The men exchanged contact information, relieving Ali of the awkwardness of asking.

Before Ajmal and Ali departed, Salim suggested they visit the Lodhipura neighborhood, the so-called *bāzār-e-ḥusn*—the "bazaar of beauty." The families of the reputed courtesans living there were the custodians of a rich and varied repertoire of classical music. The Abdullah Wala *ta'ziyah* of Lodhipura ranked number two, after the Haji Wala. Some vestige of the neighborhood's grand musical history could still be glimpsed in their *'azādārī* practices. Lodhipura was only a few furlongs away; Salim recommended they take the main roads to Pak Gate, the next gate southeast from Haram Gate, and seek further directions from there—the direct route would have lost Ajmal in unfamiliar back lanes.

As Ajmal and Ali found their way into the infamous *muḥalla*, they were detained by a group of neighborhood youths who had noticed Ali's foreignness and were suspicious. After a brief interview, they agreed to let the two pass. Men from northern Panjabi and Muhājir backgrounds had swelled in population in recent years; their rapacious eyes disconcerted the self-respecting women of Lodhipura. The women's once-bourgeoning ranks had, as a result, begun to dwindle in the *nauḥah* gatherings on the neighborhood lanes. But from Ali's perspective, the neighborhood participation was considerable.

The lane opened into a modest square nestled within the *muḥalla*. The center of attention was a small *ziyārat* set inside an open wooden shed. The doors of the enclosure were propped open. All the wooden surfaces were freshly painted dark green and decorated with framed images and garlands like an *imambarah*. The fluorescent tube running along the top of the shed illuminated not only its contents but also the faces of about thirty girls and women standing directly in front, as well as dozens of men encircling them. The relatively small number of women Ali had seen earlier were for the most part over fifty and darkly clad. This neighborhood gathering, by contrast, included a slender, college-aged girl wearing a pink *qamīz* with a black *dupaṭṭa* around her shoulders and a moon-faced young woman who stood to her right, outfitted in lime green, with a matching scarf that kept slipping off her head. Several women wore stylish floral-patterned *shalwār qamīz*es, one purple, one brown. A few wore spectacles. These seemed to be educated, middle-class women.

As Ali and Ajmal arrived and found a place to stand on a nearby verandah, the women launched into an Urdu *nauḥah* recounting the attempted disgrace of Husain's sister Zainab (Media Example 5.3). After the soldiers returned from Karbala, celebratory music welcomed the victors. Yazid ordered his men to impale the severed heads of Husain and the other slain men atop spears and march them through the city of Damascus. The women, trailing behind, were forced to walk through the bazaars without their hijabs. Ali wondered whether the women "of the bazaar" in this neighborhood identified with Zainab's response to this forced exposure.

The second couplet in this poem focused on Husain's daughter, Fatimah Kubra, who was left without anywhere to go. She had lost her new husband Qasim as well as her brother Ali Akbar.

ey ġairat-e maryam terā bāzār meṉ jānā
na bhūl sakegā tujhe tā ḥashr zamānah
ey ġairat-e maryam terā bāzār meṉ jānā

mar jā'eṉ jo shauhar to panāh dete haiṉ bhā'ī
kubrá kahāṉ jā'e nah rahā ko'ī ṭhikānā

Oh, honor of Maryam [Zainab], your journey through the bazaar
The world will not be able to forget you until the final day.
Oh, honor of Maryam, your journey through the bazaar.

If [one's] husband dies, then [one's] brother gives protection.
[But] where may Kubra go? No refuge remains.

As Ali stood listening, Ajmal chatted up a college student named Nasir, the grand nephew of the famed *ḍhol* player Allah Wasayah. Although the men in Nasir's generation had given up the family music profession in favor of more lucrative pursuits, Nasir knew the local music scene very well. Ali learned that this was one of an increasing number of *nauḥah*s sung in Urdu. The tune is a popular one for *nauḥah*s in Lahore and Multan, so it was a simple matter to fit the text composed by the poet Ali Akhtar to this tune. Nasir pointed out a sturdily built, clean-shaven man in his thirties standing to the right of the woman dressed in lime green, poking his head in closer than the other men nearby. "That is Shaukat. He holds all the *nauḥah* notebooks and feeds lines to the lead singers. His sister is standing to his right, wearing the tortoise shell glasses and dark brown clothes. Although they are Muhājirs their family has been here so long it is as if they are now Multanis."

The women began to sing a different *nauḥah*, this one in Saraiki. Nasir called it a *marṡiyah*, even though it was not in the poetic form of five or six lines associated with the *marṣiyah*s Ali knew in Urdu. "This *marṣiyah* was composed by Ghulam Rasul Hasrat. He lived in this neighborhood and resided in the household of Suraiya Multanikar for a period. He is one of our greatest poets—he composed *kāfī*s, *doṛhā* love-songs, *ġazal*s, *marṣiyah*s, all these. If he had been from Lahore or one of the bigger cities he probably would have been famous throughout India and Pakistan." Ali made a mental note: the Muharram repertoire in this neighborhood is deeply entwined with all the genres of song in Saraiki.

"How do these women learn the songs?" Ali asked.

"In my house they begin with the poetry. My mother meets with a group of women before Muharram and they craft the tune together. They might also re-use a melody from a previous year, or base their melody on a tune heard on cassette."

As the *nauḥah*s and *mātam* abated, many of the men and women vacated the square. Nasir suggested the visitors wait for the *sej* procession, which would be arriving soon. In the clearing to the right of the green shed, a few youths were laying burlap on the ground and covering it with thick bleached cloth. Two men settled their voluminous *naqqārah*s into cloth-covered rings on the ground and began testing their sounds. Piling recycled newspaper remnants, school notebook pages, and rotting lumber from a dilapidated kiosk against a deteriorating brick wall across the lane from the *naqqārah* players, someone built a small fire. The dry, hot air of the day had left the *bam* head taut and resounding well when struck. One musician pressed the heel of his hand into this large bass drum to warm and stretch it out, alternately striking and pressing. Finding the voice of the *zīl*—the treble drum of the *naqqārah* pair—a bit dull, the junior player carried it to the fire and carefully turned the head toward the flame.

Mārū reverberated from a distance, at first only the pumping of the bass, and then gradually a rich blend of timbral registers—more substantial than Ali had heard in Bheḍi Potra. The wailing of two *shahnā'ī*s pierced through the thicket of drum strokes and trickled through the narrow lanes now as the procession approached. Several women and men seen here earlier were now returning via the alley on the right, closely followed by a slightly stooping *shahnā'ī* player with long, gray hair and a beard, and his younger playing partner. Next came a pair of *ḍhol* players and, to Ali's surprise, two elderly but nimble *tāshā* players. By this time, the two *naqqārci*s were playing their version of *mārū* as well, creating together such a magnificent volume that it was impossible for Ali to communicate with Nasir without reading his lips.

The music stopped for a few minutes as about a dozen young men positioned the gilded *sej* to the left of the shed, while others shouted directions and cleared obstructions. The *tāshā* players took that moment to tauten their drum head by the glowing embers of the smoldering rubbish. Ali asked Nasir who the *tāshā* players were. Nasir said, "These men belong to families of Lodhipura. They did not play last year and I'm surprised to see them now. They are probably the last *tāshā* players left in Multan."

Ali took this moment to ask Nasir in whose honor the *sej* was supposed to be. Nasir merely reported the standard interpretation: this *sej* represented the nuptial bed of Qasim.

Three women then began to sing a "mārū wala nauḥah"—a *nauḥah* for *mārū*, set, according to Nasir, in the classical *rāg, raṇa*. This *nauḥah*, more than any of the others Ali had heard, resembled classical *k̲h̲ayāl* performance in slow tempo. Nasir said, "The drummers are playing a fourteen-*mātra* pattern we call a *ṭhekā* in Saraiki; it is part of *mārū*. Only the best of our musicians know how to make the melody and the drumming patterns fit together. See the *ḍholī* on the left? That's Mehr; he's one of Multan's musical treasures. His family is responsible for passing the art down orally, *sinah-ba-sinah*, from generation to generation; it's a shame that none of his sons are learning now. Mehr has the rare ability to lay down the appropriate *ṭhekā* immediately upon hearing one of these slow *nauḥah*s. The other drummers follow his strong lead. The singers are able to draw out their syllables against this framework, returning to the metric cycle at each return of the *sam*. The *nauḥah* does not necessarily dictate one particular drum pattern in and of itself. Here Mehr is helping the singers fit the melody to a fourteen-*mātra* pattern. In a concert, this *cīz* [composition] is often sung to sixteen-beat *tīntāl*. It all depends on how the singers stretch or compress their melodies."

Ali heard the pattern of beats, 3 + 4 // 3 + 4, articulated sparsely on the three kinds of drums as the women wove their melody fluidly, yet in near-perfect unison, around the structural drum strokes. A few women standing nearby tried unsuccessfully to keep *mātam* during this part of the performance. The *sam* did not arrive until the syllable *vāg* at the end of the first line. The three singers brought their right hands to their collarbones as all of the drummers joined together to mark the *sam*. The momentum of the women's sturdy arms, combined with the pressure of their voices, created a blunt thud accompanied by a small voicing of the displaced air—like the staccato punching of a car horn.

Ali could only understand a few words of the text—*shah* and *grave*. Nasir filled in the rest of the text and translated it into Urdu for Ali.

asthāyī
hay vay maiṉ muṭhi hai pora
kahīn na valā'ī shāh dī vāg

I am devastated!
There was no one to grasp the Shah's reins.

antara
mo gānī badhṇā hay mār ghateo ne hai
qabar nimāṇi de nāl

Oh! [they have] killed the bridegroom
Near the graveyard of tyranny.

The voice was that of Qasim's mother, Umm-e Farwa. The presence of the stylized nuptial bed made this *nauḥah* particularly fitting. Standing to Ali's left, an older man with dark rings under his eyes shook visibly as he sobbed. As one of the *tāl* cycles neared completion, the maroon-clad lead singer doubled the speed of the line "There was no one to grasp the reins," bringing the melody to a powerful articulation of the *sam.* Several other women joined in and sang the *nauḥah* in "double *lay*," this time anchoring their melismas on and around *mātam* strokes (which are indicated by boldface syllables and asterisks): "**hay** vay maiṉ **muṭhi hai** po**ra**; **kahī**n na va**lā**'ī **shāh** dī **vāg**; **mo** gānī **badhe** * ṇā * hay **mā**re gha**teo** ne * **hai; qa**bare ni**mā** * ṇi de **nāl.**" Even at this accelerated tempo, the piece was more subtle and intricate than the forceful *nauḥah*s the men had been singing while performing *mātam* earlier.

The lead singer began another. Nasir commented, "This is also an old Saraiki *nauḥah.* It is in *malkauns* *rāg* and *dīpchandī tāl*—a fourteen-beat *ṭhekā.*" Its text was close enough to Urdu for Ali to gain a general understanding.

asthāyī
hur shāh di ḵẖāṭir kahāṉ gayā
hur shāh di ḵẖāṭir kahāṉ gayā

Hurr, where did you go for the sake of the Shah [Husain]?
Hurr, where did you go for the sake of the Shah [Husain]?

antara
mangaṇ saḵẖiyāṉ tun dān gayā
chaṛh murshad di dīd dhyān gayā

Begging, you went for forgiveness from the magnanimous one [Husain].
Rising high in the Master's [Husain's] sight, you came into [moral] consciousness.

asthāyī
hā naukar baṇ sultān gayā
hā naukar baṇ sultān gayā

Having been a servant, you became a sultan.
Having been a servant, you became a sultan.

Hurr was the Umayyad general known for experiencing a change of heart as preparations were under way for the siege of Karbala. He sought out Imam Husain and begged his forgiveness. By the time the battle began, Hurr had chosen to fight on the side of Husain and was one of the first to be slain by Yazid's forces. The last line expressed Hurr's transformation metaphorically: he rose from being one under Umayyad control to one who, like a king, could control his own fate. He lived up to the meaning of his name in Arabic, "free."

Ali, Ajmal, and Nasir continued to listen to and discuss the music of Lodhipura until about 2 A.M. Then they began to stroll further around other nearby neighborhoods, relishing select *nauḥah*s and catching short snippets of Urdu and Saraiki *majlis*es. At Haram Gate, *ta'ziyah*s from each of the neighborhoods and guilds stood in a line. In the ritual of calling out the names of each, one man shouted: "Here is the *ziyārat* of the potters" (shouts and cheers); "of the ironworkers . . . the Durbar *ta'ziyah* from the shrine of Musa Pak. . . ." Each float had arrived according to its prescribed route and was lined up according to license number. Nasir explained, "After performing *mātam* and chanting *nauḥah*s, the constituencies will carry their *ziyārat*s to their respective *asthānā*s [home stations]."

Nasir led them to the home of his grand-uncle, Allah Wasayah, the aged *ḍhol* player. Although Wasayah was ailing and unable to play this year, he agreed to sit with the men and discuss times past. Sipping from a cup of *kāva*, green tea with cardamom, Wasayah recalled, "A man named Wali Muhammad [b. 1860?] came to Multan from Iran in the late nineteenth century. At that time the *ta'ziyeh* theater [Shī'ī passion play] was flourishing under the patronage of the Qajar dynasty. Wali Muhammad brought his knowledge of literature, music, set design, costumes, and everything to Multan. He was a brilliant musician. We all called him Master. In those days we also had theater in Multan, our own version of *ta'ziyeh*. All of that began to deteriorate after Master Sahab died, about thirty-five years ago; but we still perform the *nauḥah*s he composed.

"Wali Muhammad wrote a special *nauḥah* for each of the first eleven days of Muharram. You know, just like some neighborhoods launch their *'alam* processions on the fifth of Muharram in honor of Husain's half-brother Abbas, and on the sixth they carry the *ziyārat* of Ali Asghar's cradle, and on the seventh the *mehndī*? Like that Wali Muhammad created musical and theatrical pieces tied to the traditional themes of each day. His attention to art and narrative left a lasting impression on the culture of Muharram in this area. If you go back to Lodhipura at about 5 A.M., you'll witness the lifting of the Abdullah Wala *ta'ziyah* and hear some *nauḥah*s that are special to that time—some of them composed in Wali Muhammad's era or even earlier."

The three men took Allah Wasayah's suggestion. The exhaustion of a long night had left its mark not only on the bodies of Lodhipura's men and women but on their attire as well. Cloth that once billowed or crinkled sharply from a freshly washed and ironed *qamīz* or *dupaṭṭa* now clung to the flesh. Damp fabric had sucked dry particles of Multan's red soil from the still-smoldering air of the night. On the exposed skin of men and even some women, perspiration blended with the blood of vigorous *mātam*, which had begun to ooze from the skin—some participants had used their fingernails as well as their hands.

The lead female singer from the night before was less bedraggled than the others. Her voice had, if anything, become thicker and more potent overnight. She sang with a voice seemingly impervious to the stress. Her vocal chords, like the bodies of pious *mātamdār*s, were anaesthetized. As the men prepared themselves for another round of strenuous lifting, the women began to sing one of the *nauḥah*s prescribed for this ritual moment:

> *asthāyī*
> o vārī vecca taḍe lāl banrā voh hā'ī hā'ī
> ho lāl ve allah tenūn̲ maut dā gā gāna badhā
>
> Oh! I would sacrifice myself for you, dear bridegroom.
> Oh, dear one! God has given you the beads of death.
>
> *antara*
> shāh tān̲ merā hai yatīm shahzādā hai
> o tan tukre sar hai judā vo hā'ī hā'ī
>
> The King—the orphaned prince—is mine!
> Oh! his trunk in pieces, his head rent asunder, hā'ī hā'ī!
>
> jaikūn̲ pahcān naīn̲ sagdī mā vo hā'ī hā'ī
> ho lāl ve allah tenūn̲ maut dā gā gāna badhā
>
> I can't recognize you, hā'ī hā'ī;
> Oh, dear one! God has given you the beads of death.

Ali had been scribbling the poetry in his notebook and annotating the text with explanations of the words with which he was unfamiliar. The *nauḥah* in *raṇa* from the previous night had used an expression for bridegroom, "gānī badhṇā," that meant something like "one bound by a necklace of beads"—like the *shahnā'ī* player he had seen earlier wearing a garland as a sign of his dedication to a saint. This metonym relied on knowledge of the local wedding ritual of tying a chain of beads. "Beads of death" was the poet's way of setting into motion a range of metaphorical relations among worldly and mystical forms of attachment and bondage.

In the hazy light just after dawn, Ali chanced upon two *malaṅg* mendicants, *baddhā*s dressed in black and wearing the characteristic multicolored necklace. One carried a conch shell (*saṅkh*); Nasir called it a "nād-e 'alī'"—"that which evokes Ali." The *malaṅg* blew it in a distinct pattern. First his partner shouted, "na'rah-e haidarī" (exclaim, "Ali!"). Those surrounding responded "Yā 'Alī" in unison. The conch player tooted a high pitch about fifteen times, accelerating with each iteration until he could play no faster. There was a pause, then a pattern: two articulations of the same upper note and one an octave below. Several more iterations of the upper note followed. The *malaṅg* then launched into a rapid pulsating pattern of short-long-long (roughly 𝅘𝅥𝅯𝅘𝅥𝅮. 𝅘𝅥𝅮.). Each burst of air caused the sound to swell and the pitch to rise a few microtones. The octave and pulse patterns returned. Finally a new rhythmic pattern appeared, played twice: a short blast on the original high note, followed immediately by a long note about five times the duration of the previous, and then a single staccato burst followed by a pause (𝅘𝅥𝅯𝅗𝅥 ‿ 𝅘𝅥𝅯𝅘𝅥𝅯). The logic of this latter pattern was immediately affirmed when the other mendicant reiterated *na'rah-e haidarī* to the same initial rhythm (he pronounced "na'rah-e" as "nār-e") (Media Example 5.4 ⎗).

Later in the morning, the three men found themselves at Haram Gate again. *Mātamdār*s, chanters of *nauḥah*, and enthusiastic devotees blanketed the pavement that transected rows of secured shopfronts far up and down the street. The first in the growing line of *ta'ziyah*s surpassed the grandeur of any *ziyārat* Ali had yet seen. Its three stories were familiar in form: two gilded cubical stories on the bottom held minarets on each corner and faux archways on each flank. The octagonal shape of the third story provided a transition to the structure's crest—not so much a dome as an enormous, virid teardrop. The carving and luteous inlay shone magnificently as a simultaneous background and foreground, a stencil that brought out leaflike patterns on the green tear. A golden pole, just slightly taller than the surrounding buildings, rose from the tip. Ali realized now that this was the Haji Wala *ta'ziyah*, parts of which he had seen being assembled at the time of his arrival in Multan. The *ziyārat* he had seen in Bheḍi Potra the previous night must not have been a *ta'ziyah* at all, but a *sej,* its strings of flowers forming a kind of nuptial canopy.

The throngs were largely but not exclusively male, and judging from the full heads of black hair and the resonance of the *nauḥah*s, relatively young. Although the clothing was not completely uniform, the preponderance of black-, white- and gold-attired masses created a dramatic visual effect. From Ali's vantage point, two groups were prominent. On the right, a cluster of men in their twenties consulted a bound volume of *nauḥah* texts as they projected their voices above the considerable din. On the left, about thirty bare-chested men stood facing one another in two rows. The *nauḥah* reciters were executing *mātam* strokes after their own fashion, reinforcing the act of singing more than creating percussion. As the singers angled their torsos slight upward for the *antara*, some of them shifted the targets of their *mātam* strokes from their chests to their heads. Several men held their hands up high, opening their fists and jerking their fingers outward in time, as if flicking water into the air.

As the main singers returned to the *asthāyī*, the *mātamdār*s took their turn, their resonating pairs of chest cavities creating a tight stereo effect. Most of the shirtless men had by now developed palm-sized patches of crimson just below each collarbone. Each heavy episode of *mātam* corresponded to the entry of a new line—a description from the scene of battle from a witness's perspective. The thwacking of vigorous *mātam* gave way to moderate timekeeping with the return of the line "karbal tuṉ pay likhdā hun vaqt rihā ko'ī na'īṉ." This refrain conveyed the image of someone physically present at Karbala writing down his observations, with an urgency carried in the phrase "there is no time left" (vaqt rihā ko'ī na'īṉ).

A richly resounding voice emerged amid this spirited antiphony. The bearded young source of this sound faced a semicircle of *nauḥah* reciters. From this distance, Ali could hear only select words of his melodically stirring *doṛhā:* "Akbar dī . . . Sayyadāt . . ." and long extensions of the vowels /ī/ and /o/. His liquid voice would enter with a forceful syllable on the fifth degree, touch a step below, return to the fifth, and then embark on an elaborate, crooked descent to the tonal center. The invigorated singer would launch in again directly on the fifth or transition back up from the tonic with an extended florid melisma.

All this time he was manipulating his hands and arms, expressively emphasizing the rhythm or melodic contour. At one point he lifted his arm and pointed his forefinger upward. This gesture of bodily engagement, common to singers and listeners, also carried a mystical connotation, Nasir told him, especially in Sufi contexts. A single finger means Hazrat Ali is "number one," the first Imam and the figure through whom most Sufi orders in South Asia trace their lineage. The singer held his finger raised as if projecting his sound into the air. And then, with the crisp conclusion of the line, he pulled his hand back and down sharply. His companions began to follow his lead, although the tune seemed difficult to follow, and their collective volume was dwarfed by the power of his voice. The central group and the participants surrounding the spot more broadly then returned to the *antara* of the original *nauḥah* and continued as before (Media Example 5.5 ⬗).

This was a high point for Ali. The *doṛhā* singer seemed to act spontaneously in a context in which such individualism tended to be precluded. In the North Indian public sphere, no such space or genre for soloing existed amid *nauḥah* and *mātam*. The occasional *soz*- or *marṡiyah-k̲h̲wān* leading responsorial recitations in front of a *ta'ziyah* would be overpowered by the massive crowds singing *nauḥah*s. Even though Ali could not hear the words of the *doṛhā* clearly, the singing conveyed to him a kind of authenticity and truth that the scripted group performances could not. At some level, Ali equated the *doṛhā* reciter with the *tāshā* player. The *tāshā*'s virtuosic potential provided a venue for the player's creativity; at the same time, it communicated a verbal message that was, for some, more felt than heard.

Ali had found a compelling angle for the first installment of his Muharram series. He felt duty-bound to remain for the rest of the sensational goings-on that day but was both too distracted and too exhausted to be impressed by much—even by the train of dozens of *ta'ziyah*s. One exception was the forced march of the gargantuans: the Ustad and Shāgird *ta'ziyah*s, painted uniformly in gold and perhaps four times larger than the Haji Wala. Functionaries sprinkled water liberally to settle the dust on the hastily cleared streets. A *ḍhol* player and a *shahnā'ī* player heralded the arrival of these monsters (Media Example 5.6 ⬗). About twenty vigorous young men struggled and strained to lift the Ustad. They literally ran from one resting point to the next, while others herded the rather bovine onlookers in the street clear of harm's way.

In another arena young men were engaged in *zanjīr kā mātam*, flailing themselves with chains fitted with sharp metal blades. Unlike the tightly choreographed *mātam* accompanying the *nauḥah* chants, this was an individualistic enterprise. The youths and young men stood hunched over, some with one hand held to the posterior of the cranium for protection and perhaps stability. The other hand traced the scourge through a smooth arc around to the back as the body rocked in contrary motion. Although Ali had never ex-

Boy performing *zanjīr kā mātam*, flailing himself with a scourge strung with blades. Ashura (10 Muharram), May 18, 1997. Multan, Pakistan. Photo by the author.

ecuted this kind of *mātam* himself, he knew from some of his more ardent and demonstratively Shī'ī former classmates that it involved a special technique. You need to hit the skin at just the right angle to create superficial wounds which bleed a lot but are not injurious. In Aminabad, someone would be on hand to sprinkle rosewater—cooling the sun-baked men as well as enhancing the flow of blood. No such person was in evidence here.

Although the actions were not coordinated by a common musical referent, a variety of sounds punctuated their movements. First were the cymbal-like sounds of the flails themselves, each to its own regular rhythm. The slightly different rate of each made multiple cycles of metallic swishing seem to slide in and out of phase—as if the flayers were aware of and approximating one another's scourge rhythms. Another prominent sound projected from a large metal loudspeaker affixed to a three-wheeled vendor's cart. The cart, which had been repurposed for the occasion with a ten-foot-tall black canopy, seated some fourteen boys and a *ẕākir*. His *doṛhā,* blasting from the crude speaker, provided a mobile feast of distorted vocal sound. Other amplified chants and shouts arrived from the left and the right, but the onlookers were comparatively silent.

This was not an atmosphere comfortable for even the most liberal Sunni. Ajmal had returned home shortly after arriving at Haram Gate; now Ali, too, decided to find his way back for a rest, long overdue.

Ali spent two more days in Multan poring over his notes, filling out details from memory, and querying Ajmal and others whom he had met in

Multan about the past days' events. In Bheḍi Potra he met with members of the hereditary family of musicians who held the license for the Haji Wala *ta'ziyah*. Paying a courtesy call to Bashir Husain Mazhar, who was recovering well, he found that Salim and Sufiya had already left town. In Lodhipura he bid farewell to Nasir and his grand-uncle and attempted to track down the *tāshā* players. They had vanished. Nasir wrote to Ali a few months later saying that both men, brothers, weakened by the strain of playing night after night, had succumbed to an undiagnosed "fever." They died within a week of one another. With their demise, the line of *tāshā* players in Lodhipura had come to an end.

Ali began drafting his article on the train to Lahore, took a break for some light reading while making the short but bureaucratically tedious journey from Lahore to Amritsar on the Samjhauta Express, and enjoyed something that passed for a night's sleep on the train to Delhi. A railway strike left Ali stranded in Delhi. He forced himself to complete a rough draft of his piece during the day so that he could unwind with his former classmates in the evening. While conscious of his rather weak and aestheticized engagement in religious matters, he did not exactly chide himself for lack of commitment. Despite his ease of rapport with Ajmal, Ali felt he had been on duty as a faithful family member and a journalist twenty-four hours a day since arriving in Lahore. He was now grateful for the Black Label that Arjun, the old friend with whom he was staying, had procured from the Duty Free in Dubai. He borrowed a typewriter one day to prepare a fair copy of his work. Sitting with a lit cigarette to one side and a cup of South Indian coffee to the other, Ali chuckled at his jaded appearance—an Indian caricature of an American journalist. He allowed his thoughts to drift to Sufiya. What would she think of him? Giving in to a moment of vanity, he asked Arjun to snap a photo on the Kodak he had carried, underutilized, on his trip.

The strike ended, but the backlog of passengers promised more delays. Ali ultimately reached Lucknow after a grueling twelve hours, bumping and jostling over the pitted Uttar Pradesh roads on a bus that was Super Deluxe in name only.

CHAPTER 6

Shah Jamal

It was March; clear skies, 20 degrees. All electrical phases were working and there was no water shortage. Since returning from Pakistan in mid-October, Ali had been asked to write snappy copy for stories in the local news: "Five Die in Mustard Oil Adulteration Case, Mustafabad"; "Twelve-Year-Old Girl Rescued from Temple Dedication Scam."

This had been the arrangement. Still, Mr. Chandlal felt guilty as he reached out to receive Ali's latest report. His tongue slid against the leafy juices of betel and masticated tobacco pooling in his mouth, but all he could come up with was a platitude: "True journalism knows no shortcuts."

Ali was not bothered: in a short article he could experiment on a small scale. This wasn't a punishment but an opportunity: as a wordsmith he needed time to tinker. Chandlal had honored his word—even welcomed Ali's return without complaint, despite the second-rate temporary replacement Ali had secured for himself.

Chandlal was, in fact, impressed with Ali's draft of "The Drums of Islam in Multan." It conveyed "immediacy and charm." But the piece could stand improving—and it could be more timely. Chandlal decided to run it prior to Muharram the following year. In the meantime he wanted to cultivate the young man's loyalty. Ali was the most promising if idealistic writer ever to come under his watch. Chandlal, for his part, was approaching retirement and mindful of his legacy; he wanted to be remembered as someone who encouraged Ali. He even offered to provide a modest subsidy for Ali's projects.

Ali hoped to return to Lahore for the *'urs* of Madho Lal Husain, the so-called Festival of Lights, Mela Cīrāġān, scheduled for the end of March. "This is no ordinary festival," he pointed out. He went on to recount the festival's somewhat racy back story and its implications for an Islam in Pakistan that was more inclusive than many Indians might have thought possible. Shah Husain was a sixteenth-century mystic remembered for his Panjabi poetry, his absorption in music, and his transgressive love for Madho, a Brahmin boy. So intertwined were their bodies and spirits that Panjabis refer to Shah Husain and his lover jointly as Madho Lal Husain. The festival combines the commemoration of the saint with remnants of what was once a celebration of spring in Lahore that included Hindus. It retains some of the ludic excesses of the Hindu rite of Holi.

"If I may make a suggestion," chanced Ali, "we can link our coverage of Holi with the piece I propose by publishing a note a few weeks in advance. Something like, 'Our special correspondent Muharram Ali will travel to Lahore to cover Holi, recast as a Sufi festival. Check back in April for his report.'" Chandlal saw no harm in this. Ali wrote to Ajmal in Multan, his uncle Qasim in Lahore, and to both Salim and Sufiya. He departed for Lahore a few weeks after the Holi holiday.

Qasim, who had acquired a second vehicle this year, generously offered to share both his old Daihatsu (with its broken air conditioner) and his driver, Ali Muhammad. The latter, an impoverished immigrant from the Northern Areas, now had a tremendous command of Lahore's geography and was a valuable asset for Ali. The weather was still fair and dry, much like Lucknow's—here peaking at about 32° in the heat of the day and cooling to 17° at night. Ali picked up the phone to contact Salim and was promptly invited over for tea the next day.

Salim's widowed mother occupied a large first-floor flat in Shadman Colony.* Ali Muhammad cut across Shadman Road from Fatima Memorial Hospital and found the powder-green building, fronted by a row of bicycles, about fifty meters from the Shī'ī cemetery. Salim greeted Ali warmly at the foot of the stairs and invited him into the large spare front hall, lined invitingly with earth-toned kilims. They settled themselves comfortably on a dusty brown couch in the corner. Salim unfolded a map of the city and handed Ali a laminated newspaper article. Salim's mother, Nuriyah, carried in a scratched metal tray with cups, saucers, sugar bowl, and teapot made of delicate china ornamented with fine curved blue lines.

*The "first floor" in South Asia means the second story.

Salim presented a plan: "This is a convenient home base. First we should hear the *ḍhol* players Pappu Sain and his partner Jhura on Thursday night—this article was published in the *Dawn* newspaper. . . . It'll give you an idea of who Pappu is. The Shah Jamal shrine is only a short walk." Salim pointed out the shrine on the map, only half a kilometer south of the flat. "If possible we'll find a way to talk with Pappu Sain. He lives in Baghbanpura, near the shrine of Madho Lal Husain. Every week he makes the seven-kilometer journey on foot—no small feat with that heavy *ḍhol* hanging from his neck. Sufiya is arriving from England tomorrow. Her parents live here, in Rehmanpura. You would have passed her neighborhood on your way from Model Town. Maybe she'll join us."

"The plan sounds great. I'd also like to contact Shahid and Niamat Ali, the *ḍhol* players who performed at my cousin's wedding last year. They are regulars at the Mela Cirāġān." Ali pulled out a slip of paper with the name of a neighborhood, a phone number, and the letters "pp," standing for "particular person." Salim projected his voice to the next room: "Mushtaaaq! 'Phone' le kar ā'o." The houseboy brought a hefty black dial phone from the next room, uncoiling its long, heavy, stiff cord. Ali dragged his finger in the recalcitrant dial to each digit and chuckled, thinking of his brother. The number belonged to the owner of a small provisions shop, who said he would pass on Ali's message and phone numbers.

On Thursday Salim and Ali set out for Shah Jamal. Sufiya demurred. At about 9 P.M. they turned off Shah Jamal road onto the street leading to the shrine. Auto rickshaws, a few cars, bicycles, hawkers, and shrine-goers of many descriptions muddled their way through the lane, pushing against and around one another. A muffled thumping of *ḍhol*s reverberated from the shrine tucked into the raised ground above the street. The two men ascended a stairway to the left and entered a walled courtyard some sixteen hundred square meters. A whitewashed wall of brick, rising in tall, right-angled projections like giant stairs from the sloping ground, bounded one part of the square. The remaining sides, cement panels, bore rough lattice-work of diamond-shaped perforations. Long-standing trees, trunks branched low to the ground, rose from two of the corners and overhung crowds of men and a few women sitting around the edges or behind perforated cement screens.

Zulfiqar Ali, known as Pappu Sain—probably in his mid-twenties—was the elder of the two drummers. His wavy hair flowed onto his back just below his neckline, his thick beard covering most of his face. Pappu's aubergine *shalwār qamīz* stood out against the glimmering shade of maroon favored by most of the dancers and other mendicants present. His clean-cut playing partner Manzur Sain, known as Jhura Sain, outfitted himself in a sage-colored *shalwār qamīz* that reminded Ali of the largely muted hues of Lahori men's attire in general.

The drummers were still warming up. Ali recognized the *ṭhekā* for *tīntāl*, which Pappu was outlining crisply with the *tīlā* held in his left hand. Both drummers joined in energetically and loudly with an extended pattern returning to the *sam.* Pappu followed with a cycle emphasizing subtle undulations, pressing the bass head's skin with the curved *kūṇḍi* to produce a tabla-like wavering of pitch. The two men joined for a simple, loudly resonating *tihā'ī* whose cadential function was magnified by a brief silence at its conclusion. The audience roared enthusiastically—many of them producing the explosive sounding syllable *'ī*. Some said "Jhūle Lāl," others yelled "Husain" (Media Example 6.1 ⛐).

"'Ī," Salim informed Ali, "is the name of Hazrat 'Alī, collapsed into a single syllable."

The ranks of those in attendance varied considerably in age and social class. A quiet, elderly man whose whiskery white beard barely covered his pockmarked skin stood in the background under his olive flat cap. Salim recognized this regular visitor to the shrine—a retired postal worker. Many others came mainly for the Thursday night spectacle. A small uniformed outfit from the Lahore police sat together affably in the inner ring of viewers. A college-aged youth in tight, faded jeans fired up six cigarettes, arranged them between the fingers of one hand, and created a smoke trail as he distributed the fags among his companions. This fellow had emerged earlier from a car that had pushed its way close to the shrine. Salim pointed out the distinctive regional headgear of some attendees: a Sindhi *ṭopī* with inset green, blue, and amber glass pieces, and yellow-and-green embroidery; a Chitrali or Pathan *pakol* cap of thick wool, its sides rolled up. Some men wore bandanas to hold their hair back and soak up the sweat of the day.

Ali struck up a conversation with a lorry driver in his mid-fifties who said he often came to see Pappu Sain, whom he considered the best of all *ḍhol* players. Pappu's *ḍhol* playing made him sense God's 'compassion' and feel 'proximity to God.' He could hear the 'voice of the *qalandar*' from Pappu's *ḍhol*. Ali learned that this latter referred specifically to saint Lal Shahbaz Qalandar in Sindh and to the *qalandar* figure in general—an accomplished type of world-renouncing, dreadlocked mystic.

Pappu and Jhura, who had stopped for a moment, suddenly regained everyone's attention with a thunderous beat. Ali's ear was deafened momentarily with the cascading cries of "*'ī*" all around. Amidst this thick series of punctuations, someone yelled, "Jhūle Lāl" (darling/ruby of the cradle/swing). Who was this? One person said, "That is Lal Shahbaz Qalandar in Sindh." Someone else said, "No, Jhūle Lāl is Uḍero Lāl, a different saint."

The mystics present at this gathering, mendicants called *malaṅg*s or faqirs, were on the Sufi path but not *qalandar*s themselves. Some of the *malaṅg*s had arrived in their crimson finery, with their upper garments, kurtas or *qamīz*es, falling below their shins. Loose pants or pantlike waistcloths (*lācā*) made of white or red-striped smooth or gauzy material peeked out from underneath. The heavily accessorized among them wore ponderous belts with metal attachments; one belt was covered with egg-shaped brass bulbs—possibly bells. One man wore a peculiar turban, matching the red of his robe but with a black rim. Most of the *malaṅg*s, and the dancers especially, wore *ghuṅgrū*s—ankle bells arranged in rows on a band of cloth or leather about five centimeters wide. One man toted a green bag over his shoulder and kept three brass cylindrical receptacles of different sizes hanging from his shoulder strap. The *malaṅg*s were wearing necklaces, often several at a time, of white and blue beads or of large and small wooden beads, and thumb-sized mountings of amber, rose, and black stone or glass affixed to chains.

Seeing Ali taking notes and asking questions, a smartly dressed young man named Shahbaz sidled up, introduced himself as the brother and manager of Pappu Sain, and started offering unsolicited information: "This is *tīntāl* . . . the *dhamāl* pattern will start after Shah Jamal enters into Pappu's body. . . . Now it has begun . . . Watch this man," he said, "Muhabbat Sain is Pappu Sain's oldest *dhamālī*. Nasir Sain is his disciple. Pappu Sain made Nasir's *dhamāl* perfect through own his bodily movements while playing the *ḍhol*. Muhabbat Sain and Nasir are addicted to doing *dhamāl* in front of Pappu Sain and Jhura. If they hear *ḍhol* and do not do *dhamāl* they will feel destitute. When they 'play' *dhamāl* they feel a direct line to Qalandar Pāk (Lal Shahbaz Qalandar)."

Ali observed a variety of *dhamāl* styles: with one drum groove, a dancer kept his wrists angled tightly inward and then rapidly bent his arms upward in front of him, making an upward slicing motion with his hands while simultaneously agitating his head from side to side and jogging in place; another dancer kept his hands pointing outward and alternately drew his forearms across his body—when his right arm bent, his head went to the right, when his left arm bent, his head went to the left. This was coordinated with a drum groove emphasizing each movement distinctly. Sometimes a *dhamālī* who was dressed in green with a red sash rapidly tipped his head from side to side, stepping softly and pushing one hand down as

Pappu Sain (left) playing the *ḍhol* while *dhamālīs* (right) dance, propelling their long, wavy hair from side to side. Shah Jamal Shrine, Lahore, Pakistan, February 15, 1998. Photo by the author.

if he were repeatedly closing a jack-in-the-box. A favorite move of some was to keep their hands at their sides, eyes closed, and raise each knee high into the air in alternation while making small circles or taking large steps across the arena.

Having heard now the names of Lal Shahbaz Qalandar, Uḍero Lal, and Shah Jamal, all connected with *dhamāl,* Ali now asked Shahbaz, "Who is Shah Jamal?"

"Shah Jamal was a Sufi who lived in the time of Shah Jahan [the seventeenth century]. See this mound where the shrine is? It is called Damdamah. Shah Jamal's durbar rose seven stories above it. Across stood a queen's palace and the royal garden and pool. As the palace did not reach the height of the durbar, women and girls of the royal family were visible bathing from Shah Jamal's vantage point on top. The queen asked Shah Jamal to leave. His abode, she said, should not rise higher than her palace. Shah Jamal became 'intoxicated' and 'shook' *dhamāl* until his durbar came crashing into the ground. Four stories sank beneath the earth, burying Shah Jamal. But he didn't die. No one saw him die, in fact."

"You said that Shah Jamal enters into Pappu Sain . . ."

"Yes, that's what he says . . . after about fifteen minutes or half an hour."

"I was hoping to talk to Pappu Sain about his experiences as a drummer. Could you help me arrange that?"

"Yes, but not tonight. We will meet on Sunday, inshallah. Phone me at this number . . . we can go together to pick up Pappu Sain from his room. We'll confirm it on Saturday."

Ali continued to observe Pappu Sain, aware now that the drummer, like the *malaṅg*s, had entered into *mastī* or *ḥāl*. The entire gathering had become increasingly interactive. Pappu's playing was not rhythmically complex in the sense of presenting intricate metrical changes: most of the performance was in a cycle of four or eight *mātra*s. Rather, it consisted of virtuosic elaboration on simple motives: he used changes in dynamics, contrasts in timbre, and displays of speed to create musical interest. With a rapid filler pattern in the background, he might play a two-stroke bass gesture a few times, then add a third, fourth, and fifth stroke, finally blending fore- and backgrounds together. The boldness and simplicity of the foregrounded material made it seem particularly accessible to this assembly—as if Pappu were placing jewels on a silk pillow and offering them up to a nobleman.

In the transition from *tīntāl* to *dhamāl*, the motive ♩. ♪♩ ♩ was particularly prominent and instigated the crowd's response, "mast qalandar," to the same rhythm. Sometimes Pappu would follow this motive with a resonant stroke and a rest, prompting the onlookers to chant "mast qalandar mast . . ., mast qalandar mast. . . ." At other times he would fill out the motive, playing the whole basic pattern of *dhamāl*. Shahbaz identified this as the "real" *dhamāl* and uttered its associated words, "dam-ā-dam mast qalandar" (figure 6.1).

The words meant, "With each breath, [utter] 'mast qalandar' [intoxicated mystic]." Sometimes the crowd assigned the words "Jhūle Lāl" to the first

Figure 6.1.

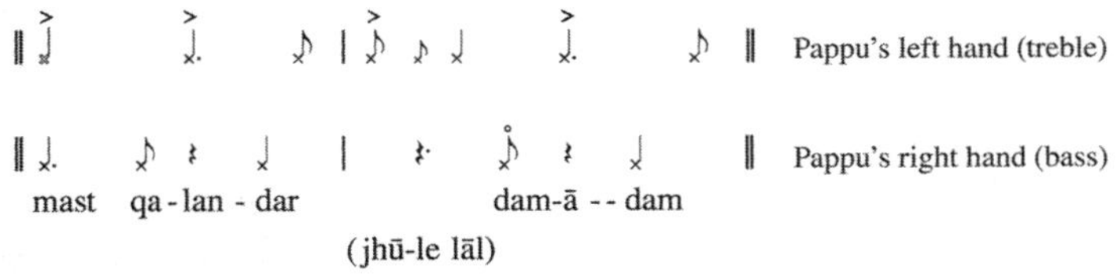

Simplified representation of the *dhamāl* pattern played on the *ḍhol* by Pappu Sain and the way the verbal phrase "dam-ā-dam mast qalandar" aligns with it. Small type indicates a very light stroke; the small circle above an eighth note indicates a damped stroke.

three prominent treble strokes in the second half of the pattern, creating an antiphonal effect: one group chanted the words "mast . . qalan . dar ." in a mid-register, husky voice, while another provided the high-pitched response, "jhū-le-lāl." Occasional vocalizers would intone words at a different rate than their implied articulation on the *ḍhol* but keeping the same rhythmic idea. One man sang/spoke "dam mast qalandar," rising about a step to the word *mast*, dipping indefinitely below his home pitch for the syllables *qalan*, and melodically resolving on *dar* before resuming.

Every so often, when the playing was soft, the chanters would raise the energy level. One man yelled "qalandarī **lā-ā-ā-ā-ā-l** qaland**a-a-a-a-a-r**," to which dozens provided a chorus of prolonged *o-o-o-o-h* and staccato '*ī* sounds. Pappu and Jhura then took hold of the roar, playing loudly and thickly themselves. Then they began to alternate between forceful and gentle strokes at a rate approximating that of human respiration. One man matched the tempo with breathy utterances of the word *mast*. After pushing the word out, he inhaled deeply, and repeated the cycle until he began to hyperventilate.

Pappu began to spin, then Jhura, both while playing the *ḍhol*. Ali laughed to himself, remembering a Ram Lila procession in Lucknow in which members of a group calling themselves *Panjabi ḍhol* made a show of spin-

Drummer advertising himself as a member of a "Panjabi *ḍhol*" party lifts a drum over his head and begins to spin without playing. Ramlila procession, Lucknow, Uttar Pradesh, India, October 13, 1998. Photo by the author.

ning with their instruments—a slovenly, fat drummer clunked, hefting a not-very-large *ḍhol* to his head and turning on his axis. He could barely accomplish this, even without playing. This was Ali's first experience of the *aṣlī cīz*, the real thing.

As the *ḍhol* players at hand ceased their rotations, the dancers took their turns. One dressed in a white *shalwār qamīz* spread his arms straight out. As he began to rotate faster and faster, his *qamīz* rose up to his waist like the top of a mushroom. At half speed he looked like a snow angel Ali had seen in an American children's book. At full speed the dancer resembled a white pencil trisected by spinning disks. Some of the *dhamālī*s began to fall to the ground. Others stabilized themselves. A muscular, bald *malaṅg* who at nearly two meters' height towered over the others looked upward, pointed a single finger into the air, and repeatedly shouted "yaktā'ī (oneness)."

Pappu and Jhura played for more than two hours before putting the *ḍhol*s down for the night. Pappu, like the recently collapsed *dhamālī*s, was drenched in dampness from his vigor and looked upon the scene with glassy eyes. Ali thought of epileptics after a seizure and patients after electroshock therapy. Shahbaz introduced Ali and Salim to Pappu, who responded with alacrity—his rapid return to an ordinary state came as a surprise to Ali. Pappu would be glad to meet them on Sunday.

: : :

Nuriyah was leaving for Multan to visit her brother that weekend. With the flat clear, Salim offered to host the interview at home. Since, in the end, Shahbaz decided to come to Shadman directly, Ali and Salim set off to fetch Pappu themselves. Shahbaz had given hasty verbal directions to Ali Muhammad over the telephone. The three men located Pappu's place in Baghbanpura with difficulty. Leaving the car and driver, Ali and Salim proceeded on foot across an uncultivated field of weeds, stagnant water, mud, and discards. The room Pappu rented from a small family in a modest two-bedroom house contained little more than a rough-wool-blanketed bed low to the floor, a shabby but unsoiled gray-green footlocker, a few books in Panjabi, his instrument, and a single mineral-stained glass tumbler.

When everyone had reached the Shadman flat, the time for lunch was approaching. Salim and Ali had tried their hand at cooking rice and mustard greens. But they relied on the Boti Tikka House for a selection of kabobs and a favorite stall for *roġani nān*, seeded flatbread baked in a wood-fed clay oven. Pappu was touched that the men had taken the trouble to prepare food themselves and took an instant liking to them. Shahbaz, who had been on the scene for about a year, was looking out for Pappu's interests. Because Pappu tended to take people at face value, he had been the victim of exploitation; surreptitious recordings had been made and marketed; Pappu had been invited to participate in studio recordings and cheated out of any fees or royalties. This convivial welcome helped dispel any lingering fears with regard to the men's motives. As the four men ate and engaged in small talk, Muharram Ali explained what had drawn him to Lahore and to Pappu Sain.

Pappu found in Ali's story something that resonated with his own: "My parents were childless, so my father asked his pir to pray on their behalf. Shah Wali Sarkar prayed and told my father, 'You will have a son; he will be a *ḍhol* player; and you will name him Farid Muhammad.' Actually, my real name is Zulfiqar Ali. But I was born by virtue of that pir's prayer. Now there is a shrine for that pir, Sayyad Baba Mehar Shah Wali Sarkar, in Hoshyarpur, India.

"My father Baba Luḍan Sain was a great classical *ḍhol* player. He and one uncle were the only *ḍhol* players in my family. All the *ḍhol* players in Lahore would copy my father's 'compositions.' There was also a *ḍhol* player named Bao from Amritsar—this was before Hindustan existed [that is, before Partition]—he used to play with my father. People used to come and go to India freely at that time. Back then people didn't even play *bhāngṛā* here—they only half knew it—and they didn't know how to play *dhamāl,* either. My father would play *relā*s and *mukhṛā*s (rhythmic patterns) for the faqirs; the faqirs would match his playing with the sounds of their *ghuṅgrū*s. In this way the faqirs 'acquired musicality' or 'immersed themselves in sound' [came into *sur*]. My father was the one who introduced *dhamāl* to this area [presumably having picked it up through Bao]; for that matter, he was the one who made the *ḍhol* popular in this part of the Panjab.

"I used to sit and listen to him. But he wanted me to be educated, so he sent me to school, and he sent me to do this and that job. But I would run away from school and avoid doing any work. My father beat me severely. I said, 'Go and ask your pir.'

"My father heard me playing one day. Hoping that I would lose interest, he had a *ḍhol* made for me that was so large and heavy that I couldn't carry it. I would put the *ḍhol* around my neck and when I found it difficult to walk, he would walk beside me supporting the instrument with one hand. So this way, as God wished, by the grace of Allah and the Prophet, it happened.

"My 'teacher's teacher' Shaukat Sahab had a student, Ghulam Qadir, who was a close friend of my father and a 'hereditary musician.' Ghulam Qadir was listening to me one day when my father said, 'Pappu is not disciplined enough to learn from me and it pains me to beat him. Would you teach him?' So in this way, with the blessings of the pir and *murshid*, I underwent training. My teacher even used to give me 'gifts' and money to spend. What he would teach me in the morning I would play for him in the evening. The ability to do this was a gift to me from my pir—no one could teach that. I just had it."

"Did your father teach you anything?" asked Ali.

"I play by the 'grace' of my father and my ustad. A person has just two fathers: one is the real father, who sows the seed, and the second father is the ustad. *Bas jī*, but what I tell you is this: nobody 'made me pick it up,' it is just a gift from Baba Pir. When I play, I do not remember what I am supposed to do; when I pick up the *ḍhol* my '*murshid* enters me.' 'Rapture' falls upon me. *Bas, mastī* comes. In that state of *mastī* I play."

"As I told you on Thursday," explained Shahbaz, "Pappu Sain was not there when he was playing. It was another person, inside Pappu Sain, who was playing the *ḍhol*."

"So who is actually playing?" asked Ali, clumsily.

"I have my pir and *murshid* before me, and Allah and the Prophet . . . that's it. This 'vision' is the only thing that comes to me. An ordinary person who spins will fall down. Only Allah's 'strength' keeps me going. When I play for *S*arkār [Master], Shah Jamal's *dīdār* [spiritually beneficial vision] is there for me. I'm immersed in my 'passion' for him. Last week Sarkār Shah Jamal came to me in a dream telling me I would not be doing 'duty' for him this past Thursday. Sure enough, someone came to me that day offering me a large sum to participate in a recording session. But I said, 'No, I am being pricked by a needle inside: I have to go to Shah Jamal.' Jhura and I are '*āshiq*s [lovers] like that."

"Does Sarkār enter you from the minute you lift the *ḍhol* to play?" Salim asked.

"No. At first I look at the 'people around me.' When I get away from them, I enter into *mastī*, the *mastī* of *sur* [sound, resonance, musicality]. Then Sarkār calls me. My work takes a lot of 'strength,' to stand and play *ḍhol* well, with *sur*, with *lay* [sense of time], with 'rhythm.' Baba comes inside me and grabs me, he guides me, tells me where and when to go.

"'Concordant music is the true calling.' 'Knowledge of music' is the 'pure/true thing'; there is no 'defilement/falsehood' in it. Whatever *ṭhekā* is being played, that very *ṭhekā* must continue. Because the *ṭhekā* is pure, some other person cannot just go off in another direction. It is true that some '*dhamāl* shakers' and *ḍhol* players 'gear their performances to the temperament of those around them.' They play with their eyes open; they focus on the money. But others play as they should, immersed in *mastī*.

"Salim, I'll tell it to you straight in Panjabi. I can't speak Urdu correctly. If we are true Muslims, when we prostrate to do *namāz* prayers we should not lose focus even if someone tries to cut our throats. But if we are 'immature prayers,' we will look back even if someone says we have dropped something. The *namāz* for Sarkār is similar. There is a 'dance' in which a *kanjarī* [courtesan] looks into the viewer's eyes and tries to trap him. She plays and displays her body from different angles. One who dances for Qalandar with *mastī* doesn't look for anything. He looks forward, in the direction of the *murshid*. Only the one whose eyes are looking forward, and who is 'attached' to Allah, to the Prophet and to his pir and *murshid*, can be said to be doing *dhamāl*. . . . Have you been to Sehwan Sharif [in Sindh]?"

Salim and Ali spoke at the same time: Salim had visited several times. Ali had never been to Sindh.

"They play *naubat* [*naqqārah*] in the morning. The drums say 'mast qalandar, mast qalandar.' That is the *qalandar*s' call to prayer [*az̲ān*]. When people do *raqṣ* [dance] they come to know this. When the *naubat* is playing, people enter into *mastī*, dance, and say *dam-ā-dam mast qalandar, 'alī har dil ke andar* [with each and every breath, mast qalandar, 'Ali is in every heart]. This is the continuously repeated practice [*vird*] of *mastī*."

Shahbaz added, "You have to say *mast qalandar*. It is a kind of 'praise of God.'"

"No one says *mast qalandar* of their own accord, in fact," said Pappu. "On Thursday nights, for instance, Baba Shah Jamal must first enter into my heart and then, through the *ḍhol*, ask the people to say *mast qalandar*. They get *mast* and utter *mast qalandar* between their lips without self-awareness."

"There is that song Lāl Merī Pat that Nusrat Fateh Ali Khan sings," began Salim.

"Reshma sang it earlier," inserted Shahbaz.

" . . . in which the line *dam-ā-dam mast qalandar, 'ali dam dam de andar* appears," Salim continued. "Did chanting *mast qalandar* become more popular with that song?"

"Listen," said Pappu, "we all consider Nusrat Fateh Ali Khan to be great; his 'impact' is such that everyone knows how to say *mast qalandar*. He has used his tongue [*zabān*] and instruments [*sāzān̲*] to make *mast qalandar* reach every house. I am doing it with two sticks and a 'dead thing'—the leather on my drum. God has conferred language upon human beings, and by means of words a person can attract an audience. If one recites the words of God, the listener will have to sit and pay attention. But to force a person to listen to a dead thing is more difficult. I plan to release a cassette so that *mast qalandar* may be heard on the *ḍhol* in every home."

"Did Nusrat's song change the way you thought about *dhamāl*?" asked Ali.

"I have been playing *ḍhol* since the time Nusrat began singing the *qawwālī* Jogi Nāl Jāna, which was before he began singing Mast Qalandar. *Mast qalandar* has been my *vird*, my *ẕikr-fikr* [recited formula and thought], right from the beginning. I know what *dhamāl* is and who are its authentic practitioners. The 'real basis' of *dhamāl* is this: | **dhāg** . . da nāg . din . **tāg** . . da nāg . din |. Any 'Muslim hereditary musician' in the 'outside world' will tell you this. The faqirs have made their own *bol*s for this, | **dīn** . . pa ṇā . da ma **dīn** . . pa ṇā . da ma |. This means 'Maula Husain provided refuge [*panāh*] for the faith of Islam [*dīn*],'" explained Pappu. "The faqirs do *ẕikr* like that with *dhamāl*."

Ali registered the convergence of Shīʿī and Sufi concerns in this *ẕikr* and hastily noted down the *bol*s as Pappu continued speaking.

"We play | **dhā** . . da nāg . din . **tāg** . . da nāg . din . | and the faqirs do the *ẕikr*, 'mast qalandar, dam-ā-dam mast qalandar . . .'" Pappu continued.

"'*Alī dā pahlā* number [Ali is number one]," Salim added, drawing on the rhyming phrase in the second half of a popular version of the chant.

"'*Ali dā pahla* number is wrong!" protested Pappu. "Somebody said it wrong. Hazrat Ali himself assigns ranks among human beings, but in calling Ali *number one* we become the ones assigning numbers. We faqirs do not accept the line 'Ali is the first' because the Prophet and Hazrat Ali are the ones who assign positions to human beings, 'saints,' and 'prophets.'"

"Where did this phrase come from, if it is wrong?" queried Ali.

"I heard this phrase when sitting among faqirs. I have been in the company of esteemed faqirs in the *qalandar* 'tradition.' One master Baba Lal sat among them. They all said that Ali is not in the numbering system, nor is Muhammad, because Muhammad and Ali have the power to assign whatever number they want. We Muslims believe in them . . . stand at their doors, Ali's and Muhammad's, as beggars. The biggest door is Allah's, of course, but he has introduced himself through them."

"What about *dhamāl* itself? Where did that originate?" Salim interjected.

"*Dhamāl* started when the Prophet raised 'Ali's hand and said, 'for whom I am *sarkār* 'Ali is also *sarkār*' (*man kunto maula, fahāza 'ali-un maula*). Hearing this, 'Ali 'spun three times.'" Pappu traced his finger counterclockwise in the air.

Muharram Ali entered this point in his notebook. As a Shī'ah, he knew that the *hadis̱* to which Pappu had alluded is a key source of authority for both Shī'ahs and the many Sufi orders that trace their lineage through Hazrat Ali. This important text and its associated melody, together called the *qaul*, play a prominent role as the first or last piece in *qawwālī* performances—particularly at shrines. In linking *dhamāl* with the *qaul* Pappu had made a strategic rhetorical move.

"Out of happiness that the Prophet Muhammad had chosen him from among all the other 'prophets,' Ali entered into a state of *mastī* and danced [*raqṣ kiyā*]. Later the *qalandarī* tradition began. Lal Shahbaz Qalandar took up that *dam-ā-dam mast qalandar dhamāl,* and later so did Shah Husain . . . and there is Shah Jamal's 'tradition' to consider as well. These traditions are all 'in mutual agreement.' One becomes a qalandar by dancing.

"When Lal Shahbaz Qalandar was in a state of *mastī* he would lie on a bed of thorns. Bleeding made him feel happy. Sarkar Qalandar did both *dhamāl* and *mātam* for Imām Pāk [Imam Husain]. Becoming *mastī* with the beat of the *naubat,* he used to dance and fly like an eagle [*shahbāz*]. Once a *ḍhol* player asked Qalandar for something to eat or drink and he said, 'When I fly, you will find a ruby [*la'l*] on the ground. When you play with *mastī* and *josh* [passion], I will come. No matter how much you play, you can't bring me down, as I am an eagle and I fly high. But the one who says *dam-ā-dam mast qalandar* correctly can bring me down.'

"[The saint] Baba Bulleh Shah also 'shook' *dhamāl*. He went to live among the *kanjar*s [courtesans] for twelve years, washing their pots and pans, carrying tablas and other instruments. He learned *sur* and how to dance [*nācnā*] with *sur*. 'A person lacking *sur* is not favorably received even by Master Allah.'"

Ali wrote feverishly in his notebook: remarkable statement by Pappu Sain, implying that unmusical people are somehow tarnished in the eyes of God; must follow up on Bulleh Shah story.

Salim asked, "Sain Sahab, is *dhamāl* the only 'rhythm' [English word] that induces *mastī,* or are there others?"

"Not every rhythm can do this. There are other *tāl*s that people play with *mastī*. But the *tāl* that causes *mastī, dam-ā-dam mast qalandar*, is the one that plays the same inside a person's heart as it does on the outside." Pappu struck his chest with the heel of his firm hand and caused his neckwear to jangle. "This is the tradition of Sarkār, of Qalandar. With other *tāl*s the player may even keep his eyes open! He might be able to enter into *mastī* through his own agency, but he will not be able to cause others to become *mast*. Only the *dhamāl* of Qalandar causes *mastī,*" insisted Pappu.*

"Shahbaz bhai, didn't you say at one point on Thursday night that Pappu Sain had switched from *dhamāl* to Sindhi [another pattern]?" asked Ali.

"I made a mistake; it was Baluchi Lava," Shahbaz said.

"Does that also cause *mastī?*" Ali continued. "After all, it is played on the *ḍhol* as well."

"Of course, it is connected with that pattern also," said Pappu.

"How about *luḍḍī*?" Salim added.

"No, *luḍḍī* is different. *Luḍḍī* and *bhāngṛā*"—Pappu lifted his hands to clap over his head, in imitation of the dances—"these are Panjabi 'culture,' lifting the legs . . ."

"Like disco," Shahbaz added.

"And there is *jhūmar* also. . . . 'Passionate' people shake *bhāngṛā* at weddings, shouting 'hā! hā!' *Bhāngṛā* is Panjabi 'culture.' People get 'excited' similar to the way they respond to the wrestling pattern on the *ḍhol*, which has its own style. If I play it, an old wrestler will recognize it in a minute," Pappu went on, "but nowadays people play *bhāngṛā* for wrestling and for 'fencing' also. *Bhāngṛā* is played on such occasions. Faqirs 'play *dhamāl.*'"

"You have mentioned *tāl*s that can induce excitement and happiness. Do any *tāl*s bring about a condition [*kaifiyat*] of sorrow or dispiritedness [*udāsī*]?" Ali wanted to coax the discussion in the direction of Muharram.

"Certainly, why not! Suppose a person starts to play *jhaptāl*, but doesn't really make a connection—'it's really a matter of connecting with the moment.' On the surface the playing may be 'insipid' but at base the *tāl* is 'sweet.' The player may have rehearsed a lot, but when he reaches the venue he may not remember because the time is not 'ripe.' At a certain point *udāsī* comes. The player should be good but the 'time' should also be ripe.

"All *tāl*s are 'frightening,' in fact. *Tāl*s are all 'intimidating'—how to 'handle' them, how 'to play' them, how to 'come and go' through them—all these are intimidating. Music is frightening. But there are some souls [*rūḥ*] who play by 'intuition,' with the help of Allah. I'm like that. This Thursday I'm going to play *uṣūl*, a five-*mātra tāl*. Well, I'm just threading my beads to it, threading my beads to it." Pappu cradled the string of beads hanging from his neck, evincing the composure of a master.

---

*See the chapter notes for the original statement in Urdu from which this important passage is drawn.

"Once Jhura and I were playing at the shrine of Pir Pak Farman . . . there were many *ḍhol* players there. Jhura began to play *tīntāl* and a fire broke out behind us! We ran away with our *ḍhol*s. Music causes rain also, you know . . . singing *rāg malhār* causes rain. Many people have caused rain or fire. All of music, both singing and playing, is fire [*āg*]! One has to begin with 'control.' Those without 'control' are lacking in *tāl* and musicality [*betālā, besurā*]."

Pappu had been shifting between Panjabi and Urdu, making it necessary, at times, for Salim or Shahbaz to clarify terms. He had turned to English for the word *culture* and now for *control.* Ali's friends in the Subaltern Studies Collective in Delhi would have made much of this—particularly in light of Bernard S. Cohn's recently published article "The Command of Language and the Language of Command."

"In that case, which *tāl* would you use to cause others to feel sadness [*ġam*]?" asked Ali.

"*Tīntāl* is a good *tāl*, for whatever purpose . . . the same *tāl* 'gives birth to dispiritedness'; *nā-dhin-dhin-nā* creates sadness." Pappu recited *bol*s in a very slow tempo. "When played in another way, it can also produce *josh* [excitement]." Pappu recited in a medium tempo, swinging the *bol*s significantly and emphasizing the undulating bass. "It is sad when the 'player delineates sad *bol*s,' but he can also make the *bol*s *josh*. The composition can be sad while the *mukhṛā* [the portion of the composition that returns to the *sam*] is *josh*. The *mukhṛā* may be 'flying' while the composition, which is sad, 'remains on land.'"

"*Ṭhīk*, I understand now that through your artistry you can produce *josh* and *ġam*. I wondered whether there are particular rituals that call for sad playing. Funerals, for instance. Is *ḍhol* played at funerals?" asked Ali.

"I played *ḍhol* at my father's funeral. He was a *walī* [friend of God, a Sufi], a faqir; so he asked me to play *ḍhol* when he left this world. I played *tīntāl*, *nā-dhin-dhin-nā*, and *phumniyā̱n* of Sakhi Lalah Sarkār. My father instructed me what to play and how to perform his funeral rituals, and told me he would never forgive me if I did not carry out his wishes. I did as he requested."

"Did you play anything else?" asked Salim.

"Qalandar's *dhamāl*. He was a faqir, no? a faqir. He predicted the day of his death," said Pappu.

"How did you feel, playing at his funeral?" Shahbaz asked, helpfully.

"My father had died. How would I feel? I was grieved at the 'duty' my father had assigned me. He didn't seem dead to me. He appeared to be sleeping, liable to wake up at any time."

"And the *tāl*s?" Shahbāz continued.

"They were sad, of course. I played one *mātamī ḍhol* [mourning *ḍhol*, *ḍhol* for *mātam*]. The faqirs composed this *bandish*, 'caṛhe duldul kaṭe kāfir' [mounted Duldul, unbelievers were killed]":*

caṛ he dul dul ka ṭe kā fir

The basic configuration of strokes matched that of seven-pulse *mārū* in Multan, with the text outlining ♪ ♪ 𝄾 here, instead of ♪ 𝄾 ♪.

"On *ḍhol*," Pappu added, "the *bol*s are"

𝄆 da ṇa na dhā . dhā . | da da ga dhi na ta ka 𝄇

Once again, Ali's interest was piqued by the depth to which the *qalandar* 'tradition' drew upon ostensibly Shī'ī themes. "So do they play this for Muharrram?" inquired Ali.

"Previously they played it," replied Pappu.

"Here?" asked Ali.

"They play it in Sehwan but they don't play it here anymore. In Lahore, the 'elders' used to play *mātamī* with the faqirs. On the tenth of Muharram they used to play it when they took out the *ta'ziyah*s. I saw it in Lahore only once when I was a small child. My father played as they took out a *ta'ziyah* and *sehrā* [that is, for Qasim's wedding]. Now they don't let us play because of 'sectarianism.' For ten days I don't even touch a *ḍhol*."

"Because of animosity between Shī'ahs and Sunnis, they don't allow *ḍhol* playing during Muharram in Lahore anymore," said Shahbaz, to make it perfectly clear.

"Forgive me for asking, but what is your affiliation?" ventured Ali. "As the offspring of a Sunni father and a Shī'ī mother, I consider myself neutral."

"I have no affiliation and he has no affiliation. He is a Sā'īṉ [mendicant]. Just a Sā'īṉ," said Shahbaz, defensively. He closed off direct inquiry into this dangerous territory and effectively blocked Pappu from answering.

Getting at the question in a different way, Ali inquired, "*Sain jī*, do you participate in Muharram?"

"I do. 'I participate in the mourning' for Imam Pāk, Maula Husain. 'I sit and mourn.'"

*This refers to Imam Husain's climbing onto his horse and battling at Karbala against Yazid's forces.

"Ali asks because he and I were in Multan on Ashura at the beginning of this year and heard drums and *shahnā'ī*; on the *shahnā'ī* they played *marsiyah* and *nauḥah*," Salim offered. "They were also observing the traditions of mourning for Imam Husain."

"Yes, they play in Multan, in Sindh . . . everywhere but Lahore. They are right to play *mātamī*. On the ninth and tenth in Sehwan, they play *mātamī*. On the tenth of Muharram in Sevan, if a son is born to any Sayyad family of Qalandar, they will also play a 'happy drum pattern' to announce the birth. Playing *ḍhol* at Shah Jamal is also a way of doing *mātam*. One person does *mātam* this way. Another person does it with *zanjīr* [chains with blades], and yet another does it with tears. But someone may do it with the dance [*raqṣ*] of *dam-ā-dam mast*, shaking *dhamāl* with *mast qalandar*. For him it is *mātam*. Shaking *dhamāl* is also *mātam* when one keeps the 'image' of Karbala before one; then the intention [*maqṣad*] of *dhamāl* is *mātam*."

Ali thought back on some of the recurring issues in Pappu's statements—the intentions of the performer versus the needs and interpretations of the listener; the capacity of the performer to acquire musical skills and to draw upon those skills at a given moment, to bring "outside" what is "inside"; and the delicate balance between music as a professional craft and as a Sufi discipline. The men took a tea break. In the meantime a student of Pappu's arrived. When they resumed the conversation, Ali followed up on these thoughts and asked, "*Sain jī*, what makes a good *ḍhol* player?"

"To learn music, you need ears [*kān*] and tongue [*zabān*]. When my teacher recites *bol*s, I need to be able to produce the same with my tongue and on my drum. In Lahore there are two or four such boys who play. They are our students. One learned from my father; his brother Shabbir is with me. Some Gakkhaṛs also play *ḍhol*. They live in 'rough tents' like itinerants. The guy who plays in the upper area of Shah Jamal is a Gakkhaṛ. He is deaf and dumb. He can't play. You need ears and a tongue to play!

"Normally I play alone, without distraction, or with Jhura. No one can 'match' us. But one day when Shabbir and his brother were playing I said to Jhura, 'They're quick on the uptake [*tez*]; we are, too. Let's join them.' We 'challenged one another' with *mukhṛā*s and enjoyed it a lot. I said, 'Your playing attracted my soul.'"

"What do you call it when you and Jhura play together, like *jugalbandi* . . ." Ali struggled for words, "but when both of you fit one another's strokes together?"

"It is just matching [*milāp*], matching *bol*s. I say [that is, play] these *bol*s [demonstrating]; he says these *bol*s [demonstrating]."

Ali captured these on his tape recorder and noted Pappu's use of the word *milāp*, "matching, meeting, encounter," which connotes not merely replication in musical terms but also artful variation. It also embraces question-answer forms of interplay. As Pappu recited the *bol*s he ascribed to himself, he concluded on a raised pitch; as he recited Jhura's response, he finished on a low pitch. "*Sawāl-jawāb* [question and answer]," Ali said.

"Exactly. We 'mix' within the 'tempo,'" said Pappu, "and then, when I have 'laid down' a *ṭhekā*, say, in *rūpak*, he will play a *mukhṛā* or a *tīyā* over it. Then, I've already set the *naġmah* ['tune,' here, the same as *ṭhekā*], no? Then I am exploring ['moving back and forth']; then I play double [*dogun*] or quadruple [*caugun*] that which is set as the base speed [*thallā*]. Then when I play the *mukhṛā* and the *tīyā*, then I 'sit' [play the background pattern]. I make a 'round' [*cakkar*] and then it is his turn to explore it. Then we both play *thā* at the same time. That is a *gol* ['ball']; they call that *sam*. Sometimes they also call it *k͟hālī* and *bharā* ['empty' and 'filled']." Pappu asked his student and Shahbaz to recite the *naġmah* of *rūpak* as he continued to improvise *bol* patterns over it.

"I heard the term *chēṛ chāṛ* ['mischief'] for what you are calling *phir tuṛ rahnā* ['moving back and forth']; do you use that term?" asked Ali, following up on terminology he had picked up in Multan.

"I call it *laggī, parṇ, gat, toṛā,* or *qaidah*. It is also called *thā dhun*, *bol*s which are done over the ground pattern [*thal*] . . . [*demonstrating*]. All of this I am explaining as if a tabla player has set the *ṭhekā* and you are a *sitār* player or someone, exploring over that. The *toṛā* that I play once, I will not play again, understand? I play a new one every time. Now I am doing *chēṛ*, now I'm 'talking.'" Pappu demonstrated.

Pappu referred back to the term *chēṛ,* which Ali had suggested, implying the meanings perhaps, of "incitement" or "interchange." After referring to the foregoing *bol* patterns as talking, Pappu instilled a sentence-like set of intonations into his recitation, also maintaining the relative lengths of words, phrases, sentences, and pauses between sentences. The demonstration reminded Ali of the way the enormously famous *kathak* dancer Birju Maharaj would turn a *bol* pattern into a narrative, using not only his voice but also his face, hands, and bodily movements.

"*Sain jī*, many of the terms you use are common in classical music. Are there any expressions you use that are particular to the *ḍhol* tradition?" asked Ali.

"No, actually the original purpose [*aṣīl maqṣad*] of *ḍhol* is straight *bhāṅgṛā*." Pappu recited the *bol*s | dhā . ga nā . ga nā . ga dhī . ga |. "We have put tabla inside the *ḍhol*. We play"—Pappu recited a rapid set of *bol*s for *bhāṅgṛā*—"which are actually tabla *bol*s, *bol*s for the fingers. There were some great *ḍhol* players who raised the level of musicianship on the instruments. There was the *mirās̱ī* Baba Khadim Husain, and 'Ali Hayat

Khadim . . . and there was Baba Lal Magpur. Great, great *ḍhol* players. Now dead. Baba Lal was from Gujrāt, the original place for *ḍhol*. He was the one to introduce the round *tīlā*. Previously players used a 'flexible' flat stick made of cane, like the ones used in kites. The sound of that was 'grrrrrr [recites *bol*s] grrrrrr [reciting more *bol*s].'"

Ali had already been thinking that the barrel-shaped Panjabi *ḍhol*, with its interacting patterns on the bass and treble sides, was like the paired cylindrical *ḍhol* and the *tāshā* all rolled into one. Pappu's description of the way the old flexible stick was used on the treble side matched closely the way the flat stick on the *tāshā* is often used to create drum rolls.

"In Lahore everyone used to use the flat stick. Here, in Lahore, Pakistan . . . in Panjab culture, our Lahore . . . I told players about the round stick. It lets me play the *bol*s for the fingers on the *ḍhol*. Some people who don't know play *dhamāl* like this." Pappu recited first in an unadorned manner. "Ones who are skilled will play a lot more like this." He recited rapid strings of syllables. "I listen to good tabla players and then I play. That is my 'interest.' I like listening to classical singers and players. That is what dwells within me."

That evening Ali pored over his notes, contemplating the dimensions of musical competence in this tradition: the fluid relationship between verbal and manual articulations of patterns, the emotional subtleties and speech-like qualities created through manipulations of tempo and intonation, and the spiritual and musical hierarchies.

Lesser musicians are mere imitators. Qualified musicians must transcend mere replication to produce an appropriate variation or response—and yet they must never violate music's *truth* by deviating from the ground pattern. The terminology for performance gets at the agonism and affection in this interchange, as well as its spatiotemporal imagery of making circles, moving back and forth, flying over, and remaining below. Pappu was an interesting personality, all right. At one moment a lump of clay in the hands of his pirs, at the next an agent in absorbing the latest techniques and forms from classical musicians. At one moment a pious devotee for whom the pursuit of fame and money is anathema, at another, a discerning practitioner with a clear sense of his own value as a musician.

As Ali struggled to think how he might write this up, he realized this would all be more than Chandlal had bargained for.

CHAPTER 7

Madho Lal

Ali spent several days after the interview exploring the area around the Madho Lal Husain shrine as preparations were under way for the *'urs*. Ali Muhammad deposited Ali and Salim on Goray Shah Road and the two men wended their way north through Baghbanpura. They passed the shrine of Abdul Ghani and its graveyard. They ambled down a market road. The vendors who sharpened knives and other metal tools created such a rumbling screech that the two were forced temporarily to suspend their conversation.

A wide footpath beyond the market traced a curve from one shrine and graveyard toward another. It led them past an uneven brick wall outside the bend, which bordered a patch of burlap-toned earth. The soil rose in mounds over the graves of a saint's deceased followers. The wooden grave markers—cement if the family could afford them—framed white plaques engraved in black, green, and red.

Standing opposite the cemetery was a wall twelve meters long and two meters tall covered in white indoor-outdoor tiles. Segments of Arabic calligraphy on the smooth wall conformed neatly to the tile boundaries. Devotees could perform ablutions while sitting on cement stumps along the wall's base. A metal pipe with individual spigots ran along it, while a trench at the base of the wall contained the spilling water and provided a space for bathers to place their legs.

A single man with hooded eyes now huddled over the trench washing his face. The man's white *shalwār* was crinkled, hitched up to his knees;

a faded, roughly woven plum towel rested loosely on his left shoulder. He rose as Ali and Salim passed.

"Salām aleikum."

"Wāleikum as-salām."

Ali made a spurious request for directions to Shah Husain's shrine. Muhammad Mushtaq, his *shalwār* back in place, offered to lead the way—he was on his way there himself. Ali represented himself as doing *ziyārat* (visitation/pilgrimage) at the city's famous *mazār*s (shrines). Mushtaq seized the opportunity to expound on the saint's role in his life.

"When I was eighteen I hadn't even a paisa in my pocket. One day, by the blessings of Sarkār [Shah Husain], a man invited me to work in Dubai. In the days of Bhutto [Zulfiqar Ali Bhutto, prime minister 1971–77] everyone could get a passport for twenty-five rupees. Within three days I had a passport, money in my pocket, and a plane ticket. For ten years I worked as a welder for the *goṛa*s [Caucasian employers] and sent money home. I had earnings but no peace, so I returned home. My children had been idly eating and drinking, frittering away our only source of family income. After all that hard work I came home to nothing. Mālik [Shah Husain] gave me a jolt and I was off again to Dubai. I returned a few years later and started working in an automobile-spare-parts shop in Misri Shah [a nearby neighborhood]. I come here on my way to work in the morning and on my way home after work. Now I have everything. I don't need money. There is always great *sukūn* [peace, tranquility] here.

"The *kāfī*s of Shah Husain are very powerful for setting human beings on the straight path," he went on. "Everything will accrue to those who listen to the words of these *kāfī*s and act accordingly, following their hearts. Those who approach the shrine with coarse material demands, saying 'I want money, I want this, I want that' will not be blessed with anything."

Salim commented, "I'm an admirer of Shah Husain's *kāfī*s." Then to Ali he said, "Some say Shah Husain was the originator of the *kāfī*. Supposedly the name comes from '*kāfī*' [enough]. Much meaning packed into few words." Then back to Mushtaq. "They're hard to follow. How did you learn them?"

"I'm not literate. At the Shah Husain Sangat on Thursdays a knowledgeable person reads out a *kāfī* and explains the meaning of difficult words. We sit around him cross-legged in a circle and listen. Then on Sundays a music-*wālā* comes to sing."

"So on Thursdays, first they hold the Sangat and then Pappu Sain walks to Shah Jamal," prompted Salim.

"Pappu Sain . . . Sarkār has given his family so much, but they squandered it—they never 'covered' themselves [saved money]! Pappu's father was a competent musician himself—a strong man with a large mustache, a native of Hoshyarpur. He was blessed with a son when he arrived at the shrine of Sarkār," Mushtaq explained.

So Pappu's background was common knowledge. Ali scribbled: *Pappu and Mushtaq, each in his own way, criticized devotional action with the intent of material gain. Was praying for a son different? Mushtaq himself owed his financial comfort to the agency of the saint, but not because he asked for it, and he chided Pappu for not being financially responsible with what came his way.*

Ali returned to the subject: "Do you have any favorite *kāfīs*?"

Although Mushtaq protested that he could not remember any in their entirety, he was persuaded to recite what he could of his favorite. He liked the theme and thought its words were 'straightforward':

> Oh mother! To whom can I tell
> The condition of pain that separation has caused?
> The smoke of my master descends
> And when I look it's red inside.
> The bread of happiness, the broth of the gallows, and the tinder
> of my sighs.

"This is about Sarkār's love for his mother. He is hurting very badly, and he sees everything burning around him," explained Mushtaq. "My mother is a widow. She roams around here and Sarkār comes to visit her. She's happy. People think she's a *malaṅgnī*. It's been that way for years and years. This *kāfī* really 'pulls' you from the inside, even if you don't fully understand the words. But the 'music' must be set properly in order to produce the desired effect."

"I have heard Pathane Khan sing this one. It's wonderful!" said Salim. He proceeded to recite, with a hint of a tune, a version of the whole *kāfī* he had memorized from a book:

māye nī maiṉ kīnoṉ ākhāṉ		dard vichoṛ dā ḥāl
dhuvāṉ dhukhe mere murshid vālā		jāṉ phūlāṉ tān lāl
sulāṉ mār dīvānī kītī		birhauṉ peyā sāḍe ḵẖayāl
dukhāṉ di roṭī	sūlāṉ dā sālan	āhīṉ dā bālan bāl
jangal bele phire ḍhuṇḍendi		aje nah pāyo lāl
rānjhan rānjhan phirāṉ ḍhuṇḍaindi		rānjhan mere nāl
kahe ḥusain faqir nimānā		shoh mile tāṉ thīvāṉ nahāl

Oh mother, to whom can I tell		The condition [ḥāl] of pain that separation has caused?
The fire of my master smoulders.		If I poke, it is red [lāl].
The poking of spikes drives me mad.		Separation consumes all my thoughts [ḵẖayāl].
Bread of sadness	Broth of the gallows	Ignite [bāl] the tinder of my sighs.
I searched the forest		But could not find the ruby/red/darling [lāl].
I wandered searching for Ranjhan;		Ranjhan is near [nāl] me.
Says faqir Husain the destitute:		Meeting God would be ecstasy [thīvāṉ nahāl].

"Wāh wāh," responded Mushtaq. "That was really 'pithy.'"

Later Salim was to explain some of the 'nuances' of the poem, matters of local significance, and words and figures of speech not found in Urdu. Of the portions he recited, Mushtaq had colloquialized the pronunciation, added vowels appropriate only to singing, and replaced a number of words—in one case with an antonym. According to Salim, many Panjabis reduce the meaning of this poem to Shah Husain's love for his mother, possibly because of the way they hear it performed. The first line, the only line in which the word *mother* appears, is sung as a refrain. The impact of line one is further magnified in performance because singers only select some of the other lines when they render the *kāfī*.

At that later point Salim wrote out the whole poem, noting that the story of Hīr and Ranjhā (alluded to at the poem's end but not included in Mushtaq's version at all) has taken many forms over the centuries. Among them, he explained, Waris Shah's version holds an exalted status in Panjabi literature. The impoverished Ranjhā falls in love with Hīr, the daughter of a wealthy headman; she reciprocates his affections, but class differences prevent the two from marrying. Shah Husain's tortured love for Madho, itself a metaphor for divine love, formed the basis for his adopting the persona of Hīr.

Ali reflected, Is Shah Husain confiding in his mother, like a girl to her mother, about a secret love? Might *mother* also refer to Shah Husain's own pir, who would, by the logic of Sufi devotion, be not only like a parent, but also like a female lover in relation to God? Is it a sign of his master's spiritual success that Shah Husain could see the redness of his master's fire, the visible evidence of his own spiritual burning? Husain's own sustenance (bread and broth) cooks over the heat generated by his sorrow, but he cannot find the color red (*lāl*) in the embers of his own tinder. Might someone read the second occurrence of the word *lāl* not merely as meaning red but as a specific reference to one of the rubies (*la'l*) that Lal Shahbaz Qalandar had dropped in the forest for his ardent follower? *Lāl* is obviously also Ranjhā: Hīr cannot find her *darling* (*lāl*), who is lost or dead in the forest (the forest plays a prominent role in many redactions). But like the allegorical search for the mythic Simorgh in Fariduddin Attar's Sufi classic, *The Conference of the Birds*, this quest has led Hīr and Shah Husain not to the other, but to a discovery that the other is the self. Shah Husain is Lal Husain.

In Mushtaq's presence, barely losing eye contact, Ali scratched out the basis for some of these later reflections: follow up on 'mother' theme . . . how performance affects interpretation . . . how poems relate to life experience . . . simultaneous meanings of lāl and semantic parallels set up by rhyme.

At this juncture he simply asked, "What does this mean, 'searched the forest but I could not find the *lāl*'?"

Ignoring the poem's context, Mushtaq summarized Shah Husain's story: Madho used to live across the river from his friend, the faqir Shah Husain. Madho's mother used to give him money to procure groceries from town; he used to meet Shah Husain on the way and give him the money. When Madho returned home he was empty-handed. One day Madho's mother complained and word reached Shah Husain. He instructed Madho, "Take your basket and heap it up with earth clods." When Madho and his mother uncovered the basket at home they found a huge pile of red rubies *(la'l)*.

Salim added what he'd heard: "They called him Lal Husain because he wore red clothes and danced. Madho ran away from home to be with him, and when his parents took him away, the saint lost his power to perform miracles. The orthodoxy accused Shah Husain of homosexuality, but those who followed him called it 'pure love.' Now they're buried together in the same shrine. Lal Husain's a patron saint of Lahore's gay community, among others."

The shrine of Madho Lal Husain at night. The gray-haired man holding the notebook is the late Dr. Adam Nayyar. December 26, 2003. Photo by the author.

Arriving at the shrine a few minutes later, the three men entered the compound through a red brick Tudor arch. Stretching away from them to the immediate left was an open-fronted, squat, rectangular pavilion with green-painted grillwork. Men sit there, Mushtaq said, reciting the poetry of Shah Husain and Waris Shah over loudspeakers throughout the *'urs*. Along the right side of the passageway was another graveyard—this one more well-endowed, with gracefully hewn tombs of white and burnt-red marble resting above ground. Rectangular soil beds upon many of the tombs nourished live greenery or were at least strewn with rose petals.

Salim pointed to a freshly installed sepulcher for the celebrated Panjabi poet Ustad Daman (1911–84) directly opposite the right side of the shrine. "Even Faiz," Salim explained, referring to Pakistan's acclaimed Urdu poet Faiz Ahmad Faiz (1911–84), "deferred to the Panjabi poets Shah Hussain, Bulleh Shah, and Ustad Daman. This place is drenched in Panjabiyat!"

Again the mention of Bulleh Shah. Ali checked the name from his earlier notes and asterisked it with the current date.

In preparation for the *'urs*, hundreds of thousands of tiny lights and ornaments were strung onto filaments woven into an elaborate net overhead. Vendors had also set up for the occasion. On the ground to the right, a ginger-turbaned man sat beside a tall stack of brightly-colored cloth blankets and floor coverings—only the metal grille bordering the graveyard kept the heap from tipping over. Along the left was a long, flat tent with merchants proffering cheap jewelry, gaudy plastic toys, rose petals, and cassettes; the wares hanging along the front of the tent were uniform all the way down, rendering one stall indistinguishable from the next. Faqirs, beggars, drummers, pirs and their disciples, and entire families were camped out on mats along every available wall, around every tree, and amongst the tombs in the graveyard. Men and women shuffled in and out as children laughed and scampered about.

The corridor led straight on to the two layers of rounded archways making up the gateway to the inner courtyard of the shrine. The rounding of the first arch was given texture by symmetrical but varied scallops, joining at the top with a head-sized arch topped by a light. A man stood to the left of the opening behind neatly strung masses of rose and orange flower petals, displayed for sale. Yellow-gold streamers with crimson bulbs or faux flowers adorned the top and sides of the arch. Suspended above the flower seller, red and green blankets (*cādar*s) hung invitingly as offerings to the saint. These ones were inscribed with the Arabic word *qul* (say!). The final letter of this word, *lām*, looped around and under to the left to cradle a finer inscription of verses from the Qur'ān. Yellow, red, and green flags along the top and sides of the archway framed the view of the shrine's green dome.

A *malaṅg* walking by the shrine of Madho Lal Husain shortly before the *ʻurs*. A bit of the fire pit (*cirāġdān*) is visible to the left of and behind the tree. Behind the fire pit is the wall of the shrine itself, plastered with announcements of the *ʻurs*. In the upper right corner of the photo, the word *qalandar* can be seen in Urdu/Panjabi script at the end of a sign that reads, "Ḥaẓrat sak̲h̲ī mādho lāl ḥusain mast qalandar." Above the sign is part of the painting depicting the *ka'bah*, with streaks of light issuing from a ball in unseen hands. The entrance to the main shrine is below the painting and sign. March 25, 2005. Photo by the author.

The top of the archway was dominated by a large sign in Arabic that read: "Māshā'llāh, yā 'allāh, lā il-lāha illa'l-lāh muḥammadur rasūl 'allāh, yā muhammad (Praise God, Hail Allah! No god but God, Muhammad is the Prophet of God, Hail Muhammad!)."

"No indication of whose shrine this is!" Salim pointed out. He went on to explain the role of Shah Husain's shrine as a lodestone for Panjabi chauvinism. Some find this separatism threatening to national and Islamic unity. Such persons not only deny Shah Husain's status as a Muslim but also disseminate their views in school textbooks. Placing the *Kalmah* right at the entrance to the shrine, he argued, is a gesture designed to encourage inclusion of Shah Husain in representations of mainstream Islam. But it masks the ecstatic and transgressive undercurrent of the shrine and narratives of the saint.

Just then, two men climbed up on ladders to cover the Arabic sign with a colored poster of Shah Husain, "designed and manufactured by Saeed Glass Company." On it, a bald and gray-bearded Shah Husain sits in front of his *mazār*, flanked by images of the *ka'bah* and Jerusalem floating in an emerald glow. A saffron-clad boy—presumably Madho—bows slightly over the old man and holds a dazzling ball of light in his two hands; perhaps he's giving the light, or perhaps he's drawing the light from Shah Husain's heart. A calligrapher was now inscribing in red, below the picture, "Ḥaẓrat sak̲h̲ī mādho lāl ḥusain mast qalandar." Had Shah Husain's name now acquired the epithet for Lal Shahbaz as well? Did the very act of reading this new sign constitute a performance of *mast qalandar*?

Off to the left was the *cirāġdān*, where a bonfire is lit during the *'urs*. Resembling a well, its vertical earthen shell was over a meter high and nearly three meters in diameter. Dozens of old and new oblong clay lamps lay distributed on the thick rim alongside brass structures with similarly shaped lamps attached to their trunks or branches. One stood leaning a bit to the right with chandelier-like arms, five at the lower level, four at the second, and two at the top. Another looked like a bicycle: two wheels with lamps welded onto the spokes, the tires, the frame, and the seat. Spilled oil, clarified butter, and paraffin left sticky dark patches and drips along the rim and down the sides of the lamps and *cirāġdān* alike.

Salim, observing Ali as he inspected the motley collection, said, "This *'urs* is popularly known as the Festival of Lights (*Melā Cirāġān*). Thousands of people bring lamps and candles, tossing them into the *mac* [bonfire]." Ali immediately supposed there was a connection with the ball of light in the poster and with the mystical idea of *nūr,* the divine light Muhammad has passed on through his legitimate spiritual successors. He shared his thoughts with Salim, who said, "Could be. Some say the fire combines Zoroastrian and Hindu elements. It's a thing the Shī'ī *malaṅg*s keep alive." But what did locals think?, Ali wondered.

Approaching from the left was a bearded, orthodox-looking man who turned out to be the imam of the mosque of the shrine, an official of the Panjab Auqāf Department (Ministry of Religious Affairs). This shrine was one of the last holdouts after the Pakistani government, initially under the orders of Ayub Khan (r. 1958–69), undertook to nationalize all the Sufi shrines in the country, thereby reducing the political potency of individual religious figures (Ewing 1997, 72). The shrine had come under the Auqāf only a few years back, Salim had told him earlier, after years of court cases. Ali was sensitive to the tension between *sharī'at* and *ṭarīqat*, the law and the way, evidenced in so many ways around here—the covering of the sign earlier being only the most obvious. What did the maulvi make of this place?

Maulvi Hafiz Muhammad Ramzan had just emerged from the mosque, some twenty or thirty meters beyond the *cirāġdān*. The four men greeted one another, and Mushtaq introduced his new acquaintances. After preliminary small talk, Ali asked the maulvi what 'impression' this shrine had made upon him. Ramzan hedged at first: "We are at the door step of the *buzurg*s [elders, that is, the saint]; Allah has given us everything: children and a good life."

More pointedly, Ali asked, "Is there some connection between the fire and the *buzurg*s?"

"*Kuch nahīn*,* the people are celebrating the marriage of Sarkār. They are expressing their 'happiness' in their own individual manner. They hope to 'coax' Sarkār into turning his attention toward them and that their actions will make him happy."

Open-minded maulvi, thought Ali, thankfully.

"Happiness is 'compulsory and essential,'" said another man, joining the conversation in Urdu. His name was Muhammad Asif Alim Lodhi, and he had been drawn to Lahore from Karachi "like a magnet," just as his late father had prophesied.

"The lamps are *mannat*s [fulfillments of vows]," said yet a sixth man.

"The lamps are for the sake of the faqirs," argued Lodhi. "As Shah Husain's poetry says, 'Neither of the rich, nor of the poor, the lamps burn only for the faqir'; they go on burning, eternally. You will never see lamps burning even for the graves of wealthy men or kings. There aren't enough lamps for everyone to light them individually, so the *cirāġdān* counts for everyone. It's the biggest lamp of all."

As the conversation lost focus, Mushtaq directed Ali and Salim to a cement platform about twenty-four square meters, midway between the *cirāġdān* and the pavilion they had seen when entering. Chalky floral designs enlivened the red-oxide surface of the smooth cement. At the end facing the mosque, a chest-high brick wall (also called a *cirāġdān*) supported several more of the curiously shaped verdigris lamps.

"This area," Mushtaq indicated with a restrained sweep of his hand, "is the domain of the *malaṅg*s." Some of the *malaṅg*s sitting, crouching, or standing there looked the part, but many were unextraordinary in their dress and bearing. "Despite its benign appearance," Mushtaq explained discreetly, "this is a delicate piece of turf with its own hierarchy and means of establishing consensus." It may have been a little awkward for Mushtaq, but he made a few tactful inquiries to determine the pecking order. Then he

*Literally, "nothing at all." Here, merely a transitional expression that evades the direct question and focuses on the *'urs* in general.

introduced Ali, who was by now openly identifying himself as a journalist from Lucknow interested in music and the Sufi *ṭarīqat*.

Ali was directed to Muhammad Aslam, aka Baba Manna, a sinewy septuagenarian dressed in khaki with a fringed light-blue checkered cloth tied around his head. A bit intimidated, Ali decided to start simply and resume his earlier line of inquiry. Pointing to the fire hole at the base of the wall, he asked, "What's that for?"

"So far as I'm concerned, the purpose of the *mac* is to cook and to take support from the fire night and day." Having himself raised the topic of cooking, Babaji now took the opportunity to state in his best English, "I am Cook-Man, Army." Carefully reaching into the pocket of his *qamīz*, he produced a laminated testament to his ability: "He cooked the food and eatables of such a High Standard that it was personally appreciated by General Officer DP Army and also by guests and all others who have attended this auspicious occasion . . . Administrator and Coordinator Ali Jawahar Khan, from the Directorate of Procurement, Army, Ministry of Defense, Block #8, Liaqat Barracks, Karachi, 12 July 1979."

"Wāh, wāh," responded Salim.

Mushtaq looked into Ali's eyes, poker-faced.

This was the second time Ali's preconceptions about the state of being a faqir or *malaṅg* were unsettled. Feeling more confident now that the chief *malaṅg* had taken the opportunity to distinguish himself, Ali announced, "I've come here to learn about *dhamāl* and about the fine men who have dedicated their lives to the Friends of Allah [Wali-Ullah, that is, saints]. Now it is my honor to meet all of you and I wondered if you could tell me, what is a *malaṅg*? I really don't understand."

Babaji explained as if to a child, "*Malaṅg*s are people who have run away from their homes and native places. Some are hurt by the police and run away. Some are destroyed by drugs and run away. Some suffer from hunger and roam from door to door. Some are completely wiped out by intoxicants and seek sanctuary at the shrine. But the real *malaṅg*s are those who have made a name for themselves and who have historical festivals in their honor."

Another *malaṅg* waxed bucolic, saying, "A true *malaṅg* is out there in the wilderness, in the mountains, in the forest, in the streams, and the sea."

Ali suppressed a smile as he tried to envision the latter.

As Babaji-the-cook warmed to his subject, he included himself: "We do not practice what we preach, we've run away from our families. We have been disobedient and then we have come here."

Shehzad, a voluntary servant of the shrine wearing a bright red and white cap with vertical sides, added ruefully, "We have lice in our pubic hair."

Babaji, opting for a more elegant tone, offered a line of poetry. "'Difficult is the life of a faqir, ascending the gallows, to beg from door to door, and to call every woman a sister.' This is how Miān Muhammad Baksh Jhelumin, the Rumi of Kashmir, put it. He's buried in Khaṛi Sharif with his master, Hazrat Baba Pir-e Shah Ghazi Bu 'Ali Qalandar—also known as Damṛi Wāle Sarkār, because he will not allow the sun to set unless at least 25,000 small coins [*damṛi*] are donated at his shrine each day."

Saghir Ahmed, a reputed *ḍhol* player who happened to be visiting the shrine that day, overheard the conversation and added, "Singers use special *rāga*s to sing Mīān Muhammad Baksh Jhelumin's epic *Saiful Maluk* [Sword of Kings]. It's a common pastime in our Panjab countryside to hold

A likeness of Saghir Ahmed accompanied by the words "King of kings of *dhamāl* Saghir Ali Khan." On a building near the residence of Saghir Ahmed. Jhelum, Panjab, Pakistan, December 25, 2003. Photo by the author.

special gatherings dedicated to singing this poetry. As drummers we know to accompany it with either *cañcal, dādra,* or *bhāṅgṛā*. Like that, each style of singing has its own *ṭhekā* and *rāga*. When you come to the *'urs*, you'll hear Waris Shah's *Hīr-Ranjhā*, which is always sung to Panjab Bhairavi, although it has no drummed support."

Glad for the input of a musician, Ali turned the question to Saghir. "What's a *malaṅg* in your view?"

"A true *malaṅg* must be *majẕūb* [lost in the love of Allah] and in a state of *mastī*. Anyone who is just tired of poverty or has a fight at home and puts on a bunch of beads and comes over here is not a real *malaṅg* but pretends to be one."

There was a brief ripple of tension.

"Is it possible for a true *malaṅg* to be a musician of any kind?" Ali asked.

Saghir sort of laughed and said, "I know what you're talking about. I think Pappu is great, but if you are a *darvesh* you don't need to play. Getting high on cannabis is not a good way to become a skilled musician." He enacted a caricature, wagging his head and smiling. "What do you think?"

Ali avoided the question. "Babaji, you just mentioned the name of Bu 'Ali Qalandar. What is the difference between a *malaṅg* and a *qalandar*?

"*Qalandar* means . . . there have only been two-and-a-half *qalandar*s in this world. Lal Shahbaz Qalandar is one. Bu 'Ali is one. And Rabia Basri in Iraq (being female) is half a *qalandar*. You know about Baba Farid and Rabia Basri?" Babaji asked. He continued without waiting for a response: "Baba Farid goes over to meet her and when he's entering her domain he hears birds chirping and gets irritated by the sounds. He says, 'May you [birds] die,' and they die.

"So here stands Rabia Basri, scooping water out of the well, spilling it and spilling it. Baba Farid makes a sign asking for water. He says, 'You're not quenching the thirst of my heart and you're spilling full scoops of water!' Rabia Basri replies, 'I know you murdered those birds on your way here.' Baba Farid asks, 'Where do you get your information?' She answers, 'The same place you do. The hut of my beloved is burning one hundred miles away. And I have to extinguish these fires!'"

Ali felt like this was a much more satisfying explanation of the *mac* than he had yet heard, even if it wasn't meant to be.

Then, enigmatically, Babaji quoted Iqbal, got up, and left: "Go into your self and find out the secrets of life. If you can't be mine, then at least be your own."

On that philosophical note, Ali and Salim decided it was time for them to leave as well. They thanked Mushtaq, the maulvi, and the others and said they would return in the coming days for the *'urs*. Ali took Saghir's contact information, hoping to meet him again at the *'urs*.

: : :

Saturday morning, March 30. Ali woke to the sharp bouquet of burning garbage. It stung the eyes even more than the smoky acridity of everyday air in Lahore, which was already almost as bad as Delhi's. A jet roared high in the air, cutting a wake in the mackerel sky. But he had no complaints. Sufiya had arrived to join the men for chai, omelettes, and butter toast before the three of them headed off to the *'urs*. Ten busy days in Lahore did nothing to bestill Ali's incipient feelings of desire for Sufiya—who was, after all, staying only ten minutes away. Sufiya, with fresh self-confidence owing to a new gym routine, had decided to dress like the cosmopolitan she was. Her black designer jeans traced her hips smoothly while her red silk blouse accented her "proportions"—partly veiled by her black *dupaṭṭa*. Set off by ruby earrings and gold sandals, her skin positively shimmered. Ali complimented her, very politely, and when she blushed, fumbled for words to soften the impact of his obvious attention.

She deflected his near-apology, saying women in Lahore are not delicate flowers. Northern Panjabi men do not hesitate to say what they like and what they want. "They think we appreciate comments on our 'physique,'" she said. "I, for one, prefer subtlety and respect. I decided to dress like a foreigner today, by the way. I'm out of place as it is, and would prefer to be seen as a Pakistani living abroad if I'm to be pushing through the crowd with you two."

"But," she continued, "while we're on the subject, you're looking quite smart yourself."

He'd shaved, bought a white silk *shalwār qamīz*, and even had his hair cut. "The herpetologist grows to resemble his subject," he said dramatically, cupping his hands above his ears. "I was starting to look like a *malanġ* myself, so I thought I'd spruce up. 'Difficult is the life of a faqir, ascending the gallows, to beg from door to door, and to call every woman a sister,'" he added, his attempt at Panjabi slain by the *lehja* of his Urdu.

This time Sufiya didn't blush, but took Ali's hand, grasped it tightly, and let it go just as Salim entered the room with chai. "My mother's still out of town and our houseboy has taken leave for the *'urs*. We'll have to manage on our own."

No one was complaining.

Ali Muhammad dutifully transported them to Shalimar Gardens. They decamped and dissolved into the throng.

The first thing Ali felt was disorientation. There were more small tents and cooking sites, with smoke streaming thickly from several directions, landmarks from his earlier visits giving way to previously unnoticed features—trees, gravestones, cement structures, and grillework. With the *cirāġdān*, many other fires spanned his field of vision, from small hand-held oil lamps, to modest kerosene stoves, to an enflamed tree stump. This latter was perched on boulders off to the shrine's left toward the mosque, its hollow core a chimney for burning shafts of wood fed to the fire below. For all Ali knew, it might have been a sapling in Shah Husain's time.

From his courtyard vantage point, the multitude of attendees expanded outward farther than Ali could see. The swarming bodies were like cells under a microscope, some congregating, others streaming past. Drummers with their *dhamālī*s maintained their stations (*thān*s, places/turf). Aside from functionaries, most of the others present were either fixed in place watching the *dhamālī*s or trying to squeeze from one place to another.

Ali had read somewhere that Maharaja Ranjit Singh, the nineteenth-century Sikh ruler of the Panjab, used to patronize a spring festival here. The *'urs* became a multifaceted event that drew pilgrims from many religious backgrounds, including Hindus, Sikhs, and Christians. Partition had put an end to most of the religious diversity, and Islamization under the rule of General Zia ul-Haq since 1978* had severely dampened women's participation at most shrines, but even now Ali could see attendees from all sectors of Lahore's population: a rough-handed, lean man in green propelled to the left; a fresh-looking pear of a man strolling to the right; a mother in her long white *dupaṭṭa*, talking animatedly; a black-shirted man slipping by quickly with an infant at his chest; teen-aged children laughing and pushing one another; a tired-looking, wiry volunteer in soiled clothing stirring a communal pot of rice; an eight-year-old, wedged between a tree and a table, cleaning a pile of chickpeas; a tall boy in a black business suit filing past a lonely drummer; the backs of fifty people's heads, capped, *dupaṭṭa*ed, turbaned—whether bald or blessed with hair, long or short, curly or straight, soiled, oiled or hennaed.

The eyes of the latter crowd were locked on a pir and his disciples: on the left, a mother—dressed in albescent, diaphanous layers of fabric—joining hands in movement with her child; next, the father, chained in roses, raising his hands and crying, "Jhū-ū-ū-ū-le Lā-ā-ā-ā-l." On the right, a young boy, whipping his head forward and shoulders back, chest forward and head back, to the hand and finger movements of a grinning, toothless pir.

*He was in power until 1988.

The bald master, reposed in the shade of a massive tree, wore a garland of yellow flowers over a sweater geometrically designed in white, maroon, and mauve. He faced the shrine. His *ḍhol* accompanists and the boy faced him. Not everyone can attend the shrine at the same time. Ali walked closer and inquired about the man in the sweater. Salim and Sufiya trailed behind.

"That's Baba Rashid Sain from Burewala," said Khurshid Ali, one of his disciples. "We accompany our pir sahab here every year and sing songs of Babaji."

"Babaji is doing *dhamāl* with his hands. He sits because he is crippled," added Parvez Bhat, another *murīd.* "He's training that little boy"—as if it weren't obvious.

Behind him Ali heard a familiar voice of cynicism. It was Shehzad, Mr. Lice. "The kids are doing *dhamāl* because money is being thrown. If a five-rupee note drops they'll bend down and pick it up."

"That lady is dancing with her child in fulfillment of a vow to Sarkār," said Khurshid, ignoring or not hearing Shehzad's comment.

The boy *dhamālī*-in-training suddenly collapsed. Two men carried him away, arms and legs still splayed and convulsing. "They lift him off the ground to break his *ḥāl.* It's dangerous. He's not ready," Parvez said.

Behind Rashid Sain, the sound of overdriven speakers projected a man's shouting, hectoring voice. Ali couldn't make much of the distorted Panjabi, but it sounded like speeches on Hazrat Ali—just like a Shī'ī *majlis.* Badgering gave way to melismatic singing in a *rāga* Ali recognized as Sindh Bhairavi. Ali turned to Salim, but it was Sufiya who said, "This is Waris Shah's *Hīr-Ranjhā.* He's reciting Hīr."

"This is Panjab Bhairavi," Salim reminded Ali. "*Hīr-Ranjhā* is always sung in this *rāga.*"

"Sounds like Sindh Bhairavi to me."

"In the Panjab it's Panjab Bhairavi!" Sufiya retorted, with a wink.

Ali wormed his way to the flaming tree-trunk. Niamat and Shahid Ali were playing with their backs to a magnificent banyan tree. Something plunked down from above. A bearded *goṛa* in a purple *shalwār qamīz* scrunched and contorted himself among the branches, looking for his video camera's eyepiece. Shahid motioned for Ali to draw near. He handed the *goṛa* the small black cylinder and joined Shahid. A third man played the *ciṃta* (long steel tongs) and, with another youth, collected the rupee notes that devotees were showering on the drummers and the *dhamālī*s. Two *dhamālī*s 'played' *dhamāl* in the foreground: one in his twenties or thirties with a green outfit and a crimson sash, the other in his sixties in a saffron outfit with a green sash. His shoulder-length hennaed hair almost matched.

Green ripped his head from side to side, his slightly long hair obscuring his face. Then he made a dance move out of the conventional salute to the shrine, elbow bent, fingers to forehead. Saffron took small steps in place, turning slowly, making graceful moves with his open right palm. Then he froze, arm straight out, finger pointing to the shrine, gaze fixed. Behind him was a mentally feeble twig of a man with shorn head who had been counted among the *malaṅg*s on Ali's earlier visit. His chartreuse top nearly reached his skinny naked ankles.

Shehzad had managed to follow Ali and was probably wanting money. Shehzad took it upon himself to comment on the authenticity of the *dhamāl*. "See, the true *dhamālī* will have *lagan* [attachment] and will show attention to Sarkār. He will be in a state of *mastī* in his *lagan*."

A youth with adolescent mustache—sporting black trousers, blue shirt, and shiny gold watch—dragged his male companion before the drummers. Interlocking their hands together overhead, they began to dance. Then the friend broke loose with a string of *bhāṅgṛā* moves—raising and lowering his bent forearms from the elbow while throwing his head forward and back, raising one leg and hopping, and then the other. A corpulent charcoal-dressed man with stiff wavy hair chased the boys from the *thān*.

"He's a *baddhā* of Shah Jamal," said Shehzad, making a motion around his neck to indicate the beads. "Those boys were just making 'drama' for themselves, doing a disco and a bit of this and a bit of that. A true *malaṅg*, you see, whether he's straight upside down or right side up, he will keep on turning, he'll keep on turning until he falls down unconscious."

An older faqir stooped to stick his face into the flame under the stump before entering the arena. His impressive gray locks and his formidable beard did not catch fire but stood out against his knee-length, elaborately embroidered cerise *perahan* (frock) and white *dhoti*.

"That guy always scatters embers from the fire to mark his territory (*thān*) so that 'non-entities' stay away," said Shehzad.

Everyone stood back or was pushed back by the *baddhā*. The new man was Arif Sain, Shahid and Niamat's dedicated *dhamālī*. For a moment, they thinned the texture of their *dhamāl,* emphasizing the motive:

Sain jī began to swing his outstretched arms forward and back and, in alternation, bend his knees and lift his widely spaced heels. At first it seemed his steps matched the drumming simply—the left foot touching the ground at the beginning of the pattern, the right in the middle. But no, Arif Sain was dragging; after a few rounds the right foot fell where the left had once done. Then, as the *ḍholī*s executed cross-rhythms in anticipation of the first accented stroke in the *tīyā*, Arif Sain threw his shoulders and head back to join them with a bodily accent.

Ignoring the other two parts of the *tīyā*, Sain began his next routine. Bending his neck, he rotated his head, which began both to transform his hair into a propeller and to drag his body, which had the uncanny appearance of spinning more slowly than his head. His feet, spread wide, clunked stiffly from his sharply crooked knees. Finally his outstretched arms rose. Again he synched at the beginning of the *tīyā*, reoriented himself, and began once more. This time he combined the previous move with up-and-down head movements, outward-bent wrists, and slightly flapping arms. The falcon returned to kiss the stump.

Sufiya had by this time caught up with Ali and squeezed Shehzad away, the warmth and perfume of her presence registering itself in Ali's anatomy with more than a shiver. Salim, who appeared on Ali's other side, said, "*dekh-udhar,* look at that family over there!"

A burly mother accompanied an attractively full-faced woman in her mid-twenties and her younger sister, both of whom were dressed in black, with black chiffon draped over (and slipping from) their heads and green scarves over their shoulders. Men and boys of several generations sat assembled around them, a few tending to large pots of food. A man with a saffron *pagaṛī* waved a handful of rupee notes around the food before him, encircled his party behind him, and handed it to the *ciṃta*-player. (The blessings of the saint, it would seem, travel to the givers along the reverse path.) Salim had directed Ali to the scene as the young woman was becoming increasingly animated, her head bobbing and lolling sideways in time to the music.

Arif Sain, inserting a variation, raised the corners of his *perahan* as if he were carrying grain or cradling an infant. Someone belted out, "*'ī* ." A new greybeard appeared from the right in a fancy rose-and-yellow robe which hung open slightly, revealing a full-length white outfit underneath. A stiff cap and puce scarf completed the finery. The box of wares he was toting looked like the wooden cage an Indian astrologer would use for his fortune-telling parrot.

"That's the Perfume Baba," Shehzad exclaimed. "He's been coming here from Jallo ever since I can remember. He's an *aṣl dhamālī.*"

Perfume tipped his head subtly in acknowledgment of Arif Sain, went to place his "cage" next to the stump, and took a deep draft of the smoke escaping from underneath it before entering the *thān*. Arif Sain stepped aside. The graceful movement of Perfume's hands and hips gradually gave way to the moves of an inspired Niamat Ali, who began to spin while playing the *ḍhol*. The Perfume Man moved aside, manipulating his fingers and arms as if in conversation with Niamat.

Shehzad commented, "These guys will do anything for money. That *ḍholī* will lie down on the floor and pick up a banknote with one eyelid, then turn on the other side to pick up another, and catch a third with his mouth."

The *ḍholī*, pace Shehzad, resumed his position next to Shahid Ali. Now Arif Sain arrived flying through the air from the left (how an old man could jump so high Ali did not know). Arif and Perfume played *dhamāl* each according to his own style. Perfume, holding the end of a silk handkerchief in one hand and placing his other hand behind his back, shimmied sideways seductively.

"You know about Bulleh Shah, *nā*?" asked Sufiya.

"*Bolo*. Tell me."

"Bulleh Shah lived in the Panjab in the late-seventeenth, early-eighteenth century. He somehow offended his pir sahab and went into exile. For twelve years he took up residence with the *kanjar*s"—as Pappu had said. "You see, his pir was a great lover of music and dance. One day, Bulleh Shah dressed up as a courtesan in ankle bells, dance costume, the works. He appeared before his master, dancing and singing seductively. His master didn't recognize him at first, but was taken by the bait."

"What happened then?"

"He'd redeemed himself. Bulleh Shah resumed his discipleship and became one of the most important poets of the Panjab."

"So these *dhamālī*s, wearing anklets, fancy clothes, wiggling their hips . . ."

"All quite aware," she said, reading his thoughts.

Suddenly the presence of transvestites, their farinaceous makeup and exaggerated femininity, made new sense. He had seen three of them dancing in an area all their own—only for money, he'd thought.

" . . . *matlab*: 'I'm a prostitute before you. I've no honor. If I can make you happy with my movements, that's fine by me.' The aim is love, however it might be obtained. For that matter, actual prostitutes come here, too. Their *'ishq* for the saint is genuine. In Sehwan, you'll see whole tents of them camped out. There's a special ritual in which courtesans dance before the shrine. The background is, when Lal Shahbaz Qalandar came to Sindh from [present-day] Azerbaijan, he settled in a brothel area. Lal Shahbaz and Lal Husain are connected like this, it's all *pyār* (love)."

The attractive woman Ali and Salim had noticed before now smiled brightly and mimicked the raised arm movements of Perfume, who faced her from the other side of the smoking stump; she continued the movements and elaborated, twisting her wrists, even as he turned away. She held rupee notes over the head of the elder next to her until a helper collected the *vel*. Then she stood and stretched her arms in an arch up and down with one shoulder forward, then the other—a sexy, filmy, *bhāngṛā*-type movement. The *ciṃta* player collected another offering from her. The mother offered two notes in succession, circling each note over another man's head. The daughter's motions increased in intensity.

"She's a *malaṅgnī*," said Shehzad, who saw the object of Ali's attention, "a Behāran (from Bihar, India) . . . comes every Thursday."

Perfume and she locked into a more extended exchange of shoulder, arm, and hip movements and then Perfume took a rest, stepping around the stump to sit close by her. Arif resumed, torso nestled horizontally between his bent knees, head down, arms pumping.

"Raqṣ-e-bismillah," said Salim, who thought Arif looked like a headless chicken. "Mehr Ali sings in his *qawwālī*, 'doing the dance of *bismillah* (sacrifice)'—like the Sufi image of the seeker, wandering the world, directionless."

"Overinterpreting," said Sufiya, confident in her role as arbiter of meaning.

Now the *malaṅgnī*'s *mastī* impelled her into the *thān*, her movements not as refined as the others,' repetitive but not neat. Her face assumed a dull expression and her hair fell free, flying around, sticking to her face. She was hopping and jogging with floppy, ill-controlled, asymmetrical hand and arm movements. Then her arms went straight to the sides, elbows bending, sweeping her hands toward her chest and back.

"Fuck me," someone uttered, sotto voce, near Ali's ear.

The *malaṅgnī* traced a large circle with her right arm, ending it abruptly but exhaustedly with the first articulation of the *tīyā*. Sensitive to the cadence, she repeated the movement three times with the *tīyā*. Then she collapsed. Kneeling, she resumed the *dhamāl* with her head shaking and torso spiraling.

Her mother entered the *thān* with long arm and leg movements using all the space available . . . put her hands directly into the fire . . . raised her pointer fingers in the air . . . skipped with an imaginary rope. Returning to the double pointing motion, she bent over with her arms stretched forward like horns. Left and right she shook like a buffalo. Her arms flopped free and, as she twisted, her limp right arm got hoisted over her left shoulder. This turned into *zanjīr kā mātam*, sans scourge, no doubt about it.

"I had a feeling those women were Shī'ī," said Salim, "especially with the black dress."

Ali choked on the overpoweringly thick smoke of the *mac*, which had just blown in their direction from behind. People hurled candle after candle into the blaze from more than a meter away, and black clouds tumbled out. Ali could see why these *malaṅg*s had chosen the flame under this stump for their loving attention.

They mutually agreed it was time to leave. On their way out they saw those who'd been marginalized. Here was a drummer on the side, not called upon to accompany anyone. "His drum's too big, and he's not playing 'in tune.'" Some boys were fooling with dance movements in another area, the two drummers practicing their *bhāṅgṛā* pattern. "Disco," said Shehzad. When they were almost at the outer archway, Shehzad said, "You know, I sweep the floor for Sarkār and for his sake somebody gives me five, somebody gives me ten [rupees] . . . and some give me fifty and some give me a hundred." Ali pressed a few fresh notes into his hand and Shehzad smiled with genuine satisfaction.

: : :

In Pakistan, despite tensions in some government shrines between the mosque and the shrine proper,[1] understanding music, movement, poetic recitation, and other forms of action in Sufi shrines involves more nuanced categories than those of "scriptural Islam" and "Islam on the ground." Even a rough map of the Madho Lal Husain complex would suggest this with its dedicated *malaṅg* space, with its centers and peripheries created through performance, and with the ongoing transformations of the shrine as Panjabi nationalists, the Auqāf, and other interest groups struggle for their piece. Texts and jurists are just as embedded in social action and dialogue as local practitioners—of whatever literacy—are mindful of the Qur'ān and the *hadith*. The latter engage with Qur'ānic sounds and mediated jurisprudence and find responses to these sounds and rulings embedded in ritual, poetry, narrative, and debate.

Members of all these Muslim cultural groups are as engaged as any other in ongoing processes of "entextualization" and "contextualization," picking up the "precipitates of continuous cultural processes" (Silverstein and Urban 1996, 1) and inserting them into new contexts—generating in turn new "sedimentations" (texts) for others to contextualize in new settings. Sung forms of *kāfī* emerge through processes of contextualization.[2] Someone sets a short poem to music—or alters an existing song—omitting or substituting verses, changing pronunciation or vocabulary. In time the new sung version takes on a life of its own, registers on the minds of listeners, becomes a new kind of not-merely-verbal text. Mushtaq, in the version of the poem he cited, invested perhaps excessive significance in line one because of the particular section of the *kāfī* with which he was familiar. In Mushtaq's life, the poem presented a powerful message about love for one's mother. Another listener or reader might contemplate the poem in light of Waris Shah's *Hīr-Ranjhā*, a move which would likely reduce the impact of the mother theme dramatically and emphasize the parallels between Shah Husain's narrative and the myriad of allegories in Sufi poetry for the human love of God.

As-yet-unrealized contextualizations form part of the horizon potentials of any text. These might be dangerous. The *mārū* pattern in Multan, in the obscene verbal form hostile Sunni children propagate, could easily be deployed in a polarized public space, for instance, to instigate communal violence. In Ali's story, however, it merely serves as fodder in his exploration of how actors invest drumming with verbal significance. The children's chant is, for his purposes, equivalent to the two verbalizations that Pappu provides, the faqir's and the classical musician's. Ali examines these with clinical distance; he reflects upon himself with similar remove, wondering why he lacks religious conviction.

Individuals negotiate the positions of themselves and others in the world by means of a commonly held pool of images and ideas, which circulate as texts constantly undergoing reconfiguration and rematerialization. These "common terms of understanding"[3] consist of the ideas, the poems, the images to which all relevant actors have access, whether or not they are in agreement about what they in fact, or ought to, mean or do. A common set of phenomenological forms, with horizon potentials never fully realized, are part of the everyday experiences of those living in a shared environment. Interpretations of a dance like the *raqṣ-e-bismillah*—and interpretations of the image of the headless chicken itself—for instance, linger as possibilities to be considered, mentioned, or rejected, because both the form of the physical dance and the image of the acephalous avian lend themselves to mutually convergent deformation (or not) by a reflective actor. James Fernandez's pithy definition of metaphor as "the predication of a sign-image upon an inchoate subject" (Fernandez 1986, 31) is doubly apt here, with respect to the *malaṅg*'s splayed kinesis, and the fowl.

Ali and those he encounters relate what they see and hear to (stereo) typical forms: the *ta'ziyah* in relation to cenotaphs and Hindu temples; Muharram *mehndī*s and Sufi *'urs*es in relation to everyday weddings; lives of ordinary humans in relation to those of model figures like Hazrat Ali—or negative archetypes like Yazid; the actions of *malaṅg*s in relation to *qalandars*; *dhamāl* in Lahore in relation to that at Sehwan; Muharram drumming in relation to that at funerals and celebrations; drum patterns in relation to verbal rhythms and tone-melodies; incidents from everyday life in relation to shared poetry; poetry as remembered and recited in relation to that which is taught and inscribed in chapbooks and family manuscripts; subject positions and actions of actual men and women in relation to gender roles idealized in mystical thought. It is not the perfect likeness among these sets but the lack of perfect fit that gives rise to contemplation and possible action. Entextualization implies not only iconic replication but also selection. Contextualization, which has unpredictable consequences, does not rely on essential meanings.

Through these forms of implicit comparison, individuals engage in countless acts of inclusion and exclusion. These may implicate the state, as when Zia ul-Haq erected a barrier separating men from women in the Baṛi Imām shrine in Islamabad, where he declared that there shall be no mixing of genders in state shrines. They may implicate the purveyors of religious iconography—as in a popular poster I saw in Islamabad which included all the major saints of Pakistan except Shah Husain. They certainly embrace the *qawwāl*s and *malaṅg*s and Sufi enthusiasts who all pile the three big Lals into one giant *qalandar* pot: Lal Shahbaz Qalandar, Lal Husain, and Jhūle Lāl. Acts of inclusion and exclusion are obviously carried out by proponents of Panjabiyat, who place literary masters of the Panjabi language, Shah Husain, Bulleh Shah, Ustad Daman, and Waris Shah—and the *kāfī* song style, and Panjab Bhairavi *rāga,* and distinctive forms of dress, the list goes on—together through their poetry, performance, and symbolism at the Madho Lal Husain shrine for an *'urs* of tremendous political potency. Performing acts of inclusion or exclusion on the basis of such comparisons—which always involve decisions about likeness—is part of the process Herzfeld (2005) describes as social poetics.

As complex agents, individuals exercise freedom to choose among favored identity categories, some of which may seem incongruous: Pappu Sain is a disembodied agent of Shah Jamal and a consciously active classical musician; Baba Manna is a proud "Cook Man" and a senior *malaṅg*. The mother of the *malaṅgnī* mimes the most male and Shī'ī form of bodily action possible, while men put on the airs of a whore. The models for such action are all out there, available to these actors—they are common background knowledge, common terms of understanding: the Auqaf's signs and personages; the saint's hagiographies in pictures, in words, and in deeds; Bollywood films; Qawwālī lyrics.

Mimesis, in Davis's (1999; 2002) interpretation of Aristotle, and social poetics, in Herzfeld's (2005) framework, entail exaggeration or deformation, a form of framing that requires also breaking the frame. Drummers (and other musicians who learn by imitation) must be able to match the strokes of their masters, their competitors, and their partners perfectly. But to be a real musician means to step out of the frame. "Fly above" the *ṭhekā*, but never violate its truth. According to a Sufi way of phrasing this idea of mimesis, "the original is born from the imitation" (*naql se aṣl paidā hotā hai*) (Qureshi 2009, 177, translation mine). Indian classical musicians learn, initially, by imitating their masters; eventually the playing is no longer merely imitative. But progress on the Sufi path, like musical learning, requires pacing, timing. The boy who collapsed before Baba Rashid Sain broke through a subjective barrier too fast; he didn't transcend, he crashed.

The line between conformity, transcendence, and, in someone's eyes, transgression or incompetence is a fine one. Charles Keil (1994) has made much of "participatory discrepancies," the variations from grid-like time patterns and conventional pitch values that render much music musical.[4] It is nevertheless possible to be wrong, to be too "out of time" and too "out of tune." So, too, with *dhamāl.* One charged with patrolling the *thān* of the *dhamālī*s may accept or reject participants according to his own sense of a dancer's behavior in relation to a range of possible, normative models or according to his subjective sense of the participant's character. But he cannot control the reactions of onlookers. In Lahore, he could not control whether the *malaṅgnī* was perceived as drenched in the love of God (*majẕūb*) or as a slut—nor, arguably, could she. Those who look to Shah Husain as a patron saint cannot control whether his story humanizes their own or enhances grounds for dismissing the whole scene as a degraded and crass excuse for homosexuality and prostitution.

In part because no actors in the world can completely determine how their behaviors will be received, they may wish to limit who and what may be seen or heard. The internet and social media, notably, have brought this issue into particular prominence at the beginning of the third millennium. Chapter 8 is, in part, an attempt to reveal the broader political context in which Muslim drummers and the receivers of drumming negotiate what should be manifest, visible, or external (*ẓāhir*) and what is, or could be, concealed, invisible, or internal (*bāṭin*) in contemporary Pakistan.

CHAPTER 8

The Manifest and the Hidden

Ali's departure the next day was in equal measures dreadful and inevitable. After returning to Salim's flat from Baghbanpura for much-needed rest and tea, the trio had planned to dine stylishly in Model Town. Sufiya now complained of a headache and exhaustion and didn't want to go out. Salim dispatched himself to a nearby Afghan kabob stall for more modest victuals, leaving Ali to tend Sufiya. The two now alone, Sufiya owned up to her ruse: she was feeling just fine, thank you very much. So much had been communicated between the two. The touch of digits and limbs, the heat of proximity, the movement of eyes. Pious Sufiya was also practical-minded and frank—no moral coward, no frail-petaled bloom.

The two devised a plan.

If Salim noticed any change when he returned, he didn't let on.

: : :

Ali's journey home, however emotionally complicated, had been proceeding without incident.

On the very last leg, traveling from the Lucknow railway station to Aminabad, his bus suddenly lurched and bumped.

Passengers rushed to their windows. Passersby gathered at the front end.

By tragedy, by sickening coincidence, Ali's mother Sakina was no more.

: : :

November 1995

Over the course of the following decade the violent death of Ali's mother had set his father on a devil's course. The first thing to go was his "gift of the gab." The once-lively, eccentric raja became morbidly obsessive as his quick-wittedness gave way to senescence. Events transpired in the household that Ali could not grasp. Ali's father would sigh with regret, saying he should never have left Sakina in the dark for so long. Although neighbors spoke in hushed tones, Ali took away lurid impressions of his mother rushing from the house the very day of his return—her indigo sari rent, exposing a raw, scratched shoulder; her gray hair springing from her head in a tortured mass; and her eyes, strained wide, unfocused, as if sightless.

Ali's louche brother Sajjad, meanwhile, had degenerated from a winsome ne'er-do-well to a repulsive opium addict, a pallid figure with thinning hair and sunken eyes, angles and sticks suspended in loose clothing. Sajjad's unfortunate wife had to support the family working long hours as a nurse. Then there was the distaff labor: cooking, minding three children, keeping the place in order. There were no servants to manage. Ahmed Ali Khan, no longer compos mentis, could not prevent the dissipation of his family fortune. Would-be friends and trusted servants boldly looked him in the eye as they relieved him of lucre. He was in no position to help either son or the offspring of his three remaining wives.

Ali had fared better. First, his assignments at home grew to be regular and more interesting. Then the publishing of his article "The Drums of Islam in Multan" prompted a flurry of responsive letters. Ali's write-up on the *'urs* of Madho Lal Husain, for its part, became so involved that he was obliged to write two pieces: a breezy piece of sensationalist reportage for the newspaper and an academic experiment, which he sent to *Eastern Anthropologist*, the flagship journal of an anthropological society based in Lucknow.

The editorial board was not prepared to publish the overwritten product. Still, several of its members praised aspects of the ethnography and encouraged Ali to pursue formal anthropological training at Lucknow University. Ali took this advice, sailing ahead of his provincial classmates to earn a PhD in anthropology in record time. Driven by his passion and success, Ali now also undertook classical Hindustani music training at the Bhatkhande School of Music. Talentless on the drums and merely adequate in singing, Ali was nevertheless a quick study, able to develop sharp listening skills. Fancying himself something of an ethnomusicologist after a few years, he wrote a letter to Professor Qureshi, recalling that childhood day of marbles and bats in Mehmudabad.

The year following its publication in Lucknow, the Multan piece was, with Salim's help, republished in Lahore. Its reception was mixed. Some letters to the editor praised the sensitivity of this Indian journalist to the creativity and multifacetedness of Islam in Pakistan. Others complained, in effect, "What's this Hindu-disguised-as-a-Muslim, dancing-girl-loving Indian doing in our midst, poisoning the minds of our children with the praise of music? Celebration of this kind doesn't befit us as Muslims honoring Husain."

Worse than this was an incident on the street. According to the *Dawn* newspaper, a gang of three Shīʿī men living near Chawk Wazir Khan in Lahore's old city, outraged to hear of Muslims celebrating Muharram with *shahnāʾī* and drums, bused themselves to Multan on *Cānd Rāt*, located Bheḍi Potra, and instigated a public skirmish. They were not experienced fighters. The AK 47 one of the Lahoris kept under his cot was useless in his untrained hands: he feared the weapon more than the confrontation. The toothless fight was broken up shortly after it began, the perpetrators escaping with minor injuries. But news of this incident spread and ramped up the already escalating communal tension in Multan.

Ali fell reluctantly into his new role as resident head of the family. His elder brothers and sisters from his father's other wives lived further afield. Samina's family sent Ali money discreetly to look after the family's interests in Aminabad. Her side of the family had been able to hold on to their earnings as extensive landholders before Partition. Although nominally occupying the nearly crumbling family haveli in Lucknow, Ali would travel to Hyderabad and Delhi on a regular basis to report, lecture, consult, and publish. By 1993 his prize-winning reporting and academic credentials had secured him modestly remunerative affiliations with Lucknow University, the Delhi School of Economics, and Hyderabad University.

Chandlal had retired in 1990 and, poor fellow, contracted the dread febrile disease *Chikungunya*, which left him nearly paralyzed and in extensive pain for two years until a bout of pneumonia, on top of his asthma, finished him off. His successor, Biswas "Bunty" Sengupta, a self-satisfied, pomaded, oily little man, was less enthusiastic about Ali's diverse interests and would not subsidize his field trips—but he was obligated by his predecessor's agreement to allow Ali time for brief research stints. Sengupta's status as The Boss did little to ameliorate his insecurity in the face of Ali's worldliness, erudition, and professional success. Owing to all the personal and professional upheaval, Ali had put his formal travels for research on hold for a number of years. In the meanwhile, he made quiet inquiries and continued to fill his notebooks with observations and queries during free moments while on brief professional visits to Delhi and Hyderabad (Andhra Pradesh).

Sufiya had also suffered setbacks. After completing her MPhil at Cambridge and taking a job as an editor while contemplating her next move, she was forced suddenly to return to Rehmanpura to look after her mother. The previous year, her father had snagged a lucrative position as an engineer for a Swedish firm, working in Iran's oil industry near the border with Iraq. One day, though, he failed to show up at the drilling site. . . . Before leaving Pakistan—and while Sufiya was still abroad—he had been negotiating possible marriage alliances for Sufiya with a Naqvi family in Multan. Nothing was etched in stone, but Sufiya nevertheless encountered difficulty in extricating herself from the awkward family entanglements. She certainly could not do so immediately upon returning from England after the tragedy.

The *plan* had been for Ali to make his way back to England—somehow, as a journalist, as a tourist, anything. Away from their parochial milieux they were sure to find a way to stay together. No less intent on this outcome, the two were forced to postpone, and postpone again, and again. The boldness of their youth, their derring-do, gradually gave way to soberminded acknowledgment of their ponderous responsibilities. Susceptible to romantic excess, they found some solace in contemplating their own lives as if fictionalized under someone else's authorship. They read Somerset Maugham. Their lingering pain had become a habit, an injury, an aching tooth around which they needed to chew the activities of daily life. There was no sweetness in this pain, and none of that Sufi "burning" stuff—for either of them.

A short-term solution was to rendezvous in Karachi, where Ali planned to launch his next research excursion in June based on a tip from some Sindhi friends in India. Since launching this project he'd grown frustrated with the increasingly sectarian attitudes and actions of many Shī'ahs and Sunnis. Money from Iran and Saudi Arabia, respectively, fueled initiatives to pursue stricter forms of religious education in South Asia, creating a generation of young leaders averse to generations-old musical customs. Yet according to his friends, to this day, Shī'ahs and Sunnis were joining together for musical rituals in Hyderabad, Sindh. Was this so? How did they conceptualize their roles in the current political climate? Muharram season extended into the Muslim months of Safar and Rabi ul Awwal, so there might still be time to attend a *majlis* or witness a procession.

In the other Hyderabad, in Andhra Pradesh, India, a number of folklorists and anthropologists were busily documenting Muharram observances.

More even than in Sindh, in the Telangana region surrounding the city of Hyderabad, the range of communities who participated peacefully in Muharram was extensive. The faculty on the Golden Threshold Campus had managed to secure a major national grant for research on the theme of Muharram and national integration. Several people must have overlooked the fact that Ali proposed to go to the Pakistani Hyderabad when they approved a small stipend for his trip.

Sufiya, now in her late thirties, didn't need an excuse to travel on her own. Nevertheless, she reported to her family that she was visiting old classmates (who indeed lived in Karachi).

They met by moonlight.

: : :

Muharram Ali: Drumming Project Notebook #17

Entry, Tuesday 10 June 1997

. . . In Hyderabad. Trudged from the bus after sleepless night. Modest accommodations—Hotel Midway. Excellent fish from the Indus. Exceptional mangoes. Wish I had a beer. Sindh Agricultural University contact in Tando Jam: Vice-Chancellor Rafiq Anwar Memon . . .

: : :

Rafiq Anwar Memon generously placed the university public relations officer, Rajab Ahmed Pathan, at Ali's disposal for the duration of his brief visit. In consultation with R. A. Pathan, he formulated a plan to interview two sets of consultants, ethnic Sindhis and Mujāhirs. On Wednesday, he set out with Rajab for his first interview.

Ali had brushed up on the history of the region. He was reminded that more than forty-five hundred years earlier, some of the world's first city dwellers had resided in what is now the Mohenjo-daro archaeological site, located on a flood plain of the River Sindh in the north of the province. The language of Sindh is similarly ancient, deriving from a variant of Prakrit, the group of old Indo-Aryan spoken languages closely linked to Sanskrit. Ali knew Hindus of Sindhi background in Lucknow and Delhi, many of whom maintained their language. What struck Ali most in reading up on the language was its vast variety of sounds, including four implosives which, he thought, would be terribly difficult to articulate while singing.

Lower Sindh had come under Umayyad control as early as 712 CE, when Muhammad bin Qasim had, after several incursions, overtaken the ruler of Sindh.[1] Umayyad sovereignty over Sindh, and eventually the territory stretching to Multan, was primarily political. The Umayyads retained existing Sindhi governmental structures and did not undertake forced conversion of the local people to Islam. The locals practiced forms of Buddhism and what came to be called Hinduism. So long as the existing inhabitants paid tax, they could worship their own gods and retain their lands. There was a measure of accommodation: bin Qasim banned the slaughter of cows (perhaps for economic reasons), and a Hindu raja had the Qur'ān translated into a local language.

Even in modern Pakistan, whence most Hindus had fled, Ali observed for himself Sindh's relatively heterogeneous population. Many Hindus, he learned, still remained in Sindh after Partition, although their temples were now often hidden from public view, occupying unassuming spaces in ordinary domestic buildings. Many of the older ones were crumbled, suggestive ruins. Pakistanis of African descent, meanwhile, frequently but not exclusively employed as household servants, were often seen in urban Karachi and Hyderabad. Despite the diversity of the population, a strong sense of insidership seemed to betray the identity of indigenous Sindhis. The more public components of Sindhi weddings, Ali discovered, would take place on the borders of the village, not in the interior. And the hinterlands, even as Ali monitored the situation in the early twenty-first century, had their own unbridled dominance owing to the power of local landlords. The feudal structure allowed landowners to function as Mafia dons, sending their toughs out to extort money from the local population and especially to kidnap and hold for ransom other wealthy or prominent figures—whether Sindhis, Mujāhirs, or vulnerable outsiders. Ali was accustomed to the chaotic and unsafe environment of feudal thuggery from Bihar, but the situation here was worse. He could hardly afford the armed guards he had been advised to employ.

But he was lucky to have the guidance and companionship of the lanky Rajab Ahmed Pathan, even if he was obliged to profess patience as the latter Public Relations Officer recited a rehearsed series of figures and facts. Rajab continued spewing the information out as he jerked shut the door of his white Toyota Crown. They headed to an *imambara*, called a *peṛh* in Sindhi.

"After Partition," pronounced Rajab in his sharp English, "many Indian Muslims fled to the new capital city of Karachi, located advantageously on the coast. Before Partition, Karachi's population was roughly two hundred thousand. As its population swelled Karachi became cosmopolitan. Those who'd flocked to Karachi from India eventually formed the Muhājir Qaumi

Mahaz [MQM].* You must have heard of it. Initially the party supported the Pakistan People's Party, first chaired by Zulfiqar Ali Bhutto. The MQM and PPP were mutually supportive for a brief time in the 1980s, when the PPP was under the leadership of Zulfiqar Ali Bhutto's daughter Benazir. They helped Mujāhirs join forces with indigenous Sindhis. The two groups together opposed the Pathans, along with the Panjabis who'd immigrated in the 1960s.

"My name is Pathan," he clarified in a stentorian tone, "but my family migrated south to Sindh long ago. Now we are included as Sindhis, actually, not as Pathans.

"Unfortunately, the relationship between Mujāhirs and the PPP deteriorated," Rajab continued. "The alliance between Mujāhirs and Sindhis got broken. Now Muhajirs, Sindhis, Pathans, and Panjabis go on fighting one another.[2]

"Many Mujāhirs also came to Hyderabad," Rajab added as he squeezed his car into a makeshift parking space between the road and a stationery shop. "This place has a deeper history than Karachi." He went on to recount how one of the Kalhoras who ruled Sindh in the eighteenth century, Ghulam Shah, constructed a fort for what he envisioned as the future city of Hyderabad.[3] As they emerged from the car, Rajab rapidly explained that successive governments held the Hyderabad fort as a stronghold until the British took over in the mid-nineteenth century.

Walking around the corner to the modest Peṛh Muhammad shrine, Pathan turned to music. "We have three important Muharram instruments in Hyderabad: the *naqqārah,* the *ḍhol,* and the *gazī* [double reed]. The *naqqārah* and the *gazī* date from the Kalhora period, but the musician groups, Manganhārs, are known from ancient times. They are descendents of the Samma people who welcomed Muhammad bin Qasim. You see, the Manganhārs were a people before the coming of Islam. That's why we have both Shī'ī and Sunni musicians here."

This was the kind of thing Ali *wanted* to hear, but Rajab's glibness put him on guard.

Rajab led the way into this *peṛh*, where the Hanafi (Sunni) caretaker, a slight man with modest white raiment and turban, was seated on a carpet. Next to him several *naqqārah*s, nearly a meter in diameter, were overturned. The smooth, graceful terra cotta bodies of these drums supported heads whose hide latticework was as visually pleasing as it was functional. The

*Founded in 1984 under the leadership of Altaf Husain. In 1997, the word *Muhājir* was replaced with *Muttahida* (united) to make the party name more inclusive.

*Naqqārah*s stored in a corner of the Peṛh Muhammad shrine, Hyderabad, Sindh, June 11, 1997. Photo by the author.

bottom of each instrument was a kind of bulb or knob molded from the same clay and painted orange.

Lala Gul Sanubar Pathan spoke awkwardly with Ali in Urdu, interspersing occasional English words and directing some of his responses in Sindhi to Rajab. His family had been overseeing this Peṛh Muhammad shrine since its founding in the eighteenth century. "This is a shrine of butchers," he said. "This is the butchers' quarter." Every year, Lala Gul would invite the same troupe of twelve Manganhārs to perform for Muharram. He bore the two-to-three-thousand-rupee fee for this service himself, and the musicians would play for as long as was necessary, about eleven hours in total for the rituals connected with this shrine on Ashura and other key days of commemoration.

Lala Gul's way of talking about Muharram reminded Ali of Lucknow Shī'ahs—and of the rare Sunnis, like his father, for whom the exploits of Husain and his party were a frequent topic. The diminutive man rehearsed the commonplaces of Shī'ī history as if they belonged to the uncontested heritage of all Muslims: Zainab initiated the institution of the *majlis-e-'azā* (mourning assembly) to mourn the loss of her brother Husain. Timur (Tamerlane) introduced the practice of involving *ta'ziyah*s in Muharram ceremonies, as he was a great lover of the Prophet's family.

"How do customs [*rasm*s] of this shrine relate to those of the Fiqah-e Jafriya?" asked Ali, referring to Shī'ahs tactfully not as partisans—the literal meaning of *Shī'ah*—but as those who follow the jurisprudence of the sixth Shī'ī imam (also revered by Sunnis).

Rajab fielded the question, emphasizing that Shī'ī and Sunni practices are identical in Sindh. "Here they play the *naqqārah*, *ḍhol*, and *gazī* and chant *nauḥah;* they perform rituals with the *sej,* the *ta'ziyah,* and with many *zuljinah* horses; they hold *majlis*es and recite *qaṣīdah*s and *marṣiyah*s; they even do *mātam* here, striking their heads with their hands and their bodies with knives and chains [*zanjīr kā mātam*]."

Ali took all this in with skepticism. As much as Rajab might downplay differences, the fact that the *peṛh*s as institutions are identified as Shī'ī or Sunni suggested that the two groups also identify themselves separately. Was it more a matter of *qaṣā'ī*s (butchers) versus other quasi-castes than Sunnis versus Shī'ahs? Surely their embrace of *mātam* couldn't be explained by their trade alone.

Lala Gul delved deeper, without prompting, into the motivations underlying these customs. "*Mātam* performed by walking over hot coals is laudable," he explained. "*Mātamdār*s might know a fraction of the pain that Husain's sister, Zainab, felt when she had to step through fire to find her children after the battle."

Ali scratched in his notebook assiduously, Lala Gul exhibits a strong impulse to integrate and explain practices in light of the received wisdom about the battle of Karbala.

"What about poetry recitation. Do they do *marṣiyah*, *nauḥah*?"

"Yes, and *qaṣīdah.* It's all the same thing. First the *ẕākir* comes and delivers a sermon, then the recitation begins."

This reversed the order familiar to Ali, in which poetry recitations preceded the sermon. At home, sometimes the sermon part would be omitted entirely, and *qaṣīdah*s did not carry a tragic enough emotional tone.

When Ali asked whether reciters would deliver *majlis* poetry in the *tarannum* (chant) or the *taht-ul lafẓ* (spoken) style, Lala Gul was vague. He directed Ali to a place where he could listen for himself. Audio cassettes of such star reciters as Nadeem Sarvar and Hasan Sadiq and even video cassettes showing bloody *mātam* were freely available at a "Music Centre." Lala Gul didn't seem to be bothered by the moral grouping this name implied.

Music shop near a *mazār* (Sufi shrine). Note the mixture of religious images and paraphernalia with electronics and storage media. This is the kind of shop to which Lala Gul alluded, although the one depicted was located in Multan, not Hyderabad, Sindh, and reflects technology of a later period. July 2, 2007. Photo by the author.

Ali's confusion grew as Lala Gul continued. In part, his words were unclear. In part, they lacked specificity. Was Lala Gul now talking about practices at his own *peṛh* in particular or had he proceeded into generalizing, commenting on the tradition at large?

Underscoring the unity of Shī'ī and Sunni approaches to Muharram in Sindh, Lala Gul explained, "Our people do all different kinds of *mātam,* and when the processions join on the ninth and tenth of Muharram there is *zanjīr kā mātam*. The instruments are silent at that time—only bloody *mātam*."

Yes, *zanjīr kā mātam* seemed always to be . . . Ali searched for a term . . . idiometric??—each flagellant moving to his own rhythm. There was little concern with coordination and the drum was, at the very least, unnecessary. It could be otherwise. Ali gathered from a French-made film he'd seen that *zanjīr zanī* (as they called it in Farsi) was highly coordinated in parts of Iran.

Remembering the *mātam* with swords Muhammad Baksh had discussed in Multan, and its association with *ḍhol-tāshā*, Ali asked if "sword-*mātam*" was practiced here. too.

"Sindhi speakers don't; only Urdu speakers 'play fencing.' It's on Ashura while drummers beat on the *ḍhol* and *tāshā*. Urdu speakers also erect paper *ta'ziyah*s and submerge them in water at the end. Sindhis don't do all that water-immersion and all. We just keep the *ta'ziyah* in place. We treat it respectfully. Although the Urdu speakers have different styles of *mātam* and drumming, 'we all share the same end': remembering Husain. And we both have 'music parties,'" Lala Gul explained.

Lala Gul had used the English phrase *music party*. Ali flipped it back into Urdu. "So the Manganhārs play *mūsiqī* for Muharram in Sindh?"

"No, no, that's separate. The Manganhārs perform *mūsiqī* for weddings. They use a 'dance style' and they play *sharnā'ī* and *ḍhol*. For Muharram they play in a 'mourning style.' They use a special *sharnā'ī*. In our Sindhi *zabān* we call it *gazī*. It has a higher pitch, like wailing. On the *ḍhol* [the mourning style] is called *ḍanḍ*. That sad playing is *ḍanḍ*," Lala Gul explained. "They say the *naqqārah* was used as a war drum, to welcome the army of Husain. Here it welcomes the procession when it stops at each *peṛh*."

"Tomorrow is the anniversary of the martyrdom of Sakina. If you return here tonight at around 9:30 P.M. you'll see all this for yourself," said Lala Gul.

A Manganhār musician named Vasant Faqir entered the *peṛh* at this moment. He'd been alerted by Lala Gul via an eight-year-old boy who was serving them tea. Ustad Faqir explained that the *naqqārahs* are played in pairs. One person maintains the *ṭheko* (Sindhi for *ṭhekā*)—a role called *pahlūdārī* ("acting from the sidelines," or "supporting"). The other person plays an imaginative arrangement of cross-rhythmic patterns called *ṭhā dhunī* and *toṛā* against that ground, and completes each episode with a tripartite cadence called a *ṭiko*.

"Anyone can play the *naqqārah*," explained Lala Gul. "The Manganhār group will be leading the procession through the streets and bylanes accompanied by the *ḍhol*. It's quite splendid, *māshallah*, there will be ten or twelve *gazī* players performing simultaneously as they walk. When they arrive, people from the community will be here taking turns on the *naqqārah*, welcoming them."

"It's a communal affair," affirmed Vasant Faqir, "but we Manganhārs are the musical masters. *We* play the patterns on the *ḍhol* and the *naqqārah* and gradually other nonprofessional participants pick up a few basic techniques and patterns. During Muharram members of the public have the chance to try playing. If you come tonight, you'll even see small boys playing the *ṭheko* part." Finishing his tea, he looked haggard, his eyes begging permission to leave.

Ali scribbled, Participation of community in drumming valued here, as in Lucknow, but both Shī'ahs and Sunnis here.

He reflected: LALA GUL, AS A NONSPECIALIST, HAD BEEN USING *ḌAṆḌ* GENERICALLY FOR ALL MUHARRAM INSTRUMENTAL PERFORMANCE. VASANT FAQIR, A PRACTICED MUSICIAN, INTIMATED THAT *ḌAṆḌ* WAS ONLY ONE (MUSICAL) ITEM AMONG MANY. LALA GUL DENIED *ḌAṆḌ*'S STATUS AS *MŪSIQĪ* WHILE IMPLICITLY ACKNOWLEDGING ITS MUSICALITY—IT BEING A GENRE PERFORMED BY MUSICIANS.

Ali jotted, If the term *mūsiqī* for Muharram performance is taboo, is the English word music more neutral? *Music* indirectly included everything sold in the "Music Centre" and played by musical groups.

Ali and Rajab thanked Lala Gul and made plans to meet Vasant Faqir the next day in an open cement courtyard where Muharram processions regularly lingered. Ali went back to the hotel to rest before the evening's rituals. He bought batteries for his ailing cassette recorder and made sure the flash on his camera was operating.

: : :

At about 9 P.M. the two men returned to the courtyard. The moonlight and lamp shadows drew Ali's attention to the odd mixture of architectures. A dusty brick building, probably the loading dock behind a shop, issued no invitation with its locked-down corrugated metal door. A rust-colored box affixed to the bricks presumably measured the flow of current coursing through vine-like cables along the wall. Random swaths of whitewash bespoke slapdash attempts to hide something. Above the ground floor of a multistory modern apartment with pale-green and beige siding, awkward, steplike corbels supported a shallow projection of the outer wall. Here was another tallish apartment, with rough-textured walls with some kind of filigree pattern. It had mismatched features: faux archways about two meters tall along the top, rectangular triple windows with a gabled façade on each floor below. Two contrasting vertical patterns on each side of the windows shot up from the ground: left, a fluid hexagonal pattern; right, cement molded to look like two chains.

The *peṛh,* viewed from the back with its familiar minarets, was lodged between two of these tall apartment buildings. For the first time, Ali noticed the inflorescent pineapple pattern on the dome, a white star painted in the center of each green segment. Behind the *peṛh* (in front of Ali) was an *'alam* permanently fixed in its own gated compound, about nine square meters. Was this *'alam* style peculiar to Sindh? More than four stories tall, it towered above the *peṛh* and peaked above the surrounding apartments. Its green teardrop foundation with red and yellow details matched the dome; the *'alam* projected upward in contrasting geometrical blocks, balusters, and chandeliers, one or two meters in height each.

Illumination from the chandelier branches and the oval crest radiated out into the courtyard.

At moments, everything would go black, the rumble of the generator would compete with the sounds of the drums, and bright lights would come on. Ali made his way around the courtyard, each step surrendering precious foot space to men, boys, girls, and several dandified prancers who didn't necessarily enjoy their exalted status as *zuljinah*s this year (Media Example 8.1). The *gazī* players leading the procession had not yet reached the compound, but Ali could hear their instruments' acute keening. In the compound, two *naqqārah* players sat facing away from the *'alam*. Their drums, propped on broken pieces of concrete, faced one another at acute angles. The *bam*s (larger bass kettle drums), nestled obliquely, resounded toward the players' flanks; the *zīl*s, nearly horizontal, rewarded the raps of the players' wands with firm resistance and tintinnabulation. His view obscured at first, Ali noticed only the drummers' hands alternating right and left, now joining together, now separating, crossing, moving together again. It was a brisk ten-beat *ṭhekā* not yet audibly related to the advancing processional music.

Squeezing by an imposing cameraman who blocked his view, Ali watched a mustached player in his forties begin to elaborate on the pattern. He substituted strokes—high for low, low for high—and densified the texture. A slim youth in his late teens or early twenties held the basic pattern for a while, then the two switched roles. Ali outlined the pattern in his notebook: four strokes and a gap, four strokes and a gap, 5 + 5 = 10.

After tautening the skin of another *zīl* before a small fire, a young man replaced one that had lost its vibrancy. Ali now drifted toward the procession entering from the left of the *peṛh*. The *gazī* players with their piercing woodwinds entered first. It was curious that those following behind them were stepping backward, facing the other way. Was this to avoid the bright light a camera crew had trained on the incoming group? Maybe not. They continued to pace in reverse even after clearing the bright light. Now came the rear of the procession, facing front. Most of the men and boys were striking the top of their heads, but without force, raising and lowering the palms of their right hands. He could just make out the chant of "Yā Husain" these *mātamdār*s were shouting over the sounds of the *ḍhol*s and *gazī*s.

At first, with languid pace and sparse strokes, the *ḍhol* players outlined a pattern of seven counts, | ♩. 𝅗𝅥 | and | ♪♩ 𝅗𝅥 |. The stressed strokes on 1 and 4 corresponded to "Yā" and "'sain." If the processioners meant their hand movements to coordinate with the chant or the drums, only some of them succeeded. The *ḍhol* drummers then increased the intensity and drive with a set of patterns that, combined with the "Ya Husain" chant, created a three-against-four cross rhythm. Now chanters coordinated their *mātam* strokes perfectly. They shouted "Ya" in time with their head-strikes and "sain" as they released their arms on the intervening beat.

Reduction of one left (bass) pattern on *ḍhol*	$\mid {}^{12}_{8}↓.\quad ♪↓\quad ↓.\quad\mid$
Rhythm of "Yā Husain Yā Husain" syllables	$\mid {}^{12}_{8}↓\quad ♪↓.\quad ↓\quad ♪↓.\mid$
Palm strikes alternating with releases	$\mid {}^{12}_{8}↓.\quad ↓.\quad ↓.\quad ↓.\mid$

Ali could not make out how or whether the *naqqārah* players had adjusted their patterns. Indeed, he could not hear the *naqqārah*s at all. He couldn't help but note the effectiveness of the metric shift from seven to four, however—he was recalling *mārū* in Multan. The groove of the infectious new pattern successfully solicited the participation of parties who had been, up to that moment, dégagé. The *mātamdār*s clustered, rank and file, facing the *peṛh*. One of the crimson-velvet-draped *zuljinah*s, bedecked in silver finery, stepped and bobbed impatiently, as if in time to the music. Ali chuckled at the illusion. At home . . . television with the sound off . . . his father playing 78 r.p.m. records of Begum Akhtar and Amir Khan in the next room. The characters, like the horse, seemed to know the music.

The crowd began to thin as some of the men and boys streamed out to join other processions. Ali, who could now observe beyond his immediate vicinity, counted among those remaining several young Sidi men, Pakistanis of African ancestry. One of these stunning black youths wore white, silver, possibly pearl studs in his ears. Probably 5–10 percent of the other participants were children between the ages of ten and fifteen; several had their heads shaven. One man in his twenties wore a lettered cap, visor facing backwards: "Captain Midas."

A sixty-year-old mustached man wearing an olive *shalwār qamīz* began *ālāp*-like forays on the *gazī*, with occasional references, at cadential moments, to the tune the group had been playing. Ali sensed the sound with the skin of his face, so palpable was the instrument's intensity at short range. A vein leading from the player's right eye socket throbbed before branching off and disappearing into the gray roots of his cropped, hennaed hair. As he blasted into the shrill reaches of the *antara*, the musician raised his right eyebrow as if to help raise the pitch; sharp ripples rose in the russet skin of his forehead. The ten-count pattern of the *naqqārah*s across the courtyard seemed to provide a loose frame for the *gazī* player's flowing melodies. After a minute or two, another *gazī* player from behind took his turn and returned to similar points of cadence. The *mātamdār*s, lost following threes and fours, gave up.

: : :

The next day Rajab and Ali returned to the empty courtyard at the appointed time. There was no sign of the night's magic, and no sign of Vasant, either.

:

After forty-five minutes, Rajab began—hopelessly, in Ali's view—to inquire around the neighborhood. They ran into the little boy who had brought them tea the day before. For five rupees and a mangled piece of toffee he agreed to go in search of Vasant. Claiming to have fallen ill, Vasant sent his relative and former student Faqir Husain Baksh in his stead. A recalcitrant, unschooled thirty-two-year-old, Faqir had studied *sharnā'ī* with Vasant from the age of eight and played regularly at Peṛh Muhammad.

Once Rajab and Ali introduced themselves, Ali tried awkwardly to put Faqir at ease. "*K̲h̲air* . . . I am a music enthusiast, not a critic, and I have great respect for Bismillah Khan and others who play your instrument. I admire your profession."

Faqir Husain emitted a grunt in response and adjusted the rough, dingy cloth wrapped around his head.

Ali tried to warm him up. "What was it like learning from Vasant Faqir?"

Faqir Husain reservedly explained that it had taken him six or seven years to master the instrument.

PERHAPS THIS LOCAL TRADITION WAS NOT AS DEEP AS THE HINDUSTANI CLASSICAL TRADITION? NO TEACHER AT THE BHATKANDE SCHOOL WOULD HAVE CLAIMED TO HAVE MASTERED HIS OR HER ART IN SUCH A SHORT TIME.

Prompted to continue, Faqir explained, "There are three basic playing styles: Muharram, 'classical,' and wedding. Classical concerts on stage do not pay well. We make our money at weddings."

"Why do you play for Muharram?" asked Ali.

"Our performance improves the rituals. It is not exactly *mūsiqī*, you know, because it is a sad occasion. We play to announce the procession—like when the *zuljinah*s come out. Our family has been doing this for ten generations and our forefathers have been maintaining this for fourteen hundred years. It's a duty."

"How lucrative is it compared with, say, classical concerts?"

"We go of our own accord, not for money," he said.

WHO HAD POCKETED THE MONEY LAST NIGHT?

"May I ask, what is your own religious affiliation?"

"Maulā'ī. We are followers of 'Ali and Imam Husain," said Faqir. His sixty-year-old father, Faqir Nathu, joined him as they all sat on the stone verandah of a building at the courtyard's entrance. The helpful chai-boy returned, asking if he could bring them cool drinks. Rajab peeled off some rupee notes and the khaki-clad *baccā* bounded off soundlessly on his calloused feet.

Rajab explained to Ali that the designation *Maulā'ī* is, in Sindh, equivalent to Fiqah-e Jafriya. The term seemed to neutralize possible sectarian implications.

"Does your playing have any connection with your being Maulā'ī?" asked Ali.

"As I said, it is a duty. Some people say Muharram rituals are a protest against tyranny. I suppose that's true," said Faqir Husain, without commitment.

Ali recognized this freely circulating idea as one of the political ideas emphasized by the Iranian revolutionary Ali Shariati (1933–77).

WHY IS THIS SO FORCED?

"Well, what, for instance, do you play on the *gazī*? Where do the tunes (*ṭarz*es) come from?" asked Ali.

"There are *marsiyo*s, you know . . . *marsiyo*. In Sindhi. And in Urdu, Panjabi, and Saraikki. But on *gazī* only the (*ṭarz* comes."

"Can you give me an example of the *marsiyah*s you play?"

"I call to mind what to play by thinking of the melody, not the poem."

Faqir Husain's father, Faqir Nathu, then retrieved a single line of Panjabi from the recesses of his memory. Clearing his throat, he began to sing: "'Oh, grandfather, listen to my "condition," I have come leaving my brother behind without a shroud.'"

"Actually," Faqir Nathu continued, "the *naqqārah* does the real work, the 'performance.' The supporting instrumentalists like the *ḍhol* and the *gazī* just keep repeating the same thing over and over. It is the *naqqārah* player who does the *tīyā*, *tabl* and such like. Qasim Shah is the *naqqārah* player who leads our group. He'll help you."

Rajab jotted down information on how to reach Qasim Shah as lightly carbonated umber liquid arrived in jaded Coke bottles. The taste reminded Ali of the homemade stuff from the hinterlands of India with colorful names like *Love-O* and *Kiss-O*. After taking a moment for refreshment, Ali resumed.

"What are the important things to keep in mind when playing?"

"You have to know when to play the proper *vajat* [pattern]," said Nathu.

"For example . . ."

"For Muharram, we start with Ya Husain, then we play *ḍaṇḍ*, and then we finish with *tā'ū* [literally "dispersal"]. In the wedding there is no special order: we play *jhūmar* and other *vajat*s for dancing and we accompany songs. For classical, we know things like *tīntāl, jhaptāl* and *dhamār*."

"Do you also play different *dhun*s [tunes] for these different occasions?" asked Ali.

"Of course . . . that is, for Muharram we don't have *dhun*s, we only have *zārī*s."

After some clarification, he wrote, Zārī: a kind of short nauḥah in Sindhi. Dhun and kalām: light, cheerful melodies appropriate for weddings. Tarz: any melody, buoyant or grave.

Though it had been slow going, Ali felt he had made moderate progress with this interview. Taking Faqir Nathu's advice, Ali and Rajab sought out Muhammad Qasim, known as Qasim Shah.

: : :

Qasim lived in Kotri, a town across the Indus River from Hyderabad. A trim, clean-cut man with triangular face and patrician nose, Qasim looked to be in his late thirties or early forties Dressed snappily in black, Qasim welcomed Ali into the spacious front room of his single-story home. Waiting for his arrival and ready to talk music were the fleshy, mustachioed Aijaz Ali—Qasim's bespectacled playing partner on *naqqārah*—as well as some other members of the ensemble, *surnā'ī* players Abdullah Khan and Imam Bux, and the youthful *ḍhol* player Amjad Husain.

Unlike the musicians Ali had met the previous day, Muhammad Qasim was well versed in Hindustani music and could communicate the structure of his music to Ali clearly using familiar Hindustani musical terms. Ali sensed that Qasim was someone with whom he could be frank. "Qasim Sahab, when I spoke to Lala Gul Sanubar Pathan, he insisted that what you play for Muharram is not music, it is *ḍaṇḍ*. I can understand why he would say such a thing, but I'm curious as to your view as performer."

"Yes, of course we are not supposed to call these Muharram items *mūsiqī*. What to do?" asked Qasim ruefully. "They come from the same source. The drumming is 'classical.' Most of the *marṣiyo*s we play on the *gazī* are in *rāg* Puriya Dhanasri. They're also in Jaunpurī, Husainī, Bhairavi, Kedāro, Lauṛāu, Pahāṛi, Sindhi Jog, Koyārī. . . . Whichever *rāg* pleases a composer at a given time, he'll make a *ṭarz* from that *rāg*."

"Is the same *marṣiyo* text sometimes sung to different tunes?" queried Ali.

"*Bilkul ṭhīk* [absolutely right]."

"Do *gazī* players know the words to the tunes they are playing?"

"Not usually, but, for example, this person does." Qasim gestured toward an old man who had recently entered and seated himself in a folding chair with nylon webbing.

"Only with the *sharnā'ī.* I can't do *āvāz* [sing it independently]."

"We have a tough time remembering the words because no one sings them anymore," Qasim explained. "They were composed before we were born, some of them two hundred years ago."

"If possible, I'd like to record an example of a poem used on the *gazī.*"

"We can try."

"I'm trying to get a clearer picture of the *vajat*s you play for Muharram. How do you begin? How many *mātra*s are in the drum patterns?"

"We begin with this." Qasim demonstrated a continuous, dense stream of strokes with two pencils on a book. "It's called *tabl.* Then the *gazī-wālā*s play *osāro*—kind of like *ālāp*, in Husaini" (Media Example 8.2).

"What does *osāro* actually mean?"

"Lamentation. Wailing and lamentation at Sindhi funerals. The piercing sound of the *gazī* reminds us of women's wailing. We get affected by that sound. Then there's *ḍaṇḍ.* We've been playing it on the drums for funerals since ancient times. For Muharram we have two types, one with ten *mātra*s and one with four *mātra*s."

"So the sequence is . . ."

"After the *tabl* and *osāro,* we perform the *vajat* 'Ya Husain' while people shout those words. Then we play the ten-count version of *ḍaṇḍ.* We alternate the two versions of *ḍaṇḍ* during the procession and when we stop at a *peṛh.* We can also play the *vajat* 'Husain Husain.' Both the Ya Husain and Husain Husain *vajat*s are linked to the rhythm of chant. We have another *vajat*, called *tā'ū*, which we use whenever we go from here to there. In Sindhi the word means 'disperse, or move ahead.' The *naqqārah* plays

dhān			gi	nā		din		tan			gi	nā		tin	
X	2	3	4	X	6	7	8	O	10	11	12	X	14	15	16

Table 8.1. Muharram *vajats* played in Hyderabad, Sindh

1. *tabl* and *osāro* (introduction on drums and double reeds) said to be in Husaini *rāga*
2. Ya Husain *ṭhekā* (4 *mātra*s)
3. Shah Panjatan (8 *mātra*s)
4. *ḍaṇḍ* (10 *mātra*s)
5. *ḍaṇḍ* (4 *mātra*s)
6. "Husain Husain" (2 *mātra*s)
7. *tā'ū* (4 *mātra*s)
8. *lolī* (14 *mātra*s)

[Qasim recited, clapping on the Xs and waving on the O], and the *gazī* plays a special tune."

THE FUNCTION IS LIKE THAT OF SAVĀRĪ SOME PLACES, THEY USE IT WHEN PROCESSIONS GET MOVING. THE TĀL STRUCTURE IS EQUIVALENT TO DHAMĀL. THE TUNE AND CONTEXT SET THIS ONE APART.

"One *vajat* is for *naqqārah* alone, not *ḍhol.* It's called Shah Panjatan, in honor of the Panjatan Pāk. The last *vajat,* fourteen *mātra*s, is called *lolī,* which means lullaby in Sindhi," explained Qasim.

OBVIOUSLY RELATED TO ONE OF THE MANY "LULLABIES" (LORĪS) ADDRESSED TO HUSAIN'S SLAIN INFANT.

Qasim and his group began assembling to demonstrate their repertoire in a courtyard nearby. Ali made a rough recording and went through it with the performers.

THIS IS THE SAME SHIFT FROM A SEVEN-COUNT TO A FOUR-COUNT PATTERN FOR "YA HUSAIN," BUT I DON'T HEAR THE CROSS-RHYTHMS IN ABSENCE OF THE CHANT.

One of the listeners, Sayyad Alam Shah Bukhari, began to sing the tune softly. Ali turned off the tape recorder and gently requested the retired government servant to repeat the words. He sang, "Momin karyo mātam (o allah . . .) karyo karbala jo" ["Believers! perform *mātam*, oh God, the one for Karbala"] (Media Example 8.3 ⛟). He tried to remember the *marṣiyo* for the previous *osāro* section, "Husain ʿe husain-e ʿaẓam" ["Husain, O great Husain!"] (Media Example 8.4 ⛟).

CALLS FOR A STRETCH OF THE IMAGINATION. I CAN'T REALLY HEAR IT. QASIM AND THE OTHERS ALL SEEM TO GO ALONG WITH THIS READING. IS IT THIS TEXT THAT MAKES THE OSĀRO "IN HUSAINI"? MELODY NOT CLEAR ENOUGH TO ME TO BE IN, OR NOT IN, RĀGA HUSAINI.

Ali stayed with Qasim Shah until early evening listening to the ensemble's recording and discussing their favorite classical musicians.

Muharram Ali: Drumming Project Notebook #17

Entry, Friday, June 13, 1997

The manganhār repertoire demonstrated by Qasim Shah belongs clearly to a rich, vibrant musical tradition tied both to specific ritual practices of Sindh and to the art music of North India and Pakistan. As members of a manganhār community that comprises both Shīʿahs and Sunnis, Qasim and his fellow musicians are effective mediators. Qasim's art militates against social and religious distinctions.

As Ali reviewed his notes the next morning, he realized how strongly he was projecting his values onto Qasim; he began annotating his write-up with critical questions. Looking back at his discussions with Lala Gul, he remembered that although Sindhis downplayed the distinction between Shī'ahs and Sunnis, not just in relation to music but in terms of ritual practice as well, this move did not represent a global outlook. It was a Sindhi-centric one. Urdu speakers, migrants from India, were not embraced in this integrative worldview.

: : :

Rajab showed up at about 11 A.M. at the Hotel Midway with contact details for several Mujāhir groups and direction to neighborhoods where they play during Muharram.

"Are any of these professional musicians?" asked Ali, as he reached gingerly for the searing car-door handle.

"I don't think so," opined Rajab. "They're neighborhood groups who play only for Muharram. A man named Abdul Samad heads a big Mujāhir family, some 250 persons. He amassed a fortune in the satellite-dish business and sponsors local Muharram processions."

"Do Fiqah-e Jafriya participate?"

"I'm fairly certain they don't. Muhajirs are different from Sindhis. That Shī'ah-Sunni conflict is there, no?"

Rajab drove to the first site, Khata Chowk; nearby, in repose, was a *naqqārah* so enormous Ali didn't think he could reach across it even with the fingertips of his outstretched hands. A couple of young men were idling around, evidently looking out for Ali and Rajab. When the two pulled up in the Crown, one of the young men trundled off to inform an elder. Ali

In some regions of South Asia, *naqqārah* playing has declined; this may reflect changes in fashion or the waning of performance knowledge. In the village of Paryawal, east of Lucknow in Uttar Pradesh, this old metal *naqqārah* shell has been repurposed as a whitewash mixing bucket. October 24, 1998. Photo by the author.

wasted no time in introducing himself to one of the remaining fellows. Qamar was a bulky, clean-shaven man about two meters tall.

"Qamar Sahab, I'm glad to meet you. I'm a reporter from Lucknow." Then, pausing, he added, "You're also from Hindustan, no?"

"Actually, my family is from Ajmer, but I've never been there myself."

"I've heard there are large *naqqārah*s like this in that part of Rajasthan, too. Were you playing this last night for the *shahādat* of Hasan?"

"No, *jī*, our people drum for the first ten days of Muharram. We play this *naqqārah* only on the seventh. For the mehndi. We brought it out for you to see, *bas*."

"Who plays such a large drum?"

"We all do. Sometimes we beat on it, one person after the other. Sometimes four or five play at the same time from different sides. *Tāshā-wālā*s and *ḍhol-wālā*s move around here and there and drum as well. One guy sounds the *jhānjh* [cymbals] and another one rattles the 'shakers.'"

"What items do you play?" asked Ali

"Items? I think we play three *cāl*s [here, percussion patterns]. The ones who know start us going, then we join in. These streets get packed with people. Lots of people want to play, so we take turns."

IMPORTANCE OF COMMUNITY PARTICIPATION . . . BUT NO APPARENT BODY OF SPECIALISTS AS AMONG THE SINDHIS.

The elder now approached. Qamar explained the presence of the two newcomers to his ustad and relayed their questions.

"We play *ek kī cāl, tīn kī cāl,* and *mātam kī cāl,*" clarified Muhammad Shafi.

"What's the difference between *ek kī cāl* and *tīn kī cāl*?

"*Ek kī cāl* has one *ḍankā* [beat] and *tīn kī cāl* has three." Shafi demonstrated the *ḍhol* pattern with a stick against a cement block.

"I see why the other two are named with numbers, but why is this one called *mātam*?"

"It's just a name," insisted Shafi.

Ali scratched in his notebook, The name *mātam* seems to indicate that this *cāl* is a Muharram pattern, a token of a type rather than an index of a specific mourning function.

Resisting Shafi's implication that the name is not relevant to the function, Ali pursued the issue of religious motivation in a different way. "Why do you think it is important to drum?"

Shafi, looking away, chose his words carefully before turning back to Ali and replying, "We play the drums at Muharram to keep the 'drumbeat of religion' continuing, to keep our name illuminated."[4]

"*Māshallah*, this is a grand philosophy," Ali gushed in spite of himself. "Where does it come from? Is this your own idea?"

"It was like this. My father was reciting 'supererogatory prayers' at night, after doing *namāz*. He had a vision. A voice said, 'You are my *'āshiq* [lover]; try to keep my name alive through this form [of drumming].'"[5]

As usual, a "voice" appears, not a visible presence.

"So," asked Ali, "does this mean drumming is a religious [*mazhabī*] activity?"

"*Bas*, men perform because they have *shauq* [a penchant]," said Shafi, somewhat evasively.

"Let me put it in another way. When some people where I come from chant poetry, they are very emotionally affected. They cry. They are religious people."

"It's not like that. Our people are excited and lost in their passion and ardour [*dhun*]."[6]

Qamar interjected, "He's saying that their passion is directed toward the act of playing the drums, not toward their faith."

"Does this mean playing will earn them no merit?" asked Ali.

"They are just fond of playing, there is no purpose [*maqṣad*] in it, just a predilection [*shauq*],"[7] explained Shafi.

Rajab chatted further as Ali wrote, *These musicians, unlike Lala Gul, are reluctant to relate the content or purpose of their playing to the historical or emotional implications of Muharram ritual. Shafi grants that drumming is good for propagating Islam, without acknowledging it as an Islamic or religious activity.*

Twenty minutes later, Rajab indicated to Ali it was time to move.

"*Ijāzat* . . ." asked Ali, formulaically requesting permission to take his leave. Shafi and a few other men shook his hand good-naturedly and followed them to the car in the manner of good hosts.

Rajab drove briskly to Ladies Park in the Pakka Qila neighborhood, a Mujāhir stronghold in Hyderabad city. Rolling down the window and asking directions to the unmarked street number six, Rajab navigated to a canopy about a hundred square meters fronting a corner electronics shop and a few houses. A pride of youths gathered next to three sizable *ḍhol*s, these ones reminiscent of marching bands' bass drums, their double-sided heads more than a meter in diameter. The metal rim betwixt the heads measured in at the width of an average man and sported synthetic covers of glittery yellow and green.

A beetle-browed man introducing himself as Ahmad came forward to greet Ali and Rajab. He guided them to the group leader: "This is

Muhammad Ikramuddin Sahab. He came to Hyderabad from Agra when he was about eleven years old." The bald Ikramuddin, in white *shalwār qamīz* and skull cap, stood about 170 cm tall, almost trapezoidal with his low paunch.

After briefly explaining his project, Ali learned that Ikramuddin's family members were butchers and merchants. He and five of his nine fellow players were introduced as Sheikh Siddiqis, while two called themselves K͟han Sahabs and two Rājputs. Ikramuddin grew up observing his family members constructing the drums and playing them during Muharram.

"What was it like during Muharram in Agra?" Ali inquired.

"My father and uncles would make the drums themselves. They'd fashion a bamboo frame for the skin on each side and then affix the frame to a wooden shell. Here in Hyderabad, we cut a metal chemical drum in half and bolster it with a metal rod. Then we attach the skins on metal frames. When I was a child in Agra, *ḍhol* players would stand in lines stretching for miles. You couldn't see the end of them. Here we have only 10 percent of that participation."

"It must have been a sight to behold," marveled Ali. "Why are so many people attracted to it? What's the purpose?"

"*Hamārī k͟hālī shauq muharram kā* . . . we play merely out of interest during Muharram, not for any particular purpose. Abdul Samad Sahab calls us. We don't ask why. 'Our extended family from India used to play'; we received *ta'līm* [training] there, so we carry it on here."

Ahmad reiterated the point and added, "Just as some people do *mātam* because of their faith, there is also the custom [*ravāj*] of playing *ḍhol* during Muharram. No one knows about its being good or bad or about its benefits [*fā'ida*] and defects [*nuqṣān*]. They play out of interest [*shauq*], as a pastime [*shuġl*]."

As Ahmad continued, Ali wrote furiously in his notebook: Mention of 'benefits and defects' significant . . . a resistance to interpret drumming in the context of Islam. Contrast Ajmeri group: drum sounding beat of religion. Why 'benefits and defects'? Defensiveness toward possible criticism? Avoids staking a position. Ahmad argues for ignorance—or for absence of meaning. Drumming is its own reward, provides personal satisfaction. Connected with family's past, history in India, but not with Muharram specifically.

Ahmad went on in a defensive and defiant vein, "People say many different things about the meaning of drumming during Muharram, but there is no authentic evidence that would give the answer as to whether people actually play to mourn the Karbala matter or not; in fact what happened at Karbala was a matter of three hundred years ago."[8]

MAYBE AHMAD REFERS TO THE GAP BETWEEN THE EVENT AND THE FIRST WRITTEN RECORDS? . . . NOW-FAMILIAR DEFENSIVENESS: LOCAL PRACTICE VALUED, SO LONG AS NOT CONSTRUED AS ISLAMIC.

"It's like this," Ahmad elaborated. "There are three 'categories.' One is *ḍhol* players. They have their own way [*rujḥān*], Then there is a separate category of *marṣiyah* reciters, and then there are the ones who do *mātam*. The *ḍhol* players have no connection with the *marṣiyah* reciters."[9]

"When you play the drums, do other people shout out slogans or chants [*na'rah*]?" prompted Rajab, helpfully.

"Only Shī'ahs cry out 'Husain' and such things," claimed Ikramuddin. "As for us, we just mind our own business, play *ḍhol*, and keep walking straight."

Ahmad acknowledged that Sunnis too will chant such slogans, but those were other Sunnis, and their actions have nothing to do with drumming. "There are both Shī'ahs and Sunnis who call out 'Husain.' These people are taught that Husain is brave. Like that, one category of people expresses the idea that Husain was oppressed. Because he was wronged they do *mātam*. But *ḍhol* playing comes in none of these categories."[10]

While Ahmad resisted any notion that drumming could be integrated into the themes of Muharram, Ali continued to probe to understand what motivated these musicians to perform and why they think Muharram activities are performed at all, considering Ahmad's dismissal of their historical validity.

"As I told you," Ahmad said impatiently, "Muharram rituals have nothing to do with religion. It is not related to history because the historical record was written three hundred years later. Nobody saw how Husain and his party were martyred and wrote about it. In their [Shī'ī] books it was written that their women's scarves were pulled off in such and such a way, and that there was *marṣiyah* reciting. Other books say different things. Different scholars wrote differently, and people, because of lack of education . . ."[11]

" . . . went on practicing in a historically unsupportable fashion," inferred Ali.

THIS IS THE POLAR OPPOSITE TO LALA GUL. AHMAD DOES NOT ALLOW FOR AN INNER (BĀṬIN) MEANING, A HIDDEN TEXT, OR THE EXPECTATION THAT THE KARBALA MARTYRS ARE SPIRITUALLY PRESENT.

"I'll tell you the reason," said Ahmad, getting to his next point. "Before Pakistan came into being and the British government was in India, the ones in the majority used to benefit. Because of this they were divided. Some [that is, Sunnis] went with the *ḍhol* players and some [that is, Shī'ahs] went with the performers of *mātam*. The rich divided the people in order to prove their communal majority to the British government. '*We* have the majority . . . or *we* have the majority.' For example, after these Shī'ī people started doing *mātam* here in Pakistan the Sindhi people also started doing it. Sindhis don't know what *mātam* is but they do *mātam*! They don't know what Muharram is but they do *mātam*! They have no connection with either Shī'ahs or Sunnis."[12]

Ali wrote, Ahmad believes cooperation among Sindhi Shī'ahs and Sunnis results from ignorance about Muharram. Adoption of external practices. Sharing of *mātam* masks the Sindhi lack of understanding.

"Shī'ahs do *mātam* just because of opposition. They are only 20 percent but they make a lot of noise to make it look like they have a majority. The category of those who did *mātam* was smaller in India. When those people came to Pakistan they gathered others [Sindhis] to perform in public to make it look like the Shī'ī population was larger. The Sindhis are not Shī'ahs, but the Vaḍeras [feudal lords] fed them hashish and asked them to do *mātam*. They don't even know what *mātam* is but they make *zuljinah*s because they got training from the Shī'ahs. Those wishing to show themselves in the majority grew in number."[13]

AHMAD ARGUES FOR POTENTIAL OF PUBLIC, OSTENSIBLY RELIGIOUS, DEMONSTRATION TO ENABLE REAL-WORLD POLITICAL POWER. THIS POWER LIES BEHIND ACTIVITIES SUCH AS DRUMMING AND *MĀTAM* THAT ARE ONLY SUPERFICIALLY JUSTIFIABLE BY A STORY LINKED TO KARBALA.

Now the drummers were ready to demonstrate. Ali drew up a list of drum patterns—each one a *cāl* prefixed by a number. Except for two patterns, named one-and-a-half and two-and-a-half, all the others were named for the number of stressed strokes. The patterns were built from such a common set of building blocks (see Chapter 4) that as the number of stressed strokes increased it was possible for Ali in most cases to predict what each successive *cāl* would sound like.

With Ikramuddin leading and correcting the others, the group demonstrated each *cāl* individually. During Muharram, Ali learned, the leader would mix and match these numbered *cāl*s at will. Isolating each pattern to play individually exposed several of the players' weaknesses. During Muharram lesser players might have followed along in a constantly shifting series of *cāl*s, but their errors wouldn't necessarily have been noticed or corrected. Here it was taking the musicians a few tries to play each pattern correctly; Ikramuddin had to start, stop, correct, and restart the performance several times until the group could play all the patterns properly. There were no variations or opportunities for improvisation within the patterns.

Both the clinical way in which this group named its repertoire and the tightly circumscribed repertoire itself, Ali noticed, distinguished this tradition from that of the Sindhis, whose pieces were evocatively named and called for improvisation. Even the Ajmeri group's pattern named *mātam* was contextually significant, despite Shafi's insistence that it was "just a name."

By the time the Agra-*wālā*s successfully demonstrated all the patterns it was about 4:30 P.M. Rajab needed to attend to some university business, so he dropped Ali at the hotel. They were to resume the next day.

Muharram Ali: Drumming Project Notebook #17

Entry, Saturday 14 June 1997

Reflections on the Ajmer and Agra Muhajir groups recorded today. Members of the Agra group willfully resist the notion that their drumming bears any organic relationship to Muharram. They derive pleasure from playing and are proud to maintain the tradition of their forefathers in Agra. The repertoire must have been carefully constructed by someone with musical training. The generative procedure of augmenting a rhythmic pattern by adding modules is not unlike the way *ṭhekās* are constructed for *tāls*. The specifics of these patterns fall into a self-contained micro-system unlike anything I've seen. Was this distinctiveness intentional? Did someone devise this mathematical system, with its numbers for names, consciously, as a way to avoid religious connotations? These drummers are able to intervene loudly in the public Muharram proceedings as Muhājirs from Agra. Yet they do so while professing nothing at all regarding the occasion or the place of either drumming or Muharram in the observance of Islam. The Ajmer group is on the fence owing to their vision justifying the use of drumming to propagate Islam. Yet like the Agra group, they deny explicit connections between what they do and Muharram. The Sindhi-Urdu contrast is one of integration versus disjunction. The Sindhis tended to present integrative views of music and Muharram; these fellows hold disjunctive views.

: : :

Rajab picked Ali up on Sunday for their final interview and recording session in Hyderabad. They drove first to a run-down apartment complex near Hali road, south of the Pakka Qila. There they met Allaudin, at eighty years old the most senior musician in the group, who had agreed to arrange for the interview and recording session. They spoke at the threshold of his doorway for ten minutes. Rajab was verifying the time and place: this evening in the open ground of an industrial compound. Allaudin responded with welcome alacrity to Ali's initial questions about his *qaum,* ancestral home in India, and training on *ḍhol* and *tāshā*. A Sheikh Siddiqi from Bharatpur (west of

Agra), Allaudin trained under a Hindu drummer. Ali anticipated an interesting conversation about cultural intermingling of Hindus and Muslims.

When Ali and Rajab entered the dented, scraped, dull-green steel doors of the compound at 8 P.M. they were met by eight players ready for business: five *tāshā* players and two *ḍhol* players ranging in age from twenty to sixty-five, plus Allaudin. The *ḍhol*s, smallish Western tom-toms about 40 cm in diameter and breadth, were encased in blue aluminum and hung from the players' necks. The *ḍhol*s' small size made it easy for players to strike them forcefully with hard, rubber-headed mallets on one side and make both subtle and penetrating sounds with the fingers of their hand on the other. As the musicians warmed up, Ali was surprised at how loud and deep these small drums could sound; the large *ḍhol*s and huge *naqqārah* he'd seen the previous day were impressive to see, but produced little loudness (one of the Ajmer men had beaten on the *naqqārah* to demonstrate its deep sound). The *tāshā*s were of the old-fashioned terra cotta variety, manufactured by the local artisan Muhammad Ishaq on Tando Mir Mehmood Road. Shallow bowls 25–35 cm in diameter, the drums were covered with hide and decorated with five to six ochre spots, four or five around the edge and one in the center.

Muharram drummers whose leader traces his ancestry to Bharatpur, India (see also Media Example 4.31). Hyderabad, Sindh, Pakistan, June 15, 1997. Photo by the author.

Even before they began to demonstrate, Ali was affected by the apparent professionalism of these players. This impression only deepened over the course of the evening. Drawing up a list, Ali noted the combination of contextually and analytically relevant (that is, numerical) names.

The labels *kalmah* and *dauṛ* each refer to a single pattern; *gintī*, *tāla*, and *kairvā* admit of two varieties; there are three patterns labeled *mātam*. Must observe whether *chautāla* and *ek tāla* are equivalent to their Hindustani classical counterparts. Do these fellows perform concerts?

Ali switched on his Walkman Professional and attempted to resume the earlier conversation: "Allaudin Sahab, before you begin the demonstration, would you mind telling me more about how you learned this art [*fan*]?"

Ali remained patient as this master politely derailed his line of questioning, transforming a personal question of training into a tradition-wide question about the origin of Muharram drumming.

"Shah Timur had great love and respect for Imam Husain. When visiting Husain's tomb, he beheld a 'vision.' 'Timur, you always come here. You can take a copy/image of this tomb back home and do *ziyārat*.'* So he made a replica of the tomb at his place and did *ziyārat*. This is history and not a false story! People came there for *ziyārat*, which in time created a problem: a 'rush' started pulling and pushing for want of space. So they started to take the *ta'ziyah* out on procession. People from different neighborhoods could see it when the procession walked past. But when the procession went by many people weren't aware of its presence. They heard the 'slogan' but didn't realize it was a procession. They 'solved the

Table 8.2. Names of patterns in the repertoire of a *ḍhol-tāshā* group with roots in Bharatpur, India

kalmah
das kī gintī
bīs kī gintī
ek kā mātam
do kā kairvā
tīn kā mātam
cheh kā mātam
dauṛ
chautāla
ek tāla
chaltā hū'ā kairvā

*The name *Tamerlane* in English derives from Persian *Timur-e-lang*, or Timur-the-lame. The story hereby alludes to Timur's difficulties in making a long pilgrimage.

problem' with an instrument, a *ḍhol*. By hearing the *āvāz* [voice/sound] of the *ḍhol* people could know of Imam Husain's *ta'ziyah* procession."

"And what is your connection with this?"

"In those days, all people who had love and respect for Imam Husain used to play. We have been fulfilling this *ḥāẓrī* [offering] until today. But we play only during Muharram because it is not our profession [*pesha*]."

Ali scribbled, Allaudin accounts for drumming via story of Timur and ta'ziyahs. Integrative view in this respect. Evades question of training. Calls playing a ḥāẓrī, as something "presented" (pesh karna), and, less often, as "playing instruments" (bajāna).

"How do you all remember so many *tāl*s when you play so infrequently?"

The forty-year-old Shaikh Akram responded, "It's 'under faith's authority,' not ours."

Allaudin expanded on this. "You see, our first item is always *kalmah*. One becomes Muslim only after reciting [*paṛhna*] the *kalmah*. If one doesn't say the *kalmah* one can't be a Muslim. So during our *fan* we first present the *kalmah*. This *uṣūl* [rule] will be kept up so long as we are Muslims."

SEEMS UNUSUALLY PREOCCUPIED WITH PROVING HE'S MUSLIM. MAYBE BECAUSE SHEIKH SIDDIQIS ARE RELATIVELY RECENT CONVERTS TO ISLAM?

With this, Allaudin signaled for his group to begin (Media Example 4.31). Ali heard the mallet strokes on the *ḍhol* combine with accents on the *tāshā* to outline the rhythm of **lā** il-**lā**ha **illa**'l-**lāh** mu**ḥam**ma**dur** ra**sūl 'al**l**ā**h. The *ḍhol* players completed each "statement," which consisted of a pattern played twice (one for each half of the *kalmah*), with an additional stroke; that is, eight counts for the verbal statement plus one more downbeat leading into *tāshā* solos. Within the statement, *tāshā* players took turns inserting rapid flams, drags, and buzz rolls. Between statements, four *tāshā* players kept a steady (swung) pulse while a fifth player improvised solos. The *ḍhol* players, maintaining eye contact with the current lead *tāshā* player, returned to the *kalmah* statement after a series of off-beat cues (figures 8.1a, b, and c; see the chapter notes).

Ali notated the rhythm with a series of X's and points and observed, The interval between successive sets of kalmah phrases seems to depend more on the dynamics of interaction than on counting beats; usually a multiple of four between iterations of the kalmah but not always; different from ṭhekā idea.

After another cue, the drummers sped up and transitioned into a pattern called *das kī gintī* (count of ten); the perceptual effect was one of stretching and flattening out the beats of the *kalmah* (Media Example 4.31 ⭮, at 3:00). Ali could not immediately grasp how this pattern could be construed as ten. This, too, was a riff-based pattern, not a *ṭhekā*. Ali counted thirteen beats in a complete rendition of the pattern—or twelve if the final stroke was, as in the case of the *kalmah*, a marker of the ending of the pattern. Counting emphasized strokes only, Ali perceived a pattern of six strokes, a gap, three stressed strokes, a gap, three stressed strokes, a gap, and the final stroke. Occasionally they played the three-stressed-stroke motive three times, a *tihā'ī*:

1	2	3	4	5	6	7	8	9	10	11
x . X .	. X . .	X . . .	x . X .	. X . .	X . . .	x . X .	. X . .	X . . .	. . . .	X

Coincidentally or not, this version could be counted as ten emphasized strokes by including the final stroke or as ten *mātra*s by reckoning the final stroke as the downbeat of the next section. But it was a variation, not the main pattern. The group followed *das kī gintī* by *bīs kī gintī*, "count of twenty," which was the same patterns as the former, played (apparently) as fast as possible. The significance of *ten* and *twenty* in these pattern names remained opaque to Ali.

Since Ali had by now encountered several instances of texts lurking behind drumming or *shahnā'ī* playing, he asked, "Allaudin-*jī*, are there any other *tāl*s with 'words'?"

"*Jī*?" responded Allaudin, trying to catch Ali's point.

"For example, during Muharram, some *bajāne-wāle* perform *marṣiyah* poetry on their instruments."

"They know their art; we have nothing to do with that."

Allaudin signaled for the group to continue, calling out the names of the *cāl*s one by one: "The *mātam* of one! . . . the *kairvā* of two! . . . the *mātam* of three! . . . the *mātam* of six! . . ."

Ali listened to these patterns with attention to what was being counted. Each of the four patterns could be heard as spanning eight *mātra*s. The three *mātam* examples provided clear instances of the number of stressed bass strokes corresponding to the number in the name. In *ek kā mātam* each cycle began with a single strong bass stroke. *Tīn kā mātam* presented the strong strokes on counts one, two, and three. *Cheh kā mātam* (the *mātam* of six) consisted of the same three stressed strokes on counts one, two, and three, balanced by three softer combination strokes on five, six, and seven. The combinations involved double striking (on five and six) and damping (on seven). Ali contemplated the position of "the *kairvā* of two" within this sequence. This was clearly a variation of the classical *kehervā ṭhekā,*

1	2	3	4	5	6	7	8
dhā	ge	nā	tī	nā	kā	dhin	nā

the key point of similarity being the sense of drive created in moving from count seven to count one. On the tabla, these strokes are emphasized with resonant strokes on the bass, or *bāyāṉ*, drum. On the *ḍhol*, these performers brought out count seven with a bare-handed stroke and count eight with a mallet beat. Ali thought that the emphasis on these two points in the *tāl* could account for the name. But as far as he knew, this was not a standard naming practice; rather, it seemed designed for the sequence played by this group. Perhaps, Ali considered, numbering is one way of remembering the pieces.

The *tāshā* players took a break to tauten their drum heads by a small fire fashioned of rotted furniture pieces and broken cartons.

Ali gently persisted with his earlier line of questioning. "Where did the name of these items originate? *Mātam,* for instance."

"This *mātam* is not *that mātam*, the 'lamentation' *mātam*; it's merely the *cāl* name. The names are mine."

"Did you compose them?"

"No, sir, the art of 'singing' was started by Tansen but now there are thousands of singers. This is how it goes. First some people use some art, then others take it up. Like now we have learned a little bit, but we are nothing in comparison to the people who had these in the past."

Ali continued to probe Allaudin about his knowledge of the repertoire's origin and his own training. Allaudin evaded discussing his Hindu teacher and finally came right out and said that his teacher was not Hindu. At this point, Rajab joined the conversation impatiently.

"Dear old man, you told us this morning that you had learned from some Hindu."

"There is no question of learning from a Hindu. If I had learned from a Hindu, then why would I have come here? It is our religious matter.[14] I told you this—didn't I?—that before everything we present the *kalmah*. We play the *kalmah*. No? So that before everything we make manifest [*ẓāhir karte heṉ*] that we are Muslims."[15] He reiterated that his connection with Muharram is a matter of faith, comparable to the way Timur used to show his faith by making a pilgrimage to Imam Husain's tomb, and then later effected the same end by attending to a replica of the tomb, the *ta'ziyah*.[16] "Drummers now feel 'passion,' just as they did in Timur's time. Others may feel like they are on the battlefield. We feel as if we are standing before the tomb of Imam Husain."[17]

Ali dropped the matter. If Allaudin had learned from a professional musician of any sort, that would help explain why their repertoire contained classical items. "Do you play all these items for Muharram, or are there other occasions, too?"

"We don't play for any other function. We don't know as to whether it will be considered bad or good, but anyway, we don't play."[18]

PROFESSION OF IGNORANCE RECALLING THE AGRA-WĀLĀS' VIEWS YESTERDAY.

"Has anyone objected to your playing?"

"The *mullahs* object to *mūsiqī*. That music has become something different from what we play, hasn't it? I told you that first of all we present *kalmah*. *Kalmah* is not a music item. But we play it because of faith. Those who understand this art of music understand this thing that we play also as music. In any case, it is our faith to present *kalmah* the first of all."[19]

The group now played *ek tāla* and *chautāla* (Media Example 8.5 ⎘).

Obvious affinity with the eponymous tabla ṭhekās in Hindustani classical music; even the khālī strokes are marked by subdued or damped strokes on the ḍhol. Clearly somebody with knowledge of the classical tradition, perhaps the concealed Hindu teacher, created a version of these tāls for the ḍhol. The knowledge was transmitted to these players in isolation: they have no conscious knowledge of the classical system.

"Is this classical music?" inquired Ali.

"There is classical also in it. Those who understand classical music consider this classical also. Those who don't understand classical think of it as clattering, *dhūm-dhaṛkkā*. We consider it only a faith. Otherwise, to us, it is neither classical nor any other thing. We do it only out of faith."[20]

Now it was getting to be about 9:30. Several drummers asked permission to leave. Shaking Allaudin's hand, Ali pressed an envelope with six thousand rupees into his palm: "*Bacco̱n ke liye* [for the children]."

Muharram Ali: Drumming Project Notebook #17

Entry, Sunday 15 June 1997, 10:30 p.m.

Today I worked with a Muhājir group whose leader, Allaudin, migrated from Bharatpur. He acknowledged associations between his drumming tradition and Islam in broad terms, as well as Muharram in particular. The kalmah and Allaudin's diffuse notion of "faith" indexed Islam broadly; the Timur story tied drumming to Muharram. But Allaudin stopped short of identifying specific parts of the repertoire with markedly Shī'ī rituals or practices—namely the drum pattern mātam. Mātam is, like kairvā, merely a cāl name. The kalmah is qualitatively different from the numbered cāl patterns in that it refers to a specific text and is performed in response to the tāshā players' cues rather than at a specific point in a regularly recurring cycle. Allaudin finds it important to make manifest (ẓāhir) the inner (bāṭin) meaning of the kalmah. Perhaps this stems from a desire for these Sheikh Siddiqis to proclaim their status as Muslims in Pakistan, where they continue to be regarded as migrant-outsiders and recent converts to Islam. Connected with proclaiming and reclaiming the status of being Muslim is the rejection of a specific learning process. Allaudin's disavowal of his Hindu teacher also serves to disconnect what his group plays from the highly developed system of music found throughout north India and Pakistan.

On Monday morning Ali caught the first bus to Karachi. The four hours transitioned him from the warm but not unpleasant climate of Hyderabad to the stifling humidity of Karachi. His bachelor cousin Ilfaz (related through his father's second wife) picked Ali up at the bus station and brought him to his posh rented flat near Zamzama Park. Sufiya, who was staying nearby in the same neighborhood, Clifton, joined them for tea in the afternoon and Ali dominated the conversation, describing what he had seen and the issues he felt had been raised. He tried explaining the concepts of *integration* and *disjunction* as attitudes expressed by drummers and other participants regarding the relation of their practices to religious sensibilities.

Trying to grasp these abstractions, Sufiya asked, "So would you call me an 'integrationist'"?

"I guess when it comes to my friends, these labels are overly simplistic. But yes, as one dedicated to the Panjatan Pak who responds to Muharram arts as part of your religious sensibility, I would."

"And I'm Sunni. Does that mean I have a disjunctive attitude?" asked Ilfaz.

"Your religious affiliation doesn't dictate whether you have more or less integrative or disjunctive views. It's more a matter of cultural upbringing and the current political situation. You know our folks in Lucknow, Ilfaz. We're heavily integrationist. The interrelationships of peoples, histories, and arts have been my father's hobbyhorse since as early as I can remember. It's hard for me to step out of that world and understand the objections and resistance of others. Listen, everyone knows at least some of the stories that circulate about Karbala. The association between Muharram drumming and war music is pretty obvious. What interests me now is what people make of these circulating associations. Disjunctive attitudes are not ones that fail to acknowledge the similarities between rituals and supposed historical events. Rather, they're attitudes that resist linking such associations to their own identities as Muslims."

"I don't get involved with Muharram at all, so I don't know where that puts me. But I know a singer named Asad—he's not a Shīʿah, but he's hooked on singing *sozs* and *salāms*. In our circle some are more religious than others, but there are no *kaṭṭar* [hard, severe] Shī'ahs. Still, when this guy sings, we all are moved. I'm not a fan of the poetry; Anis and Dabir are nothing compared to Ghalib. I respond to Asad's rhythms and tunes. But I can tell from the way my Shī'ī friends talk to one another that they respond at a whole different level. Would you say Asad has this disjunctive thing?"

"It's hard to know without getting to know him better. I'd have to know something about his own piety. If he's a religious guy but sings just for *shauq*—that is, if he locates his piety outside of singing—then yes, that's the kind of disjunction I mean. Whereas, if he somehow sees singing itself as an expression of love for God, the Prophet, the Prophet's family, that sort of thing, like some Sufis do, then I would see him as integrationist. It's not the practice itself, but the relationship of the practice to the person."

"I see what you're getting at," said Sufiya, "but if you're uncomfortable labeling your friends and relatives shouldn't you also give the same respect to the people you've only recently met?"

"Particularly given the history of your family," Ilfaz added gravidly, "attitudes change."

This last comment was lost on the chastened Ali. The conversation drifted to local politics in Karachi, updates about the family in Karachi, and food. At about 11 P.M. the three of them shared an exquisite meal by the seaside. Unbeknownst to the couple, Ilfaz had arranged to stay at a friend's flat for the night, and surprised Ali and Sufiya by dropping them off at his own flat, saying *k͟hudā hāfiz*, and speeding off.

CHAPTER 9

The Voice in the Drum

Ali awoke at 5:30 A.M., damp and intoxicated in the pungent, salty, heavy Karachi air. *Shalwār*-clad Sufiya was draped in a matching black tee shirt foraged from Ilfaz's neatly fitted almirah. She looked up from her newspaper. Peering over her half-frame reading glasses, she caressed the blue rim of her steaming cup of chai with parched lips.

"What, no butter-toast, no omelette, for me, my dear?" Ali queried cheerily from beneath his sleep-swollen eyelids.

The edges of Sufiya's firm smile rose imperceptibly—her expression inscrutable, reserved—the enigmatic Sufiya, glimpsed through the weather-worn teak shutters in Multan. Then as now, Ali found himself at once excited and disquieted. Sufiya pressed her palm into the rattan seat on her left, beckoning. Close. In silence, Ali poured himself tea.

: : :

It was evening. Sufiya herself was the one to revisit Ali's project. "Asma was telling me about a Muhājir group in Jacob Lines." Asma was Sufiya's schoolmate and host in Karachi. "Their families migrated from Nizamuddin *bastī* in Delhi and they celebrate Muharram grandly with *ta'ziyah*s, *'alams*, and drumming. And there's Shī'ī involvement."*

*This is significant because the families in charge of the Nizamuddin 'Auliya shrine, after which the neighborhood was named, are Sunni.

"I've heard about these people."

"You'll need to be careful. Jacob Lines is a volatile neighborhood."

The next morning, Ilfaz didn't hide his skepticism about Ali's proposal to show up in Jacob Lines and "make inquiries." Ali couldn't quite convince him that ethnographers often rely on serendipitous encounters. Ilfaz implored him to be vigilant. "Why not visit the Pakistan National Council of Arts office in Karachi first? Maybe the music angle will work in your favor. Let me accompany you; I need a break from work anyway."

The local director of the PNCA, an affable, sturdily built, clean-cut man in his late forties, sat with his fleshy hands outstretched on his large, uncluttered desk. "I don't recall ever having invited artists from Jacob Lines. But regarding Muharram arts you should contact Asghar Husain—he knows a lot and has a strong voice." This Shī'ī *soz k͟hwān*, it turned out, was regularly invited to recite in Jacob Lines and knew a number of local people. He lived on Manora Island, just offshore west of Ilfaz's flat. After a quick call on the mobile, they agreed to meet up near the ferry.

In Jacob Lines, Ilfaz parked his car near the Husaini blood bank and the three men proceeded down Nizami Road. Asghar recognized a stolid, broad-shouldered man in his mid-forties on the street as a *ḍhol* player and struck up a conversation, introducing his two companions. The *ḍhol* player, Hashim, was pleased to learn that Ali had visited the Nizamuddin *dargah* in Delhi. He explained that the rituals here in Karachi were exactly the same as those there and encouraged Ali to attend Muharram celebrations in both places. Ali inquired about the drummers and the drum patterns. Attracted by the conversation, a small cadre of drummers gathered. Ali executed a quick survey: Hashim the unschooled floor-maker, a master tailor and several junior tailors, a mason, and a packer working in a glue factory. Some had studied up to the tenth standard and others had acquired very little education.

Hashim described how he and the other players would take turns beating the four *t̤arz*s: *savārī, mātam, kalmah,* and *dhīmā*. To Hashim's surprise, Ali clapped out the *kalmah* pattern he'd heard the Bharatpur group perform. Hashim insisted that someone from the Nizami tradition must have taught them, because according to his relative Muhammad Razaq, the Nizami people invented this pattern to pass the time during procession. For the Nizamis it was a matter of *shauq*—it alleviated the tedium of playing the other patterns, when, "ẕehn bhar jāta hai," the mind gets filled up.

Ali raised for discussion the Bharatpur group's idea about the *kalmah* pattern. Hashim's view was simply that those on procession get enjoyment (*mazah*) out of Muharram drumming in general and that such drumming alerts those in the area to what is going on.[1] More pointedly, Hashim said, "A rhythm gets built inside the *marṣiyah*."[2]

A man named Nasir, short in stature with a black, collared shirt and mustache, joined the group and listened attentively. He explained that when Hashim's group plays *mātam* his people do *sīnah zanī* with their hands and shout 'Husain, Husain.' Ali ascertained that several *k̲h̲āndān*s are involved in the proceedings. These included the descendants of Nizamuddin Auliya and some of his other followers. Ilfaz picked up on the fact that Nasir was Shī'ī and subtly conveyed that crucial bit of information to Ali. "Our people used to live side by side with them in Delhi," explained Nasir.

"So, Hashim-sahab, Nasir's people strike their chests while you play." Ali asked, "What do your people do . . . *matlab*, how do you feel about this *mātam* drumming?"

"People are very, I mean like this, in a 'languid state'; they listen, deeply immersed . . . and many begin weeping also . . . they shed tears . . . their hearts are moved."[3]

Ali maintained eye contact while noting his impressions: Hashim's emotional expression uncommon among Sunni Muhājirs. He uses the term sust—slow, heavy, languid, weak. Draws connection between slowness in time, weight, and bodily condition. Contrasts strongly with the way Urdu-speaking Shī'ahs usually represent Sunni attitudes. Could his view relate to his specialization on the ḍhol? Could infrequent bass attacks connote weight and slowness?

Ali was curious as to whether participants' emotional responses were keyed to the specific texts but found that Hashim did not actually know how the texts fit the patterns. Rather, he was tuned in to the 'feeling' that would tell him which *marṣiyah* is 'inside' a particular drum pattern. The discussion of emotionality led Ali to inquire whether Shī'ahs also play *marṣiyah*s on the drums. Hashim indicated that not all Shī'ahs know about the *āvāz* (voice) of the drums—only those, such as Nasir, who hailed from his area. A procession used to come from Nasir's place in India. One famous musician Hashim referred to as Ustad Sheikh used to be invited to play in Nasir's Delhi neighborhood. Nowadays these Shī'ahs lived across from Hashim's place, nearby. They participated in one another's rituals in Karachi. The Shī'ahs had continued to maintain 'faith' in the Nizami rituals.[4]

Nasir turned to Hashim wistfully and recalled how Hashim's group would play the drums and his Shī'ī family would weep, and both contingents would recite *marṣiyah*.[5] Ali continued to press the question of whether Shī'ahs ever played the *ḍhol* and *tāshā*. Nasir maintained that his people only did *mātam* but pointed out that one relative, Wajid Khurshid Ali (d. ca. 1952), was a great tabla player who used to perform on Radio Pakistan.

He had a 'real sensitivity to' classical music. Though he didn't play *ḍhol* or *tāshā* himself, he supported the art.

Ali jotted, *Fellows like Wajid Khurshid Ali, involved in both classical music and ritual music, could have helped teach a few tabla ṭhekās to ḍhol-tāshā groups without them ever undergoing classical training per se.*

By this time the conversation had drawn the attention of Muhammad Razaq himself. In his late seventies, Razaq, clad in a charcoal green *shalwār qamīz*, wore his hennaed gray hair long. His scraggly, longish beard, fanning out like rays from the sun, barely covered a scar along his left jaw, mottled flesh on his spare neck, and a birthmark above his adam's apple. The wiry *tāshā* master recalled, "There was one Shī'ī *ta'ziyah* that used to be taken out at Nizamuddin Auliya, the Khurshid-wālā *ta'ziyah*, sponsored by Wajid Khurshid Ali. We would play the drums on one side of the *ta'ziyah* and they would do *sīnah zanī* on the other."

Ali asked if there used to be Shī'ī *tāshā* players in Delhi, as there had been in Lucknow.

"Only a few. I remember Ansar Husain—a peculiar fellow. When he talked to you he always looked like he was glancing over your left shoulder. A physical disorder. Unnerving. Anyway, his playing was a matter of controversy. Some people thought it was a *gunāh* [sin] because they believed Yazid's side played the war drum [*jangī tabal*] and blew the trumpet [*ṣūr*] to celebrate their victory whenever they slew a member of Husain's tribe."

Nasir, also partly responding to Ali, pointed out that the important thing is not that Shī'ahs play themselves but that they help maintain the *silsilah*. Their interest and patronage keep the drumming tradition viable and foster the continued cooperation between Sunnis and Shī'ahs. Hashim pointed out that there have been obstacles. Other Urdu-speaking Shī'ahs have moved into Jacob Lines and objected to what they're doing. So after a decade of walking together in processions, Hashim's and Nasir's people now have separate processions. But their relations are still cordial. Relations with outsiders, however, are strained.[6]

Nasir waxed philosophical. "In each era [*har daur meṉ*] opponents [*mukḫālifīn*] keep coming to block our paths."

"For example?"

"Suppose the Sīpah-e-Sabah* or the ISO† want to make trouble for

*"The army of the companions of the Prophet," a virulently anti-Shī'ī militant organization.

†The Imamia Students Organisation, a group committed to an ideology of purist Shī'ism.

us," explained Razaq. "They won't have the courage to do so directly. Rather, when Nasir's people and our people are joining together in a *julūs* [procession] or something, they'll throw a stone, or tear the *ḍhol*, or hit one of drummers, and then disappear into the crowd. After incidents like this, Shī'ahs and Sunnis here began to perform their rituals separately."

Asghar elaborated. "Anti-Shī'ī groups spread propaganda that Shī'ahs are *kāfir*s. The Nizamis were subjected to the same criticism through their association with Muharram. Opponents would tell the Nizamis that they were committing *gunāh*s by playing the drums."

Ali wondered aloud whether this controversy would prevent them from demonstrating. Hashim said that it might be possible indoors. There were restrictions on when and where they performed. It could never be during *namāz*. If they diverged from this schedule, their opponents would pelt them with stones.[7]

Ali's cousin Ilfaz, in his role as guide for the day, took this opportunity to interject, rather formally, in English, "The neighbors dislike the drumming because it presents a public vision of Islam—a music-loving Islam—lacking decorum and sobriety. Drumming draws attention to *ta'ziyah* rituals and blurs the distinction between Shī'ahs and Sunnis. Of course," he went on, "Chishtis have suffered criticism from many kinds of orthodox or reactionary parties over the centuries."

"*Saccī bāt hai* [Ain't it the truth]," agreed the septuagenarian Razaq.

"When these noble people from Nizamuddin migrated from Delhi to Karachi, the power and influence they once held in Delhi declined. They are now a politically weaker, more economically depressed, minority community in Karachi. That's not to say that Muhājirs in general are less educated or affluent than their Sindhi and Pashtun counterparts. The different Muhājir subgroups, the Sindhis, and the Pashtuns all compete for economic and political resources here. This fragile Nizami-Shī'ī coalition makes them particularly vulnerable to attack."

Hashim the floor-maker and Razaq caught the gist of Ilfaz's lecture but not its sententious tone.

"We have one book," Razaq began, "which explains all our Chishti customs, our drumming, our poetry, everything." He sent a small boy to fetch it. "Sayyad Ali Abbas Nizami wrote it in Urdu and our Nizami Institute published it here about seven, eight years ago." Razaq invited the three visitors to his place for tea and biscuits and asked Hashim discreetly to arrange for a set of drums.

The boy produced the book—actually a fifteen-page Urdu pamphlet: "Code of laws [*dastūr-e 'amal*] and faith of the Nizami lineage: 'urses of the great religious people and others." Ali flipped through it and hastily paraphrased key passages in Urdu, hoping to procure a copy for himself later:

> The dastūr-e 'amal responds to a fatwa against members of the Nizami k͟hāndān for engaging in 'unauthorized religious innovations'; defends criticisms against celebrating 'urses and listening to musical instruments as part of 'spiritual audition'—including qawwālī sessions; also reacts against the accusation of shirk [recognizing God's attributes in others] as evidenced by ta'ziyah rituals. Counters by proclaiming Chishti order's great esteem in many lands. Asserts that conducting 'urses and listening to pure, mystical poetry constitutes worship and that denying this 'reality or truth' amounts to straying from the path.

Ali noted a disjunctive tone in a passage that denied the 'religious' status of rituals with *ta'ziyah*—including drumming and recitation of poetry—on the grounds that no Muslim regards the *ta'ziyah* as God. The fact that these community members nevertheless hold the *ta'ziyah* in great esteem runs counter, Ali observed, to Lala Gul's insinuation that Sindhis treat their *ta'ziyah*s more respectfully than do Urdu speakers. The author also made explicit the emotional complexity of the rituals, which create 'impressions' of 'happiness and sadness mixed together.' The acknowledgment of affective mixing in this document embraced a dangerous ambiguity in the contemporary political climate, noted Ali.

"*Baṛī dilcasp.* Fascinating document," said Ali.

"It's for you," replied Razaq.

"Very kind of you. I didn't notice much about music here. And I couldn't find the texts of the *mars̱iyah* poetry you mentioned."

"It's not there? It must be in some other book. You come back next week. Definitely I'll find it for you," promised Razaq.

Hmm . . .

"My *keseṭ rikārḍar* is with me. Would you mind reciting one *mars̱iyah*?"

"I can't recall exactly. . . ." Razaq lowered his eyelids pensively for a minute or two. From the rusty depths of his larynx, a gravelly tone began to emerge. Gaining strength, settling on a comfortable *sur*, Razaq launched into a *soz.* Ali could perceive the seven-count musical structure, even though it was occasionally interrupted. The musical timing fit well with *ramal* meter, the *'arūz* of the text:

ran me jis dam subha 'āshūrā āyā̱n hone lagī
lashkar-e shāh-e shahīdā̱n me az̤ān hone lagī
yā̱n namāze̱n aur kamar bandī vahā̱n hone lagī

is taraf tadbīr katl-e tishnegān̲ hone lagī
tāl o jangī kī ṣadāen̲ jā sunī ma'ṣūm nē
tā lagī talvār bhī haidar ka kabzā cūmne

The moment the morning of Ashura dawned in the battlefield,
The call to prayer issued amidst the army of the King of Martyrs,
Where prayers and battle preparations were under way.
On the other side, they schemed to slay those thirsting ones.
The blameless one stood simply listening to the sound of drums
    and battle
Until an enemy sword itself stole close enough to kiss the hilt of
    Haidar's sword [which Husain had].

Ali scribbled as quickly as he could, "Tāl" is paired with "jangī" (battle) and serves as the object of Husain's listening. Tāl o jangī rhymes in a diminished form with "tā lagī"—"until . . ." at the beginning of the next line. The text does not specify whether drumming is good or bad, then said, "Wāh, Wāh Muhammad Razaq Sahab, Subḥāna'llāh [Praise God]!"

"Why we play this is . . . you see, Timur had a dream . . . you've heard about it?"

"Yes, about making a *shabīh* of his mausoleum so he wouldn't have to make a long pilgrimage with his lame leg."

"*Vahī* [that very one]. In that dream, Timur heard a voice saying, 'Husain, Husain.' It's that *ṣadā* [voice] that comes from the drums—'Husain, Husain.' When we play the *mātam ṭarz* [pattern] and those people do *mātam*, everyone chants 'Husain, Husain.' The *mars̱iyah k̲h̲wān*s can't read those *mars̱iyah*s for everyone—they can't be in so many places, and their voices aren't loud enough. So to reach the crowds, *mars̱iyah*s have come to be played on *ḍhol* and *tāshā*."[8]

"Excuse me, Cācaji, but could you explain a little bit more how you make the *mars̱iyah* syllables sound on the drums?"

"The stick of the *ḍhol* falls at the places where the words come; the *tāshā* just goes on playing."[9]

During the conversation, another man of his generation entered carrying a *tāshā*. He stood a few centimeters taller than Muhammad Razaq. In a white *shalwār qamīz* and skullcap overlapping his receding hairline, he sported a full and neatly trimmed pepper-and-salt beard and mustache. Soft-spoken, with craggy visage and tight hollows under his cheekbones, the man appeared somber.

"This is Sarir Ahmed Nizami," said Razaq.

"We've been playing *tāshā* for over 450 years, ever since Amir Timur brought the *tabarrukāt** to our place," said Nizami.

"Do you belong to the same family?"

"No, I am a Sayyad," replied Nizami.

"I'm Sheikh," said Razaq. "All different *qaum*s play. All that's required is 'love.'"

"Hashim Sahab was telling me that you express the words of *mars̱iyah*s in your drumming patterns. Then Muhammad Razaq Sahab sang one of them for me. I don't understand; do you sing the words of the *mars̱iyah* while you play?"

"We don't say the words with our mouths, we say them with the sticks. If we try to go by the words we'll get derailed from the *tāl*," replied Muhammad Razaq.[10]

Nizami explained, "The *tāshā* is for *ḥisāb* [counting]. We go according to the *mātra*s."

"The slow one, *dhīmā*, is the most difficult," added Razaq.

"The *mars̱iyah* we play on *tāshā* is this one." Nizami sang, "āj ṣug̱rā yūṉ madīne meṉ haiṉ rotī bhar ke nain [Today Sughra cries in Medina like this with eyes full of tears]" (Media Example 9.1).

Ali waited for the next line. "And?"

"That's all I remember. There are so many *band*s [stanzas]; it's a large *marsiyah*. Our forefathers wrote this a long time ago. My father brought this one back from Bengal. It was written by Faṣīḥ [b. 1780]."

"Muhammad Razaq Sahab sang this tune with a different text a few minutes ago."

"No . . . the *mars̱iyah* for *dhīmā* is this one."

Razaq's eyebrow twitched, but he remained otherwise stone-faced.

"When would *ran me jis dam subha 'āshūrā āyāṉ hone lagī* be sung?"

"Some *mars̱iyah*s like this are recited with melody [*tarannum*] at *majlis*es," explained S. A. Nizami, "and others are recited by groups of men standing before the *ta'ziyah* each time the procession stops. We don't play at those times, and they don't recite while we play."

"Tell me the words of the one you just sang again, please, one by one."

Ali jotted down the Urdu. "So when do you play *dhīmā*?"

"We play it in an open area. People stand around respectfully, thoughtfully. It creates the impression of the day Sughra heard of her father's

---

*Sacred relics—probably something from Imam Husain's shrine used in connection with the *ta'ziyah* rituals.

A crowd in the Nizamuddin neighborhood listening attentively to *ḍhol-tāshā* drummers performing *dhīmā*. The *ḍhol* player in the center with his arm raised is Ghulam Hasnain Nizami. Directly to his right playing *tāshā* is Mamraj. Eve of Ashura, Nizamuddin, New Delhi. December 27, 2009. Photo courtesy of Nathan Tabor.

martyrdom. You know she was ill—she'd been left in Medina when her family traveled to Karbala. If you keep the 'memory' of this *marṣiyah* in your 'heart,' when you hear *dhīmā*, it will come into your 'consciousness' that this is the *marṣiyah* being played."

Ali began to scribble an emerging insight: If you already have the topic of the poem in your head, hearing the appropriate drum beat seems to set off an emotional trigger.

"Dhīmā bajā'enge!" Nizami called to the others to start playing *dhīmā* along with him.

Muhammad Razaq started them off playing a slow, even set of strokes on the *tāshā* (slower than 60 mm, a beat per second; Media Example 9.2). Two strokes and a rest, four strokes, then S. A. Nizami joined, both of them playing at twice the density. The *ḍhol* entered at what seemed at first to be irregular intervals. Ali found the relationship of the *ḍhol* strokes to the *tāshā* pattern confusing. (When he later reviewed the recording, Ali began to hear a cycle of 3 + 4 beats outlined by *ḍhol* strokes and by the onsets of *tāshā* patterns. Some cycles lacked a clear internal articulation of 3 + 4 beats, but the performers maintained a seven-count cycle consistently throughout their demonstration.)

Ali heard Nizami start to play a figure on the *tāshā*  which, if iterated three times, would have been a common *tihā'ī* in an eight-beat *tāl* ($3 \cdot 3 = 9$, with the last beat falling on the first beat of the next eight-beat cycle). But he played the figure five times, the final iteration corresponding with a *ḍhol* stroke. That is, it occupied fifteen beats, with the last beat falling on beat one of the seven-beat *ḍhol* cycle.

As the performance progressed, Ali searched for other regularities, but they were few. It sounded like the *tāshā* players were improvising, but he could not understand how they were coordinating with the *ḍhol*. Judging by their limited manual capabilities, and the fact that these drummers played so very infrequently, Ali was hesitant to draw conclusions based on this one performance. The performers could only vaguely explain what they were doing with reference to the *marṣiyah*. The 3 + 4 metric structure was common to the poem's poetic meter, its sung rendition, and the drummed version, and Ali had to satisfy himself with that explanation for the time being.

When Razaq, Nizami, and the others had played *dhīmā* for some minutes, they moved seamlessly into *mātam* (end of Media Example 9.2 and Media Example 9.3).

Keeping the same pace, the metric frame shifted from the 3 + 4 beat cycle ($\frac{7}{4}$)—which Ali had not yet grasped during the performance—to a two-beat cycle ($\frac{2}{4}$), whose regularity was immediately evident to Ali. One of the *tāshā*s maintained the pattern

The other *tāshā* improvised phrases and rolls cutting across this pattern. The *ḍhol* outlined the short metrical unit through an alternation of center and rim strokes:

 *cob* (stick) in right hand, playing in center, ♪, and rim, , of the *ḍhol*

 bare left hand, interlocking soft or damped strokes

The switch to *savārī* was just a matter of speeding up the same pattern slightly. After the onset of *savārī*, Nasir and a few others started to strike their hands on their chests and chant "Husain, Husain":

 "sain," the emphasized syllable, fell on each eighth note; "Hu," barely audible, preceded "sain" by about a 32nd note

Finally the drummers proceeded to *kalmah*, which was largely the way the Bharatpur group had played it, except it did not include the additional "downbeat" at the conclusion of each two iterations. As in the Bharatpur

example, the *tāshā* players cued the return of the signature pattern with a cadential formula, and, also as with the Bharatpur group, no large-scale metric frame governed the span of time between each return. Again, Ali spotted the drummers' tentativeness. If he had not already heard the Bharatpur group exercise rhythmic flexibility when playing the *kalmah*, Ali might have judged the Nizami group incompetent.

At the conclusion of the short demonstration, S. A. Nizami added, "Like that *kalmah* I told you about, no? 'Ali kī zarbeṉ is also played. This is the poem we expressed with our drum sticks when we played 'Ali kī zarbeṉ."

jangal pahāṛ kahte haiṉ nād-e 'alī 'alī
mushkil ko merī hal karo mushkil kushā 'alī yā 'alī yā 'alī

The forest and mountains ring with the cry Oh Ali, Ali!
Alleviate my difficulties, problem-solver, Ali, Oh Ali! Oh Ali!

Ali could not ascertain exactly where this text fit in—as part of the *kalmah*, perhaps the *tāshā* part, or as an independent pattern they had not discussed previously. He couldn't get a clear answer. Perhaps this was another text used in the *majlis* but not necessarily beat out on the drums. Ali thought he recalled hearing this text called out as a *na'rah* (slogan) in a *majlis* in Lahore ten years earlier.

Ali was eventually able to coax Nizami into providing the so-called *marṣiyah* text associated with *mātam* (Media Example 9.4)—which served also, at a faster tempo, for *savārī*. Although Nizami could only provide two lines, Ali recognized the style of rendition as *salām*—not *marṣiyah*—because of the refrain following each line. This text also sounded familiar, but he couldn't place it. The refrain, *maẓlūm ḥusainā*, projected forward a pattern of double longs and double shorts set up in the poetic meter of the poem proper.

– – ◡/◡ – – ◡◡ – – ◡/◡ – – | – – ◡ ◡/– –
jab fāṭimah firdaus se kahtī hu'ī ā'īṉ maẓlūm ḥusainā

– – ◡/◡ – – ◡/◡ – – ◡/◡ – –|– – ◡ ◡/– –
marne se tere luṭ gaī muj mā kī kamā'ī mazlūm husainā

When Fatimah came from paradise saying, "Oppressed Husain"
because of your [Husain's] dying, all I [Fatimah]
had invested as a mother was plundered, Oppressed Husain.

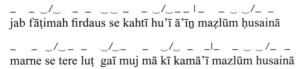

While singing, Nizami emphasized four-syllable units that made semantic sense, for example, "when Fatimah . . . from paradise . . . saying"; but this arrangement also obscured the poetic meter, making it sound more like repeated feet of _ _ ⏑ _ (for example, "*jab fāṯimah*" with "*mah*" treated as a long syllable). He concluded the melody of each line, before the refrain, with a long melisma on the syllable *ī* (nasalized in the first case).

Ali said, "How does this text relate to your drum strokes?"

Razaq replied, "You listen again, you'll hear it. We play it *jalad* [fast]."

After repeated listenings that evening, the only similarity Ali could perceive was the persistence of four-syllable units. Where there were two-syllable units—at the end of each line and the end of the refrain—the prolongation in singing could theoretically be reckoned as completing the four-syllable time unit.

Line:	jab fāṯimah / firdaus se / kahtī hu'ī / ā'īn̲ (+ melisma)
Refrain:	maẓlūm ḥu / sainā (+ pause between lines)

The four-syllable units were at least congruent with the length of the metric cycle and the durations created by chanting "Husain, Husain."

Muharram Ali: Drumming Project Notebook #17

Entry, Wednesday, June 18, 1997, 8 p.m.

Challenging interaction with Nizami drummers and Shī'ī 'partners' today . . . strong insistence that all their drum patterns were grounded in texts. Several kinds of texts (which they call marṡiyah) are in evidence: marṡiyah, salām, kalmah, and slogans. The sound pattern of kalmah on drums is obvious. Others require a leap of imagination. Are these fellows merely relaying their forefathers' assertions that the texts and drumming patterns are related, without actually knowing themselves how this is the case? I'm worried they've produced whatever poetry they could remember just to please me—that would mean any relationship with drumming I perceived was simply the product of my creative listening. Must travel to Delhi . . .

: : :

The next morning, Ali, Ilfaz, and Sufiya sat together consuming toast, jam, and tea in Ilfaz's flat, speculating on what it means to express the words of the *marṡiyah*s with drumsticks. Ali recalled the Bharatpur group's use of the *kalmah*. "There, it was the only pattern with a verbal counterpart . . . it was like a proclamation, 'Hey, we're Muslim,' which gave them license to play other drum items. For the Nizamis it was different. Even though they claimed to have invented the *kalmah* pattern on the drum, they downplayed its importance."

"Still," said Sufiya, "don't you think the *idea* of text plays a similar role here?"

"Yes," responded Ilfaz. "The thing is, they were particular about the texts—the meanings behind them."

"And yet they can't quite tell you how the drums play the texts . . . and most of the players say they don't know the exact words, either," said Ali.

"I'll see if I can enlist Asghar Husain's help to get the book S. A. Nizami kept referring to," promised Ilfaz.

Sufiya and Ali flew to Lahore that afternoon. Before returning to their respective hosts in Lahore, the two dined at the Village Restaurant, a lavish simulacrum of Panjabi folk culture. Its dhoti-clad waiters, waterwheel and terra cotta pots, and station after station of chefs cooking rices, breads, kabobs—*sarson kā sāg* (mustard greens) and *makā'īn kī roṭi* (cornmeal flatbread), *gol gappa* (deep fried, puffed bread served with onion and chickpeas), and other street food—were much to take in.

"I've always wanted to try this place," said Sufiya, looking almost apologetic.

"It's like a movie set . . . talk about making a business out of nostalgia, but I guess I shouldn't talk."

"You're more willing to be inconvenienced than these types in order to experience the *aṣlī cīz*—but yes."

"Problem is, I'm not sure that what I have on offer can keep up with the market. Seriously, Sufiya, I don't know how often I'll be able to return to Pakistan. Bunty is making things difficult for me at work . . . and I'm ambivalent. I still feel the newspaper should be a window to a wider world, but I'm constricted. The turnover's quick. We have to assume our readers' attention span is short."

"You've been veering this way for years now; I wondered when you'd make the leap."

"Friends at the Delhi School of Economics have been making noises about a position at the Institute of Economic Growth working alongside one of our country's leading social anthropologists. It's a truly international place. It'd be good for me to get out of Lucknow.

"There are other matters too. The family is crumbling, along with our property in Lucknow . . . many decisions to make. It's impossible for me to imagine a settled life without you . . ."

"So, just like that, I'm supposed to leave Pakistan . . . renounce my citizenship . . ."

"I didn't say . . ."

"But your plans don't seem to provide for another option."

Sufiya stiffened, then resumed the conversation coolly.

It was not the farewell Ali had hoped for. But what could he expect? he thought, as he boarded the flight to Delhi.

: : :

Ali decided to spend a few days in Delhi with his slick, slender, still-bachelor friend Arjun—who was, unfortunately, fresh out of liquor. They dispatched themselves to the United Coffee House in Connaught Place. Pressing the heels of his palms against the edge of the table with its stained maroon cloth, Ali stretched his neck and shoulders. By the time the Golden Eagle beer was served, lightly chilled, he had already begun updating his friend on events of the past few years.

"Ali, I keep meaning to tell you, you left a roll of film with me about ten years back. There's a nice shot of you at my flat, typing away about one of your earlier visits to Pakistan. Then there are some blurred pictures of *ta'ziyah*s and musicians. And look here. Who is this fetching young woman in purple? Isn't there a law," goaded Arjun, "about taking pictures of women in Pakistan?"

"I thought I'd lost that roll! She's the reason I'm single." With relief, Ali unraveled the story he'd thus far withheld from friends and family in India.

"Can't say I know how you feel, *yār*. I've four brothers and five sisters, all married with kids. I'm quite glad to be on my own. Easy enough to find a sheila around here." Arjun sounded silly to Ali, retaining this bit of Australian slang that was popular among their circle of friends in the 1980s. "No attachments. Still, there must be a solution for you. You shouldn't take my advice. I'm better at offending than reconciling." But Arjun didn't hesitate to counsel Ali anyway. "The thing with women, see, is you need to demonstrate what you're willing to do for them. . . ."

" . . . despite being disingenuous," Ali finished the sentence silently.

"Right now, I'd like to follow up on my work in Karachi. I need to visit the Nizamuddin shrine."

: : :

The next morning Ali decamped from Arjun's flat in Jangpura and strode to the southern part of the Nizamuddin neighborhood over a footbridge and along a weather-worn stone wall. After a few false turns, he navigated through a small network of lanes and deposited his *cappal*s (sandals) with a custodian near the shrine. The entrance opened into a multilevel courtyard in front of the grave of the thirteenth- or fourteenth-century poet-musician Amir Khusrau, Nizamuddin's favorite disciple. Ali wandered through the *dargah* complex, past Khusrau's tomb and toward that of Nizamuddin, and approached a sturdy, middle-aged man with a green *zarī*-bordered swath of tulle tied about his head with one corner projecting backward at an acute angle. The *pagaṛī-wālā* asked a young man to bring Ali to Kabiruddin Nizami, who was seated quietly on the verandah outside Hazrat Nizamuddin's mausoleum. Ali explained what he'd been doing in Karachi, the community he'd been in touch with there, and his excitement over Shī'ī participation.

"There's no connection with Shī'ahs here . . . they may attend . . . no, they don't perform *mātam* . . . they don't disturb us."

Puzzled, Ali probed Kabiruddin for historical information, for evidence of the intercommunal cooperation he had been told about in Karachi, but learned nothing.

"I thought you might like to see this pamphlet." Ali handed him the *dastūr-e-'amal*, thinking this document might trigger his interest. "I obtained it from the Nizamis in Karachi."

Glancing at it perfunctorily, Kabiruddin returned it to Ali. "People are always coming up with these objections . . ." Kabiruddin began to ramble, and Ali attempted to extract himself from this fruitless lead.

Eventually Ali was able to meet Farid Ahmad Nizami, grandson of the former Sajjāda Nishīn, Shamsul-Mashaikh Hazrat Pir Zamin Nizami Syed Bokhari, who had died about four years earlier. "My grandfather Pir Zamin Nizami," he told Ali, "was a great scholar and poet, wrote many *marṡiyah*s, and did real research on the history of Muharram in Nizamuddin. No one knows for certain when the tradition started, but there is no evidence that it is more than 250 years old. What is it you'd like to know?"

"Two things, Farid-sahab: one is about the drumming that takes place during Muharram here."

"Drumming is just . . . to inform people of the procession."

"OK, but I heard something about *marṡiyah* texts connected with them."

"Yes," admitted Farid Ahmad reluctantly, "some people say so."

"Who are the drummers?"

"You should talk to Mamraj. He lives in the old city—Basti Julāhan, Sadar Bazār."

"Is he a follower of Nizamuddin?"

"He's a professional Hindu drummer whose father used to drum at the shrine, too. They learned from our *baṛe baṛe* ustads [great masters] from before Partition. Many of our people left. Now Mamraj and his family are the specialists."

"Is there anyone among the pirzadahs who might know about the drum texts?"

"Ghulam Hasnain Nizami studied with one of the same masters. If there is anything to what people say, he should know. What was your other question?"

"In Karachi, Sunni Nizamis cooperate with Shī'ahs who used to live in this neighborhood. Those Shī'ahs walk in the Nizami processions and vice-versa, and they do *mātam* to the beat of the drums."

"We have no such thing. Shī'ahs are welcome—they sometimes come from the old city—but there is 'no connection' between the way they and we observe Muharram. We Sunnis celebrate it as the *'urs* of the Grandson of the Prophet. We consider it a victory. Shī'ahs emphasize the tragic aspects of the *vāqe'ah-e-*Karbala."

"But not all Sunnis actively participate in Muharram. What is the Nizamuddin association?"

"We're Sayyads. Hazrat Imam Husain belongs to our lineage. Hazrat Shah Niaz be-Niaz in Barelvi also wrote in praise of Imam Husain—the Niyazis are also Chishti, but are more constrained. Barelvis and Naqshbandis don't observe Muharram. Some Qadiri order shrines celebrate Muharram. The main difference among Sunnis is between the Jam'ātīs and the Khānaqāhīs.* Over the past few years, many pirs in Ajmer [a shrine in Rajasthan] have begun to turn to Shī'ism, and more and more Shī'ahs are turning up for our Muharram celebrations."

Ali and Farid continued to converse until one of the other pirzadahs invited Ali to pray at the grave of Nizamuddin. Ali stepped out of the shrine complex to a vendor, next to the *cappal-wālā* keeping guard over their sandals, to purchase some rose petals for sprinkling on the dark-green *cādar* covered tomb. He stood in the saint's sepulcher solemnly with his hands upturned. Later invited into one of the many chambers in the shrine complex for tea, Ali inquired after Ghulam Hasnain Nizami but learned he wasn't in Delhi and wasn't expected for several weeks. One of his hosts gave him a card and asked him to enter his name and address in a guest log. "We'll send you an invitation to the *'urs*. Inshallah you will join us." Ali realized he should have offered a *niyāz* earlier.

A man named Naveen, who'd gone in search of Ghulam Hasnain, handed Ali his own calling card with three other numbers written on the back. "These are the numbers we have for Mamraj the *tāshā* master. One is in Gurgaon. The other two are for his flat in the old city."

---

*That is, between conservative Islamists and those belonging to Sufi orders. However, Farid Ahmad Nizami is explaining here that even among the Sufi orders, there are those who do not celebrate Muharram.

Ali walked back to Arjun's flat, reheated some mediocre leftover *dāl* and *roṭī* from the night before, and took refuge from the unforgiving noonday sun. He began dialing Mamraj's numbers. For the first one, there was a stream of beeps, buzzing, and disconnection. The second led to one ring followed by a loud hiss. The third produced a busy signal or the message "yeh nambar maujūd nahīn hai" followed by the same woman's emotionless voice saying in English, "This number does not exist." Frustrated, Ali took a nap. At 3 P.M. he awoke, covered in sweat—the power had been cut. The phone was still in operation. He tried again, with the same result. Finally, the Gurgaon number gave way to ringing after the long series of beeps.

"Hello? . . . Hello, hello . . ."

"Hello . . . Hello . . . *Hello.*"

"I'm trying to reach Mamraj . . . yes . . . the *tāshe bajāne wālā* . . . My name is Ali."

"I'm his son, Ram Babu. Mamraj is in Delhi."

They arranged to meet early the next morning at the family's flat in Sadar Bazar, when, Ram Babu was sure, his father would be home.

: : :

Ali walked up the narrow, uneven, winding cement steps to Mamraj's flat. Bharat Singh, a meaty fellow in his mid-thirties, greeted him at the door, introducing himself as Mamraj's son. Square-jawed Mamraj sat cross-legged to the left, his thick black hair and mustache providing a striking background for his gold earrings. Prominent cheekbones and folds of skin below the eyes seemed to make Mamraj's shrewd gaze even more intense. With a crimson lower lip projected upward to keep his mouth from overflowing with masticated betel, Mamraj muttered something incomprehensible. Ali responded as if the statement were directed toward him. Several other younger men and youths, presumably family members, were moving about the house. Ali launched into his usual spiel, took a census—family of tāshā, ḍhol and shahnā'ī players . . . Mamraj . . . unschooled . . .—and then, after receiving permission to turn on his tape recorder, said, "I find it fascinating that Hindu *log* play *tāshā* at Nizamuddin."

"I don't believe in religious boundaries," replied Mamraj, who had discharged his load. "All Muslims are my friends. When we play at Muharram, walking from Nizamuddin to the Jorbagh Karbala there are Sunnis, Shī'ahs, Sardārs [Sikhs], Hindus . . . and there's a brass band that plays *marṣiyah.*"

"Muharram is like Ram Lila for Hindus," said Bharat Singh.

Ali thought of the Ram Lila processions he'd seen in Lucknow, the tableaux vivants with young children decked out in costumes and makeup making the rounds of even the most heavily Muslim neighborhoods of the old city, little deities in front of painted panels. And then, in the same locality and playing for the same festival, there was the decrepit, talentless, but somehow endearing *tāshā* player, Rafiq, who used to live under a rusted metal sheet laid against a wall on a lane off Victoria Street in the old city.

In response to a series of Ali's questions, Mamraj explained that he and his family 'attend to or believe in' the *ta'ziyah* and other objects connected with Muharram observance. They play also for Ram Lila and for Hindu and Muslim—but not Christian—weddings. "At the wedding of [the god] Shankar Bhagwan," he added with conviction, "[sage] Nārad Mundi played the *tāshā*."

Tāshā playing is a 'meritorious service' in the name of Nizamuddin Auliya, Mamraj went on to explain. Far from being rejected by Muslim religious authorities, his role as a *tāshā* player was lauded—he held the position of leader (first turban) and his son Ram Babu was second in command. Their role in the shrine grew out of the network of discipleship at the shrine. Mamraj

Tableaux vivants in the Ramlila procession, Lucknow, India, October 13, 1998. Photo by the author.

learned from Ustad Muhammad Sheikh (the musician Hashim had mentioned in Karachi as being invited by Nasir's family—in Delhi—every year to play during Muharram). Muhammad Sheikh played at Nizamuddin until his death at the age of sixty-four. Mamraj took over in about 1964. Mamraj heard that his ustad had studied under Ustad Til but knew nothing further about the lineage. Mamraj's father also played at Nizamuddin but had learned under a different master, one Ustad Karimullah, who went to Pakistan. Ali realized that some of the differences between the current traditions in Delhi and Karachi might be traced to differences in the tradition as transmitted by Muhammad Sheikh and Karimullah, respectively. Mamraj identified himself as a member of the Ustad Sheikh *gharāna.*

"Even my grandfather used to play at Nizamuddin," Mamraj offered proudly. "There are five generations of players in my family now because my grandchildren play *tāshā,* too."

Ali began to inquire about *tāl*s that might be specific to their tradition.

"Indeed. We have many *tāl*s," explained Bharat Singh. "Take *savārī,* for instance—not the *savārī* for Muharram, this one is like *dīpchandī* on tabla. We begin a program with this. It is like the *naġmah* played as an introduction to a vocal program. . then we have *nā-din-din-nā, bhaṅgṛā, caukaṛi, bāsaṭh jarbeṉ, batīs jarbeṉ, bārah jarbeṉ, terah jarbeṉ . . .*"

"*Bāsaṭh . . .* ?"

"*Jarbeṉ* [beats]," said Mamraj. "This has sixty-two beats, for instance: *mora aṭṭhā* twenty-four, *chakka* twelve, *tirī* nine, *durī* six, and *langṛa nauba* eleven." Mamraj recited the *bol*s and then played the *tāshā* part with a pair of flat *tāshā* sticks on a stack of books. Bharat Singh lowered his finger to show the *ḍhol* strokes and how they added up to the string of numbers Mamraj had just run off.[11]

Ali asked how the parts fitted together.

"Well, the *ḍhol*, that gives you the main tune—like the *naġmah* on the harmonium," explained Bharat Singh.

"Then the *tāshā*"—Mamraj started playing riffs after Bharat Singh's virtual *ḍhol* strokes—"provides the *badal* [response] to the *ḍhol.*"

Ali noted, A double analogy, "introduction" and "tune": the naġmah is the introductory melody played on the harmonium before the singing starts, just like the *ḍhol* begins and then the *tāshā* joins. And naġmah is also word for "tune," here the pattern on the *ḍhol.*

"Sometimes I've heard several *tāshā* players beat out a continuous pattern, like a *ṭhekā*, while one *tāshā* player does *chēṛ chāṛ*," observed Ali.

"It's like this, if there's a vocal program, you'll have two *tānpūra* players sitting beside you—a-a-a-a-h." Bharat vocalized the drone. "The tabla will go on playing"—he imitated undulations of the tabla—"the harmonium goes on playing the *naġmah* . . . these all 'keep the support going.'"

"So the *ḍhol* is . . ."

"*Naġmah,*" Bharat Singh and Mamraj said in unison.

"And the *tāshā* playing the simple *ṭhekā?*" Ali prompted.

"Tick, Tick, Tick . . . that is *tānpūra,*" replied Bharat Singh as he tapped it out.

Mamraj explained that their group plays with a Western band, but only during Muharram, and at that time the band's trumpets and clarinets play only *marṣiyah*. Mamraj hummed the tune, then inserted the words "karbalā meṉ mehndī voh, kar ga'ī savārī vakṛi, ab bajāo husain kā mātam (That's the *mehndī* in Karbala: the *savārī* variation [or procession] is completed, now play the *mātam* of Husain)," which reflexively commented on the process of celebrating Muharram, and provided (unnecessary) directions to the musicians. (Media Example 9.5). The sixteen-count *Imām Husain kī Mātam,* Mamraj said, accompanies the tune. He played the pattern and hummed the tune again. Ali recognized it as the *mātam/savārī ṭarz* from Karachi, but the band melody Mamraj had just sung bore no resemblance to S. A. Nizami's *salām*.

YET ANOTHER TEXT BUT THIS ONE SOUNDS TO ME LIKE DOGGEREL.

"We play it only on the days in which there is *mātam,*" Mamraj added.

Mamraj clarified this by explaining that no one performs *mātam* on their bodies, but some people cry. First a group of men will sing *marṣiyah*; after they pause, Mamraj's group plays. "It's not the sound of the drums but the occasion that makes them sad," he explained. Ali came to realize Mamraj was neither interested in, nor informed about, participants' specific religious affiliations, so it was unclear who would cry and who would sing—or, for that matter, whether Shī'ahs participated at all anymore.

At Ali's request, Mamraj and the others began, with great precision and virtuosity, to demonstrate *dhīmā* (Media Example 9.6). But Ali found it to be in eight, not seven. Ali asked Mamraj if there were words to *dhīmā,* and Mamraj proceeded to hum a tune wordlessly—the melody was different from the one S. A. Nizami and Ghulam Hasnain Nizami had sung. This one had points of emphasis at intervals of four counts (Media Example 9.7). Being unable to provide text, Mamraj offered as an alternative "lā illāha illa'llāh . . .," pounding a book to show how the *kalmah* pattern fitted the well-known declaration of faith.

When Ali finally took his leave, he barely reached the railway station in time to board the Gomti Express to Lucknow—and slip one of the ticket collectors a few hundred rupees for a seat.

: : :

Back in Lucknow, Ali returned to his unremarkable job. Bunty had arranged punitive assignments for Ali and reorganized the office, encroaching on his work space. The air conditioner on his side of the room had been replaced with a noisy, old, ineffectual model.

Ali had dinner at his elder brother Sajjad's home in the "trans-Gomati" neighborhood of Nirala Nagar, close to where his wife Amina worked as a nurse. Sajjad's condition had improved in the past few years, after a stint in the hospital and the support of a close doctor friend. He'd started singing again, reviving his popularity with Lucknow's elite by peppering their soirées with cleverly chosen songs and tales. During Muharram, he'd even bring some cash to the household from donations made in appreciation of his *soz k̲h̲wānī.*

"Abbā jān has been saying some odd things lately, Ali," said Sajjad. "You ought to look in on him."

"I had planned to see him tomorrow. What do you mean?"

"He's seldom lucid these days. Half the time he doesn't know who I am. Sometimes he calls me Latif, gets very angry, speaks of a land dispute. Over and over he goes on asking things like 'Have you spoken with Abbas and his people? What have they said?' Even when he's lucid, he's not entirely of this world. Once I asked him who Latif was. He almost fell off his chair."

They continued to talk about their father's bizarre behavior and other family matters, and then Sajjad said, "I never told you about the day mother died. We were in the Aminabad haveli and I heard *mammi* wail—a ghostly sound, really. I ran to the study, where father had spilled his scotch and looked very confused. Mammi was pale and shivering. She shooed me out and made us all tea. Before I could talk to her alone, she had left the house."

Willfully putting aside the awkward questions stirred up by mention of these tense domestic scenes, Ali shared with Sajjad the work he'd been doing in Pakistan. How long it had been since they'd spoken! Sajjad showed the same support, the same genuine enthusiasm, that had first helped Ali muster the courage to undertake music research. Ali was on the verge of opening up about Sufiya when Sajjad said, "Ali, you probably know about this, but I remember when I was a child that there were government servants hanging around asking our father questions about his sponsorship of Muharram processions in Aminabad. I think there are Census of India studies published of Muharram in the Lucknow area, and I believe in Delhi as well. You might be able to fill in some of the historical gaps in your study if you can catch hold of these publications."

In the months that followed, Ali made inquiries in all the libraries he could think of in Lucknow. He even asked the son of Mehmudabad Uncle if he kept these studies in his library. Finally, through his associates at *Eastern Anthropologist*, Ali was able to track down the volumes in question.

Muharram Ali: Drumming Project Notebook #18

Entry, Tuesday, July 15, 1997, 4 p.m.

Notes and comments on Census of India report, 1961, Delhi and Lucknow, re: Nizamuddin:

The Census of India sponsored studies on Muharram in Delhi, Lucknow and Hyderabad. The Delhi study—evidently carried out in May 1964 despite the printed publication date of 1961—seems to corroborate the story of cooperation told by the Sunnis and Shīʿahs in Jacob Lines, Karachi. The first of two sections follows processions and *majlises* of Shīʿahs, the second, of Sunnis (primarily the Nizamis). The Shīʿī section also documents instances of non-Shīʿī participation in Shīʿī rituals.

> On the 20th of Safar [Chehllum day, 40 days after Ashura], a *tazia* procession stopped at Dargah Shah-e-Mardan where about 1,000 people had gathered. A formal function took place there in which various scholars and government officials representing different religious groups participated; it was obviously designed to highlight the universal truths raised by the events at Karbala, pertinent to Hindus, Muslims, Sikhs, and so forth (Government of India 1965?, 70–72).

Whether such a gathering was an annual occurrence is not mentioned. I wonder whether the census study itself might have directly or indirectly motivated the organizers to emphasize communal harmony.

On the 7th of Rabi-ul-avval, the last major procession was accompanied by two "band parties," one from Amroha, Uttar Pradesh, whose participants were not identified, and one from Delhi, who were Sunni and played the *tāshā*. This being the only explicit mention of *tāshā* drumming in conjunction with the Shīʿī ceremonies, I'm guessing that the drummers were connected with the Nizami tradition. Nizami participation was explicitly mentioned at one of the prominent halting points of the Shīʿī procession, the Jama Masjid, where Pir Zamin Nizami Syed Bokhari—Farid Ahmad's grandfather—delivered half-an-hour's speech. He said that some might be suprised that he, being a Sunni, was speaking in a gathering of the Shīʿahs. But there was nothing strange in that. The political, economic and religious condition of the country demanded that the Hindus, Muslims and Sikhs of all sects share in each other's joys and sorrows. There was a special need for the Shī'ahs and Sunnis to come closer to each other as both were based on some common principles. (Government of India 1965?, 73)

The geography of the Nizami rituals provides a possible clue into the history of Shī'ī and Sunni interaction prior to Partition. The drawing on p. 57, "notional place of Karbala ground, Ali Ganj, Delhi, and adjoining dargah shah-e-mardan, showing the places of various activities connected with the performance of moharram" delineates how most of the places for "burial of tazias by Sunnis on Ashura day" are spatially segregated from those of the "burial of tazias by Shiahs on Chehellum day and 8th Rabi-ul Awwal." The notable exception is the Sunni *ta'ziyah* from the Nizamuddin *imambara* (p. 78), which is grouped in the Shī'ī area.

According to the report, "division of the ground for burial of tazias by Sunnis and Shias was effected during British rule some 30 years ago" (p. 57). This would have been in the mid 1930s, preceding the time of Partition by more than ten years. I suspect the bulk of Shī'ī and Sunni burial places were segregated to avoid outbreaks of violence. Maybe the harmonious relationship between Nizami Sunnis and Shī'ahs made this unnecessary in their case. This description from 1964 seems to concern the Nizamuddin processioners, although it is not entirely clear:

> Near Gali Kasim Jan, two *tazias* taken out by Fakhruddin alias Kallu and his brother Alauddin were waiting. The *tazia* of Alauddin was much smaller in size and was taken out for the first time. Though these two *tazias* were taken out by Sunnis, they were accompanied by 50 Shias who were beating breasts and wailing "Husain!" "Husain!" before the *tazias*. There were also three drummers in the party. They were showing their skill in beating the drums while dancing in a circle. Some of the spectators rewarded the drummers by giving them one to five rupee notes. (Government of India 1965?, p 77).

The chanting of "Husain! Husain!" and performance of *mātam* conforms to what Nasir described last month in Karachi. The census evidence and my fieldwork contradict Nizami statements in Delhi today about the insignificance of Shī'ī participation in the past.

: : :

Ali passed through Delhi several times over the following nine months in connection with his forthcoming job offer at the Delhi School of Economics. Unfortunately, Ghulam Hasnain Nizami seemed always to be out of town or unavailable. Ali hoped to gain a better understanding of how the Delhi and Karachi drum repertoires were related to one another and to their respective texts or tunes by attending Muharram celebrations at Nizamuddin the coming year. Bunty had become so rude and condescending that Ali decided to resign effective April 26—the day before *Cānd Rāt*. Because of his father's unstable condition and other family obligations during Muharram, Ali was likely going to have to shuttle back and forth between Lucknow and Delhi. He hired a videographer, Bhaskar, the son of a childhood friend, who was to remain on site in Delhi shooting scenes that Ali himself might have to miss.

Muharram activity each day began and ended not at the *dargah* but at the Nizamuddin Imambarah around the back of the *dargah*—a courtyard Ali estimated to occupy four hundred square meters with a shrine centered along one side. The enclosed area contained *ziyārat*s—a *ta'ziyah* and small *mehndī*s. The top of the central shrine wall was decorated with slabs of whitewashed cement shaped like pointed arches and meter-high flags of either green or white. The shrine entrance bore the familiar crescent archway outlined in gold paint culminating in a medallion at the crest. Several arbors provided shade and visual relief from the generic symmetry of the architecture. Next to one of them, on the wall beside the shrine entrance, was a stylized painting of a tree. Ali recognized this as a *shajarah* tracing the Chishti lineage to the Prophet via Ali, his cousin and son-in-law. To the right of the tree, painted on the compound wall perpendicular to the front, was the *kalmah* in white calligraphy set against a black rectangle.

Ali followed processions on several of the days and nights. Having a videographer with him made him conspicuous, but it also led the "in-charges," shrine functionaries who wore prominent badges, to direct Ali where to go and when. One of these men pointed Ali to a group of men entering select homes and, reading from a common book, reciting *mar̤siyah*. Ali, spoiled by the wonderful *soz k̲h̲wān*s of the Lucknow area, was aesthetically disappointed at the heterogeneous mix of voices—all singing, but tunelessly, and matching neither in pitch nor timing. The man said, "Where they go, you should go." Ali and his companion had to squeeze their way in and find stairs, stones, or other items on which to stand in order to be able to see what was going on. Mamraj and his group often entered with the reciters to play a *salāmī* (drum pattern of salute). The sound was almost unbearably loud in the tight, roofless enclosures.

On some of the early days, there were at least two other *ḍhol-tāshā* groups, not nearly as skilled, who followed behind the same procession—their *ḍhol*s also thundered in the streets quite impressively. And there were children, in one case dressed in shiny green with matching turban, who were making their first efforts at playing *tāshā*—reminding Ali of what his brother must have looked like as a young boy. These small children were already starting to get the hang of it.

The procession on the seventh was particularly splendid—red and green banners (*'alams*) seven meters tall, inscribed in gold and silver with the names of the Panjatan Pāk, garlanded in red, white, and orange flowers and carried about the neighborhood, beneath the network of wires and other overhead impediments, and into the *imambarahs* of individual household compounds. The band Mamraj had described, composed of clarinets and trumpets, accompanied Mamraj's family and various Sunni processioners who took turns playing the *tāshās*, and particularly the *ḍhols*, which were quite heavy. Ali could hardly miss the mehndi song Mamraj had croaked out in their first session—it was one of the only tunes the band played, and it continued for hours and hours.

At night, on the ninth of Muharram (May 6, 1998), Ali stood waiting in the main Nizamuddin *imambarah* as adults decorated the Mughal-period *ta'ziyah* with flowers, jewels (at least some of them presumably faux), and other ritual items. He had seen a number of community members participate in drumming but had not yet been able to ascertain which one was Ghulam Hasnain. The procession wasn't to begin for several hours yet. Ali searched for familiar faces. He caught the attention of Naveen, the man who'd helped Ali search for Ghulam Hasnain earlier. He and Ali quickly slipped through the crowd to find Ghulam Hasnain, leaving Bhaskar at the ready for the procession.

Serwer Sadiq Hussain Nizami, Ghulam's son, welcomed them into the courtyard of their family home, asymmetrically floored with ivory, sable, and ochre mosaic tiles. Serwer cut a striking figure with his long black hair, mustacheless beard, and black *sherwānī* with white cloth peeking out from his wrists and lower legs. This courtyard and front area of the house, like those of many other pirzadahs on the processional route, looked like the Nizami *imambarah* in miniature: the building end of the compound was open toward the courtyard and lined with white cloth, highlighting a flower-covered *mehndī* sitting on an ornamented red box. A middle-aged and a younger drummer playing long, narrow metal *ḍhols* followed Serwer and Ali into the courtyard. Another youth held the center of attention with a metal disk attached to wires and battery-powered lights such that when he spun the disk, he created a whirl of lambency, which he proceeded to hold over his head, around his body, vertically, and diagonally. All of this activity was directed toward the *mehndī* and Ghulam Hasnain Nizami, who was sitting nearby. A few minutes later, a man entered carrying a meter-long staff and a round shield barely wider than an outstretched hand. Serwer took up the challenge. Grabbing his own lathi, he lunged at the man. They advanced and parried, cracked lathi against lathi. Serwer backed up the stairs, the shield hand held back for balance—then down he came, pushing his rival back like a hero swordsman in some black-and-white Hollywood film. Both men grinned and gritted their teeth competitively. Ali had heard of such mock battles but never seen one for himself.

Eventually the excitement died down and Ali was able to converse with Ghulam Hasnain Nizami. The latter, he learned, had the same ustad as Mamraj—Muhammad Sheikh—but unlike Mamraj, he was aware of the association between the Nizami drum repertoire and *marsiyah*s. He told a familiar story: "I can't remember them . . . we have a book . . . it tells all about our music. It's a big book, it tells about the origin of the tabla . . . everything."

Ali tried to get specific, naming a few.

"'Ali kā Panja is like this." Ghulam Hasnain vocalized the drum sounds and counted one finger for each stressed stroke, adding up to five (and creating a fist in the process). His recitation contained too many pauses and ambiguities for Ali to be able to follow it.

"What about *dhīmā?*"

"*Dhīmā* . . . I don't remember it properly." He thought for a few moments. "Serwer, get the book and come."

They conversed, and Ali wondered whether talk of this book was a smokescreen.

After a few minutes Ali asked, "How about *mātam*?"

More time passed.

"In Karachi, they sang, *jab fāṭimah* . . ."

Ghulam Hasnain unhesitatingly took up the languid melody Ali had heard before: "jab fāṭimah firdaus se kahtī hu'ī ā'īn maẓlūm ḥusainā / marne se tere luṭ gaī muj mā kī kamā'ī mazlūm husainā."

Ali, pleased with himself, said, "Yes, that's it."

"But that's not the *marsiyah* for *mātam*. That one's sung for *majlis*es."

Ali tried not to register his disappointment.

"The one for *mātam* is . . ."

Ghulam Hashnain strove but came up with nothing. Finally: "*Kalmah*, that one you must know. 'lā illāha illa'llāh.' That's not a *marsiyah.*"

"*Jī han* [yes, sir]."

Serwer returned. "The book is not available right now. We will find it, God willing, next time you come."

"*Dhīmā* is like this," Ghulam said suddenly. "Āj ṣughrā yūṉ madīne meṉ haiṉ rotī bhar ke nain [Today Sughra cries in Medina like this with eyes full of tears]." He used he same text and tune that S. A. Nizami had sung in Karachi!

"Wāh, wāh! Now, can you show me with your hands how the drum strokes play this *marṯiyah*?"

Ghulam Hasnain had a great deal of trouble coordinating his singing and his hand clapping, but eventually he was satisfied with his execution of a version in which each of three *ḍhol* strokes corresponded to a word in the text (Media Example 9.8). Ali wrote the text in his notebook and confirmed that Ghulam Hasnain meant to emphasize the three syllables *yūṉ*, *meṉ,* and *nain*: Āj ṣughrā **yūṉ** madīne **meṉ** haiṉ rotī bhar ke **nain** (Today Sughra cries **in** Medina **like this** with **eyes** full of tears).

It was still unclear to Ali how the whole pattern fitted together, for Ghulam sang the text in the same flowing *soz* style as had his counterpart in Karachi. At least now Ali knew what to listen for. Visitors continued to flow in and out of the house and courtyard, and father and son were soon engaged in greeting the stream of guests. Ali thanked them warmly and departed.

Returning to the intricate web of lanes, Ali followed the sound of drums to the main *imambarah*, where the *ta'ziyah* was being taken for a round that night. Only on the next evening, Ashura, he was told, would it be taken to the ritzy Karbala in the Jorbagh neighborhood and its pearls and flowers sprinkled with rose water and buried two meters underground. Ali and Bhaskar the videographer wriggled to the front, walking backward before the procession, ascended a stairway to one side, and gained vantage points from within the procession itself. Ali snapped amateur photographs along the way and logged them. With few exceptions, the drummers played Imām Husain kī Mātam continuously.* Every so often, when the *ḍhol* player passed his instrument ponderously to another, the pattern changed slightly. At first Ali thought this was merely a glitch as the musicians paused for the handover. But then Ali noticed that they inserted a single iteration of the *kalmah* at this point (Media Example 4.29). This reminded him that in all these days, he had not yet heard a continuous performance of the *kalmah* pattern.

The procession emerged from the confines of the narrow lanes into a clear, wide area surrounding a now-emptied intersection. Two adolescents peered out from the third story of a modernist black-and-white apartment

*In Karachi this is the pattern called *mātam* at the slow speed and *savārī* at a faster tempo.

building that combined arches and pillars at the windows with painted squares, rectangles, crenels, and diamonds. Opposite was a large red sign for Baba Tours and Travels, and there were a number of other travel shops—Bengali Travels, a shop advertising overnight video coaches. "It must be a clearing for tourist buses to load up passengers and turn around," thought Ali. The flock of processioners gathered patiently around Mamraj and Ram Babu on *tāshā*, Ghulam Hasnain Nizami on *ḍhol,* and some others; the *ta'ziyah,* about fifteen meters away, was completely covered with cream and red flowers, pearls, and red and green streamers. Mamraj held the gaze of Ghulam Hasnain and struck the *tāshā* . . . two strokes and a rest . . . the others joined in; Ghulam raised the *ḍhol* stick high into the air and lowered it with conviction; the *ḍhol* bellowed. Ali tried to count the number of *mātra*s between the *ḍhol* strokes. A couple of times it seemed as if the pattern was six beats, eight beats, and then sixteen beats, but it was not rigorously maintained (Media Example 9.9 ✎).

Ali noted quickly, The "7"s of Karachi might be implied by the 6 + 8, and the "8"s of Mamraj's demonstration are supported by the 16s. But neither rules govern the meter. Nothing else, at first hearing, suggests the pattern of three emphasized syllables Ghulam Hasnain had demonstrated earlier.

Ali and Bhaskar packed up their equipment after a few more hours and Ali returned to his pal Arjun's house for the night.

Bhaskar returned to his modest office and, at Ali's request, made an S-VHS copy of this night's footage for review. This and footage from the other days served as the basis for Ali's further speculation about the way the drums encoded the words of the *salām* and *marṣiyah* poetry. Back in Lucknow, over the following months he assembled charts collating the different texts his consultants offered in connection with the drum patterns, noted the ways the poetic meter was manipulated, and hypothesized that the *dhīmā* drum pattern, as played and verbalized by Ghulam Hasnain, outlined hypermetric relations within the poetic text—a sequence of short-long-prolonged intervals on the *ḍhol.** The exact *mātra* value of the durations varied from cycle to cycle, but the relative lengths remained constant.

Ali was forced to acknowledge that there was no single code to crack. The verbal meanings of the drum patterns were cloaked in clouds of subjectivity and hazy memory.

These insights emerged later, however. On the morning of Ashura, Ali received a call at 2 A.M. in Arjun's flat. Aminabad. Ali hastily departed on the first bus he could catch.

---

*Ali's efforts to work through these problems appear in Appendix A.

CHAPTER 10

A Silver Box

Ahmed Khan sat in his jade velveteen teak-framed wing chair, facing away from the hearth and its uncleared char and ash. Strands of thin, oily gray hair strayed across his brow, and the raja's right hand gripped the seat to quell his trembling. Ajmal and Huma, who'd arrived that morning, planted themselves on the worn matching couch, and with each movement puffed dust into the frowsty chamber. Huma was urging Ahmed Khan to drink a crisp glass of ruhafzah, glimmering like fresh-sliced watermelon.

"Kevṛa! I can't bear the taste."

Huma looked puzzled. It was a signature ingredient in Avadhi cuisine.

The residents of Aminabad were calling on the raja almost every hour, bringing fruits and other small gifts, peeking into the house with scarcely restrained curiosity. Ahmed Khan, slipping in and out of an aguish delirium, confused and paranoid, felt safe only in his bedroom and parlor. Operating from a tiny room behind the kitchen, a young Hindu couple from mountainous Kumaon—the two servants left in his retinue—labored at their charge cheerfully. Despite their and Ali's efforts the haveli had been deteriorating rapidly. Fatimah, in from London, supervised a facelift for three rooms long abandoned to dust, mold, and cobwebs. Arriving family members—Ajmal and Huma, Ilfaz, Samina, and others—shared these rooms.

Ahmed Khan spoke to Huma. "Sakina, where's Abbas?"

"Bahno'ī, this is Huma, my wife—you attended our marriage in Multan in 1975."

Ahmed Khan's febrile, cataract stare lit up his sallow countenance as he said, "Of course, of course." And then, as if to underline the point, the bibulous raja downed the red liquid and said, "Well done."

Ali entered the room. "Hello, Baba."

Seeming to tune in, Ahmed said, "Ali, my son. You're looking well! When did you return from London?"

"I was in Karachi, father, researching a story. I work in Lucknow now."

Ajmal embellished Ali's statement with forced cheer, "We've been unearthing the treasures of Muharram together in Multan as well. Ali's become quite the anthropologist."

"Muharram . . . a waste . . . nonsense . . . Where's your wife?" demanded Ahmed.

"I've not yet"—Ali caught a gravid glance from Huma—"brought her here."

The Kumaoni servant Kunwar entered. "Raja Sahab, food is ready."

Spared a moment of awkward conversation, the group repaired to the large dining table in the adjoining room. It had not yet benefited from Fatimah's oversight. As the smell of fresh pheasant from the estate drifted through the musty air, Ali wondered if others felt the same sense of unsettling anachronism, of absurd misplacement.

The clan shared a few bottles of another red liquid Samina had procured, the ill-advised libation being enough to send Raja Sahab to bed for the afternoon. The family returned to the parlor.

"How long has my brother-in-law been in this state?" Ajmal hadn't been in India since his childhood in 1947. His sister Khadija, older by fifteen years, had already married Ahmed Khan by the time of Partition and was obliged to remain in India. Ajmal never saw her again.

"It's been a slow decline . . . since mother's death. But the last three years have been the most dramatic," explained Sajjad. "He's plagued by nightmares and doesn't sleep properly. He's sometimes lucid when he wakes up. Then during the day he sweats and shivers, then his mouth goes dry and his lips crack—we have to hold his head for him to sip water. Today he's better than usual."

After an interval, Samina said, "What's this 'Latif' business? When you were a *baccā* your Aya sometimes called you Sajju, but I don't remember anyone using a different name—especially not your father."

Cousin Ilfaz's eyes darted about the room.

"It's a mystery to me. In the morning Abbu usually knows who I am. As the day drags on and he loses his grip, it's as if he is looking through me. I become Latif."

Ali added, “And then there’s Abbas . . . who’s that?”

In walked Sana, Ahmed Khan’s ‘discarded Begum,’ his issueless first wife who’d been pensioned off forty years earlier to live on a piece of land near Barabanki and had hardly set foot in Aminabad since. The hearty octogenarian declared in chaste Urdu, “Abbas’s family owned my home and land in the 1930s, but your father claimed that the property was rightly his on the basis of some papers left in your grandfather’s estate.”

“I remember some Abbas, from when I was a young child,” said Sajjad. “The impoverished fellow would come by looking for a handout. Father would never come to see him, but Khadija-mā would treat him kindly, feed him, send him away with some second-hand clothing and cash.”

“That was him. Khadija knew about his unfortunate circumstances. Your own mother did not. Your father seized his land,” revealed Sana, ominously.

“This doesn’t sound like our father,” responded Ali with trepidation.

“You didn’t know your father,” Ilfaz blurted out.

“He’s alive, *yār,*” protested Sajjad.

“Before the two of you were born, before the time of Pakistan,” Sana began.

“It was never proven that Latif was murdered, *k͟hālā-jān,*” averred Ilfaz.

“Your father’s character was different,” Sana continued. “He was ambitious and competitive. What he couldn’t achieve through his own abilities, what he couldn’t acquire legitimately, he’d cheat and steal for—even cause harm to others. In those days, he put on a show of being religious merely to secure the support of Abul Ala Mawdudi’s followers and the like. He foresaw the movement’s power and wanted to benefit from the groundswell of popular emotion.”

“How could that be?” asked Ali. “You’re talking about the roots of the Jam’āt-i Islamī.”

“How do you explain his marriage to our mother? Those people couldn’t possibly have supported his marrying a Shī‘ah,” Sajjad pointed out.

“Exactly. Every alliance he made from the political to the marital was a stratagem of some kind,” affirmed Ilfaz.

“Your father was staunchly sectarian in those days,” Sana said, “and for the worst reasons—profit, greed, blind grasping for power. His father Fazal-ud-din, then raja of Aminabad, had by the late 1930s begun to lose his mental capacities. Ahmed was scheming for a land grab.”

“What was the issue? Presumably he had what he needed and when his father died, the estate would have accrued to him,” reasoned Ali.

“He had an elder brother,” said Sana.

"Latif," revealed Ilfaz.

"The court cases went on until 1947. The family split and somehow the violent death of one Muslim disappeared in the wash of communal bloodshed at the time," Sana explained. "I couldn't have a child with that man . . . did everything possible to avoid it . . . and after what he did to me, I could no longer bear children."

"I don't understand," said Sajjad.

"He had what he wanted. He'd seized the land from Abbas, applying pressure through powerful neighbors and business contacts. The chaos of the new India provided a smokescreen. He could make himself anew. At first it was a ploy to ingratiate himself with local politicians. He was afraid to migrate to Pakistan, to lose everything he'd striven for here—after all, it was material benefit and not religion that drove him. In India, it was expedient to be a secular Muslim. He invented the persona you've grown up with—that romantic wallowing in the nineteenth century, that ecumenical view of humanity, that artistic dilettantism. He's never been a person of conviction, and eventually he came to believe his own lies. Sakina married an utterly self-deluded man. I've no idea how he kept the scandal a secret from her parents—or perhaps he paid them off.

"About five years ago your father contacted me. His nightmares had already begun. He knew his mind was beginning to slip. We talked about those early years. He apologized and cursed his weakness. He told me that you, Ali, became everything he never had the moral compass to be . . . that idealism was your strength. He begged me to help him keep his past a secret while he lived. I could never forget who he was, but something kept drawing me to him. We'd meet in Lucknow or at my place. He had nobody else from his former life. In his cafard, he'd sometimes forget what year it was. The visits stopped when Sakina died.

"Just now he called Muharram 'nonsense.' But he seemed to take genuine pleasure in our Aminabad processions and *majlis*es when we were kids," Ali countered tenuously.

"His former personality is reasserting itself. But as I said, Ali, your father came to believe his own lies—and after all, Muharram in Aminabad is also a celebration of royalty, patronage, territory. The camels, the drums, the masculine *nauḥah* and *mātam,* the music—all that boosted his prestige and made religious ritual far more tolerable. The staid life of praying at the *masjid* was never his style anyway; the trappings of Shī'ī ritual, without commitment to genuine lamentation, suited the figure of the liberal Sunni raja he wished to adopt."

"What do the doctors say about his condition?" asked Samina.

Sajjad responded, "The specialists disagree. One implied venereal disease, another thought malaria might be a component, a third insists it's a genetic form of dementia. Diabetes has complicated the picture. His vital signs have been very weak for the last several days, and all the doctors agree he's unlikely to survive another ten days."

The assemblage was at a loss for words.

"What plans are in place for the estate?" Samina broke the silence.

"This is something we need to confer about. Though obsessed with death, father hasn't made plans for the future. He's discussed nothing with us. *Bāt suni'e* (listen), I'm not ready to become the raja of Aminabad. Father knew it . . . I know it . . . but it falls to me unless I abdicate," Sajjad explained.

After some thought, Ajmal ventured the obvious. "It sounds like your father would have supported Ali assuming the mantle."

"Ali has been doing the needful for some years now; he should at least get the credit," Samina pointed out.

The others nodded in assent.

"How would this jibe with your own plans, Ali?" Huma asked.

Ali remembered that Huma and Sufiya were distantly related.

"Join the ranks of the part-time rajas . . . ?" offered Ali weakly.

"A figurehead, not a potentate . . . someone the people of Aminabad can look up to, count on to carry on the annual cycle of Muharram ceremonies and performances. All rajas these days are part-time," Sana said matter-of-factly.

A metallic sound pealed from the raja's bedroom. Kunwar hurried back first and found the raja clanging on the metal pitcher in his wash basin with his cane, calling for his sons. Ali and Sajjad joined him in the room and closed the door at his request.

"Sajjad, Ali . . . I have something to tell you . . . about your mother. It wasn't exactly an accident . . ."

"Father, it's all right. This isn't necessary now," said Ali.

"Who will carry on here?"

"You don't need to worry about this, father, please take your rest. We've been urging Ali to fill your shoes," said Sajjad.

As if expecting this response, Ahmed turned his eyes to Ali. "Ali, beneath a slit of wood under the left drawer of that writing table you'll find a key. Use it to open the inner compartment of this almirah."

Ali found two old volumes: a thick leather-bound folio with flaking gold foil and a handsomely bound diary.

"The big one is our *rūbakār,* Ali. It contains information for organizing Muharram in Aminabad. Munir will help you manage everything." Munir had been the raja's steward until his death about ten years earlier; the position had been handed down in the family, but Ali wondered whether Munir's son Anwar was up to the task.

Flipping to a random page in the *rūbakār*, Ali found specifications for the *ziyārat*s—measurements, types of wood, paper, and colored cloth, a recipe for wax. It even gave several options for artificial blood to sprinkle on the *tābūt*. Another section, dating back more than a hundred years and ending a decade ago, specified the Aminabad families traditionally tasked with responsibilities in the procession. A page dated 1898 listed the order of participants in the *julūs*—far more elaborate than Ali had witnessed in his lifetime—along with annotations in another hand:

1) Banner: black and white bearing royal insignia
2) Shāhī bāja: *ḍhol, tāshā*, karnal, jhānjh, *for memory "Sain-Imām-Husain-Haidar"*
3) Raushan Chauki—cart carrying shahnā'ī and nagāra players who play *nauḥah* tunes.
4) Elephant decorated with shawl
5) Māhī Mārātib—*Avadhi royal insignia, silver: crown, fish, barking lion, sun, moon*
6) Camels with banner—*relatives of Husain brought on camels*
7) Camels with 'alams
8) Mātamī band
9) Silver-handled jhandīs—*red, yellow, black, green flags*
10) 'Alam Hazrat Abbas and other 'alams
11) Soz k̲h̲wāns and mars̲iyah k̲h̲wāns.
12) Jarīde—item which bears name of the relatives of the Prophet, Fatimah, 12 Imams
13) Zuljinah
14) Tābūt
15) Zarī akdas (wax)
16) Anjum-e-mātamī—*each anjuman receives 50 rupees (1910)*

"The smaller one is my journal. Upsetting stories may circulate after my death. I don't expect you to forgive me, but this diary might help you understand the kind of person I was as a young man. After my death, you must place my diary in the *Muk̲h̲āfir k̲h̲ānah,* our family archive. There is a locked cabinet, partly blocked by my writing table, containing select whiskeys and cognacs. Five generations of personal family history are hidden behind a false panel. You'll find a key to the cabinet in a silk pocket within the binding of my diary. Ali and Sajjad, you are not to open this cabinet to our relatives, to visiting researchers, and especially not to journalists or government officials. Like generations of rajas before you, Ali, from today, you must tell your own story.

"Behind the panel you'll also find a silver box with the personal possessions of Latif . . . he was your uncle . . . he looked after me as a child . . . and I shamed him." Ahmed Khan's right hand began to tremble violently and his left eye welled up. Sajjad unfolded a small packet of paper containing a powder the family *ḥakīm* (doctor) had provided, stirred it into a cup of warm water, and helped his father sip it. The tremors ceased and the raja's vacant stare returned after a few minutes. Ali looked at the collection of powders and potions on the shelf with skepticism.

Ahmed Khan's anatomy held out for two more weeks.

: : :

1 Muharram 1419 AH (April 27, 1998)

Salim, Sufiya's cousin, showed up in Aminabad on the first of Muharram, sending a shiver of emotion through the body of the new raja. Salim had made quite a name for himself in Pakistan as an energy resource analyst, and after spending a few years in the United Arab Emirates, he was offered a job in Manchester—energy consultant, South Asia region. He found a way to conduct business in Kanpur and Lucknow and took leave on religious grounds to visit Ali.

"My friend . . . Raja Sahab . . . I've been hearing about you through Huma. Reader in Anthropology. Mubarak on all your successes."

"Thank you, *bhai*. Professor now, actually. Congratulations to you as well! In fact, I've been thinking of you lately—" Ali tightened his abdomen as if to strangle the visceral stirrings, to suppress the twinges—"now I'm the one to decide on the musical artistry in this town. I was thinking about our talks on music in Multan. I hope you'll come to the *majlis* at our haveli tonight. I've selected some of the finest *soz k̲h̲wān*s of Lucknow and Rampur."

"If it's anything to compete with what I hear from the *naubat k̲h̲ānah,* I'm sure to be in for a treat. Odd, though, there's only that one *tāshā* player over there. Doesn't seem to have much to do." He pointed to a lanky young man dressed in a tattered mango *shalwār qamīz*.

"That's the state of affairs. Majid is the last of the hereditary *tāshā* players in Aminabad; the townspeople don't take up the drums to participate anymore. In a few days, more players might drift in from the countryside, but they're often decrepit. Who'd want to join their ranks? These fellows get no respect."

"Someone seems interested," said Salim, noticing a bearded, light-skinned man in a blue Pakistani-style *shalwār qamīz*, animatedly talking to Majid.

Sajjad, standing nearby, joined the conversation. "That's an American ethnomusicologist. He followed his wife to Pakistan and then India for her doctoral research on the Urdu *mars̱iyah*. He's latched onto the *tāshā* . . . can't imagine why. But I told him he'd come to the right place."

"We can hardly turn him away," said Ali with the first grin he'd allowed himself in a long time. But it was short-lived.

"Look, Ali, I know this is not the moment, but we need to meet privately," said Salim. "Something's happened."

: : :

Sufiya's mother had died in Lahore the previous week after a yearlong battle with non-Hodgkin's lymphoma—it was the infection from the hospital and not the disease itself that ultimately killed her. After the standoff in The Village, Ali had not been in touch with Sufiya since leaving Lahore, and she had not written or phoned. Sufiya had over the course of that year founded her own small publishing company specializing in progressive, English-language writing by Pakistani authors. As editor-in-chief, her new occupation devoured her time—and with the attention she devoted to her mother during the year, there was little time left for sleep. Her health suffered. The death of her mother unlocked the emotions she had been successfully holding at bay through desperate immersion in her work. Salim knew his cousin well and was able to pry from her the feelings she herself had refused to acknowledge. Salim described Sufiya's distraught state to Ali, reminding him of her strength of character. She had established herself in Lahore, no longer bound to her mother but to her own passion.

Ali phoned Sufiya the next morning, and they spoke for hours. When Muharram was over, Ali took the extraordinary step of traveling to Lahore and marrying Sufiya. They were never to live in the same country together.

: : :

Although Ali's father warned him never to share the family secrets locked behind the Black Label and Glenfiddich, he trusted me. Occupied with teaching anthropology in Delhi, acting as little more than a cipher in Aminabad, occasionally lecturing in Hyderabad and Lucknow, and traveling once a month to Lahore, Ali had time only to sketch bits and pieces of his story in his volume of the family journal collection. With my fieldwork and analysis and his memory for places, feelings, and events, we collaborated on this narrative. I met Sufiya, who visited Delhi every two months. Tough as leather and sharp as a whip, she was everything Ali described and more. She was our editor.

Richard K. Wolf, April 7, 2013

APPENDIX A

Dhīmā and Mātam

The vocal renditions of *dhīmā* fit more or less in the framework of the Hindustani *rūpak tāl* of seven counts—assigning one count for a short and two counts for a long syllable for the first few feet:

Basic *ṭheka* (defining drum pattern) for *rūpak tāl*

0			+			
| tin	tin	na |	dhi	na |	dhi	na
1	2	3	4	5	6	7

0 = k̲h̲ālī, "empty," or section indicated by a hand wave
+ = tālī (or bharī, "full"), indicating a hand clap

But the rhythm is not metronomic. It's not clear whether each line should be analyzed in isolation or whether a flexible metric framework is meant to hold continuously throughout.

The drum pattern on *tāshā* for *dhīmā* as played in Delhi is symmetrical and duple, which seems to be entirely unconnected with the asymmetrical *rūpak*. The distinctive feature in *dhīmā*, according to Muhammad Razaq, Sarir Ahmed Nizami, and Ghulam Hasnain Nizami, is the sequence of emphasized *ḍhol* strokes. But these lack clear periodicity; the distance between the strokes varies within a performance and from performance to performance. One possibility is that the musicians have lost the knowledge to perform this pattern properly—they all complain of its difficulty. Are inconsistencies in the sequence of stressed strokes a vestige of something once more systematic, something that involved exact repetition?

Another possibility is that the *ḍhol* strokes have always been flexibly distributed, marking out prominent positions in the *ḍhol* player's subjective sense of melodic-poetic unfolding—abstracted to the point where even those who don't actually know the words can reproduce and convey the "feeling" of a poetic passage. When singing, Sarir Ahmed Nizami and Ghulam Hasnain Nizami completed the melodic line with something like a *mukhṛā*[1] culminating on the syllable *nain*. In classical terms, this is ambiguous because the *nain* can be heard as either beat one or beat four of a seven-count cycle (see table A1).

The *ḍhol* strokes, though separated in each cycle by an inconsistent sequence of *mātra*s at the syllabic level, are consistent at the hypermetric level in that they articulate relations of short, long, and prolonged.[2] That is, if one counts syllable values in (a slightly adjusted version of) the poetic meter, allotting 1 for a short syllable and 2 for a long syllable, the sequence is as follows:

yūn̲ + 7 metric units = short
men̲ + 10 metric units = long
nain + 11 metric units = prolonged

The 11 units include an adjustment (the parenthetical long below) that makes the last foot a full 7 units rather than the 5 units contained in the poetry itself. The singers pause at this point, and the underlying *rupak tāl* also encourages this adjustment in performance.

Hyper meter:	⌣ (7) _ (10) ___(11)
Poetic meter	_⌣ _ _ / _ ⌣ _ _ / _ ⌣ _ _ / _ ⌣ _ (_)
Stressed syllables	āj ṣuġrā **yūn̲** madīne **men̲** hain̲ roṭī bhar ke **nain**

The relation between these three sets of durations was indeed maintained by Ghulam Hasnain Nizami when he played *dhīmā* during Muharram, in close interaction with Mamraj. In Richard Wolf's video of 2009, Media Example 9.9, the intervals between *ḍhol* strokes were mainly counts of 3, 4, and 7 but the "prolonged" value sometimes extended to 8 or 10 counts.

If one were to ignore Ghulam Hasnain's assignment of *ḍhol* strokes to particular words, it would be tempting to adjudge the 3 + 4 + 7 version as the correct one, corresponding well to the structure of *rūpak tāl* and the poetic meter. If that were the case, though, one would have expected Mamraj's group to be able to master the simple pattern on their own. But on their own, they often placed a *ḍhol* stroke every 8 counts (Media Example 9.6). My sense is that they merely gave the impression of *dhīmā* when performing it for me but, in context, relied on someone like Ghulam Hasnain Nizami to perform it on the *ḍhol* properly.

Mātam

Setting aside the fact that Ghulam Hasnain Nizami denied that the text S. A. Nizami sang was the correct one for *mātam*, it is significant that both that text (Media Example 9.4) and that of the song sung by Mamraj (Media Example 9–5), as well as the chant "Husain, Husain," can easily be accommodated by the structure of the drumming (Media Example 9.3). In syllabic terms, both texts outline the same

Table A1. *Dhīmā* text arranged in possible rhythmic relationships with *rūpak tāl* based on the performances of the text in *soz* style

1	1̲	2	3	**4**	5	**6**	7	1̲	2	3	**4**	5	**6**	7	1̲	2	3	**4**	5	**6**	7	1̲	2	3	**4**	5	**6**	7
2	ā		j	ṣu	ġ	rā		**yūn̲**		ma	dī		ne		**men̲**		hain̲	ro		tī		bhar		ke	**nain**			
	-----11 units										*7 units*									*10 units*						-----------		
3	ā		j	ṣu	ġ	rā		**yūn̲**		ma	dī		ne		**men̲**		hain̲	ro		tī					bhar			ke
											7 units											*14 units*						
4	**nain**				ā		j	ṣu	ġ	rā		**yūn̲**		ma	dī		ne		(etc.)									
						11 units																						
5	ā		j	ṣu	ġ	rā		**yūn̲**		ma	dī		ne		**men̲**		hain̲	ro		tī					bhar			ke
											7 units											*14 units*						
6	**nain**							ā		j	ṣu	ġ	rā		**yūn̲**		ma	dī		ne	(etc.)							
								14 units																				

Top row: Four cycles of *rūpak tāl* (7 counts). The *k̲h̲ālī* beat (beat 1) is indicated with an underline and the *tālī* beats (4 and 6) are in boldface.

Row 2: The text is lined up as if one foot of poetry corresponded to one *tāl* cycle—that is, with one beat of the *tāl* corresponding to a short syllable and two beats to a long. The last syllable of the fourth foot is made extra long here to complete a four-foot cyclical structure. This creates a hypermeter composed of 7, 10, and 11 metric units. Each unit is counted from the syllables (in boldface) that are supposed to be supported with *ḍhol* beats: *yūn̲*, *men̲*, and *nain.* For *nain*, one must count to the end of the fourth cycle and then back from the beginning of the first cycle until one reaches the place of the syllable *yūn̲* in the chart, i.e., beat one of the cycle after a round of the *tāla* has passed.

Rows 3–4: An approximation of the manner in which text is actually sung in Media Example 9.1 with *rūpak tāl* superimposed. This yields hypermetric relations of 7, 14, and 12. Note the long melisma on *tī* and the cadence-like resolution on beat 1. Recordings of the same tune (with different text in the same meter) that continue, do so from somewhere in the middle of the next cycle and not at the same point each time.

Rows 5–6: A possible "correction" that would preserve both the melisma on *tī* and a prolongation of *nain* and still adhere to *rūpak tāl*. This would yield hypermetric relations of 7, 14, and 14.

total number of counts, although they do not begin in exactly the same place in the drummed structure. In the first text ("jab fāṭimah . . ."), the long and short syllables can theoretically be projected onto the resonant bass strokes and short-duration rim strokes of the *ḍhol,* respectively, rather than onto actual long and short durations on the drum. In this configuration, each syllable would be rendered on the drum with an equal duration in the overall rhythmic pattern; only the differences in timbre and decay would distinguish long from short syllables in the model text. When this text is actually recited musically in *salām* style, however, it does not resemble the version played on the drums. It sounds as if the poetry is made up of a repeating foot of _ _ ⏑ _ . That is to say, every fourth syllable in the first twelve gets a melodic extension which pulls against the scansion of that syllable (which is short). Sarir Ahmed Nizami's recognition of this apparent mismatch was implied by his explanation that, when the text is performed on the drums, it is rendered "quickly" (*jalad* [his pronunciation]); the rhythmic patterning of the sung version is reconfigured to flatten out the syllabic durations, however, and not merely sped up.

The brass band song (which does not follow the *'arūz* metric system) provides a better analogue of the surface rhythm, with the text as sung providing primary and secondary accents in logical positions within the drumming pattern. Table A2 shows how the text "jab fāṭimah . . ." correlates with the poetic meter, bass and rim strokes

Table A2. Relationships between the *mātam/savārī* drum pattern and the texts with which it is associated

jab	fā	ṭi	ma	fir	dau	s	se	kah	tī	hu	'ī	ā	'īṉ	(pause?)		maẓ	lū	m	ḥu	sai	nā	
–	–	⏑	⏑	–	–	⏑	⏑	–	–	⏑	⏑	–	–	(⏑ ⏑)		–	–	⏑	⏑	–	–	
C	C	R	R	C	C	R	R	C	C	R	R	C	C	R	R	C	C	R	R	C	C	
rl	r.	rl	r.	rl	r.	rl	r.	rl	r.	rl	r.	rl	r.	rl	r.	rl	r.	rl	r.	rl	r.	
x	x	x	x	x	x	x	x	x	x	x	x	x	x	x	x	x	x	x	x	x	x	
.hss	.hss	.hss	.hss	.hss	.hss	.hss	.hss	.hss	.hss	.hss	.hss	.hss	.hss	.hss	.hss	.hss	.hss	.hss	.hss	.hss	.hss	
	kar.	ba	*lā*	meṉ	**mehn**	dī	*voh*		**kar**	ga'ī sa	*vā*	ri	**va**	kṛi		ab ba	**jāo**	hu	*sain*	kā	**mā**	tam

Top row: The first line of *salām* for the *mātam* pattern, according to S. A. Nizami (Media Example 9.4 ⯑).

Row 2: The scansion of this line.

Row 3: From the demonstration of *savārī*, June 8, 1997 (Media Example 9.3): the pattern of the right-hand stick (*cob*) on the *ḍhol*. The left hand plays the center of the head with the bare hand bisecting each stick stroke and is not notated here. C = center, resonant stroke; R = rim stroke.

Row 4: From the *savārī* demo: the *tāshā* pattern, two pulses per syllable: r = right hand; l = left hand; . = rest.

Row 5: From the *savārī* demo: strikes on the chest indicated by *x*s.

Row 6: From the *savārī* demo: the chanting of "Husain" (presented as continuous for analytic purposes, but in actuality episodic), four pulses per syllable; . = rest; h = hu (almost silent); ss = sain (loud for two pulses).

Row 7: Mamraj's rendition of the text to the *mātam/savārī* song as played on brass instruments during Muharram. Primary accents are in boldface and secondary accents appear in italics. An incomplete version of the same text in Media Example 9.5 ⯑ substitutes "*cal ga'ī*" for "*kar ga'ī*."

on the *ḍhol*, right and left hand strokes on the *tāshā* (the ostinato, not the improvisation), strikes on the chest of those performing *mātam*, the chanting of "Husain, Husain," and the text of the song associated with the brass band tune. The only text actually uttered during a performance—and only in Karachi—is "Husain, Husain." The other texts are hidden or remembered, at best. Each column receives a count, logically grouped into fours based on the drum strokes. The doubled column marked "pause?" is a suggestion of how one might account theoretically for the projection of the repeating _ _ ⌣ ⌣ unit continuously from the main text of the poem into the refrain (which should not technically figure into the scansion). The first four syllables of the text provide a template for the entire drum pattern (Center Center Rim Rim on the *ḍhol*).

APPENDIX B

Summary of Commemorative Themes on Particular Days of Muharram in South Asia

Many of the specifics vary by region. The rough framework below is meant to contextualize the details mentioned in the book. For a more detailed outline of commemorative themes and ritual activities during Muharram in South Asia, see Bard 2002.

Event	Date of Islamic Calendar	Special or Representative Poetic Forms and Rituals
Cānd rāt; Sighting of Muharram Moon	Eve of first of Muharram	*Nauḥah*s and *mātam* (breast-beating); drumming to announce sighting of moon; some Shīʻahs refrain from making or listening to music from this day (10 days or more)
Onset of Muharram	1st of Muharram	*Marṣiyah*s about the martyrdom of Husain's messenger, Muslim, or about Imam Husain setting out on his journey to Kufa. Processions, including royal parades in Lucknow and Hyderabad, Andhra Pradesh
Husain's arrival in Karbala	2nd of Muharram	*Marṣiyah*s and speeches about portents of doom at Karbala

Event	Date of Islamic Calendar	Special or Representative Poetic Forms and Rituals
Martyrdom of Hazrat-e Abbas	5th or 8th of Muharram	*Nauḥah*s about 'Abbās and about his relationship with his niece, Husain's daughter, Sakina. *'Alam*, battle-standard of 'Abbās, brought out in procession. Funeral food, *hāzirī*, and blessings distributed in 'Abbās's name
Martyrdom of 6-month-old Ali Asghar, son of Imam Husain	Eve of 6th Muharram and 6th of Muharram	*Salām*s or *nauḥah*s that incorporate lullabies; presentation of new *nauḥa*s and competition among *anjuman*s (recitation clubs) in Lahore. Procession of *jhūla*s (cradles)
Martyrdom of Ali Akbar, 18-year-old son of Imam Husain	6th, 8th, or 9th of Muharram	*Marṣiyah*s about Ali Akbar's prowess in battle or about Husain searching for his son's body on the battlefield; *nauḥah*s about the funeral of Ali Akbar. Procession of and obeisance to *tābūt* (coffin) of Ali Akbar
Mehndi (pre-wedding henna ceremony) for Husain's nephew Qasim and daughter Kubra	7th of Muharram	*Salām*, *soz*, *marṣiyah,* and *nauḥah* about wedding rituals and a bridegroom slain on the battlefield. Procession of henna, fruits, sweets, and bridegroom's flower-veil (*sehra*); special prayers and vows related to marriage (e.g., obtaining a good husband), children, and family matters; procession of Zuljinah (Imam Husain's horse, which returned riderless to the camp after Husain's death)
Eve of the battle of Karbala; *shab-e 'ashūr*	9th of Muharram	*Marṣiyah*s on the martyrdom of Imam Husain. Processions with *jhūla*s, *tābūt*s, *zuljinah*

Summary of Commemorative Themes

Event	Date of Islamic Calendar	Special or Representative Poetic Forms and Rituals
Battle of Karbala; imprisonment of the women of Husain's family	10th of Muharram	*Marṣiyah*s on the martyrdom of Imam Husain. Processions with *'alam*s and/or *ta'ziyah*s. Stick fighting; *zanjīr* and *talvār kā mātam* (flagellation with scourges and swords)
Third day post-death ceremony, *sevvum* or *soyyam*	12th of Muharram	*Marṣiyah*s emphasizing endangerment of the women of Imam Husain and the pride of Zainab, Imam Husain's sister; emphasis on Zainab's establishment of mourning practice
Death of Sakina, the young daughter of Imam Husain, in Yazid's prison	20–22 Muharram or 2–3 dates in the month of Safar	*Marṣiyah*s about Sakinah, her relationship with Imam Husain and her mother, and about the many tortures she suffered at the hands of Yazid and his henchmen. Processions with coffin within households or neighborhoods
40-day post-death ceremony, *Chehlum* or *'arabein*	20 Safar	*Marṣiyah*s on the return of the women to Medina after their imprisonment. Processions with *'alam*s and/or *ta'ziyah*s; often miracles (blinding lights, visions of the *Panjatan Pāk*) are said to occur in *chehlum majlis*es
Martyrdom of the 11th Imam, Hasan Askari, and concluding mourning assemblies of the Muharram cycle	8 Rabi-ul-awwal	Many *nauḥah*s with intense breast-beating. long final *majlis*es
Death of Shimr and other enemies of Husain; Zain-ul-Abidin smiled for the first time 40 years after the Karbala tragedy	9 Rabi-ul-awwal	*Tabarra'* or ritual cursing of the enemies of the *Panjatan Pāk* in poetic couplets. Burning of an effigy of Shimr or Umr; wearing of red clothing, jewelry, and make-up; community members dressing as bride and groom

APPENDIX C

Cast of Characters by Chapter; Key Figures in the Karbala Story

All characters are fictitious unless specified otherwise; names listed here are limited to those that appear repeatedly in the story.

Cast of Characters by Chapter

Chapter 1

Ahmad Ali Khan: raja of Aminabad (fictitious principality outside Lucknow), husband of Sakina, father of Ali and Sajjad, Sunni religious background

Kannamma: Ali's South Indian Hindu ayah

Muharram Ali: Protagonist, journalist, son of Sakina and Raja Ahmed Ali Khan, brother of Sajjad

Raja of Mehmudabad: Actual historical figure, included fictitiously in the narrative

Regula Qureshi: Ethnomusicologist who conducted research in Lucknow in 1968–69 and worked with Maharaj Kumar (Amir Hyder Khan), second son of the famous maharaja of Mehmudabad at the time. The actual situations described are fictitious.

Sajjad: Elder brother of Muharram Ali, first son of Sakina

Sakina: Wife of Raja Ahmed Ali Khan, mother of Muharram Ali and Sajjad, Shīʿī religious background

Chapter 2

Ajmal Ahmed Khan: Brother of Ahmed Ali Khan's second wife, Khadija. A Sunni Muslim, *pakhavaj* and tabla player, living in Multan, Pakistan. A few statements are quotations from a real drummer from Multan named Ajmal, but the character in the story is not based on any one person.

Chandlal: Ali's editor at the *Times of India* in Lucknow
Fatimah: Ali's cousin; lives in England
Qasim: Sakina's elder brother; lives in Lahore and hosts Ali on some of his visits
Muhammad Baksh Multani: (Real) *mīrāṣī* performer of the *naqqārah, ḍhol,* and *tāshā* (appears briefly in the analytic section and substantially in the narrative section of Chapter 4)
Niamat Ali: (Real) *ḍhol* player in Lahore (statements based on interviews conducted in 1997) placed in a fictitious context
Saeed Naqvi: Renowned journalist who currently resides in Delhi. His speech at Founder's Day is fictitious.
Shahid Ali: (Real) *ḍhol* player in Lahore (statements based on interviews conducted in 1997) placed in a fictitious context
Sibte-Jafar: (Real) well-known *soz-k̲h̲wān* and college principal who lived in Karachi until he was gunned down while riding his motorcycle home from work on March 13, 2013. The incident, widely believed to be sectarian, sparked demonstrations and impassioned outcries in the Shī'ī community.

Chapter 3

Pappu Sain: (Real) *ḍhol* player in Lahore; given name Zulfiqar Ali. Appears substantially in Chapter 6.
Gunga Sain: (Real) *ḍhol* player in Lahore
Arif Sain: (Real) *dhamālī* in Lahore

Chapter 4

Nazir Ahmed: (Real) *ḍhol* player in Multan (plays with Muhammad Baksh Multani)
Huma: Wife of Ajmal Ahmed Khan
Mīān Allah Dīvāyā and Mīān Rahīm Baksh: (Real) Illustrious *nagāra* players of the past; teachers of Muhammad Baksh Multani
Allah Ditta: (Real) Muhammad Baksh Multani's grandfather
Ustad Mamraj: (Real) *Tāshā* master in Delhi. He appears in the analytic section of this chapter and as part of Ali's narrative in Chapter 9.

Chapter 5

Saleem Gardezi: (Real) Shī'ī professional singer in Multan placed in a fictitious context
Syed Karrar Haidar Zaidi: (Real) *soz k̲h̲wān* in Multan. He is placed in a ficitious context, but the description pertains to an actual performance in 1997.
Bashir Husain Mazhar: (Real) resident of Multan, some of whose verbatim statements from 1997 are used in the narrative; some were originally in English, others in Urdu/Saraiki. However, in the text his personal background, his familial relationships, and his actions are fictitious. In the story, his sister's son Salim is related to Ajmal's wife, Huma. Sufiya is his sister's granddaughter.
Sufiya: Woman with whom Ali eventually falls in love. She is the granddaughter of Mazhar's sister.

Salim: Mazhar's nephew, distantly related to Huma. He strikes up a friendship with Ali and figures later in the narrative.

Nasir: Fictitious grand-nephew of the famed real *ḍhol* player Allah Wasāyah. Some of the identifications of performers Nasir makes and some of his statements on the history of the tradition are taken from interviews with Suraiya Multanikar; the names of performers and composers refer to actual historical figures. The source of some of his statements is the late Adam Nayyar.

Suraiya Multanikar: Hailed from the Bheḍi Potra neighborhood and made her career as one of Pakistan's leading female vocalists. She wouldn't have been present in the time frame of the narrative, and would not plausibly have been able to strike up a conversation with Ali on the street, and so is not included as a character. But her family did host the composer Ghulam Rasul Hasrat in their home.

Arjun: Old friend of Ali's, with whom Ali stays in Delhi from time to time

Shahbaz: (Real) man who saw himself as Pappu Sain's manager in the 1990s (not in the 1980s, when this narrative takes place). Statements he makes in the story are based on conversations in 1997.

Chapter 6

Nuriyah: Widowed mother of Salim. She lives in Shadman Colony, Lahore.

Jhura Sain: (Real) playing partner of Pappu Sain. His given name is Manzur.

Chapter 7

Muhammad Mushtaq: (Real) devotee who regularly visits the Madho Lal Husain shrine. Statements are taken largely from interviews and conversations with him in 2003; the time period is adjusted to the 1980s and context of the conversation is altered for the sake of the narrative.

Maulvi Hafiz Muhammad Ramzan: (Real) imām of the mosque of the Madho Lal Husain shrine in 2003. The conversation is based on his actual speech but recontextualized to the 1980s and Ali's story.

Muhammad Asif Alim Lodhi: (Real) devotee at the Madho Lal Husain shrine in 2003, originally from Karachi

Baba Manna, "Babaji," known as Muhammad Aslam: (Real) malaṅg at the Madho Lal Husain shrine in 2003

Shehzad: (Real) voluntary servant and devotee at the Madho Lal Husain shrine in 2003

Saghir Ahmed: (Real) highly skilled *ḍhol* player based in Jhelum, Panjab. Some of his comments are drawn from an interview in 2003, but not at the Madho Lal Husain shrine.

Baba Rashid Sain: (Real) pir from Burewala who attended the *'urs* of Madho Lal Husain in 1997

Parvez Bhat: (Real) disciple of Baba Rashid Sain who attended the *'urs* of Madho Lal Husain in 1997

Khurshid Ali: (Real) disciple of Baba Rashid Sain who attended the ʻurs of Madho Lal Husain in 1997

Perfume Baba: (Real) *dhamālī*, perfume merchant, who was a frequenter of the *ʻurs*es of Madho Lal Husain as of 1997 and likely would have been on the scene during the time frame depicted

Chapter 8

Biswas "Bunty" Sengupa: Ali's new boss, editor of the *Times of India* in Lucknow

Rafiq Anwar Memon: Vice-chancellor, Sindh Agricultural University, Tando Jam, Sindh-fictitious

Rajab Ahmed Pathan: University public relations officer, Sindh Agricultural University, Tando Jam, Sindh. Much of his speech is based on that of an ethnographic consultant. His name has been changed here.

Lala Gul Sanubar Pathan: (Real) Sindhi caretaker of Peṛh Muhammad in Hyderabad, Sindh

Vasant Faqir: (Real) Manganhār *sharnā'ī* ustad, teacher of Faqir Husain. In this narrative his words and actions are based on those of others. He was not an ethnographic consultant of mine.

Faqir Husain Baksh: (Real) *sharnā'ī* and *gazī* player in Hyderabad, Sindh, who studied with Vasant Faqir. Some of his statements are based on interviews.

Faqir Nathu: Father of Faqir Husain Baksh in the story. Someone by the same name played *sharnā'ī* and *gazī* along with Faqir Husain Baksh in real life. Statements by this character are those of others.

Qasim Shah, known as Muhammad Qasim: (Real) *naqqārah* player in Hyderabad. Statements in the narrative are taken from interviews.

Sayyad Alam Shah Bukhari: Based on a (real) musician present at the (real) Muhammad Qasim interview

Qamar: Fictitious member of *muhājir ḍhol-tāshā* group hailing largely from Ajmer. Now residing in Hyderabad, Sindh, Pakistan.

Muhammad Shafi: (Real) elder, leader of *muhājir* group hailing largely from Ajmer. Now residing in Hyderabad, Sindh, Pakistan. Statements in the story are derived from interviews in Urdu.

Muhammad Ikrammudin: (Real) elder, leader of *muhājir* group hailing largely from Agra. Now residing in Hyderabad, Sindh, Pakistan. Statements in the story are derived from interviews in Urdu.

Ahmad: (Real) member of *muhājir ḍhol-tāshā* group hailing largely from Agra. Now residing in Hyderabad, Sindh, Pakistan. The name is changed owing to several inflammatory statements.

Allaudin: (Real) elder, leader of *muhājir* group hailing largely from Bharatpur. Now residing in Hyderabad, Sindh, Pakistan. Statements in the story are from interviews in Urdu.

Ilfaz: Ali's cousin related through his father's second wife. Resides in Karachi.

Chapter 9

Asghar Husain: Based on a real Shī'ī *soz k̲h̲wān* who assisted with research in Jacob Lines. The name has been changed.

Hashim: (Real) *muhājir ḍhol* player in Jacob Lines, Karachi, Pakistan

Muhammad Razaq: Elder *tāshā* player who migrated to Karachi from Delhi. He is a real figure whose name is changed here to avoid confusion with another character in the book.

Nasir: (Real) Shī'ī living in Jacob Lines. The name has been changed.

Muhammad Sheikh or Ustad Sheikh: (Real) historical figure who played *tāshā* for Muharram in Nizamuddin before and after Partition. Teacher of Mamraj.

Wajid Khurshid Ali (d. ca. 1952): (Real) historical figure who used to perform tabla on Radio Pakistan and sponsored a *ta'ziyah* procession in India before Partition.

Ansar Husain: (Real) Shī'ī *tāshā* player in pre-Partition Delhi, according to the memory of one man in Jacob Lines in 1997. Personal details about Ansar Husain are fictive.

Sarir Ahmed Nizami: (Real) elder *tāshā* player who migrated to Karachi from Delhi; a member of Nizami *k̲h̲āndān*.

Farid Ahmad Nizami: (Real) grandson of the former Sajjada Nishin Pir Zamin Nizami Syed Bokhari, and (in 2010) son of one of the two men claiming status as Sajjada Nishin at Nizamuddin Dargah. His statements are adapted from a personal conversation but are not verbatim.

Ghulam Hasnain Nizami: (Real) *Ḍhol*-playing member of Nizami *k̲h̲āndān* in Delhi said to hold special knowledge of Muharram drumming and the texts that lie behind them.

Naveen: Fictitious helpful man at Nizamuddin Dargah

Bharat Singh: (Real) son of Mamraj. A *shahnā'ī* player.

Ram Babu: (Real) son of Mamraj. A *tāshā* player.

Amina: Sajjad's wife

Serwer Sadiq Hussain Nizami: (Real) son of Ghulam Hasnain Nizami

Karbala Narrative, Selected Characters

Husain's Side

By tradition, the warriors of Husain's party consisted of about 72 family members and supporters

Husain, grandson of the Prophet Muhammad and son of 'Alī, the first Shī'ī imām

Muslim bin 'Aqil, Husain's cousin and the messenger sent to Kūfa to rally support for Husain against Yazīd. Muslim was beheaded by the henchmen of Ibn Ziyād.

'Abbās 'alamdār, Husain's half-brother and standard-bearer in the army. 'Abbās lost his life after the gruesome torture of having his arms severed while he tried to bring water from the Euphrates for the suffering children of Husain's party.

'Alī Akbar, Husain's eighteen-year-old son, who fought heroically against the enemy's massive forces. Many *marṣiyah*s take as their themes Akbar's prowess in battle and the anguished scene of Husain bringing his battered body back to the camp.

Qāsim, son of Husain's brother Hasan (the third Shī'ī imam), who was said to have been wedded to Husain's daughter on the battlefield and was slain immediately thereafter. The rich rituals and dramatic elements surrounding Qāsim's wedding are extremely popular in South Asian Muharram observances, but this is one of the events in the Karbala chronology that is not historically attested.

Sajjād/Zain-ul Abidin, son of Husain who was too ill to participate in the Karbala battle. He survived to become the fourth imam in Twelver Shiism.

Sakina, the young daughter of Imam Husain. She died in Yazid's prison.

Sughra, daughter of Husain. She was too ill to leave Medina when her father departed for Karbala.

Zainab, Husain's sister, who proudly sacrificed her sons in the battle of Karbala and made fearless speeches in Kufa and Damascus after Husain's martyrdom to apprise Muslims of Yazīd's atrocities.

Yazīd's Side

Yazīd, Ummayad caliph of Islam, who ruled from Damascus from 680 CE. He is considered by Shī'ahs to be the usurper of the Caliphate that should have been Husain's.

Ibn Ziyād, governor of Kufa, who sent massive armed forces to fight Husain. Ziyād's commander cut off Imam Husain's encampment from the Euphrates River, so that even the women and children suffered without water in the desert for three days before the battle of Karbala.

Shimr, the soldier who dealt the death blow to Husain, decapitating him.

Notes

An Essential Note from the Author

1. This is one solution to a problem that all ethnographers potentially face. For a discussion of similar issues in other ethnographies, see Herzfeld (1997, 7) and Needham (1972, 15 and passim).

Note from the Editor

1. Disclaimer: Any similarity between the name of the above-named editor and persons real or fictitious (with the exception of one appearing in the story to follow) is entirely coincidental. The Note from the Editor does not express the views or editorial procedures of individuals associated with the University of Illinois Press.

Chapter 1. Drumming, Language, and the Voice in South Asia

This is the first of four chapters in which the story of Ali precedes a longer section that contextualizes and analyzes aspects of drumming and voice in South Asia. The first-person voice of section two of each of these four chapters is always that of the author of this book, Richard Wolf. Some of the quotidian details of Ali's and Sajjad's life histories were inspired by incidents in the lives of personal acquaintances of mine, but none of the characters in this section are real people disguised with false names. The tale of Karbala, however, is retold here in a manner consistent with the ways Shī'ahs themselves tell it.

Sources for section I (Ali's story)

Kazim, Ali Muhammad. 1887/1307 H. Biography of Ghaziuddin Haider (in Persian). Nayyar Masud consulted this work from his personal library and read out passages, translating them into Urdu. Details from these passages are reframed in the descriptions of this chapter. According to Masud, Kazim's published work of 1887 consists of his own eyewitness accounts of nawab of Awadh, Ghaziuddin Haider, who lived from 1769 to 1827.

Masud, Nayyar (professor in the history and literature of Persian and Urdu at Lucknow University), interview with Richard Wolf, June 24, 1998, Lucknow, India. He provided descriptions of Muharram based on his lifetime of attending Muharram observances and the sources he has consulted in Urdu and Persian.

Sharar, Abdul Halim (1965, 1994) provides extensive descriptions of Muharram rituals and processions.

Korom (1999) suggests that the *tassa* of Trinidad also carried verbal messages in the context of Hosay (Muharram).

Chapter 1 notes

1. In contemporary Buddhist traditions of ritual music as well, "melodic instruments . . . usually play adaptations and elaborations of vocal song melodies" (Ellingson 1986, 332; see also Ellingson 1980, 434–35 and passim).

2. I borrow the term *vococentrism* from film and media studies, in which the word refers to emphasis on the vocal medium relative to other elements of sound in audiovisual productions.

3. Local populations were allowed to practice their own religion, provided they paid tax (Ikram 1964).

4. Professional groups perform at the Chennai Sangamam, a folk festival conceived and organized in part by Tamil Maiyam, the daughter of N. Karunanidhi, Tamil Nadu's chief minister, and sponsored by the government of the state. The Dravidianist politics of the Tamil Nadu government favor non-Brahmin castes because, according to party ideology, they represent the true Tamil people. In advertisements for the festival in 2010, large color tableaux were painted on compound walls on Radhakrishnan Salai and other roads in Chennai depicting colorfully clad frame-drum players. Part of the message was obviously championing the arts of the oppressed. Ironically, in May 2011 the Dravida Munnetra Kazhagam was criticized for diverting funds meant for scheduled caste welfare to fulfill Karunanidhi's 2006 campaign promise to deliver color televisions to the needy.

5. *Gāyaki ang* means literally vocal "limb" or "subdivision," implying that branch of music making that is vocally oriented.

6. More specifically, *gāyaki ang* also may refer to Vilayat Khan and his disciples' rendering of a medium-speed *k̲h̲ayāl* melody in *tīntāl* or *ek tāl* on an instrument, with an effort to preserve the rhythm of the text (George Ruckert, pers. comm., May 18, 2011).

7. With the rise of sectarian clashes in Lahore and the bombing of prominent Sufi shrines, Pappu's Thursday night performances were banned for a period and activities at the shrine limited. Whether these performances will continue remains uncertain at the time of this book's publication.

8. *Formants* are clusters of overtones, visible on a sonogram, which give vowels, for example, their distinctive characters. These clusters of overtones, which are numbered, correspond to resonating cavities. F1, or the first formant, corresponds to an area that begins where the tongue is closest to the roof of the mouth and extends into the throat cavity. F2, or the second formant, is the cavity in the front of the mouth.

Within the speech of any given speaker, certain vowels are intrinsically higher in pitch than others. The vowel /i/, for instance, is higher than /a/, and /a/ is higher than /u/. The complex reasons for these differences involve the relationship between the frequency of the vocal chords and the resonant properties of the mouth and throat cavities.

Relative pitch refers to the relationship between pitches rather than the absolute value of a pitch such as C, D, or E.

9. A few other examples include Tamil ritual drumming ensembles, including combinations of *tappaṭṭai, tājā, mattaḷam,* and other drums; some *ḍhol-tāshā* ensembles; and Nilgiri tribal instrumental music.

Chapter 2. Emotional Agents

Muharram Ali's education is modeled after that of the prominent Indian journalist Saeed Naqvi, who did attend La Martinière College but did not deliver the address.

The first day of Muharram, which is used as a point of temporal reference in this chapter, fell on September 27, 1984.

The full Urdu text for the *nauḥah* mentioned as being sung at the wedding *majlis* can be found in Sayyid Ġulām Ḥaidar Tirmiz̲ī, *Majālis-e k̲h̲atūn (jadīd): har do ḥiṣah kāmil* (Women's majlises (modern), the complete two volumes), in Urdu (Lahore: Kutubk̲h̲ānah-e is̲nā ʻasharī, n.d., 62). I thank Amy Bard for the reference and the suggestion of a plausible *nauḥah* for the occasion.

The real Sibte-Jafar rendered the *soz* mentioned in the text for a *majlis* arranged for Amy Bard, which I videotaped on June 16, 1997, in Karachi (Media Example 2.1).

Shahid and Niamat Ali are real performers, although they were playing as a pair in the 1990s, not the 1980s, when Shahid would have only been about ten years old. I met the two drummers after videotaping them (while sitting above them in a banyan tree) performing at the *'urs* of Madho Lal Husain in 1997. After collecting their contact information, I invited them to my residence on April 23, 1997, for an extended interview and demonstration. The statements that they make in this chapter and the next are based on that interview. Their scene in the story, however, is set ten years before my fieldwork took place. Ali needed to be born closer to the date of the partition of India and Pakistan to make the chronology of the larger narrative work, and I did not detect anything in what I chose to include that would have been implausible ten years earlier.

The overview and analysis in the second section are, as in Chapter 1, the original work of Richard Wolf. The first-person singular pronoun refers only to him.

The fictive Ali returns briefly in the section titled Complex Agency—in the present tense—to present a hypothetical example. Ajmal's responses are based on actual statements of a drummer named Ajmal. To avoid redundancy, the encounter is not duplicated in the main narrative.

Original Terms for Selected Passages in Single or Double Quotation Marks (Urdu Unless Noted Otherwise)

the way plants intertwine and grow into one another—paiwand ho jāna
refined—bārīk kā kām
[Qadar Baksh Mazari described] falling in love with and going crazy over the voice—us kī āvāz peh ʻishq ho gayā . . . dīvānah ho gayā
dense, loud instrument[al sounds]—keṭṭi mēḷam (Tamil)
to ridicule—maẕāq uṛāna
rites and services—lāg (Saraiki)

Selected Interviews

Muhammad Baksh Multani, Multan and Islamabad (March 27, 1997; April 9, 1997; May 16, 1997)
Nathan, Ṭhaṭṭah district, Sindh (May 30, 1997)
Javed Ali, Lahore (April 23, 1997)
Muhammad Urs Bhatti, Karachi (May 31, 1997)
Qadar Baksh Mazari and Bashir Ahmed, Islamabad (April 11, 1997)
Allaudin, Hyderabad, Sindh, Pakistan (June 15, 1997)

Chapter 2 notes

1. Bharāins (the same word is also pronounced *Piraī* in Panjabi) are "said to take their name from the fact that the Prophet gave his coat (*pairdhan*) to one of their ancestors as a reward for circumcising a convert after a barber had refused to do so" (Ibbetson 1916, 229).

2. *Ḍom* is the term these people used for themselves in Hunza in the 1930s; the surrounding Burusho people called them Bēricho (Lorimer 1939, 1).

3. I thank Margaret Mills for this final point. I am not certain that all or many locals think of Viśvakarma caste members in general terms as "transformers."

4. Nasir-ud Din Tusi (d. CE 1274) and Mulla Sadra (d. CE 1640), for example, drew on the philosophies of Ibn Sina and Aristotle in their theological contributions to what became modern Shiism (Momen 1985, 94, 113). Much of the knowledge of Aristotle and other Greek sources in the Latin Middle Ages was first made available through Latin translations of Arabic translations and commentaries. These latter included original interpretations of al-Fārābī and others (Randel 1976, 187 and passim).

5. During my fieldwork among the Kota people in the Nilgiri Hills of South India, I was told repeatedly that the difference between a double-reed melody for worshipping and one for a funeral could be felt, even though there is no systematic difference between the two (Wolf 2001, 396).

Chapter 3. Tone and Stroke

Muharram Ali's initial statement in this chapter about the best *tāshā* players living in the countryside is lifted directly from statements of numerous research consultants in Lucknow and other cities of North India. Even though the precise conversation has been crafted to fit Ali's story, Niamat and Shahid Ali's demonstrations, technical discussions, opinions, and life histories continue to derive almost exclusively from my interview with them on April 23, 1997 in my Lahore residence. Only selected words and phrases, not long verbatim quotes, are reproduced from their original statements in Urdu and Panjabi. The aim is to highlight Ali's process of discovery of the Lahore *ḍhol* repertoire and performance scene, as one who had grown up in Lucknow. The original interview and demonstration, as well as the video of the *'urs*, are available for consultation at the Archive of World Music at Harvard University and at the Archive and Research Centre for Ethnomusicology in Gurgaon.

Original Terms in Urdu or Panjabi for English Words in Single Quotation Marks

surface things—ūtliyāṉ cīzāṉ
sharp—tez
[he] will show [teach] him—dassde naiṉ
weighty—gahrā'ī
chief—muḍh
judges—parkhan vāle
keeping [to maintain (the *tāl*)]—rakhnā
raising [to raise]—uṭhāna
general gathering—pancāyat (this term often refers to a body of decision makers, like a town council)
noble birth—ashraf
gathering of affection—pyār dī caukī
spirit bolstering—ḥosalah afzā'ī

Technical Notes, Section I

The five-beat version of *fāḵẖtah aṣūl*, or *sūrfāḵẖtah*, is evidently more well-known than the six-beat version in the Pakistani Panjabi tabla repertoire (Lybarger 2003, 188). The ten-beat *fāḵẖtah*s appear in Arabic and Persian theory from Safi-al din (mid-sixth century CE) onward. Maraghi's *fāḵẖtah sağir*, vocalized "tan tananan tananan," divides the ten beats into 2 + 4 + 4. Depending on their tempo of rendition, these historical *fāḵẖtah*s might have been perceived as patterns of five. By the same token, the structure of *panj tāl* in figure 3.3 can be heard as 2 + 4 + 4. The initial *dhin dhin* would comprise the first two beats and the syllables *nā nā* would initiate each of the two four-beat units. Further research is needed to determine the extent to which *fāk̲h̲tah*s persist in the Panjab merely as names for metrical units, or as names musically linked with the metrical entities described by these early theorists. Sources which discuss the *fāk̲h̲tah*s include the following:

al-Urmawī, Ṣafi al-Dīn. 2001. *Kitāb al-adwār fi 'l-musiqā* (Persian translation and Arabic text), edited by Āryu Rostami. Tehran: Mirās-e Maktub, 183–84 (Arabic), 81 (Persian trans.)

al-Urmawī, Ṣafi al-Dīn. 1984. *Book on the cyclical forms of musical modes: Kitāb al-adwār,* ed. Fuat Sezgin, intro. Eckhard Neubauer. Reproduced from MS Nuruosmaniye 3653, Istanbul. Series C, Facsimile Editions 6. Frankfurt-am-Main: Institute for the History of Arabic-Islamic Sciences at the Johann Wolfgang Goethe University, 89–90.

Marāghi, 'Abd al-Qāder Ebn Gheybi Hāfez. 2009. *Jāme' al-alhān*, ed. Bābak Khazrā'i. Tehran: Iranian Academy of Arts. *Fāk̲h̲tah kabir* and *saġir* are discussed on 244–45.

(I am grateful to Stephen Blum for providing these valuable historical references.)

When "Niamat . . . elaborated the groove with a denser stream of strokes" he employed a technique sometimes referred to in English as "doubling." *Ḍhol* players in Eastern Panjab (India) call this *tirakaṭ* (Schreffler 2002, 67–68). *Dugun* refers to a structurally equivalent technique (Lybarger 2003, 220; Kippen 2006, 96). Both involve elaborating the content of a pattern and not merely playing the same material at twice the speed.

Select Interviews and Recordings

Interviews with members of several ensembles in Hyderabad, Sindh, June 14–15, 1997

Mamraj and Bharat Singh, Delhi, August 13, 1998

Interviews, demonstrations, and videotapes of Nanda Devi festival in Almora (at that time, part of Uttar Pradesh), August 26 to September 3, 1998

Runza Yadagiri, Rudraram village, Andhra Pradesh, November 27, 1998

Interviews and demonstrations with several drum groups in Dharmapuri, Tamil Nadu, December 29, 1998 to January 3, 1999

Figures

Figure 3.1. Fāk̲h̲tah aṣūl of six *mātra*s (counts) (see Media Example 3.1 ⭍)

1	2	3	4	5	6
dhin dhin	nā nā	din din	nā nā	kat tā	tiṭakiṭa

Figure 3.2. Tihā'ī in Fāk̲h̲tah aṣūl, recited by Niamat Ali (see Media Example 3.1 ⭍)

taṛaṛa deñ . dañ . de teñ . . . taṛaṛa deñ . dañ . de teñ . . . taṛaṛa deñ . dañ . de (dhin din nā nā, etc.)

Figure 3.3. Panj tāl

1	2	3	4	5
dhin dhin	nā nā	din din	nā nā	kat tā

Figure 3.4. Muġala'i (see Media Example 3.3)

1	2	3	4	5	6	7
tā .	ni ta	ni ta	dhin dhin	da da	dhin dhin	da da

Chapter 3 notes

1. I thank Margaret Mills for the apt expression "technician of emotion" and for suggesting its broader theoretical significance in thinking about musicians' roles.

2. For instance, *ek tāl* (meaning "one *tāl*") in Hindustani music has four claps. In South India, *eka tāḷam* (also meaning "one *tāl*") is represented by a single hand clap followed by a variable number of finger counts. For further discussion of the evolution of Hindustani *tāl* names and structures see, e.g., Kippen 2000, 1988; Clayton 2000; Stewart 1974.

3. *Cāl* can also mean "a move, a strategy, or a trick."

4. *Ṭhīk* probably derives from the Sanskrit *sthirā,* whose range of meanings includes "firm, hard . . . not wavering or tottering, steady . . . unfluctuating" (Platts 1884, s.v. *ṭhīk*; Monier-Williams 1990, s.v. sthirā).

5. "Brōvabarāma" is a song, or *kriti*, in South Indian classical music. Composed by the "saint" Tyagaraja, it is set to the eight-count *tāla* called *ādi tāla.*

6. The notion of tonal patterning as subordinate to rhythmic patterning is expressed in the classification system of the ninth-century Arab musician Isḥāq al-Mawṣili, whereby "every rhythmic mode is considered a genus, which is subsequently subdivided into types according to the melodic modes used in conjunction with it, and these melodic modes do indeed serve as differentiae" (Sawa 2009, 5).

7. The former is usually a drum groove in $^{6}_{16}$ or $^{7}_{16}$, while the latter is in $^{8}_{8}$.

8. Elsewhere versions of this drum are called *paṟai.*

9. I worked with these two groups twice: once in April 1991 in the context of a *jātra* (festival) and once in their own villages in December–January 1998–99.

10. The Toṭṭi Paṟaiyars are so named for their traditional role as scavengers or messengers (University of Madras 1924–16, s.v. *tōṭṭippaṟayaṉ*); Nataraj from Menaci described their role as those who play for all occasions, good and bad.

11. The twelve variations idea has currency among a number of folk drummers in the area.

12. A consensus was reached that *tiruppu* means "beat" in English, but the English word *beat* is itself ambiguous, since it can refer to a rhythmic pattern or an individual strike.

13. He may have meant "for one of them," or "for the first one," or "for the variation called *one*, characterized by one stressed stroke." Chapter 4 considers patterns

organized by the number of stressed strokes and includes one *mēḷam* example (Media Example 4.9 ⎗) that illustrates a sequence of increasing numbers of stressed strokes.

14. One other pattern seems not to be part of the aforementioned *brijj* system. That pattern, called the *allā cāmi mēḷam* (Media Example 3.11 ⎗) (pattern for the God Allah), is played exclusively on the *tappaṭṭai* and *tāshā* and is reserved for Muharram. It involves only two variations on the *tappaṭṭai*. The overall effect mimics the *ḍhol-tāshā* texture found elsewhere in India and Pakistan.

15. The names of many more *haríip*s can be found in Schmid (1997, 253–54) and in the Colin Huehns Asia Collection at the British Library, http://sounds.bl.uk/World-and-traditional-music/Colin-Huehns-Pakistan, accessed January 5, 2014.

16. Schmid was presumably focused on the second meaning when summarizing the *haríip* style as one in which "the melody played on the wind instrument expresses the musical content [and] the bass drum reinforc[es] and dramatiz[es] the texture" (2000, 795).

17. The outline of the Ḍūmaki language by the British Iranist and military and intelligence officer D. L. R. Lorimer describes *haríip* simply as music (Lorimer 1939, s.v. hari·p).

18. About two hundred miles south-southeast of Sust in the region of Baltistan is a classification of fifty-two tune types called *harīb*. Played on the *sorna* (i.e., *surnā'ī*), these tunes bear such names as *ushak, bhasan, sindhṛī, mokhālef, yagāh, dugāh,* and *segāh*. These names suggest possible links with Iranian dastgāh and Central Asian *shashmaqām* music (Faruqi et al. 1989, 18).

19. Another version of this *haríip* can be downloaded from http://karaoke.esnips.com/doc/1565be56-5aee-491e-9bde-e8a6c4288190/Tambal-Hareep. http://brushaskimusic.blogspot.com/2009/07/dowload-hareeps-for-freeenjoy-them.html, accessed January 5, 2014.

20. Another version can be heard at http://karaoke.esnips.com/doc/af560b7d-adb4-4266-9185-51f01f781350/Algani-%5Bspecial-hareep%5D. http://brushaskimusic.blogspot.com/2009/07/dowload-hareeps-for-freeenjoy-them.html, accessed January 5, 2014.

21. *Ġalawáar* is played to mark the beginning of the game and again each time there is a goal (Schmid 1997, 184, 253)—a function similar to that of *bóote haríip*. Perhaps it was this contextual similarity that led Haidar Bek to switch the order of *haríip*s at the point we reached *ġalawáar* and insert *bóote* instead. They wanted to play *ġalawáar* near the end. According to local Web sites on Hunza, *ġalawáar* is also used for the sword dance. http://www.ideeaz.com/altithunza/dances.htm, accessed July 4, 2011. http://www.achunza.org/Dances.html, accessed September 2010, indicated the same.

22. For a more general discussion of this set of relations among parts, see Huehns 1991, 384*ff.*

23. Reis Flora's observations that the "*naubat* genre and style" can be identified by "rhythmic patterns on the *naqārah*" and that the "*śahnāī* has a secondary role" (1995, 60) support the ideas presented here, as do Carol Tingey's findings in Nepal that items of occasional repertoire for the *pancāl bājā* are identified either by melody or by *cāl* (Tingey 1994, 120).

Chapter 4. Beyond the Mātra

The descriptions of Multan come from the observations I made when visiting Multan several times in 1997 and again in 2007 and are also inspired by a large variety of photographs. The descriptions and statements regarding Muharram rituals and music in this and the next chapters are drawn from my own observations and experiences, statements of participants on the street during Muharram in 1997, and follow-up interviews with the musicians of the Bheḍi Potra neighborhood, with the famous vocalist Suraiya Multanikar (originally from Lodhipura *muḥalla*), and with several others in 2007. The drummer Muhammad Baksh Multani, discussed in this chapter, is the same person mentioned in Chapter 2 and elsewhere, and this characterization is based very closely on the real musician of the same name. Some of Ajmal's statements and explanations are drawn from those of a drummer named Ajmal, even though the fictional character is not meant to represent the real Ajmal.

Because of the sensitivities involved, I do not provide the names of sources for the following details in the text, which are ethnographically reliable, at least as stories: Iqbal Husain is a Lahori painter famous for depicting the women of Hira Mandi, the red-light district. This anecdote was related to me in Multan. The playful scenario of a girl fretting over her exams as the subject of a *majlis* is based on the schoolgirl antics of one my Shī'ī friends. According to a Multani contact in 2007, the obscene chant in Saraiki was one that Sunni kids in Multan genuinely were using to provoke Shī'ahs.

The etymology of the word *dab* is more complicated than that which the character Ajmal (at this moment completely fictional) provides in the text. *Dab* derives from the Sanskrit root *dam*, "to tame, subdue, or overpower." See Platts (1884) s.v. dabnā and Monier-Williams (1990) s.v. dam. However, since *dab* is sometimes used in South Asia in vocal imitations of drum rhythms, it is plausible that a listener, particularly a drummer, would make this connection in this context. The anecdote was not related to me by a musician, and it would have been awkward (if not offensive) for me to bring up the meaning of *dab* in this chant with a drummer in Multan.

Rohtak, currently a district in Haryana, India, was established in 1824 as part of the domain of the British Resident in Delhi. In 1858, following the Indian Rebellion of 1857, Rohtak became part of Panjab.

Technical Matters Discussed in Section I

Compare *panj tār dī savārī* with similar organization of tabla *tāl*s in Lybarger (2003, 205–6) and both tabla and *pakhāvaj tāl*s in Kippen (2006, 120–21, 299, 311). Notation in figure 4.2 is after Lybarger (2003). Ability to perform in this *tāl* is an important sign of musicianship for a classical percussionist in North India and Pakistan. The word *savārī* can refer to a form of conveyance, a cavalcade or retinue. The English word *suite* perhaps best captures the connection between the image of a principal figure traveling with his or her company and the musical idea of a composition with several parts. The *savārī* travels, as it were, through five parts, or five constituent *bol* patterns.

Baksh said, "I used to play | jhā . ṇe ke nā . ke ne / dā . ṇe ke nā . ke ne |" without mentioning the fact that this *bol* pattern corresponds with *dhamāl*. He referred to the sword fighters as Katkis. According to Schreffler (2002, 120), Nihang Sikhs and others interested in the *gatkā* martial art of fencing perform their displays of swordsmanship to the *dhamāl* pattern in India. In Hallaur, Eastern Uttar Pradesh, where Shī'ahs predominate, I was told in 1997 that Hindus and Sunnis at that time engaged in *gatkā khel* (swordplay) and also employed lathis and shields (*ḍhāl*) in the procession on Ashura; their activities were some distance from the drumming, which was performed by Shī'ahs and other communities together.

Terms in Urdu and Saraiki for English Words in Single Quotation Marks

make the tempo sit—lay biṭhāna
classical—English word *classical*
horse ride—ghuṛ savāri
hold the *vājā* (drum pattern) steady—qā'im rakhnā
recite *bols*—paṛht paṛhnā (lit. "recite a reading")
[those who first recite and play are] genuine—ṣaḥīḥ
to transform [a basic pattern]—tabdīlī karnā
to make [a pattern] beautiful—k͟hūbṣūratī karnā
[to go one cycle around the *tāl*, that is, take a] round—cakkar
place [position within the *tāl*]—jagah
fun—majāgīrī
[when] the procession departs—jaṇj caṛhṇ
palanquin—ḍoli
new fashion—jīven̲ jīven̲ ravāj
cloth (held out by Hindus as part of the wedding ritual)—pallu
procession departure—jaṇj caṛhī
The sound of the *ḍhol* extends a long way—ḍhol dī āvāz baṛī dūr tak jāndī 'ai
The sound of the *tāshā* resonates only in the immediate area—tāshe dī āvāz . . . maujūdah jagah tak

Other Terms

Kirāṛ can be a derogatory term for a Panjabi Hindu merchant (Rose 1911–19, 2:552); in this case Baksh is using what he understands to be the Saraiki term for a Hindu.

Karaṛ's literal meaning, "a type of seed," does not shed light on the musical meaning. It is possibly related to the Panjabi word *karār* (Arabic *qarār*), "a promise or agreement." Also, the word for Hindu, Kirāṛ, may also be pronounced karaṛ, but these speakers used the two as distinctly different words. *Karaṛ* is used onomotopoeically in *karaṛ karaṛ karnā*, to grind the teeth, break a bone, or make a noise as of breaking a bone (Vanguard 1983 s.v. karaṛ), so it may refer to the clamor of a procession starting. None of these are satisfactory etymologies, in my view.

Ḍāḍkeyāṉ ālī jhūmar is a variety of *jhūmar*. I have not been able to translate "*ḍāḍkeyāṉ ālī.*"

Ḍoliwālā vājā is the *vājā* (pattern) played during the procession of the palanquin (*ḍoliwālā*).

Select Interviews and Recordings (not Otherwise Specified by Date in the Main Text)

Muhammad Baksh Multani, Multan and Islamabad (March 27, 1997; April 9, 1997; May 16, 1997)

Figures

Figure 4.1. Mārū drum pattern and obscene jeer

	♩	♪	♩	♩	♩	♪	♩	♩
Right hand (with *cob*)	CR		CD		CR		CR	
Left hand (bare)	EF	EF	EF	ER		EF	EF	ER
	dab .	te	piṭ .	ṭo .	bheṇ .	ḍe	cu .	ḍo .

Key:

Right-hand strokes on bass head with the stick (*cob*):
- CR = Resonant stroke on center of head
- CD = Damped stroke on center of head

Left-hand strokes on treble head with the hand:
- ER = Resonant stroke with palm and fingers open, edge of head
- EF = Stroke with fingertips, edge of head (the stroke resonates but is softer and has fewer upper partials)

Figure 4.2.

Base speed (1 cell = 1 *mātra*): *pandrāṉ mātre dī panj tār dī savārī*

X	jā .	. nā	. .	
2	ka .	te ke	ta .	te ke
3	jhā .	tij jhā	ge de	ge de
4	gi .	nā .		
5	ge de	ge de		

Half speed (1 cell = 2 *mātras*): *tīh-mātre dī panj tār dī savārī*

X	jā .	. nā	. .	
2	kā .	. .	tā .	. .
3	tā .	. .	(a) .	. .
4	ge .	jhā .		
5	(a) .	ge de		

Panj tāl dī savārī demonstrated by Muhammad Baksh Multani Key:

X = *sam* (= beat 1)

2, 3, etc. = *tāṛī* (= *tālī*), claps

cell = 1 rhythmic unit (number of *mātras* determined by tempo)

(a) = continuation of vowel without a clear consonant attack in the demo

Figure 4.3. *Bol* pattern for *Shādmānah*

ghinã.ta kitata. **jha.jha**. kita.na

Figure 4.4. *Bol* pattern for *Jhūmar*

dhā.dhin.natinak. **trā.tin**.natinak.

Figure 4.5. *Bol* pattern for *Karaṛ*, *ḍhol* part

Recited by Muhammad Shabbir, March 27, 1997, Multan, Panjab, Pakistan. Compare with Media Example 4.1, the same pattern with slightly different *bol*s, points of emphasis, and intonation.

ghinata**ki**natakina **ja**ge**ja**ginaja**ja**gina

Figure 4.6.

Bol pattern for "grand" *vājā* played at a Sayyad's wedding

jhai . . ge . ne . ta . . . . ta . . . / jhai . . ghi . . ghi . ne . ge . ne .

Bol pattern for "small" *vājā* played at a Sayyad's wedding

gin . nā . kit . ta . / gin . nā . vij . jā .
gīn . . kit . tā . / gīn . . vic . cā .

The two patterns above are called *mārū* when they are performed during Muharram.

Figure 4.7. Two parts of *Choṭā Mārū* recited and played on the *ḍhol*

	♩	♩	♩	♩	♩	♩	♩	♩
Right hand (with *cob*)	CR		CD		CR		CR	
Left hand (bare)	EF	EF	EF	ER	EF	EF	EF	ER
	gin .	nā .	kit .	ta .	gin .	nā .	vij .	jā .

	♩	♪	♩	♩	♩	♪	♩	♩
Right hand (with *cob*)	CR		CD		CR		CR	
Left hand (bare)	EF	EF	EF	ER		EF	EF	ER
	gīn .	.	kit .	ta .	gīn .	.	vic .	cā .

Key:

Right-hand strokes on bass head with the stick (*cob*):
- CR = Resonant stroke on center of head
- CD = Damped stroke on center of head

Left-hand strokes on treble head with the hand:
- ER = Resonant stroke with palm and fingers open, edge of head
- EF = Stroke with fingertips, edge of head (the stroke resonates but is softer and has fewer upper partials)

Figure 4.8. Approximate scansion of Baksh's recitation of mārū text

– – ‿ – – – – ‿ – – ‿ ‿ – – –(‿)
velā valī vay shāh sayyadā ā-j ay ẓulam dī rāt

– – – – – ‿ – –(‿)– – ‿ – – ‿ ‿ – – –
dekh rabbā tayryān̲ be-parvā'yān̲ kambiyā 'arsh 'i lā hī dā

Vertical alignment shows metric parallelism between the two lines. The italicized words "Oh God, see" do not fall within the parallel structure and may have been appended to the original poem. Performed in Media Examples 4.4 and 4.5.

Figure 4.9. *Ḍhol* and *tāshā bol*s for Karaṛ (Media Example 4.6)

Counts:	1	2	3	4

ḍhol: || **gi**na **ta**gita **ta**gina **tā**ge **nā**gina **tā**gena ||

tāshā: || ti ki **ta** kati ki **ta** ka ti ki **ta** ka ti ki **ta** ka || (*ṭhekā*)

| trrr diridiri tā.tā. trrr diridiritā.tā. trrr diridiri | (*tihā'ī*)

Muhammad Baksh Multani recites these *bols* very quickly and briefly in Media Example 4.6. This figure shows how the basic *ḍhol* pattern and basic *tāshā* pattern align; notice the alternating alignment of the accents on the two drums. The second line of *tāshā* notation shows an example of a *tihā'ī*. The phrase "trrr diridiri" is uttered three times, with the two-stroke "ta.ta." serving as a timekeeping device and the "trrr" representing a 4 pulse trill, so that the phrase returns to the *sam* (beat one). In the audio recording Muhammad Baksh improvises, sometimes with extended rolls, sometimes with fragments of the *tihā'ī* he recited.

Chapter 4 notes

1. This list is not meant to be exhaustive. Drum patterns are frequently tied to the movements of dancers, for instance, and drum patterns are often named for dances. The relationships between dance steps and drum pattern within any given tradition might merit a study in its own right. Steps or prominent movements might be accentuated on a regular basis in a drum pattern in a manner befitting the first category, the number of stressed beats. Other ways in which drum patterns may be grounded in dance may involve ongoing cues and responses that drummers and dancers exchange in many kinds of South Asian folk and classical traditions.

2. The anthropologist David Mandelbaum recorded in his fieldnotes in the mid-1930s the participation of a local Dalit as a drummer in a Kota festival, and I was also informed of such participation in the early 1990s.

3. For information on this demon, see Claus 2003, 329.

4. The best-known melody for this *bhajan*, and the one performed for funerals in Hyderabad, Andhra Pradesh, was composed by Vishnu Digambar Paluskar. The song is widely known as a favorite of Mahatma Gandhi, possibly because it praises God using both Hindu and Muslim terms.

5. The performers were unable to execute a ninth *cāl* called "two-and-a-half" (*ḍhaī cāl*) or explain how it is organized. They named this piece and attempted to play it, however.

6. Sharma notes that *ādi tāla* and *jhampatāla* are listed in the *Saṅgītaratnākara*, but their forms are different from those that bear these names today in Karnatak music. *Simhanandana tāla* is cited as a *tāla* with a legacy dating to the thirteenth century or earlier, but it does not form part of contemporary concert practice (Sharma 2000, 204).

7. Only after the *Saṅgītanatnākara* did particular drum syllables begin to be prescribed for each *tāla* (Sharma 2000, 217–18). Even in the fourteenth century, when *ṭhekā*s were first coming to define *tāl*s, theorists of the time might not have considered the *cāl*s played by this Hyderabadi group *tāl*s.

8. *Lehrā*, mentioned earlier, is another word for this kind of melody. It wasn't entirely clear whether what these musicians referred to as the *naġmah* was the combination of the basic *tāshā* pattern with the *ḍhol* pattern or the *ḍhol* pattern alone.

9. I could not locate a dictionary definition for *ḍhaburī*. Mamraj or one of his group members wrote this word in parentheses next to the name of one of the *tāshā* players who demonstrated for me in 1999. In an interview in Delhi on August 13, 1998, Mamraj and Bharat Singh explained the three layers to me and likened this middle layer to the "*tānpūra*." I doubt that *ḍhaburī* is a corruption of *tānpūra*. As of the time of this writing I have not been able to clarify what *ḍhaburī* means; I mention it here for the reference of future scholars and employ the term in the main text for convenience.

10. In Hindustani music, *upaj* may refer broadly to improvisation and more narrowly to the systematic elaboration of a phrase (Rahaim 2011). Mamraj also mentioned that this *tāshā* part will perform *chēṛ chāṛ* and *cakkardār* (compositions; see Kippen 1988, 206).

11. He beats his hand in time with the recitation but does not take care to replicate the *ḍhol* pattern precisely.

12. Note that the fourth unit in the first phrase, "lal," is only a hypermetric "short" because it is pronounced as a contraction. If pronounced the way it is spelled in Arabic, lā 'al, it would take more time and would scan as 2 + 2.

13. The examples she gives are *cautāl* and *dhamār*. In *cautāl*, five of the twelve *mātra*s are represented by doubled syllables (in bold; *tālī* and *k̲h̲ālī* not shown):

dhā dhā / dhīn tā / **kiṭa** dhā / dhīn tā / **tiṭa kata** / **gaḍi gina**

In *dhamār*, each *mātra* is represented by a single syllable, except in two cases (in bold; *tālī* and *k̲h̲ālī* not shown) where a single syllable stands for two *mātra*s:

ka dhi ṭa dhi ṭa / **dhā -** / ga ti ṭa / ti ṭa **tā -**

14. Music scholars have maintained an abiding interest in the composition of musical areas. In 1958 Bruno Nettl defined a musical area simply as one "exhibiting a degree of homogeneity in its music." A number of ethnomusicologists attempted to track the geography of musical styles by mapping the distribution of musical features such as melodic contour, rhythms, and harmonies. In 1959, A. M. Jones published *Studies in African Music* with a map showing the distribution of African harmony. Documenting the distribution of instruments and repertoire continues to be valuable in ethnomusicological fieldwork, although it is becoming less common. Eric Charry's

remarkable and thoroughgoing study of Mande musical culture in Mali, Senegambia, and Guinea-Bissau is a recent exception.

15. In addition to superficial word borrowings, languages in these families came to share pervasive phonological features like "retroflex, cerebral, or domal consonants in contrast with dentals" and morphological ones such as "constructions in which verb stems or nonfinite verb forms are strung together in series which are closed by a finite verb form" (Emeneau 1956, 9). The evidence Emeneau amassed militated against Sapir's controversial view at the time that morphological "influences" of one language upon another have almost always been "superficial" and not "profound." Sapir regarded language as "probably the most self-contained, the most massively resistant of all social phenomena. It is easier to kill it off than to disintegrate its individual form" (Sapir 1921, 220; Emeneau 1959, 4).

Chapter 5. Muharram in Multan

The descriptions of places, people, music, and atmosphere of Muharram in this chapter are based closely on my own experiences attending events from the eighth to the tenth of Muharram in Multan (May 16 to May 18, 1997) as well as on interviews with Muhammad Baksh Multani (1997), Suraiya Multanikar (2007), and others about Muharram of Multan earlier in their lifetimes. The first of Muharram in the year when the story takes places, 1984, fell on September 26; the tenth, Ashura, fell on October 5. Although no one gave me a precise date after which the *tāshā* performances ceased in the Bheḍi Potra neighborhood, the year 1984 is plausible as one in which the last hangers-on in this dying performance tradition could have participated—and it fits Ali's chronology.

The sensual, descriptive details included here are based on my specific observations in Multan—sometimes complemented by relevant observations made elsewhere (the miscellaneous trash used in the fires, for example). The musical descriptions, other than those of the *tāshā* players, are mainly based on my documentations of specific Muharram performances in context. A few of the songs were originally sung for me by Suraiya Multanikar as illustrations of what she used to sing with others in her Lodhipura neighborhood in her childhood. The historical personages mentioned in the text are all genuine; some of those about whom I have only heard appear as living figures in the narrative. Others are described to Ali in the narratives by fictional intermediaries (see the cast of characters at the back of this book for details on real and fictional characters). In attending these kinds of massive ceremonial events throughout India and Pakistan, I've found it common for one or another man or youth to latch on to me, supply information (whether or not I ask for it), and suggest I direct my video camera this way or that. Some of the characters in this narrative are based on the general figure of the "helpful intermediary."

Ali's thoughts about asymmetrical rhythms evoking woundedness and death are meant to suggest the kinds of interpretation one might find among reflective Muslims in South Asia. A close analogue to this can be found in funeral music of the Bartan and Roshan districts in Tajikistan, where songs of the *falak* genre set to asymmetrical rhythms called *shikasta* ("broken") are accompanied by dance movements said to represent "broken" parts of the body (Azizi 2012, 371).

The comparisons Ali makes with Muharram at home in Uttar Pradesh are based on my own experiences attending Muharram observances in Lucknow and Mehmudabad in 1998, on numerous written and personal sources concerning Muharram's history in the region, and on interviews with drummers from cities and towns in eastern Uttar Pradesh.

Regarding the intermingled symbolism of Ali Akbar and Qasim and discussion of the *sej* (saige) in the Muharram processions of Chiniot, Pakistan, see G. Abbas (2007, 38).

The Sunni Islamic religious scholar and son of Shah Waliullah, Shah Abdul Aziz, lived in Delhi from 1745 to about 1824. Aziz led an influential group of reformist thinkers in Delhi from 1763 to 1824 and published an extensive if somewhat vicious and ill-informed diatribe against Shiism that was completed in about 1790. He also railed at such practices as singing or listening to singing at graves. See Wolf (2003); Rizvi (1982); Aziz (1926).

The singer Saleem Gardezi of Multan, a genuine historical figure, was indeed shunned by his family. The Ajmal whose words are occasionally used for the fictive Ajmal elsewhere in the text was Saleem's friend and introduced me to him. However, the specific events described here involving these two men are not versions of real events in their lives. I never had the opportunity to hear Saleem sing, and mention of his conventional singing here is not meant to blemish his memory. I was grateful to Saleem for introducing me to a number of musicians, including Muhammad Baksh Multani. I portrayed Saleem in this way in the text because I was moved by his sad familial predicament and his untimely death sometime early in the twenty-first century.

I met a man named Bashir Husain Mazhar in Multan during Muharram in 1997, and the quotations in the narrative are based on what he said to me and sometimes (in Urdu) to unnamed interlocutors. His profession, family details, and activities are otherwise fictional.

Regarding the issue of Zainab's humiliation, opinions vary as to whether this treatment caused her to experience humiliation; some Shī'ahs maintain that she maintained her noble and proud bearing despite being subject to this tribulation.

The identification of poems, poets, singers, and the prompter in the performance descriptions are all ethnographically accurate. Suraiya Multanikar viewed my 1997 video of Muharram and provided the details included in the text.

In "**hay** vay maiṉ **muṭh**i **hai** p**o**ra; **kah**īn na val**ā**'ī **shāh** dī **vāg**; **mo** gānī **badh**e * ṇā * hay **mā**re gha**teo** ne * **hai; qa**bare ni**mā** * ṇi de **nāl,**" *mātam* strokes fall on the boldface syllables and in between syllables where boldface asterisks appear.

The "na'rah-e haidarī" call and the "Yā 'Alī" response pattern are common at Sufi shrine gatherings and Shī'ī *majlis*es alike.

English Terms in Single Quotation Marks Translated from Urdu and Saraiki Field Transcripts

custom—rasm
traditional practice—rivāyat
remembrance—yād
music—mausiqī

Technical Notes

The scale positions in *rāg malkauns* are C E♭ **F** A♭ B **C**. The tonic is underlined and other important scale degrees of the *rāg* are indicated in boldface. Compare with *dhani*: F **A♭** B **C** **E♭** F.

Ali alludes to the *āṭāwālā* tabla of the Panjab, with wheat paste added to boost the bass of the *bāyāṉ* (the left-hand drum of the tabla pair) and no black spot; both drums in a pair of ordinary tablas have a black spot made of iron filings, lamp black, and a binding agent.

Selected Interviews and Recordings

Suraiya Multanikar, June 30 and July 2, 2007
Musicians of the Bheḍi Potra neighborhood, July 3, 2007
Qaisar Naqvi, July 1, 2007
Adam Nayyar, June 30 to July 3, 2007
Conversations with Bashir Husain Mazhar and others in Bheḍi Potra during Muharram, and audio and video recordings of the rituals and processions, May 16–18, 1997

Other Sources

Police manual for *ta'ziyah* processions in Multan, 2006 (Urdu).

Chapter 6. Shah Jamal

The descriptions of activities at Shah Jamal shrine are based on my experiences visiting there on numerous Thursday nights in 1997, twice in 1998, and once on Christmas night in 2003. Comments of informants at and around the shrine are either taken verbatim from field recordings or are reconstructed from remembered conversations. The interview with Pappu Sain is drawn largely from verbatim transcripts of our conversation at my home. The extensive list of local words Pappu and others used, included below, are glossed in the main text in English (in single quotation marks unless otherwise noted).

The Hindu celebration of Holi at the time Ali proposed to visit Lahore would have fallen on March 7, 1985. The Madho Lal Husain *'urs* that year would have been held on approximately March 30.

Many impoverished men migrated from what was in the period of the story called the Northern Areas (now Gilgit-Baltistan) of Pakistan for whatever work they could find, including work as household servants and drivers.

Ali met Pappu Sain much as I did, through the mediation of Shahbaz Bhatt.

Ali's comparisons to Lucknow are based on specific observations of mine in Lucknow (the order was reversed for me, as I spent a year in Lucknow after my year in Lahore).

When Salim adds *'Alī dā pahlā 'number'* as a popular rhyming complement to Pappu Sain's *dam-ā-dam mast qalandar*, he approximates how I interacted in the interview situation. Early in my fieldwork, a Bharāin player of the *ḍholak* (small barrel drum) recited these words to me as *bol*s for *dhamāl*.

Several times in Pappu's discussion he plays upon a classic distinction in Islamic philosophy between the external or manifest (*ẓāhir*) and the internal or hidden (*bāṭin*). The story as it continues to take shape in Chapter 8 thematizes this distinction.

Pappu's discussion of fire here should be understood in the context of his belief in the extraordinary power of music, in general, in the hands of an able performer. He is not commenting on, for example, music in relation to anything Islamic. His discourse on this topic is informed by a larger tradition of lore connected with classical music—*rāga*s more than *tāla*s—in the Indian subcontinent.

Regarding the chant *Caṛhe duldul kaṭe kāfir*, in South Asia, *Duldul* is often used interchangeably with *Zuljinah*; in this instance, the name *Duldul* is probably chosen for rhythmic reasons. According to other lore in the larger Muslim world (and also parts of India, see Hiltebeitel 1999, 343), Duldul is the name of either a mule or a horse given to 'Ali by the Prophet Muhammad.

Pappu's allusion to "the guy who plays in the upper area of Shah Jamal" referred to Gunga Sain, a deaf and dumb *ḍhol* player who later received wide acclaim as a *ḍhol* player. At the time of this writing, Pappu and Gunga are both international celebrities. Pappu's awareness, and jealousy, of Gunga's rise in popularity are reflected in his statements—originally made in 1998. Pappu may have not spoken in this manner in 1985 (the time of the story), but I believe, despite the anachronistic detail, his statements about musicianship need to be included here.

Urdu or Panjabi Terms Glossed by English Words in Single Quotation Marks (Except Where Noted)

compassion—raḥmat
proximity to God—Allah dī qurbat
voice of the *qalandar*—qalandar dī āvāz
play (*dhamāl*)—khelnā (this verb, meaning literally "to play," is not ordinarily used for musical instruments or dancing)
intoxicated—mast
shook *dhamāl*—dhamāl ḍālī hai
composition—bandish

acquired musicality or immersed themselves in sound—apne sur meṉ āte the, literally "came into their *sur*"
teacher's teacher—dād ustād
hereditary musician—mīrāṣī
gifts—nazrāṉ
grace—ṯafīl
made me pick it up—pakṛāyā
murshid enters me—murshid mērē meṉ ā jāte haiṉ
rapture—wajd
vision—naẓr
Allah's 'strength'—ṯāqat
passion—lagan
my work takes a lot of 'strength'—zor
people around me—dunyā
concordant music is the true calling—sur-sangīt hai jo voh saccā kām hai
knowledge of music—'ilm-e mūsiqī
pure/true thing—saccā kām
defilement/falsehood—jhūṭ
dhamāl shakers—dhamāl ḍālne vāle
gear their performances to the temperament of those around them—jaise kissī kī ṯabi'at hai voh aise bajāte hai
immature prayer—kacce namāzī
attached—from the verb *lagna*, to be attached
praise of God—tasbīh
impact—aṣr
dead thing—murdah
real basis—aṣal maqām
Muslim hereditary musician—kḫān sāhab
outside world—dunyā
saint—walī (lit. friend, i.e., of God)
prophet—nabī
tradition—rivāyat
spun three times—tīn cakkar lagā'e haiṉ
took up . . . *dhamāl* (not in single quotation marks in the text)—dhamāleṉ pā'ī heṉ
in mutual agreement—ek milāp hai
correctly (not in single quotation marks)—ṣaḥīḥ bolnā (to say correctly)
A person lacking *sur* is not favorably received even by Master Allah—be surā te allah mīyāṉ ko bhi nahīṉ bandeh qabūl hota hai.
[passage beginning "not every 'rhythm' can do this," marked by asterisk]:
dusrā ridhim hotā hai. tāl bajānā, us meṉ mastī meṉ, voh mastī ke sāth hī voh bhī bajātā hai. jo tāl bande meṉ jo bajegā, andar jo us ke dil meṉ bajegā nā, andar jo, jaisā, aisā bāhar nikalegā. aur jis, jitnī ridhim hai, voh nahīṉ. yeh sarkār kī rivāyat bajā'ī jātī hai. qalandar kī, jo mastī meṉ le ātī hai dam-ā-dam mast qalandar.

culture—English word *culture*
fencing—gatkā
[Faqirs] play *dhamāl*—dhamāl vajdī 'e
passionate—having *jazbah*
get excited—have *josh*
it's really a matter of connecting with the moment—vaqt bannhaṉ dī gal
ripe—baṉyā
insipid—phīkā
sweet—mīṭhā
make a connection—lagā'o
frightening—k͟haufnāk
intimidating—ḍar wāle
handle—hatth pāyā
to play [*tāl*s]—kheḍnā
to come and go [through the *tāl*s]—phirnā ṭurnā
intuition—āmad (literally, "coming")
control—English word *control*
to give birth to dispiritedness—udās paidā karnā
[it is sad when the] player delineates sad *bol*s—bajāne wālā ġamgīn bol kaṛh rahā hai
flying—parvāz
remains on land—thale
duty—English word *duty*
elder—buzurg
sectarianism—firqah vāriyat
I participate in the mourning [for Imam Pāk, Maula Husain]—ġam vaj sharīk hūnāṉ
I sit and mourn—sog meṉ baiṭhā hota hūṉ
happy drum pattern—joshī kā ḍhol
image—naqshah
rough tents—pakhivāj
[to] match; [to be equal to]—milāp honā
challenged one another—*muhn peh mār rahā hai*, literally, "hit one another's faces"
your playing attracted my soul (single quotation marks only for the self-quotation in text)—rūḥ lagāyā hai
[to] mix—ralāna
tempo—English word *tempo*
[to] lay down [a *ṭhekā*]—lagāna
moving back and forth—phir ṭur rahā āṉ
sit—baiṭhā huṉ (here, play background pattern)
talking—bāte kar rahā hūṉ
flexible—lacak
interest—lagā'o [note earlier usage of this term to mean "make a connection"]

Other Terms

yaktā'ī—literally oneness or unity; refers here to the oneness of God and perhaps to the peak experience of feeling connected to God

laggī, parṇ, gat, toṛa, qaidah—types of compositions. The uses of the terms vary from tradition to tradition. It is not clear from Pappu's explanations the extent to which he differentiates among the terms.

Selected Interviews and Recordings

Pappu Sain and Shahbaz Bhatt, Lahore, February 7, 1998

Recordings of conversations and of Pappu Sain performing at Shah Jamal, February 5, 1998 and February 12, 1998

Chapter 7. Madho Lal

The descriptions of the *'urs* of Madho Lal Husain is based on what I witnessed and videotaped on March 29, 1997, and on subsequent visits to the shrine that year, as well as December 26–27, 2003, and March 25, 2005. The geographic and neighborhood details were accurate in the late 1990s and early 2000s. The quoted statements were drawn from interviews with those named. The late Adam Nayyar accompanied me to the shrine in 2003 for a set of feedback interviews using an edited version of the video I'd made at the *'urs* in 1997. The results of this research process are further discussed in Wolf (2006). The present chapter delves more deeply into the content of those interviews and the sensorium of the shrine environment.

Some explanations by Saleem and others to Ali in this chapter are based on the phrasing of Adam Nayyar as he interpreted local Panjabi speech during our interviews. I was only able to communicate in Urdu.

Regarding *Panjābiyat*, or sense of Panjabiness, at the shrine of Shah Husain, see Hasan (2002, 115). In 1954 the secretary of the Punjab Youth League staged a demonstration at this *'urs* to make Panjabi an official state language (Rahman 2001), and this site continues to be used by Panjabi organizations to promote Panjabi exceptionalism (Rahman 1996, 201*ff.* and passim). Regarding the ambivalence of Pakistanis toward Shah Husain, see also Jalal (1995), who discusses the role of the educational system in Pakistan in excluding such figures as Shah Husain from the official canon.

The character Saghir is based on a highly respected *ḍhol* player by that name. I met him in the context of organizing his visit to the United States (which did not work out) and took the opportunity to interview him about *ḍhol* playing, music philosophy, Sufism, and his opinions of other musicians.

Terms and Phrases Glossed by English Words in Single Quotation Marks in the Main Text

straightforward (words)—sīdha sīdha lafuz

pulls—hangūra

music—English word *music*
pithy—ṭhōs
nuances—bārīkī
pure love—muḥabbat
impression—as̱r
happiness—k̲h̲ushī
coax—*manāna*; refers to one "coaxing" his or her way back into a lover's affection after having caused annoyance or other displeasure
compulsory and essential—lāzmī
to play *dhamāl*—dhamāl khelna
drama—English word *drama*
non-entities—lallu panju
in tune—sūr vic

Other Terms

matlab—meaning (used in conversation to mean, "that is . . .")

Select Interviews

Muhammad Mushtaq and others at the site of the Madho Lal Husain shrine December 26, 2003
Shehzad and *malaṅg*s at the Madho Lal Husain shrine, December 27, 2003
Saghir Ahmed (*ḍhol* player), Islamabad, December 29, 2003
Shahid and Niamat Ali, April 23, 1997.

Chapter 7 notes

1. A shrine complex may include a building enshrining the grave of the main personage being honored, perhaps another such building for a disciple (e.g., Amir Khusrau at the famous Nizamuddin Auliya shrine in Delhi), and features such as a mosque, a graveyard, living quarters, and office space.

2. Shah Husain supposedly sang his *kāfī*s, but today's renditions are not an unbroken continuation of this practice.

3. Common terms of understanding are "structures, themes, or scenarios that are in clear currency—either redundant, passed down from generation to generation, or acute, achieving relevance at particular historical moments." I continue to maintain that "[m]any subjects filter or shape their understandings through commonplaces drawn from Sufi [Shī'ī and other] poetry, stories about saints [and Imams] and *'urs*es, and spiritual interpretations of music and movement" (Wolf 2006, 246).

4. A major problem with Keil's formulation concerns the entity against which any musical gesture displays "discrepancy." In short, discrepancy from what? Mathematical precision cannot be a universal norm from which deviance is a discrepancy.

Chapter 8. The Manifest and the Hidden

This chapter is based on fieldwork I conducted in Hyderabad, Sindh, June 11–16, 1997, and the vast majority of field consultants' statements are transcribed nearly verbatim—although rearranged and shortened to maintain readability. Some of the original statements appear in the endnotes. For others, keywords are provided below in the manner of earlier chapters. Some parts of this chapter appear in a different format in "The Manifest and the Hidden: Agency and Loss in Muslim Performance Traditions of South and West Asia," chapter 6 of *Music, Culture and Identity in the Muslim World: Performance, Politics and Piety*, edited by Kamal Salhi (New York: Routledge, 2013). The attitudes I have termed "integrative" and "disjunctive" are analyzed in light of the semiotics of Charles S. Peirce in that version of the chapter, and Ali's story is, of course, absent.

Regarding Ali Shariati, his collected works, in thirty-five volumes, stressed that "the true essence of Shi'ism is revolution against all forms of oppression" (Abrahamian 2008, 144).

The assertion attributed to Faqir Nathu in the narrative regarding the *naqqārah* player's doing the real "performance" was adapted from the words of *naqqārah* player Muhammad Qasim (Qasim Shah), "Ḍhol bas us kā yahī kām hotā hai. Voh ṣirf pahlūdārī pakaṛ ke khaṛā hotā hai. Kām jo kartā hai jo 'performance' kartā hai voh ṣirf nagārevālā kartā hai. Tīyā to vaġairah vohī kartā hai. Ṯabl vaġerah vohī kartā hai" (June 14, 1997). The original quotation doesn't mention the role of the *gazī*, because it focuses only on the relative importance of the improvising *naqqārah* player in relation to the *ḍhol* player. I have taken the liberty of extending this statement to encompass the *gazī* player, who usually provides a repeating melody.

Regarding Muhammad Shafi's statement that *mātam* is just a name for a *cāl*, he also said that *mātam kī cāl* has "four or five" *ḍanka*s (beats). It is not clear what this means.

Original Terms for Those Appearing in English in Single or Double Quotation Marks in the Text

sword-*mātam*—talvār kā mātam
play fencing—ā'ī doz kheltā hai
we all share the same end—āḵẖirī 'eṇḍ' vo'i hai, yād vo'i hai
dance style—*raqṣ* style (English word style)
mourning style—*mātamī* style
classical—English word *classical*
condition—ḥāl
performance—English word *performance*
classical—English word *classical*
shakers—English word *shakers*
drum beat of religion—dīn kā ḍankā
supererogatory prayers—tavajjud

our relatives from India used to practice this—"hamare vahīn̲ Indiā se, hamāre bhā'ī band banāte the." Literally, "ours there, from India, our bound-brothers [relatives, caste-mates], used to make/build." The verb *banāte the,* "used to build/make," was somewhat ambiguous in the original context. It could have meant that his relatives played or developed the tradition of playing which Ikramuddin brought with him to Pakistan when he migrated. This would have made sense in terms of the question I originally asked, viz., "How did you learn?" However, the original interview then turned in some detail toward the manufacture of the drums themselves. So Ikramuddin might have meant "my family members used to make" the drums and only implied that they also played them.

vision—bashārat

copy/image—taṣvīr

false story (not within single quotation marks)—jhūṭī bāt nahīn̲

rush—English word *rush,* i.e., crowd

slogan (not in single quotation marks)—na 'rah bāzī

solved the problem—nikālā

under faith's authority [not ours]—sirf 'aqidat ke taḥt

words—alfāẕ

lamentation (*mātam*)—sog wālā (*mātam*); this is somewhat redundant, as *mātam* itself means "mourning or lamentation." The drummer is trying to divorce *mātam* from its everyday meaning and use it as a simple name for a pattern.

singing—gāyakī

passion—jaẕbāt

Other Terms

tabl—generic term in Sindhi meaning to strike *naqqārah*, but also meaning the introductory rapid drum rolling and, here, implies a wider range of creative embellishment.

dhun—both an intense emotional state of passion and ardour and melody or drum pattern. The meaning is determined by context.

ziyārat—here, to visit the replica of a shrine in place of a long-distance pilgrimage

bajāne-wāle—instrumentalists

Selected Interviews, Field Recordings, and Demonstrations

Hyderabad, Sindh:

Interview with Lala Gul Pathan, Peṛh Muhammad shrine, June 11, 1997

Procession at Peṛh Muhammad shrine, June 11, 1997 (audio and video)

Interview with Faqir Husain Baksh, June 12, 1997

Demonstration with Muhammad Qasim, June 13, 1997 (audio and video)

Feedback interview with Muhammad Qasim, June 14, 1997

Interviews and recordings with Muhammad Shafi, Ikramuddin, and Allaudin and their respective groups, June 14–15, 1997 (audio and video)

Figure 8.1.

a. The *kalmah* pattern as played by a *ḍhol-tāshā* group in Hyderabad, Sindh whose lead member traces his origin to Bharatpur, India. Counts are indicated by numbers in the top row. *X*s show the basic outline of stressed strokes for the *kalmah* pattern on the *ḍhol*. The third row shows how *ḍhol* strokes correspond to stressed syllables in the verbal *kalmah* (Muslim statement of faith): "There is no god but Allah and Muhammad is his Prophet" (see also Chapter 4). The final, boldfaced *X* is the return to count one and may be followed by a variable gap of time. Fig 8.1b shows the cue the lead *tāshā* player initiates after his solo to bring the group back to the *kalmah* signature pattern (Media Example 4.31 ⛟).

1				2				3				4				5				6				7				8				*1*
X				X				X		X		X				X				X				X		X		X				**X**
lā			il	lā	ha			il		lā'		lāh			mu	ḥam			ma	dur			ra	sūl		'al		lāh				

b. The cue and cadential phrase for the same *kalmah.* Numbers in the first line indicate counts. *R* stands for the emphasized stroke in a roll or some other variation of a roll; *r* stands for varieties of rolled strokes on the *tāshā*; *x* represents a discrete stroke of the *tāshā;* dots represent rests or variable strokes that occupy the same interval of time. A lead *tāshā* improvises while the other *tāshā*s maintain a basic background pattern. When the lead *tāshā* player wishes to conclude his solo, he cues the *ḍhol* players with a version of the pattern below and all return to the *kalmah.* The interval between successive sets of *kalmah* phrases is entirely dependent on the dynamics of interaction (Media Example 4.31 ⛟).

1				2				3				4				5				6				7				8			
R	r	r	r	R	r	r	r	R	r	r	r	R	r	r	r	x	.	.	x	.	.	x	.	.	x	.	.	x	.	.	.

c. Using the cue notated in fig. 8.1b, drummers may also transition to *das kī gintī* ("count of ten"), notated below. It, like the *kalmah,* is a riff rather than an ostinato. When one listens to this pattern right after the *kalmah,* it sounds as if *das kī gintī* takes the first five strikes in the *kalmah* pattern and flattens out their durational differences. This creates a rhythmic tension with the underlying count, which resolves on count five. Then the pattern continues with two sets of three closely spaced strokes that are reminiscent of those in the *kalmah* (corresponding to the syllables "il lā' lāh") and closes with a strike on count 13. Lowercase *x*s indicate unstressed *ḍhol* strokes (Media Example 4.31 ⛟). *Bīs kī gintī* ("Count of 20") is the same pattern, played faster.

1				2				3				4				5				6				7				8				9				10				11				12				13			
	X			X			X			X			X			X				x		X			X			X				x		X			X			X								X			

Chapter 8 notes

1. The provocation, ostensibly, was a pirate attack off the shores of present-day Karachi on a ship of Arab widows and children. These survivors were being sent back to Arabia with placatory gifts from the rulers of Sri Lanka, under whose watch the Arab sailors had inexplicably perished.

2. See Burki 2006, s.v. Sindh; Bose and Jalal 2004, 196. The different perspectives regarding Muharram and music adopted by the Muhājir and Sindhi groups with whom I worked in 1997 (exactly when the story takes place) need to be understood in their contemporary political climate. They are not necessarily longstanding views maintained from one generation to the next.

3. See Memon 1994, 4.

4. Ye dīn kā ḍankā chālu rakhne ke liye. . . . ye hamāra nām roshan rahe, dīn kā ḍankā bajtā rahe.

5. Ye hamāra bāp ko beshārat huī thī ke hamāra nām zinda rahā. Jab vo tahajjud paṛhte the rāt ko, rāt ko namāz ke ba'd tavajjud paṛthe the to un ko beshārat huā thā kih tum hamāre 'ashiq ho. Lihāẕā hamāra nām jārī rakhte kī shakl yeh paida karo.

6. Bas voh ek apne josh meṉ hote apne dhun ke andar hote haiṉ voh.

7. Nahīṉ, voh to bas shauqīn hote haiṉ, bajāne ke, us kā ko'ī maqṣad to hai nahīṉ, bas shauq.

8. Log ṯaraḥ ṯaraḥ ke, ko'ī mustanad ko'ī bāt nahīṉ alasī ke jis kā javāb de sakeṉ kih karbalā ke us meṉ bajāte haiṉ nahīṉ, bajāte haiṉ—jis ṯaraḥ kih ye to karbalā kī bāt to tīn sau sāl kī bāt thī.

9. Yeh tīn kaiṭīgarī hoti haiṉ. Ek yeh ḍhol vāle ek alag. Un kā apnā ek rujḥān. Ek marṡiyah vāle, ek alag. Ek mātam vāle, ek alag. Yeh ḍhol bajāne vāle un kā marṡīye se ko'ī ta'luq nahīn.

10. . . . ahl-e sunnat jamā 't haiṉ, voh shujā't ke nām se husain ko pukārte haiṉ ye ta'līm hai kih husain kī shujā 't thī. Ek us ṯaraḥ se ek "category" 'aisī hai kih maẕlūm bayān karte haiṉ husain ko, kih maẕlūm the, to voh mātam. Ek yeh kisī us meṉ nahīn āyā ḍhol bajānā.

11. . . . us kā maẕhab se to kō'ī ta'luq hī nahīṉ. Is liye ta'luq nahīṉ ke tārīq tīn sau sāl ke ba 'd likhī hu'ī. Kissi ne kuch nahīṉ dekhā ke shahādat kyūn kyūn, kis ṯarīqe se hū'ī—un kī kitāboṉ meṉ likhā kih is ṯaraḥ dūpaṭa khīnce marṡīye ḵẖvānī hū'ī. Kisī kī kitāboṉ kuch likhā jis ṯaraḥ muḵẖtalaq 'ulamā likhte rahe haiṉ. Log ta'līm kī kamī ki vajah se log. . . .

12. Hāṉ, jis kī vaja maiṉ bata'ūn āp ko, jab hindustān pākistān nahīṉ thā, jab hindustān pākistān nahīṉ thā. "Briṭish government" thī to jis ke "majority" ziyādah hotī thī, to is kā bhalā hotā thā—ye do ḥaṣūl meṉ bhī—kuch ḍhol bajāni vāloṉ meṉ ā'e, kuch us meṉ mātam karne vāloṉ meṉ ga'e. To briṭish government ko yeh dikhānā kih akṡaryat merī zyādah hai. Yā kih akṡaryat merī zyādah hai—vahān log sarmāya dār jo the, vo apne akṡaryat dikhāne ko logoṉ ko taqsīm do ḥaṣūl meṉ taqsīm karte the—kih log mere zyādah haiṉ. Log zyādah haiṉ. Jise kih ab yahāṉ pākistān meṉ ye Shī 'ah ḥaẕrāt mātam karte the. Yahān sindhī, vo samajhtā hī nahīn haiṉ kih Muharram

kyā cīz hai, lekin mātam kartā hai vo. Us ko ahl-e tashī‘ se sunnat va al-juma‘t se kō'ī vāsṯa nahīn̲ hai.

13. Ẕid kī vaja se—apnī aks̲aryat dikhāne ke liye vo ek . . . lekin ye "category" kam thī. Hindustān men̲ mātam vālon̲ kī—yahān̲ jab, "automatic" pākistān jab ā'e to yeh sindhī yahān̲ kā, sindh ke rahne vālon̲. Vo Shī'ah nahīn̲ hain̲. Voh to vaḍeron̲ ne caras pilā'ī us ko. Mātam karo, us ko nahīn̲ pata mātam kyā cīz hai. Duldule banā rahā hai, in ko us se tarbiyat milī, ek āke do se milī nā? To aks̲aryat baṛha ga'ī gyārah, aur pānch aur cheh hī gyārah honge.

14. Us men̲ hindū kā to mas'alah hī nahīn̲ ātā jab . . . agar hindū se sikhā jātā to kal kyūn ātā yahān̲? Ye, ye to hamārā maz̲habī mas'alah hai. (In the original interview, Allaudin had mentioned learning from a Hindu the day before the demonstration.)

15. Main̲ ne āp ko ye batāyā na kih ham sab se pahale kalmah pesh karte hain̲ - kalmah bajāte hain̲. Na to ham yeh sab se pahle yeh ẓāhir karte hain̲ kih ham musalmān hain̲.

16. Voh jis ṯaraḥ ke a'e, shahanshāh tīmūrlang ko 'aqīdat thi, aur vo ḥāẕirī dene ke liye har sāl jāte the . . . is ṯaraḥ ham ko 'aqīdat hai.

17. Yeh maḥsūs karte hain̲ kih ham ḥaẕrat imām ḥusain ke rauẕe ke sāmne rahe hain̲.

18. Ham magar ham nahīn̲ bajāte ye hamīn nahīn̲ ma'lūm burā samjhā jā'egā, acchā samjhā jā'egā ba har ḥāl ham nahīn̲ bajāte.

19. Voh mūsiqī kuch aur ho ga'ī nā? Main̲ ne āp ko sab se pahle 'arẕ kiyā ke sab se pahle ham kalmah bajāte hain̲. Kalmah mūsiqī ki cīz to nahīn̲ hai. Lekin 'aqīdat ke taḥt ham log voh bajāte hain̲. Us ko mūsiqī men̲, jo us ko samajhte hain̲. Jo is fan ko samajhte hain̲ to voh is cīz ko bhī samajhte hain̲. Varnah [va agar na] hamārā 'aqīdah voh hai jo main̲ ne pahle 'arẕ kiyā. Sab se pahle kalmah pesh karte hain̲.

20. Is men̲ klāsīkal bhī ātī hai. Is men̲ klāsīkal bhī ātī hai. Jo us klāsīkal ko samajhte hain̲ voh is klāsīkal bhī samajhte hēn, aur jo klāsīkal ko nahīn̲ samajhte hain̲ vo k̲h̲ālī dhūm-dhaṛkkā samajhte hain̲. Ham to ṣirf 'aqīdat samajhte hain̲. Bāqī hamāre nazdīk na ko'ī klāsīk hai, na kuch hai, ṣirf ham to 'aqīdat ke taḥt karte hain̲.

Chapter 9. The Voice in the Drum

This chapter is based both on research in Karachi in June 1997 and on research in the Nizamuddin neighborhood in 1998, 1999, 2009, and 2010. A chapter based on some of the material used in this chapter, titled "The Musical Lives of Texts: Rhythms and Communal Relationships among the Nizamis and Some of Their Neighbors in South and West Asia," will appear in *Tellings and Texts: Singing, Story-Telling and Performance in North India*, edited by Francesca Orsini and Katherine Schofield.

As in previous chapters, much of the dialogue (other than banter among the fictitious characters) derives from statements by musicians or other participants in the rituals described. I, like Ali, was aided by the Pakistan National Council of the Arts in Karachi.

In the *dastūr-e ʻamal* (Nizami 1989), which I did indeed receive from members of the Nizami *k̲h̲āndān* in Karachi, the discussion of rituals creating an "impression of happiness and sadness mixed together" is on page 3.

I originally met Mamraj via an official at the Nizamuddin shrine, and all the information he provided is musically and ethnographically sound. Mamraj's group performs from the sighting of the moon (*Cānd Rāt*) until the eleventh of Muharram, and then on the twentieth and fortieth days of the Muharram season (see Appendix B for the significance of some of these dates). Mamraj reported that his was the same schedule to which his ustad used to adhere. In addition to the musical terminology Mamraj used in the main text, he also used the terms *upji* (*upaj*, improvisation), *chēṛ chāṛ* (mischief; see glossary), *cakkardār* ("circular"—a composition containing a *tihā'ī* that is itself repeated thrice), and *tīyā* (tripartite cadence) for types of response and extemporization on the *tāshā*.

Technical Notes

The first poem is in the six-line poetic form with rhyme scheme aaaabb, called *musaddas*, most common in Urdu *marṡiyah* poetry. The *qāfiyah* of this poem is the syllable *āṉ* and the *radīf* is *hone lagī.* It scans as follows:

_ ⏑ _ _ / _ ⏑ _ _ /_ ⏑ _ _ /_ ⏑ _
ran me jis dam ṣubḥa ʻāshūrā ayāṉ hone lagī
_ ⏑ _ _ / _ ⏑ _ _ /_ ⏑ _ _ /_ ⏑ _
lashkar-e shāh-e shahīdāṉ me az̲ān hone lagī

yāṉ namāzeṉ aur kamar bandī vahāṉ hone lagī
is taraf tadbīr katl-e tishnegāṉ hone lagī
tāl o jangī kī sadāeṉ jā sunī maʻṣūm nē
tā lagī talvār bhī haidar ka kabzā cūmne

Each foot is counted with proportional units, 2 for a long syllable, 1 for a short: 2 + 1 + 2 + 2 = 7. The last syllable of each line is often lengthened in performance, as it is in this case, to fit a common musical meter—here one of seven counts.

The "thirsting ones" (*tishnegāṉ*) mentioned in this poem are both literal, because Husain's party was blocked from getting water from the Euphrates, and metaphorical, in that they were thirsty for battle, for martyrdom, and so forth.

I thank Amy Bard for her translation of this poem.

: : :

The single line from the second poem scans in the same way:

_⏑ _ _ /_ ⏑ _ _ /_ ⏑ _ _ /_ ⏑ _ (_)
āj ṣuġrā **yūṉ** madīne **meṉ** haiṉ rotī bhar ke **nain**

See Appendix A for more extended musical discussion of this in light of what Ali discovers after traveling to Delhi.

: : :

A methodological point regarding the fourth poem, "jab fāṯimah firdaus se": Originally, S. A. Nizami (of Karachi) provided the first line of this text and told me it underlay *mātam*. Then Ghulam Hasnain Nizami of Delhi provided the second line, to the same tune. But Ghulam Hasnain insisted this was a *marṣiyah* sung in *majlis*es and not the one used for *mātam*. They are combined here so that the reader has a richer sense of the poem's content. The meter, named for each individual foot, is *hazaj musamman ak̲h̲rab makfūf maḥẕūf.* (The foot called *hazaj*, for example, is _ _ ᴗ.)

English Terms in Single Quotation Marks

languid state—sust kaifiyat
feeling—(from verb) meḥsūs karna
inside—andar
faith—'aqīdah
real sensitivity to—*shauq* for
pure, mystical poetry—pākīza 'arfanah kalām (not indicated in single quotation marks in text)
unauthorized religious innovations—bida't
spiritual audition—sama'
reality or truth—haqīqat
religious—maẕhabī
impressions—ta'aṣṣurāt
happiness and sadness—k̲h̲ushī and ġam
mixed together—mile jhule
love—muḥabbat
memory—yād
heart—dil
consciousness—ẕehn
no connection—ko'ī ta'luq nahīn̲
attend to or believe in—mānte hain̲
meritorious service—sevā
keep the support going—qā'im rahta

Other Terms

log—folks, people

Select Interviews and Recordings

Hashim and other drummers from Jacob Lines, Karachi, June 2, 1997
S. A. Nizami and others from Jacob lines, Karachi, June 8, 1997
Mamraj, Bharat Singh, and others, Delhi, August 31, 1998
Mamraj and party, March 13, 1999
Ghulam Hasnain Nizami, Mamraj, and others, New Delhi, December 27–29, 2009

Chapter 9 notes

1. Aṣal men̲, us kā jo mazah ātā hai, voh julūs ke sāth ātā hai, sunne kā aur dekhne kā. Ādmī ko patah caltā hai ke kyā cīz hai.

2. Ṣirf . . . mars̱iyah, us ke andar ek lay banā'ī jātī hai.

3. Logon̲ ki bahut . . . maṯlab yeh kih, sust kaifiyat hoti hai, sunte hain̲, us ko ġor se . . . aur bahut so ke ānson̲ bhī ā jāte hain̲, rone lag jāte hain̲, dil hil jāte hain̲ (June 2, 1997).

4. Nahīn̲. Maṯlab yeh kih har Shī'ah log nahīn̲ bajāte. Jo hamāre 'alāqe ke hain̲ jaise yeh hain̲ in ke hān̲ se julūs nikaltā inḍīa men̲. To vahān̲ par ustad shaik̲h̲ bajāte the jāke. Bulāte the yeh log. To, yahān̲ par bhī, hamāre ghar ke sāmne qarīb hī hain̲. Yahān̲ par bhī yeh log bulāte hain̲, ham jāte hain̲, in ke yān̲ bhī. In kā 'aqīdah hai.

5. This conversation is pieced together from very rapid speech not clearly captured on the recording. Ellipses here are sections that can't be heard, not parts that were intentionally omitted. I have attempted to make Nasir's statements clear, inferring the subject of certain verbs and changing the word order: Yeh jo batāyā men̲ ne, yeh log 45 sāl se bajā'e rahe hain̲ vahān̲ par. Tāshā . . . 45 ho ga'e the, 45 sāl ho ga'e, vahān ek in ke bhā'ī the aur rishtedār the, voh, sharū' se yeh silsilah calā ā rahā hai . . . ham log bulāte hain̲ yeh hamāre hān̲ dillī se calā ā rahā hai. Inḍīa se calā ā rahā hai yeh silsilah kih jahān̲ muharram sharū' ho, 'azādārī aur cānd kī 29 tārīk̲h̲ apne . . . bulāyā, kih āp . . . salāmī len̲ . . . ro paṛe. Mātam kiyā . . . mars̱iyah paṛhain̲ge. Us ke ba'd ro'en̲ge, āp mars̱iyah paṛh len̲ yā phir mātam ke dinon̲ men̲, tāshā bajā'en̲ge (June 2, 1997).

6. Nasir: Yeh silsilah calā ā rahā hai. Usī silsile ko qā'im rakhā, keh yeh mas̱lan in kih jo bāp dādā the, voh calā ga'e to ab un kī aulād ne sharū' kar diyā. Jo ek k̲h̲āndanī kām thā vo caltā calā ā diyā hai. Kām bhī in ko is silsile se bulāte hain̲ jo hamāre buzurg bulāte the, usī silsile se ham bhī in ko bulāte hain̲, kih bha'ī jo rasm caltī calī ā rahī hai voh caltī rahegī. Ham apne baccon̲ ko batāte hain̲ kih bha'ī yeh kām karnā hai . . . marnā jīnā to lagā huā hai. Ham mar jā'en̲ to āp . . .

Hashim: Ham log Inḍia men̲, maṯlab ek sāth rahte the . . . donon̲, hamāra in ke ta'luqāt acche the. Bāt cīten̲ maṯlab sārā kuch thā. To yeh is cīz ko mānte the. Āte the. Hamāre julūs men̲ bhī yeh log āte the . . . ham in ke julūs men̲ cale jāte the. Isī ṯaraḥ se maṯlab yeh kih silsile yeh cālu the . . . ab yahān̲ āke jo inhon̲ ne, Karācī me kuch 'arṣe ham log sāth calen̲. Taqrīban ko'i āṭh, nau sāl, das sāl, taqrīban sāth julūs calte rahe. Us ke ba'd men̲ tabdīlī ā'ī hai ke alag alag ho ga'e. In kā julūs pahle nikālta hai, maṯlab bahut si tabdīlīyān̲ ā ga'ī hain̲. Yeh jo hain̲ . . . hamāre jo purāne hain̲, maṯlab yeh jo sāth men̲ cale āne hain̲, to abhī bhī vohī hai. Ham logon̲ ke hān̲—lekin jo kuch log aur jagah ke hain̲ voh bilkul alag hue ve hain̲ (June 2, 1997).

7. Shī'ahs call Nizami drummers to play on the twenty-ninth of Dhu al Hijjah (*Cānd Rāt* or the night before), the seventh and tenth of Muharram (Mehndi for Qasim's wedding and the martyrdom of Husain, respectively), and the twentieth of Safar (the fortieth-day mourning ceremony). Nizami drummers play for themselves all day outdoors on the ninth and tenth of Muharram and in their own homes for

thirty to sixty minutes each day from the first to the ninth. See Appendix B for more details regarding significant days of Muharram.

8. Sunne vāle bhī ziyādah hote haiṉ. To ab marṡiyah har daf'ah to nahīṉ kah sakte, na, is vajah se yeh marṡiyah ḍhol tāshe meṉ āyā, vahāṉ par, hamāre hāṉ.

9. Voh ḍhol kī cob—tāshā jo baj rahā hogā—ḍhol yeh cob jo paṛegī, jahāṉ in kā lafẓ ā'egā vahāṉ ḍhol ki cob paṛegī.

10. Marṡiyah paṛhenge to apne tāl se phisal . . . nikal jā'enge.

11. Refer to Chapter 4, pages 106–110, for an analysis of some of these patterns.

Appendix A

1. This is a cadential phrase in Hindustani music, often following a sparser, flexible rhythmic texture and providing rhythmic drive to the *sam*. Martin Clayton defines *mukhṛā* as "anacrusis" (Clayton 2001, 213 and passim).

2. This representation of language through the drums is an extreme example of what Theodore Stern (1957) called an abridgement system.

Glossary

Each headword in the following list of terms is spelled as it is first encountered in the text (more than one spelling may be employed). If the South Asian language of the headword is not specified, it is Urdu or Urdu/Hindi, although there will be cognates in other South Asian languages as well. Etymologies and other pronunciations are provided, when useful, in parentheses. Persian is usually the conduit language for Arabic terms. I have avoided cluttering the text with chains of derivations, but some of the brief etymologies are enlightening. Most of the etymologies of Urdu words are adapted from Platts 1884.

Urdu/Hindi words that have worked their way into the English language and are defined in many English dictionaries appear without diacritics or italics in the text unless they are part of a transliteration of a poem or quotation or denote a special usage (see mehndi, below). Such words include Muharram, nikah, ustad, tabla, mela, raja, nawab, ashram, mehndi, bhajan, roti, kabob, purdah, Holi, kurta, durbar (pronounced *darbār*), inshallah, pir, faqir, imam, maulvi, haveli, dhoti, and shah. (I decided against the English "shalwar kameez" for *shalwār qamīz*). When words are derived from these terms, in adjectival form, for example, they are similarly left in roman type and without diacritics, for example, nawabi, not *nawābī*. Some usages mix transliterations and English conventions. Plurals are always English plurals. The word *Sunni* appears without diacritics while the word *Shī'ah* retains diacritics (because 'ayn, signified by ', is a letter and not merely a diacritic).

For the adjective, Shīʿī is employed (instead of Shiite), but no diacritics are used for Shiism. Certain frequently used terms, such as imambarah, are presented in the text without diacritics; their variations in spelling and transliterations are provided below.

I use the form Sahab for the word sometimes written Sahib in English (Arabic, *ṣāḥib*), meaning, in the context of this book, "sir." It is usually pronounced as one long syllable: "Sāb." Similarly, the respectful form of address Janāb is written Janab here, for simplicity's sake. A number of words are pronounced with either long or short vowels, depending on the region. The specialist may notice the presence of a long initial vowel in *bhāṅgṛā* here, since that is a typical Western Panjabi pronunciation. *Bhaṅgṛā* is also correct for pronunciations elsewhere in South Asia.

Abbā jān—dear father
acchā (Hindi)—OK, yes, well . . . (used as a transition in a response)
aḍi—see *aṭi*
ʿalam (Arabic علم, "mark, sign"; "spear, flag")—a banner, pole, or insignia atop a pole, carried in Muharram processions. Generally considered a sign of Hazrat Abbas, the standard-bearer in the battle of Karbala. *See pages* 4, 67, 138, 199, 200, 222, 246, 255, 266, 267, 273
ālāp (< Sanskrit, "discourse")—rhythmically elastic, improvised exploration of a *rāga* in Hindustani music (*ālāpana* in South India)
alġozah (Persian الغوزه)—two end-blown flutes played simultaneously; common in Rajasthan and Sindh. *See page* 42
alu paratha (ālu parāṭhā)—a kind of flatbread stuffed with potatoes
anjuman (< Persian, "assembly")—social clubs for chanting *nauḥah*. *See pages* 122, 130, 255, 266
antara (< Sanskrit, "different from")—second part of a song, usually focusing on the upper tetrachord or octave. Contrast with *asthāyī*. *See pages* 26–27, 126, 128, 130, 137, 139, 141, 142, 201
Aruntiyar—a Telugu-speaking Dalit caste that, in Tamil Nadu, is associated with leather work and drumming. Also known as Cakkiliyar. (In some regions they may be Tamil-speaking.)
ʿarūz—Perso-Arabic system of quantitative meter (i.e., prescribed sequences of long and short syllables). *See pages* 18, 104, 227–228, 262
aṣal (other forms used in text: *aṣlī, aṣl, aṣīl;* < Arabic)—actual, true, original, genuine
ʿāshiq (Arabic)—lover. *See pages* 155, 209
Ashura (*ʿāshurā'*, Arabic, from the verb "to make ten")—the tenth of Muharram, commemorating the martyrdom of Imam Husain. *See pages* 88, 92, 122–143 passim, 284
asthāyī (*sthāyī,* < Sanskrit, "standing, staying")—the first part of a song, usually focusing on the lower tonic register. Contrast with *antara*. *See pages* 126, 130, 137, 138, 139, 141

aṣūl (uṣūl; Arabic اصول, "roots, foundations")—foundation or cyclical pattern; more specifically, a pattern of five or six counts performed by Panjabi *ḍhol* players. *See pages* 56–58, 61, 279–280, 325

aṭi (Tamil, "hit, beat" [pronounced *aḍi*]; Kota, *ary*)—beat; generic term for percussion pattern in several kinds of Tamil folk drumming. *See pages* 62, 63, 65, 68–74, 94, 106

āvāz (Persian)—voice, sound. *See pages* 42, 125, 205, 216, 224, 278, 284, 292

'azādār (from Arabic 'azā, infinitive noun of "to be patient")—one in mourning or performing mourning practices associated with Muharram

'azādārī (Persian)—mourning practices, especially those associated with Muharram. *See pages* 29, 124, 131, 133, 304n5

aẕān (Arabic)—call to prayer. *See pages* 156, 227–228, 302

baccā (Persian)—boy

baddhā (Panjabi and Urdu from Sanskrit, *baddha,* "bound, tied, fixed")—a devotee bound to a religious figure. *See pages* 124, 139–140, 180

bam (Persian, "bass in music")—bass drum of a *naqqārah* pair. *See pages* 135, 200

band (Persian)—stanza

bandish (Persian, "construction, composition")—instrumental or vocal composition in North India and Pakistan. *See pages* 154, 161, 292

baṛā—large, grand, long. *See pages* (for musical references only) 67, 87, 88, 89, 125, 286

baṛā k̲h̲ayāl—"grand k̲h̲ayāl," a genre of Hindustani classical vocal music. A performance in this genre begins slowly and speeds up, proceeding for about 45 minutes or longer. *See page* 67

barādarī (Persian)—brotherhood, community. *See page* 39

barāt—wedding procession

bas—enough, that's all

bashārat (< Arabic)—vision, divine inspiration, happy news

bastah (Persian بسته, "parcel, bundle of papers")—a collection of poetry

bastī—inhabited place, neighborhood

bāyān̲—"left"; bass drum of the tabla pair. *See pages* 218, 291

bāzu—(Persian بازو, "arm, companion, one who accompanies in a song")—vocal drones supporting a tuneful reciter of *soz*, *salām*, and *mars̱iyah*. *See pages* 26, 120–122

beat (English)—In some cases beats are like counts. In European terms, a $\frac{4}{4}$ measure consists of four beats, counted as quarter notes. In South Asian music, local terms for "beat," like *tālī* or *aṭi*, make the Western musicological usage of the term *beat* ambiguous. Beats in South Asian music may refer to a kind of hypermeter. For example, in *tīntāl* the "beats" or *tālī*s fall on counts 1, 5, and 13 in a slow cycle of 16 *mātra*s or they fall on counts 1, 2, and 4 in a fast cycle of 4 *mātra*s. When the difference between beat and count is important, I emphasize it in the text. *See* main index

beṛā (Hindi, from Sanskrit बेडा, *beṛā,* "boat")—ship, raft. Float used during Muharram, metaphorically providing a conveyance for the oppressed over a sea of troubles. *See page* 116 bhāṇḍ (Hindi, "jester, bufoon, actor")—One of several names for a community of mimicks, buffoons, singers, dancers, storytellers and actors; would in earlier times (in the lifetime of Ali) participate in Muharram processions in Lucknow. *See pages* 35, 38, 116

bhāṅgṛā (*bhaṅgṛā*)—A collection of four- or eight-count drum patterns, one basic version of which is | **dhā** . ga **nā** . ga **nā** . ga **dhī** . ga | (four counts indicated in boldface). Also a set of related dance moves. The drum pattern is strongly associated with weddings in the Panjab but is also associated more generally with Panjabi music. The international remix music by this name grew out of these folk drum patterns and dances. *See pages* 29–31, 58, 63, 98, 111, 154, 159, 163, 176, 184, 240

Bharain (Bharāin)—a low-ranking class of musicians, especially drummers (see Chapter 2). Also known as *Bharāin Sheik͟h*. *See pages* 29–38 passim, 41, 43, 58, 278n1, 292, 322

bharā, bharī (< Sanskrit *bhara*, "carrying")—filled. Sections of a *tāla* that are not structurally "empty" (*k͟hālī*). *See pages* 20, 58, 163, 259

bismillah (Arabic بسم الله *bi'smi'llāh*, "in the name of God")—phrase uttered at the beginning of important activities; in some contexts a metaphor for sacrifice

bol (Hindi, "word")—syllable used to represent drum strokes or to create stroke-melodies verbally. Also used occasionally to refer to a drum pattern. *See pages* 16, 20–22, 39, 57, 85–91, 95–98, 107–112, 157, 160–164, 240–241, 283, 284, 286–287, 292

bunyād (Persian)—foundation. In music, a pattern serving as the basis for something more complex, possibly played by a second performer. *See page* 87

buzurg (Persian)—great. Term in North India and Pakistan sometimes used to refer to elders and saintly figures.

cācā—uncle. Term of respect for older male.

cādar (Persian)—a large sheet of cloth, sometimes embroidered; commonly an offering at the grave of a personage at a *dargah*. Also a strip of cloth covering a woman's head. *See pages* 59, 170, 237

cakkar (< Sanskrit *cakra*)—circle. Used here in the context of a *tāla* cycle; to make a "round" means to go through a *tāla* cycle once.

Cakkiliyar—Caste name. See *Aruntiyar. See pages* 34, 68, 71, 93, 94

cāl (Hindi, from *calnā*, "to move, flow)"—gait; percussion pattern; timbral and accentual qualities of a percussion pattern; the change from one dance movement or drum pattern to another. *See pages* 65–66, 74, 99–100, 102, 111–112, 208, 212, 217–219, 281n3, 282n23, 288n7, 297

cañcar (Hindi, cañcal चंचल, "unsteady, fickle, playful")—name of an up-tempo *tāl* with seven *mātra*s. *See pages* 88, 89

cappal—sandal (footwear)

caugun (*cau* [4] + *gun* < Sanskrit *guṇ*, "times")—quadrupling the base speed of a drum pattern

cauk (Hindi चौक, many meanings stemming from "an aggregate of four")—a major traffic intersection caukī (Hindi चौकी, many meanings stemming from "an aggregate of four")—a group of musicians

chand (< Sanskrit *chandas*)—poetic meter; accentual and timbral qualities that lend a rhythmic pattern its uniqueness (and several other, not necessarily compatible, meanings). *See page* 112

cānd rāt—moon night. The eve of the first of Muharram, determined by the sighting of the new moon. *See page* 115

chēṛ chāṛ—mischief; in a musical context, making (rhythmic) variations, often in a spirit of competition to throw off another musician. *See pages* 87, 163, 240, 288n10, 302

choṭā—small, short (in length). *See pages* (for musical references only): 87–88, 125, 286

ciṃta (Panjabi)—long steel tongs played by musicians and blacksmiths. *See pages* 34, 179, 181, 183

cirāġdān (Panjabi from Persian *cirāġ*, "lamp, light"; *cirāġān,* "display of lamps")—fire pit. *See pages* 171, 172, 173, 178

cīz—thing; composition

cob—sturdy stick used to play the *ḍhol*

count (English)—refers here to homogeneous durations, such as *mātra*s, that are counted in reckoning a *tāl*. Some people would call these beats. See *beat.*

dādra—tāl of six counts. *See page* 31

daf (Arabic *daff*)—a frame drum. *See pages* 40, 63, 98

dāk (Kota, from *dākl*, "type"; or Tamil *tākku-,* "to beat")—generic Kota term for drum pattern. *See pages* 63, 65, 68, 94

Dalit (Marathi, "broken or reduced to pieces" [Molesworth s.v. dalita])—term in current use in English and across Indian languages to refer to scheduled castes (also known as Harijans or untouchables). *See pages* 14, 34, 36, 65, 67, 68, 93–98, 105, 106, 287n2

ḍaṇḍ (Sindhi [Mewaram s.v. *ḍhaṇḍh*])—Sindhi genre of instrumental music for mourning. *See pages* 198–200, 204–205

ḍankā (Hindi, "drum stick, kettledrum")—beat or stroke (on the drum). *See pages* 63, 65, 208, 297, 300n4

dargah (Persian *dargāh,* "portal")—Sufi shrine

darśan (Sanskrit *darśan*)—critical action of seeing and being seen by a divinity in the process of Hindu worship; also, the act of seeing an important living figure. Also used by Muslims in some parts of India and Pakistan in the compound *dīdār-darśan,* meaning "to see somebody." *See page* 33

darvesh (Persian)—dervish, *malaṅg*. *See page* 176

deśī (Sanskrit)—Of the country, provincial. Term used in a variety of ways. In the history of Indian music theory, *deśī* referred to the diverse practices of the locals as opposed to the codified "way" (*mārga*) associated with status and learning. *Deśī* can be roughly translated as "folk" when it appears in Ali's story, in that many musicians contrast *deśī* with "classical." *See pages* 85, 101, 112 ḍhaburi (?< Hindi *dhab*, "sound of a drum" or *ḍhab*, "style, manner")—term possibly referring to the steady, recurring *tāshā* part in a *ḍhol-tāshā* performance. At least one person holds this part while another player improvises. This is equivalent to the "fuller" in Indo-Trinidadian practice. Information about this term is ambiguous in my notes from Mamraj and his group in Delhi as of this writing. The meaning and possible etymologies I provide are speculative. *See pages* 102–103, 106, 108, 111, 112, 288n9

dhamāl (Hindi *dhammāl,* "jumping into or running through fire" [Platts s.v. dhamāl])—name of a set of related eight-count drum patterns, normally performed at Sufi shrines. Also the name of the dances performed to these patterns. See Chapters 6 and 7 for extended discussion. *See pages* 18, 58–59, 63, 86, 133, 149–154, 157–164, 178–182, 187, 206, 283, 284, 292

dhamālī—someone who dances *dhamāl. See pages* 59, 133, 149–153, 178–182, 187

dhamār—a fourteen-beat tāl. *See pages* 58, 204, 288n13

dhīmā (Hindi, "slow")—pattern played by Mamraj *tāshā* group for Muharram in Delhi

ḍhol-tāshā—an ensemble consisting of cylindrical (or occasionally barrel) drums called *ḍhol*s and shallow bowl-shaped drums called *tāshās*. This combination of drums is widely used for Muharram observances and weddings in South Asia, Trinidad, and elsewhere. *See pages* 4–5, 7, 277n9

ḍhol (tol, dol, dohol; Sanskrit *ḍhola*)—double-headed barrel or cylindrical drum found widely in South and West Asia. *See pages* 18–19, 21, 29–32, 40, 66, 71, 85, 87

ḍholak—small barrel drum. *See pages* 16, 28, 34, 35, 292

ḍholī—ḍhol player. *See pages* 41, 128, 132, 136, 181, 182

dhoti—waistcloth or cloth tied between the legs in the manner of pajamas

dhun (Hindi धुन < Sanskrit *dhvan*, "to sound"; or Sanskrit *dhū*, "shaking, agitating")—passion, ardour, tune. *See pages* 8, 64, 80, 204, 209, 298, 300n6

dīdār (Persian)—spiritually beneficial viewing (c.f. *darśan*), e.g., when Ismaili Muslims see their spiritual leader, the Aga Khan. *See page* 155

dīndār—"person of the faith." One of several term for Muslims whose families converted to Islam (from Hinduism) in recent generations. *See pages* 25, 41

dogun (do [2] + gun < Sanskrit *guṇ,* "times")—doubling the base speed of a drum pattern

ḍoli (< Sanskrit *dolikā*, "litter")—palanquin. *See pages* 87, 90, 285

doṛhā (cf. Hindi *doha* possibly from *drohāṭ,* Hindi poetic couplet form)—Saraiki genre of poetic recitation with elastic rhythm. One type is sad and associated with Muharram; the other type is a love song. *See pages* 127, 135, **141–142**, 143

du'ā (Arabic)—prayer. *See page* 126

du'ā-e-k̲h̲air—Prayer for the welfare of someone. Muslim ritual drummers in Multan used to recite this for Hindu and Muslim patrons alike. *See page* 90

dugga (possibly related to Telugu డుగ, *duga*, "double")—a narrow cylinder drum found in Andhra Pradesh and perhaps elsewhere. *See pages* 95–98, 319

dupaṭṭā (Hindi, "double-width")—long, fine scarf used to cover a women's chest and sometimes her head. Completes a matching set with a woman's *shalwār qamīz.*

faqir (*faqīr* < Arabic, "poor")—religious mendicant. *See pages* 41, 149, 154, 157, 159, 160, 161, 166–176 passim, 179–187 passim, 294

fan (< Arabic *fann*, from the verb "to adorn")—art, craft, skill. *See pages* 46, 215

Fiqah-e Jafriya (< Arabic, *fiqh,* "knowledge, understanding")—term for *Shī'ah*s, those who follow the jurisprudence of the sixth imām, Imām Jafar. *See pages* 196, 203, 207

gali (Hindi)—narrow lane, often in the historical part of a South Asian city

ġam (Persian)—sadness, grief, mourning

ġarāra—a type of Muslim women's garment consisting of a tunic, scarf, and wide-legged pants.

ġazal (< Arabic verb غزل, "to talk in an amatory and enticing manner")—poetic form in *'arūz* (classical Perso-Arabic poetic meter) with the rhyme scheme aa ba ca, etc. Rhymes use *qāfiyah* and (optionally) *radīf.* Mystic love themes. *See pages* 28, 135

gazī (Sindhi)—a Sindhi double-reed instrument, shorter in length than the *sharnā'ī,* that is used exclusively during Muharram. *See pages* 194, 196, 198, 200–206 passim, 272, 297

gharāna (Hindi, "household, lineage")—a sociomusical term for musicians who learned from masters in a musical lineage. Usually implies a shared musical style. *See pages* 36, 82

ghuṅgrū—small bell or set of bells on wrists or ankles. *See pages* 149, 154

gintī (Hindi, "enumeration, counting, reckoning")—term used in *tāl* names such as *das kī gintī*, "count of ten." In Kathak *gintī* refers to the practice of verbally counting beats (as opposed to reciting *bol*s) as part of the performance. *See pages* 63, 65, 215–217, 299

gol (Sanskrit *gola*, "anything round")—ball. The actions of two drummers taking turns improvising against one another's background patterns and coming together on the first count of the *tāl*, the *sam*, together.

hadis̱ (Arabic *hadith,* "narration")—source for authority in Islam based on bodies of sayings and actions attributed to the Prophet Muhammad. *See pages* 29, 184

ḥāl (Arabic, "state or condition")—mental state or disposition; elevated state of consciousness as a result of performing a discipline such as *z̤ikr*, dancing, listening to music, or (other forms of) prayer. *See pages* 16, 17, 151, 179

Hanafi—one of the four schools of Islamic jurisprudence. Also an adjective for a follower of this school. *See page* 194

havelī (Persian *ḥawelī*)—in South Asia, a large house, usually with courtyard and compound wall, originally sheltering an extended family. A villa. *See pages* 4, 81

ḥāz̤rī (Arabic *ḥāz̤irī*, "presence")—offering (said of music in this case). *See page* 216

Hindustānī music—the classical music of North India and Pakistan. *See pages* 15, 16, 38, 67

ḥisāb (Arabic)—counting, accounting. *See page* 229

Holi (< Sanskrit *holākā,* poss. from "cry or shout in singing")—Hindu celebration that involves building a large bonfire, sprinkling colored powder on one another, and creating mischief. It commemorates the escape of Lord Vishnu's devotee, Prahlad, from the fire of the demoness Holika.

hypermeter—as used in this work, a meter abstracted from a sequence of accented syllables or drum strokes and the durations separating them. It is abstracted in the sense that durations are telescoped into the ideal-typical categories short, long, and prolonged. The meter is *hyper* in the sense that the performance of accents may not correspond to the onset of feet in a poetic meter or to long syllables; and it may not replicate the alternation of strong and weak beats of meter in conventional Western terms. Hypermeter is used to explain how durations between drum strokes could relate to formal duration patterns in prosody. *See pages* 104, 110, 249, 260, 288n12, 309

iktāla—twelve-beat tāl played by Panjabi *ḍhol* players (comparable to ek tāl in Hindustani classical music). *See pages* 58, 67, 215, 219, 276n6, 281n2

imambarah (imāmbārah, imāmbāṛa, imāmbargah; Urdu امامباڑہ)—shrine commemorating Husain and other Karbala martyrs where *ta'ziyah*s, *'alam*s, and other ritual artifacts are kept. *See page* 4

'ishq (Arabic)—love. *See page* 182

jalad (*jaldī,* < Arabic *jald*)—fast

jān—dear (added to forms of address)

janab (*janāb,* Arabic)—respectful way of addressing or referring to a man

jaẕbah, jaẕbāt (Arabic)—passion, fury, violent desire. *See pages* 159, 218, 294, 298

jhānjh (< Sanskrit *jhaṇajhanā*, onomatopoeia for the sound of cymbals)—cymbals. *See pages* 208, 255, 63:VB

jhaptāl (< Sanskrit *jhampa,* "a jump")—a *tāl* of ten *mātra*s. *See page* 31

jhol (Panjabi, "a wrinkle in clothing")—lilt or swing of a drum pattern that renders it distinct. *See pages* 56, 57, 61, 66, 74, 112

Jhūle Lāl—literally, "beloved (or ruby) of the cradle." As used in the Panjab, refers to one of a number of saints associated redness in Sindh.

jhūmar (Panjabi, Hindi, "a gathering, a troupe")—name of a Panjabi dance and the accompanying drum pattern. *See pages* 29–31

jī—suffix indicating respect to the addressee

josh (Persian *jūsh*, "boiling, agitation, enthusiasm")—passion, frenzy. *See pages* 158, 159, 160, 209, 294, 300n6

julūs (Urdu from Arabic, "accession to the throne, pomp")—procession. *See pages* 124, 226, 255, 304n1, 304n4, 304n6. *See also* processions

ka'bah—One of the most holy Islamic sites and the destination of pilgrims on the *hajj*. A cubic structure located in the Masjid al-Haram in Mecca. *See pages* 116, 171, 172

kāfī—Genre of Sufi poetry sung in Sindhi, Saraiki, and Panjabi. Some say it derives from the word *kāfī*, meaning "sufficient"; the idea is that the brief texts of these compositions are packed with meaning. *See pages* 61, 135, 166–168, 184–186 passim, 296n2

kāfir (Arabic)—infidel. *See page* 226

kaifiyat (Persian)—condition, state of mind

kalmah (Arabic)—word, specifically the Muslim declaration in Arabic that there exists only one God and that Muhammad is the Prophet of God. Also refers to an item in *ḍhol-tāshā* repertoire associated with the same Arabic text and emphasing the bold syllables: lā il-lāha illa'l-lāh muḥammadur rasūl 'allāh. *See pages* 47, 48, 50, 103–105, 111, 171, 215–219, 223, 231–233, 241, 245, 247–248, 299, 301n15, 301n19

kanjar, kanjarī (Hindi)—courtesan. *See pages* 156, 158, 182

Karnatak music (Karnāṭak or Carnatic music)—the classical music of South India. *See pages* 12–14, 67, 281n5

kaṭh—nine-*mātra tāl* played by Panjabi *ḍhol* players. *See page* 58

kehervā (*kervā, kairvā*)—Hindustani classical *tāl* with many variations, also present in a variety of folk traditions. *See pages* 63, 110, 111, 215, 217, 219

kevṛa—essence made from the male inflorescence of *Pandanus fascicularis;* a characteristic flavor of Avadhi cuisine

k̲h̲air (Arabic)—an expression appearing at the beginning of a sentence, or after a pause, meaning roughly "well . . ."

k̲h̲ālā—aunt (also a polite way of addressing older female)

k̲h̲ālī (Arabic)—"empty." The section of a *tāl* in Hindustani music and related genres indicated by a wave of the hand (or marking the beat with the back of the hand). *See pages* 21, 58, 66, 163, 219, 259, 260

Khan Sahab (K̲h̲ān Sāhab)—Respectful way of referring to a Muslim, especially a hereditary musician. One of a number of terms low-status drummers whose families converted to Islam in recent generations have adopted for themselves when asked their *qaum* or *barādarī. See pages* 59, 210, 293

k̲h̲āndān (Persian)—family, lineage. *See page* 36

k̲h̲ayāl (< Arabic, "to think, fancy")—genre of Hindustani classical music. *See pages* 15, 20, 67, 119, 136

k̲h̲ushī (Persian)—happiness

k̲h̲wān (Persian)—tuneful reciter of a genre such as *soz* (e.g., *soz k̲h̲wān*)

klāsikal (English)—classical, as pronounced in Urdu, Panjabi, and other languages. *See page* 85

koḷ (< Tamil *kul̲al*, any tube-shaped thing)—Kota double-reed instrument with conical bore

kriti (< Sanskrit *kriyā*, "doing, performing")—song genre, usually with three sections, that comprises the bulk of South Indian classical compositions. *See page* 281n5

kūṇḍi (Panjabi, possibly from Persian *kundah*, "arm of a paper kite" [Steingass s.v. كنده])—curved stick for playing bass strokes on the *ḍhol* in the Panjab. *See page* 56, 148

lācā (Panjabi)—Panjabi men's waistcloth

lahja (*lehja,* Arabic, "tongue")—(speech) accent

lahrā—see *lehrā*

langṛā (Persian لنگ, "lame")—lame. Refers to asymmetrical rhythmic patterns such as 3 + 4. *See pages* 107, 240 lay (lai; laya; pl. in Panjabi, layvān; < Sanskrit *laya,* "to stick or cling to")—used variously to refer to aspects of rhythm, including sense of rhythm, tempo, and particular rhythmic patterns. *See pages* 103, 304n2

lay biṭhāna—To make the *lay* sit. A systematic process for cutting the speed of a *tāl,* changing the *bol*s of the *ṭhekā* but leaving the overall structure of the *tāl* intact. *See pages* 86, 284

lehrā (lahrā, Hindi)—Generally in North India and Pakistan, a repeating melody or percussion pattern that outlines a metric cycle and often serves as the steady background for dance or drum improvisation. More specifically, it is a version of *bhāṅgṛā* in the *ḍhol* playing of Panjab; the second half of the pattern employs a variation on the bass side of the drum. Schreffler (2002, 140–41) identifies this pattern in East Panjab as Lahirīā. *See pages* 9, 30, 62, 67, 86, 288n8

lolī (cognate with Urdu *lorī*)—lullaby, the concluding item in a sequence of Muharram *vajat*s (drum patterns) in Sindh. *See pages* 205, 206

luḍḍī (Panjabi)—a type of Panjabi dance and *ḍhol* pattern. *See page* 31

mac (Panjabi)—fire, bonfire. *See pages* 172, 174, 176, 184

maqṣad (Arabic)—aim, intention

majlis (Arabic مجلس, a noun of place from the verb "to sit")—Assembly. Short everywhere in this book for *majlis-e-'azā,* mourning assembly associated with Muharram and Karbala (the term can be used in Urdu and Persian for many kinds of gathering, the type being clear from context). These are held frequently during Muharram season and occasionally throughout the year. The mourning assembly features poetic recitation and often a sermon. *See pages* 15, 26–29, 53–54, 91, 118–122, 179, 196, 229, 277

majẕūb (< Arabic "to draw, pull")—drawn, attracted; lost in the love of God. *See pages* 176, 187

malaṅg (f. malaṅgnī) (< Persian, poss. prohibitive of *langidan*, "do not limp")—Sufi mendicant. *See pages* 18, 26, 41, 59, 76, 140, 149, 151, 153, 166–176 passim, 179–187 passim, 271, 296

mālik (Arabic)—master, proprietor, respectful form of reference to a Sufi saint

mannat (Hindi, "vow, intention")—vow. *See pages* 1, 173, 179

mār (Hindi, "beating, thrashing")—Beat. Generic term for drum pattern among some *Dalit* groups in and around Hyderabad, Andhra Pradesh, made more specific by preceding with a number, e.g., *do* mār, "two-beat." *See pages* 65, 95–98

mārga (Sanskrit, "road, path, way")—Path or way; way in a moral sense. The codified theoretical "way" described in early Indian theoretical treatises and contrasted with *deśī.*

marṡiyah (Sindhi *marṡiyo*; Persian مرثیه, "elegy, lament for the dead")—Generic term in South Asia for an elegiac or heroic poetic narrative on the Karbala theme. Recited at *majlis*es with or without melody. The classical Urdu form consists of six-line stanzas with the rhyme scheme aaaabb. *See pages* 27, 88, 120–122, 134–135, 162, 196, 203, 204, 211, 217, 224, 227–233 passim, 236, 238, 241, 245, 247–249, 265–267, 274, 300, 302, 304n2, 304n5, 305n8, 305n10 marsiyah-go—reciter of *marsiyah*. *See pages* 82, 122, 142, 211, 228, 255

mārū (Hindi, "striking, warlike, fatal"; Saraiki *māṛū*)—name of a drum pattern played during Muharram in Multan. *See pages* 52, 63, 83, 84, 88–90, 123–125, 128, 135, 136, 161, 185, 201, 285–287

māshā'llah (Arabic, "what God wills")—Well done!

mastī (Persian)—intoxication (drunkenness from alcohol or drugs, also can be a spiritual "high"). *See pages* 17–18, 151, 155, 156, 158, 159, 176, 180, 183, 293

mātam (Persian ماتم "grief"; from the Arabic term for misfortune)—metric striking of the hands on the chest while chanting *nauḥah* in a *majlis* or Muharram procession. Connotes the suffering of the Karbala martyrs. Term includes other forms of self-mortification, with or without chanting. Select entries: *See pages* 52, 142, 158, 161–162, 196–198, 201, 208–248 passim

mātamdār—one who performs *mātam*. *See page* 140

mātamī—pertaining to mourning or *mātam* (e.g., *mātamī ḍhol*, drum pattern on the *ḍhol* for a funeral). *See pages* 161, 162, 198, 297

mātra (Hindi [mātre is the oblique form] < Sanskrit)—a count in a *tāla* cycle. *See pages* 34, 56–58, 65, 85–114 passim, 136, 151, 159, 205–206, 217, 229, 249, 260, 280, 283–288 passim, 309

maula (Arabic)—Lord. Used as a respectful term of reference for saints, imams, and other personages.

Maulā'ī (Sindhi < Arabic)—religious designation used in Sindh; equivalent to Shī'ī. *See page* 203

maulvi (Arabic)—Muslim cleric. *See pages* 2, 172, 173, 176, 271

mazār (< Arabic *zār*, "to visit")—Sufi shrine. *See pages* 58, 166, 172, 197

mazhabī (< Arabic, "to pass along")—religious

mehndi (*mehndī,* common pronunciation of Hindi मेंहदी *menhdī,* the henna plant)—Henna, especially in reference to the South Asian wedding ritual of decorating the bride's hands. During Muharram in South Asia, sometimes a reference in the context of Qasim's weddding. Small floats also called *mehndī*s are among the *ziyārat*s (floats) carried on procession in parts of India and Pakistan. Because *mehndi* has been adopted into the English language, I use the transliteration *mehndī* only in reference to the float. *See pages* 27–28, 29, 35, 39, 116, 122, 130, 139, 185, 208, 241, 245, 246, 266

mēḷam, moḷam (Tamil < Sanskrit *mela,* "meeting, union")—ensemble of double reeds and drums or drums alone. *See pages* 63, 64, 66, 68–74, 79, 278, 282n13, 282n14

mīrāsī (f. mīrāsan)—hereditary musician. *See pages* 34, 37–39, 41–42, 85, 91, 154, 163, 270

mridangam (Tamil < Sanskrit मृदङ्ग, mṛidaṅga)—double-headed barrel drum used in South Indian classical music. *See page* 20

muġala'i ("of the Mughals")—a seven-beat *tāl*. *See pages* 31, 57, 58

muḥabbat (Arabic)—love. *See pages* 296, 303

muhājir (Arabic)—migrant, in this work, Muslims who migrated to Pakistan at the time of the partition of India in 1947. *See pages* 25, 41, 46, 47, 65, 90, 98–102, 120, 134, 193–194, 207, 219, 223–234, 300n2 muḥalla (Arabic)—neighborhood

Muḥarram—the first month of the Hijri (Muslim) calendar and the name of the commemoration of the events at Karbala in 680 CE. In the history of South Asia, this has traditionally involved a large-scale public procession often including Sunnis and Hindus as well as Shī'ahs. Some Sufi orders that are nominally Sunni celebrate Muharram as an *'urs*. *See pages* 1, 4, 67

mukhṛā (poss. < Sanskrit *mukhara*, "resonant, sounding, expressive")—rhythmic or melodic cadence that drives toward the *sam,* or first count of the *tāl*. *See pages* 154, 160–163, 260, 305n1

murshad (*murshid,* Arabic, from "to cause to take a right way or course")—preceptor, guide, or director of a religious order. *See pages* 91, 137, 155, 156, 167, 293

musaddas (Arabic, "made into six")—Technical term in poetry and music referring to six of some entity. Musaddas form, the most important form for classical Urdu *marṡiyah* poetry, consists of six lines with the rhyme scheme aaaabb. *See page* 121

mūsiqī (*mausiqī;* from Greek μουσικὴ, "music," via Arabic and Persian)—music, especially with musical instruments. *See pages* 15, 125, 198, 199, 202, 204, 219, 293, 301n19

nā-dhin-dhin-nā—name of a Panjābi *ḍhol tāl* in Pakistan consisting of eight counts. *See pages* 58, 111, 160, 240

nāgasvaram (*nākacuram, nātacuram, nāyaṉam,* Tamil)—name of a long double-reed instrument in South India used in classical and various folk musics. *See pages* 14, 32, 33, 68, 70, 71

naġmah (Urdu and Persian, from Arabic نغم, "to read or sing in a low voice")—melody, signature tune, percussion pattern. *See pages* 16, 80, 102, 163, 240, 241, 288n8

namāz—Muslim prayer

naqqārah (naqārah, nagāṛa, nagāra; Persian نقاره)—kettledrum, often a pair consisting of bass and treble. *See pages* 21, 29–30, 38, 85–87, 90

naqqārcī—player of *naqqārah*

naql (< Arabic, "to transport")—transmit, copy. *See pages* 31, 35, 187, 302

na'rah (Arabic, "to burst out with a gushing noise")—slogan. *See pages* 50, 211, 232, 298

na'rah-e haidarī—The slogan of Ali. A call to shout the name of Ali. Common in *majlis*es and other Shī'ī contexts as well as at some Sufi shrines. *See pages* 140, 290

nātacuram—see *nāgasvaram*

naubat (< Arabic, "to supply the place of [another]")—see *naqqārah*. Also "time" or "turn"; the kettledrums are played to announce events and times of day. *See pages* 156, 158, 282n23

naubat k̲h̲ānah—House of drums. A tower where *naqqārah* and *shahnā'ī* players sit and broadcast their music at key times. *See pages* 3, 5

nauḥah (Persian نوحه, from the Arabic verb "to lament")—passionate dirge in couplet form chanted while standing or walking in procession, often accompanied by metric strikes of the hand on the chest (*mātam*). *See pages* 27, 35, 82, 116, 122, 128–142 passim, 162, 196, 153, 255, 265, 266, 277

navāz (Persian)—performer on an instrument, e.g., sarangī navāz, "sarangi player"
niyāz (Persian, "request, supplication")—offering
nūr (Arabic)—light, especially the quasi-divine light transmitted via Muhammad to his descendents. *See page* 172
pāgal (Hindi)—crazy
pagaṛī (Hindi)—Turban, mark of distinction. A turban can be bestowed upon a person as a form of honor. The *tāshā* player Mamraj said that he holds the first *pagaṛī* at the Nizamuddin Shrine for his role in leading Muharram processions from there.
pahlavān (Persian پهلوان, "champion, wrestler")—a term often used in South Asia for a master instrumentalist or vocalist. *See page* 58
pahlūdārī (Persian)—Acting from the sidelines, supporting. In music, maintaining a basic pattern while another musician performs variations. *See pages* 198, 297
pāk (Persian; Sanskrit *pāvaka*)—pure
pakhāwaj—double-sided barrel drum associated with *dhrupad* and other genres of Hindustani music. *See pages* 20, 31
panāh (Persian)—refuge
pangūṛa (Saraiki)—float representing Husain's son Ali Asghar, who was killed by an arrow to the neck. *See page* 116
panj tāl dī savārī (panj tār dī savārī)—a fifteen-beat compound tāl consisting of five parts. See *savārī. See pages* 48, 85, 86, 283, 285
Panjabiyat—sense of being Panjabi. *See pages* 170, 171, 186, 295
panjatan (Panjatan Pāk)—five, specifically the five "pure" (*pāk*) ones, Muhammad, Fatimah, Ali, Hasan, and Husain. *See pages* 1, 4, 29
parṇ (Hindi)—genre of improvisation and composition in Hindustani music that *ḍhol* players in Panjab, Pakistan, employ in their demonstrations of knowledge and skill. *See pages* 58, 163, 295
peṛh (Sindhi)—Imambarah in Sindh. *See pages* 193–205 passim, 272, 298
perahan (*pairāhan, pīrāhan*, Persian, "robe")—long, loose robe or tunic
pir (pīr, Persian, "old")—Muslim spiritual guide, saint, deity, the last in limited cases. For example, in the Telangana region of Andhra Pradesh, members of some scheduled castes use *pīr* to refer to Hasan and Husain, whom they worship as deities during Muharram. *See pages* 60, 91, 92, 154–156, 164, 168, 170, 178–179, 182, 237
pirzadah (*pīrzādah;* Persian, "offspring of *pīr*")—functionaries at a Sufi shrine who belong to one of the authorized lineages associated with the saint
Pōta Rāju—Protector deity found in Tamil Nadu and Andhra Pradesh (see Hiltebeitel 1989). Dancers in Andhra Pradesh wear costumes and makeup to dance the Pōta Rāju dance, accompanied by *dugga* and *tāshā* players. *See pages* 95, 97, 98
purāne shehr—old section of a South Asian city
pyār (< Sanskrit *priya*, "beloved")—love. *See page* 182
qāfiyah (Persian, from Arabic قافية *qāfiyat,* verbal noun of "to follow")—In poetry of the greater Indo-Persian tradition, the final or penultimate rhyming syllable or syllables in classical poetry. If penultimate, the word or words following the *qāfiyah* (called *radīf*) are the same in each rhyming line. *See pages* 120, 302

qalandar (Persian)—type of ascetic Sufi mystic; capitalized when referring specifically to the saint Lāl Shāhbāz Qalandar of Sindh

qamīz (*kamīz*, < Arabic *qamīṣ*)—South Asian long-sleeved tunic, typically worn with *shalwār*

qaṣā'ī (< Arabic)—butcher community. *See page* 196

qaṣīdah (Arabic)—Normally a type of panegyric or epic poetry in South Asia with *'arūz* (meter) and end rhyme in each line. Derives from a pre-Islamic genre in Arabic. Though in practice quite diverse, in *majlis* contexts *qaṣīdah*s are seen affectively to contrast with tragic *marṡiyah*s. *See page* 196

qaul (< Arabic, "to say or tell")—in *qawwālī* music, the traditional saying of the Prophet (*hadiṡ*) "for whom I am master Ali is also master" (*man kunto maula, fahāza 'ali-un maula*) along with the particular melody to which it is sung. *See pages* 16, 157, 158

qaum (< Arabic, "to stand")—community, caste, occupation, or other category for identity among South Asian Muslims. *See pages* 43, 213, 229, 315

qawwāl (< Arabic, *qawl*, "to say or tell")—singer of *qawwālī*. *See pages* 16, 38

qawwālī—genre of Sufi devotional music in India and Pakistan. *See pages* 16, 17–18, 26, 28, 117

qul (cf. *qaul*)—say

rabāb (*rubob* < Arabic)—plucked or bowed lute with either protrusions or notches at the intersection of the neck and the resonating chamber. *See pages* 43, 65

radīf (Arabic, "one who rides behind")—monorhyme, a word or words that return at the end of each rhyming line of poetry in the Indo-Persian tradition; contrast with *qāfiyah*

rāg (*rāga, rāgam;* Sanskrit, "color, melody")—tune, tune type, melodic framework for improvisation. *See pages* 16, 26, 67, 77, 80

Rājput—A martial caste in Rajasthan, India. Low-status communities in South Asia—including those of some drummers discussed in the present work—commonly stake claims to Rājput status. *See pages* 39, 41, 210

ramal (Arabic)—the name of one kind of foot in the *'arūz* poetic metrical system in the pattern long-short-long-long. Such a foot may be combined with contrasting feet, but a common meter encountered in this text consists of three full *ramal* feet plus one shortened (apocopated) foot: _ ◡ _ _ / _ ◡ _ _ / _ ◡ _ _ / _ ◡ _. *See pages* 227–228, 231

raqṣ (Arabic)—dance. *See pages* 156, 158, 162, 183, 185, 198, 297

rasm (< Arabic, "to mark, trace, delineate")—custom, practice, usage. *See pages* 125, 130, 196, 291, 304n6

rauẓah (< Arabic, "to break, or train")—garden; tomb of a revered personage; mausoleum. *See pages* 4, 115, 116

ravāj (< Arabic, "to have a ready sale")—practice, custom. *See pages* 89, 210, 282

relā (Hindi, "a line of animals, rushing, streaming")—genre of improvisation and composition in Hindustani music that *ḍhol* players in Panjāb, Pakistan, employ in their demonstrations of knowledge and skill. *See pages* 58, 154 rūbakār (Urdu from Persian, *rū-ba-kār*, "matters-for-work, proceedings")—record and manual of rituals and upkeep related to the maintenance of a royal estate in North India. *See page* 255

runza (Telugu)—type of vertical barrel drum played in the villages surrounding Hyderabad, Andhra Pradesh. *See pages* 37, 63, 64, 65, 67

rivāyat (< Arabic, "recital, narrative, history")—custom, tradition. *See pages* 125, 291

roṭi (< Sanskrit *roṭikā*)—flatbread

rūḥ (< Arabic, "to be entered or cooled by the wind")—soul. *See pages* 126, 159, 162, 294

ṣadā (Arabic, "echo, sound")—voice, sound

Sajjāda Nishīn (Persian, "sitting on the prayer carpet")—the presiding authority in a Sufi shrine

Sain (*sā'in*, Panjabi, from Sanskrit, *svāmikaḥ,* "king, spiritual preceptor, image of deity")—religious mendicant, *malaṅg*

salām (Arabic سلام, "to be or become safe")—Poem in couplet form, usually with a refrain, that is recited melodically at *majlis*es. Tends to be more syllabic than *soz*. *See pages* 26, 27, 120, 232–233, 241, 247, 249, 261–262, 266, 303

sam (< Sanskrit *sama*, "identical or homogeneous with")—first beat of a *tāla* cycle (which is "identical or homogeneous with" the last beat of the cycle). *See pages* 56, 74, 87, 136, 137, 148, 160, 163, 285, 287, 305n1, 313, 318

sama' (< Arabic, "to hear")—spiritual concert, especially listening to music at a Sufi gathering. *See pages* 16, 39

saṅgat (< Sanskrit *saṃgata*, "come together")—gathering (e.g., for music and poetry). *See page* 59

sangīt (< Sanskrit saṃgīta)—music. *See page* 56

Saṅgītaratnākara—thirteenth-century treatise by Sarngadeva that, among other things, provided an inventory of *deśī tāla*s. Only after this treatise appeared did particular drum syllables come to be prescribed for particular *tāla*s. *See pages* 12, 101, 288n6

saṅkh (< Sanskrit *shankh*)—conch shell; sometimes carried and blown by Sufi mendicants in antiphony with chants in honor of Ali. *See page* 140

Saraiki (Sarā'ikī)—Language related to Panjabi and Sindhi spoken in southern Panjab, Pakistan. Also called Multani. *See page* 28

sāraṅgī (Sanskrit)—vertically held, bowed lute with waisted resonating chamber. *See pages* 37, 42, 82

sārinda (< sāraṅgī)—vertically held, bowed lute with waisted resonating chamber

sarkār (Persian *sar-e-kār,* "head of work")—Master. Often used as a term of respect for a Sufi saint; appears in capital letters here when substituting for a proper name.

savārī (Persian)—Ride or cavalcade. A name commonly used for a *tāl* and especially for a compound *tāl* like the "*savārī* of five *tāl*s." The term is also used to refer to a person in an altered mental state, "ridden," as it were, by a spirit or divinity. *See pages* 58, 63, 67, 69, 85, 86, 103, 105, 111, 206, 223, 231, 232, 240, 241, 248fn, 262, 283, 284, 285

sawāl-jawāb (Persian)—question-answer, musical call and response sayyad (sayyid)—honorific for descendants of the Prophet's family. *See pages* 87–89, 91

sāz (Persian)—generic term for musical instrument in many regions of South, West, and Central Asia. *See pages* 56, 156

scheduled caste (English)—administrative term for Dalits or so-called untouchable castes. *See page* 14

sehrā (*sahrā* < Sanskrit *śekhara*, "wreath, diadem")—North Indian or Pakistan wedding song; wedding garland; music accompanying the ritual of garlanding at a wedding. *See pages* 38–39, 87, 161, 266

sej (Hindi *sej,* "bed")—nuptial bed of Qasim (or Ali Akbar) used as a *ziyārat* float in some South Asian Muharram processions. *See pages* 116, 122, 130, 135, 136, 141, 196, 290

shabīh (< Arabic شبیه *shabīh*, "resembling")—*Ta'ziyahs* and other ritual items and places that resemble their models. Closely related to the concept of *ziyārat* in that ritual involvement with the likenesses is tantamount to making a pilgrimage to a holy site. *See pages* 117, 132, 228

shādī—wedding or other happy occasion

shādiyānah (Persian شادیانه, relating to marriage and rejoicing)—music and gifts, usually at weddings; can be a specific ritual, as that described by Muhammad Baksh Multani. *See page* 87

shādmānah (Persian *shādmān*, "pleased, happy")—drum pattern played for weddings in the Panjab. *See pages* 87, 286

shāgird (Persian)—disciple

shahādat (< Arabic, "to give evidence")—martyrdom

shahnā'ī (*shehnai,* Sindhi *sharnā'ī;* Persian شہنائي, "large pipe")—double-reed aerophone with conical bore found in a variety of forms in South Asia and elsewhere. *See pages* 3, 4, 29–30, 82–92 passim, 123–129 passim, 135, 140, 142, 162, 190, 198 (sharnā'ī), 217, 238, 255

shajarah (< Arabic, "to be intricate")—genealogical tree, often passed down in Muslim religious orders

shalwār (Persian)—Thin trousers, wide and held by a drawstring at the top, and narrower by the ankles. Worn with loose-fitting *qamīz* in North India and Pakistan.

sharī'at (< Arabic, "to make apparent")—Muslim law. *See pages* 91, 172

sharnā'ī—see *shahnā'ī. See pages* 40, 61, 198, 202, 205, 272

shauq (Arabic شوق, "desire, excite")—interest, inclination, penchant. *See pages* 25, 209, 210, 221, 223, 225, 300n7

sheik̲h̲ (Arabic, "venerable old man")—Term that normally implies noble status or a position of authority in a Sufi shrine. Also one of a number of terms low-status drummers whose families converted to Islam in recent generations have adopted for themselves when asked their *qaum* or *barādarī.* Often short for *Bharāin Sheik̲h̲* or *Sheik̲h̲ Siddiqi* in the Panjab (see *bharāin*). *See pages* 41, 43, 229

sherwānī—a kind of long coat; formal Muslim dress that grew from an amalgam of Indian and British sartorial styles

shirk (Arabic, "partership")—The sin of acknowledging "partners" of Allah—that is, recognizing God's attributes or powers in others. The term is often wielded to

condemn polytheists. In this case the implication is that, in carrying out rituals with the *ta'ziyah*, Nizamis consider the structure itself to be infused with divinity, much in the way Hindus consider their *murti*s more than mere statues.
shīrmāl—saffron-flavored *roṭi* (flatbread)
silsilah (< Arabic)—chain (here, of transmission)
sinah-ba-sinah (Persian, "chest-to-chest")—face-to-face oral instruction by master to disciple. *See page* 136
sinah zanī—breast-beating (*mātam*). *See pages* 122, 224, 225
soz (Persian سوز, "burning, inflaming")—Lamentational genre sung at *majlis*es, usually employing one stanza of a *marṡiyah* poem. May be chanted solo with vocal support or in chorus. *See pages* 15, 26–27, 32, 38, 120, 227
śruti (Sanskrit, "hearing, listening")—tone, sound, that which is heard, minute tonal interval
sthān (from Sanskrit, "place")—place
sthāyī—see *asthāyī*
subḥāna'llāh (Arabic)—"Praise God." An expression of praise and encouragement.
sukūn (Arabic)—peace, tranquility
sur (*sūr*) (< Sanskrit *svara*, "sound, noise")—pitch, understanding of music (see *svara*). *See pages* 31, 56, 155, 158
surnā'ī (*sorna*)—Gilgit-Baltistan and other regional variants of the word *shahnā'ī*. *See pages* 76–79, 204, 282n18
svara (< Sanskrit *svara*, "sound, noise")—pitch, or, in Karnatak music, a unit of musical thought consisting of pitch and the context-sensitive oscillations associated with that pitch in a given *rāga*. *See page* 10
tabal—see *tabl*
tabarruk (< Arabic تبرك)—blessed food, shared at the end of a *majlis*. *See page* 122
tabarrukāt (plural of *tabarruk*)—here, sacred relics
tabaṭk (Kota)—Kota frame drum (see *tappaṭṭai*). *See pages* 93–95
tabl (*ṭabl* Arabic طبل, "drum"; tabal)—one of a variety of possible drums; the act of striking a drum; name of introductory item in Sindhi Manganhār repertoire. *See pages* 63, 66, 203, 205, 225, 297, 298
tābūt—coffin (here, representation of Husain's coffin in Muharram rituals)
tāl, tāla (from Sanskrit *taḍ-*, "to beat or strike")—Metrical framework. Sometimes used to mean "percussion pattern." *See pages* 8, 20–22, 31, 62, 63, 67, 86, 95, 101, 105–106, 112, 215, 281n2, 288n6, 288n7, 292
tālī (cf. tāṛī; < Sanskrit, "slapping the hands together or against one's arm")—in the gestures associated with Hindustani classical music and related genres, a clap. *See pages* 57, 62, 66, 259, 260, 285, 309
ta'līm (< Arabic, "to know")—training. *See pages* 210, 300n10
tāṛī (cf. tālī)—Clapping gestures and emphasized strokes associated with *naqqārah* and *ḍhol* traditions in Multan. The basis for identifying *tāl*s before the *mātra* conception became common. *See page* 85
ṭarīqat (< Arabic, "road, path")—way, especially according to the orders of Sufism. *See pages* 17, 172, 174

tambūra (*tānpūra;* Hindi)—lute with a gourd or wooden resonator providing the drone in much South Asian music. *See pages* 102, 240, 241, 288n9

tānpūra—see *tambūra*

Tansen—celebrated sixteenth-century singer and composer in the court of Akbar. *See page* 218

tappaṭṭai (*tappeṭa, tabaṭṭa, tabaṭk* in various Dravidian languages, from Tamil *tampaṭṭam,* DEDR 3082)—a frame drum. *See pages* 14, 64, 66, 70, 73, 93–95, 277n9, 282n14

ṭarz (Urdu, from Arabic طرز, "form, shape")—melody, drum pattern. *See pages* 79, 80, 203, 204, 223, 228, 241

tāshā (*ṭāsah, tāsha, trāsa, tāsa, tāja, tāza, tassa;* Arabic طاس, *ṭās*)—shallow, bowl-shaped drum hung from the neck and played with two, often flat, sticks. *See* main index

tā'ū (Sindhi)—Dispersal. Item of Sindhi *manganhār* drum and *gazī* repertoire. The name probably refers to the dispersal of the crowd that gathers at a shrine, one stop in a sequence of several during processions. *See pages* 204, 205

tavajjud (*tahajjud,* Arabic)—supererogatory nighttime prayers. *See pages* 209, 297, 300n5

tawā'if (Arabic طوائِف, "peoples, troops, dancing girls")—Female well versed in the arts of singing and dancing. In South Asia the term connotes a courtesan as well as a dancer-singer. *See pages* 28, 37

ta'ziyah (< Persian تعزیه)—In South Asia, a float representing the mausoleum of Imam Husain, grandson of the Prophet, Muhammad. Not to be confused with *ta'ziyeh. See pages* 4, 81–83, 116–117, 123–144 passim, 161, 185, 196–198, 215–249 passim, 267

ta'ziyeh (Persian تعزیه)—An Iranian passion play, usually centered on an episode in the Karbala story. Not to be confused with South Asian *ta'ziyah. See page* 138

tez (Persian)—intelligent, quick on the uptake

ṭhā dhunī (Sindhi) (*thā dhun*, Panjabi)—a type of drum pattern variation. *See pages* 163, 198

thallā (Panjabi)—base speed of a drum pattern. *See page* 163

thān (Panjabi)—place, turf (see *sthān*). *See pages* 178, 180, 181, 183, 187

ṭhekā (Hindi, from *ṭhīk*, "firm, strong")—pattern of drum strokes (stroke-melody) that defines a *tāl* in several genres of North Indian and Pakistani music. Scholars trace the contemporary Hindustani practice of specifying a *tāla* by its specific *ṭhekā* (and not merely its beat structure) to the fourteenth-century treatise *Saṅgītopaniṣat-sāroddhāra*, which was apparently the first to provide specific drum syllables for all the *tāla*s (Sharma 2000, 206; Simms 2000, 44). *See pages* 56–58, 62, 64, 66, 73–75, 78, 86, 95–99, 105, 110–112, 136–137, 148, 155, 163, 176, 187, 200, 216, 217, 240, 241, 259, 288n7, 294, 316

ṭheko (Sindhi)—*ṭhekā*. *See page* 198

ṭhīk (Hindi, "firm, strong")—short for ṭhīk hai, "OK". *See pages* (in etymological sense): 66, 281n4 tihā'ī—a pattern repeated three times, usually concluding on the *sam* (beat one) of a *tāl*. *See pages* 56, 148

ṭiko (Sindhi)—Sindhi musical term for *tihā'ī*. *See page* 198

tīlā (Panjabi, "stalk of any grain with ear attached" [Bhai Maya Singh, s.v. tīlā])—thin stick for making crisp, often rapid treble strokes on the *ḍhol*. *See pages* 56, 148, 164

tīntāl (tīntār)—Literally "three tāl," referring to the three *tālīs* (beats or claps) in the structure. A tāl of 4, 8, or 16 counts depending on tempo; a fourfold structure of *tālī—tālī—k̲h̲ālī—tālī*, and a *ṭhekā* appropriate to the tempo. *See pages* 57–58, 136, 148, 151, 160, 204, 309

tīntār—see *tīntāl*. *See pages* 58, 86

tiya (*tīyā*)—see *tihā'ī*. *See pages* 103, 163, 181, 183, 203, 297, 302

toṛā (Hindi, "break, interruptions")—a kind of rhythmic variation. *See pages* 163, 198, 295

udāsī (Hindi)—sorrow or dispiritedness. *See page* 159

upaj (*upji*, Hindi, "produce, product")—musical improvisation. *See page* 103

'urs (< Arabic, wedding)—Death anniversary of a revered personage ("saint") celebrated as a festival. Metaphorically, a celebration of the marriage of the deceased's soul to God. At some Sufi shrines, such as that of Nizammudin Auliya in Delhi, the martyrdom of Husain is celebrated as an *'urs*. *See* main index

ustad (*ustād*, Persian)—master. *See pages* 25, 59

uṣūl (< Arabic, *aṣl*)—Rule. For music, see *aṣūl*. Also, cyclical pattern, often performed on a frame drum, that forms one of the rhythmic layers of Turkish and Central Asian music. *See pages* 57, 61, 159, 216

vāh (wāh; Persian, Arabic)—bravo!

vājā (Sanskrit *vādya*, "to be said or spoken; musical instrument")—Saraiki term used to refer to drumming patterns (prior to use of the word *tāl*). *See pages* 63, 66, 68, 86–90, 93, 106, 284, 285, 286

vajat (Sanskrit *vādya*, "to be said or spoken; musical instrument")—Sindhi term for an item of repertoire on nagāra, ḍhol, and shahnā'ī. The verb *vajjāirnu* means "to cause a sound, to strike, or to wield a sword" (Mewaram 1910 s.v. vajjāirnu). *See pages* 63, 64, 203–207

vāqe'ah-e Karbala—the events at Karbala

vazan (vazn; Arabic *vazn*, "weight")—Poetic meter. Stylistic practice of deforming the ideal-typical version of a rhythmic pattern. *See pages* 111–112

vel (Panjabi)—offering, especially money given to a musician or dancer. *See page* 183

vibhāg (Sanskrit *vibhāga*, "distribution, apportionment")—section of a *tāl* demarcated by hand claps or waves. *See pages* 66, 105

vīṇā—Currently the name of a long-necked lute (Sarasvati *vīṇā*) in South India and a stick zither (*rudra vīṇā*) in North India; historically, instruments called *vīṇā* also included harps. *See pages* 10–13

vird (< Arabic, "practice, habit")—continuously repeated practice. *See pages* 156, 157

-wālā (-vālā; < Sanskrit *pāla*, "protector, keeper")—something or someone pertaining to the aforementioned, e.g., a rikshāvālā is one who drives a rickshaw.

walī (Arabic)—friend (of God); saint; Sufi
yād (Persian)—remembrance. *See pages* 125, 291
yakka (poss. < Persian *yak,* "one")—a *tāl* of six *mātra*s. *See page* 58
yār (Persian)—friend; beloved (in poetry); term of male sociality (like "man" in the expression "hey, man" in American slang). *See pages* 235, 252
zabān (Persian)—tongue, language. *See pages* 156, 162, 198
ẕākir (Arabic, "rememberer"; see *ẕikr*)—one who delivers sermons at a *majlis*. *See pages* 84, 127, 143, 196
zanjīr (Persian)—chain; *zanjīr kā mātam*, self-flagellation with blades attached to chains. *See pages* 142, 183, 196
ẓarb (Hindi *jarb* < Arabic, "to beat or strike")—beat, name of drum. *See pages* 63, 65, 106–111, 240
zarī (Persian)—anything woven with gold thread, used as a border for fabric
zārī (Persian, "lamentation, cry for help")—brief dirge in Sindhi (similar to *nauḥah* but shorter in length). *See page* 204
ẕikr (ẕekr; Arabic ذكر, "to remember, to mention")—verbal formulas recited aloud or silently by individuals or groups as a means to fix the mind on God. *See pages* 17–19, 47, 50, 65, 104, 156, 157, 313
zīl (*zīl,* Persian, "treble in music")—treble drum in a pair of *naqqārah*s. *See pages* 135, 200
ziyārat (Persian; < Arabic, "to visit")—Pilgrimage, visit to tomb or shrine, float, or other emblem associated with Muharram. Also, Arabic salutation to the Karbala martyrs performed at the end of a *majlis*. *See pages* 91, 116–118 passim, 133, 138–141 passim, 245, 255; as pilgrimage, 166, 215
Zuljinah (Arabic, *dhuljanāḥ*)—name of the horse used in South Asian Muharram processions to represent Husain's riderless steed, whose appearance signaled Husain's slaughter. *See pages* 84, 119, 126–129 passim, 196, 200–202 passim, 212, 255, 266, 292

References

Abbas, Ghulam. 2007. *Tazias of Chiniot*. Lahore: Tarikh.

Abbas, Shemeem. 2002. *The female voice in Sufi ritual: Devotional practices of Pakistan and India*. Austin: University of Texas Press.

Abrahamian, Ervand. 2008. *A history of modern Iran*. Cambridge: Cambridge University Press.

Alter, Andrew. 2008. *Dancing with* devtās*: Drums, power and possession in the music of Garhwal, north India*. Aldershot: Ashgate.

Ansari, Ghaus. 1960. *Muslim caste in Uttar Pradesh: A study in culture contact*. Lucknow: Ethnographic and Folk Culture Society.

'Aṭṭār Nīshābūrī, Farīd al-Dīn Muḥammad. 1991 or 1992 [1370 H]. *Manṭiq al-ṭayr* (*Conference of the birds [Persian]*). 7th ed. Tehrān: Shirkat-i Intishārāt-i 'Ilmī va Farhangī, vā'bastah bih Vizārat-i Farhang va Āmūzish-i 'Ālī.

Ayoub, Mahmoud. 1978. *Redemptive suffering in Islām: A study of the devotional aspects of 'Āshūrā' in twelver Shī'ism*. The Hague: Mouton.

Aziz, Shah Abdul. 1926. *Fatawa-e Azizi*, vol. 1 (The fatwas of Aziz). Urdu translation by Haji Muhammed Said. Calcutta: n.p.

Azizi, Faroghat. 2012. Falak: Spiritual songs of the mountain Tajiks. In *Music in Central Asia: An introduction*, ed. T. Levin and E. Köchümkulova, 370–80. Pilot ed. Bishkek, Kyrgyzstan: Aga Khan Music Initiative and the University of Central Asia (commerical edition to be published by Indiana University Press, 2014).

Baily, John. 1988. *Music of Afghanistan: Professional musicians in the city of Herat*. Cambridge: Cambridge University Press.

Balocu, Nabī Bak̲h̲shu K̲h̲ānu [N. A. Baloch]. 1975. *Musical instruments of the lower Indus Valley of Sind*. 2d ed. Hyderabad, Sindh: Zeb Adabi Markaz.

———. 1978. *Sindhī mūsīqī jī mukhtaṣiru tārīkha*. Bhiṭ Shāh: Shāha ‘Abdullaṭīf Bhiṭ Shāh Saqāfatī Markazu.

Bard, Amy Carol. 2002. Desolate victory: Shī‘ī women and the marsiyah texts of Lucknow. PhD diss., Columbia University.

———. 2010. Turning Karbala inside out: Humor and ritual critique in South Asian Muharram rites. In *Sacred play: Ritual levity and humor in South Asian religions*, ed. Selva Raj and Corinne Dempsey, 161–84. Albany: SUNY Press.

Berger, Hermann. 1985. A survey of Burushaski studies. *Journal of Central Asia* 8(1): 33–37.

———. 1998. *Die Burushaski-Sprache von Hunza und Nager.* Wiesbaden: Harrassowitz.

Berreman, Gerald D. 1978. Ecology, demography and domestic strategies in the western Himalayas. *Journal of Anthropological Research* 34(3): 326–68.

Bharata Muni. 1986. *Nāṭyaśāstra*. English translation with critical notes by Adya Rangacharya. Bangalore: IBH Prakashana.

Blum, Stephen. 1978. Changing roles of performers in Meshhed and Bojnurd (Iran). In *Eight Urban Musical Cultures,* ed. Bruno Nettl, 19–95. Urbana: University of Illinois Press.

———. 2002. Hearing the music of the Middle East. In *The Garland encyclopedia of world music,* vol. 6, *The Middle East,* ed. V. Danielson et al., 3–14. New York: Routledge.

———. 2012 [1391]. Ta’ammolāti tārixi bar bāb-e davāzdahom-e Jāme‘ al-alhān (Historical reflections on chapter 12 of the Jame‘ al-alhān). In *Gozideh maqālāt hamāyeš-e beyn al-melali-ye ‘Abdolqāder Marāği* (Selected papers from the international conference on ‘Abdolqāder Marāği), ed. Daryush Talā’i, 9–21. Tehran: Čāp-xāna-ye Dijitāl Mo‘asese Matn.

———. 2013. Foundations of musical knowledge in the Muslim world. In *The Cambridge history of world music*, ed. Philip V. Bohlman, 103–24. New York: Cambridge University Press.

Booth, Gregory D. 2005. *Brass baja: Stories from the world of Indian wedding bands.* New Delhi: Oxford University Press.

Bose, Sugata, and Ayesha Jalal. 2004. *Modern south Asia: History, culture, political economy*. 2d ed. New York: Routledge.

Brăiloiu, Constantin. 1984. *Problems of ethnomusicology.* Cambridge: Cambridge University Press.

Buehler, Arthur F. 1998. *Sufi heirs of the Prophet: The Indian Naqshbandiyya and the rise of the mediating Sufi Shaykh*. Columbia: University of South Carolina Press.

Burki, Shahid Javed. 2006. *Historical dictionary of Pakistan*. 3d ed. Lanham, MD: Scarecrow.

Burrow, T., and M. B. Emeneau. 1984. *A Dravidian etymological dictionary*. 2d ed. Oxford: Clarendon.

Burton, Richard Francis, Sir. 1851. *Sindh, and the races that inhabit the valley of the Indus.* London: W. H. Allen.

Charry, Eric S. 2000. *Mande music: Traditional and modern music of the Maninka and Mandinka of Western Africa*. Chicago: University of Chicago Press.

Chaudhuri, Shubha. 2009. The princess of the musicians: Rāni Bhaṭiyāṇi and the *Māngaṇiārs* of western Rajasthan. In *Theorizing the local: Music, practice and experience in south Asia and beyond,* ed. Richard K. Wolf, 97–111. New York: Oxford University Press.

Claus, Peter. 2003. Kāṭama Rāju. In *South Asian folklore: An encyclopedia*, ed. M. Mills, P. Claus, and S. Diamond, 329–30. New York: Routledge.

Clayton. Martin. 2000. *Time in Indian music: Rhythm, metre, and form in North Indian rāg performance.* Oxford: Oxford University Press.

Cohn, Bernard S. 1985. The command of language and the language of command. In *Subaltern studies IV: Writings on South Asian history and society,* ed. Ranajit Guha, 276–329. Delhi: Oxford University Press.

Dahiyat, Ismail M. 1974. *Avicenna's commentary on the poetics of Aristotle: A critical study with an annotated translation of the text.* Leiden: Brill.

Davis, Michael. 1999. *The poetry of philosophy: On Aristotle's* Poetics. South Bend, IN: St. Augustine's.

———. 2002. *Aristotle:* On Poetics. Trans. Seth Benardete and Michael Davis with an introduction by Michael Davis. South Bend, IN: St. Augustine's.

Djumaev, Alexander. 2002. Sacred music and chant in Islamic Central Asia. In *The Garland encyclopedia of world music,* vol. 6, *The Middle East,* ed. V. Danielson et al., 276–329. New York: Routledge.

Douglas, Mary. 2002. *Purity and danger: An analysis of concepts of pollution and taboo,* with a new preface by the author. London: Routledge.

Ellingson, Ter. 1980. Ancient Indian drum syllables and Bu Ston's Sham Pa Ta ritual. *Ethnomusicology* 24(3): 431–52.

———. 1986. Buddhist musical notations. In *The oral and the literate in music,* ed. Tokumaru Yosihiko and Yamaguti Osamu, 302–41. Tokyo: Academia Music.

Emeneau, M. B. 1956. India as a linguistic area. *Language* 32(1): 3–16.

Ewing, Katherine. 1997. *Arguing sainthood: Modernity, psychoanalysis, and Islam.* Durham, NC: Duke University Press.

Faruqi, Farhana, Ashok Kumar, Anwar Mohyuddin and Hiromi Lorraine Sakata. 1989. *Musical survey of Pakistan: Three pilot studies*. Adam Nayyar, general ed. Islamabad: Lok Virsa Research Centre.

Faruqi, Lois Ibsen al-. 1985. The suite in Islamic history and culture. *World of Music* 27(3): 46–66.

Fernandez, James W. 1986. *Persuasions and performances: The play of tropes in culture*. Bloomington: Indiana University Press.

Flora, Reis. 1995. Styles of the *śahnāī* in recent decades: From *naubat* to *gāyaki ang*. *Yearbook for Traditional Music* 27:52–75.

Gorfain, Phyllis. 1986. Play and the problem of knowing in *Hamlet*: An excursion into interpretive anthropology. In *The anthropology of experience,* ed. Victor W. Turner and Edward M. Bruner, 207–38. Urbana: University of Illinois Press.

Government of India. 1965[?]. *Muharram in two cities, Lucknow and Delhi.* Census of India 1961. Monograph 3, vol. 1, pt. VII-B.

Hasan, Mubushar. 2002. Of nationalism and taxes: Translation of "Ustad" Daman's Punjabi verse. *NIPA Karachi Journal* 7(4): 113–15.

Henry, Edward O. 1988. Social structure and music: Correlating musical genres and social categories in Bhojpuri-speaking India. *International Review of the Aesthetics and Sociology of Music* 19(2): 217–27.

Herzfeld, Michael. 1997. *Portrait of a Greek imagination: An ethnographic biography of Andreas Nenedakis.* Chicago: University of Chicago Press.

———. 2005. *Cultural intimacy: Social poetics in the nation-state.* 2d ed. New York: Routledge.

Hiltebeitel, Alf. 1989. Draupadi's two guardians: The buffalo king and the Muslim devotee. In *Criminal gods and demon devotees: Essays on the guardians of popular Hinduism*, ed. Alf Hiltebeitel, 339–71. Albany: SUNY Press.

———. 1999. *Rethinking India's oral and classical epics: Draupadī among Rajputs, Muslims, and Dalits.* Chicago: University of Chicago Press.

Hodgson, Marshall G. S. 1974. *The venture of Islam: Conscience and history in a world civilization.* Chicago: University of Chicago Press.

Huehns, Colin. 1991. Music of northern Pakistan. PhD diss., King's College, University of Cambridge.

Hughes, David W. 2000. No nonsense: The logic and power of acoustic-iconic mnemonic systems. *British Journal of Ethnomusicology* 9(2): 93–120.

Hughes-Buller, Ralph. 1906. *Baluchistān district gazeteer series,* vol. 7, *Makrān: Text and appendices.* Bombay: Times Press.

Hujwiri, Ali ibn Uthman al-. 1976. *Kashf al-maḥjūb: The oldest Persian treatise on Sufiism.* Trans. Reynold A. Nicholson. Lahore: Islamic Book Foundation.

Ibbetson, Denzil. 1916. *Panjab castes*. Lahore: Printed by the Superintendent, Government Printing, Punjab.

Ikram, S. M. 1964. *Muslim civilization in India.* Edited by Ainslie T. Embree. New York: Columbia University Press.

Jairazbhoy, Nazir Ali. 1999. *The* rāgs *of North Indian music: Their structure and evolution.* Bombay: Popular Prakashan. (Orig. pub. 1971.)

———. 2008. What happened to Indian music theory? Indo-Occidentalism? *Ethnomusicology* 52(3): 349–77.

Jakobson, Roman. 1960. Linguistics and poetics. In *Style in language*, ed. T. A. Sebeok, 350–77. Cambridge: MIT Press.

Jalal, Ayesha. 1995. Conjuring Pakistan: History as official imagining. *International Journal of Middle East Studies* 27(1):73–89.

Jones, A. M. 1959. *Studies in African music.* Oxford: Oxford University Press.

Joshi, Varsha. 1995. Drums and drummers. In *Folk, faith and feudalism: Rajasthan studies*, ed. N. K. Singhi and Rajendra Joshi, 112–48. Jaipur: Rawat.

Kazim, Ali Muhammad. 1887. [1307 H]. *Biography of Ghaziuddin Haider* (in Persian). [From the collection of Nayyar Masud; publication details not obtained.]

Keil, Charles. 1994. Participatory discrepancies and the power of music. In *Music grooves*, ed. Charles Keil and Steven Feld, 96–108. Chicago: University of Chicago Press.

Khalilian, M. A., and Stephen Blum. 2007. Musical ontology of the Naqshbandi order in eastern Iran, Annual Meeting of the Society for Ethnomusicology, Columbus, Ohio, October 26.

Kippen, James. 1988. *The tabla of Lucknow: A cultural analysis of a musical tradition.* Cambridge: Cambridge University Press.

———. 2000. Hindustani tala. In *The Garland encyclopedia of world music,* vol. 5, *South Asia: The Indian subcontinent.* ed. Alison Arnold, 110–37. New York: Garland.

———. 2001. Folk grooves and tabla *tāls*. *Echo* 3(1). http://www.echo.ucla.edu/Volume3–Issue1/kippen/index.html. Accessed January 23, 2014.

———. 2006. *Gurudev's drumming legacy: Music, theory and nationalism in the* Mṛdang aur Tablā Vādanpaddhati *of Gurudev Patwardhan*. Aldershot: Ashgate.

Korom, Frank J. 1994. The transformation of language to rhythm: The Hosay drums of Trinidad. *The World of Music* 36(3): 68–85.

Kramrisch, Stella. 1958. Traditions of the Indian craftsman. *Journal of American Folklore* 71(281): 224–30.

Kroeber, A. L. 1952. *The nature of culture.* Chicago: University of Chicago Press.

Kūfī, 'Alī ibn Ḥāmid. 1939. *Fāthnāmah-'i Sind: al-ma'rūf bih Chachnāmah (*The conquest of Sindh: The famous Chachnāmah [in Persian]). Hyderabad, India: Majlis.

Kugle, Scott, comm. and trans., and Aditya Behl, poetic trans. 2000. Haqiqat Al-Fuqara: Poetic biography of "Madho Lāl" Hussayn (Persian). In *Same-sex love in India: Readings from literature and history,* ed. Ruth Vanita and Saleem Kidwai, 145–56. New York: St. Martin's.

Kumar, Pushpendra, ed. and M. M. Gosh, trans. 2010. *Nāṭyaśātra of Bharatamuni: Sanskrit text, romanized text, commentary of Abhinava Bhāratī by Abhinavaguptācārya and English translation by M. M. Ghosh.* 2d ed., rev. and enlarged. Delhi: New Bharatiya.

Leitner, G. W. 1996. *Dardistan in 1866, 1886, and 1893: Being an account of the history, religions, customs, legends, fables, and songs of Gilgit, Chilas, Kandia (Gabrial), Dasin, Chitral, Hunsa, Nagyr, and other parts of the Hindukush, as also a supplement to the second edition of the Hunza and Nagyr handbook and an epitome of part III of the author's The languages and races of Dardistan.* New Delhi: Asian Educational Services.

Link, Hilde K. 2003. Geomancy. In *South Asian folklore: An encyclopedia,* ed. Margaret A. Mills, Peter J. Claus, and Sarah Diamond, 246–48. New York: Routledge.

Lorimer, D. L. R. 1939. *The Ḍumāki Language: Outlines of the speech of the Ḍuma or Bēricho, of Hunza.* Nijmegen: Dekker and van de Vegt N.V.

Lybarger, Lowell H. 2003. The tabla solo repertoire of Pakistani Panjab: An ethnomusicological perspective. PhD diss., University of Toronto.

Maceda, José. 1974. Drone and melody in Philippine musical instruments. In *Traditional drama and music of Southeast Asia*, ed. Mohd. Taib Osman, 246–73. Kuala Lumpur: Dewan Bahasa dan Pustaka.

Madian, Azza Abd Al-Hamid. 1992. Language-music relationships in Al-Farabi's "Grand book of music." PhD diss., Cornell University.

Marāghi, ʻAbd al-Qāder Ebn Gheybi Hāfez. 2009. *Jāmeʻ al-alhān*. Critical ed., edited by Bābak Khazrā'i. Tehran: Iranian Academy of Arts.

Massoudieh, Muhammad Taqi. 1980. *Mūsiqī-e torbat-e jām*. Tehran: Surush.

Memon, Siddique G. 1994. *The tombs of the Kalhora chiefs in Hyderabad.* Karachi: Oxford University Press.

Merriam, Alan P. 1964. *The anthropology of music*. Evanston: Northwestern University Press.

Mewaram, Parmanand. 1910. *A Sindhi-English dictionary.* Hyderabad, Sind: Sind Juvenile Co-operative Society. http://dsal.uchicago.edu/dictionaries/mewaram/.

Mijit, Mukaddas. 2012. The Uyghur *muqam.* In *Music in central Asia: An introduction,* ed. T. Levin and E. Köchümkulova, 251–60. Pilot ed. Bishkek, Kyrgyzstan: Aga Khan Music Initiative and the University of Central Asia (commerical edition to be published by Indiana University Press, 2014).

Moffatt, Michael. 1979. *An Untouchable community in South India: Structure and consensus.* Princeton: Princeton University Press.

Mohammad, Mahboob Ali. 2010. Following the pir: Shared devotion in South India. PhD diss., University of Wisconsin, Madison.

Molesworth, J. T. 1847. *A dictionary: Marathi and English.* 2d ed., rev. and enl. Bombay: Printed for government at the Bombay Education Society's press.

Momen, Moojan. 1985. *An introduction to Shiʻi Islam: The history and doctrines of twelver Shiʻism*. New Haven: Yale University Press.

Monier-Williams, Monier. 1990. *A Sanskrit-English Dictionary.* Delhi: Motilal Banarsidass. (Orig. pub. 1899.)

Natavar, Mekhala Devi. 2000. Rajasthan. In *The Garland encyclopedia of world music,* vol. 5, *South Asia: The Indian subcontinent,* ed. Alison Arnold, 639–49. New York: Garland.

Nayyar, Adam. 1988. *Qawwali.* Islamabad: Lok Virsa Research Centre.

———. 2000. Punjab. In *The Garland encyclopedia of world music,* vol. 5, *South Asia: The Indian subcontinent,* ed. Alison Arnold, 762–72. New York: Garland.

Needham, Rodney. 1972. *Belief, language and experience*. Oxford: Blackwood.

Nelson, David P. 2000. Karnatak tala. In *The Garland encyclopedia of world music,* vol. 5, *South Asia: The Indian subcontinent,* ed. Alison Arnold, 138–61. New York: Garland.

Nettl, Bruno. 1958. Notes on musical areas. *Acta Musicologica* 30(3): 170–77.

Neuman, Daniel M. 1990. *The life of music in north India: The organization of an artistic tradition*, with a new preface. Chicago: University of Chicago Press.

Neuman, Daniel M., and Shubha Chaudhuri, with Komal Kothari. 2006. *Bards, ballads and boundaries: An ethnographic atlas of music traditions in West Rajasthan.* Calcutta: Seagull.

Nicholson, Reynold A., trans. 1996. *The Kashf al-Mahjub: The oldest Persian treatise on Sufism, by 'Ali B. 'Uthman Al-Jullabbi Alhujwiri.* Lahore: Sang-e Meel.
Nizami, Sayyad Ali Abbas. 1989. *K͟hāndān-e niẓāmī kā 'aqīdah va dastūr-e 'amal: 'urās buzurgān-e dīn va dīgar.* (Urdu; Code of laws and faith of the Nizami lineage: *'urs*es of the great religious people and others). Karachi: Idār-e Niẓāmī.
Pickthall, Muhammad M., trans. 1977. *The meaning of the glorious Qur'an: Text and explanatory translation.* New York: Muslim World League.
Platts, John T. 1884. *A dictionary of Urdu, classical Hindi, and English.* London: W. H. Allen.
Powers, Harold. 1970. An historical and comparative approach to the classification of ragas (with an appendix on ancient Indian tunings). *Selected Reports in Ethnomusicology* 1(3): 1–78.
———. 1980. India: I, The region, its music and music history, 69–91; II, Theory and practice of classical music, 91–141. *The new Grove dictionary of music and musicians*, ed. Stanley Sadie. London: Macmillan.
Qureshi, Regula. 2009. *Sina ba sina* or "from father to son": Writing the culture of discipleship. In *Theorizing the local: Music, practice and experience in South Asia and beyond,* ed. Richard K. Wolf, 165–83. New York: Oxford University Press.
Rahaim, Matt. 2011. Beethoven as Khyaliya, Nagarjuna as musicologist: Are Indian and Western compositions comparable? *Punyaswar.* http://www.shadjamadhyam.com/are_indian_and_western_compositions_comparable. Accessed January 21, 2014.
Rahman, Tariq. 1996. *Language and politics in Pakistan.* Karachi: Oxford University Press.
———. 2001. The learning of Punjabi by Punjabi Muslims: A historical account. *International Journal of Punjab Studies* 8(2): 187–224. http://www.apnaorg.com/articles/IJPS/. Accessed January 21, 2014.
Randel, Don M. 1976. Al-Fārābī and the role of Arabic music theory in the Latin Middle Ages. *Journal of the American Musicological Society* 29(2): 173–88.
Reddy, William M. 2001. *The navigation of feeling: A framework for the history of emotions.* Cambridge: Cambridge University Press.
Rizvi, Saiyid Athar Abbas. 1982. *Shah Abd Al-Aziz: Puritanism, sectarian polemics and jihad.* Canberra: Marifat.
Rose, Horace Arthur. 1911–19. *A glossary of the tribes and castes of the Punjab and North-West Frontier Province: Based on the census report for the Punjab, 1883.* Lahore: Printed by the superintendent, Government printing, Panjab.
Rowell, Lewis. 1992. *Music and musical thought in early India.* Chicago: University of Chicago Press.
Roy Chaudhury, M. L. 1957. Music in Islam. *Journal of the Asiatic Socety* 23(2): 43–102.
Russell, R. V., and Hira Lal, eds. 1916. *The tribes and castes of the central provinces of India.* London: Macmillan.
Sakata, Hiromi Lorraine. 2002. *Music in the mind: The concepts of music and musician in Afghanistan.* Washington, DC: Smithsonian Institution Press.

Sapir, Edward. 1921. *Language: An introduction to the study of speech.* New York: Harcourt, Brace.

Sawa, George Dimitri. 2009. *Rhythmic theories and practices in Arabic writings to 339 AH /950 CE: Annotated translations and commentaries.* Ottawa: Institute of Mediaeval Music.

Sax, William. 1991. *Mountain goddess: Gender and politics in a Himalayan pilgrimage.* New York: Oxford University Press.

Schmid, Anna. 1997. *Die Dum zwischen sozialer Ohnmacht und kultureller Macht: Interethnischen Beziehungen in Nordpakistan* (The Ḍom between social stigma and cultural power: Interethnic relations in northern Pakistan). Wiesbaden: Franz Steiner.

———. 2000. Northern Areas of Pakistan. In *The Garland encyclopedia of world music,* vol. 5, *South Asia: The Indian subcontinent,* ed. Alison Arnold, 792–801. New York: Garland.

Schreffler, Gibb. 2002. Out of the *ḍhol* drums: The rhythmic "system" of Punjabi *Bhangṛā*. MA thesis, University of California, Santa Barbara.

Sells, Michael Anthony, trans. 2007. *Approaching the Qur'án: The early revelations.* 2d ed. Ashland, OR: White Cloud.

Shah, Waris. 1921. *The story of Hîr and Rânjhâ, 1776 A.D.* Trans. G. C. Usborne, with prefatory remarks by R. C. Temple. London: B. Quaritch.

Sharar, Abdul Halim. 1994. *Lucknow: The last phase of an Oriental culture* (Guẕishtah lakhnau). Trans. and ed. E. S. Harcourt and Fakhir Hussain. Delhi: Oxford University Press. (Orig. pub. 1975.)

———. 1965. *Guẕishtah lakhnau yā mashraqī tamaddun kā āḵẖarī namunah (tārīḵẖī va jaġrāfī yā'ī halāt).* Lucknow: Nasim Book Depot.

Sharma, Premalata. 2000. Śastra and prayoga: Contemporary tāla practice vis-a-vis śāstraic tradition; with special reference to Hindustani music. In *Indian aesthetics and musicology: The art and science of Indian music, compiled articles of Prof. (Miss) Premalata Sharma,* ed. Urmila Sharma, 1:201–22. Varanasi: Āmnāya-Prakāśana, Bharata Nidhi.

Sherinian, Zoe. 2009. Changing status in India's marginal music communities. *Religion Compass* 3(4): 608–19.

Silverstein, Michael, and Greg Urban. 1996. The natural history of discourse. In *Natural histories of discourse,* ed. Michael Silverstein and Greg Urban, 1–17. Chicago: University of Chicago Press.

Simms, Robert. 2000. Scholarship since 1300. In *The Garland encyclopedia of world music,* vol. 5, *South Asia: The Indian subcontinent,* ed. Alison Arnold, 42–59. New York: Garland.

Singh, Maya. 1972. *The Panjabi dictionary.* Patiala: Languages Dept.

Snell, Rupert. 1991. *The eighty-four hyms of Hita Harivaṃśa: An edition of the Caurāsī Pada.* Delhi: Motilal Banardsidass; London: SOAS.

Stern, Theodore. 1957. Drum and whistle "languages": An analysis of speech surrogates. *American Anthropologist, n.s.,* 59(3): 487–506.

Stewart, Rebecca. 1974. The tabla in perspective. PhD diss., University of California, Los Angeles.

Terada, Yoshitaka. 2000. T. N. Rajarattinam Pillai and caste rivalry in South Indian Classical Music. *Ethnomusicology* 44(3): 460–90.

Thurston, Edgar, and K. Rangachari. 1909. *Castes and tribes of southern India.* Madras: Government Press.

Tingey, Carol. 1994. *Auspicious music in a changing society: The Damāi musicians of Nepal.* London: School of Oriental and African Studies, University of London.

Tirmiẕī, Sayyid Ġulām Ḥaidar. n.d. *Majālis-e k̲h̲atūn (jadīd): har do ḥiṣah kāmil* (Women's majlises [modern]: The complete two volumes [in Urdu]). Lahore: Kutubk̲h̲ānah-e is̲nā 'asharī.

Toynbee, Arnold. 1961. *Between Oxus and Jumna.* New York: Oxford University Press.

Trimingham, J. Spencer. 1998. *The Sufi orders in Islam,* with a new foreword by John O. Voll. New York: Oxford University Press.

Turner, Victor. 1986. Dewey, Dilthey and drama. In *The anthropology of experience,* ed. Victor W. Turner and Edward M. Bruner, 33–44. Urbana: University of Illinois Press.

University of Madras. 1924–36. *Tamil lexicon.* Madras: University of Madras.

Urmawī, Ṣafi al-Dīn al-. 1984. *Book on the cyclical forms of musical modes: Kitāb al-adwār,* edited by Fuat Sezgin. Reproduced from MS Nuruosmaniye 3653, Istanbul. Series C, Facsimile Editions, vol. 6. Intro. Eckhard Neubauer. Frankfurt-am-Main: Institute for the History of Arabic-Islamic Sciences at the Johann Wolfgang Goethe University.

———. 2001. *Kitāb al-adwār fi'l-mūsiqā* (Persian translation and Arabic text), edited by Āryu Rostami. Tehran: Mirās-e Maktub.

Vanguard Books. 1983. *Vanguard Panjabi-English Dictionary.* Lahore: Vanguard Books.

Wegner, Gert-Matthias. 1986. *The dhimaybaja of Bhaktapur.* Wiesbaden: F. Steiner.

———. 2009. Music in urban space: Newar Buddhist processional music in the Kathmandu valley. In *Theorizing the local: Music, practice and experience in south Asia and beyond,* ed. Richard K. Wolf, 113–40. New York: Oxford University Press.

Wehr, Hans. 1976. *Arabic-English dictionary: The Hans Wehr dictionary of modern written Arabic,* ed. J. Milton Cowan. 3d ed. Ithaca: Spoken Language Services.

Weidman, Amanda. 2006. *Singing the classical, voicing the modern: The postcolonial politics of music in south India.* Durham: Duke University Press.

Wolf, Richard K. 2000. Embodiment and ambivalence: Emotion in south Asian Muharram drumming. *Yearbook for Traditional Music* 32: 81–116.

———. 2000–1a. Mourning songs and human pasts among the Kotas of south India. *Asian Music* 32(1): 141–83.

———. 2000–1b. Three perspectives on music and the idea of tribe in India. *Asian Music* 32(1): 5–34.

———. 2001. Emotional dimensions of ritual music among the Kotas, a south Indian tribe. *Ethnomusicology* 45(3): 379–422.
———. 2003. Return to tears: Musical mourning, emotion, and religious reform in two south Asian minority communities. In *The living and the dead: Social dimensions of death in South Asian religions*, ed. Elizabeth Wilson, 95–112. Albany: SUNY Press.
———. 2005. *The black cow's footprint: Time, space and music in the lives of the Kotas of South India*. Delhi: Permanent Black; Urbana: University of Illinois Press, 2006.
———. 2006. The poetics of "Sufi" practice: Drumming, dancing, and complex agency at Madho Lāl Husain (and beyond). *American Ethnologist* 33(2): 246–68.
———. 2007. Doubleness, mātam, and Muharram drumming in South Asia. In *Pain and its transformation*, ed. Sarah Coakley and Kay Kaufman Shelemay, 331–50. Cambridge: Harvard University Press.
———. 2009a. Introduction to *Theorizing the local: Music, practice, and experience in South Asia and beyond*, ed. Richard K. Wolf, 5–26. New York: Oxford University Press.
———. 2009b. Varnams and vocalizations: The special significance of some musical beginnings. In *Theorizing the local: Music, practice, and experience in South Asia and beyond*, ed. Richard K. Wolf, 243–302. New York: Oxford University Press.
Youssefzadeh, Ameneh. 2002. *Les bardes du Khorassan iranien: le bakhshi et son répertoire*. Paris: Institut d'études iraniennes.

Index

This index concerns figures and concepts of academic relevance. Entirely fictional characters and events in the plot do not appear in this index unless they embody a fieldwork-based generalization pertinent to the academic messages of this book. Names of academically relevant figures whose names have been disguised are not indexed. The names of real people whom I neither met nor interviewed but who speak in the text are not indexed. The names of important historical figures who are mentioned in the text (but are not characters in the text) are indexed. Because chapters 5–10 are primarily narrative, significant information appears in the chapter notes and endnotes and for this reason, unlike in standard indexes, references to authors mentioned exclusively in the notes are also indexed. It is common for individuals to be known by a single name. If only a single name is known, it is indexed as such.

This work includes two types of index, the main index, which provides entries, subentries, and sub-subentries, and the glossary, which provides most of the page numbers on which a given term is mentioned. Entries appear in both the main index and the glossary only if it is necessary to provide subentries or sub-subentries. Cross references to the glossary are provided where appropriate.

Parentheses are (occasionally) used for page numbers in this index to indicate that the given pages are relevent to the subentry but do not fit the category precisely. Foreign language terms are not italicized in this index. Page numbers on which a given term or concept is defined appear in italics. If a long list of page references are provided, those in bold indicate the most detailed or relevant treatment of the entryword.

Abbas, Ghulam, 290
Abbas, Shemeem, 17–18
Abrahamian, Ervand, 297
accentuation(s), 56, 93–114 passim; alternating, of ḍhol and tāshā, 287; bodily, 181; combinations of, to articulate texts, 216; complexity of, in Hunza, 76; in defining tāls, cāls, ṭhekās, etc., 57–58, 61, 66, 74, 104, 310; irregularity of, in vājā-based system, 93; notation of, xx; primary and secondary, 57, 262–263; in relation to dancing, 76; stressed beats, 93–114 passim; in tags, 99–102
acrobats, 25, 33, 35. *See also* Bāzīgar
action: contemplation of, 54; dance transitions, 66; devotional, 167, 173, 186; human, as mimetic, xiv, 48–49; not coordinated by common time referent, 143; physical, in names of drum repertoire, 61; rhetoric of, 47; stereotypical, 185–186. *See also* agency
aḍi. *See* aṭi in glossary
affect(s), 51–54; conventional, 51–52, 54, 89; musical sound as label for, 52, 54; system of, 92. *See also* emotion; emotional contour and texture
affection. *See* love
Afghanistan, 33, 119
Afzal, Muhammad (Mīrā͟sī drum ustad), 34
agency, 44–51, 164; complex, 45, *46*, 52, 186; of Imam Husain, 121; of musician, 41, 43, 158; of saint, 156, 167
Agra (Uttar Pradesh, India): drum patterns associated with, 64, 100; drummers' ancestry in, 98–102, 209–213, 272
Ahmadi, Sarvar, 19
Ahmed, Bashir (sārinda player), 43, 278
Ahmed, Nazir (ḍhol player), 85, 87, 88, 91, 270
Ahmed, Saghir (ḍhol player), 175–176, 271
Ahsan (poet), 35
Ajmer, Rajasthan: drum terminology from, 63; pirs in, turning toward Shiism, 237; music of Muhājirs whose families migrated from, 65, 208–214
"Āj Ṣuġrā yū͟n madīne me͟n hai͟n roṭī bhar ke nain" (text underlying dhīmā), 229–230, 248, 260, 261, 302; demonstration of text's relation to dhīmā drum strokes, 248
Akhtar, Ali (poet), 134
Akhtar, Begum (singer), 28
Akram Ali, 59
aksak. *See* rhythm: asymmmetrical time patterns. *See also langṛa in glossary*
Ali, Aijaz (naqqārah player), 204
Ali, Hazrat (nephew and son-in-law of the Prophet Muhammad), 7, 116fn; as assigner of human ranks, 157; dance of, 158; as leader of Muslim faith, 29, 142, 157; in song texts, 17–18; syllable *'ī*, called using, 148; in ẕikr, 156, 157
Ali, Javed (singer), 38, 278
Ali, Shahid and Niamat (ḍhol players). *See* Shahid Ali; Niamat Ali
Ali Akbar (son of Husain), 116, 130, 134, 266, 273–274, 290
Ali Asghar (son of Husain), 116, 139, 266
" 'Alī har dil ke andar" (a ẕikr), 156
Allaudin (drummer in Hyderabad, Sindh), 46–47, 49, 213–220 passim, 278, 298, 301n14
Alter, Andrew, 21, 35, 36
Ampaṭṭan (Tamil caste/occupational category), 32–33
anachronisms in text explained, 277
anchoring, 97, 137, 201
Andhra Pradesh, 32, 33, 34, 63, 64, 65, 67, 95, 97, 191, 265, 280, 287n4. *See also specific cities and regions*

Ansari, Ghaus, 33, 35, 38, 41
'aqīdah. *See* faith
Arab culture, 125. *See also* bin Qasim, Muhammad
Arain (cultivator caste), 59
architecture, recursion in Shī'ī/Islamic, 118
Arif Sain (dhamālī), 59, 180–183, 270
Aristotle, 48–49, 51–54 passim, 278n4
artistry, drumming described in terms of, 46
aṛy (Kota: beat), 94. *See also aṭi in glossary*
ashrāf (those of noble birth), 41, 42, 279
assonance, 50
Attar, Fariduddin, 168
Auqāf (Ministry of Religious Affairs), 172, 184, 186
auspiciousness, 33, 34, 63, 74
authenticity, 164, 187
  doubting of, 179, 180, 182
  of malaṅg, 176
  sameness, internal and external, in terms of, 158, 162
  terms, local: aṣal maqām, 157, 293; aṣl dhamālī, 181; aṣlī cīz, 153; saccā kām, 155–156; ṣaḥīḥ, 86
āvāzia (vocalist), 16
Ayoub, Mahmoud, 53
Azerbaijan, origin of Lāl Shahbāz Qalandar in, 182
Aziz, Shah Abdul. *See* Shah Abdul Aziz
Azizi, Faroghat, 290

Bachak, Muhammad (sāraṅgī player), 42
Baghbanpura (Lahore), 147, 153, 165
bagpipes, 4, 9, 75, 79, 87
Baily, John, 33
bājā/bajāna (ensemble type and related verb "to play"), 63, 64, 66, 216; gūnlābājā, 37; mangal bājā, 33; noun or verb, used as, 241, 293, 294, 300n7, 300n8, 300n9, 300n10, 300n12, 301n15, 301n18, 301n19, 304n4, 304n5; pancāl bāja, 282n23; shāhī bājā, 255
Baksh, Faqir Husain, 202–203
Baksh, Mīān Rahīm, 85, 270
Baloch (ethnonym): musicians, stylistic omnivorousness of, 43
Baloch, Ghulan Shabbir, 83
Baloch, N. A. *See* Balocu, Nabī Bak̲h̲shu K̲hānu
Balocu, Nabī Nabī Bak̲h̲shu K̲hānu, 39, 40, 41
Baltistan, 36, 280n18. *See also* Gilgit-Baltistan
Baluchi: language, 42; name of drum pattern, 87
Baluchistan, 18
Bao (name of ḍhol player), 154
barāt. *See* processions: wedding (barāt)
barbers, 32–34, 36, 43, 278n1
Bard, Amy, 54, 265, 277, 302
"Baṛe be murawwat hain̲ yeh ḥusn wāle," 28
bass, the (ḍhol in Trinidad), 103
bāṭin, 187, 211, 219, 292. *See also* hiddenness/interiority
"Baun maut jahān ic thindeh nain̲," 130
bazaar: women (i.e. courtesans) of, 133–140 passim; Zainab paraded through, 133–134
Bāzīgar, 34. *See also* acrobat
beat, 62, 105
  ambiguities in naming by, 96
  beat-based pattern, 105–113 passim
  k̲h̲ālī, 21; on ḍhol, 219
  mātam, of, in relation to drum, 237
  off-beat: cues, 216; throwing opponent off, 76
  onomatopoeia of, 84–85
  perceiving, 56, 72
  relation to, in: gesture, 101; metaphors, 56–57, 60, 208, 210; voice and (tone) melody, 125

beat (*continued*):
strength of: organization by number of stressed beats, 93–113, 287n1; strong versus weak, 50
terms related to, 62–66, 72, 73, 94, 125, 240, 281n12, 297; "beat" in Pakistan, 125; ḍanka, 65, 208, 297, 300n4; large scale conceptions, 106 (*see also glossary*)
versus count, 64
Beda, 34–35
beggars as devotees, 157
beginning(s): bass stroke initiating measure, 98–102; bol group onset, 86; collective process of song composition, 135; foundational belief/knowledge, 157; marked musically, 77, 87, 115, 282n21; musical control at outset, 160; musical sequence, of, 63, 68, 205, 240; patterns, of, serving as definitive, 94; qaul introducing qawwālī performance, 158; ritual of, 87; steady pattern preceding improvisation, 86, 106
Berger, Hermann, 75, 77
Berreman, Gerald D., 36
bhajans, 97, 98, 287n4
bhāṅgṛā dance, 31, 159; inappropriate in dhamālī thān, 180; woman, of: bhāṅgṛā-like moves accepted as dhamāl, 183
Bharāin Sheik͟h, 41. *See also individual glossary entries for Bharain and Sheik͟h*
Bharatiya, 35
Bharatpur, India: musical tradition associated with muhājirs from, 46, 63, 64, 105, 213–220 passim, 231, 232, 233, 272, 299
Bhatt, Shahbaz (Pappu Sain's former "manager"), 149–163 passim, 271, 292, 295
Bhatti, Urs (alġozah player), 42
Bheḍi (musician), 126
Bheḍi Potra (neighborhood, Multan), 81–83, 91, 123–144 passim, 190, 271, 283, 289
Bhutto, Benazir, 194
Bhutto, Zulfiqar Ali (prime minister of Pakistan), 166, 194
bin Qasim, Muhammad, 10, 40, 192–193, 194
blacksmiths, 36, 37, 310
Blum, Stephen, 19, 20, 33, 35, 51, 280
body, the
emotional-physical states: crying and osāro genre, 205; listeners, of, correlated with weight and time, 224
knowledge: drumming terminology, 62, 66, 107, (125); embodied, relating music to text, 17–19; grounding of, 60
parts of: finger-pointing, 141–142, 153, 183; heartbeat and musical rhythm, 56–57
Bohar Gate (Multan), 118
bol(s). *See also bol in glossary*
disguising, 87
recitation of: while humming, 97; in performances, 86
reckoning tāl by patterns of, 86
bondage, symbolism of, 124, 140, 298
Bose, Sugata, 300n2
Brăiloiu, Constantin, 99
breath, 17–19, 56, 60. *See also under* body, the
brijj (in reference to drum patterns), 72–73, 282n14
British imperial period, musical developments during, 75
broadcasting, radio and television, 115–116, 119, 224

Bu ʻAli Qalandar, Hazrat Baba Pir-Shah Ghazi (aka Damṛi Wāle Sarkār), 175, 176
Buddhism: Buddhist musicians, 37; music in, 10, 11, 21, 276n1; South Asia, in, 83, 193
Buelher, Arthur F., 60
Bukhari, Sayyad Alam Shah, 206
Bulaydi, Mahmand Murid (singer), 42
Bulleh Shah (saint), 158, 170, 182, 186
burning. *See* fire, symbolism related to
Burton, Richard Francis, Sir, 39, 40
Burushaski (language), 64, 75, 77
Burusho (native Burushaski-speaking people), 77, 278n2
butcher community (qaṣā'ī), shrine of, in Hyderabad, Sindh, 195. *See also* Peṛh Muhammad (shrine)

cadence (as musical closure), 8, 95, 105, 260
  "ball (gol)," as, 163
  danced, 183
  drum strokes, on: ḍhol, of, with ambiguous function, 108; thā, 163
  melodies, in: asthāyī, in, 126; dramatic, 136, melodic return, 201
  structural aspects, other: anacrusis, relation to 305n1; deśī tāls, 101; formulae, 232, 299; silence following cadence, 148
  See also tihā'ī, ṭiko, tiya, and mukhṛā in glossary
cadence (as flow of music or language), 43
"Cahrah chupā liyā hai kisī ne hijāb meṉ," 28
calligraphy, 170
cāls. *See* tāls, cāls and related entities, specific, discussed; tāls and cāls. *See also cāl in glossary*
Camār, 34
"Caṛhe duldul kaṭe kāfir" (text to mātamī ḍhol), 161
cassettes, audio: "mast qalandar," to propagate, 157; mindless reproduction, as signs of, 31; use of, 28
caste: boundaries of, musicians traversing, 41; classifications, super and sub-, of, 35–39; mobility, upward, in, 41; music making and, 14–15, 32–43 passim. *See also* rank: social
Cat-1, Cat-2 and Cat-3, 35–43 passim
celebration, issues surrounding, in mourning contexts, 29, 92. *See also under* funeral(s)
Central Asia, music of, in comparative perspective, 57, 65, 282n18
ceremony/ies, musical constitution of, 52, 54. *See also* rituals: musical structuring of
Chachnāmah, 40
chandas, 112
chanting. *See* recitation
chants. *See* exclamations
Charry, Eric S., 288–189n14
Chaudhuri, Shubha, 39
Chennai Sangamam, 276n4
children: processions of, during Muharram 119 (photo); Shī'ī, behavior of, informal, at majlis, 119; Sunni, taunting Shī'ahs, 84
Chishti (Sufi order): customs, 226–227; inclusiveness, 117; Muharram of, 237, 245; music of, 16, 132; status, 226. *See also names of specifi Sufi saints*
circumcision, 33, 34, 278n1
clapping: non-tāla, 16, 68, 76; rhythmic cycle, showing divisions of, 85–86, 93. *See also* gestures; krīya
classical music, South Asian
    identification of, a matter of perspective, 219

classical music, South Asian (*continued*):
North Indian and Pakistani: ḍhol-tāshā ensembles, transmitting knowledge of, to, 46, 110, 215, 217, 219, 225; knowledge of, by folk and ritual drummers, 31, 164, 204; rhythmic system of, and practice in, 31, 57, 86; South Indian, compared to, 20–21, 105–106, 113; vocalists versus instrumentalists, 15–16, 37–38, 41
relation to folk, 60, 85, 163–164
South Indian: colkaṭṭu (drum syllable recitation) in, 20; North Indian, compared to, 20–21, 105–106, 113; tāla in, 62, 106; tempo stability of, in, compared to folk drumming, 95; text, articulation of, in, 14; voice, ideology of, in, 12–13
terminology, 85, 86, 163, 302
See also Hindustānī music; Karnatak music in glossary
Claus, Peter, 287n3
Clayton, Martin, 112, 281n2, 305n1
clustering as conceptual basis for pattern-naming, 107–110
Cohn, Bernard S., 160
colonialism, 75; division of ta'ziyah burial grounds under, 244; favor, gaining under, through mātam and drumming, 211–212, 300n12; social ranking and, 14–15
color symbolism: red, 167–169
"common terms of understanding," 185, 186, 296n3
communal antagonism, Shī'ah-Sunni, 91, 123, 185, 190, 207, 211. *See also* sectarianism
community/ies: religious backgrounds, of different, co-participating in an event (*see under participation*); skills and roles, as defined by, 33
competition(s): drumming at, 77; drumming, 6, 39, 58–59, 85, 87, 162; nauḥah and mātam, 266; professional/social rivalry at, 34; wrestling, 60
composition(s): cakkardār, 288n10, 302; ḍhol bandish, 154, 161; gat, 163, 295; laggī, 163, 295; parṇ, 58, 163, 295; qaidah, 163, 295; through-composed, 93, 106; toṛā, 163, 198, 295. *See also names of specific kinds of composition*
conch shell used as musical instrument, 140
connoisseurship, musical, 31, 39, 58–59
consensus building, 58
context(s): differences in, articulated musically, 10; irrelevance of, for ḍhol genre, 99; Islam as a musical, 99, 210, 213; metric, multiple, for melodic ideas, 88, 126; musical items and groupings defined by, 76, 111, 206, 215; names of musical items referring to, 61, 63, 66, 69, 71, 76, 98, 110, 112, 215; political, 187; recitation and musical performances, conferring meaning on, 50, 91; stroke-melody versus tone-melody, shifting emphasis on, depending on, 9, 68, 75; "work" (toḻil), as 72–73. *See also* drum performance, contexts for
contextualization, 184–186
continuity, musical, 13
counting, act of (rhythmic), 56, 62, 65, 86, 89, 93, 106, 111, 112, 229, 247, 249
count versus beat, 64 (*see also* beat)
drum pattern names related to, 61, 64, 66
reckoning, 86, 217, 233; (ḥisāb), with tāshā, 229
speed of, 57
terms for, 63–64; chakka, 107, 240; durī, 107, 240; mora aṭṭhā, 107, 240; tirī, 107, 240
unclear basis for, 216–217

See also gintī in glossary
courtesan, 37, 133, 156, 158, 182. *See also names of courtesan communities*
cues, musical, 79, 105, 216, 219, 232, 287n1, 299
customary practice /fashion. *See ravāj in glossary*
customs/rituals. *See rasm in glossary*
cutter (top, improvisatory layer of Indo-Trinidad ḍhol-tāshā ensemble), 103
cycles, rhythmic: overlapping, of zanjīr kā mātam, 143; periodicity of, 73; pulses, without fixed number of, 93–164, 249, 260; "round" (cakkar), as a, 87, 163; tone-melody in relation to, 51, 79; units, syllabic, in relation to, 233; ẕikr, 65. *See also* tāls and cāls

ḍaámal (kettledrums), 77–79
dab, 84, 85, 283
ḍaḍáṅ (drum), 76–79
dādehāl, 38. *See also* genealogists
Dahiyat, Ismail M., 51
dam-ā-dam mast qalandar (ẕikr underlying dhamāl), 17–18, 151, 152, 156, 157, 158, 162, (172), 292, 293
Daman, Ustad (Panjabi poet), 170, 186
dance:
  conceptualizations: category, as high level generic, 68; courtesan (nācnā), as that of, 158; intentionality of (maqṣad), 162
  drumming, relation to: steps of, coordinating with drumming, 180–181; sticks, using 87, 90; Tamil drum patterns, 69; "voice of the drum," understanding through dance, 156
  money offered for, 59
  names of specific: bhāṅgṛā (*see bhāṅgṛā dance*); choliyā, 74; ḍāḍkeyāṉ ālī jhumar, 87, 285; jhūmar, 29–31, 87, 90, 159, 204, 285, 286; kathkī, 90; lion (sher), 98; luḍḍi, 159; Pōta Rāju, 98; sammī, 31 (*see also dhamāl dance; kathak dance*)
  regional styles and contexts: Gilgit-Baltistani, 76; Kota, 68, 94; Sufi, 17, 59, 169, 179–183
  See also raqṣ in glossary
dancers, relations with drummers, 59, 66, 76, 77, 149. *See also dhamālī in glossary*
dappu, 63, 66. *See also tappaṭṭai in glossary*
darśan, 33
daruvu (Telugu, to beat), 65
"Dastūr-e 'amal" (Ḵẖāndān-e niẓāmī kā 'aqīdah va dastūr-e 'amal: urās buzurgān-e dīn va dīgar), codes of laws for Nizamuddin followers regarding 'urses, 226–227, 236
Data Sahab. *See* Hujwiri, Ali ibn Uthman al-
David (biblical King), 11
Davis, Michael, 48–54 passim, 186–187
death
  commemorations: Ali Akbar, of, 130; wedding, as (*see 'urs*)
  drum patterns for announcing, 69, 72, 79, 125
  predicting day of, 160
  symbolic relations with: asymmetrical rhythms, 125, 289; beads, 139–140; divinity, as opposite, 72; leather of drum head, 156, 157; māru (drum pattern), 52, 125
  See also funeral(s)
debba (Telugu, "beat, blow"), 65
defilement, 155. *See also* pollution; tīṭṭu
deformation, 47–51, 185; deviation from models, 88, 164, 185–187, 263; drum pattern sequence, in, perceptual effect of, 216; poetic meter in performance, of, 232–233; variation and expression, musical, as, 72, 112

deities: embodiments of, in symbolic battle standards ('alams), 67; Hindu, 3, 69, 239; likenesses of, 75; music indexical of, 9, 69, 94. *See also* God
Delhi
  Islamic reformers in, 117, 290 (*see also reformism*)
  music and musicians: classical music, 37–38; ḍhol-tāshā players in, 93, 102, 225, 230, 237–244, 259, 288n9, 303; qawwāls of, 132
  Nizamuddin neighborhood in, 222, 224, 226, 230, 237–238 (*see also under Nizamuddin Auliya*)
density (of drum strokes), 205
  altering, 57, 93, 95; thickening, 33, 69, 278 (*see also keṭṭi mēḷam*)
  clustering by, 107, 108
  doubling, 230; dogun, 163; double lay, 137, tirakaṭ/dugun, 280
  quadrupling, 57; caugun, 163
Detha, Vijaydan, 40
deviation. *See* deformation
dhamāl dance
  authenticity: adjudicator of, 180, 187; criteria for, 156, 180
  conceptualizations: mātam, as, 162; origin story of, 157–158
  styles of, 149–150, 153, 179–183; with hands, 179
  See also dhamāl and dhamālī in glossary
dhamāl drum pattern
  content of: bols for, 157; tā'ū of Sindh, similarity to, 206–206; texts for, 157
  history of: introduction to Lahore, 154
  mourning associations: funeral, played for, 160–161; mātam, as, 162
  See also under tāls, cāls and related entities, specific, discussed. *See also dhamāl in glossary*
dhamauñ/damāũ (drum), 21, 75
Dharmapuri, Tamil Nadu, 62, 68, 71, 94, 280
ḍhol
  construction and parts, 40, 210, 214; frame, bamboo 210; frame, metal, 210; mallet, rubber headed, 214; shell, split chemical drum, 210; shell, wood, 210; stick, flat versus round, 164
  effects and meanings: emphasis, reinforcing verbal points of, 18, 104, 105, 232, 299; ġamnāk (sadness) of, 91; naqqārah, distinction from, 125
  history of: bhāṅgṛā, as original repertoire, 163; development in Lahore, 154; migration from Agra to Hyderabad, Sindh, 98–102, 209–213; popularization, 154
  performance of: naġmah on harmonium, compared to, 240–241; strength (zor) involved, 155
  sound of: resonance of, 91; tabla, imitation of, 148; volume of, 214 (*see also sounds(s): undulation*)
  types: Panjabi barrel, compared to cylindrical ḍhol of ḍhol-tāshā ensemble, 164; wide diameter, 209–213
  See also ḍhol in glossary
ḍhol players
  identified: Lahore, living in, 58–59, 154; named, 38, 154, 163–164
  interactions among: competitions, 58–59; faqirs, with,154; mātam performers, with,128; participation in Agra, vast, 210
  perspectives of: contexts, appropriateness of, 91; origin of ḍhol, on, 40; Mīrāṣīs and Bharāis, 38
  See also (*ḍholī in glossary*); drummer(s); *names of particular players*

ḍhol-shahnā'ī ensembles, 82, 91
ḍhol-tāshā ensemble(s), 4–5
instruments: carriers of musical styles and ideas, as, 113; described, 214 (photo); multiple ensembles, 245; Western band during Muharram, with, 241
places, venues and contexts: Choṭa Imambarah, 7, 84; "fencing" (ā'ī doz khelnā), 197; Hyderabad, Sindh, 65; Muharram exclusively, 46
players: actions of, moving around while playing, 208; members of lineage, Nizamuddin shrine, 240; Muhājir, Sheiḵẖ Siddiqis, 41
sound: functional layers in, 102–103, 240–241; imitation of, 37
See also ḍhol; tāshā
dhrupad, 15, 20
dhrupadiyā, 15
Dumāki (language), xix, 64, 75–80, 282n16
dhus (drum), 6
directionality: devotee facing shrine of saint, 156, 179
discipleship: master-disciple relations, 60, 91, 92, 149, 154–156, 178–179, 182; rituals of, 42. *See also under* learning/training/development
discourse, analysis of, 45–54 passim
"disjunctive" attitudes, 208–213; contrast with integrative impulse, 213, 220, 297; "ways" (rujḥān) of performers unconnected, 211, 300
distortion: electronic, of sound, 143, 179; omission, as, 47. *See also under* deformation
Ditta, Allah, 85, 270
Divāyā, Mīān Allah, 39, 85, 87, 270
Djumaev, Alexander, 65
dol. *See* ḍhol
Ḍom, 36, 75–80, 278n2
door: metaphor of devotee standing at that of God, the Prophet or the Saints, 157, 173
dotār (Iranian lute), 19
double-reed instruments. *See under* instrument(s); *and names of individual instruments*
Douglas, Mary, 33
Dravidian languages, 112, 113; politics of, 276n4
drones, 71, 120, 126, 203, 240. *See also bāzu in glossary*
drum-making, 33, 210
drum parts
drum head: "dead thing" (murdah), as, 156, 157, 293; material on, 291
drumsticks, 65, 111, 233; innovation in tīlā, 164; kūṇḍi (curved bass stick), 56, 148; tīlā (thin treble stick), 56, 148; VD, 65; words for drumstick also meaning kettle drum (ḍankā/ḍamkā), 63
snare, 37
See also under ḍhol: construction and parts
drum pattern(s), 8, 93
conceptualizations, 71, 73–74, 85–86, 89, 93–114; differentiae, primary repertorial, as, 69, 74, 75, 79; gestalts/composites, as, 66, 68, 70, 73, 89; "happy" (joshī), 162, 292 (*see also under emotion or condition [kaifiyat]*); indexical with rituals (*see rituals: drumming for [specific]*); mathematical formulae describing, 99–102, 110, 213; patrons, for particular, 87; rāgas, likened to, 64 (VI.A.5), 77, 80, 106; recognizing/identifying, 18, 73, 87, 93, 105, 106, 110, 159, 282n23; terms for, 62 (*see also naming, practice of*)

drum pattern(s) (*continued*):
functional roles and organization: bass drum/part, 36, 95, 102, 105, 107, 218; beat-based pattern defined, 105; interlocking (*see interlocking drum patterns/strokes*); mātra-based pattern defined, 105; mixing and matching of patterns, 212; motivic basis (Dalit drumming), 68–74, 93–98; riff-based pattern defined, 105
genres/types, not conceptualized in cyclical terms: keṭṭi mēḷam (*see keṭṭi mēḷam*); salāmī (drummed salute), 245, 304n5; tabl (*see tabl in glossary*)
textual associations: corresponding to ẕikr, 18–19; linked to texts, 7, 9, 17, 18, 22, 84–85, 93; linked to texts via song melodies, 93, 97; marsiyah as "inside" (andar) drum pattern, 224
vocalizations, 20, 56–58, 70–75 passim, 85–88, 90, 96–97, 152, 247, 279 (*see also under recitation*); models for syllable sequences, 20
See also bol(s); stroke melody; tāls, cāls and related entities, specific, discussed
drum performance, contexts for
agonistic contexts: ā'ī doz khelnā (fencing), 197; gatkā (fencing), 159, 284; polo matches, 75, 78; war, 125, 198; wrestling, 159
bifurcation of, based on mourning or non-mourning function, 72, 111
celebratory occasions, other; festivals, non-funerary, 72; rituals and folk festivals, 40; visits of officials, 75
commemorative ceremonies: funerals, 14, 72, 98, 125; Muharram, 42, 98, 102, 111, 142; Sufi shrines (mazārs), 58, 59 (*see also under names of individual saints*)
Hindu deities and festivals, 14, 33, 69, 74–75, 94, 102, 239; Ganesh pūja, 98; Navarātri, 98; Ram Lila, 239
weddings, 58, 69, 73, 86–90, 102, 239; procession (barāt), 29; reception venue (shādī hall), 25
drum techniques: damping, 20, 56, 96; resonance, creating, 20, 56, 96
drummer(s)
activities of: dance teaching, 149; multiple occupations, 32–43 passim; singing, 39
motivations for becoming a, 42
qaum (community) names of: K̲h̲ān Sahab, 59, 210 (*see also K̲h̲ān Sahab in glossary*); Rājput, 41 (*see also Rājput in glossary*); Sheik̲h̲ Siddiqi (*see Sheik̲h̲ Siddiqi*)
social positions: relationship with dancers, 59, 149; status of, 14–16, 34, 37, 41
See also names of particular musicians and under names of drums
drumming
amateur, 42, 198, 216
descriptions of, 29–32, 151; analogies with classical melody-drum relations, 102, 163, 240–241, 288n9
emotional associations: happiness, 125; inherent, 92; passion (josh) and ardour (dhun), 209; sensitivity (shauq), 224–225; sorrow, 125, 159
evaluation of, 29–32, 39, 58–59; creating musical interest, 151
moral associations: benefits (fā'ida) and defects (nuqṣān), 210, 219; meritorious, 59

motivations for: duty, 160; enjoyment (mazah), 223; lack of purpose (maqṣad), 209, 210; penchant (shauq) for drumming, 209, 210, 223
religious considerations: communal, during Muharram, 198, 208; Islam, irrelevant to, 210; Muharram processions, historical, 125; prohibitions during Muharram, 44, 92; religious (maẕhabī), 209
status as music, 41, 219; "to present" rather than "to play," verbs used, 216
voice of, 125, 156
duhl, 40. *See also* ḍhol
Duldul, 161, 292, 301n13. *See also Zuljinah in glossary*
Ḍumāki (language), xix, 64, 75, 77, 282n17
duzarb, 65

economics (of music, recitation, and dance), 14, 16, 25, 30, 39, 42, 59; invitations to play, 26, 39, 59, 154, 195, 223, 224, 240; material gain, focus on, 155, 179, 182; money, showering on ḍhol players and dancers, 179; weddings as lucrative, 202. *See also* payments and tips
economy: reformist criticisms of expenditure on ritual, 92
ecstasy, 16, 18. *See also* (*ḥāl in glossary*); mastī; possession; wajd
education: general, in tension with musical training, 154; primary and secondary school, 43
Ellingson, Ter, 10, 276n1
embellishment, musical: "mak[ing] it beautiful," (ḵẖūbṣūratī karnā), 87; playful/competitive (*see chēṛ chāṛ in glossary*)
embodiment: ẕikrs, of, 17. *See also under* body, the
Emeneau, Murray B., 113, 289n15
emotion or condition (kaifiyat)
causes, expressions, and associations: drum, created by deep undulation on 160; drums and drumming, associations with, 7, 10, 31, 44, 60, 88, 91, 159, 160; emotional state of performer, 60; "felt" (meḥsūs) presence of underlying texts, 224, 303; happiness as essential to one's comportment at an 'urs, 173; majlis performances, association with, 27, 29, 89; musician as "technician of" emotion, 60, 281n1; occasion, not drum sound, induces sadness, 241; qaṣīdah, insufficient sadness of, 196; text and context, emotion related to, 91–92; vowels, expressed in, 50
emotional descriptors: anger, 124; attachment (lagan), 156, 180; destitution, 149; dispiritedness (udāsī), 159, 160; excitement (josh), 159, 160; fear, 88, 159 (ḵẖaufnāk, frightening); happiness, 125; "hearts moved" (dil hil jāte haiṉ), 224, 304n3; intensity of, 52–53, 92; interest (lagā'o), 164, 294; intimidation (ḍar), 159; intoxication (with God/saint/love) (*see mastī*); languidness (sust kaifiyat), 224, 304n3; love (*see love*); passion/ardour (dhun) 209, 298, 300n6; passion/attachment (lagan), 155; passion/desire (jaẕbāt) 159, 218, 298; passion/frenzy (josh), 158, 209; pulling (hangūra, "pulls"), 167; sadness, 52, 89, 91, 92, 125, 159, 160 (ġam), 167, 227, 302; tranquility (sukūn)

emotion or condition (kaifiyat) (*continued*):
process and combinations: changes in, 27, 51; complexity/mixtures of emotion, 29, 31, 32, 35, 51–54, 89, 125, 227, 302, 303; signposts for emotional experiences in time, 53
See also affect
emotion, physical signs of: crying, 31, 127, 137, 205, 224; enthusiasm, 89, 92; somberness, 60
emotional contour and texture, 51–54, 60
emotives, 53–54
energy, divine, 60
ensembles, musical
content of: gazī-ḍhol-naqqārah, 198; number of instruments equaling, 7, significance of, 90; tāshā-dugga, 95–98
terms for, 76, 198; naming of musical repertoire, significance for, 66, 72
See also ḍhol-tāshā; ḍhol-shahnā'ī
entextualization, 184–186
errors, musical: correcting, 212; revealing musical system, as, 99, 100
essentialism as social strategy, 47
ethnography, strategies in carrying out, 44
etymology, local concern with, 40, 85, 283
Euro-American musical genres, allusions to: Rock and Roll, 98; Disco, 76, 159, 180, 184
Europe: comparisons with, 9; Rom of, 36; thought in, history of, 48, 50
European(s): expatriate employers, 166; interactions with, consequences of, 15, 92; terms of, classical musical, used for folk drumming, 98
Ewing, Katherine, 45–46, 172
exaggeration, 48, 186
exclamations: Husain, 148; Husain Husain, 224, 244;'ī (short for 'Alī), 148, 152, 181; Jhūle Lāl, 148, 149, 151, 178; mast qalandar (*see also dam-ā-dam mast qalandar*), 152; qalandarī lāl qalandar!, 152; Ya Husain, 200. *See also na'rah in glossary*
expectations: musical, deviations from 96, 121; musical, of listeners, 51, 56; poetry, in, 121; social, 46, 49
exteriority/outwardness/manifestation: relation of internal to external, 158, 162, 188–221 passim. *See also* ẓāhir
"Ey ġairat-e maryam terā bāzār meṉ jānā" (nauḥah), 134

faith, 25, 46–47, 298, 303, 312; declaration of, 50, 104, 216, 241, 299 (*see also kalmah*); drumming as expression of (aqīdat), 219; Shī'ahs for Nizami rituals, of, 224
Faiz, Faiz Ahmad (poet), 170
fāḵẖtah, 56–57, 279–280
Fārābī, al-, 48, 51, 278n4
Farid, Baba: story of, 176; 'urs of, 132
Faruqi, Farhana, 34, 38, 282n18
Farwa, Umm-e (wife of Hasan and mother of Qasim), poem in voice of, 137
Faṣīḥ (poet), 229
father, roles of, in transmitting arts, 25, 55, 85, 154–155, 160, 202, 236, 240; discouragement, 42; drums, constructing, 210; encouragement, 59; metaphorical, 155; poetry, providing, 229, 236; vision, realizing his, 209
Fatimah, "Bibi" (daughter of the prophet Muhammad), 4, 29, 40, 110, 121–122, 255, 319
Fatimah Kubra (Husain's daughter), 130, 134, 266
fatwa (against members of Nizami family) and response, 227
fayḍ. *See* energy, divine

Fernandez, James W., definition of metaphor, 185
festivals, folk, 40, 276n4
feudalism, 42, 193, 212. *See* Vaḍera; zamīndār
fieldwork. *See* methodological issues and fieldwork
film music: melody-centrism of, 68; songs, 28, 98; style of, 28. *See also* music, mass mediated
film(s): "50 50," 98; Armān, 98; Badnām, 28; Jai Santoṣī Mām̐, 98; Nikāḥ, 28; Shahnoor (film studio), 32
fire: dhamālīs interacting with, 180, 181, 183; firepit (cirāġdān), 171 (photo); mac (bonfire), 172, 174, 176, 184; music as, 160; symbolism related to, 167–168, 173, 174, 176; Zainab stepping through, to find her children, 196
Flora, Reis, 282n23
flying: metaphor, musical, 160, 164, 187; saint, of, 158
folk music, 67; Panjabi, 27–28; Saraiki, 85; Sindhi, 17–18; South Indian, 14
formants, 20, 277n8
formulae, verbal, 17–19. *See also* ẕikr
frame(work):
  analytical/interpretive, xiii, 7, 44–48, 186–187
  musical: departing from, 187; melodic, 16, 318; rhythmic/metric, 8, 31, 57, 136, 201, 231–232, 259
frame drums, 14, 40, 63, 70–71, 93–94, 276n4, 311, 323. *See also names of individual drums*
fuller (middle layer of Indo-Trinidad ḍhol-tāshā ensemble), 103
funeral(s): barbers at, 34; bhajan for, 97, 288n4; celebration of, 92; Dalits as functionaries at, 34, 72, 95; drumming at Arab, 125; drum repertoire at, 60, 63, 69, 72, 74, 79, 97, 98; food, special for, 266; Kota music at, 15; melody, Kota, for, 279n5; music of, in Tajikistan, 290; musicians at, 14, 15, 34, 60, 72, 95; Pappu Sain, at father's, 60, 160–161; Sindhi, 205

"gait" (as generic term for rhythmic pattern). *See cāl in glossary*
Gakkhaṛ (ethnic group in Panjab), 162
gamaka (integral ornament in Karnatak music), 12
gānā (singing), 15
Gardez, Shah Yousef. *See* Shah Yousef Gardez
Gardezi, Saleem (genuine and fictionalized), 42, 119–120, 270, 290
gawaiyā, 15
gāyaki ang, 15, 16, 276n5, 276n6
gender issues: dhamāl in public, female dancing of, 182–183; divorce, social commentary on, 28; headscarves (historic), forced removal of women's, 134, 211, (290); instrumentalists, male, relation of women singers to, 128–129; Panjabi men, intimidation from northern, 133, 177; persona, female, 17–18; shrines, women's participation at, 178; spatial configuration, 118, 129; vowels, expressed in, 50
genealogies: Arabian descent, 41; claimed relations of descent, 34, 40; tree representing, 322
genealogists, 38, 40
genre(s): definitions of, ambiguities in, 68, 73, 76–77, 79, 93, 111; Euro-American (*see Euro-American musical genres, allusions to*); names of tāls and patterns as, 111
genuineness. *See* authenticity
geomancy, 37
gestures: responsory, 27, 120; tāla, 21, 56, 57, 60, 62, 101
Ghani, Abdul (saint), 165

gharāna: Delhi, 15, 37–38; membership, claiming, in, 38. *See also gharāna in glossary*
Gilgit-Baltistan (Pakistan), 36, 64, 76–80, 292
glottal articulations, xxiii, xxiv, 96
God: compassion of, felt through ḍhol's sound, 148; death, in opposition to, 72; drum pattern for, 72, 73; energy of (*see energy, divine*); identification with, emotional, 16; mind, focusing, on, 17; musical performance, intuitive, assisting in 159; name of, money collected in, 40; name of, uttering the, 19; strength (ṯaqāt) of, to support human strength, 155, 191; unity of, 47, 50, 153. *See also kalmah in glossary*
goldsmiths, 37
ğoṭhu (patron village in Rajasthan), 39
graves, worship at, 117. *See also* mausoleum[s]; *rauẕah in glossary*
Greece, philosophy of ancient. *See* philosophy: Greek
groove, 9, 29, 57, *66*, 106, 111, 149, 201, 280, 281n7
ground, musical, 8–9, 62, 86–87, 93–114, 163; naġmah as, 163, 240; "sitting" as (baiṭhnā), 163, 294; ṭhekā as, 163; *See also bunyād in glossary*
Gujrat (Pakistan), drummers from, 58, 164
Gunga Sain, 59, 270, 292
gũnlābājā (Newari genre), 37

Habibi, Habib (Iranian dotārist-singer), 19
hadis̱-e kisa, 29
Haider, Ghaziuddin (Nawab), 276
Haidar Bek (drummer), 76, 282n21
Hājī Bek (surnā'ī player), 76
Haji Wala ta'ziyah, 81, 83, (123), 130, 133, 140–141, 142, 144
Ḥajjām, 36. *See also* Mangali
Hallaur (Uttar Pradesh, India), 284
Haq, Zia ul- (former president of Pakistan), 123, 178, 186
Haram Gate (Multan), 81, 83, 91, 118, 123, 130, 133, 140, 143; lining up of ta'ziyahs at, 138
harīb, 282n18
haríip, 36–37, 64, 75–80, 282n15, 282n16, 282n19, 282n21; as music, 282n17
harmonium, 16, 35, 38, 82, 102; ḍhol compared to, 240–241
Hasan, Imam (Al-Hasan ibn Ali ibn Abi Talib, grandson of the Prophet Muhammad), 29, 116; birth of, 40
Hasan, Mubushar, 295
Hashim (ḍhol player), 223–226
Hasrat, Ghulam Rasul (poet), 135, 271
"Hay vay maiṉ muṭhi hai pora" (nauḥah), 137
healing, 127
hegemony, agency and, 45
Henry, Edward O., 32, 34
Herzfeld, Michael, 46–50, 186, 275n1
hiddenness/interiority, 2; external, relation to, 158, 162; rhythmic idea, disguised, 87. *See also* bāṭin
Hiltebeitel, Alf, 292
Hindi (language), 74; film, 98; musical terms in, 8, 30, 65, 74, 107, 109, 112 (*see also under Urdu for terms listed as both Hindi and Urdu)*
Hinduism: fire in, 172; history of, in Multan and Sindh, 83, 193; Holi in, 146, 291
Hindu(s)
  associations with Muslims;
    Hindu(s): festivals of, Muslims drumming for, 69, 95, 98; Karbala martyrs, possessed by spirits of, 67; Mela Cīrāġān, at 147, 178; Muharram, perceptions of, 67, 117; music, playing, with Muslims, 46; patrons, as,

39; religions, members of other, cooperation with, 244; teacher of Muhājir, as, 46–47, 214, 218–220, 301n14
music, musicians, and musical contexts: bhajan, famous, 287n4; drummers, 92, 102–111, 236, 238–240; material culture, 117; swordplay, 284; weddings, 90
representations of: deities, Kota drum patterns for Hindu, 94; Kirāṛs (ethnonym), 87, 90, 284; stereotypes, 46–47
Hindustani (language), 74. *See also* Hindi (language) and Urdu/Hindi (language)
Hīr-Ranjhā (epic), 167–168, 176, 179, 185
history: legendary versus historical events, 211, 215; South Asian music, of, 113–114
Hodgson, Marshall G. S., 17
horse, symbolism of, 126. *See also Zuljinah in glossary*
Huehns, Colin, 76, 77, 282n15, 282n22
Hujwiri, Ali ibn Uthman al-, 11, 26; 'urs of, 59, 132
Hughes, David W., 20
Hughes-Buller, Ralph, 43
Hunza (Norhtern Pakistan), 36, 62, 75–80, 278n2, 282n21
Hurr (Al-Hurr ibn Yazid al Tamimi, Ummayyad general), 137, 138
"Hur shāh di k͟hāt̤ir kahāṉ gayā" (nauḥah), 137–138
Husain, Altaf (MQM founder), 194fn
Husain, Ansar (Shī'ī tāshā player): controversy surrounding, 225
Husain, Imam (grandson of the Prophet, Muhammad), 1, 7, 116fn; birth of, 40; bravery of, expressions of, 211; Duldul, riding on, 161fn (*see also Zuljinah in glossary*); oppression of, expressions of, 211; poetry, in, 26–27, 92, 121–122; tragedy versus victory, death of, as 237
Husain, Shabbir (ḍhol player), 59
"Husain 'e husain-e 'aẓam" (osāro), 206, media example 8.4
Hyderabad, Andhra Pradesh (India), 17, 33, 65, 67, 93, 95–98, 191–192, 265, 287n4, 316, 321
Hyderabad, Sindh (Pakistan), 40, 45–46, 192–220, 272, 278, 280, 288n7, 297–299; Muharram of, Muhājir participation in, 41; procession, children's, in, 119; repertoire of, drum, 63–65, 98–102, 105

Ibbetson, Denzil, 33, 34, 278n1
Ibn Rushd, 48
Ibn Sinā, 48, 51, 278n4; "imaginative assent" of, 50–51
iconicity, 18, 20, 22, 43, 48–49, 51, 96, 116–117, 119; imperfection of, giving rise to contemplation, 186; perceptions in relation to typical forms, 185–186. *See also* imitation; mimesis
identity/ies: categories of, 47–51; overlapping, 48
Ikram, Sheikh Mohamad, 276n3
Ikramuddin, Muhammad (ḍhol player), 210–212, 298
Ilakkiyampaṭṭi (Tamil Nadu), 69, 70, 71
imambarah. *See imambarah and peṛh in glossary*
Imambarah Māsumīn (Multan), 118
imagination, xiii; Aristotle's *Poetics*, in, 49, 54; dhamāl, in dancing, 183; improvisation, drummed, against musical ground, 198; models, vocal, imagined, 7, 88, 98; Muharram Ali, of, 1–2, 6; practice, relation to, in 56. *See also* Ibn Sinā, "imaginative assent" of; improvisation

imitation: ḍhol-tāshā ensemble, of, 37, (282n14); "Gāon dafalī tāl," of daf ensembles, 98; learning, role of, in 187; Panjabi ḍhol playing, of 152–153; valuation, negative, of, 31, 35, 164
improvisation, 56, 58, 74, 105, 163, 231, 287, 288n10, 299, 302, 308, 312, 313, 316, 319, 320, 325
examples of: around kalmah theme, 216; departing from and returning to nauḥah melody, gazī player, 201; during nauḥah and procession, of shahnā'ī, 128; placement of tāshā theme, 106–107
terms relating to: chēṛ chāṛ, 87, 163, 240, 288n10, 302; "moving back and forth" (phir ṭur rahnā), 163; upji/upaj, 103
individual, role of in relation to group, 32, 44, 52–54, 142, 173, 185. *See also* agency
Indo-Aryan languages, 112, 113, 192
Indo-Caribbean(s), 113, 45; tassa and bass of, 103 (and photo)
"Ins o malak o jin ke madadgār haiṉ shabbīr" (marṣiyah), 121–122
instrument(s), musical: associations of, emotional, 91; double-reed, 9, 33, 34, 39, 63, 68, 71, 76–79, 194, 205, 279n5, 313, 318, 315, 322 (*see also names of individual instruments*); names of, related to repertoire names, 62, 66, 68, 72, 77 (*see also under ensembles, musical*); repertoire for particular, specificity of, 90
"integrative" impulse, 195–199, *196*, 206–207, 216; contrasted with disjunctive attitude, 213, 220, 221, 297
interaction, musical, forms of, 128–129, 162–163; in chēṛ chāṛ, chēṛ as interchange/incitement, 163 (*see also chēṛ chāṛ in glossary*); eye contact, 76, 121, 216; "to lay down" (lagāna) ṭhekā or naġmah over which someone improvises, 163; "to mix" (ralāna), 163; "question-answer" (sawāl-jawāb), 163
interlocking of drum patterns/strokes, 75, 79, 231
interpretation, musical. *See* transformation: musical
intoxication. *See* mastī; ecstasy
Iqbal, Muhammad (poet), 176
Iran: art forms of, brought to Multan, 138; 'azādārī, history of, in 124; instruments of, 65; Islamic revolution of, 35, 123, 203; music, dastgāh, of, 282n18; musicans of, 19, 33, 35, 138; Shiism, financial support for, from, 191; ẕekr practices in, 18, 19; *See also names of specific regions*
Irula (Nilgiri tribe), 94
Ishaq, Muhammad (tāshā maker), 214
Islam: dichotomy of "scriptural," versus "on the ground," transcending, 184; distancing of drumming from, 210–211; music in, 11, 13, 17, 219; politics of, in Pakistan, 47, 184; recent converts to, 41
Ismaili Muslims, 75, 312

"Jab fāṭimah firdaus se kahtī h'ī ā'īṉ maẓlūm ḥusainā" (salām associated with savārī and mātam), 232–233, 247, 262–263, 303
Jacob Lines (Karachi), 110, 222–233; education and professions of ḍhol-tāshā ensemble members, 223
Jafar, Imam (Ja'far ibn Muḥammad al-Ṣādiq, 6th Shī'ī imam), 196
jāgar/jāgariya, 74–75
Jairazbhoy, Nazir, 113
jajmānī. *See* service specialists: customary compensation of
Jakobson, Roman, 48–50

Jalal, Ayesha, 295, 300n2
Jamali, Misri Khan (ustad), 42
"Jangal pahāṛ kahte hain̲ nād-e 'alī 'alī " (text for 'Alī kī zarben̲), 232
jarb(en̲). *See ẓarb in glossary*
Jhelumin, Mīān Muhammad Baksh, 175–176
Jhūle Lāl, ambiguous identity of, 149. *See also under* exclamations
Jhura Sain (Pappu Sain's playing partner), 147, 148, 149, 152, 153, 155, 160, 162, 163, 271
"Jogi Nāl Jāna," (song sung by Nusrat Fateh Ali Khan), 157
Jones, A. M., 8, 288n14
Joshi, Varsha, 41
Jyothi Band (Hyderabad, Andhra Pradesh), 95–98

kalām: light, cheerful melody, 204; Sufi poetry, 227, 303
Kalāwant, 37
Kalhora (rulers of Sindh), 194
Kāḷiyamman̲ (goddess), 69, 94
kalmah: identity as muslim and playing pattern, connection between, 216; inserted at time of exchanging drums, 248; invention of, as drum pattern, 223; music, as not a piece of, 219; notated with cue and text, 299. *See also (kalmah in glossary)*; tāls, cāls and related entities, specific, discussed
Kamin (caste), 36
Kammari (blacksmiths), 37
Kaṃsāli (gold and silver workers), 37
Kancari (copper- and brass-smiths), 37
Karachi, 41, 110, 264, 273; Delhi, compared with, 237, 240–249 passim; Hyderabad, compared with, 194; India to, migration from, 193; Jacob Lines, musicians of, 222–233; Lahore from, migration to, 173; Pakistanis of African descent in, 193
Karbala, 1, 67; events at, government of India uses, to highlight university truths, 243; martyrs of, devotion to, 42; poetry, story of, in 26–27; story of, recounted on street, 124
"Karbalā men̲ mehndī voh, kar ga'ī savārī vakṛi" (song played to accompany mātam), 241
Kārlu (caste), 38
Kasbī, 38
Kāsi (stone workers), 37
kathak dance, 67, 90fn, 163, 313
Kaveri (drummer, Ilakkiyampaṭṭi), 70–73
Kazim, Ali Muhammad (chronicler), 6, 276
Keil, Charles, 187, 296n4
keṭṭi mēḷam, 33, 69, 278
kettledrum, 3, 4, 6, 30, 63, 65, 71, 75, 77, 125, 200, 311, 318
Khadim, 'Ali Hayat (ḍhol player), 163
Khadim Husain, Baba (ḍhol player), 163
k̲h̲alīfah, musical, 38
Khan, Ali Akbar, 15
Khan, Ayub (Pakistani president), 172
Khan, Chand, 37–38
Khan, Iqbal Ahmed, 15, 38
Khan, Nusrat Fateh Ali, 17, 132, 156; impact on dhamāl, 157
Khan, Pathane (original name, Ghulam Muhammad; Pakistani singer), 115, 167
Khan, Vilayat, 276n6
Khan as high-status name, 41
Khaṛi Sharif (Azad Kashmir, Pakistan), 175
Khata Chowk (in Hyderabad, Sindh), 207–209
k̲h̲ayāliyā, 15
Khorasan, 19, 33, 35
Khurshid Ali, Wajid (Shī'ī tabla player), 224–225; sponsor of ta'ziyah in Delhi, 225

Khusrau, Amir (poet), grave of, 235–236, 296n1
Kippen, James, 20, 21, 63, 64, 66, 112, 280, 281n2, 283, 288n10
Kirāṛ (Hindus in Pakistani Panjab), 284; as patrons, 87, 90; special vājā for, 87, 90
"Kisī ne kūfe ke raste meṉ" (soz), 26–27
knowledge: ability to recite bols, indicated by, 86, 162 (*see also recitation: of drum/rhythmic syllables, importance of*); access to, differential, 7, 224; audience, of, 87; background, 44, 46, 186; musical ('ilm-e mūsiqī), 155; special, of great musicians, 58; textual underlay for drum patterns, regarding, lack of specific, 224 (*see also under memory*)
Koḷāḷ (caste), 94
Kolmel (Kota village), 93–94
Korom, Frank, 276
Kota (Nilgiri tribe), 9, 14–15, 63, 65, 68, 93–95, 279n5, 287n2
Kothari, Komal, 40
Kotri (Hyderabad, Sindh), 204
koṭṭu, 73. *See also aṭi in glossary*
Kramrisch, Stella, 37
krīya (hand gesture), 21
Kūfī, 'Alī ibn Ḥāmid, 40
Kurumba (Nilgiri tribes): Ālu, 94; Beṭṭa, 94; Kāṭṭu Nāyaka, 94; Mullu, 14–15

lagan (passion/attachment), 155, 180, 293. *See also* emotion or condition (kaifiyat)
Lahore: Ashura, drumming on, in, 161; cultural center, as, 11; Liberty Circle, 25; Lucknow, compared with, 26–27; Sufi shrines in, 18
"lā il-lāha illa'llah muḥammadur rasūl 'allah": drummed text, offered as example of, 241, 247; notated, aspects of drummed version, 104, 216; sign, on, 171; uttered by drummer, 241, 247. *See also* kalmah; (*kalmah in glossary*)
Lal, Baba (esteemed faqir), 157
Lal, Hira, 33, 35
la'l (ruby), 149, 158, 167, 168, 169, 315
lāl/la'l, multiple meanings of, 17–18, 168, 186
Lal Magpur, Baba (ḍhol player), 164
"Lāl merī pat," (folk song), 17–18, 156
Lāl Shahbāz Qalandar, 17–18, 149; dancing dhamāl, through, feeling a connection to, 149, 156; dhamāl taken up by, 158; Sindh, settlement in, 182. *See also* Sehwan (Sindh)
lamentation/weeping, 27; reflection on, 29, 31
lamp black, in black spot of tabla, 291
lamp(s). *See* lighting and lamps
language(s)
  cultural identity and relations: code-switching/loanwords, 160; influences, morphological, between, 289n15; intelligibility of regional, 74; language(s), affect, limitation of, in describing 52; Panjabi literature vis-à-vis Panjabiyat, 186; Sindhi versus Urdu, speakers, cultural differences, 197–198, 207
  music and poetry: areas, linguistic and musical, 113–114; instruments "speaking," 43, 156; multiple, performing in; 42–43; poetic function of language, 48; shift of, in poetry, 26–27; "to speak" and "to play," etymological connection between, 66; variations, drum, as "words" (vārttai), 72
lay bandhnā (build rhythm), 103
leading, role in drum ensemble of, 70, 71, 76, 93–95

learning/training/development
institutional training: reading and listening,167; state textbooks, 171
musical learning, 42–43; family, within versus outside, 25, 55, 85, 154–155; haphazard and informal 21, 55; metaphor for mutual development, 25; periods of study compared, 202; training sequence, 58, 61
pir (roles of pir and ustad overlap): controlling progress, 179, 187; imitating hand movements of, 55; mimetic, 178–179, 187; roles of, 154, 178–179
ustad: attending competitions with, 58; faiths, across, 47, 218; oral learning from, 86, 166; physical punishment, meted out by, 154; reciting drum syllables, 86, 93; roles, other, of, 46, 55–58, 86, 154–155
lehrā (Panjabi ḍhol pattern), 30
Leitner, Gottlieb William, 36, 77
licensing, colonial, 123, 130, 138, 144
light, symbolism of, 172, 173. *See also nūr in glossary*
lighting and lamps, 123, 129, 170, 171, 172, 173, 178
Link, Hilde K., 37
listening, 15, 31, 91
local, the, access to understandings of, 44
Lodhi, Muhammad Asif Alim (devotee), 173, 271
Lodhipura (Multan), 133, 136, 139, 144, 283, 289
Lok Virsa, National Institute of Folk and Traditional Heritage, 40
Lorī (ethnonym), 43
lorī (musical genre). *See* (*lolī in glossary*); lullaby
Lorimer, David Lockhart Robertson, 36, 278n2, 282n17
loudspeakers/amplification, use of, 143, 170
love
discourse and poetry: dāstāns, in, classic lovers, 168 (*see also Hīr-Ranjhā*); discourses on, regarding musicians, 42, 59, 60, 120, 129, 155, (162), 229; genuineness of, 182; human love as metaphor for divine love, 168, 185; songs, 135, 312
love of or for: beloved, the, 18, 176; God, of, 155, 176, 187, 209, 221; mother, for, 167–168, 185; pir, of, 182; Prophet's family, of, 196, 215, 216, 221; same-sex, 146, 169, 182, 187
See also muḥabbat; pyār; 'ishq; 'āshiq; majẕūb; *yār in glossary*
Lucknow, 17; Lahore, compared with, 26–27; processions of, 35
Luḍan Sain, Baba, (father of Pappu Sain), 154–155, 160, 161, 162, 166–167
lullaby, 34, 206. *See also lolī in glossary*
Lybarger, Lowell H., 279, 280, 283

Madho Lal Husain, 'urs of, 59, 133, 146, 165–187 passim, 275; area around shrine of, described, 165. *See also* Shah Husain
Madian, Azza Abd Al-Hamid, 48, 51
Mādiga (caste), 34
magicians, 37
Maharaj, Birju, 163
Maiyam, Tamil, 276n4
majlis-e-'azā: description, 120–122, 196; food at, 122; order of, compared, 196; voice quality of ẕākir at, 179; wedding related practice at, 29, 89

malaṅg: definitions of, 174–176; domain of, 173; musician, as, 176; qalandar, versus, 176; subjectivity, complex, of, 174. *See also malaṅg in glossary*
malaṅgnī, 167, 182–183, 187; Shī'ī, 183. *See also* malaṅg
Mamraj and ḍhol-group, 63, 65, 93, 102–112, 230, 236–249, 263, 264, 270, 273, 280, 288n9, 288n10, 302; religious boundaries, view opposing, of, 238
Mandelbaum, David G., 287n2
"Man kunto maula, fahāza 'ali-un maula" (the qaul), 157
mangal bāja (drums), 33
Mangali, 32–33
manganhār and māngaṇiār: 39–41, 194–206, 272; Shī'ī and Sunni, musicians as effective intercommunal mediators, 206
maṉmattaḷam (spherical drum), 14, 71, 277n9
mansuriya, 88, 91, 92. *See also marṣiyah in glossary*
Manzur Sain. *See* Jhura Sain
Marāghi, 'Abd al-Qāder Ebn Gheybi Hāfez, 279–280
marginalization: barber and other musicians, of, 33; drummer at 'urs, of, 184; Shī'ahs, Ahmedis and others as result of Islamization, of, 123; Urdu speakers in Sindh, of, 207
marṣiyah
  performance: configurations of reciters of, different, with and without drums, 229; drums, on, to reach crowds, 228; recitation of, heterogeneous group, in Delhi, 245; sticks, saying with, rather than mouth, to maintain tāl, 229, 305n10; tune of, played on trumpets and clarinets, 241
  poets, poetry, and terminology: dhīmā, impression conveyed by, via marṣiyah, 229–230; Muharram poetry/songs, marṣiyah as generic term for, 233, 241; Sufi poet of, 236; text of, on tāshā, 229
  See also marṣiyah in glossary
marṣiyo: classical rāgs, gazī, played on, in, 204; rāgs, different, any sing text sung to, 204; ṭarz (tune/rāga) of, set according to composer, 204; 200 years old, used for Sindhi vajats, melodies of, 205. *See also marṣiyah in glossary*
martyrdom, desire for, 26. *See also* self-sacrifice
masakbīn. *See* bagpipes
Massoudieh, Muhammad Taqi, 19
master. *See* pir(s); (*pir in glossary*)
master-disciple relationship. *See* discipleship
mastī: cause of, 158, 159; causing, in others, 158–159, 293. *See also* ecstasy; (*ḥāl in glossary)*; possession; wajd
Masud, Nayyar, 35, 276
mātam
  motivations, representations and configurations: commercial videocassettes of, 196; drum pattern called mātam, denial of link with, 218; "end" same, style different, 198; Shī'ahs performing, on one side of ta'ziyah and Sunnis drumming on the other, 225; women, performed by, 128–129; wronged, Husain was, performed because, 211
  types of: bed of thorns, lying on, as, 158; choreography of, 141; ḍhol playing as, 162; head, hands striking top of, 200–201;

Lāl Shahbāz Qalandar, of, 158; nauḥah text, coordination with, 130, 137, 141; sinah zanī, 122; swordplay as, 90, 197; tears as, 162; walking over hot coals as, 196; Ya Husain chant, coordination with, 200–201; zanjīr kā (*see zanjīr kā mātam*)
See also mātam in glossary
matchmakers, 39
materialism, local critiques of, 155, 166, 167
mātra(s): alternatives to, 93–114; cāls, difference of, with same number of, 111; counting, 85–86, 89, 93; history of, 85; reckoning systems, hybrid, mātra- and non-mātra-based, 98–102; tāshā, counting (ḥisāb) with, 229. *See also mātra in glossary*
mattaḷam. *See* maṉmattaḷam
mausoleum(s), 4, 228, 236
Mawṣili, Iṣhāq al-, 281n6
"Māye nī maiṉ kīnoṉ āḵẖāṉ" (kāfī by Shah Husain), 167–168
Mazari, Qadar Baksh, 42–43, 278
meaning(s): fields through which negotiated, 44–46. *See also* semiotic relations
mediation: drummer, of, between devotee and saint, 34
mehndi: drumming, 208; lack of, lamented, 130; music of, 27–28, 35
Mehr (historical drummer in Multan), 136
mela(s), 59, 63, 146, 147, 172
melody/ies, 8; articulation of, 76; defining role of, 67; meter, poetic, fitting, 227–228; nauḥah, flexibility of, in relation to tāl, 136; nauḥah, of common, 134; nauḥah, zārī, dhun, kalām and ṯarz, distinctions among, 204; rhythm of, drummer following, local view on, 125; rhythm, separability from, 8–9, 79; (ṯarz) on gazī from marṡiyo, 203. *See also* tone melody/ies; stroke melody; *ṯarz in glossary*
Memon, Siddique G, 300n3
memory: sustaining, of repertoire when performed only during Muharram, 216; texts underlying instrumental melodies or drum patterns, issues of regarding memory of, 203, 204–205, 227–228; text, underlying, shahnā'ī melody stimulating memory of, 205; (yād) of marṡiyah is kept in heart, if, one can recognize poetry in drum pattern, 230
Menaci (Tamil Nadu), 69, 70, 71, 281n10
mendicants, 18; becoming, 59; described, 26, 149; musicians as, 41; unaffiliated with any sect, as, 161. *See also* (darvesh in glossary); (faqir in glossary); malaṅg; qalandar
merit, spiritual: 29, 59, 131, 209, 239, 303
Merriam, Alan, 33
metaphor, 19, 56–57, 58, 155, 160, 164; definition of James W. Fernandez, 185
meter
processes: clash in, creating, 200; musical, shifts in, 125, 126, 201, 205; responses to, 51; syllables, emphasizing important, in, 65. *See also under* poetry; (*'arūz in glossary*)
types of poetic: hazaj, 303; quantitative, 18, 88, 104, 112, 231–233, 249, 260–262, 287, 288n12, 302; ramal, 227–228, 231; varṇika and mātrika, 112
methodological issues and fieldwork, 44–45, 73, 215, 226, 277
Mevlevi (Sufi order), 17
midwives, 32–33

milād, 53
milāp ("matching, meeting, encounter": musical joining and interplay), 162–163
mimesis, 48–49, 186, 187; acting as dancing girl, Bulleh, of 182; mental image (naqshah) of Karbala, dancer keeping, 162; training of disciple, by pir, in 178–179; zanjīr kā mātam, dhamālī imitating, 183. *See also* semiotic relations
Mīr Ālam, 38
mīrāsan, 27, 28, 116. *See also mīrāsī in glossary*
Mīrs (aristocracy in Hunza), 78
Mīrzāda, 38
mnemonics, musical, 20. *See also* bol(s)
models: musical, 7, 9, 12, 20, 98; religious, 4, 119, 185–187, 321 (s.v. shabīh); textual, 7, 261. *See also* deformation; iconicity
modernity, 12; critique of notion of, 45; Islam, and, 131; processes, historical, in relation to 114. *See also* reformism
modulation, musical, 89; "come and go" [phirnā ṭurnā] through tāls, 159
Moffatt, Michael, 33
Mohammad, Mahboob Ali, 67
mohri (lead singer in qawwālī), 16
Momen, Moojan, 278n4
"Momin karyo mātam" (text for "Ya Husain"), 206, media example 8.3
moral behavior, discourses on, 166
mother, theme of, in poetry, 167–168
motives, drum pattern, 93, 106, 113; combined, motivic units, 99–101; conservative use of, 99–102; Hyderabad, Andhra Pradesh, in, 95; Panjabi, 151, 180, 217; "riff" in "riff based pattern," as, or signature phrase, 18, 105, 232, 299; Tamil, 70, 73, 74, 75; ṭhekā, compared to, 73
mourning, meritorious, 29; lack of among Sunnis, 46. *See also* lamentation/weeping
MQM (Muhājir Qaumi Mahaz), 193–194, 194fn
Mu'āwiyya (Ummayyad Caliph), 116fn, 124
Muftiyān Masjid, 122
Muhājirs: assimilation of, into local populations, 134; female, from Bihar, 182–183; resources in Pakistan, economic and political, competition for, 226; Sindhis and PPP, relations with, 194; status of in Pakistan, 220. *See also Muhājir in glossary*
Muhammad (the Prophet): story of the cloak (hadis̱-e kisa), 29
Muhammad, Wali (historical figure in Multan), 138–139
Muḥarram
  controversies: historical evidence, lack of, for Muharram practices, 210; music during, issues regarding, 44, 53, 82, 89–91, 134, 161, 225, 207–249 passim; sectarianism during, 161; tyranny, as protest against, 203
  local traditions: Delhi and Lucknow, Census of India report on, 243–244; discourses on, 195–199; Multan, in, 115–144 passim, 162; Sindh, in, 195–221 passim
  multicommunity participation in: Hindu celebration of, 67, 69; identical Shī'ī and Sunni observances of, in Sindh described, 196, 197; Sunni participation in, 42, 90, 196–199, 207–249
  music and drumming: classical "music" during, in Hyderabad, Sindh, 204; ḍhol playing as a "pastime" (shuġl) during, 210; ḍhol playing during, as "custom"

(ravāj) 210; drumming during, 1, 33, 42, 53, 95–99, 161, 162; gazī, special instrument for, 198; kalmah pattern during, 104–105; Lahore (formerly), mātamī ḍhol during, in, 161; mātamī style of performance for, 198; Shī'ī drumming during (*see Shī'ah[s]*); subjectivity of musician, music in relation to 203–221 passim
significance of days of, 29; ninth, 246; rituals on particular days of, 83, 115, 138–139, 265–267, 304n7; seventh, 122, 246
themes, other: humor in connection with, 84; mock battles in (*see also play/playfulness: swordplay/fencing*), 247; royalty, celebration of, as, 253
Multan (Pakistan), 283; Bheḍi Potra neighborhood, 82; fieldwork in, 42, 283, 289–290; history of, 83, 92; Muharram, music of, in, 44, 52, 53, 91, 92, 115–144, 162, 197, 201; music in, 38–39, 42, 63, 161, 185, 285–287; musicians in, 270; recitation, majlis poetry, special style of, in 120–122; terminology, musical, in, 163; tilework of, 81
Multani, Muhammad Baksh (drummer), 38, 85–92, 270, 278, 283, 285–287, 289, 290, 321
Multanikar, Suraiya, 28, 135, 271, 283, 289, 290, 291
Munda languages, linguistic interaction with, 113
Mushirabad (Hyderabad, Andhra Pradesh), 33, 67
Mushtaq, Muhammad (devotee), 166–174 passim, 184–185, 271
music
concepts: affect, music as label for, 52; classifying, principles for, multiple, 68, 73, 76–77, 79, 93, 111; craft versus discipline, as 162; definitions of, 1, 15–16, 125, 198, 199, 202, 204; duty, as, 202; functionality versus artistry of, local views on, 38, 125; metaphors describing, 56–57, 58, 155, 160, 164; moral implications of, 11, 15, 16, 48–49, 91; soul, human, effect on, 48–49; understanding/knowledge, musical, 31, 155
economics of (*see economics [of music, recitation, and dance]*)
qualities of: fire (āg), performance as, 160; fire, causing, 160; "insipid," as, (phīkā), 159, 294; rain, causing 160; "sweet," as (mīṭhā), 159, 294
types of: instrumental, 7, 11, 68; mass mediated, 67–68; practice, historical changes in, 82; styles, playing, three Sindhi, 202
music, functions of: announcement/heraldry, 79, 115, 142, 202, 224; calling people for assembly, 77; honoring victors, 77; improving the rituals, 202; marking otherness, 94; praise, 77, 156, 287n4; welcoming, 198
"Music Centre," 196, 199
musician(s): becoming a, 41–42; categories, social, of, 32–43; classification, grades of generality in, of, 35–39; hierarchies among, 14–16, 32–43 passim, 77; interactions among (*see interaction, musical, forms of*); Manganhārs as master, 198; powers, social, of, 35, 38, 76; "profession" (pesha) of, as connected with repertoire, 216; quick wittedness of, 38; Shī'ī and Sunni, 40, 82; stigma of being a, 42; terms for, 15–16, 29–31, 32–43 (*see also individual names of musicians communities*)

musicianship: acquiring, 154; assessments of, 29–31, 38; "control," musical 160; criteria and definitions of, 7, 41, 160, 162; focus necessary for, 156; hereditary, as, (*see also mīrāṣan; individual names of musician communities;* (*mīrāṣī in glossary*), 32–35, 37–41, 43, 75, 82, 91, 129, 144, 154, 157, 257; resistance/sensitivity to notion of hereditary, 41, 43; tez--quick on the uptake, 162; unmusical person disfavored by God, 158
Muttahida Qaumi Mahaz, 194fn. *See also* MQM
mystic. *See* (*faqir in glossary*); malaṅg; qalandar

nād-e 'alī, 140
Naī, 33. *See also* barbers
naming, practice of: drum patterns, 7–8, 61–80 passim, 91–114 passim, 208, 212–219, 280, 281n2, 287n1, 288n6, 297, 298; higher status, adopting, of, 41; historical implications of, 113–114; hybridity of, within a repertoire, 98, 215; mātam as "just a [drum pattern] name," 208; repertoires, connection among, through, 282n18; respect, conferring, 40
Nanda Devi (goddess), 74–75
Naqqāl, 35–36
naqqārah: large, associated with Ajmer and Muhājirs therefrom, 207, 208, 214; parts of, 135, 200; performance practice in Sindh, 198, 200–206; players (naqqārci), 39, 135; preparation, performance, 135; repurposed, disused naqqārah (photo), 207; role, key, of, 203; Sindh described, of, 194–195 (photo); vajat for, Shah Panjatan, 206. *See also naqqārah in glossary*
"Naql se aṣl paidā hotā hai," (The original is born from the imitation), 187
Naqshbandi (Sufi order): Mojaddedi, 19; silent ẕikr of, 19
Nārttampaṭṭi (Tamil Nadu), 70, 71, 94
Natavar, Mekhala Devi, 39
nauḥah: descriptions of performances with mātam, 122, 130, 141–142; relation with shahnā'ī melody, 128–129; women's public performance of, 128–129, 133; "mārū wala," 136–137; in k͟hayāl style, 136; for each of first 11 days of Muharram, 138–139; for ta'ziyah-lifting, 139–140. *See nauḥah and zārī in glossary*
"Navigation of feeling, the," 32, 51–54
Nathan (ḍhol player), 40, 278
Nathu, Faqir, 203–204, 272
Nayyar, Adam, 16, 34, 38, 43, 169 (photo); credited, ix, 271, 295
Nazimabad (Gilgit, Pakistan), 76
Needham, Rodney, 275n1
Nettl, Bruno, 288n14
Neuman, Daniel, 14, 15, 37, 39
Newars, music of, 21, 37
Niamat Ali (ḍhol player), 25–26, 30–32, 34–35, 38, 55–60, 73, 111, 179–182, 277, 279, 280, 296
Nilgiri Hills, tribal music in, 14–15
nizam of Hyderabad, 67
Nizami (family of followers of Nizamuddin Auliya). *See* Nizamuddin Auliya
Nizami, Farid Ahmad, 236–237, 243
Nizami, Ghulam Hasnain (pirzadah and ḍhol player), 230 (photo), 237, 241, 246–249, 259–261, 303
Nizami, Sarir Ahmed, 228–233, 234. 241, 248, 262–263, 303
Nizami, Sayyad Ali Abbas (author of dastūr-e 'amal), 226–227, 302

Nizami, Serwer Sadiq Hussain (son of Ghulam Hasnain Nizami), 246, 247, 273
Nizami Sayyad Bokhari, Shamsul-Mashaikh Hazrat Pir Zamin (religious leader at Nizamuddin shrine), 236, 243
Nizamuddin Auliya, 117; ḍhol-tāshā playing at, 450 year history, 229; followers of, in Karachi (see also Jacob Lines [Karachi]) 110, 222–233; power and influence of followers of, declining after migration to Pakistan, 226; rituals, Muharram, associated with shrine of, 102–110, 235–241; shrine of saint, 38, 102, 235–237, 296n1; "sins" (gunāh), drummers at shrine accused of committing, 226. *See also under* Delhi
Nizamuddin Imambarah: description of, 245
noise: conceptions of sound as, 91; dhūm dhaṛkkā (clattering) 219; making of, to get attention, 212
norms: behavioral, 187; discrepancy in relation to, 296n4; musical 114; religious, 48
Northern Areas of Pakistan. *See* Gilgit-Baltistan (Pakistan)
notation, issues of, 21, 106–107
Nur Jahan (Queen), 124
Nuru, Mullah (manganhār ancestor), 40

occupational specialists, 32–43. *See also* service specialists
offering(s)
  art and material: cloth, 90; music (as ḥāẓrī), 216
  monetary: niyāz, 237; vel, 183
oil pressers, 37
orientalism, 12, 45
orientation, musical, 77, 79, 93, 181
osāro ("lamentation," ālāp-like item), 205
ottu (double-reed drone), 71
"O vārī vecca taḍe lāl banra voh hā'ī hā'ī" (nauḥah), 139–140

pace, metrical, 57, 200, 231
Pahāṛi languages, 74
Pak Gate (Multan), 133
Pakka Qila (Fort area, Hyderabad, Sindh), 209–219
Pakistan: classical music in (*see under classical music, South Asian*); Muslim place, as, 50; ẕikr in, 18. *See also names of individual cites and provinces*
Pakistan National Council of Arts (PNCA), 40, 42, 223, 301
palakai. *See tappaṭṭai in glossary*
Paluskar, Vishnu Digambar, 287n4
pampai (drum), 14
Panasa. *See* Runzavānlu
Panjab, India, 17
Panjab, Pakistan: "culture," Panjabi, luḍḍi and bhāṅgṛā as, 159; dhamāl in, 18; surnames of musicians in, 41
Panjab gharāna, 82
Panjabi (language): musical terms in, 56, 58, 66, 74, 156, 278n1, 279, 310, 313–315, 317, 322, 327; poetry, sung, in, 130, 167–168; poets, 146, 170, 186; speakers, culture of, 159, 170, 171, 186, 295
Panjabi (people): in Sindh, 194
Pappu Sain (Zulfiqar Ali), 18, 59, 60, **147–164**, 150 (photo); Bulleh Shah story as told by, 158, 182; chapter notes regarding, 270, 271, 276n7, 291, 292, 295; subjectivity, complex, of 186; verbalizations, drum pattern, 185; views of others about, 148, 166–167, 176
paṟai (drum), 14, 281n8. *See also tappaṭṭai in glossary*

Paraiyar: 34, 35, 68; Toṭṭi Paraiyar, 71, 281n10
parallelism, 48, 50–51, 168, 185; melodic, 8; metric, 287
paronomasia, 26–27
participation: communal drumming, 198, 208; multicommunity, in events, 90, 122, 178, 196, 224, 236, 243
Partition (of India and Pakistan in 1947), 24, 25, 41, 46, 50, 98, 316; Hindus in Sindh after, 193; "Hindustan existed, the time before," as, 154; interaction, Shī'ī-Sunni, prior to, 224, 244; Karachi after, 193; musical traditions before, 236, 273; religious diversity, end of, after, 178
Parveen, Abida, 17
Pashto (language): instrument speaking in, 43
Pathan (ethnic group, speakers of Pashto): jhūmar dance, version of, 87; Sindh, in, 194
Pathan, Lala Gul Sanubar (peṛh caretaker), 195
patronage, 35, 38, 39, 40, 87, 89, 91, 138, 178, 312; of majlis, 119
pattern as link for melodic/rhythmic terms, 80. *See also* drum pattern(s)
payments and tips, 59; awards for playing one new bol after the other, 87; peṛh, at, caretaker financing musicians, 195; "spirit bolstering," 59; vel, 183; ways of giving money to performers, 179, 181, 183. *See also* economics (of music, recitation, and dance); offering(s)
Peirce, Charles Sanders, 297
"Perfume Baba" (dhamālī), 181–183
Peṛh Muhammad (shrine), 194–201 passim
periodicity: absence of, 102, 106, 259; drone, of, 8; motives, of, 73
periya mēḷam (ensemble in Tamil Nadu), 32
permutation, 8, 73, 94, 98–102
Persian (language), musical terms derived from, 75
Perumal (drummer of Ilakkiyampaṭṭi), 70–73
Perumal (drummer of Nārtampaṭṭi), 70
pesha (profession/vocation/business), 216
philosophy: cross fertilization of, Greek-Arabic, 48; Greek, 47, 48–51, 278n4; Islamic, music in, 11, 15, 16
photographs: role in this book, 49, 283; teaching through, 117
pir(s): poems alluding to relationship with, 168. *See also pir in glossary*
Pirla Paṇḍaga, 67
pir-murīdī. *See* discipleship
pitch: bol recitation, of, creating question-answer effect, 163; high, connoting wailing, 198; intrinsic, 20, 277n8; relative, 20, 277n8
place: domain of malaṅgs, 173; musical, (jagah), sam as, 87; thān (turf) of ḍhol players and dancers, 178
Plato, 48
play/playfulness, 34, 38, 42, 87, 283, 284, 310; courtesan, of, 156; dancing dhamāl as, 149, 179, 182, 292, 294, 296; "fun," as (majāgīrī), 87; musical (*see also chēṛ chāṛ in glossary*); swordplay/fencing, 74, 90, 159, 197, 297
poetics theory: Aristotle and, 48–51; contributions to, Greek and Muslim, 48; poetic function, 48. *See also* social poetics
poetry
  poetic and musical genres, in: dhrupad, 15; qasīdah at majlis, 196; soz, 26–27
  treatment of texts: building of rhythm (lay) inside (marsiyah), 224, 304n2; disagreement over which poem underlies drum pat-

tern, 229; melody on gazī during Muharram, sung poetry as basis for, 203; scansion in relation to music, 18, 88, 112, 231–233, 260–262, 287, 288n12, 302
understanding: interpretations, local, of, 167–168; musical setting of poetry required for proper effect, 167; semantic implications of musical setting of mars̱iyah, 121–122
See also specific poetic forms and techniques
poets: Panjabi, 170; Urdu, 170. *See also names of individual poets*
Politics (of Aristotle), rhythms and songs in relation to human character, 48–49
pollution, 33. *See also* tīṭṭu
popular music. *See under* music
possession, spirit, 67; of Pappu Sain by Shah Jamal, 151, 155. *See also* ecstasy; (*ḥāl in glossary*); mastī; wajd
posters: announcement, majlis, 118; images, Sufi on 49, 172, 186
Powers, Harold S., 11–12, 113
PPP (Pakistan People's Party), 194
prayer: maturity of those engaging in, compared to that of musicians, 156, 293; Muslim, music in, 15; procession, in, Muharram, 127. *See also du'ā in glossary*
prayer leader, 127. *See also ẕākir in glossary*
preacher. *See ẕākir in glossary*
processions, 67, 69
music: drum pattern to initiate, 206 (*see also savārī in glossary*); music to announce, 215–216, 236
organization and contents: list of items in a Muharram procession (originally Mehmudabad), 255; routes, 130, 291 (police manual); segregation of once unified Shī'ī-Sunni processions, 225
terms for, 284, 285, 309, 314
types of, by event or participant: "Arab," 125; children's, 119; Muharram, 4, 5, 6, 35, 84n1, 102, 104, 122, 124–126, 130, 135, 138, 197–198, 200–202, 205, 206, 207, 215–216, 223–226, 229, 237, 241, 243–246, 248–249, 265–267, 290; Newari, 37; Ram Lila, 152, 238–239; wedding (barāt), 29, 30, 63, 87, 90
prolongation, rhythmic, 99, 101, 233, 249, 260–261, 313
prompter, textual, 16, 134
prosody, 18–19, 104. *See also specific techniques*
prostitutes and prostitution, 182, 187. *See also* courtesan
public sphere: artistic individualism in, 142; awareness of behavior in, 92
puja, 4, 75, 98
pūnakam, 67

Qadir, Ghulam (ḍhol teacher of Pappu Sain), 154–155
qalandar, 17–18; call to prayer of, from kettle drum (naubat), 156; malaṅg, distinct from, 149, 176; tradition (rivāyat) of, 157, 158; voice of, from ḍhol, 148. *See also* Lāl Shahbāz Qalandar
Qasim, Muhammad (aka Qasim Shah, naqqārah player), 203–207
Qasim (nephew of Husain), 35, 67, 116, 122, 130, 134, 136, 137, 161, 266, 270, 274, 290, 304n7
qawwālī: āṭāwālā tabla in Panjabi, 132, 291; names used by musicians, 41. *See also qawwālī and qawwāl in glossary*
Qur'ān: remember God, injunction to, in, 17; translated into local languages, 193; verses from, posted, 170

Qureshi, Regula (cited for her scholarship, not for her fictional role in the story), 60, 187

Rabia Basri (qalandar), 176
rāgas
historical relation among, 113
mentioned: Bahudāri, 67, 281n5; Bhairavi, 26, 204; Husainī, 204; Jaunpurī, 204; Kedāro, 204; Koyārī, 204; Lauṛāu, 204; Malhār, 160; Malkauns, 137; Pahāṛi, 204; Panjab Bhairavi, 176, 179, 186; Puriya Dhanasri, 204, Raṇa, 136; Sindh Bhairavi, 179; Sindhi Jog, 204
"Raghupati Rāghava Rāja Rām" (bhajan), 97
Rahaim, Matt, 288m10
Rahman, Tariq, 295
rāj (domain of patron villages), 39–40
Rajasthan, music of, 30, 39–41, 63, 208, 237; alġozah, 308. *See also individual cities*
raja tappaṭṭa (lead frame drum), 72–73, 93–95
Raman, S. (Kota musician), 94
Ram Babu (tāshā player), 239
Ram Lila (Hindu holiday) 152, 239 (photo); ḍhol-tāshā playing for, 239; drum patterns for, 111; Muharram, compared to, 238
Ramzan, Maulvi Hafiz Muhammad Ramzan, 172, 173, 271
Randel, Don M., 278n4
"Ran me jis dam subha 'āshūrā āyāṉ hone lagī" (marsiyah), 227–228, 229, 302
Rangachari, K., 33, 37
rank: assignment of, 157; social, 14–15, 33, 37, 38, 41; of ta'ziyahs, 130, 133. *See also* caste
raqṣ-e bismillah, 183, 185
Rashid Sain, Baba (pir), 178–179, 187
rationalism, 45
Razaq, Muhammad, 223–233 passim, 259
recitation: drum/rhythmic syllables, of, important, 55–58, 60, 73, 86, 93, 162 (*see also under drum pattern[s]*); life story of goddess Nanda Devi, of, 74; lines, selection of, in performance, 168; meaning of, shaded by context, 50; singing, versus, 15–16; taht-ul lafẓ (declamation), 196; tarannum (chant), 196, 229; terms for, 15. *See also* poetry; singing
recording(s), musical: attitudes toward, 34; circulation, as modes of, 17; surreptitious, marketed, 154
Reddy, William, 53
redemptive suffering, 53
reformism, 29; communal boundaries, reinforcing, 92; discourses of, in South Asia, 92; Islamic reformers in Delhi, 117, 290; prohibition of Muharram drumming, 90–91
rehearsal, absence of, 46
relationships among musicians, expressions for, 25
religion(s): connection with, lacking, view of Muharram as, 211, 227; multiple, accommodation of, 193 (*see also participation: multicommunity, in events*); support religion (dīn), to, drumming (ḍankā), 208–209, 297, 300n4
remembrance, 17, 26, 125. *See also* (*yād in glossary*); ẕikr
repertoire: defining items of, 9, 68; hybridity of, 98, 215; size of, in relation to context(s), 46
repetition, 19; avoiding, 39, 163; verbal formulas, of, 156. *See also* ẕikr; *vird and ẕikr glossary*

requests, musical: drum/dance repertoire at weddings, 87, 89
Reshma (Pakistani singer), 17, 156
responses: music, to, 27, 152, 163, (*see also musician[s], interactions among; variations, creating*); poetry, to, 27; Qur'ānic sounds and jurisprudence, to, 184; ritual sequence, elements in, to, 32; tāshā, response (badal) of, to ḍhol, 240
reversal, 48
rhetoric (verbal and non-verbal), 46–50, 158
rhyme: analyzed, 50, 228, 302; change in, effect of, 26–27; drum, 85; "imaginative assent" and, 51; semantic parallels of: 156 (zabān-sāzān̲), 157, 162 (kān-zabān), 168; tension, performative, preceding, 120
rhythm, 7, 8; asymmetrical time patterns, 76, 78, 99–102, 107, 125, 201, 240, 259, 289, 290, 315; bodily, 60 (*see also body, the*); changes in, 57, 95; cross-, 78, 79, 102, 181, 198, 201; elastic, 76, 79, 89, 121, 136, 201, 312; groove in relation to, 66 (*see also groove*); melody, relation to, 8–9, 67–80; pattern definition, 67–80; soul, relation of, to, 48–49; structural, 8; surface, 62; tension, rhythmic, 74, 103, 299; textual (*see text, rhythms of*). *See also* beat; counting, act of (rhythmic); periodicity; stroke melody; tāls and cāls; tone melody/ies
rhythms. *See* drum pattern(s)
riff-based pattern, 102, 105, 216–217. *See also* beat: beat-based pattern; motives, drum pattern
rituals
  interpreting rituals: complex, public rituals, 44–54; controversies, 29, 52; efficacy, 54. *See also rasm in glossary*
rituals (music and song): drumming for specific, 17, 21, 41, 73; musical structuring of, 32, 74, 75 (*see also ceremony/ies, musical constitution of*); singing, mīrā̲s̲ī, for, 39; songs/nauḥahs for mehndi, 116; South Indian temple music, 14
  specific rituals and ritual events: birth of a son, 162; ruk̲h̲satī, 31, 60; ta'ziyah-lifting, 139; ta'ziyahs, calling out names of, 138; wedding of Qasim, commemorating, 122
  Sufi rituals, 17; courtesans, of, at Sehwan Sharif, 182
Rizvi, Saiyad Athar Abbas, 290
Rohtak (district in India), muhājir musicians from, 90–91, 283
Rom, relation to Ḍom, 36
Rose, Horace Arthur, 34, 35, 284
Rowell, Lewis, 8, 10, 101
royal(ty): processions, 5, 6, 7; ritual and music, evoked through, 67, 126, 253, 255, 265
ruby. *See* la'l (ruby)
Ruckert, George, 15, 276n6
Runzavānlu, 37, 65, 67, 280
Rupayan Sansthan, 40
Russell, Robert Vane, 33, 35

Sadiq, Hasan, 196
"Saiful Maluk" (epic, Sword of Kings), 175–176
Sain, Pappu. *See* Pappu Sain (Zulfiqar Ali)
saint(s), Sufi, 17–18, 34; affections of, "coax, to" (manāna), 173; devotion to, as motivation for becoming a musician/drummer, 42; relationships with, accounts of devotees', 166–184 passim
Sajjād (Zain-ul Abidin, son of Husain), 127, 274

Sakata, Hiromi Lorraine, 33, 34, 38, 282n18
Sakina (Husain's daughter), 27, 198, 266, 267
salām: text associated with savārī and mātam drum patterns, 232–233, 247, 261–262, 303
Samad, Abdul (Muhājir patron), 207, 210
Samma (Rajasthani Rājput clan), 39, 40, 194; sammatka, 40. *See also Rājput in glossary*
Sangaṛ Veṛah (near Delhi Gate, Multan), 122
Sanskrit (language): musical terms and derivations, 62–64, 66, 67, 68, 112, 281n4, 283, 308, 310, 312–317, 319–323
Sapir, Edward, 289n15
Saqfi, Mukhtar (historical figure), 124
Saraiki (language): chant imitating drum, 84; instrument speaking in, 43; majlises, 138; nauḥahs, 122; poetry, 82, 88, 137, 139; sermons, 127; terms, musical, 63, 64, 66, 86, 127, 136, 312, 314
sartorial conventions, 26, 27, 30; notable, of women, 133; red clothes, 169; turban-wearing, 31
Sarwar, Nadeem, 196
Sarwar Sultan, Sakhi, 34
Satan, 11
Sawa, George Dimitri, 281n6
Sax, William, 74
Schmid, Anna, 36, 76, 77, 78, 282n15, 282n16, 282n21
Schreffler, Gibb, 21, 34, 66, 280, 284, 315
script, musical notation and sonic relations with, 21
sectarianism, 92, 117, 123, 203, 207, 225, 270, 276n7, 290; euphemisms, use of, to deemphasize, 196, 203; exacerbation of, by mutual "opponents" (muk͟hālifīn), 225; financing of violent, 191; firqah vāriyat (Urdu for sectarianism), 161, 294
Sehwan (Sindh), 17–18, 156, 161, 162, 182, 185
self-sacrifice, 92; desire for, 26; personal, as resource for artistry, 120
Sells, Michael Anthony, 50
semiotic relations
  processes: drum patterns, pertaining to, 69, 79; potentials, interpretive, unrealized, 185; speech acts, self-altering, 53; text, single, differing emotional implications of, 91–92;
  types: iconicity (*see iconicity*); metaphor (*see metaphor*); metonymy, 140; non-arbitrariness, 20; self-referentiality, 241; synecdoche, 18, 173; token, 53, 208
  See also meaning(s)
seniority, musical, 59
sermons, majlis, 49, 54, 84n§, 91, 116, 127, 196, 315, 324
service specialists: customary compensation of, 39, 40, 90; musical and non-musical, 32–43
Seshagopalan, T. N., 13
"set" (Ḍom musical ensemble), 76–79
Shabbir (ḍhol player), 162
Shabbir, Ghulam (procession patron), 122
Shafi, Muhammad (ḍhol ustad), 25, 65–66, 213, 297, 298
Shah, Anwar, Pir, 91
Shah, Ghulam (historical figure), 194
Shah, Wajid Ali (nawab of Lucknow), 5–6
Shah, Waris (poet), 168, 170, 176, 179, 185, 186
Shah Abdul Aziz, 117
Shah Husain: biographical details, 146, 169; dhamāl taken up by, 158; kāfī,

inventor of, credited as, 166; kāfīs of, 166–167; poetry/sayings attributed to, 173; status, controversial, of, 169, 171. *See also* Madho Lal Husain
Shah Husain Sangat, 166
Shahid Ali (ḍhol player), 25–26, 30–32, 55–60, 73, 111, 179–182, 277, 279, 296
Shah Jahan (Mughal emperor), 150
Shah Jamal (saint), 158; agent of, Pappu Sain as, 149, 151, 156, 186; baddhā of, 180; dīdār of, 155; shrine of, 18, 59, 147, 162, 166, 291, 292, 295; story of, 150; voice of, speaking through ḍhol, 156
"Shāh kehte the, 'bas zyādah ġam nah khā'o sakīnah'" (nauḥah), 27
shahnā'ī performance, description of, 126. *See also shahnā'ī in glossary*
Shāh Nāmeh, 35
Shah Wali Sarkar, Sayyad Baba Mehar (Sufi saint), 154
Shah Yousef Gardez (11th c. saint), 118, 119; descendants of, 119–120
shaker (one who does, literally "shakes" dhamāl—dhamāl ḍālne vāle), 155
shakers (maracas), 208
Sharar, Abdul Halim, 6, 276
Shariati, Ali (Iranian revolutionary), 203, 297
Sharma, Premalata, 101, 112, 288n6, 288n7, 322 s.v. ṭhekā
Shaukat (teacher's teacher of drummer Pappu Sain), 154
Shehzad (devotee/shrine service volunteer), 174, 179–184 passim
Sheikh, Ustad Muhammad (historical musician), 224, 240, 247
Sheiḵẖ Siddiqis, 210, 213; converts to Islam, as recent, proving status, 47, 216, 220; Muhājirs, as, 41. *See also Sheiḵẖ in glossary*
Sherinian, Zoe, 14
Shī'ah(s): drumming for Muharram, views on, 90, 224–225; "faith" ('aqīdah) in Nizamuddin rituals, 224; mātam, Shī'ahs of Sindh accused of using, for political favor, 211–212; Maulā'ī, 203; Nizami Sunnis, relations with, during Muharram, 237; weeping of, upon hearing Nizami drumming, 224. *See also under Sunni regarding Shī'ah-Sunni relations*
shields (ḍhāl) for mock battles, 247, 284
Shiism, 1; arrival of, in Multan, 119; drumming/instrumental music, views of, in, 44, 53, 92; partisans of, interfering with intercommunity participation in Muharram, 225–226; recitation, concept of, in, 16, 20; themes of, in qalandari tradition, 161; themes of, shared with some Sunnis, 195–196
Shina (language), 76, 77
shops, music, 30
shrines: Data Sahab/Hujwiri, 26, 132; imambarah (*see glossary*); nationalization of Sufi, 172; peṛh (*see glossary*); Pir Pak Farman, 160; Sufi, 18, 25. *See also names of individual saints and shrines*
Sibte-Jafar, 26–27, 270, 277
Sidis (Pakistanis of African descent), 193, 201
Sikhs, 178, 238, 243, 244, 284
silversmiths, 37
Silverstein, Michael, 184
Simorgh, 168
Sindh: 'alam, style of, in, 199; dhamāl in, 18; history of, 192–193; Khaipur district, 42; Manganhārs of, 39–41; muslim conquest of, 10, 40, 192–193, 194; population, heterogeneous, of, 193; Ṭaṭṭah district, 40; ẕikr in music of, 17

Sindhi (language): instrument speaking in, 43; speakers, practices of, 212–213, 227; terms, musical, in, 63, 64, 66, 198, 203–206, 298, 311, 312, 314, 315, 321–324
singer: drone, of (*see bāzu in glossary*); versus reciter, 16. *See also* vocalist
Singh, Bharat (ḍhol player), 238, 240, 241, 273, 288n9
Singh, Maharaja Ranjit, 178
singing, 15; kāfīs, 166; overlapping style of, 120; reciting, versus, 15; shahnā'i, with, 85, 88; styles of, with specific ṭhekās and rāgas, 176. *See also* gānā
slogan, 50, 140, 211, 232, 233; "Husain" and other, crying out, tied to identity claims, 211; na'rah bāzi insufficient for heralding ta'ziyah, 215, (298); played on drums, 205, 232. *See also* exclamations; *na'rah in glossary*
Snell, Rupert, 112
sociality: male, 59, "sangat," 59, 60, 322
social poetics, 46–51, 186
songs: composition of, for Muharram, 135; drum patterns, as guides to, 97–98
soul, 48, 126, 159, 162. *See also rūḥ in glossary*
sound(s)
  concepts: concepts of, in religious traditions, 11, 91; inauspicious, 33; spacial conceptions of, 91
  contexts: Muharram, 116, 143; Qur'ānic, 184
  qualities: density, loudness, 33; intensity, 201; undulation, 57, 148, 160, 241; volume, attempt to increase, 40
  types: generator, 200; metal, grinding, 165; rifle shots, 29; whistling, 76
South Asia as a musical area, 133–114
South India, music in, 12–15, 17. *See also individual place names*
soz k̲h̲wān, 16, 26–27, 38, 118, 120–122
space, 184; arrangement of peṛh courtyard, 200; boundaries of, and time 37; configuration of mātamdārs and nauḥah singers, 141; geography, ritual, clue to Shī'ī-Sunni historical relations, 244; marking territory (thān) with embers, 180; moving through space, 62, 65–67, 164; positioning of instrumentalists and nauḥah singers/chanters, 128. *See also* directionality; place
speech-song. *See doṛhā in glossary*
spinning, 26, 152, 153, 155, 181, 182
"spirit bolstering" (ḥosalah afzā'ī), 59, 92, 277. *See also* payments and tips
"śruti māta laya pitā" (musical aphorism), 67
stairs/steps, ṭhekās compared to, 58
standard, battle. *See 'alam in glossary*
standardization, 114
stereotypes, 46–47, 185
Stern, Theodore, 305n2
Stewart, Rebecca, 281n2
stress. *See* accentuation(s)
strike, to. *See* beat
stroke melody, 8–9, 17, 18, 20, 67, 74; contrapuntal, 71, 79, 87; metric contexts, different, in, 88, 126; ṭhekā and, 56; tone melody, complexly related to, 36–37, 76–79
strumming: rhythmic patterns named for stresses in, 65; textual patterns reflected in, 15
subject positions: emotional response

and, 52; introduced theoretically, 45
Sufi(s), 150; the path of becoming a, 149, 179
Sufism: hierarchies in, 180; history of, 17; justification of z̲ikr in, 17; music of, in historical sources, 11; music, philosophy of, in, 16; music, types of, in, 16 (*see also names of individual genres*); quest, spiritual, in, 168; training, spiritual, in, 60 (*see also discipleship*)
Sughra (Ṣuġrā) (daughter of Husain), 127, 229–230, 248
suites and suite-like structures, 57, 61, 67, 73, 74, 102, 212, 283; "twelve variations," 71, 281n11
Sumrah (Rajasthani clan), 39
Sunni muslims
  ambiguous social implications: Jahangir, Emperor, as, 124; participation in Muharram by, 42, 46, 90, 117, 211, 224, 238, 243, 244, 246, 287 (*see also under Muharram*); reformism among, 290
  antagonism toward Shī'ahs, 84, 123, 161, 185, 191; distinction from Shī'ahs, alleged British involvement in emphasizing, 211; partisans of, interfering with intercommunity participation in Muharram, 225–226; prohibition against Shī'ī activities among, 91, 92; sectarian divisions, events leading to, 211, 226; views on own responses to Muharram drumming contrasted with Shī'ī views on Sunni responses, 224
  categories of: Chishti sufi, 222fn; Deobandi, 123; Hanafi, 194; Jam'ātīs versus Khānaqāhīs, 237
  cooperative relations: living side by side with Shī'ahs, Nizamuddin, Delhi, before Partition, 224; relations with Shī'ahs, call for closer, 244; reverence for Imam Jafar 196; Shī'ahs, cooperation with, 191, 122, 224–225, 237; Shī'ahs, with, composing Manganhār community, 40, 194, 197, 198, 206, 207, 212
  performance by: drumming, accused of, for political gain in Sindh, 211–212; reciting mars̲iyah, 224
surgeons, 32–33
swing, rhythmic, 56, 66, 74, 106, 108, 111–112, 216. *See also cāl; (chand in glossary); jhol*
syllables, 20–22; drum strokes, relation to, 20–21, 56, 96; ease/awkwardness of sequences, 20–21; long and short, 18–20, 104; settings (syllabic/melismatic), melodic, 27; terms for drum/rhythmic syllables, 20; timbre of, 20
syntax, 49–50

tabal, 63, 66, 225. *See also tabl in glossary*
tabla: accompaniment, as, 67; "inside" ḍhol, as put, 163–164; mars̲iyah, with, 82; qawwālī, in, 16, 132; solo instrument, as, 102; syllables and strokes of, correspondence between, 20; undulation of (*see sound[s]: qualities: undulation*)
tabla player(s): caste category of, 37; knowledge of, 31
tag, musical, 99–102
Ṭa'ifah, 35
tailors, 33, 36, 37, 43, 223
Tajiki/Tojiki (language), 65
Tajikistan, 65, 290

tāls, cāls and related entities, specific, discussed
Indian and Pakistani metrical structures by name: alġāni, 76, 78, 282n20; Ali kā panjā, 64, 106, 108, 109, 110, 111, 247; Alī kī zarbeṉ, 110, 232 (performance described); Baluchi, 87; Baluchi Lava, 159; bapóe dáni, 77; baṛā (grand/big) mārū, 87, 88, 89, 125, 286; bārah jarbeṉ, 240; bāsaṭh jarbeṉ, 106, 107, 109, 111, 240; batīs jarbeṉ, 106, 107, 111, 240; bhāṅgṛā, 29–31, 58, 63, 98, 111, 154, 159, 163, 176, 184, 240; bulá haríip, 78; būti/bóote haríip, 77; cañcar/cañcal, 88, 89, 176; cār kī cāl, 99–102; caukaṛi, 111, 240; chautāla, 215, 219; cheh kī cāl, 99–102; choṭa (small) mārū, 87, 88, 89, 123, 125, 286; dādra, 31, 176; ḍaṇḍ, 198–200, 204–205; danni/dáni haríip, 77–78; dauṛ, 64, 215; ḍeṛh kī cāl, 99–102; ḍhaī cāl, 287n5; dhamāl, 18, 58, 63, 86, 149, 151, 154, 157–164, 180, 206, 283, 284, 292; dhamār, 58, 204, 288n13; dhīmā text, 229, 248, 249 (performance described), 261, 302; dhīmā, 103, 111, 223, 229 (as difficult), 230–231 (performance described), 241 (alternate tune and performance described), 247–249, 259–261; dīpchandī, 137, 240; do kī cāl, 99–102; ḍoliwālā vājā, 87, 285; drut tīntāl, 57; ek kī cāl, 64 VI:D2, 99–102 (Agra Muhājirs); 208 (Ajmer Muhājirs); ek tāl, 67, 215, 219, 276n6, 281n2; fāk̲h̲tah aṣūl, 56–57, 279–280; ġalawáar, 78, 282n21; gintī, das kī and bīs kī (*see also gintī in glossary*), 299 (notation); Husain Husain, 205, 224, 228, 231, 233, 244, 260, 262, 263; Husainī kī bārah terah, 63, 106, 107, 108, 109, 111; iktāla, 58; Imam Husain kī mātam (Mamraj group's name for the Nizami mātam drum pattern), 241, 248; jhaptāl, 31, 110, 111, 159, 204; jhūmar, 31, 87, 90, 159, 204, 285, 286; kalmah, 47, 103, 104, 105, 111, 215, 216, 217, 218, 219, 223, 231, 232–233 (performance described), 241, 247, 248, 299, 301n15, 301n19; karaṛ, 87, 90, 284, 286, 287; kaṭh tār, 58; keharvā/kairvā, 63, 110, 111, 215, 217–218, 219; lolī, 205, 206; luḍḍi, 159; mandir tāl, 75, 79; mārū (*see mārū in glossary*); mārū text, 88; mātam kī cāl, 66, 208, 297; mātam, 103, 111, 161, 162, 213, 215, 217, 218, 219, 223, 224, 228, 231 (performance described), 232, 241, 247, 248, 259, 261–262, 297, 298, 303; mātamī ḍhol, 161–161; muġala'i , 31, 57, 58; Muharram kī savārī, 103, 105, 109, 111, 223, 231, 232, 240, 241, 248fn, 264; nā-dhin-dhin-nā (or nā din din nā), 58, 111, 160, 240; palath, 90; pānc kī cāl, 99–102; panj tāl, 56, 280–281; panj tāl/tār dī savārī, 58, 85, 86, 283, 285; Panjabi ṭhekā, 111; rūpak, 57, 58, 163, 259–261; sammī, 31; sāt kī cāl, 99–102; savārī (non Muharram, Mamraj's group), 240; shādmānah, 87, 286; Shah Panjatan (for naqqārah only), 206; sīdī bārah terah, 106, 107, 111; Sindhi, 159; sūrfak̲h̲tah, 279; tāmbal, 78, 282n19; terah jarbeṉ, 240; ṭhekā, ten-beat, on naqqāṛah described, 200; tīn kī cāl, 66, 99–102 (Agra Muhājirs), 208 (Ajmer

Muhājirs); tīntāl, 57–58, 136, 148, 149, 151, 160, 204, 276n6, 309, as "chief," 58; tīntār, 58, 86; Ya Husain, (200), 204, 205, 206; tā'ū, 204, 205 (notated); yakka, 58
Metrical structures, historical, or those identified not by a proper name but by context or description only: deśī tālās, 101, 112; du'ā-e-khair ritual, drum pattern for, 90; miśravarṇa, 101; wrestling, for (akhāṛā, wrestling-ground), 87, 157
repertoires of drum patterns listed, 63–64, 69, 76, 98, 100, 205, 215
South Indian (exclusively) metrical structures by name: allā cāmi mēḷam, 282n14; cādā dāk, 68; cāmi mēḷam, 69, 73, 282n14; cāvu (mēḷam/dappu), 63, 69–71, 79; dauṛ savār mārg, 67; do mār, 95; eka tāḷam, 279n2; eyṛ dāk, 94; kalyāṇa mēḷam, 69, 73; koḷāḷ dāk, 94; mūṉḏ dāk, 94; oḏ dāk, 94; tīn mār, 95; tiruganāṭ dāk, 68, 94; Vijayawada, 95

tāls and cāls
categorizing of: cāl as generic term, 99, 111; counts, number of, in, 61, 86; multipart, 75, 86–90, 95–98, 125; naming of, 57, 64, 93–94, 101 (*see also, naming, practice of: drum patterns*); naqqārah ṭhekā, 86; repertorial items *in*, 67; subgenres of, 111 (e.g. savārī), 205 (ḍaṇḍ), 215 (e.g. gintī); ṭhekā, tāl as synonymous with, 62; vājā, 86–89
history of, 101
processes involving: actions signaled by, 205; controlling measure length, as, 95; "giving birth" (paidā karnā) to emotions, 160; "keeping the tāl," 58, 62; ordering of, ritual, 204, 205–206
qualities associated with: betālā" as unmusical (person), 160; frightening and intimidating, as, 159; patrons, status/religion/identity of, differentiated according to, 87, 90; ṭhekas as pure/true (saccā), 155

Tamerlane (Timur, Timur-the-lame), 215fn, 299n16; faith, comparison of Muharram drummer's to that of Tamerlane, 218; originator of ta'ziyah, procession and rituals, as legendary, 196, 215–216; sacred relics (tabarrukāt), as one who brought, to Nizamuddin shrine, 229; "vision" (bashārat) of, 215, 228, 298; "voice of the drum" to announce his ta'ziyah procession, 215–216; voice of, saying "Husain Husain," 228

Tamil language: political movement, 12, 276n4; terms, musical, in, 20, 63–66, 68–74, 94, 277n9, 278, 308, 311, 314, 316, 317, 322

Tamil Nadu, music in, 12–15, 276n4, 277n9; drumming, local concepts of, 71–74; stressed strokes, naming patterns by number of, in, 95–95

tānpūra: simple (ḍhaburi?) tāshā part compared to, 240–241. *See also tambūra in glossary*

tāshā, 1, 14
names and characteristics: heads, ochre spots on, of, 214; Nārada, mythical association with sage, 239; obscurity of, 31; shells, terra-cotta, of, 214; tājā (Tamil version), 14, 63, 69, 71, 277n9; timbre relative to the ḍhol, 91
places and contexts: Hindus in Panjab, played, for, 87, 90; Muharram, during, banning of, 91; Muharram, played for, 90, 102–111 passim, 135; Multan, in, 85, 87, 90, 135–136

tāshā (*continued*):
players: countryside, players living in, 55; families of, players, 85; players named, 38; Sunnis, performed by, for Shī'ī Muharram ritual in Delhi, 243
techniques and musical functions: dugga, with, 95–98; functions, musical, described, 90, 102–103; response (badal), provides, to ḍhol, 240; role, accompanying, of, 95, 106; techniques, 216
See also ḍhol-tāshā ensemble(s)
tavil (drum), 14, 32
ta'ziyah(s)
concepts and distinctions: Hindu temple, likened to, 117; numbering of, 130, 138; oldest (*see also* Haji Wala), 82
names of: Abdullah Wala, 133, 139; Darbar Pir Sahab, 130; Khurshid wālā, 225; Pir Inayat Valayat, 130; Shāgird, 83, 142; Ustad, 83, 142
rituals and processions: Multan, procession through, 129–130; names of, ritual of calling out, 138; process of lifting, 129; rituals involving, movements against, 117; submerging in water, 197–198
See also ta'ziyah in glossary
Tehrik-e-Nafaz-e-Fiqah-Jafaria, 123
Telangana (region of Andhra Pradesh), 37, 67, 192, 318
Telugu (language), speakers of: Muharram among, 67; music of, 33, 37, 63, 64, 65, 67, 71, 72, 98, 106, 312, 319
temple, Hindu (mandir), 75, 79; Pakistan, in, 193
tempo: base speed (thallā), 163; doubling, 137 (double lay), 163 (dogun); quadrupling (caugun), 163; genre subclassification based on, 77; "inflation," rhythmic, by reducing, 101; "mak[ing] the tempo sit" (lay biṭhāna), 86; rapid, mukhṛā implying excitement (josh), 160; slow, connoting sadness, 160; tāla speeds, transformation of bols for different, 85–86, 160, 285; variation in base, 95
Terada, Yoshitaka, 33
text: assignment, a posteriori, to drum patterns, 84, 93, 285; awareness/lack of awareness of text underlying drumming, 217; conch shell, mimicked with, 140; drum patterns, in, 7, 9, 17, 18, 22, 84–85, 93, 104, 161, 249 (systematicity doubted), 290 (explained technically); "fast" (jalad), played, on drums, 233; idea of, behind drumming important, 235; interpretation, dangerous horizon potentials for, 185; rhythms of, 18–19, 120, 140; strumming patterns, in, 15, 17, 19; tone-melody instruments, articulated on, 13–16, 43, 88, 203; "voice," implicating 11, 17. *See also* syllables and language(s)
texture, emotional. *See* emotional contour and texture
texture, musical: rhythmic, 305n1; soz performance, of, in Multan, 120; varying the density of, in drumming, 8, 36, 95, 180, 200, 282n14, 282n16
Thams. *See* Mīrs
theater, 138
theory and theorizing, of the voice in India, 12–14
Thurston, Edgar, 33, 37
Til, Ustad, 240
timbre: adjusting, of drumhead with heat, 135–136, 218; blend of, in mārū, 135; conceptual bridge, as

9; contrasts in, for creating musical interest, 151; discriminating, in, among tāls, ṭhekas and cāls, 61–62, 66, 74, 102; linking tone and stroke melodies, 8, 80; naming practices and 112; syllables, and, 20–22, 96, 261; vocalization of, 70
time units, homogeneous, 65
Timur. *See* Tamerlane
Tingey, Carol, 33, 282n23
Tirmiẕi, Sayyid Ġulām Ḥaidar, 277
tiruganāṭ (dance and drum pattern), 68, 94
tiruppu (drum phrase, Tamil), 72, 73, 281n12
tīṭṭu (Tamil: defilement), 33, 69. *See also* defilement
Toda (Nilgiri tribe), 14–15
tol. *See* ḍhol
tone melody/ies, 8–9; forms, 88; generic distinctions, lower-level, marked by, 68; models, as, for ṭhekas or tāls, 98; stroke melody, emphasis on, over, 36, 77; wind instrument, role of, in defining, 36, 77
Torbat-e Jam (Iran), 19
touch, 60
Toynbee Arnold, 119
trance. *See* ecstasy; (*ḥāl in glossary*); mastī; possession
transformation: musical (*see also modulation, musical*), 75, 87, 89, 284; personal, 138; powers of, artisans with, 37, 278n3; sound, power of, 38
transitions: dance, 66; musical, performing, 57, 58, 74, 79, 121, 151, 216, 299
transvestites, 182
treatises, Indian musical, 10–12; Bṛhaddeśī, 10; Ḍhol Sāgar, 21; Nāṭyaśāstra, 10, 11; Saṅgītaratnākara, 12, 101, 288n6
Trimingham, J. Spencer, 16
Trinidad, tāshā tradition in, 103
tune types, 78, 282n18, 317
turi (trumpet), 75, 79
Turkey, music of, compared, 57, 107
tuṭumpu (kettle drum, pronounce tuḍumbu), 71

Udaipur (Rajasthan), 30
Umayyad dynasty, 1, 116fn, 138, 192, 193, 274
umbrella, symbolism of, 126
units of rhythmic measure: layvān̲, 56. *See also* mātra(s)
unity: experience of, 16, 153; threats to national, 171; yaktā'ī, 295
Urban, Greg, 184
Urdu/Hindi (language): instrument speaking in, 43; poets, 170; sermons of ẕākirs in, 127; songs and sung poetry in, 28, 134, 277, 302, 315–317, 322; speakers, practices of, 197–198, 207, 213, 224–225, 227; terms, musical, and derivations in, 15, 63–67, 74, 85, 86, 107, 278, 279, 284, 291, 292–293. *See also* Hindi (language)
Urmawī, Ṣafi al-Dīn al-, 280
'urs, 34, 44, 58, 59, 296; Chishti, 117, 226–227; invitations to, 237; Madho Lal Husain, 133, 146, 165–187 passim, 277, 279, 291, 295; Misri Shah, 61; Muharram as, of Imam Husain, 237; qawwālī at, 132; Shī'ī death commemorations, compared to, 130, 237, 316; wedding, as, 173; wrestling at, 60–61
ur̲umi (drum), 14
Uttarakhand: Garhwal, 21, 34; Kumaon, 66, 74–75
Uttar Pradesh, 24, 42; mātam, women's, in, 128; Panjab, Pakistan, comparisons with, 26, 57, 120, 290; Sindh, comparisons with, 195–196. *See also names of cities and towns*

utterances: emotives as first-person, 53; musical, 47, 54; qawl as, 16; responses to, 51; salience of, in enhancing message, 50; Sufi contexts, in, 17, 152

Vaḍera (feudal lords), 212
Vaḍlangi (carpenters), 37
vādya. *See* vātiyam/vādya/vādyam
vajāuṉ, 66
vajjāirnu, 64, 66, 323
variations, creating: drum patterns, in, 70, 71, 79, 95–98, 151, 163 (*see also ṭhā dhunī in glossary*); in vocal responses to drum patterns, 152
varṇa (category encompassing castes), 36
vātiyam/vādya/vādyam, 66, 72, 323
"Velā valī vay shāh Sayyadā, āj hay ẓulam dī rāt" (mārū text), 88 scanned, 285
verbocentrism, 15, 16
versions, formal comparison of musical drum pattern, 109–110, 248, 261, 262, 279–280
violin, 13, 16
virāma, 101
Viśvakarma (collective term for artistan castes), 37, 278n3
vocalist: supporting, 16; terms for, 15–16 (*see also individual terms for vocalist*)
vocalization: bols, of, as "talking," 163; drum pattern, pitch of, 163; drum pattern, reconstruction of, based on, 96–97. *See also under* drum pattern[s]
vococentrism, 10–13, 16
"Voh jo ham meṉ tum meṉ qarār thā," (ghazal), 28
voice, 10–16; conceptions, historical, of, 12; ḍhol, of, 156; evaluation of, 42; God, (presumably) of, calling for drumming in his name, 209; instruments, in relation to, 10–22 (passim), 84–85; naqqārah/naubat drums, of, 125, 156; sound of, 7; status of, 10–16, 68; vocalness, 10, 16. *See also āvāz in glossary*
voicing, 20–21, 96
vowels: adding, to sung poetry, 168; drum, in, vocalizations, 96; drum stroke, relation with, 20–21, 104; extensions, expressive, of, 141; formants and, 277n8; intrinsic pitch of, 20, 277n8; long and short, discussed, 104; significance of, 50; variability of, length, 308
vows. *See mannat in glossary*

wajd (rapure), 155, 293. *See also* ecstasy; (*ḥāl in glossary)*; mastī; possession
Wakhan valley, 65
Wakhi (people), 77
wedding: apocryphal, of Qasim, 35, 116, 122; drum patterns for, Tamil, 69, 73; functional music at, objection to, 38; music at, 10, 25, 26–31, 33, 39, 60, 87–90, 198 (dance style); performers, status of, at, 85; rituals, 26–32, 87–90; Shī'ī, 26–32, 52–53, 89; symbolism of, 116, 123, 130, 137, 139, 173
Wegner, Gert-Matthias, 21, 37
Wehr, Hans, 35
Weidman, Amanda, 12–13, 15, 16
"weight": musical, 58, 111, 112, 279; poetic (vazn), 112; synesthetic, 224. *See also vazan in glossary*
West Asia: Muharram in, 53; music of, 7, 10, 32, 36, 45, 61. *See also* Iran
Western/Westernized/Westernization, 31
Wolf, Richard K., 18, 51, 52, 99, 112, 279n5, 290, 296n3

wrestling, 60–61; bhāṅgṛā for, 159; drum pattern for, 87, 159
Wynad region, 14–15

Yadagiri, Runza (drummer), 67, 280
Yazid, 1, 124, 134, 138, 161fn, 185, 267, 273, 274; war drum (jangī tabal) associated with side of, 225
Youssefzadeh, Ameneh, 33

ẓāhir (exteriority/outwardness/manifestation), 187, 218–219, 292, 301n15
Zaidi, Syed Karrar Haidar (soz k͟hwān), 120–122
Zainab (Husain's sister), 134, 196, 165, 274, 290
zamīndār (feudal lord), 42
zanjīr kā mātam, 143 (photo), 162, 183, 196, 197; dhamāl, in, reproducing motions of, 183; idiometricity of, 197; instruments silent during, 197; Sunnis, by, 196, 197; technique and rhythm of, 142–143
z̲at, 38
z̲ikr: unconscious recitation of, through mediation of saint, 156; z̲ikr-fiqr, 157. *See also z̲ikr in glossary*
ziyārat: processions as solution to crowding at pilgrimage site, 215. *See also ziyārat in glossary*
Zoroastrianism, 172
Zulfiqar Ali, 154. *See also* Pappu Sain

RICHARD K. WOLF is Professor of Music and South Asian Studies at Harvard University and editor of *Theorizing the Local: Music, Practice, and Experience in South Asia and Beyond.*

The University of Illinois Press
is a founding member of the
Association of American University Presses.

Composed in 10.75/13 Times New Roman
by Celia Shapland
at the University of Illinois Press
Manufactured by Sheridan Books, Inc.
University of Illinois Press

1325 South Oak Street
Champaign, IL 61820-6903
www.press.uillinois.edu